GUINNESS WORLD RECORDS 2014

Tallest usable pogo stick

When it comes to pogo sticks, one name leaps to mind. Prodigious pogo performer Fred Grzybowski (USA) displayed a 9-ft. 6.5-in.-tall (2.91-m) pogo stick at the Toronto International Busker Festival in Canada on August 7, 2011. The following year, on August 19, in St. Catharines, Ontario, Canada, he presented the **shortest usable pogo stick**—a mere 2 ft. 1 in. (64 cm) tall. And that's the long and short of it.

PENSACOLA STATE-MILTON LIBRARY

© 2013 GUINNESS WORLD RECORDS LIMITED

No part of this book may be reproduced or transmitted in any form or by any means, electronic, chemical, mechanical, including photography, or used in any information storage or retrieval system without a licence or other permission in writing from the copyright owners.

British Library Cataloguing-in-Publication Data: A catalogue record for this book is available from the British Library

US ISBN-13: 978-1-908843-35-7
US ISBN-10: 1-908843-35-7

For a complete list of credits and acknowledgments, turn to p. 268.

Records are made to be broken – indeed, it is one of the key criteria for a record category – so if you find a record that you think you can beat, tell us about it by making a record claim. Find out how on p. 10. Always contact us *before* making a record attempt.

Check the official website – **www.guinnessworldrecords. com** – regularly for record-breaking news, plus video footage of record attempts. You can also join and interact with the Guinness World Records online community.

Sustainability
The trees that are harvested to print *Guinness World Records* are carefully selected from managed forests to avoid the devastation of the landscape.

The paper contained within this edition is manufactured by Stora Enso, Kabel, Germany. The production site is Chain-of-Custody certified and operates within environmental systems certified to ISO 14001 to ensure sustainable production.

Typefaces
This edition of *Guinness World Records* is set in Myriad Pro, a beautifully proportioned and highly readable sans serif typeface designed in the early 1990s by Robert Slimbach and Carol Twombly (both USA).

The display font is a black (as in heavy) condensed version of **FLYER**, a face also designed in the 1990s, this time by Linotype.

OFFICIALLY AMAZING

Editor-in-Chief
Craig Glenday

Senior Managing Editor
Stephen Fall

Layout Editors
Rob Dimery, Jo Maggs, Lucian Randall

Assistant Editor
Roxanne Mackey

Editorial Team
Theresa Bebbington (Americanization), Chris Bernstein (indexing), Matthew White (proofreading)

Picture Editor
Michael Whitty

Deputy Picture Editors
Fran Morales, Laura Nieberg

Talent/Picture Researcher
Jenny Langridge

VP Publishing
Frank Chambers

Director of Procurement
Patricia Magill

Publishing Manager
Jane Boatfield

Publishing Executive
Charlie Peacock

Production Consultants
Roger Hawkins, Dennis Thon, Julian Townsend

Printing & Binding
MOHN Media Mohndruck GmbH, Gütersloh, Germany

Cover Production
Spectratek Technologies, Inc., Bernd Salewski (Günter Thomas)

Augmented Reality
Red Frog

Design
Paul Wylie-Deacon, Richard Page at 55design.co.uk

Original Photography
Richard Bradbury, Sam Christmas, James Ellerker, Paul Michael Hughes, Ranald Mackechnie, David Ovenden, Javier Pierini, Kevin Scott Ramos, Ryan Schude

Editorial Consultants
Dr Mark Aston, Iain Borden, Dick Fiddy, David Fischer, Mike Flynn, Marshall Gerometta, Ben Hagger, David Hawksett, Alan Howard, Dominique Jando, Eberhard Jurgalski, Justin Lewis, Christian Marais, Ralph Oates, Ocean Rowing Society, Glen O'Hara, Paul Parsons, Dr Karl Shuker, Samppa von Cyborg, Matthew White, Adrian Willis, Stephen Wrigley, Robert Young

---

President: Alistair Richards
SVP Global Business Development: Frank Foley
SVP Americas: Peter Harper
President (Greater China): Rowan Simons
Country Manager (Japan): Erika Ogawa
Country Manager (UAE): Talal Omar

PROFESSIONAL SERVICES
EVP Finance, Legal, HR & IT: Alison Ozanne
Finance Managers: Neelish Dawett, Scott Paterson
Accounts Payable Manager: Kimberley Dennis
Accounts Receivable Manager: Lisa Gibbs
Head of Legal & Business Affairs: Raymond Marshall
Legal & Business Affairs Manager: Michael Goulbourn
Director of IT: Rob Howe
Web Applications Developers: Imran Javed, Anurag Jha
Desktop Support: Ainul Ahmed
Head of HR: Jane Atkins
Office Manager (UK): Jacqueline Angus
HR & Office Manager (US): Morgan Wilber
HR & Office Manager (Japan): Michiyo Uehara
HR & Office Manager (Greater China): Tina Shi

TELEVISION
SVP Programming & TV Sales: Christopher Skala
Director of Television: Rob Molloy
TV Distribution Manager: Denise Carter Steel
TV Content Executive: Jonny Sanders

RECORDS MANAGEMENT
SVP Records: Marco Frigatti
VP RMT Commercial: Paul O'Neill
Director of RMT Operations: Turath Alsaraf
Head of Records Management Operations (US): Kimberly Partrick
Head of Records Management Operations (Japan): Carlos Martínez
Commercial Director (Greater China): Blythe Fitzwiliam
Business Development Manager (UK): Hayley Nolan
Business Development Manager (US): Amanda Mochan
Business Development Manager (Japan): Kaoru Ishikawa
Database Manager: Carim Valerio
Operations: Alex Angert (USA), Anatole Baboukhian (France), Benjamin Backhouse (UK), Kirsty Bennett (Australia), Jack Brockbank (UK), Fortuna Burke (UK), Shantha Chinniah (UK), Michael Empric (USA), Jacqueline Fitt (UK), Manu Gautam (UK), Jess Hall (UK), Johanna Hessling (USA), Tom Ibison (UK), Sam Mason (UK), Aya McMillan (Japan), Annie Nguyen (USA), Eva Norroy (UK), Anna Orford (France), Pravin Patel (UK), Philip Robertson (USA), Chris Sheedy (Australia), Athena Simpson (USA), Elizabeth Smith (UK), Louise Toms (UK), Gulnaz Ukassova (Kazakhstan), Lorenzo Veltri (Italy), Charles Wharton (UK)
Commercial: Dong Cheng (China), Asumi Funatsu (Japan), Ralph Hannah (UK/Paraguay), Annabel Lawday (UK), Takuro Maruyama (Japan), Nicole Pando (USA), Gail Patterson (UK), Terje Purga (Estonia), Lucia Sinigagliesi (Italy), Şeyda Subaşı-Gemici (Turkey), Charlie Weisman (USA)

GLOBAL MARKETING
SVP Global Marketing: Samantha Fay
Marketing Director (US): Stuart Claxton
Marketing Director (Greater China): Sharon Yang
PR Manager (US): Jamie Panas
PR & Marketing Executive (US): Sara Wilcox
Brand Manager (Germany): Olaf Kuchenbecker
Marketing Manager: Justine Bourdariat
Marketing Executive: Christelle BeTrong
PR Directors (UK): Jaime Strang, Amarilis Whitty
PR & Marketing Manager (UK): Claire Burgess
PR & Marketing Manager (Japan): Kazami Kamioka
Senior PR Executive: Damian Field
UK & International Press Officer: Anne-Lise Rouse
Director of Digital Media: Katie Forde
Video Content Manager: Adam Moore
Community Manager: Dan Barrett
Online Editor: Kevin Lynch
Designer: Neil Fitter
Design Executive: Jon Addison
Creative & Brand Executive (Japan): Momoko Cunneen
Content Manager (US): Mike Janela
Content Manager (Japan): Takafumi Suzuki

PUBLISHING & LICENSING SALES
VP Publishing & Licensing Sales (UK & International): Nadine Causey
Publishing, Sales & Product Director (US): Jennifer Gilmour
Content Director (Greater China): Angela Wu
Senior National Accounts Manager (UK & International): John Pilley
Sales & Distribution Executive (UK & International): Richard Stenning
Brand Licensing Manager: Samantha Prosser

Guinness World Records Limited has a very thorough accreditation system for records verification. However, while every effort is made to ensure accuracy, Guinness World Records Limited cannot be held responsible for any errors contained in this work. Feedback from our readers on any point of accuracy is always welcomed.

Guinness World Records Limited uses both metric and imperial measurements. The sole exceptions are for some scientific data where metric measurements only are universally accepted, and for some sports data. Where a specific date is given, the exchange rate is calculated according to the currency values that were in operation at the time. Where only a year date is given, the exchange rate is calculated from December 31 of that year. "One billion" is taken to mean one thousand million.

Appropriate advice should always be taken when attempting to break or set records. Participants undertake records entirely at their own risk. Guinness World Records Limited has complete discretion over whether or not to include any particular record attempts in any of its publications. Being a Guinness World Records record holder does not guarantee you a place in any Guinness World Records publication.

GUINNESS WORLD RECORDS 2014

ALL-NEW 3D

AUGMENTED REALITY—HOW DOES IT WORK?

This year, readers can "virtually" meet more record holders than ever! Download the FREE app and watch records come alive before your eyes!

From the front cover to specially marked pages inside the book, you will see record holders in 3D animations, videos, and interactive features just by pointing your device at the pages of the book. If you have a smartphone or tablet device, it couldn't be easier! Just follow these simple steps and prepare to be amazed.

2 Look out for the "SEE IT 3D" or "SEE THE VIDEO" symbols throughout the book. Using the app, view the book and see record holders come to life!

SEE IT 3D WITH THE FREE APP

SEE THE VIDEO WITH THE FREE APP

1 Download the FREE "SEE IT 3D" app.

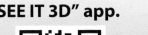

guinnessworldrecords.com/seeit3d

Available on the App Store

ANDROID APP ON
Google play

3 Take a photo of yourself with your favorite record holder and share it online with your friends and family.

TOP TIPS

• Point your device at record holders, move it around and their gaze follows you. Spooky!
• Move your device closer to the photo of Mount Everest. You will enter the Virtual Reality (VR) mode and can see the 360-degree panoramic view as if you had climbed all the way to the top!
• Tap your screen when prompted to interact with the record holders!

AUGMENTED REALITY ALERT!
ON THIS PAGE

Look for the tab— this means there's 3D on the page

Records come to life:

- *Guinness World Records 2014:* book cover
- **Tightest parallel park: pp. 10–11**
- *Dymaxion map:* **pp. 14–15**
- **Largest carnivorous dinosaur: pp. 26–27**
- **Largest spitting cobra: pp. 28–29**
- **Largest wasp: pp. 30–31**
- **Farthest distance skateboarding by a goat: pp. 42–43**
- **Shortest living woman: pp. 44–45**
- *Photo booth:* **pp. 50–51**
- **Tallest peak: pp. 74–75**
- **Most people in a Mini: pp. 106–07**
- **Tallest ridable motorcycle: pp. 156–57**
- **Largest walking robot: pp. 178–79**

AUGMENTED REALITY APP DEVICES COMPATIBILITY

Apple

Operating system: A minimum of Apple iOS 4.3 through to and including iOS 6.1.3	
The supported devices are iPhones 4, 4S and 5, iPad 2, iPad mini (3rd and 4th generation), and iPod touch (4th and 5th generation)	

Android Preferred Device List

Samsung Galaxy Tab 2 (7-inch and 10.1-inch)	Samsung Galaxy S2 and later versions
HTC One range, i.e. S, X, V	HTC Desire range
Asus Google Nexus Tab	Motorola Razr handsets from the last 18 months

For all other devices the absolute minimum specifications are:

ARMv7 Chipset	Open GL 2.0 Graphics
Android version 2.2 up to and including 4.2.2	Rear-facing camera

For more information on device compatibility, go to www.guinnessworldrecords.com/seeit3d

CONTENTS

Extraordinary images: More than 1,500 fabulous photos packed throughout the pages, including specially shot subjects and previously unseen snaps.

Augmented Reality: View the 3D video version of the record with our exclusive app. Download the free app with your mobile device and watch the page come to life! (*Find out more on p. 3.*)

Take 10: Ten related topics in bite-size chunks, including top 10s and time lines.

¡QUOTE
"Wit and wisdom straight from the horse's mouth—or the dinosaur's jaws!"

LOOK OUT FOR CROSS-REFERENCES TO RELATED RECORDS

GUINNESS WORLD RECORDS 2014

In review: A summary of recent key events on each of the sports pages.

Color-coded sections: The new, distinctive design makes it easier than ever to find your favorite records.

Tables and charts: At-a-glance stats and facts at your fingertips in data-rich tables, charts, and lists.

Trivia: Mind-blowing minutiae and behind-the-scenes stories associated with featured records.

Measurements: Startling number-base stats about the record holders and their achievements.

4,000 entries: Fully revised with more than 3,000 new and updated superlative achievements.

Free eBook

So that you can take *Guinness World Records* wherever you go, we're offering a free eBook for you to download to your digital device. Packed full of extra bonus content on your favorite records and with a behind-the-scenes look at Guinness World Records, you'll also get the inside track on how you, too, can be a record-breaker! Learn about how the incredible Augmented Reality was made and don't forget to test your knowledge by entering our competition.
To unlock this free eBook, go to: www.guinnessworldrecords.com/freebook or point your QR reader at the code above.

GWR DAY

Every year in mid-November thousands of people around the world try to set or break records for Guinness World Records Day. Look out for the **GWR Day** logo around the book for records set on 2012's GWR Day.

FOR THE RECORD

Check out **For the Record** boxes—these snippets provide background on record holders and their chosen field of excellence. Get another angle on the most outstanding records of this year and put superlative stats in context.

Actual size: Photos as big as real life! And what's record-breaking about this cockroach? *Turn to p. 32 to find out.*

ACTUAL SIZE

EDITOR'S LETTER

48 number

managed ... ania
before her record
attempt.

Welcome to *Guinness World Records 2014*! As ever, we've been inundated with thousands of claims from all around the world over the past 12 months, and here we bring you the best of the records that made it through our verification process. You'll find a tightrope-walking dog, a bearded woman, a giant motorcycle, and even a vegetable orchestra. It's also been a year of firsts, from Felix Baumgartner's epic skydive from the edge of space to PSY's billion-view pop video, via the first ever solo circumnavigation of the globe using nothing but human power ...

Meet the record holders

Talk show host Wendy Williams greeted new record holders in September 2013 alongside Guinness World Records' Stuart Claxton. Kazuhiro Watanabe (Japan) has the **tallest mohican**. How high? Turn to p. 55 to find out. Zeus is the **tallest dog ever**—and there are more canine capers on pp. 40–41.

To put together a book as packed and as comprehensive as *Guinness World Records*, we've had to sift through 50,000 claims and enquiries, watch countless hours of video footage, adjudicate live at hundreds of events in places as diverse as Siberia and Mauritius, and organize 100 photoshoots around the world.

The USA makes the biggest contribution to record-breaking with 211 claims accepted from 13,268 applications. So congratulations to the likes of Steve-O Gratin for the **most wins of the Mashed Potato Wrestling Championships** (*p. 220*), Scott A. Robb for the **heaviest cabbage** (*p. 136*), and Joshua Mueller for the **largest collection of Converse shoes** (*p. 98*): your country is proud!

Other outstanding Americans in this edition include Olympic stars Michael Phelps (**most**

Most consecutive pirouettes

Sophia Lucia (USA, b. September 7, 2002) completed 55 pirouettes at the San Diego Dance Centre in Poway, California, on March 30, 2013. Sophia, who has performed on TV as a dancer, was just 10 years old when she set her record. There are more Performing Arts records on pp. 114–115.

consecutive Olympic swimming golds in one event) and Melissa "Missy" Franklin (**fastest swim, long-course 200 m backstroke** and the winner of a total of five medals in London 2012), and Andrew Luck announced his arrival in the NFL with the **most passing yards in a first season**. Samuel L. Jackson has made movies that have collectively grossed almost $10 billion, giving him the **highest box-office gross for an actor**. And while Quvenzhané Wallis has some way to go to beat that, she also has the time: born on August 28, 2003, she was the **youngest actress to receive an Oscar nomination**, for *Beasts of the Southern Wild*.

SPORTS STARS

As soon as one *Guinness World Records* book is completed, we start immediately on the next one. Work on this edition began in the summer of 2012, when London—and the world—was caught up in Olympic fever. That summer was always going to be an exciting period for us here at Guinness World Records. It was a record third time that the Olympic Games had been staged in London

Most watermelons crushed with the head in one minute

Showing on truTV from February 2013, *Guinness World Records Gone Wild!* features Commentator Zach Selwyn, Host Dan Cortese, and Adjudicators Stuart Claxton and Liz Smith (*pictured left to right*). Look out for hopefuls such as Trizzie D. (*below*), who uses his head to destroy melons. Did he beat the record previously set at 43 by Tafzi Ahmed (Germany) on May 27, 2011? *Find all of this year's food feats on pp. 62–65.*

PEG FOR MERCY
TV hopefuls try for the **most clothes pegs clipped on the face**: check out the total they're up against on p. 51.

truTV

NOT REALITY. ACTUALITY.™

Longest-running show on Broadway

The Phantom of the Opera recorded its 10,000th performance on February 11, 2012. On January 26, 2013, the musical marked 25 years on Broadway. It also has the **highest box-office theater gross worldwide**, with an estimated $5.6 billion.

circus and sideshow artists at a temporary space in London's South Bank. Multiple record holder Space Cowboy—aka Chayne Hultgren (Australia)—invited us along to various shows and performances, where we made plenty of new friends and inducted some of the more talented members into our records database. To make the most of this exciting new material, we created a special Circus chapter, which you'll find on pp. 80–91.

1957
Year in which Dr. Seuss first published the Cat in the Hat character.

Most people wearing Cat in the Hat hats

If you don't want to set a record on your own, you can always do it with a friend—or many more: like the 281 people who wore Cat in the Hat hats on February 4, 2013. The event was organized by Random House Children's Books and the Jeff Gordon Foundation (both USA) in New York. More gargantuan gatherings themed by weird and wonderful costumes—including fictional characters—can be found on pp. 106–07.

but the first time since Guinness World Records was founded in 1954. As expected, the Olympics was a record-breaking spectacular, and we were able to document hundreds of superlatives. It was a real honor to meet some of the athletes and present their Guinness World Records certificates in person, so thank you to all those who found the time. You'll find the highlights from the Olympics—and every other major sporting event—in this year's Sports chapter starting on p. 218.

Another high point of summer for us was London Wonderground—a showcase of the world's more extreme

Largest coloring book

The Hub Network and Hasbro made a book measuring 32.23 sq. ft. (3 m²) in New York on November 10, 2012. Freddie Hoff (*above right*) from GWR was there to present the certificate to actress Melissa Joan Hart— but it's not the **largest book ever**. For that and more Big Stuff, you'll have to check out pp. 96–97.

Wonderground provided our talented team of photographers— led by Picture Editor Michael Whitty—with a wide and varied pool of talent to photograph. The picture team have, once again, pulled out all the f-stops to provide some incredible imagery, traveling the world to bring you the likes of the **largest walking robot** from Germany (*pp. 178–79*), the **largest cat** from the USA (*pp. 24–25*), Ozzy the tightrope-walking dog from the UK (*p. 41*), and Vivian Wheeler from the USA, owner of the **longest female beard** (*p. 55*).

An exciting new development for Guinness World Records over the past year has been its new TV series. As well as *Guinness*

World Records Gone Wild!, which you can read more about on p. 6, there was *Officially Amazing*, hosted by Ben Shires on the UK's CBBC channel to celebrate the best records—and some valiant claims that might not have been quite so successful! These shows have provided yet more ways to receive one of those prized Guinness

Largest collection of shoes to recycle

The generous readers of *National Geographic Kids* magazine (USA) had collected a record 16,407 shoes for recycling in Washington, D.C., by February 5, 2013. Celebrity contributions included old foot furniture from the likes of One Direction, Taylor Swift, Eli Manning, Danica Patrick, Carl Lewis, and Amanda Beard. Guinness World Records' Mike Janela adjudicated.

SHOES ON SHOW
The collection was displayed at National Geographic's headquarters in Washington, D.C.

EDITOR'S LETTER

World Records certificates, alongside our increasingly popular Challengers website. Find out more—including how you can get your name in the world's **biggest-selling copyright book**—on pp. 10–11.

Most summer Olympics attended

Before you read about the oldest people (*pp. 58–59*), meet Harry Nelson (USA, aged 90), who has been to 18 Olympics (1932–2012). A fan of track and field, Harry has missed just one Olympics: the 1936 Games in Nazi Germany.

EXPERT ADVISORS

We welcomed to our team of consultants Iain Borden, Professor of Architecture and Urban Culture at the Bartlett School of Architecture at UCL in London, UK. Iain's passion for the subject inspired us to include a new chapter—Urban Life, starting on p. 138—and gave him a chance to indulge his other passion: skateboarding (*pp. 108–09*).

Other new additions to the consultants include adventures chronicler Eberhard Jurgalski, who has provided invaluable

Most frequent clapper

It's been calculated that, as of January 31, 2013, *Wheel of Fortune* hostess Vanna White (USA) has clapped 3,480,864 times during 30 seasons of the game show! The handy hostess has also appeared in all but 10 of the 5,754 episodes since September 19, 1983. You'll find more TV records on pp. 214–15.

help in our Pioneers chapter (*pp. 66–79*), Finland's extreme body modifier Samppa von Cyborg (*pp. 46–47*), and academic historian and economist Glen O'Hara, who brings his expertise to our Money & Economics records on pp. 122–23.

The consultants provide essential support—this team alone is responsible for more than 3,000 new and updated records this year alone, in addition to the new claims-based records—so a

BASKET-BALLROOM The Globetrotters started in Chicago, USA, as the Savoy Big Five, promoting the newly established Savoy Ballroom in 1927.

Tallest basketball player

Kevin Daley (Panama, *left*) and Paul Sturgess (UK), pictured with Adjudicator Stuart Claxton, both play with the Harlem Globetrotters. But at 7 ft. 7.26 in. (231.8 cm), it's Paul—ironically known as "Tiny"—who is the **tallest basketball player**, a title he has held since November 14, 2011. The **tallest basketball player ever** was Suleiman Ali Nashnush (Libya, 1943–91), who was reputed to be 8 ft. 0.25 in. (245 cm) when he played for the Libyan team in 1962. For a detailed review of the year in basketball, including all the news from the London 2012 Olympics, turn to p. 232.

Most people making sandwiches simultaneously

Restaurant cook Salvador Rodriguez (*above left*) and New York Giants' Justin Tuck (*above right*; both USA) celebrated as they led 254 enthusiastic chefs at Subway in TimesCenter, New York, on August 15, 2012. There are many more feats of food to feast on in the mouth-watering section starting on p. 62.

Largest astronomy lesson

There were 526 trainee stargazers gathered at a full-scale model of the *James Webb* space telescope (*inset*) on March 10, 2013. The star-studded event was organized by NASA, the Space Telescope Science Institute (STScI), and Northrop Grumman Corporation. The picture above is of Sara Wilcox presenting the GWR certificate to Frank Summers and Dan McCallister on the night. This year's book is packed with extraterrestrial action—Space Telescopes (*pp. 182–83*), civilians who made it off Earth commercially (*pp. 184–85*), and Moons (*pp. 186–87*).

where you spot the SEE IT 3D icon. It's your chance to be snapped alongside Jyoti Amge (the world's **shortest living woman**, *pp. 44–45*, see the full 360-degree view from the top of Mount Everest (the world's **highest peak**, *p. 74*) without having to leave the comfort of your armchair, and get close to the **largest carnivorous dinosaur** (*p. 26*).

Talking of dinosaurs, the feature on pp. 26–27 is the brainchild of our design team at 55 Design. When faced with the challenge of showing readers just how enormous dinosaurs were, artists Paul and

2004
Year of first Pogopalooza—the celebration of Xpogo sports—in Lincoln, Nebraska.

Most pogo stick jumps in one minute

Tone Staubs (USA) performed 265 jumps at Chelsea Piers in Stamford, Connecticut, on November 15, 2012. Enthusiasts of wacky sports can be found all over the world—and all over pp. 220–21.

big thanks to all our advisors and sources, old and new, who have helped with collating and approving superlatives for the book.

FREE APP

Fans of the Augmented Reality feature we introduced last year will be pleased to see that it's back again for this edition—only bigger and better than before. We've teamed up with the UK's Red Frog to bring you fully animated 3D graphics, interactive photographs, and video footage, available to readers with a tablet device or smartphone. Just download the free app and point your device at any page

Largest hamburger

Black Bear Casino Resort (USA) prepared a heavyweight burger weighing 2,014 lb. (913.54 kg) in Carlton, Minnesota, on September 2, 2012. It was topped with 52 lb. 8 oz. (23.81 kg) of tomatoes, 50 lb. (22.68 kg) of lettuce, 60 lb. (27.22 kg) of onion, 19 lb. (8.62 kg) of pickle, 40 lb. (18.14 kg) of cheese, and 16.5 lb. (7.48 kg) of bacon.

Rich took inspiration from the beautiful—and realistic—toys from the Germany manufacturer Schleich and created a fantasy scene in which these prehistoric creatures invade London's Trafalgar Square. Thanks to both 55 Design and Schleich for helping us visualize this topic.

If you want to have a go at breaking a record and perhaps raise money for charity at the same time, just turn the page to find out how to get your record registered. You don't need to throw yourself out of a balloon from space or clock up a billion views on YouTube to get your name in the book—record-breaking is free and open to anyone to have a go. Whatever you attempt, good luck! In the meantime, enjoy this year's book …

Craig Glenday
Editor-in-Chief
Follow me on Twitter:
@craigglenday

Most expensive pet wedding

Congratulations to Baby Hope Diamond (a Coton de Tulear, *left*) and Chilly Pasternak (a Virginia Poodle), whose nuptials—or puptials?—in New York's Central Park on July 12, 2012 were valued at a record $158,187.26! The bow vows were exchanged as part of an event in support of the Humane Society of New York. Want more amazing animals? Pets are on pp. 42–43 and Bizarre Beasts on pp. 36–37.

¡QUOTE
"It gets very heavy—I have to balance the mohawk and it does make me a little tired at the end of the day."

Tallest mohican

Kazuhiro Watanabe is certainly a hair-raising record holder, but how does his massive mohican compare with the largest wig or the biggest afro? We've combed our database for the best hairy records, so head over to pp. 54–55 to find out. Kazuhiro is seen here at the launch of *Guinness World Records 2013* in Washington Square Park, New York City.

BE A RECORD-BREAKER

Are you Officially Amazing? Prove it to our Adjudicators ...

With Guinness World Records books, TV shows, Web sites, digital editions, and live events, it's never been easier to showcase your superlative talents!

Record-breaking is free of charge and you can apply wherever you are in the world—visit www.guinnessworldrecords.com and tell us all about your idea. If you're successful, your record will be put on a shortlist by the Editors, so you may even see your name in next year's edition of the world's **best-selling copyright book!**

Challengers online

You can break a record right now—what are you waiting for? Head over to **www.guinnessworldrecords.com/challengers** and pick a challenge—or suggest a new one. All you need to do is video your attempt and upload it. You might achieve the **most dice stacked into a tower in one minute** (Eric Richey, *above right*, set a record of 40 on September 17, 2012) or the **fastest time to drink 0.11 gal (500 ml) of water** (Tom Maryniak, *right*, set a time of 2.6 seconds on November 15, 2011).

1: Your first task as a claimant is to soak up Guinness World Records in every format to find a record that you want to attempt; or if you have a new idea, reading the books and watching the shows will give you an idea of the kind of thing we like to see.

2: The easiest way to reach us is via **www.guinnessworldrecords.com** and use the application form to tell us as much as you can about your idea. Try to do this a few weeks before you plan to make your attempt to give us plenty of time to consider it.

3: If we like your idea (or if it's an existing record category), we'll send you the official guidelines that you, and everyone else who attempts the record, must follow; if we're not wild about your suggestion, we'll tell you why.

4: Gather your evidence and send it in to us—we'll need independent eyewitness statements, photos, video, and so on. Check your guidelines for the specific requirements for your chosen record.

We'll be the judge of that...

In the summer of 2012, we officially unveiled the new Guinness World Records Adjudicator uniforms, and pictured here are some of the team modeling the new look. You don't need to have an Adjudicator at your record attempt—you can just send us all the necessary evidence we need to assess your claim remotely. Here's our five-step guide to making an application:

Guinness World Records Gone Wild!

Guinness World Records made a welcome return to U.S. TV screens with *Guinness World Records Gone Wild!*, hosted by Dan Cortese, pictured above with Adjudicator Stuart Claxton and Canadian record holders Sweet Pepper Klopek and Burnaby Q. Orbax (*see p. 86*). As its name suggests, the show celebrates the more outrageous forms of record-breaking, such as Mike O'Hearn's (USA) epic smash through the **most sheets of tempered glass** (18 panes).

Officially Amazing

UK fans of Guinness World Records had the chance to catch our Adjudicators in action on *Officially Amazing*. This new BBC TV show came complete with its own mascots (*left*), and the team went all over the world in search of the most heart-stopping records, including the **tightest parallel park**. A tiny 5.16-in. (13.1-cm) gap was left by John Moffatt (UK), parking his old-style Mini Mayfair between two other autos on location with the show in Hereford, UK, on December 10, 2012. Check out the clip for yourself using the free Augmented Reality app (*find out how to access it on p. 3*).

SEE THE VIDEO WITH THE FREE APP

OFFICIALLY AMAZING

GUINNESS WORLD RECORDS 2014

AUGMENTED REALITY ALERT! ON THIS PAGE

KEEP ON BREAKING
Some claimants make record-breaking a way of life—meet the record addicts who just can't stop, on pp. 94–95.

28 Number of buckets in a seven-layer bucket pyramid record attempt.

5: Wait for the results; if you're not successful, don't give up! You can try again or attempt a different record. If you're successful, you'll receive your certificate for being Officially Amazing!

Guinness World Records live events

Look out for record-breaking opportunities at one of the Guinness World Records live event shows. They happen all around the world and are a chance for anyone to have a go. Why not try for the **fastest time to build a seven-layer cardboard bucket pyramid**? You'll have to beat John Ric G. Villanueva (Philippines, *not pictured*), who took just 35.72 seconds to build his seven-stage pyramid in an event at the Marina Mall in Salmiya, Kuwait, on March 16, 2013.

FACT: OMG! host Oli White (*below*) set a record for the **fastest time to eat a jam doughnut with no hands** and without licking his lips, taking 30.53 seconds during the live launch of OMG! on October 26, 2012. Well done, Oli!

Premium services

Our free record application service takes four to six weeks. The entire process—from your first application to the delivery of an official Guinness World Records certificate if your attempt is approved—is offered without charge. If you need a quicker response, however, you can apply for a fast-track service that allocates a Records Manager immediately and guarantees a response within three days. There are other premium services available—such as corporate events, marketing options, and so on. Find out more at www.guinnessworldrecords.com.

OMG!

This year saw the launch of the new Guinness World Records: OMG! YouTube channel www.youtube.com/GWRomg Hosted by a gang of famous YouTube faces, OMG! offers various strands such as "Do Try this at Home" and "Slo-Mo Test Lab." The channel has had more than 8 million views since it launched on October 26, 2012. Pictured below right are the team presenting the two-hour live launch along with Guinness World Records Community Manager Dan Barrett.

Costliest natural disaster

Tsunamis are often incorrectly called tidal waves, and they can be caused by a variety of events such as volcanic eruptions, earthquakes, glacier calvings, and asteroid impacts. The effects of a tsunami making land can be devastating, as the people of Japan learned in March 2011. The cost to the insurance industry from this tsunami, which resulted from an earthquake off the coast of the country, is currently estimated to be $32 billion.

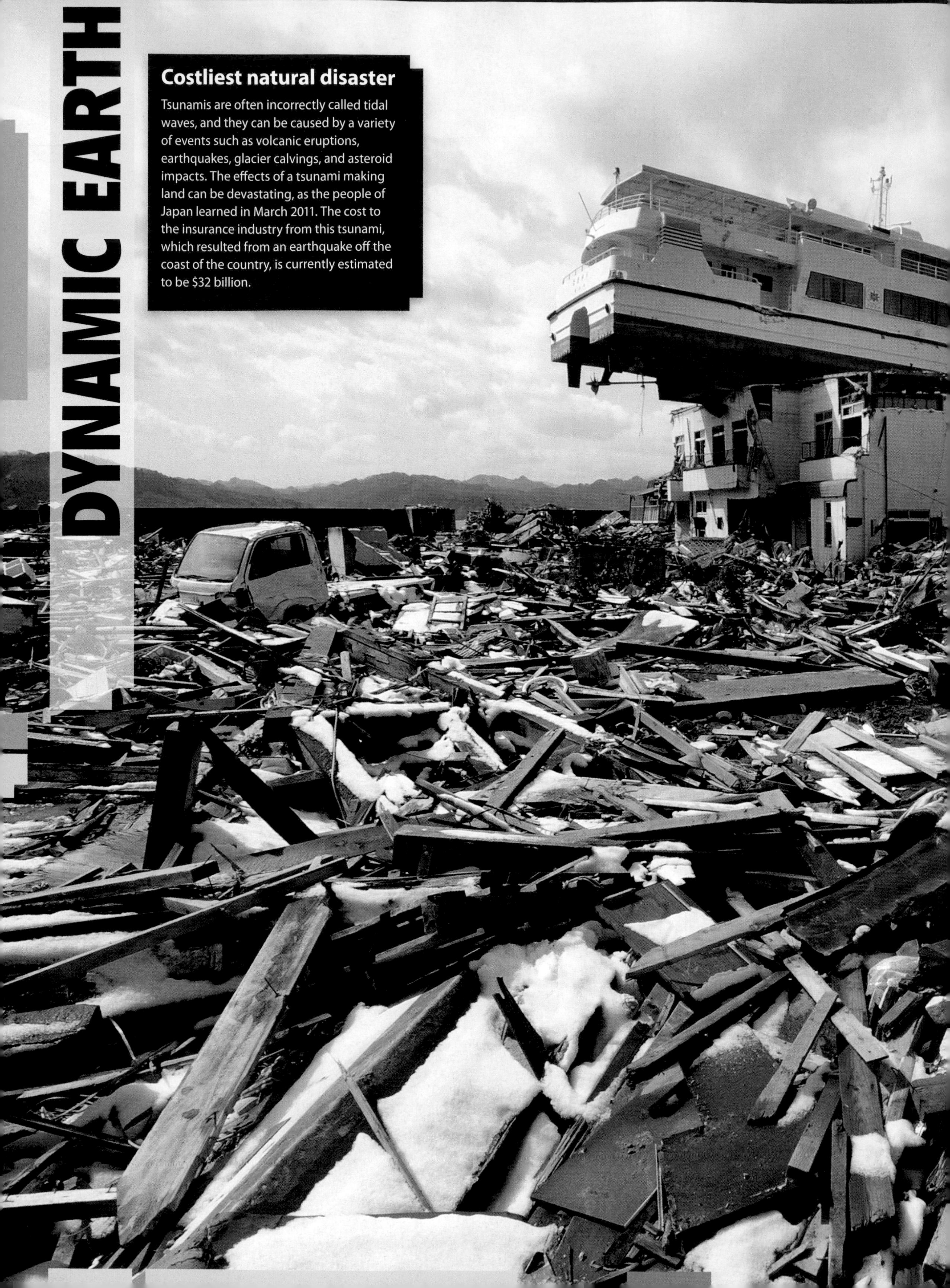

GUINNESS WORLD RECORDS 2014

WAVE OF DESTRUCTION
This image of Ōtsuchi, Iwate Prefecture, on March 24, 2011 shows a yacht stranded on a two-story building by the tsunami.

RESTLESS PLANET

Mapping the world's most extreme forces of nature

Earth is a dynamic planet: we live on an ever-shifting crust, beneath which churns an ocean of molten rock, and our climatic and environmental systems—which are unique in the Solar System—are in constant flux. Together, these forces—volcanoes, earthquakes, tornadoes, tsunamis and extremes of temperature—shape our planet and affect billions of lives.

We're shaken by 8,000 earthquakes of various intensity every day and live in the shadow of 1,500 active volcanoes. On a daily basis, we are influenced by the weather, which at its worst can be catastrophic, wiping out entire communities. Yet, despite the horrors we often see on the news, such events are responsible for just 0.06% of global deaths on a yearly basis.

Here, we map some of the major events that have made Planet Earth what it is today. "Change is," according to NASA, "perhaps the only constant in our planet's history."

Largest active volcano
Mauna Loa in Hawaii, USA, has the shape of a broad gentle dome 75 miles (120 km) long and 31 miles (50 km) wide above sea level; it has a total volume of 10,200 cu. miles (42,500 km³), and its last major eruption was in 1984.

105,000 years ago
Highest tsunami triggered by a submarine landslide
Sediment deposited by a tsunami at an altitude of 1,230 ft. (375 m) on Lanai, Hawaii, USA, following a submarine landslide.

May 18, 1980
Largest landslide (modern day)
96,000 million cu. ft. (2,800 million m³) of rock slipped down Mt. St Helens in Washington, USA, immediately prior to an eruption; also the **fastest avalanche** (250 mph; 402.3 km/h).

April 18, 1906
Worst fire damage
A fire caused by the San Francisco earthquake, USA, left the city with a repair bill of $350 million (worth $8.97 billion today).

February 13–19, 1959
Greatest snowstorm
189 in. (4,800 mm) of snow fell in a single snowstorm at Mt. Shasta Ski Bowl in California, USA.

-128.6
Record low temperature, in Fahrenheit, recorded at Vostok, Antarctica, on July 21, 1983.

May 31, 1970
Highest death toll from a single landslide
18,000+ killed in a single landslide of rock debris from Mt. Huascarán, Peru.

May 22, 1960
Most powerful recorded earthquake
M9.5 quake, near Lumaco, Chile; more than 2,000 killed, 3,000 injured, and an estimated 2 million people homeless.

April 10, 1996
Fastest wind speed
Tornado wind speed of 302 mph (486 km/h) clocked near Bridge Creek, Oklahoma, USA.

SEE IT **3D** WITH THE FREE APP

May 3, 1999
Largest tornado
Twister with a diameter of 5,250 ft. (1,600 m) measured near Mulhall, Oklahoma, USA.

October 8, 1871
Deadliest wildfire
An estimated 1,200 to 2,500 people killed as forest fires burned through northeast Wisconsin and upper Michigan, USA; more than 1,500 sq. miles (3,800 km²) of forest and farms destroyed.

FROM 3D TO 2D: THE DYMAXION MAP

The map projection featured above is inspired by the creations of the U.S. author, designer, and futurist Richard Buckminster "Bucky" Fuller (1895–1983). Typically, when three-dimensional globes are mapped onto two-dimensional surfaces, the continents become distorted. To reduce this effect, Fuller projected the continents onto an icosahedron—a regular polyhedron with 20 triangular faces and 30 edges—which could then be unfolded in various ways to create maps. With this "Dymaxion" world view, there is no right way up, producing a culturally neutral view of our planet.

January 12, 2010
Deadliest earthquake (modern day)
15.5 miles (25 km) from Port-au-Prince, Haiti; between 100,000 and 316,000 killed.

GUINNESS WORLD RECORDS 2014

Tsunami Volcano Tornado Wildfire Blizzard Flood Earthquake Heatwave Landslide

AD 130
Most violent eruption
Estimated 33 billion tons of pumice ejected in the Taupo eruption in New Zealand, flattening an area of 6,200 sq. miles (16,000 km²).

September 1, 1923
Most destructive earthquake
Greatest physical devastation from a quake; 575,000 dwellings in Kantō Plain, Japan, destroyed; death toll calculated at 142,807.

April 5–10, 1815
Greatest eruption volume
Estimated 36–43 cu. miles (150–180 km³) of matter discharged from Tambora on Sumbawa, Indonesia; caused the **greatest recorded impact on the climate for a volcanic eruption**, forcing global temperatures to drop 5.4°F (3°C), and the **largest death toll from a volcanic eruption** (92,000 killed); *artist's impression above*.

April 10, 1996
Fastest wind speed (non tornado)
Wind speed of 253 mph (408 km/h) recorded at Barrow Island, Australia.

March 11, 2011
Costliest natural disaster
Tsunami resulting from earthquake off the coast of Japan cost insurance companies approximately $32 billion.

January 23, 1556
Deadliest earthquake
Shaanxi, Shanxi, and Henan provinces, China; believed to have killed 830,000 people.

July 9, 1958
Highest tsunami wash
1,719-ft.-high (524-m) wave washed along the fjordlike Lituya Bay in Alaska, USA, following a landslip.

18,000 years ago
Greatest flood
An ancient lake in Siberia about 75 miles (120 km) long ruptured, causing a freshwater flood 1,600 ft. (490 m) deep that traveled at 100 mph (160 km/h).

October 1887
Deadliest flood
900,000 people killed when the Huang He (Yellow River) in Huayan Kou, China, flooded its banks.

December 26, 2004
Longest earthquake
The Sumatra-Andaman Islands quake, Indonesia, lasted between 500 and 600 seconds.

December 16, 1920
Deadliest landslide
A series of landslides, triggered by a single earthquake in Gansu Province, China, accounted for most of the 180,000 people killed in the event.

April 26, 1989
Deadliest tornado
1,300 people killed in Shaturia, Bangladesh, and as many as 50,000 people made homeless.

April 12, 2012
Most powerful strike-slip earthquake
M8.6 quake struck off the west coast of northern Sumatra, Indonesia.

July 10, 1949
Worst landslide damage toll
Landslide caused by a quake in Khait district of the Gharm Oblast in Tajikistan buried 33 villages and killed an estimated 28,000 people.

December 26, 2004
Worst rail disaster
Estimated 800–1,500 people killed when *Queen of the Sea* passenger train was swept off its tracks by a tsunami near the Sri Lankan village of Telwatta.

Summer 2010
Deadliest heatwave
Up to 56,000 people in Russia died as a result of overheating, droughts, forest fires, and smog.

February 3–9, 1972
Deadliest blizzard
4,000 people are estimated to have died when parts of rural Iran were blanketed in 10 ft. (3 m) of snow, ending a four-year drought.

Most tornadoes by area
The Netherlands has one tornado for every 769 sq. miles (1,991 km²) of land; the USA has one per (3,161 sq. miles (8,187 km²).

93.2
Highest annual mean temperature in Fahrenheit (over six years, 1960–66) in Dallol, Ethiopia.

AUGMENTED REALITY ALERT!
3D ON THIS PAGE

January 10, 1977
Fastest lava flow
Lava from the eruption of Nyiragongo in the Democratic Republic of the Congo traveled at speeds up to 40 mph (60 km/h); also boasts the **largest lava lake** at 820 ft. (250 m) across.

EARTHQUAKES

Most powerful earthquake

The largest instrumentally measured quake is generally acknowledged to be the Chilean earthquake of May 22, 1960, which had a magnitude of 9.5 using the moment magnitude scale and 8.3 using the Richter scale (see For the Record, opposite page). In Chile, it killed more than 2,000 people, injured 3,000 more, and left an estimated two million people homeless. The resulting tsunami (giant wave) caused great damage and about 200 deaths thousands of miles away in Hawaii, Japan, and on the U.S. West Coast.

Deadliest earthquake of modern times

At 9:53 p.m. (UTC*) on January 12, 2010, a magnitude-7 earthquake struck with an epicenter around 15 miles (25 km) west of the Haitian capital Port-au-Prince. One year after the disaster, official estimates from the Haitian government put the number of people killed by the quake at 316,000, although other estimates place the death toll as low as 100,000. Some 1.3 million people were displaced by the earthquake and 97,294 houses destroyed. Much of Port-au-Prince was reduced to rubble (pictured); to this day, vast numbers of Haitians remain homeless.

* Coordinated Universal Time, the International Telecommunications Union's global time standard

Highest estimated death toll from an earthquake

An estimated 830,000 fatalities occurred after a prolonged earthquake (or dizhen) took place in the Shaanxi, Shanxi, and Henan provinces of China on January 23, 1556.

Year with the most major earthquakes

According to data from the U.S. Geological Survey, Earth experiences an average of 16 major earthquakes with a magnitude of 7 or above each year. Since long-term records began, around 1900, the year with the most major quakes was 2010, in which there were 24 earthquakes with magnitudes measuring 7 or above.

Worst devastation caused by a quake

The quake on the Kanto plain, Japan, on September 1, 1923, had a magnitude of 7.9. In Tokyo and Yokohama, 575,000 dwellings were destroyed. The official total of persons killed and missing in what was called the dai-shinsai ("great quake") and resultant fires is 142,800.

Most powerful strike-slip earthquake

At 8:30 a.m. (UTC) on April 11, 2012, an 8.6-magnitude earthquake struck in the eastern Indian Ocean. Fears that the three-minute event would cause a major tsunami were unfounded as the quake was of a strike-slip nature, in which Earth's crust was displaced horizontally on each side of the fault instead of upward or downward.

Longest earthquake

The Great Sumatra-Andaman earthquake in the Indian Ocean on December 26, 2004 lasted for between 500 and 600 seconds. It had a moment magnitude of 9.1. These results were announced in the journal Science in May 2005.

The event also gave rise to the **longest earthquake fault rupture ever measured** in terms of distance. The rupture occurred along an estimated

FIRST SEISMOGRAPH

The earliest modern seismographs were developed in 1848, but the oldest form of earthquake-detecting equipment can be traced back to AD 132 in China. The first device was designed by the Chinese Astronomer Royal, Zhang Heng, who built a 6-in. (15-cm) bronze vessel containing a pendulum. Ground movement would cause the pendulum to dislodge balls, which would fall into the mouths of bronze sculptures formed in the shape of toads, signaling an earthquake.

DEADLIEST EARTHQUAKES OF THE PAST 100 YEARS

Dec 16, 1920:
Haiyuan, China
Death toll: 200,000
Magnitude: 7.8

Sep 1, 1923:
Kanto, Japan
Death toll: 142,800
Magnitude: 7.9

Oct 5, 1948: Ashgabat, Turkmen
Soviet Socialist Republic
Death toll: 110,000
Magnitude: 7.3

May 31, 1970:
Chimbote, Peru
Death toll: 70,000
Magnitude: 7.9

Jul 27, 1976:
Tangshan, China
Death toll: 242,769
Magnitude: 7.5

Source: U.S. Geological Survey

DYNAMIC EARTH
www.guinnessworldrecords.com

GUINNESS
WORLD
RECORDS
2014

3,000: Miles traveled by the 2004 tsunami. It reached as far as Africa.

Highest tsunami death toll

On December 26, 2004, an earthquake with a magnitude of 9.1 occurred under the Indian Ocean, off the coast of Indonesia. The resulting tsunami wave inundated the coastlines of nine countries around the Indian Ocean. The total death toll may never be known but more than 226,000 people are believed to have perished in the devastating event.

720–780 miles (1,200–1,300 km) of the boundary between the Indo-Australian Plate and the southeastern part of the Eurasian Plate. In places, the displacement of ocean floor along the fault was as much as 50 ft. (15 m).

In the wake of the event, the UK's Tsunami Earthquake Appeal received £10,676,836 ($19,863,186) in donations via the Disasters Emergency Committee Web site, from 6:16 p.m. on December 30 to 6:16 p.m. on December 31, 2004. This represents the **most money donated online in 24 hours**.

Worst tsunami-induced nuclear accident

On March 11, 2011, a megathrust earthquake struck off the coast of Japan with a magnitude of 9.03. The quake and resulting tsunami led to a series of meltdowns, failures, and releases of radioactive material at the Fukushima 1 Nuclear Power Plant in Japan. The International Atomic Energy Agency classified the event as a "Level 7," only the second nuclear disaster to ever receive this status.

Largest earthquake drill

On October 18, 2012, around 9.4 million people took part in the fifth annual Great California ShakeOut across the seismically active U.S. state.

Longest jail sentence for not accurately predicting an earthquake

On October 22, 2012, a regional Italian court gave six-year jail sentences to six scientists and a government official charged with manslaughter over the deaths of 309 people killed in the magnitude-6.3 earthquake that struck the Italian city of L'Aquila at 1:30 a.m. (UTC) on April 6, 2009. The judges decided that the seven men had downplayed the risk of a major quake in the days before it struck.

Worst fire disaster (damage toll)

The fire following the earthquake on April 18, 1906 in San Francisco, USA, cost an estimated $350 million at the time, equivalent to $8.97 billion in 2012. The devastating quake leveled about 80 percent of the city.

QUAKE STATISTICS
There are an estimated 500,000 detectable earthquakes per year, of which 100,000 can be felt and about 100 cause damage.

FOR THE RECORD

In the past, the power of earthquakes was usually assessed using the Richter magnitude scale, devised in 1935 by Dr. Charles Richter (USA, *right*). Today, the moment magnitude scale, introduced in 1979, is regarded as a more accurate system of measurement.

WHEN WEATHER GOES WILD … TURN TO P. 22

Most powerful earthquakes ever documented

Date	Location	Magnitude
Jul 8, 1730	Valparaíso, Chile	8.7
Nov 1, 1755	Lisbon, Portugal	8.7
Feb 4, 1965	Rat Islands, Alaska, USA	8.7
Jan 31, 1906	Offshore Esmeraldas, Ecuador	8.8
Feb 27, 2010	Offshore Bío-Bío, Chile	8.8
Jan 26, 1700	Present-day British Columbia, Canada, to California, USA	9.0
Aug 13, 1868	Arica, Peru (now Chile)	9.0
Nov 4, 1952	Kamchatka, USSR (now Russia)	9.0
Mar 11, 2011	East of Honshu, Japan	9.0
Dec 26, 2004	Sumatra-Andaman Islands, Indonesia	9.1
Mar 28, 1964	Prince William Sound, Alaska, USA	9.2
May 22, 1960	Nr. Lumaco, Chile	9.5

Timeline:

1990

2004

2005

2008

2010

Jun 20, 1990: Northern Iran
Death toll: 50,000
Magnitude: 7.4

Dec 26, 2004: Sumatra, Indonesia
Death toll: 226,000
Magnitude: 9.1

Oct 8, 2005: Pakistan
Death toll: 86,000
Magnitude: 7.6

May 12, 2008: Eastern Sichuan, China
Death toll: 87,587
Magnitude: 7.9

Jan 12, 2010: Haiti
Death toll: 316,000
Magnitude: 7

VOLCANOES

Most active volcano

The shield volcano Kīlauea is one of the five volcanoes that make up the island of Hawaii, USA. Its current episode of activity began on January 3, 1983. By January 3, 2013, Kīlauea had covered 48.46 sq. miles (125.5 km²) with lava flows, created 499 acres (202 ha) of new land, and erupted about 0.96 cu. miles (4 km³) of lava.

EXPLOSIVE REPUTATION
Kīlauea has seen 61 individual eruptions since 1823. No surprise, then, that its name translates as "spewing."

Oldest description of a volcanic eruption

Gaius Plinius Caecilius Secundus (aka Pliny the Younger) and his father, Pliny the Elder, witnessed the eruption of Vesuvius, Italy, in AD 79, which buried the Roman cities of Pompeii and Herculaneum, killing around 16,000 people—including Pliny the Elder. Around 25 years later, Pliny the Younger sent two letters to his friend, the historian Tacitus, providing details of the eruption and its aftermath.

Highest death toll from a volcanic eruption

A total of 92,000 people died after the Tambora volcano in Sumbawa, Indonesia (then Dutch East Indies), erupted from April 5 to 10, 1815.

Closest point to human extinction

The eruption of Indonesia's Toba supervolcano ca. 75,000 years ago, ejected some 192 cu. miles (800 km³) of ash into the atmosphere and created the **largest volcanic crater** on Earth, covering 685 sq. miles (1,775 km²). The resulting tsunamis and volcanic winter are thought to have reduced the human population to as few as 10,000.

Largest flood basalt eruption of historic times

In around AD 924, the Icelandic volcanic fissure system known as Eldgjá began an eruption that lasted between four and seven years. The eruption occurred from several vents along a 46-mile (75-km) discontinuous system of fissures and produced about 4.7 cu. miles (19.6 km³) of lava.

Most recent eruption with a Volcanic Explosivity Index of 8

The Volcanic Explosivity Index (VEI) is used to measure the relative explosiveness of volcanoes and ranges from 0 to 8. VEI 8 indicates an eruption in which more than 280 cu. miles (1,000 km³) of volcanic material is ejected. The last such event was the Oruanui eruption of the Taupo volcano in New Zealand, some 26,500 years ago. It ejected around 280 cu. miles (1,170 km³) of material and formed a huge caldera (a volcanic crater) in which Lake Taupo, New Zealand's largest lake, now sits.

Tallest volcanic columns

Devils Tower in Wyoming, USA, was formed as an underground intrusion of igneous rock more than 50 million years ago. Over time, the surrounding softer sedimentary rock eroded, leaving the monolithic landmark towering over the current landscape. It is composed of volcanic columns, formed as the molten intrusion cooled and shrank, some of which measure 600 ft. (180 m) tall.

Deadliest lahars

On November 13, 1985, the Nevado del Ruiz volcano in Colombia erupted. Hot rock and ash flows melted and mixed with ice and snow on the volcano and created four volcanic mudflows, or "lahars." These raced down the volcano's flanks at 40 mph (60 km/h), adding clay and soil from the river valleys they traveled through. Within four hours, the lahars had traveled 62 miles (100 km) and killed 23,000 people.

Largest island in a lake on an island in a lake on an island

Within Taal Lake, on the island of Luzon, Philippines, lies the Taal volcano, whose central crater is now a lake, called Crater Lake. Vulcan Point is a tiny island, some 130 ft. (40 m) across, situated within Crater Lake.

TOWERING ACHIEVEMENT
The Giant's Causeway in Ireland is another famous example of the same type of volcanic column as Devils Tower.

DEADLIEST ERUPTIONS OF THE PAST 100 YEARS

1919

1951

1951

1963

1980

Began May 19, 1919:
Mount Kelud, Java, Indonesia
Death toll: 5,115 (from mudflows)

Began Jan 18, 1951: Mount Lamington, Papua New Guinea
Death toll: 2,942 (from ash flows)

Began Dec 4, 1951:
Mount Hibok-Hibok, Camiguin island, Philippines
Death toll: 500 (from ash flows)

Began Feb 18, 1963:
Mount Agung, Bali, Indonesia
Death toll: 1,184 (from ash flows)

Began May 18, 1980:
Mount St. Helens, Washington, USA
Death toll: 57 (from ash flows)

250
Width in miles of plume of ash and gas from 1991 eruption of Pinatubo.

Smallest volcanoes

Sand volcanoes, or sand blows, are formed during earthquakes when water is squeezed out from subsurface layers, carrying sediment with it that erupts on to the surface. The largest sand volcanoes are only around a few feet across, with heights of several tens of inches.

LARGEST ...

Active volcano

Mauna Loa in Hawaii, USA, has the shape of a broad, gentle dome 75 miles (120 km) long and 31 miles (50 km) wide (above sea level), with lava flows occupying 1,980 sq. miles (5,125 km²) of the island. It has a total volume of 10,200 cu. miles (42,500 km³), of which 84.2 percent is below sea level.

Flood basalt eruption

Around 248.3 million years ago, a million-year-long eruption of lava began in what is now Siberia. Several million cubic miles of lava erupted from the Earth's crust, covering about 772,000 sq. miles (2 million km²). The Siberian Traps eruptive period was a potential cause of the Permian-Triassic extinction, the greatest in history.

The largest explosion in historic times

occurred on August 27, 1883, with the eruption of Krakatoa in the Sunda Strait, Indonesia. The ash cloud rose 30–50 miles (48–80 km) high and the explosion was heard 2,968 miles (4,776 km) away.

Island created by eruptions

The largest volcanic island is Iceland, which was formed from volcanic eruptions from the mid-Atlantic Ridge, upon which it sits. Measuring 39,768 sq. miles (103,000 km²), Iceland is essentially ocean floor exposed above the ocean surface.

Maar

A maar is a low, wide volcanic crater formed by a phreatomagmatic eruption (in which groundwater is explosively turned into steam upon interacting with magma.) The Devil Mountain Lakes maar, part of the Bering Land Bridge National Preserve on the Seward Peninsula off Alaska, USA, is a composite of two craters covering some 11.5 sq. miles (30 km²) and is up to 656 ft. (200 m) deep. It formed about 17,500 years ago, and its unusual size is due to the underground magma interacting with permafrost rather than water.

Volcanic mudflow

The Osceola Mudflow occurred 5,600 years ago and began on top of Mount Rainier in the U.S. Cascade mountain range. The mudflow is the result of a volcanic debris flow of about 0.7 cu. miles (3 km³). By the time it reached Puget Sound, more than 62 miles (100 km) away, the mudflow still had a thickness of about 100 ft. (30 m).

Largest stratospheric SO$_2$ cloud seen from space

The stratovolcano Mount Pinatubo on Luzon, Philippines, erupted on June 15, 1991 and produced a plume reaching up to 21 miles (34 km). It ejected between 16.5 and 33 million tons (15 and 30 million tonnes) of sulfur dioxide (SO$_2$) into the atmosphere, observed by Earth-monitoring satellites.

Largest active lava lake

The shield volcano Mount Nyiragongo in the Democratic Republic of the Congo contains an active lava lake in its crater some 820 ft. (250 m) across. The volcano has erupted at least 34 times since 1882.

Longest continuously erupting volcano

Mount Stromboli, in the Tyrrhenian Sea off the coast of Italy, has been undergoing continuous volcanic eruptions since at least the 7th century BC, when its activity was recorded by Greek colonists. Its regular mild explosions of gas and lava—usually several each hour—have led to it becoming known as the "Lighthouse of the Mediterranean."

1982 1985 1991 2002 2010

Began Mar 28, 1982:
El Chichón, Mexico
Death toll: 2,000 (from ash flows)

Began Nov 13, 1985:
Nevado del Ruiz (Armero), Colombia
Death toll: 23,000 (from mudflows)

Began Apr 2, 1991:
Mount Pinatubo, Luzon, Philippines
Death toll: 800 (from disease)

Began Jan 17, 2002:
Mount Nyiragongo, Democratic Republic of the Congo
Death toll: 147 (from lava flows)

Began Oct 25, 2010:
Mount Merapi, Java, Indonesia
Death toll: 353 (from gas cloud)

FORCES OF NATURE

Fastest wind speed

On April 10, 1996, a wind speed of 253 mph (408 km/h) was recorded at Barrow Island, Australia, during Tropical Cyclone Olivia—the fastest wind speed ever recorded that was not associated with a tornado.

Fastest measured derecho

A derecho is a long-lasting, straight-line windstorm associated with a band of fast-moving showers and thunderstorms. In the early morning of May 31, 1998, a derecho raced across the U.S. states of Wisconsin and lower Michigan. In eastern Wisconsin, a wind gust of 128 mph (206 km/h) was measured; gusts in lower Michigan were estimated to have reached 130 mph (209 km/h).

Farthest distance survived in a tornado

On March 12, 2006, 19-year-old Matt Suter (USA) was engulfed by a tornado while inside a mobile home near Fordland in Missouri, USA. He was knocked unconscious and awoke 1,307 ft. (398 m) away in a field.

Strongest microburst

Microbursts are a rare meteorological phenomenon characterized by a brief, localized downdraft of hurricane-force winds. They are often a threat to aircraft during takeoff or landing.

Widest tornado damage path

On May 22, 2004, the Midwestern USA was beset by around 56 tornadoes. One of them, known as the Hallam Nebraska tornado, left a swathe of destruction up to 2.5 miles (4 km) wide in some places.

The strongest microburst ever recorded occurred on August 1, 1983, at Andrews Field air force base in Maryland, USA, with a wind speed of 149.5 mph (240.5 km/h).

Highest storm surge

On March 4, 1899, Tropical Cyclone Mahina struck Bathurst Bay in Queensland, Australia. The associated storm surge—a rise in sea water level caused by a combination of high winds and low pressure—was reported to be as high as 42 ft. (13 m), with fish and dolphins found stranded on the top of 49-ft.-high (15-m) cliffs. The storm surge was responsible for the deaths of more than 400 people.

CYCLONES

Farthest measured distance by a tropical cyclone

Hurricane/Typhoon John formed on August 11, 1994 in the eastern Pacific Ocean and covered 8,250 miles (13,280 km). It lasted for 31 days, making it the **longest-lasting tropical cyclone**. John traveled from the eastern to the western Pacific; because the two regions use different labels for tropical cyclones (see below), it is known as both a hurricane and a typhoon.

Largest tropical cyclone eye

Tropical Cyclone Kerry, which lasted from February 13 to March 6, 1979 in the Coral Sea off the Australian coast, had an eye of around 112 miles (180 km) in diameter. It was measured on February 21 by reconnaissance aircraft.

Most active dust storm location

The Bodélé Depression is a dry region northeast of Lake Chad, on the southern edge of the Sahara, in a narrow divide between two mountainous regions. Winds channeled through this divide and across the depression disturb the surface sediments, whose geological evolution has made them highly erodible. On average, around 100 dust storms are whipped up in the Bodélé Depression each year, injecting some 154 million lb. (700,000 tonnes) of dust into the atmosphere each day.

KNOW YOUR STORMS

Hurricane*: Severe tropical weather system, with winds of 74 mph (119 km/h) or higher, in the Atlantic or eastern Pacific oceans.

Blizzard: Major snowstorm featuring high winds—greater than 35 mph (56 km/h)—and resulting in low levels of visibility.

Thunderstorm: Violent storm of thunder and lightning. Frequently accompanied by downpours of heavy rain and hail.

Ice storm: Storm characterized by extremely low temperatures, in which snow and rain freeze on impact with objects.

Cyclone/Tropical cyclone*: Severe thunderstorm generated over tropical or subtropical waters.

Most tornadoes in 24 hours

From April 25 to 28, 2011, a massive tornado outbreak ravaged the northeast, southern, and Midwest regions of the USA, killing as many as 354 people. From 8 a.m. Eastern Time (ET) on April 27 to 8 a.m. the following day, some 312 tornadoes were spawned by the storm activity.

Tropical cyclone formed closest to the equator

The Earth's rotation causes freely moving objects (such as airplanes, wind, or missiles) to deflect to the right in the Northern Hemisphere and to the left in the Southern Hemisphere. This is known as the Coriolis effect. Regions 186 miles (300 km) north and south of the equator have not been thought capable of generating a tropical cyclone because the Coriolis effect of the Earth's rotation is weakest here. However, on December 26, 2001, Typhoon Vamei formed in the South China Sea, just 93 miles (150 km; 1.4 degrees) north of the equator.

HURRICANES

Most hurricanes in a season

Since records began in 1851, 12 hurricanes have been recorded during the hurricane season (June 1–November 30) twice, in 1961 and in 2005.

The last hurricane of the 2005 season was October's category-5 Hurricane Wilma, the **strongest ever** on record. A hurricane hunter plane measured a barometric pressure in the eye of just 882 millibars—the **lowest ever recorded** for a hurricane. Wind

speeds in Wilma's eye wall reached a staggering 165 mph (270 km/h).

Hurricane Epsilon, which hit the USA on December 2, 2005 (two days after the official end of the hurricane season), was the 14th hurricane to reach the USA in 12 months, the **most hurricanes in a year**.

TORNADOES

Largest measured tornado

On May 3, 1999, a tornado 5,250 ft. (1,600 m) in diameter occurred near Mulhall in Oklahoma, USA.

Longest discontinuous tornado

On May 26, 1917, a tornado traveled 293 miles (471.5 km) across Illinois and Indiana, USA, although it was not continuous on the ground.

Worst flood disaster—insured losses

Hurricane Katrina, which devastated the coast of Louisiana, USA, and surrounding states on August 29, 2005, caused damage estimated to be as high as $71 billion—the greatest amount of damage ever caused by a hurricane. At least 1,833 people lost their lives in the disaster and subsequent floods.

Largest thunderstorms

Supercells are powerful storms that form around a mesocyclone—a deep, rotating updraft. Sometimes multiple miles across, they can last several hours, making them the largest and **longest-lasting thunderstorms**. They often occur on the Great Plains of the USA and can spawn tornadoes.

New York

1,370 miles (2,200 km)

Dallas

Largest tropical cyclone

Typhoon Tip had a diameter of around 1,370 miles (2,200 km) when it was studied by the U.S. Air Force (USAF) in the Pacific Ocean on October 12, 1979. The USAF flew some 60 research missions into Tip.

TITANIC TYPHOON
Although Tip never made the mainland of the USA, if it did it would have stretched between New York and Dallas, Texas!

Longest tornado path

On March 18, 1925, a tornado traveled at least 218 miles (352 km) through the U.S. states of Missouri, Illinois, and Indiana. It killed 695 people—more than any other tornado in U.S. history.

Most tornadoes by area

Perhaps surprisingly, the Netherlands has the most twisters by area, with one for every 769 sq. miles (1,991 km²) of land. By contrast, the USA has one tornado per 3,161 sq. miles (8,187 km²).

FOR OUT-OF-THIS-WORLD RECORDS, TURN TO P. 180

Snowstorm: Storm typified by heavy and persistent falls of snow. Wind speeds are lower than those in a blizzard.

Hailstorm: Thunderstorm that generates downfalls of hail (large pellets of ice).

Typhoon*: Tropical cyclone that takes place in the Indian Ocean or western Pacific Ocean.

Tornado: Violent, funnel-shape whirlwind typified by thin "funnel" touching ground and upper reaches in cloud. Can grow to several hundred yards in diameter.

Windstorm: Gale featuring high levels or violent bursts of wind, but little or no precipitation.

These are the same phenomena, but names vary according to regions in which they occur.

EXTREME WEATHER

Worst effect of weather on war

Weather always plays an unpredictable role in warfare and sometimes changes the course of history. Perhaps the most significant example is the effect of the North Atlantic Oscillation (NAO), a result of the seesaw action between the low-pressure area that sits over Iceland and the high-pressure area over the Azores islands in the Atlantic. When the NAO is strong, it drives mild, wet Atlantic winds over Britain and Western Europe, but when weak it lets cold air come in from Europe. In the harsh winter of 1941–42, when the Germans invaded Russia, temperatures dropped to at least -40°F (-40°C) and greatly influenced the number of deaths during the campaign. By early 1943, the total casualties were probably around 250,000 troops.

Most hailstorms in a year

The Kericho hills region of Kenya is subject to hailstorms on average around 132 days each year. This region is one of the top tea-producing areas in the world, and it is possible that dust particles, sent aloft by the activities of tea pickers, act as nucleation points in the atmosphere around which hailstones form.

Worst hailstorm death toll

In 1942, a forest guard in the Himalayan state of Uttarakhand, India, discovered hundreds of skeletons in the Roopkund glacial lake. In 2004, a team of scientists funded by National Geographic led an expedition to Roopkund and discovered as many as 600 individuals in the lake. A number of skeletons were discovered to have fractures in the tops of their skulls. The most plausible theory is that this group of people encountered an intense hailstorm that killed some instantly, while the rest were stunned or injured and succumbed to hypothermia.

14 MILLION
Years that Lake Vostok, far under the research station, has been isolated.

Lowest temperature on Earth

As a winter vacation destination, the Russian research station Vostok has little to recommend it. Not only did it register a temperature of -128.6°F (-89.2°C) on July 21, 1983, but oxygen is sparse at its altitude of 11,220 ft. (3,420 m), the wind can hit 60 mph (97 km/h), and its polar night can last for months.

SNOW AND ICE

Worst snow storm disaster damage toll

A "superstorm" traversed the entire east coast of the USA on March 12–13, 1993, killing 500 people and causing $1.2 billion of damage. One report called it a storm with "the soul of a hurricane."

Greatest snowfall in a year

An astonishing 1,224.5 in. (31,102 mm)—just over 102 ft. (31 m)—of snow fell on the Paradise region of Mount Rainier National Park, Washington, USA, from February 19, 1971 to February 18, 1972. At a height of 14,410 ft. (4,392 m), Rainier has a permanent covering of snow.

Largest snowflake

On January 28, 1887, at Fort Keogh in Montana, USA, ranch owner Matt Coleman reported a snowflake that measured 15 in. (38 cm) wide and 8 in. (20 cm) thick, which he later described as being "larger than milk pans." A mail courier witnessed the fall of these giant flakes over several miles.

Largest piece of fallen ice

On August 13, 1849, a piece of ice 20 ft. (6 m) long was reported to have fallen from the sky in Ross-shire, Scotland, UK. The ice was clear and composed of smaller pieces of ice or hail. Examples of these objects are now called "megacryometeors."

RAIN

Most rainy days

Mount Wai`ale`ale (5,148 ft.; 1,569 m tall) on Kaua`i island, Hawaii, USA, has up to 350 rainy days per annum. A soggy 666 in. (16,916 mm) of rain was recorded on the peak in 1982.

TEMPERATURE TANTRUMS

Coldest desert: The McMurdo Dry Valleys in Antarctica receive less than 4 in. (100 mm) precipitation per year and have a mean annual temperature of -4°F (-20°C).

Coldest permanently inhabited place: The Siberian village Oymyakon reached almost -90°F (-68°C) in 1933—the lowest temperature outside Antarctica.

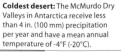

Coldest part of the atmosphere: In the mesosphere, between 30 and 50 miles (50 and 80 km) above Earth, the temperature drops with altitude, reaching around -148°F (-100°C).

Greatest temperature range: Temperatures in Verkhoyansk in the east of Russia have ranged 188°F (105°C), from -90°F (-68°C) to 98°F (37°C).

Coldest road: The Kolyma Highway in Russia passes through some of the coldest inhabited places on Earth, such as Oymyakon (see left), where temperatures as low as -90°F (-68°C) have been recorded.

Highest annual rainfall

Mawsynram in Meghalaya, India, has an average of 467 in. (11,873 mm) of rain per annum. Most of the rain occurs during the monsoon season, between June and September. Meghalaya itself means "land of the clouds."

Most in 24 hours
On March 15–16, 1952, 74 in. (1,870 mm) of rain fell in 24 hours in Cilaos on the island of Réunion in the Indian Ocean.

Most in a calendar month
A total of 366 in. (9,300 mm) of rain fell at Cherrapunji in Meghalaya, India, in July 1861.

Largest raindrops
Professor Peter V. Hobbs (UK) and Arthur Rangno (USA) of the University of Washington, USA, used laser-based equipment to image falling raindrops. They detected drops measuring a minimum of 0.33 in. (8.6 mm)

across on two occasions: September 1995 (in Brazil) and July 1999 (in the Marshall Islands, central Pacific Ocean).

Longest-lasting rainbow
Rainbows appear when sunlight passes through a raindrop. The light is refracted at different angles, causing the spectrum of colors to be seen while the sunlight is behind the viewer and the rain is in front. A rainbow was continuously visible for six hours, from 9 a.m. to 3 p.m., over Wetherby in Yorkshire, UK, on March 14, 1994. Few rainbows last for an hour.

LIGHTNING

Most strikes in one flash
Lightning is made up of a number of strokes or pulses of currents, usually too quick to follow with the naked eye. The most flickers or strikes detected in a single flash is 26, in a cloud-to-ground strike in New Mexico, USA, in 1962, recorded by Marx Brook (USA).

Most cows killed
A single bolt of lightning killed 68 Jersey cows sheltering under a tree on Warwick Marks' dairy farm near Dorrigo in New South Wales, Australia, on October 31, 2005. A further three cows were paralyzed for a few hours, but later recovered.

Worst ice storm damage

From January 5 to 9, 1988, eastern Canada and adjoining areas of the USA experienced weather that cut off power to 3 million people. Freezing rain coated power lines with 4 in. (10 cm) of ice and thousands of poles fell. The bill was estimated at CAN$3 billion ($2.1 billion).

Deadliest dust devil

Dust devil whirlwinds form from the ground upward in sunny conditions. On May 19, 2003, one caused a house to collapse in Lebanon, Maine, USA, with the death of one man. The second recorded incident was on June 18, 2008, when one caused a shed to collapse near Casper in Wyoming, USA, and a woman was killed.

Hottest place on Earth

The air around a lightning strike is superheated to around 54,000°F (30,000°C) for a fraction of a second. This is a temperature roughly five times hotter than the visible surface of the Sun. The **most powerful lightning** of all is positive lightning, in which the net transfer of charge from the cloud to the ground is positive. Positive lightning is involved in less than 5% of all strikes. It outlasts normal (negative) lightning strikes and causes a stronger electrical field, giving rise to strikes of up to a billion volts and an electrical current that may reach 300,000 amperes.

1.58
Death Valley's average yearly rainfall in inches.

Highest recorded temperature

On July 10, 1913, a temperature of 134°F (56.7°C) was measured at Greenland Ranch in Death Valley, California, USA. It was assumed that this had been beaten by a reading of 136°F (58°C) in El Azizia, Libya, in 1922. On September 13, 2012, however, the World Meteorological Organization disqualified the higher reading, restoring the record to Death Valley.

Hottest part of the atmosphere: The thermosphere starts around 50 miles (80 km) above Earth and continues to an altitude of around 310 miles (500 km). The temperature rises with altitude and can reach 3,632°F (2,000°C) when the Sun is particularly active.

Greatest temperature range in a day: On January 23–24, 1916, in Browning, Montana, USA, the temperature dropped 100°F (56°C). An Arctic cold front swept in, sending it from 44°F (7°C) to -56°F (-49°C).

Warmest ocean: Most of the Indian Ocean is in the tropics. Its minimum surface temperature is around 72°F (22°C), but can be as high as 82°F (28°C) toward the east.

Most rainfall in a minute: A figure of 1.5 in. (38.1 mm) in one minute was recorded at Basse-Terre, Guadeloupe, in the Caribbean, on November 26, 1970.

Driest place on Earth: Between 1964 and 2001, the average annual rainfall for the meteorological station in Quillagua in the Atacama Desert, Chile, was 0.019 in. (0.5 mm).

FELINE HUNGRY?

Hercules eats around 25 lb. (12 kg) of meat—about the same weight as a two-year-old child—every day, washed down with a gallon of water.

Largest living cat

Hercules is an adult male liger (a feline hybrid from a lion and tigress) housed at Myrtle Beach Safari, a wildlife reserve in South Carolina, USA. He is 10 ft. 11 in. (333 cm) in length, stands 4 ft. 1 in. (125 cm) at the shoulder, and weighs 922 lb. (418.2 kg). He is pictured here with Moksha Bybee, an animal trainer from the wildlife reserve. Ligers are generally larger than their two parental species. In contrast, tigons—hybrids resulting from the reciprocal cross (tiger with a lioness)—are often smaller.

PREHISTORIC LIFE

Visualizing the greatest creatures that ever roamed Earth

It can be difficult to appreciate fully the size of the world's largest dinosaurs and prehistoric beasts. Bone fragments and fossils unearthed by palaeontologists paint only part of the picture—skeletons are one thing, but what would it be like to encounter these "terrible lizards" face to face?

To help you get an idea of the enormity of these creatures, we asked our creatives at 55 Design (UK) to produce a composite image using models from the German toy makers Schleich that, we think, most closely match the real-life creatures. Here, then, is what it might look like if dinosaurs invaded London's Trafalgar Square …

SEE IT 3D WITH THE FREE APP

AUGMENTED REALITY ALERT! 3D ON THIS PAGE

3. Brachiosaurus
The suborder of dinosaurs called Sauropoda were herbivorous land animals that first appeared in the late Triassic, around 200 million years ago. They included the well-known *Diplodocus* and *Brachiosaurus*, but the **longest dinosaur** of all was *Amphicoelias*, estimated at around 197 ft. (60 m)—about the same length as a jumbo jet and twice as long as a blue whale (*Balaenoptera musculus*), the **largest mammal**.

9,920
Weight in pounds of the largest of all stegosaurians, *S. armatus*.

1. Spinosaurus
The **largest carnivorous dinosaur**, and possibly the **largest ever land-base predator**, was *Spinosaurus*, which roamed the present-day Sahara 100 million years ago. New examinations of skull fragments by the Civic Natural History Museum in Milan, Italy, calculated that *Spinosaurus* measured 56 ft. (17 m) long—14 ft. (4 m) longer than fellow theropod *Tyrannosaurus rex*—and weighed 15,400–19,800 lb. (7–9 tonnes).

2. Ankylosaurus
The 8,800-lb. (4-tonne) *Ankylosaurus* of the late Cretaceous period (about 70–65 million years ago) was the **largest armored dinosaur**. It was covered with thick plates and had rows of spikes running down from the back of its head to its club tail. Measuring up to 35 ft. (10.7 m) long and 4 ft. (1.2 m) tall, *Ankylosaurus* was the tank of the dinosaur world. Indeed, at 6 ft. (1.8 m) wide, it was—relative to length—the **widest dinosaur** ever discovered.

4. Stegosaurus
The **dinosaur with the smallest brain** was *Stegosaurus*, which measured 30 ft. (9 m) in length but had a walnut-size brain weighing only 2.5 oz. (70 g). This represented just 0.002% of its average 7,275-lb. (3.3-tonne) body weight (compared with 0.06% for an elephant and 1.88% for a human). Pictured is the **largest stegosaurian**, *Stegosaurus armatus*, identified by the double row of kite-shape plates running down the length of its back.

MEGAFAUNA
The term, meaning "large animal," used to describe giant creatures; the biggest megafauna on land lived around 200 million years ago.

6. *Quetzalcoatlus*
The **largest ever flying creature** was the pterosaur *Quetzalcoatlus northropi* ("feathered serpent"). About 70 million years ago, it soared over vast areas of the USA. Partial remains discovered in Texas in 1971 indicate that this reptile must have had a wingspan of 33–36 ft. (10–11 m) and weighed about 190–250 lb. (86–113 kg).

5. *Triceratops*
The ceratopsids were herbivorous dinosaurs with the **largest skulls**, characterized by huge frills and horns. The purpose of the horns is unclear, but they were probably used for defense or for mating displays. Ceratopsids included *Triceratops* (pictured), which had the **longest dinosaur horns** at up to 3 ft. (1 m) long, and *Pentaceratops*, which had the **largest skull for a land animal** at 10 ft. 6 in. (3.2 m) in height.

7. *Allosaurus*
Allosaurus was a member of the suborder Theropoda ("beast feet"), which contains the **largest carnivorous dinosaurs**, such as *T. rex* and *Spinosaurus* (*see left*). The theropods were the **most successful dinosaur group** in terms of longevity and diversity, dominating the land from ca. 200 million years ago right up to the extinction of the dinosaurs 65 million years ago.

SNAKES

Fastest snake on land

The aggressive black mamba (*Dendroaspis polylepis*) is named for the color of the inside of its mouth rather than its skin. The snake is able to reach speeds of 10–12 mph (16–19 km/h) in short bursts over level ground. Fortunately for humans, black mambas prefer to make a swift exit instead of using their speed to attack. *Find out more in the Top 10 below.*

Heaviest snake species

The green anaconda (*Eunectes murinus*) of tropical South America and Trinidad is normally 18–20 ft. (5.5–6.1 m) in length. The longest specimen recorded is a female shot in Brazil around 1960, which was 27 ft. 9 in. (8.45 m) with a girth of 44 in. (111 cm). The anaconda was estimated to have weighed 500 lb. (227 kg).

Heaviest venomous snake

The potentially fatal—although not as aggressive as reputed—eastern diamondback rattlesnake (*Crotalus adamanteus*) is found in the southeastern USA. It weighs 12–15 lb. (5.5–6.8 kg) and is 5–6 ft. (1.52–1.83 m) long. The heaviest specimen was 33 lb. (15 kg) and 7 ft. 9 in. (2.36 m) long.

Longest snake

The reticulated python (*Python reticulatus*, right) of southeast Asia, Indonesia, and the Philippines often exceeds 20 ft. 6 in. (6.25 m) and the record length is 32 ft. 10 in. (10 m) for a specimen shot in Celebes (now Sulawesi), Indonesia, in 1912. The **longest living snake in captivity**—indeed, the **longest captive snake ever**—is Medusa (*above*), who measured 25 ft. 2 in. (7.67 m) in Kansas City, Missouri, USA, on October 12, 2011.

Largest albino snake in captivity

Twinkie is not exactly a little star—at 23 ft. (7 m), she is an albino reticulated python who weighs in at approximately 370 lb. (168 kg). She is housed at the Reptile Zoo in Fountain Valley, California, USA. Quite the celebrity, Twinkie has even made guest appearances on American TV.

Longest-fanged snake

The gaboon viper (*Bitis gabonica*) is considered to produce more venom than any other snake. And it has the fangs to inject it deeper, measuring 2 in. (50 mm) for a specimen of 6 ft. (1.83 m) in length. A single adult male may produce enough to provide lethal doses for 30 individual humans. Symptoms include hypotension, hemorrhaging, cardiac arrest, and spontaneous bleeding. Docile and sluggish by nature, gaboons can be unpredictable and are capable of speed in short bursts.

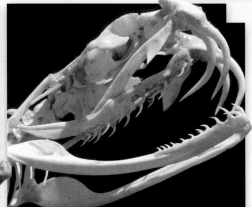

Longest sea snake

The yellow sea snake (*Hydrophis spiralis*) grows to 9 ft. (2.75 m). It is native to great swathes of the Indian Ocean, especially the northern region. It's a venomous species, although bites in humans are, fortunately, rare.

Longest species of viper

The proper name of the South American bushmaster, *Lachesis muta*, is loosely translated as "silent fate," which reflects its reputation in its native South America's equatorial forests east of the Andes, and the island of Trinidad. The bushmaster generally grows to about 6 ft. 7 in. (2 m), but can reach 10 ft. (3 m). The longest known specimen was recorded at just under 12 ft. (3.65 m).

Most venomous rattlesnake

The tiger rattlesnake (*Crotalus tigris*) is a fairly small snake (less than 40 in. (100 cm) long) and has a small venom yield, averaging 11 mg. However, its LD_{50} value—the lethal dose of venom measured in milligrams per kilogram of mass (see Top 10 below)—is just 0.6 mg/kg, making it the

FACT:

No contemporary species comes close to the **largest snake ever**, a prehistoric relative of the boa. As its name suggests, the *Titanoboa cerrejonensis* was a titan, reaching 39 ft. 4 in.–49 ft. 2 in. (12–15 m) long. It measured about 3 ft. 3.3 in. (1 m) at its thickest portion and weighed roughly 2,502 lb. (1,135 kg). Fossils date the snake back 58–60 million years.

TOP 10 MOST VENOMOUS

1. Fierce snake (aka inland taipan, small-scaled snake)
Oxyuranus microlepidotus
Australia
LD_{50} = 0.025 mg/kg

2. Eastern brown snake
Pseudonaja textilis
Australia, New Guinea, Indonesia
LD_{50} = 0.037 mg/kg

3. Coastal taipan
Oxyuranus scutellatus
Australia and New Guinea
LD_{50} = 0.106 mg/kg

4. Many-banded krait
Bungarus multicinctus
Principally mainland China, Taiwan, southeast Asia
LD_{50} = 0.108 mg/kg

5. Peninsula tiger snake
Notechis ater
Australia
LD_{50} = 0.131 mg/kg

LD_{50} measures toxicity: the lethal dose for 50 percent of test subjects in a given time, measured in mg of dose per kg of mass. The most deadly poisons need only a tiny dose to be fatal.

32
Feet that *Chrysopelea* specimens have been recorded gliding through the air.

Most aerial snake

The flying snake is native to southeastern Asia. Belonging to the genus *Chrysopelea*, these snakes do not quite live up to their common name but do glide through the air. Bent in a J shape, they launch themselves off branches, suck in their stomachs, and flare their ribs to make a concave wing shape, undulating in a typical snake movement.

most venomous rattlesnake and the most venomous of *any* snake species in the Americas.

Most venomous rear-fanged snake

Venomous snakes usually have fangs near the front of their *maxillae* (upper jaws). However, some species in the family Colubridae have fangs pointing backward and positioned at the back of their *maxillae*. These are rear-fanged snakes and the most venomous is the boomslang (*Dispholidus typus*). Native to sub-Saharan Africa, its LD_{50} is 0.06–0.72 mg/kg. The skin of a boomslang made an appearance as a potion ingredient in J. K. Rowling's *Harry Potter* series.

FASTEST SWIMMING SNAKE

The yellow-bellied sea snake (*Pelamis platurus*) has been timed at speeds of 3 ft. 3 in./sec. (1 m/sec) over short distances, sometimes with its head out of water. So evolved is it for an exclusively aquatic existence that it is totally helpless if beached on land.

HIGHEST LIVING SNAKE

The Himalayan pit viper (*Gloydius himalayanus*) is a venomous species that has been found at altitudes of 16,076 ft. (4,900 m). Pit vipers have a heat-sensitive pit organ between their eyes. The pit is used during attack to help the snake accurately aim its strike at warm-blooded prey.

SEE IT 3D WITH THE FREE APP

Largest spitting cobra

The giant spitting cobra (*Naja ashei*) lives in the coastal region of Kenya. The longest specimen on record was 8 ft. 10 in. (2.7 m) long. It has enough poison to kill at least 15 people and is the second longest venomous snake after the king cobra (*see right*).

Country with most venomous species

Australia not only contains more species of venomous snake than any other country on Earth, but is also home to five of the snakes featured in our Top 10 most venomous in the world (*see below*). These include the inland taipan

SSSHORTEST SSSSNAKE

Leptotyphlops carlae is a species of threadsnake measuring 4 in. (10 cm). The coiled snake is the size of a quarter coin and as thin as a strand of spaghetti.

ACTUAL SIZE

(*Oxyuranus microlepidotus*) at No.1, the eastern brown snake (*Pseudonaja textilis*) at No.2, the coastal taipan (*Oxyuranus scutellatus*) at No.3, the peninsular tiger snake (*Notechis ater*) at No.5, and the western tiger snake (*Notechis scutatus occidentalis*) at No.8.

Most widely distributed venomous snake

The saw-scaled or carpet viper (*see No.6 below*)—named for the patterns on its scales resembling Arabian rugs—has an unrivalled reputation for biting and killing more people than any other species. Its huge range and the fact that it is found in large numbers are responsible for its notoriety. It is very aggressive when provoked—it creates its characteristic rattle (stridulation) by rubbing its skin together before striking—and its bite causes uncontrolled bleeding.

20
Number of people—or one elephant—that the venom of the king cobra can kill.

AUGMENTED REALITY ALERT! 3D ON THIS PAGE

Longest venomous snake

The king cobra (*Ophiophagus hannah*) or hamadryad averages 10–13 ft. (3–4 m) in length. Native to India and southeast Asia, the longest on record was captured in 1937 in Malaysia and displayed at London Zoo, UK. It was 18 ft. 9 in. (5.71 m) by fall 1939. Unfortunately, it had to be destroyed, like all the zoo's venomous snakes, at the outbreak of World War II in case the zoo was bombed, which might have given the snakes a chance to escape.

6. Saw-scaled viper
Echis carinatus
Middle East and central Asia
LD_{50} = 0.151 mg/kg

7. Black mamba
Dendroaspis polylepis
Sub-Saharan Africa
LD_{50} = 0.185 mg/kg

8. Western tiger snake
Notechis scutatus occidentalis
Australia
LD_{50} = 0.194 mg/kg

9. Eastern coral snake
Micrurus fulvius
Mexico and USA
LD_{50} = 0.196 mg/kg

10. Philippine cobra
Naja philippinensis
Philippines
LD_{50} = 0.2 mg/kg

VENOM

ACTUAL SIZE

LARGEST HORNET

Native to the mountains of Japan, the Asian giant hornet (*Vespa mandarinia*) has a body length of 2.2 in. (5.5 cm), with a wingspan of about 3 in. (7.6 cm). Its stinger can grow to 0.25 in. (0.6 cm) long and inject a venom so powerful that it dissolves human tissue.

You'll find both venomous and poisonous creatures on these pages. So what's the difference between the two? It's all to do with the way the toxin is delivered: venom is injected into a victim, while poison is part of an animal's body and becomes toxic when the animal is touched or eaten.

First venomous dinosaur

Having examined a well-preserved skull from the dinosaur *Sinornithosaurus*, a team led by Empu Gong (China) reported in 2009 that this dinosaur possessed features indicating that it had been venomous, including prominent grooves running down the outer surface of its unusually long, fang-like mid-jaw teeth. This was the first time that evidence for venom production by a dinosaur had ever been presented. *Sinornithosaurus* lived in what is now China and dates from the early Cretaceous period (24.6 million to 22 million years ago).

Most poisonous frog

The poison of the golden poison-dart frog (*Phyllobates terribilis*) is toxic enough to kill 10 adult humans or 20,000 lab mice. Native American tribes sometimes tipped their blow darts with poison from these creatures—hence the frog's common name—although very few of the 175-plus species have been used for this purpose.

Most dangerous ant

Found in Australia's coastal areas, the bulldog ant (*Myrmecia pyriformis*), seen above eating a European hornet (*Vespa crabro*), attacks with its stinger and jaws simultaneously. It has caused at least three human deaths since 1936.

Most toxic species of waterfowl

The African spur-winged goose (*Plectropterus gambensis*) is native to wetlands in western Africa. This large species, which at 30–45 in. (75–115 cm) is Africa's largest waterfowl, sequesters a poison called cantharidin within its tissue from the blister beetles that it eats. Just 0.0003 oz. (10 mg) of cantharidin can kill humans; its flesh becomes so toxic that it can prove fatal to people who eat it.

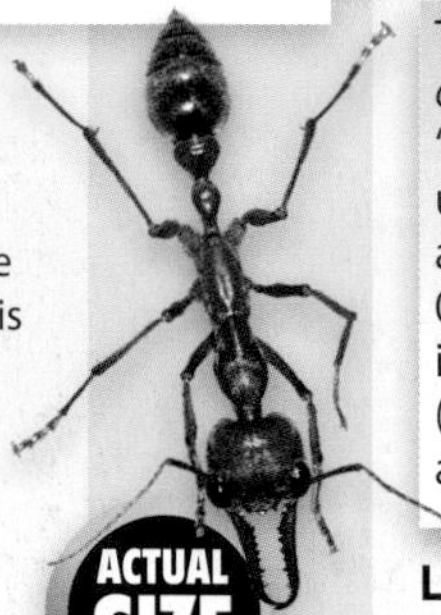

ACTUAL SIZE

MOST VENOMOUS VIPER

ACTUAL SIZE

The saw-scaled viper (*Echis carinatus*), seen above being "milked" for its venom, grows up to 31.5 in. (80 cm) long and can inject as much as 0.0004 oz. (12 mg) of venom in a single bite. Just 0.0001 oz. (5 mg) is sufficient to kill an adult human.

Longest-lived species of venomous lizard

The Mexican beaded lizard *Heloderma horridum* is a black-and-yellow forest-dwelling species that measures up to 35 in. (90 cm) long. One specimen lived in captivity for 33 years and 11 months.

Largest venomous lizard

At up to 9 ft. 10 in. (3 m) long and weighing as much as 154 lb. (70 kg), the Komodo dragon (*Varanus komodoensis*) is both the **largest venomous lizard** and the **largest species of venomous land animal**. Although scientists have long known that in the wild state its saliva contains pathogenic bacteria, it was only in 2009 that this species was also shown to possess a pair of true venom-secreting glands, present in its lower jaw.

12 Number of meals per year on which a Komodo dragon can survive.

Most venomous spider

The Brazilian wandering spiders of the genus *Phoneutria* are the most venomous spiders. The Brazilian huntsman spider (*P. fera*)—seen here consuming a frog—has the most active neurotoxic venom of any living spider. Just 0.00000021 oz. (0.006 mg) is sufficient to kill a mouse. *Phoneutria* spiders have a body-and-leg spread of around 6.7 in. (17 cm).

ACTUAL SIZE

DANGERS FROM THE DEEP

Most dangerous sea urchin: Flower sea urchin (*Toxopneustes pileolus*); toxin from spines and pedicellaria (pincerlike organs) causes pain, respiratory problems, and paralysis.

Most venomous mollusk: Two species of blue-ringed octopuses (*Hapalochlaena maculosa* and *H. lunulata*); delivers a fairly painless bite that can kill in minutes.

Most venomous marine snake: *Hydrophis belcheri* (below); has a myotoxic venom far more toxic than that of any land snake. The common beaked sea snake (*Enhydrina schistosa*) is probably equally as venomous.

Most poisonous edible fish: Puffer fish (*Tetraodon*); contains a fatally poisonous toxin called tetrodotoxin, just 0.004 oz. (0.1 g) of which can kill an adult in 20 minutes.

Most venomous gastropod: Cone shells (*Conus*); contains a fast-acting neurotoxic venom that, in some species, can be fatal to humans.

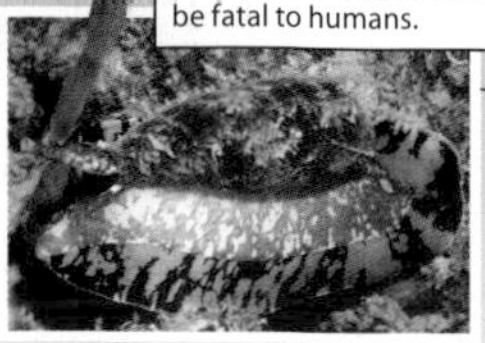

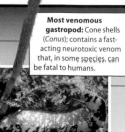

ACTUAL SIZE

Most venomous centipede

So potent is the venom of one particularly dangerous form of *Scolopendra subspinipes*—a centipede found mostly in south-east Asia—that human victims have been reported plunging their bitten hands into boiling water in order to mask the excruciating pain.

First bee venom therapy

The earliest use of apitherapy (the pharmacological use of honeybee products) to treat illnesses was by the ancient Chinese, Greeks, and Romans. Greek physician Galen (AD 129–200) is said to have used bee venom to treat baldness.

SEE IT 3D WITH THE FREE APP

AUGMENTED REALITY ALERT! 3D ON THIS PAGE

Largest wasp

The giant tarantula-hawk wasp (*Pepsis heros*) is both the largest wasp and the largest insect of the order Hymenoptera. The largest known specimen is a female from the Yanachaga-Chemillén National Park in Peru with a wingspan of 4.75 in. (121.5 mm) and a curved body length of about 2.25 in. (62 mm). Its name is a reference to the wasp's prey—the Goliath bird-eating spider and other tarantula species. The wasp grabs the spider in its jaws, paralyzes it with its sting, then drags it to its nest, lays an egg on its body, and seals it into the nest. The newly hatched wasp larvae feed on the still-living spider.

Most dangerous bee

The Africanized honeybee (*Apis mellifera scutellata*) will generally only attack when provoked, but is persistent in pursuit. It is very aggressive and fiercely protective of territories of up to a half-mile (0.8-km) radius. Its venom is no more potent than that of other bees, but because it attacks in swarms the number of stings inflicted can kill a victim.

MOST VENOMOUS LAND SNAKE

In a single strike, the small-scaled snake (*Oxyuranus microlepidotus*) can inject 0.002 oz. (60 mg) of venom, sufficient to kill a small marsupial in seconds, and more than enough to wipe out several human adults. It is native to Australia.

Most venomous jellyfish

Flecker's sea wasp or box jellyfish (*Chironex fleckeri*) is found off the coasts of northern Australia. One jellyfish produces enough poison to kill 60 humans and is responsible for one death a year on average.

In 2000, an Australian lifeguard had a narrow escape when he drank water from a bottle containing the near-transparent tentacles of one specimen. Even after death, the creature's tentacles retain their life-threatening toxicity (*see below*).

Longest spider venom glands

Each measuring up to 0.4 in. (10.2 mm) long and 0.1 in. (2.7 mm) in diameter, the longest venom glands of any spider are those belonging to *Phoneutria nigriventer*, possibly South America's most aggressive species of spider. Each gland can contain up to 0.000044 oz. (1.35 mg) of venom, which is sufficient to kill 225 mice.

Most venomous scorpion

The Tunisian fat-tailed scorpion (*Androctonus australis*) is responsible for 80 percent of stings and 90 percent of deaths from scorpion stings in North Africa. It can reach 3.9 in. (10 cm) in length and weighs up to 0.5 oz. (15 g).

ACTUAL SIZE

BIG DIGGER
Discovered in 2012 on the island of Sulawesi, the **largest digger wasp** (*Megalara garuda*) grows to 1.3 in. (34 mm) in length.

2,000
Number of scorpion species. Of these, about 30 are lethal to humans.

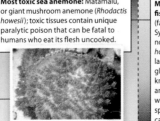

Largest jellyfish: Arctic giant jellyfish (*Cyanea capillata arctica*); enormous ocean predator—up to 7 ft. 6 in. (2.28 m) wide and 120 ft. (36.5 m) long—with a sting potentially fatal to humans.

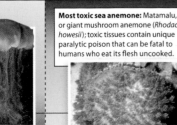

Most toxic sea anemone: Matamalu, or giant mushroom anemone (*Rhodactis howesii*); toxic tissues contain unique paralytic poison that can be fatal to humans who eat its flesh uncooked.

Most venomous fish: Stonefish (family Synanceiidae), notably *Synanceia horrida*; has the largest venom glands of any known fish, and contact with poisonous spines of its fins can prove fatal.

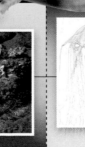

Most venomous jellyfish: Flecker's sea wasp or box jellyfish (*Chironex fleckeri*); symptoms before death include vomiting, nausea, diarrhea, shivering, sweating, aches, and pains.

Most poisonous shark: Greenland shark (*Somniosus microcephalus*); flesh contains a neurotoxin and must be boiled in several changes of water before it is safe to eat.

CREEPY CRAWLIES

ACTUAL SIZE

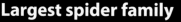

Heaviest stick insect

The females of the giant jungle nymph (*Heteropteryx dilatata*) are bulkier than the males. A female specimen was weighed at London Zoo in 1977 at 1.81 oz. (51.2 g). The species is native to rain forest in southeast Asia, including peninsular Malaysia, Sarawak on Borneo, Sumatra, Singapore, and Thailand.

FASTEST ...

Flying insect
The Australian dragonfly (*Austrophlebia costalis*) can reach up to 36 mph (58 km/h) in short bursts. In 1917, a ground velocity of 61.3 mph (98.6 km/h) was recorded for 240–270 ft. (73–82 m).

Spider
The giant house spider (*Tegenaria gigantea*) is native to North America. In 1970, an adult female attained a maximum running speed of 1 ft. 8 in. per sec. (0.53 m/s) over short distances.

Insect wing beat
A tiny midge of the genus *Forcipomyia* flaps its wings 62,760 times a minute. The insect undergoes a muscular contraction–expansion cycle in 0.00045 seconds, the **fastest muscle movement** ever recorded.

Invertebrates
Solifugids of the genus *Solpuga* have a sprint capability estimated at 10 mph (16 km/h). They inhabit north Africa and the Middle East and are also known as camel spiders or sun spiders, which is misleading because their bodies are divided into separate head, thorax, and abdomen sections, unlike the head and thorax sections of true spiders.

Fastest self-powered strike

The outer jaws of the trap jaw ant (*Odontomachus bauri*) close at 114–210 ft. per sec. (35–64 m/s). An average strike lasts 0.13 milliseconds: 2,300 times faster than a single blink of the human eye.

Heaviest cockroach

The rhinoceros cockroach (*Macropanesthia rhinoceros*) of eastern Queensland, Australia, is wingless and lives in burrows. The heaviest was an adult female weighing 1.18 oz. (33.45 g), almost double the normal weight for the species.

ACTUAL SIZE

Largest spider family

Salticidae are jumping spiders and there are more of them by classification—or taxonomy—than any other. Containing approximately 5,000 species in more than 500 types—or genera—they account for roughly 13 percent of all known spider species.

LOCKING HORNS
Male hercules beetles fight each other with their horns and they have been known to lift a hefty 4.4 lb. (2 kg).

LARGEST ...

Butterfly
Female Queen Alexandra's birdwings (*Ornithoptera alexandrae*) of Papua New Guinea have been found with wing spans exceeding 11 in. (28 cm). They can weigh more than 0.9 oz. (25 g). This is equivalent in size to a house sparrow (*Passer domesticus*).

Largest beetle

The hercules beetle (*Dynastes hercules*) of South America measures 7 in. (17 cm) long, including its horns (*left*). In terms of body length, the record holder is the titan (*Titanus giganteus*), also of South America. Specimens longer than 5.9 in. (15 cm) are rare, but one was measured at 6.6 in. (16.7 cm) when dried.

ACTUAL SIZE

TINY CREEPY CRAWLIES*

Smallest insect: Ptiliidae family of feather-wing beetle; 0.009 in. (0.25 mm); worldwide

Smallest moth: *Stigmella ridiculosa* 0.07 in. (2 mm); Canary Islands

Smallest bee: *Perdita minima* 0.07 in. (2 mm); southwestern USA

Smallest scorpion: *Microbuthus pusillus* 0.5 in. (13 mm); Red Sea coast

Smallest true fly (dipteran): *Euryplatea nanaknihali* 0.01 in. (0.4 mm); Thailand

* Not shown actual size

Largest vinegaroon

The giant vinegaroon (*Mastigoproctus giganteus*), native to southern USA and much of Mexico, can grow to 2.4 in. (6 cm) long, and the heaviest specimen weighed 0.44 oz. (12.4 g). Vinegaroons are scorpion-like arachnids that spray chemicals from their anal glands to ward off predators. The main component is acetic acid (vinegar), hence their common name.

ACTUAL SIZE

Heaviest beetle

A specimen of the full-grown larva of the actaeon beetle (*Megasoma actaeon*) of the northern regions of South America weighed 8.04 oz. (228 g) in 2009. This is almost as heavy as an adult female rat and makes it the heaviest of the nonmarine arthropods (excluding crustaceans). In other words, it's not just the world's heaviest beetle but the **heaviest insect** of any kind.

ACTUAL SIZE

Largest termite

Queens of the African warlike termite (*Macrotermes bellicosus*) can measure 5.5 in. (14 cm) long and 1.38 in. (3.5 cm) across. At this size, they can lay 30,000 eggs a day. She and her male live for as long as 20 years in huge colonies with millions of termites. The **tallest termite mound** was recorded at 42 ft. (12.8 m) in the Democratic Republic of the Congo.

Longest insect body

London's Natural History Museum holds a specimen of Chan's megastick (*Phobaeticus chani*) measuring 14 in. (35.5 cm) long. With its legs outstretched, it reaches 22.3 in. (56.6 cm). The rare species was found in Borneo, Malaysia.

Centipede

The giant or Peruvian giant yellow-leg centipede (*Scolopendra gigantea*) is 10 in. (26 cm) long. It lives in Central and South America and preys on mice, lizards, and frogs—a population hanging upside down in Venezuelan caves even feeds on bats. *See also p. 31.*

Cobwebs

Darwin's bark spider (*Caerostris darwini*) of Madagascar weaves webs that cover up to 30 sq. ft. (2.8 m²). They spin them over flowing rivers from bank to bank by a mechanism as yet unknown to make the **longest cobwebs**, spanning 82 ft. (25 m).

The **largest continuous areas of webs** are created by members of the Indian genus *Stegodyphus*. Unlike those spiders that have flat webs, they build interwoven and overlapping webs in three dimensions that can cover vegetation for a few miles.

Prehistoric insect

The dragonfly *Meganeura monyi* lived about 280 million years ago. Fossil remains of wing impressions discovered at Commentry, France, indicate a wing expanse of up to 27.5 in. (70 cm).

Most dangerous parasite

The *Anopheles* genus of mosquito contains among its species all those capable of transmitting malarial parasites. These have probably been responsible for half of all human deaths since the Stone Age, excluding wars and accidents.

ACTUAL SIZE

Noisiest butterflies

Cracker butterflies (*Hamadryas*) of Central and South America live up to their name: during their energetic courtships, their forewings collide with a crack that can be heard by humans 100 ft. (30 m) away.

Smallest wasp:
Dicopomorpha echmepterygis
0.005 in. (0.139 mm);
Costa Rica

Smallest centipede:
Hoffman's warf
(*Nannarrup hoffmani*)
0.4 in. (10.3 mm);
New York, USA

Smallest cockroach:
Ant cockroach
(*Attaphila fungicola*)
0.11 in. (3 mm);
USA

Smallest spider:
Patu marplesi
0.017 in. (0.43 mm);
Western Samoa

Smallest butterfly by wing span:
Dwarf blue
Oraidium barberae
0.55 in. (14 mm);
South Africa

033

BIRDS OF PREY

19
The number of years gyrfalcons can live to in captivity.

Largest falcon species

Sporting a wing span of 4 ft.–5 ft. 2 in. (1.24–1.6 m), weighing 2 lb. 10 oz.–4 lb. 10 oz. (1.2–2.1 kg), and measuring 1 ft. 8 in.–2 ft. 1 in. (51–65 cm) long is the female gyrfalcon (*Falco rusticolus*), resident primarily on the Arctic coasts and islands of Europe, Asia, and North America.

Smallest bird of prey

Two birds share this record: the black-thighed falconet (*Microhierax fringillarius*) of southeast Asia and the white-fronted or Bornean falconet (*Microhierax latifrons*) of northwestern Borneo. Both species have an average length of 5.5–6 in. (14–15 cm)—including a 2-in. (5-cm) tail—and weigh about 1.2 oz. (35 g).

Largest owl ever

Believed to have been flightless, or almost flightless, the now extinct Cuban giant owl (*Ornimegalonyx*) stood 3 ft. 7 in. (1.1 m) tall, with proportionately long legs, and is likely to have weighed in excess of 19 lb. 13 oz. (9 kg). This colossal creature was discovered through the study of four closely related species dating from the late Pleistocene epoch, 10,000 years ago.

Newest owl species

The Cebu hawk owl (*Ninox rumseyi*) and the Camiguin hawk owl (*Ninox leventisi*), both of which are found only in the Philippines, were documented within the same 2012 paper published by *Forktail*, a scientific journal devoted to Asian ornithology. The paper's lead author was Professor Pam Rasmussen of Michigan State University in East Lansing, Michigan, USA.

Greatest wing span for an Old World vulture

The bearded vulture (*Gypaetus barbatus*) is a somewhat atypical species with a wedge-shape tail and feathered head native to southern Europe, Africa, the Indian subcontinent, and Tibet. It boasts a wing span of up to 9 ft. 3 in. (2.83 m)—just in excess of the comparably impressive Eurasian griffon (*Gyps fulvus*) of southern Europe, northern Africa, and Asia, whose wing span can reach 9 ft. 2 in. (2.80 m).

FOR THE RECORD

Genetically, Old and New World vultures are not closely related; both families of bird are similar but this is because of "convergent evolution," in which animals develop similar traits because they live in similar environments.

Largest bird of prey

The male Andean condor (*Vultur gryphus*), a New World vulture indigenous to the Pacific coasts of South America, is the largest bird of prey in terms of weight (20–27 lb.; 9–12 kg) and wing span (10 ft. 5 in.; 3.2 m).

A weight of 31 lb. (14.1 kg) has been claimed for a California condor (*Gymnogyps californianus*) preserved at the California Academy of Sciences in Los Angeles, USA, but this species is generally smaller than the Andean and rarely exceeds 23 lb. (10.4 kg).

Smallest Old World vulture

The hooded vulture (*Necrosyrtes monachus*), native to sub-Saharan Africa, measures 2 ft.–2 ft. 4 in. (62–72 cm) long and weighs just 3 lb. 5 oz.–5 lb. 11 oz. (1.5–2.6 kg) with a modest wing span of only 5 ft. 2 in.–8 ft. 6 in. (1.6–2.6 m).

ACTUAL SIZE

Smallest falcon species

A tiny forest-dwelling species called the black-thighed falconet (*Microhierax fringillarius*) normally measures 5.5–6.3 in (14–16 cm) long, weighs only 1.2 oz (35 g), and has a wing span of just 10.6–12.6 in (27–32 cm), roughly equal to that of a sparrow.

Newest buzzard species

Formally described and named in 2010, the Socotra buzzard (*Buteo socotraensis*) is now officially recognized as a new species. It is native to Socotra, an isolated island in the Indian Ocean home to a number of other endemic species.

Highest flying birds

The highest altitude recorded for a bird is 37,000 ft. (11,300 m) for a Rüppell's vulture (*Gyps rueppellii*), which collided with a commercial aircraft over Abidjan, Ivory Coast, on November 29, 1973. Sufficient feather remains of the bird were recovered to allow the American Museum of Natural History to make a positive identification of this high-flier, which is rarely seen above 20,000 ft. (6,000 m).

ANGRY BIRDS

Northern crested caracara (*Caracara cheriway*): This bold scavenger is one of very few birds to hunt on foot and stay low to the ground, often viciously displacing and stealing from predators such as vultures.

Eurasion eagle owl (*Bubo bubo*): One of the largest and most powerful of the present-day owls, it has been known to take down foxes and even deer!

Cassowary (*Casuarius casuarius*): With a fearsome reputation for attacking humans when disturbed, this large, flightless bird can deal a fatal blow or slash with its daggerlike claws.

Red-tailed hawk (*Buteo jamaicensis*): This noisy carnivore emits a terrifying screech to ward off rival hawks during hunting and aggressively defends its territory.

Canada goose (*Branta canadensis*): This North American goose, commonly found in the urban parks of Canada, can become especially aggravated when nesting and will attack and bite anyone who comes too close.

Smallest bird of prey family

The Sagittariidae family contains just a single living species—the African secretary bird (*Sagittarius serpentarius*). Its crest of quill-like feathers and long cranelike legs instantly distinguish it from all other birds of prey. It was once classified within a family of crane-related birds known as seriemas, but has been housed in its own bird of prey family since 1935.

Most restricted diet

Under normal conditions, the Everglade, or snail kite, (*Rostrhamus sociabilis*) lives entirely upon apple snails—large freshwater gastropod mollusks native to the Everglades in Florida, USA. During droughts, when these snails become rarer, the kite will also devour crayfish to survive, but it returns to its normal exclusive snail diet as soon as typical conditions return.

Largest fish eagle species

Supreme in size, power, and aggression, the Steller's sea eagle (*Haliaeetus pelagicus*) is even more dominant than its bald and white-tailed eagle cousins. Found along the coasts of northeastern Asia, the females weigh up to 15–20 lb. (6.8–9 kg), with a wing span of 6 ft. 4 in.–8 ft. 2 in. (1.95–2.5 m).

110
Pounds of crushing pressure harpys can apply to prey using their talons.

Fastest bird dive

While diving, the peregrine falcon (*Falco peregrinus*) has an estimated terminal velocity of 186 mph (300 km/h), giving its prey little chance of escape. The fastest fully documented dive occurred during a series of German experiments, in which one peregrine falcon reached a speed of 168 mph (270 km/h) at a 30-degree angle, rising to 217 mph (350 km/h) at a 45-degree angle.

Strongest bird of prey

The female harpy eagle (*Harpia harpyja*) weighs 20 lb. (9 kg) and is capable of killing and carrying animals of equal or superior size. This apex predator (meaning it sits at the top of its food chain) is known to regularly feast on tree-dwelling mammals such as sloths and monkeys.

Largest barn owl

Distinguishable by their heart-shape masks, barn owls, or tytonids, constitute an entirely separate taxonomic family (Tytonidae) from all other owls (Strigidae). The largest of the magnificent tytonids is the Australian masked owl (*Tyto novaehollandiae*), occurring in Australia's nondesert regions and also in southern New Guinea. Females boast a mammoth wing span of up to 4 ft. 2 in. (1.28 m), weigh 1 lb. 3 oz.– 2 lb. 12 oz. (0.55–1.26 kg), and attain a height of 1 ft. 3 in.–1 ft. 7 in. (0.4–0.5 m).

Largest nest

A pair of bald eagles (*Haliaeetus leucocephalus*), and possibly their successors, built a nest 9 ft. 6 in. (2.9 m) wide and 20 ft. (6 m) deep near St. Petersburg in Florida, USA. The giant roost was estimated to weigh more than 4,400 lb. (2 tonnes) when it was measured on January 1, 1963.

The incubation mounds built by the ground-dwelling mallee fowl (*Leipoa ocellata*) of Australia may involve the mounding of material weighing up to 660,000 lb. (300 tonnes).

BIRDS OF A FEATHER
These masked mates will often keep the same partner for life and defend their territory together. The male even feeds the female for ca. 30–32 days in a row when she's incubating eggs.

Most common New World vulture

The global population of the turkey vulture (*Cathartes aura*) is presently estimated to be 4.5 million individuals, making it the most prevalent species of New World vulture or cathartid.

African crowned eagle (*Stephanoaetus coronatus*): Considered to be Africa's most ferocious eagle thanks to its taste for large prey, such as antelope, this majestic bird has been dubbed "the leopard of the sky" in Africa.

Prairie falcon (*Falco mexicanus*): A unique hunter and fast, daredevil flyer, this medium-size falcon's nervous disposition makes it unpredictable and merciless during attacks.

Ostrich (*Struthio camelus*): At 7–8 ft. (2.1–2.4 m) tall, this huge bird has powerful legs capable of a dastardly kick and a predilection for chasing humans and dogs!

Martial eagle (*Polemaetus bellicosus*): A focused apex predator with the ability to kill birds in mid-flight—it has even been witnessed successfully hunting baboons and lion cubs.

Skua (*Stercorarius*): This pirate of the skies actively harasses and steals food from larger predators and will dive-bomb any creature that dares get close to its nest.

BIZARRE BEASTS

6.56
Length in feet (2 m) of the massive horn on this beast's brow.

First hybrid shark

In January 2012, scientists revealed that the first known hybrid sharks had been recorded in waters off Queensland, Australia. They result from interbreeding between the Australian black-tip shark (*Carcharhinus tilstoni*) and the common black-tip shark (*C. limbatus*). The Australian black-tip can only exist in tropical waters, but its hybrid progeny occur in cooler, temperate seas.

Longest sea creature

Superficially similar to true jellyfish, siphonophores are very different creatures. Each individual siphonophore is actually a colony or super-organism; that is, each part of its body is a distinct, highly specialized organism in its own right, adapted anatomically to fulfill a certain function (such as floating, stinging, feeding, or reproducing). One species of siphonophore, *Praya dubia*, measures 100–160 ft. (30–50 m) and is regarded as the world's longest sea creature.

Longest wavelength of light perceived by a fish

Until recently, it was believed that fish could not see infrared light. In October 2012, however, biologists from Germany's University of Bonn announced that experiments had confirmed that *Pelvicachromis taeniatus*—a species of African freshwater cichlid inhabiting dark, shady

Largest real-life unicorn

The largest mammal with a single central horn on its head that has ever lived was a prehistoric rhinoceros known as *Elasmotherium*, or "giant unicorn." It was the size of a mammoth, its height exceeding 8 ft. 2 in. (2.5 m), its length sometimes in excess of 16 ft. 5 in. (5 m), and its weight an estimated 11,000 lb. (5 tonnes).

rivers—is able to perceive prey in a wavelength range greater than 780 nanometers. This is within the near-infrared portion of the electromagnetic spectrum.

Newest yeti crab

Yeti crabs are a specialized genus (*Kiwa*) of crablike crustaceans named after the profuse hairlike strands ("setae") on their thoracic limbs. In January 2012, scientists announced the discovery of a new species of yeti crab at a depth of some 8,200 ft. (2,500 m) on the floor of the Antarctic's Southern Ocean. This species bore abundant setae on its legs, claws, and the underside of its thorax. It has been nicknamed the "Hasselhoff," after American actor David Hasselhoff, who often displayed his hirsute chest on the TV series *Baywatch*.

50
Poitou foals born each year, making them rarer than white rhinos and giant pandas.

Donkey breed with the longest hair

The Baudet du Poitou donkey of France has a coat with hair averaging 6 in. (15 cm) long. It is often deliberately left to mat so that it yields a characteristic tangled pelage known as a *cadenette*, which the animal retains throughout its life, becoming increasingly tattered in appearance.

FOR THE RECORD

Zoe Pollock and her mother Annie (*far left*) live at Norley Farm near Lymington in Hampshire, UK, with a pack of seven Poitous. In May 2012, they treated their hairy donkeys to a cooling trim—for some, it was their first haircut in 17 years!

DEEPEST …

Scorpion: *Alacran tartarus* is found in caves more than 2,625 ft. (800 m) below the surface.

Bat colony: A colony of little brown bats (*Myotis lucifugus*) winters in a zinc mine in New York, USA, at a depth of 3,805 ft. (1,160 m).

Insect: Larvae of the nonbiting midge *Sergentia koschowi* live at a depth of 4,462 ft. (1,360 m) within Siberia's Lake Baikal, the **deepest lake**.

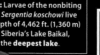

Octopus: The Dumbo octopus (*Grimpoteuthis*) lives at a depth of 5,000 ft. (1,500 m), close to the ocean floor. Its body is around 7.8 in. (20 cm) long.

Starfish: A specimen of *Porcellanaster ivanovi* was collected at a depth of 24,881 ft. (7,584 m) from the Mariana Trench in the west Pacific Ocean.

mole (*Condylura cristata*), with the fastest time being 120 milliseconds.

The nose of the star-nosed mole is covered with 25,000 mechanoreceptors, known as Eimer's organs, and is the **most sensitive animal organ**. Ultrasensitive to touch, the nose of the star-nosed mole is five or six times more sensitive than the human hand.

ACTUAL SIZE

Largest eye-to-body ratio

Vampyroteuthis infernalis can grow to 11 in. (28 cm) long, while its eyes can have a diameter of 0.9 in. (2.5 cm)—a ratio of around 12:1. Despite its fearsome name—"vampire squid from hell"—it is harmless. The **largest eye** of all belongs to the Atlantic giant squid (*Architeuthis dux*), at 15.75 in. (40 cm) wide.

Largest freshwater turtle

Carbonemys cofrinii ("coal turtle") lived 60 million years ago during the Palaeocene epoch. The first-known remains of this giant turtle were found in 2005 in a Colombian coal mine, but it was not officially named and described until 2012. Its shell was 5 ft. 7 in. (1.72 m) long—the height of an average man—and overall the turtle was almost 8 ft. 2 in. (2.5 m) long—the size of a Smart car.

Fastest mammalian eater

Research published in February 2005 by Dr. Kenneth Catania at Vanderbilt University, Tennessee, USA, recorded an average food-handling time of 230 milliseconds for the star-nosed

SLOTH GROWTH
Standing on all fours, this prodigiously sized sloth would have been taller than an adult male African bush elephant.

Oldest fossil parasites

In January 2013, scientists made public their discovery of 93 ancient tapeworm eggs in a 270-million-year-old fossilized shark coprolite (fecal dropping) from Brazil. One of the eggs even contained a probable developing larva. These fossil tapeworm eggs—from the late Palaeozoic era—are 140 million years older than any other fossil parasite.

Most teeth for a living land animal

The common leaf-tailed gecko (*Uroplatus fimbriatus*) of Madagascar has 169 teeth in its upper jaw and 148 in its lower jaw. Among nonaquatic animals, only certain prehistoric pterosaurs (flying reptiles) have ever possessed a greater teeth count.

Most fecund virgin shark

Zebedee is a female zebra shark (*Stegostoma fasciatum*) on display in a restaurant aquarium within the Burj Al Arab hotel in Dubai, UAE. Since 2007, she has produced a series of viable egg-encased shark pups, even though she has not been in the company of any male sharks. Some female sharks reproduce parthenogenetically—that is, via virgin birth (asexual reproduction)—and Zebedee is the most prolific in captivity.

Largest sloth

The Florida ground sloth (*Eremotherium eomigrans*) lived from 4.9 million years ago to the Pleistocene epoch some 300,000 years ago. It weighed more than 11,000 lb. (5 tonnes) and measured 19 ft. 8 in. (6 m) long. When standing on its hind legs, it could reach up to 17 ft. (5.2 m) high, and it had five fingers, four of which boasted giant claws almost 11 in. (30 cm) long.

EXPLORE A BUG'S-EYE VIEW OF THE WORLD ON P. 32

Crustacean: In November 1980, live amphipods were recovered at a depth of 34,450 ft. (10,500 m) from the Challenger Deep (Mariana Trench) in the western Pacific Ocean by the U.S. research vessel *Thomas Washington*.

Fish: *Abyssobrotula galatheae*, an 8-in.-long (20-cm) species of cusk eel, was collected from the Puerto Rico Trench at a depth of 27,460 ft. (8,370 m).

Sponge: Specimens from the Cladorhizidae family have been recovered from a depth of 29,000 ft. (8,840 m).

Multicellular life: A species of 0.2-in.-long (5-mm) nematode worm (*Halicephalobus mephisto*) lives some 2.2 miles (3.6 km) below the surface of the ground.

Xenophyophore: In July 2011, scientists from the Scripps Institution of Oceanography discovered examples of these unicellular lifeforms at depths of 6.6 miles (10.6 km) in the Mariana Trench.

ZOOS

Largest aquarium

The S.E.A. Aquarium in Singapore features 49 different habitats (tanks) containing a total of 10.2 million gal. (38.7 million liters) of fresh- and salt water. Part of Resorts World Sentosa, it was officially inaugurated on December 7, 2012. The aquarium is home to 100,000 animals—from more than 800 species—including manta rays, goliath groupers, and sharks.

First zoo

In 2009, archaeological discoveries made south of Luxor in Egypt included a menagerie of more than 112 animals, unearthed during excavations of the ancient settlement of Hierakonpolis. The beastly remains—of elephants, wildcats, baboons, hartebeests (antelopes), and hippos—date back to 3500 BC.

The **oldest continuously operating zoo** is the Tiergarten Schönbrunn, part of the Schönbrunn Palace in Vienna, Austria. Created in 1752 by order of Holy Roman Emperor Francis I as a crown menagerie, it was first opened to the public in 1779.

First insect house

The insect house of London Zoo, UK, opened in 1881, showcasing such specimens as silk moths and the rarer butterflies and moths from Europe. London Zoo was also home to the **first children's zoo**, opened in 1938 by six-year-old Teddy Kennedy—later Senator Edward Kennedy—of the USA.

Oldest living gorilla in captivity

Colo (b. December 22, 1956) currently lives in the Columbus Zoo and Aquarium in Powell, Ohio, USA. As of April 4, 2013, at the age of 56 years 103 days, she is currently the oldest living gorilla in captivity. Named after her place of birth, Columbus, Colo was also the **first gorilla born in captivity**.

DOME HOME

The Desert Dome exhibits plants and animals from three major deserts: the Namib desert in southern Africa, the Sonoran Desert in North America, and the Red Centre in Australia.

First aquarium

On February 18, 1852, the Council of the Zoological Society of London (UK) commissioned the building of an Aquatic Vivarium (the original term for a fish tank or fish enclosure) at London Zoo. The exhibit, which finally opened in May 1853, became known as the "Fish House," and it was here that the term "aquarium" was coined in 1894 by the English naturalist Philip Henry Gosse; the term was not initially popular with classical scholars because it actually means a watering place for cattle!

Largest indoor swamp

Part of the Henry Doorly Zoo and Aquarium in Omaha, Nebraska, USA, the largest indoor swamp occupies 24 acres (10 ha) and contains almost

Largest indoor desert

Housed under the **largest glazed geodesic dome** (spherical shell structure) in existence, the Desert Dome in Omaha, Nebraska, USA, is part of the Henry Doorly Zoo and Aquarium and encompasses 84,000 sq. ft. (7,840 m²) of exhibits spread across two levels.

Most okapis bred in captivity

Okapis remained unknown to scientists until 1901 and are very hard to breed in captivity. However, as of January 2013, Antwerp Zoo (Belgium) had bred 47 okapis. In 1954, it became the first zoo outside the Democratic Republic of the Congo to breed this rare forest relative of the giraffe.

18
Length in inches an okapi tongue can grow to—used not only to eat, but also to clean its eyes and ears!

MASSIVE MENAGERIES

Berlin Zoo (Germany): Germany's oldest zoo opened in 1844 and now boasts more than 1,500 species.

Wilhelma (Germany): Europe's largest combined zoological and botanical gardens house 1,000 species.

Henry Doorly Zoo (USA): Featuring the largest cat complex in North America, as well as the largest nocturnal exhibit, indoor swamp, and desert dome in any zoo; displays 962 species.

Antwerp Zoo (Belgium): A collection of 950 species can be found at Belgium's oldest animal park, founded in 1843.

Moscow Zoo (Russia): Russia's largest zoo spans 53 acres (21.5 ha) with animals from 927 species.

GUINNESS WORLD RECORDS 14

Largest nocturnal exhibit

Kingdoms of the Night is housed within the Henry Doorly Zoo in Omaha, Nebraska, USA, and covers an area of more than 42,000 sq. ft. (3,900 m²). The exhibit cost $31.5 million to create and opened in April 2003. It features reversed day–night cycles, allowing visitors to observe nocturnal animals, such as aardvarks, fossas (*inset*), fruit bats, and rare Japanese giant salamanders, exhibiting their natural activity patterns.

Strangest animal diet

An internal examination of a dead ostrich that had lived at London Zoo, UK, revealed that during its life it had swallowed an alarm clock, a Belgian Franc, two farthings (a British coin), a roll of film, a pencil, three gloves, and a handkerchief!

Highest-ranking penguin

Sir Nils Olav, a male king penguin, holds the rank of Colonel-in-Chief of the Norwegian Royal Guard. He resides at Edinburgh Zoo in Scotland, UK, where he was bestowed the rank on August 18, 2005, a promotion from his previous rank of Regimental Sergeant Major.

Largest reptile zoo

Originally set up as a humble one-man show by herpetology enthusiast Earl Brockelsby (USA) in 1937, the Reptile Gardens just outside Rapid City in South Dakota, USA, now house at least 225 different reptilian species and subspecies.

192,150 gal. (730,000 liters) of water. It features a beavers' lodge and cypress trees and is home to 38 species of swamp-dwelling animal, including a rare white specimen of the American alligator.

Largest game reserve

The world's largest game reserve is the Selous Game Reserve of Tanzania, with a total area exceeding 21,000 sq. miles (55,000 km²). Uninhabited by humans and boasting an area bigger than Switzerland, it is named after English explorer/naturalist Frederick Selous.

Largest exhibit of live two-headed animals

Between August 22 and September 5, 2006, the World Aquarium in St. Louis, Missouri, USA, exhibited 11 live dicephalic (two-headed) specimens, including an albino rat snake named Golden Girls.

Most zoos visited

Mark Lehman of San Bernardino, California, USA, visited 359 different zoos around the world from July 1993 to October 2000.

Most species in one zoo

The Zoologischer Garten Berlin (Berlin Zoological Garden)—Germany's first zoo—opened on August 1, 1844. The 86-acre (35-ha) site currently houses 17,000 animals from 1,500 different species, including anteaters, polar bears, and hippos (*pictured*). It is one of the most popular zoos in the world—and the most popular in Europe—and in 2011 attracted about 2.9 million visitors.

NUTTY FOR KNUT

Pictured above is Knut the polar bear (December 5, 2006–March 9, 2011), who was born in captivity at Berlin Zoo and became the first polar bear cub to survive past infancy at the zoo for more than 30 years.

HOUSTON ZOO NATURALLY WILD

Houston Zoo (USA): Welcoming 1.84 million guests each year, Houston Zoo is home to 900 species.

SAN DIEGO ZOO

San Diego Zoo (USA): With more than 800 species on show, San Diego Zoo Global also has the **largest zoological membership association** in the world with more than 250,000 member households.

KÖLNER ZOO

Cologne Zoo (Germany): Founded in 1860, this zoo in the center of Cologne houses more than 9,000 animals from 783 species.

ZSL London Zoo (UK): Established in 1826, ZSL is the **oldest scientific zoo**. It opened to the public in 1847 and now houses about 767 species.

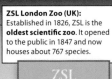

ZSL LONDON ZOO

SAN ANTONIO ZOO

San Antonio Zoo (USA): More than a million visitors a year clamor to see San Antonio's 750 species.

DAZZLING DOGS

PUPPIES ON PARADE
The St. Louis pet parade has run every year since 1994 in various guises.

Most dogs in costume

Nestlé Purina Pet Care (USA) organized a Beggin' Pet Parade for 1,326 dogs in St. Louis, Missouri, USA, on February 12, 2012. It was a Mardi Gras for all kinds of pets, although dogs were much in evidence and colorful canine costumes abounded.

Smallest service dog

Cupcake is a female long-haired Chihuahua who measured 6.25 in. (15.87 cm) tall and 1 ft. 2.25 in. (36.19 cm) from nose to tail on September 8, 2012. She is owned by Angela Bain of Moorestown in New Jersey, USA. Service dogs such as Cupcake are trained to give specialized assistance.

Dog breed with most teeth

Chow Chow puppies typically have 44 teeth, while other dogs normally possess 42 teeth or fewer.

Longest dog tail

Bentley had a tail of 2 ft. 2 in. (66.04 cm) on April 12, 2012. The Great Dane from Colorado Springs, Colorado, USA, is owned by Patrick Malcom and is the nephew of previous tallest dog record holder, Gibson.

Longest dog ears (living)

Harbor, owned by Jennifer Wert of Colorado, USA, is a Black and Tan Coonhound with ears measuring 1 ft. (31.1 cm) and 1 ft. 1 in. (34.3 cm) for the left and right ears respectively.

RAISING DANE
The average height of a fully grown Great Dane is 2 ft. 6 in.–2 ft. 10 in. (76–86 cm) for a male and 2 ft. 4 in.–2 ft. 8 in. (71–81 cm) for a female.

Tallest female dog

Bella the Great Dane, owned by Andrew and Suzanne Barbee of Chandler in Arizona, USA, measured 3 ft. 1 in. (94.93 cm) tall to the shoulder on June 27, 2012. She has won four obedience trial titles. Another Great Dane, named Zeus, is the **tallest dog** (and **tallest dog ever**). The Olympian canine measured 3 ft. 7 in. (111 cm) tall on October 4, 2011. His owners are Denise Doorlag and her family of Otsego in Michigan, USA.

3
Number of days that Rob and Davy practised in August 2012, with a best throw of 366 ft. (111.55 m).

Longest flying disk throw caught by a dog

A Whippet named Davy caught a flying disk thrown 402 ft. (122.5 m) by Robert McLeod (Canada) in Thorhild, Alberta, Canada, on October 14, 2012. Rob also set the record for the **most drink cans hit with flying disks in one minute**, striking 28 cans on January 28, 2012 in Calgary, Canada.

Dog breed with most toes

The Norwegian Lundehund, or Puffin Dog, has six toes per paw. The extras aid grip in the cliff-face caves where it hunts puffins in Norway.

Longest dog ears ever

Tigger the Bloodhound of St. Joseph in Illinois, USA, had the longest dog ears ever, measuring a total of 2 ft. 3 in. (69.1 cm) in 2004.

WORKING LIKE A DOG

Most guide dogs trained by one organization: As of 2011, the Guide Dogs for the Blind Association (UK) had successfully trained more than 29,000 dogs to provide assistance.

Fastest canine rat catcher: A "bull and terrier" dog named Billy, active in London, UK, in the early 19th century, killed 4,000 rats in 17 hours.

First animal whose evidence is admissible in court: Bloodhounds have been used to trail humans since Roman times. Their evidence is legally admissible in some U.S. courts.

Highest bounty on a dog: Agata the Golden Labrador had a $10,000 price on her head in 2004, having detected more than 660 lb. (300 kg) of cocaine in Colombia.

First canine movie star: Rollie Rover was so popular in *Rescued by Rover* (UK, 1905) that the negative wore out and the movie had to be made again.

120
Decibels of the average jet engine at takeoff—prolonged exposure can be dangerous.

Loudest bark by a dog

Charlie's bark is definitely worse than his bite—it measured 113.1 dB on October 20, 2012 during the Purina Bark in the Park event in Rymill Park, Adelaide, Australia. The big-lunged Golden Retriever is owned by Belinda Freebairn.

The **loudest bark by a group of dogs** measured 124 dB and was produced by 76 dogs in an event in Washington Park, Colorado, USA, on November 7, 2009.

Heaviest dog breed

Males of the English Mastiff and St. Bernard breeds regularly weigh 170–200 lb. (77–91 kg).

Farthest dock jump

A dock jump is a trick in which dogs run along a dock—usually some 40 ft. (12.19 m) long—and leap into water to fetch a toy. Taz, a Labrador Retriever owned by Mike Chiasson (Canada), performed a 31-ft.-long (9.44-m) dock jump on June 17, 2012 in Clayton, New York, USA. The record was matched on August 4, 2012 by Cochiti, a Whippet belonging to Diane Salts, in Ridgefield, Washington, USA.

OZZY ONLINE
A YouTube video of Ozzy balancing on his hind legs on a metal chain had more than 80,000 hits in one day!

Most intelligent breed of dog

Research published in 2009 by Stanley Coren (USA), Professor of Psychology at the University of British Columbia, Canada—and a poll of 200 dog obedience judges—revealed that the Border Collie is the brainiest breed of dog, followed by the Poodle and German Shepherd. The most intelligent dogs understand 250 words—equivalent to a child of two!

Smallest living dog

Milly—a Chihuahua owned by Vanesa Semler of Dorado, Puerto Rico—measured 3.8 in. (9.65 cm) tall on February 21, 2013.

Another Chihuahua, Heaven Sent Brandy, owned by Paulette Keller of Largo, Florida, USA, holds the record for the **smallest living dog by length**, measuring 6 in. (15.2 cm) from nose to tail on January 31, 2005.

Both tower over the **smallest dog ever**, a dwarf Yorkshire Terrier owned by Arthur Marples of Blackburn, UK. This tiny dog stood 2.8 in. (7.11 cm) at the shoulder and measured 3.75 in. (9.5 cm) from nose to tail. It died in 1945.

ACTUAL SIZE

Most tennis balls held in a dog's mouth

Augie, a Golden Retriever owned by the Miller family in Dallas, Texas, USA, held five regular tennis balls in his mouth on July 6, 2003.

Heaviest dog hair ball

Texas Hearing and Service Dogs (USA) groomed 8,126 dogs to create a ball of hair weighing 201 lb. (91.17 kg) in Austin, Texas, USA, on April 7, 2012.

Fastest crossing of a tightrope by a dog

A Border Collie/Kelpie cross named Ozzy traversed a tightrope measuring 11 ft. 5 in. (3.5 m) in 18.22 seconds at the F.A.I.T.H. Animal Rescue Centre in Norfolk, UK, on February 1, 2013. Ozzy—full name Osbert Humperdinck Pumpernickle—lives in Norwich, UK, with owner Nick Johnson.

Least hairy dog breed

The Xoloitzcuintli (Xolo for short, or the Mexican Hairless Dog) is typically bald on its body, although it may possess a few short hairs on the top of its head, toes, and the tip of its tail. This condition is due to a dominant mutant gene, which, as the Xolo is an ancient breed, probably originated several thousand years ago and may have helped it hunt in hot climates.

Highest man-dog parachute deployment: Mike Forsythe (USA) and Cara dived from an aircraft at 30,100 ft. (9,174 m) and parachuted safely to the ground.

First dog to detect cell phones: From 2006, Murphy (UK) was used to sniff out the scent of contraband cell phones in HM Prison Norwich, East Anglia, UK.

Most successful sniffer dog: Snag, a U.S. customs dog, had made 118 drug seizures worth $810 million by 2003.

First dog in space: Laika journeyed into space in November 1957 onboard the USSR's *Sputnik 2*.

SAN DIEGO PACIFIC REGION

Youngest gun dog trial winner: A 246-day-old Black Labrador puppy named Surprise of Triple Crown won the South of Ireland Gundog Club's Open Field Trial Stake in Offaly, Ireland, on December 6, 1971.

PETS

SEE IT 3D WITH THE FREE APP

AUGMENTED REALITY ALERT!
3D ON THIS PAGE

First albino pet parakeet

The aviary of Mr. E. Böhm von Bawerk of Vienna, Austria, was the 1931 breeding ground for the albino color variant of the budgerigar (*Melopsittacus undulatus*), or pet parakeet. The female budgie, the last of nine, had parents that were cobalt/whites.

Largest vocabulary for a bird

Puck, another budgerigar, owned by Camille Jordan of Petaluma, California, USA, knew an estimated 1,728 words at the time of his death in 1994. Puck's vocabulary was documented over a period of months by avian experts.

The record for the **largest vocabulary for a living bird** is 148 words, spoken by yet another budgerigar, Oskar, owned by Gabriela Danisch of Bad Oeynhausen, Germany. The blabbing budgie was tested on September 8, 2010.

The **first talking pet budgerigar** belonged to English convict Thomas Watling, who settled in Australia in 1788 after being transported. He taught his budgie—the first recorded example of a talking pet—to say: "How do you do, Dr. White?" (Dr. James White was the colony physician and an enthusiastic naturalist.) The name of the budgie was not recorded for posterity.

POLLYWOOD
One of Poncho's starring roles was alongside Jim Carrey in the movie *Ace Ventura: Pet Detective* (USA, 1994)!

Oldest parrot

The oldest living parrot is Poncho, an 87-year-old macaw who spent her "career" acting in Hollywood movies but who has since retired to Shrewsbury in Shropshire, UK. Poncho came to the UK in 2000 to appear in *102 Dalmatians* (USA/UK, 2000) but was too frail to return home and she was taken in by pet shop owners Rebecca Taylor and Sophie Williams (both UK).

Longest jump by a guinea pig

It's not quite pigs in space, but Truffles (UK) cleared 18.89 in. (48 cm) in Rosyth, Fife, UK, on April 6, 2012, beating his own record set on March 30, 2012 of 15.75 in. (40 cm).

Tallest domestic cat ever

Guinness World Records was sad to hear of the death on August 15, 2012 of Savannah Islands Trouble, who was 19 in. (48.3 cm) tall. Owned by Debby Maraspini (USA), Trouble was measured in Reno, Nevada, USA, on October 30, 2011, and remains the tallest domestic cat ever recorded.

Loudest cat purr

Despite competition from various contenders, the record for the loudest purring cat continues to be held by Smokey, owned by Ruth Adams (UK). On March 25, 2011, Smokey purred at 67.7 dB.

Largest breed of pet canary

The adult Parisian frill male measures 7.5–8.66 in. (19–22 cm) long.

GET UP AND GOAT!
Happie could have gone farther during her attempt but she hit a parking barrier!

Farthest distance skateboarding by a goat

Happie the goat lives with Melody Cooke and her family in Fort Myers, Florida, USA. There, the Nigerian dwarf cross has taken the opportunity to hone her gnarly skateboarding skills. On March 4, 2012, she hopped on a board and traveled 118 ft. (36 m), a distance she covered in 25 seconds.

ANIMALS AT WORK

Most successful chimpanzee on Wall Street: In 1999, Raven became the 22nd best money manager in the USA by choosing stocks based on throwing darts at a list of 133 Internet companies.

First cat piano concerto: *Catcerto* for orchestra and cat, composed by Mindaugas Piečaitis (Lithuania) and played by Nora the cat (USA), premiered on June 5, 2009.

Highest-ranking camel: Bert is a reserve deputy sheriff for the Los Angeles County Sheriff's Department, USA, and goes on patrol with his handler Nance Fite (USA).

Most fan mail for a cat: Socks lived in the White House during Bill Clinton's presidency from 1992 to 2000 and is said to have received 75,000 letters and packages a week.

Bravest donkey: In 1997, an Australian army donkey called Murphy was awarded the RSPCA Australia Purple Cross for animal bravery on behalf of all donkeys in the 1915–16 Gallipoli campaign of World War I. Murphy carried the wounded to field hospitals.

OLDEST ...

Cat

Creme Puff was born on August 3, 1967 and lived with Jake Perry in Austin, Texas, USA, until August 6, 2005—a total of 38 years 3 days.

Cockatiel

Pretty Boy was 28 years 47 days when he died in 2004. He was born in 1975 and belonged to Catherine Masarin of Hinckley, Ohio, USA.

Most prolific breed of rabbit

During the breeding season, the Californian (*above*) and the New Zealand White can produce five to six litters, each of which contain up to 12 kittens (young rabbits). This compares with five litters and three to seven young typically produced by the wild rabbit.

Gerbil (caged)

Sahara, a Mongolian gerbil (*Meriones unguiculatus*) born in May 1973 and belonging to Aaron Milstone of Michigan, USA, died on October 4, 1981 at the age of 8 years 4 months.

Goldfish

Tish, a *Carassius auratus* goldfish owned by the Hand family (UK), lived for 43 years after being won at a fairground in 1956.

Hamster

A hamster owned by Karen Smeaton of Tyne & Wear, UK, reached 4 years 6 months.

Parrot (stuffed)

Following the death of Frances Stuart, Duchess of Richmond and Lennox—a mistress of England's King Charles II—in 1702, her African gray parrot (*Psittacus erithacus*) soon died, supposedly of grief. The pickled parrot now perches next to the wax effigy of the duchess on display in Westminster Abbey's museum in London, UK.

Oldest rabbits

January 2013 marked the passing of Do, the world's **oldest living rabbit** (*above*). Do, who lived with Jenna Antol in New Jersey, USA, reached the age of 17 years 14 days and was less than a year away from becoming the **oldest rabbit ever**. This record is held by Flopsy (1964–83), owned by L. B. Walker of Tasmania, Australia.

42
Cat breeds recognized by the Cat Fanciers' Association, including 40 championship classes.

Longest fur on a cat

Colonel Meow, a two-year-old Himalayan-Persian cross owned by Anne Marie Avey of Seattle, Washington, USA, found Internet fame thanks to his comically angry expression. However, it's the Colonel's fur that has earned him a place in the record books. Measured on November 20, 2012, his longest strands of fur—based on an average of at least 10 hairs—reach 9 in. (22.87 cm).

Greatest mouser: A female tortoiseshell cat named Towser (UK), resident mouser at the Glenturret Distillery near Crieff in Perth and Kinross, UK, disposed of approximately 28,900 mice by 1987.

Longest-serving hearing dog: Donna, a guide dog owned by John Hogan of Pyrmont in New South Wales, Australia, completed a total of 18 years of service by May 6, 1995.

Largest animal orchestra: The 12-piece Thai Elephant Orchestra at the Thai Elephant Conservation Centre in Lampang, Thailand, weighs ca. 50,700 lb. (23 tonnes).

Most consecutive race wins by a greyhound: Between April 15, 1985 and December 9, 1986, Ballyregan Bob (UK) won 32 consecutive greyhound races.

Smallest police dog: Midge is a Chihuahua/Rat Terrier cross who measures 11 in. (28 cm) tall and 23 in. (58 cm) long. She works with owner Sheriff Dan McClelland (USA) at Geauga County sheriff's office in Chardon, Ohio, USA.

SEE IN 3D WITH THE FREE APP

ACTUAL SIZE

HUMAN BODY

iQUOTE

"Getting this record has made me feel better about myself. I feel popular, special, and important."

Shortest living woman

On December 16, 2011, Jyoti Amge, who stands at 24.7 in. (62.8 cm), turned 18 years old and became the shortest woman alive. Guinness World Records accompanied Jyoti, previously the **shortest teenager**, as she was measured at the Wockhardt Super Speciality Hospital in Nagpur, India, on her birthday. She proved to be 2.3 in. (6.2 cm) shorter than the previous record holder.

A star in the making, Jyoti is now set to act in Bollywood movies.

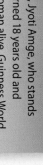

AUGMENTED REALITY ALERT!

3D ON THIS PAGE

GUINNESS WORLD RECORDS 2014

BODIFICATION

Meet the world's most extreme body modifiers

Piercing, tattooing, implanting, corseting, elongating, branding, tooth filing … there are almost no end of ways in which humans can physically modify their bodies for ornamentation and augmentation. Here, we introduce the unique characters who take this striking and sometimes controversial form of self-expression to the extreme.

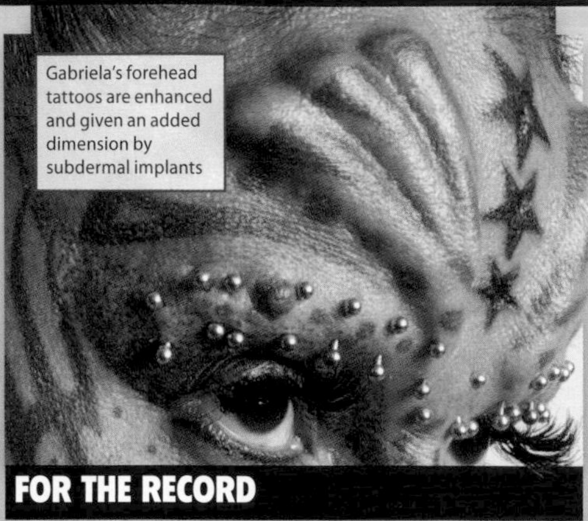

Gabriela's forehead tattoos are enhanced and given an added dimension by subdermal implants

FOR THE RECORD

An implant is a structure—typically made from metal, silicone, or coral—that is placed under the skin. There are two main types: subdermal (*above*), which sit completely under the skin, and transdermal, which protrude beyond the skin. The Peraltas have both kinds! *See table opposite.*

2 forehead implants

4 star-shape implants in the forehead and temples

10
Percentage of adults in England with a piercing located somewhere other than the ear!

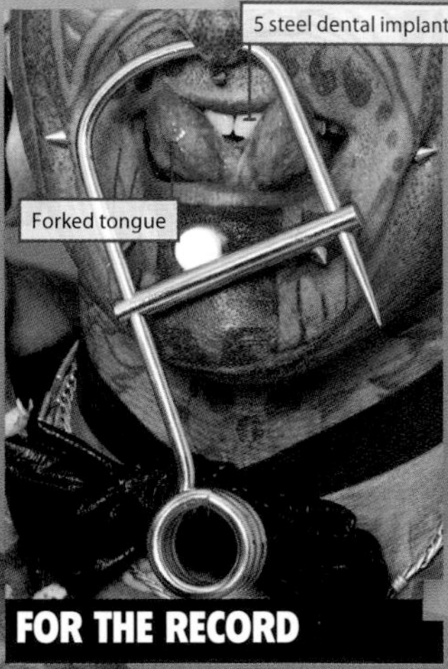

2 ear expanders, one in each lobe

30 piercings, mostly in the face and around the eyebrows

1 microdermal implant in face

60% tattoo coverage

1 diamond-shape subdermal implant in right hand

Scarification on head, left arm, and calves

Bolt through ear cartilage

2 ear expanders, one in each lobe

3 microdermal implants in face and chest; give the effect of a transdermal implant but are kept in place with an "anchor" under the skin

1 nose ring

5 steel dental implants

Forked tongue

FOR THE RECORD

Victor's tongue is "bifurcated" (from the Latin for "two-forked"). In this controversial modification—which is often banned—the tip of the tongue is sliced in two. The result is two half tongues that can, with practice, be moved independently of one another.

90% tattoo coverage

4 subdermal implants: a star and a pitchfork on left and right arms

20 piercings over the body; figure is constantly changing as new piercings are added and older ones fall out

Most modified married couple

Something old, something new, something borrowed, something tattooed! Victor Hugo Peralta (Uruguay) and his wife Gabriela (Argentina) are united by their shared love of body modification. As of November 2012, the tattooed twosome—who were married on February 21, 2008—had accrued, between them, 50 piercings, 11 body implants, five dental implants, four microdermals, four ear expanders, two ear bolts, one forked tongue, decorative scarring, and an average tattoo coverage of 75 percent.

¡QUOTE
"Most couples exchange vows and gold rings—but we pierce and tattoo each other!"

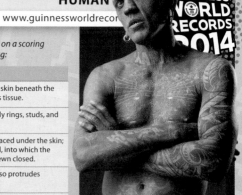

GUINNESS
WORLD
RECORDS
2014

The records for most modified man, woman, and couple are based on a scoring system encompassing a range of body modification options, including:

MODIFICATION	WHAT IS IT?
Tattoos	Indelible ink is injected into the dermis layer of the skin beneath the upper epidermis and the underlying subcutaneous tissue.
Piercings	The puncturing of the skin to add jewelry—typically rings, studs, and bars—either temporarily or permanently.
Subdermal implants	Jewelry or structures (often of silicone or Teflon) placed under the skin; an incision is made in the skin and a pocket created, into which the structure is implanted, after which the incision is sewn closed.
Transdermal implants	An implant that is placed under the skin but that also protrudes through the skin.
Microdermal implants	An implant that *looks* transdermal (i.e., on the surface) but is anchored beneath the skin; less invasive than transdermal procedures.
Dental implants	Similar to regular dental implants to anchor teeth permanently into the jaw, but usually with metal (typically titanium or steel) teeth.
Tooth shaping	The filing of teeth into extreme shapes, such as vampire fangs.
Scarring	Superficially etching the skin with a sharp edge (or, recently, laser) to form patterns of scar tissue.
Skin stretching	Most commonly performed on pierced earlobes; the skin is stretched using heavy items of jewelry or specially designed expanders.
Tongue splitting	The tongue is bifurcated (split) from the tip to an inch or so back, creating a forked effect.

Most pierced woman

When it comes to piercings alone, no one comes close to beating the colorful Elaine Davidson (Brazil/UK). Her total count is always changing because her studs and rings grow out and she adds new ones, but she has been pierced at least 4,225 times since 2000.

Most tattooed man

Lucky Rich (Australia/NZ) represents the ultimate in tattooing, having endured 1,000-plus hours of inking. New tattooes are inked over old, giving him coverage of about 200 percent.

Forked tongue

Most modified woman

Maria Jose Cristerna (Mexico) has a total of 49 body modifications, including significant tattoo coverage, a range of subdermal implants on her forehead, chest, and arms, and multiple piercings in her eyebrows, lips, nose, tongue, earlobes, and belly button.

Most modified man

You may recognize Germany's Rolf Buchholz— he appeared in the 2012 edition of *Guinness World Records* as the **most pierced man**, with 453 piercings. Since then, he has undergone a variety of modifications, including more piercings, sub- and transdermal implanting (including a new set of horns), and tattooing— giving him a grand total of 516 mods as of December 16, 2012.

¡QUOTE

"I can't really tell if my piercings have affected the way I speak, but I've learned to live with them just fine!"

2 subdermal "horn" implants on forehead

37 bar piercings through the eyebrows

8 nose piercings

111 piercings around the mouth and lips

5 chin piercings

33 ear piercings (18 in left ear, 15 in right ear) including ear expanders

9 subdermal forearm implants (6 on the right, 3 on the left)

90% tattoos; only the face and genitals are not tattooed

6 subdermal wrist implants

FOR THE RECORD

Rolf, an IT consultant, has been modifying his body for the past 13 years. He had his first piercing and tattoo on the same day, at the age of 40. Here he is in a rare photograph taken before embarking on his modification odyssey.

5 magnetic implants in the fingertips of the right hand

SIZE MATTERS

Tallest man ever

The tallest man in medical history for whom there is irrefutable evidence is Robert Pershing Wadlow (USA, February 22, 1918–July 15, 1940), who when last measured on June 27, 1940 was found to be 8 ft. 11.1 in. (272 cm) tall. His greatest recorded weight was 491 lb. (222.71 kg) on his 21st birthday and he weighed 439 lb. (199 kg) at the time of his death. He was buried in Alton, Illinois, USA, in a 10-ft. 9-in.-long (3.28-m) coffin. *See p. 50 for more.*

Tallest woman ever

Zeng Jinlian (China, June 26, 1964–February 13, 1982) of Yujiang village in the Bright Moon Commune, Hunan Province, measured 8 ft. 1.75 in. (248 cm) upon her death. This figure represented her height with assumed normal spinal curvature because she had severe scoliosis (curvature of the spine) and could not stand up straight. She began to grow abnormally from the age of four months and stood 5 ft. 1.5 in. (156 cm) before her fourth birthday and 7 ft. 1.5 in. (217 cm) when she was 13.

Shortest woman ever

Pauline Musters, known as Princess Pauline (Netherlands), was born in Ossendrecht on February 26, 1876 and measured 12 in. (30 cm) at birth. At nine years of age, she was 1 ft. 9.5 in. (55 cm) tall and weighed only 3 lb. 5 oz. (1.5 kg). She died of pneumonia with meningitis on March 1, 1895 in New York City, USA, at the age of 19. A postmortem examination showed her to be 2 ft. (61 cm).

Shortest living woman

Jyoti Kisanji Amge (India) measured 2 ft. 0.7 in. (62.8 cm) in Nagpur, India, on December 16, 2011. *See p. 44 for more.*

Most variable stature

The only person in medical history to have been both a dwarf and a giant is Adam Rainer (Austria, 1899–1950). He measured just 3 ft. 10.5 in. (118 cm) at the age of 21 but suddenly started growing at a rapid rate; by 1931, he had nearly doubled to 7 ft. 1.75 in. (218 cm). He became so weak that

GROWTH SPURT
By the age of four, Brenden was the height of an average eight-year-old; by eight, he was as tall as a 15-year-old.

Tallest teenager

Brenden Adams (b. September 20, 1995) of Ellensburg in Washington, USA, is, at 7 ft. 4.6 in. (225.1 cm), the world's tallest teen. Brenden has an extremely rare chromosomal disorder—he is currently the only known case—and at certain points in his childhood was taller than Robert Wadlow (**tallest man ever**, *see above*) at the same age.

iQUOTE
"The kids used to tease me and I found that very difficult. But now I'm really proud of being tall."

Tallest living man

Sultan Kösen (Turkey) continues to reign supreme as the tallest living man—and person—on the planet, measuring 8 ft. 3 in. (251 cm) during his last medical examination in Ankara, Turkey, on February 8, 2011. Sultan, who was born on December 10, 1982, also has the **largest hands**—11.22 in. (28.5 cm) from the wrist to the tip of the middle finger—and the **widest hand span** at 12 in. (30.48 cm).

FOR THE RECORD

The most exaggerated height claimed for a giant was 9 ft. 3.5 in. (283.2 cm) by Finland's Daniel Cajanus (1724–49). His actual height was determined *postmortem* to be 7 ft. 3 in. (222.2 cm)!

FOR MORE AMAZING ANATOMIES, JUST TURN THE PAGE!

YOUR RECORD-BREAKING BODY

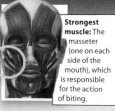
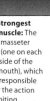

Strongest muscle: The masseter (one on each side of the mouth), which is responsible for the action of biting.

Largest artery: The aorta, which distributes oxygenated blood around the body, is 1.18 in. (3 cm) in diameter where it leaves the heart.

Largest vein: The inferior vena cava, which returns the blood from the lower half of the body to the heart.

Most mobile joint: The shoulder joint is the most mobile and, as a result, is the joint that is easiest to dislocate.

Shortest married couple

Douglas Maistre Breger da Silva and Claudia Pereira Rocha (both Brazil) measured 2 ft. 11 in. (90 cm) and 3 ft. 0.6 in. (93 cm) respectively—a total of 6 ft. 0.4 in. (183 cm)—when married on October 27, 1998, in Curitiba, Brazil.

Tallest living woman

Guinness World Records was sad to hear of the passing in late 2012 of Yao Defen of China who, at 7 ft. 7 in. (233.3 cm), was the tallest woman on Earth. In December, a records adjudicator and medical team traveled to the home of a potential successor, Siddiqa Parveen of South Dinajpur, India (*pictured*). Initial reports from a local health center had put Ms. Parveen at 8 ft. 2 in. (249 cm); unfortunately, because of ill health and Ms. Parveen's inability to stand upright, it is impossible to ascertain her exact stature. Dr. Debashis Saha, who performed the examination, estimates her standing height to be at least 7 ft. 8 in. (233.6 cm).

FACT:
When Dangi was first measured in February 2012, he was 72 years old. This makes him the oldest ever person to take the title of shortest man.

he was bedridden for the rest of his life. At the time of his death, he measured 7 ft. 8 in. (234 cm).

Tallest living married couple

Ex-basketball players Yao Ming and Ye Li (both China) measure 7 ft. 6 in. (228.6 cm) and 6 ft. 3 in. (190.5 cm) respectively, giving a combined height of 13 ft. 9 in. (419.1 cm). They married in Shanghai, China, on August 6, 2007.

Tallest married couple ever

Anna Haining Swan (Canada, 1846–88) was said to be 8 ft. 1 in. (246 cm) but her actual peak height at the age of 17 was 7 ft. 11 in. (241 cm), making her the **tallest teenage girl ever**. On June 17, 1871, she married Martin van Buren Bates (USA, 1837–1919), who stood at 7 ft. 9 in. (236 cm), making them the tallest married couple on record.

THE EIGHT-FOOT CLUB: HISTORY'S 13 GIANTS OVER 8 FT. (245 CM)

The true height of human giants is frequently obscured by exaggeration. The only people for whom heights of 8 ft. (245 cm) or more have been reliably reported are the 13 listed below.

NAME	LOCATION	HEIGHT
Robert Wadlow (1918–40)	Alton, Illinois, USA	8 ft. 11.1 in. (272 cm)
John William Rogan (1871–1905)	Gallatin, Tennessee, USA	8 ft. 8 in. (264 cm)—had ankylosis (stiffening of the joints due to the formation of adhesions) so unable to stand; measured sitting
John F. Carroll (1932–69)	Buffalo, New York, USA	8 ft. 7.75 in. (263.5 cm)—had severe kyphoscoliosis (spinal curvature); figure represents height with assumed normal curvature, calculated from a standing height of 8 ft. 0.4 in. (245 cm)
Väinö Myllyrinne (1909–63)	Helsinki, Finland	8 ft. 3 in. (251.4 cm)
Sultan Kösen (b. 1982)	Mardin, Turkey	8 ft. 3 in. (251.0 cm)
Don Koehler (1925–81)	Denton, Montana, USA	8 ft. 2 in. (248.9 cm)
Bernard Coyne (1897–1921)	Anthon, Iowa, USA	8 ft. 2 in. (248.9 cm)—had eunuchoidal gigantism (daddy longlegs syndrome)
Zeng Jinlian (1964–82)	Yujiang, Hunan, China	8 ft. 1.75 in. (248 cm)—had severe scoliosis; height estimated assuming normal spinal curvature
Patrick Cotter (O'Brien) (1760–1806)	Kinsale, County Cork, Ireland	8 ft. 1 in. (246.4 cm)—revised height based on skeletal remeasurement after bones exhumed on December 19, 1972
Brahim Takioullah (b. 1982)	Guelmim, Morocco	8 ft. 0.97 in. (246.3 cm)
"Constantine", aka Julius Koch (1872–1902)	Reutlingen, West Germany	8 ft. 0.8 in. (245.8 cm)—eunuchoidal giant; height estimated because both legs were amputated due to gangrene; claimed to be 8 ft. 6 in. (259 cm)
Gabriel Estêvão Monjane (1944–89)	Manjacaze, Mozambique	8 ft. 0.8 in. (245.7 cm)
Suleiman Ali Nashnush (1943–68)	Tripoli, Libya	8 ft. 0.4 in. (245 cm)

Shortest living man

At 21.5 in. or 1 ft. 9.5 in. (54.6 cm) tall, the shortest living man—and the **shortest man ever**—is Chandra Bahadur Dangi of Nepal, who was measured at the CIWEC Clinic Travel Medicine Center in Lainchaur, Kathmandu, Nepal, on February 26, 2012. Since attaining his records, Mr Dangi has made his first overseas trips, visiting Australia, Japan, and Italy; here he is pictured during his vacation in the Italian capital, Rome.

Longest muscle: The sartorius—a narrow ribbonlike muscle running from the pelvis to the top of the tibia below the knee—draws the lower limb into the cross-legged position.

Largest muscle: The gluteus maximus, or buttock muscle, which extends the thigh, is the bulkiest of the 639 named muscles in the body.

Smallest bone: The stapes or stirrup bone, one of the three auditory ossicles in the middle ear, measures 0.1–0.13 in. (2.6–3.4 mm) long and weighs 0.00007–0.00015 oz (2–4.3 mg).

Smallest muscle: The stapedius, which controls the stapes in the ear, is less than 0.05 in. (0.127 cm) long.

Longest bone: The thigh bone, or femur, constitutes 27.5 percent of a person's stature—e.g., 19.75 in. (50 cm) long in a man measuring 6 ft. (180 cm) tall.

Largest organ: The skin is considered an organ and is, therefore, the largest of them all, typically covering 16–21 sq. ft. (1.5–2 m²).

AWESOME ANATOMY

5,000 Calories consumed daily by Sharran in preparation for a sumo match.

failure. Minnoch's wife Jeanette (USA) weighed just 110 lb. 3 oz. (50 kg), making theirs the **greatest weight differential for a married couple** at around 1,289 lb. 11 oz. (585 kg).

Heaviest living man

Manuel Uribe (Mexico) weighed 980 lb. (444.6 kg) as of March 2012. At his absolute heaviest, in January 2006, he weighed 1,235 lb. (560 kg). Since then—and with medical assistance—he has gradually been able to lose weight. Although he has been bed-bound since 2002, Manuel married his second wife, Claudia Solis, in 2008.

Heaviest sportswoman

The heaviest female athlete currently active is sumo wrestler Sharran Alexander of London, UK, who weighed 448 lb. (203.21 kg) on December 15, 2011. Sharran is recognized by the British Sumo Federation and has won four gold medals in international competition.

Heaviest woman ever

Rosalie Bradford (USA, 1943–2006) peaked at 1,200 lb. (544 kg) in January 1987. After a health scare, she reduced her daily intake

Heaviest living woman

Pauline Potter of California, USA, weighed 647 lb. 6 oz. (293.6 kg) in July 2012, making her the heaviest living woman to have had her weight confirmed medically. Although other women have claimed to be heavier, none has been able to submit medical proof.

Heaviest man ever

In March 1978, Jon Brower Minnoch (USA) was admitted to University Hospital in Seattle, Washington, USA, where endocrinologist Dr. Robert Schwartz calculated that he must have weighed more than 1,400 lb. (635 kg), much of which was water accumulation due to congestive heart

Heaviest sportsman

Emmanuel "Manny" Yarborough of Rahway, New Jersey, USA, stands 6 ft. 8 in. (203 cm) tall and weighs 704 lb. (319.3 kg). A mixed martial artist, Manny was introduced to sumo by his judo coach; seven years later, he was ranked number one in the open sumo wrestling category for amateurs.

FOR THE RECORD

The aim of sumo wrestling is to jostle your opponent (*rikishi*) out of the ring (*dohyo*), or force any part of their body other than the soles of their feet to touch the ground. The sport is highly ritualistic, because its origins lie in Japan's Shinto religion.

to 1,200 calories and, within five years, had lost the equivalent weight of seven average women.

Heaviest person to complete a marathon

On March 20, 2011, sumo wrestler Kelly Gneiting (USA) completed the 2011 Los Angeles Marathon in California, USA, in a time of 9 hr. 48 min. 52 sec. He weighed in at 400 lb. (181.44 kg) half an hour before the start of the race; by the end, his weight had fallen to 396 lb. 3.2 oz. (179.7 kg).

BODY PARTS

Largest hands

Perhaps unsurprisingly, the hands of Robert Wadlow (USA)—the

BREATHTAKING BODY PARTS

Longest tongue (male): 3.86 in. (9.8 cm) from the tip to the middle of closed top lip; Stephen Taylor (UK), February 11, 2009.

Longest fingernails ever (female): 28 ft. 4.5 in. (865 cm); Lee Redmond (USA), February 23, 2008.

Longest nose: 3.46 in. (8.8 cm) from bridge to tip; Mehmet Ozyurek (Turkey), March 18, 2010.

Smallest waist: 15 in. (38.1 cm) corseted, 21 in. (53.34 cm) uncorseted; Cathie Jung (USA), December 19, 1999.

Largest hands: 11.22 in. (28.5 cm) from wrist to tip of the middle finger; Sultan Kösen (Turkey), February 8, 2011.

HISTORY'S HEAVIEST OVER 1,000 LB. (454 KG)

The peak weights of the individuals listed below are either taken from authenticated medical records or estimations made by medical professionals.

NAME	LOCATION	PEAK WEIGHT
Jon Brower Minnoch (1941–83)	Washington, USA	1,400 lb. (635 kg)—extrapolated by doctors from his intake and elimination rate
Manuel Uribe (b. 1965)	Monterrey, Mexico	1,235 lb. (560 kg)
Walter Hudson (1944–91)	Brooklyn, New York, USA	1,199 lb. (544 kg)
Carol Ann Yager (1960–94)	Flint, Michigan, USA	1,199 lb. (544 kg)—weight at death; peak estimated by her partner to be more than 1,600 lb. (725 kg) but not supported medically
Rosalie Bradford (1943–2006)	Sellersville, Pennsylvania, USA	1,199 lb. (544 kg)—estimated peak in 1987; confirmed at 1,053 lb. (477.6 kg) in 1989
Michael Walker, aka Francis Lang (b. 1934)	Gibsonton, Florida, USA	1,186 lb. (538 kg)—peak weight attained in 1971
Robert Earl Hughes (1926–58)	Baylis, Illinois, USA	1,067 lb. (484 kg) – also recorded the **largest chest measurement** at 10 ft. 4 in. (315 cm)
Carol Haffner (1936–95)	Hollywood, Florida, USA	1,023 lb. (464 kg)
Mike Parteleno (1958–2001)	Struthers, Ohio, USA	1,021 lb. (463 kg)—weight reported by a diet firm in 1988; prior to this, was claimed by Parteleno to be just 645 lb. (292.5 kg)
Mills Darden (1799–1857)	North Carolina, USA	1,018 lb. 6 oz. (462 kg)—had the medical condition acromegaly (gigantism)
Michael Edelman (1964–92)	Pomona, New York, USA	1,007 lb. 8 oz. (457 kg)—unconfirmed peak weight of 1,200 lb. (544.3 kg); starved to death after forming morbid fear of overeating

tallest man ever (*see p. 48*)—were also superlative. They measured 12.75 in. (32.3 cm) from the wrist to the tip of his middle finger. He wore a size 25 ring.

The **largest hands on a living person** belong to Wadlow's modern-day equivalent, Sultan Kösen (*see below left*). Sultan briefly also held the record for the largest feet on a living person—but no longer. If you want to find out who the current record-holder is, just turn the page!

Longest fingernails

Female: Chris "The Dutchess" Walton (USA, *pictured*) has fingernails measuring a total of 19 ft. 9 in. (601.9 cm).
Female (ever): Lee Redmond's (USA) nails grew to a length of 28 ft. 4.5 in. (865 cm) before she lost them in a car crash in 2009 (*see below left*).
Male: During his last measurement in February 2004, Shridhar Chillal (India) had a total nail length of 23 ft. 1.5 in. (705 cm).
Male (ever): Melvin Boothe (USA, d. 2009) had a total of 32 ft. 3.8 in. (985 cm) of nails on both hands (*see below right*).

Most fingers and toes

Pranamya Menaria and Devendra Harne (both India) each have 25 digits in total (12 fingers and 13 toes) as a result of the condition polydactylism.

The **most fingers and toes at birth**—14 fingers (seven on each hand) and 20 toes (10 on each foot)—belonged to Akshat Saxena (India). The record was confirmed by doctors in India on March 20, 2010. Akshat has since had an operation and now has the usual number of digits.

Most teeth in the mouth

Kanchan Rajawat (India) and Luca Meriano (Italy) both had 35 adult teeth as of October 17, 2008.

Sean Keaney (UK) of Newbury, Berkshire, UK, was born on April 10, 1990 with 12 teeth—the **most teeth at birth**. They were taken out to prevent possible feeding problems. Sean grew his second full set of teeth at the age of 18 months.

¡QUOTE
"When I was a child, I knew my skin was different—my uncles used to have fun showing their friends."

Stretchiest skin

Garry Turner (UK) can stretch his skin to a length of 6.25 in. (15.8 cm) as a result of Ehlers-Danlos syndrome, a disorder of the connective tissues. It also accounts for his success in another Guinness World Records category—**most clothespins clipped on a face**—as Garry can attach 159 wood clothespins to the skin of his face.

AMERICA'S GOT TALONS
Left hand: 10 ft. 2 in. (309.8 cm)
Right hand: 9 ft. 7 in. (292.1 cm)

AUGMENTED REALITY ALERT!
3D ON THIS PAGE

SEE IT 3D WITH THE FREE APP

WANT YOUR BODIES MORE SUPERHUMAN? FLY OVER TO P. 208

Longest legs (female): 51.9 in. (132 cm); Svetlana Pankratova (Russia), July 8, 2003.

Widest mouth: 6.69 in. (17 cm); Francisco Domingo Joaquim "Chiquinho" (Angola), March 18, 2010.

Farthest eyeball pop: 0.47 in. (12 mm); Kim Goodman (USA), November 2, 2007.

Longest fingernails ever (male): 32 ft. 3.8 in. (985 cm); Melvin Boothe (USA), May 30, 2009.

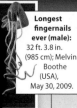

Longest tongue (female): 3.8 in. (9.75 cm) from tip to middle of lip; Chanel Tapper (USA), September 29, 2010.

AMAZING FEATS

MOST FEET AND ARMPITS SNIFFED

Madeline Albrecht (USA) tested products by foot-care and footwear firm Dr. Scholl's for 15 years at the Hill Top Research labs in Cincinnati, Ohio, USA. She smelled some 5,600 feet and an indeterminate number of armpits during the course of her work.

Largest feet ever

Robert Wadlow (USA), famously the **tallest man** ever (see p. 48), also had record-breaking feet: he wore U.S. size 37AA shoes for his 1-ft. 6.5-in.-long (47-cm) feet.

Longest toes

There's no record of Robert Wadlow's toes being measured, but those belonging to Matthew McGrory (USA, 1973–2005) were documented in the 1990s. The owner at the time of the largest feet on a living person—his right foot was 17.5 in. (44.45 cm) long, equivalent to a U.S. size 29½—Matthew had halluces (big toes) measuring 5 in. (12.7 cm). His little toes were "just" 1.5 in. (3.81 cm).

Largest pair of socks

Not even Wadlow or McGrory would be able to fill the world's biggest socks. A nylon pair measuring 45 ft. (13.72 m) from top to toe and 10 ft. (3.05 m) wide were created by Michael Roy Layne

Longest toenails

Louise Hollis (USA) gave up trimming her toenails back in 1982. When measured at their longest in 1991, the combined length of all 10 toenails came to a whopping 7 ft. 3 in. (220.98 cm)!

(USA) in October 1986 to mark the Boston Red Sox baseball team winning the American League Championship and entering the World Series.

Largest clogs

Peter de Koning (Netherlands) crafted a pair of wooden clogs 9 ft. 11 in. (3.04 m) long, 3 ft. 6 in. (1.08 m) wide, and 3 ft. 7 in. (1.10 m) tall. They were carved from a single block of poplar wood and measured in Halsteren, Netherlands, on October 20, 2012.

Largest feet on a living person

If cases of elephantiasis are excluded, then the biggest feet currently known are those of Brahim Takioullah (Morocco, b. 1982), whose left foot measures 1 ft. 3 in. (38.1 cm) and right foot measures 1 ft. 2.76 in. (37.5 cm). The measurements were taken in Paris, France, on May 24, 2011.

Brahim is pictured with Jyoti Amge (India), the **shortest living woman**. To find out more about the remarkable Jyoti, turn to p. 44.

turn to p. 44.

SKY-HIGH GUY

It's no wonder Brahim has such large feet—after all, at 8 ft. 1 in. (246.3 cm) he's the second-tallest man, after Turkey's Sultan Kösen.

GREATEST FOOT ROTATION

Moses Lanham (USA) turned his feet through 120° on the set of Lo Show dei Record in Milan, Italy, on March 10, 2011. He also set the record for the **fastest time to walk 20 m with the feet facing backward**—19.59 seconds!

PHENOMENAL FOOTWEAR

Largest shoelace mosaic: 64 ft² 130 in² (6.03 m²). Created by ECCO Shoes HK, in Hong Kong, China, on April 20, 2013.

Longest line of socks: 10,446 ft. (3,184 m). Created by The Sir Peter Blake Trust in Wellington, New Zealand, on June 30, 2011.

Largest hiking boot: 23 ft. 5 in. (7.14 m) long, 8 ft. 2 in. (2.5 m) wide, 13 ft. 9 in. (4.2 m) tall, by Schuh Marke (Germany). Presented in Hauenstein, Germany, on September 30, 2006.

Longest chain of shoes: 24,962, by the Shoeman Water Projects at Stankowski Field, University of Missouri, Columbia, USA, on May 7, 2011.

Largest collection of tribal and ethnic footwear: 2,322 pairs of footwear from 155 countries, by William (Boy) Habraken (Netherlands).

First woman to fly an airplane with her feet

Jessica Cox (USA) was able to gain her pilot's license on October 10, 2008, in spite of being born without arms. She accesses the controls with one foot and delicately guides the steering column with the other.

Largest high-heel shoe
Edmund Kryza (Poland) made a stiletto 6 ft. (1.84 m) long and 3 ft. 8 in. (1.12 m) high from artificial leather on May 8, 1996.

Largest footprint painting
On June 3, 2012, IN56 and Loving Power (both Hong Kong) created an 18,134.49-sq.-ft. (1,684.75-m²) footprint painting in Hong Kong, China. The image depicted a parent and child crossing a rainbow bridge.

Longest line of footprints
A line of 15,200 footprints measuring 14,711 ft. (4,484 m) was created at an event arranged by WA Newspapers in Perth, Western Australia, on December 10, 2005.

Longest set of dinosaur footprints
The Cal Orck'o quarry near Sucre, Bolivia, contains more than 5,000 individual dinosaur

footprints—the **most dinosaur footprints in one place**. More than 250 trackways have been identified, made by a therapod dinosaur 68 million years ago.

MOST ...

Beer bottles opened with the feet in one minute
Zlata, aka Julia Günthel (Germany), opened seven beer bottles in a minute in Beijing, China, on August 16, 2011. She adopted the contortionist's "elbow stand" position for the attempt.

NEAT FEAT
Rob removed two bread slices from a bag, the rind off the bologna, and the plastic wrap from the cheese with his feet!

Fastest time to make a sandwich with the feet

Using just his feet, Rob Williams (USA) made a bologna, cheese, and lettuce sandwich—complete with olives on toothpicks—in 1 min. 57 sec. on November 10, 2000, in Los Angeles, USA.

Skips on one foot in 30 seconds
On July 2, 2012, Stefano Vargiu (Italy) skipped 113 times on one foot in 30 seconds in Quartu Sant'Elena, Italy.

Socks worn on one foot
Fiona Nolan (Ireland) wore 152 socks on one foot in Shannon, Ireland, on March 25, 2011.
The **most socks put on one foot in one minute** is 35, by Shaun Cotton (UK) in Paignton, UK, on November 13, 2012.

Toe Wrestling World Championships won
Male: Six, by Alan "Nasty" Nash (UK) in 1994, 1996–97, 2000, 2002, and 2009.
Female: Four, by Karen Davies (UK) in 1999–2002.

Farthest distance to shoot an arrow into a target with the feet

Using only her feet while balanced on her hands, Claudia Gomez (Argentina) hit a target with a bow and arrow from 18 ft. 0.53 in. (5.5 m) on the set of *El Show de los Récords* in Madrid, Spain, on November 15, 2001.

YOUR FEET ARE OFFICIALLY AMAZING!

PUT YOUR FOOT IN IT AND HELP SET A TOE-TALLY FANTASTIC WORLD RECORD!

IT'S YOUR CHANCE TO GET YOUR NAME (AND FEET) IN THE RECORD BOOKS!

To celebrate your fascinating feet—be they big, small, cheesy, or hairy—we're asking you to put your best foot forward for a very special Guinness World Records challenge and become a record-breaker along the way.

We're creating the **largest online foot photo album** and need a minimum of 50,000 feet-ographs to make everyone who takes part a Guinness World Records title holder. Just take a photo of your feet or create your own footprint then upload it to www.officiallyamazing.tv/feet—if we break the record, you could be the proud owner of a Guinness World Records certificate!

Largest collection of shoehorns: 1,594 shoehorns, by Martien Tuithof (Netherlands). Housed in the Zijper Museum, Schagerbrug, Netherlands.

First leather shoe: 5,500 years old. Discovered by archaeologists in Areni-1 cave in Vayots Dzor Province, Armenia, in 2008.

Largest collection of shoe-related items: 15,665 different items as of March 20, 2012, by Darlene Flynn (USA).

Heaviest shoe walked in: 323 lb. (146.5 kg), worn by Ashrita Furman (USA) at Potters Fields, London, UK, on Guinness World Records Day, November 18, 2010.

Most socks sorted in 30 seconds: 18 pairs, by Silvio Sabba (Italy) in Pioltello, Milan, Italy, on May 5, 2012.

HAIR

Greatest weight lifted with the hair

Suthakaran Sivagnanathurai (Sri Lanka) hoisted 143 lb. 4 oz. (65 kg) at St. Mark's Catholic Primary School in Brisbane, Queensland, Australia, on December 8, 2012, using his hair. The weight was held for more than a minute. He has also endured the **longest time suspended by the hair**, spending 23 min. 19 sec. aloft at Uniting Church hall in Brisbane on December 18, 2011.

Heaviest vehicle pulled with the hair

Ajit Kumar Singh (India) used his hair to pull a truck weighing 20,700 lb. (9.38 tonnes) in Nawada, Bihar, India, on September 21, 2010. Singh pulled the truck for a distance of 180 ft. (55 m).

Widest wig

Annie Woon (China) made a wig measuring 5 ft. 5.2 in. (1.65 m) wide and 1 ft. 3.6 in. (39 cm) high in Hong Kong, China, on January 7, 2013.

The **tallest wig** was made by Emilio Minnicelli of Bologna, Italy, out of real hair. It measured 46 ft. 11 in. (14.3 m) tall on May 15, 2004.

Longest hair

Male: Swami Pandarasannadhi (India) had hair measuring 26 ft. (7.93 m) in length in Madras, India, in 1948. From photographs, it appears that he was affected with *Plica neuropathica,* which causes matting of the hair.

Female: Xie Qiuping (China) had hair of 18 ft. 5.54 in. (5.627 m) when measured on May 8, 2004. She stopped cutting her hair in 1973.

Longest body hairs

Chest: 9 in. (22.8 cm), Richard Condo (USA)
Leg: 7.48 in. (19.01 cm), Guido Arturo (Italy)
Arm: 7.44 in. (18.90 cm), Kenzo Tsuji (Japan)
Ear: 7.1 in. (18.1 cm), Anthony Victor (India)
Eyebrow: 7.1 in. (18.1 cm), Sumito Matsumura (Japan)
Back: 5.11 in. (13 cm), Craig Bedford (UK)
Eyelash: 2.75 in. (6.99 cm), Stuart Muller (USA)

Most wins at the World Beard & Moustache Championships

Karl-Heinz Hille (Germany) won eight contests between 1999 and 2011. He competed in the Imperial Partial Beard category, a style honoring Kaiser Wilhelm I of Prussia (1797–1888). Guidelines stipulate that the beard be grown on the cheeks and upper lip. The ends must point upward and not curl over.

¡QUOTE
"I like to visit schools, especially schools with children who are different. It is OK to be different."
– Jesus Manuel Fajardo Aceves

Largest hairy family

Pictured (*from left to right*) are Luisa Lilia De Lira Aceves, Karla Michelle Aceves Diaz, Luis Abran Aceves, and Jesus Manuel Fajardo Aceves (all Mexico). They are four of a family of 19 with a rare condition called congenital generalized hypertrichosis, characterized by excessive facial and torso hair. Women are covered with a light-to-medium coat of hair while the men have thick hair on some 98% of their body.

COLOSSAL CUTS AND CLOSE SHAVES

Most heads shaved in one hour by an individual: John McGuire (Ireland) used his clippers on 60 people at Today FM in Dublin, Ireland, on February 18, 2010.

Most heads shaved in an hour by a team: 10 hairdressers shaved 318 heads at the Style Club in Dublin, Ireland, on February 18, 2011.

Most heads shaved in an hour (multiple venues): The "funrazor" event for the Child Cancer Foundation shaved 722 heads at nine different locations around New Zealand on December 7, 2006.

Most consecutive haircuts in 24 hours by an individual: Nabi Salehi snipped 526 heads of hair at A&N Style in London, UK, on June 4, 2011.

Most consecutive haircuts by a team in 12 hours: Stylists at Great Clips in Springfield, Ohio, USA, cut 392 hair styles on May 14, 2011.

Largest ball of human hair

Henry Coffer (USA), a barber in Charleston, Missouri, USA, began saving hair at a customer's request. More than 50 years later, Henry made a hair ball weighing 167 lb. (75.7 kg), as of December 2008.

Heaviest object removed from stomach

A trichobezoar is a hair ball resulting from trichophagia—the eating of one's own hair. A hair ball weighing 10 lb. (4.5 kg) was removed from the stomach of an 18-year-old woman at Rush University Medical Center in Chicago, Illinois, USA, in November 2007.

Largest collection of hair from historical figures

John Reznikoff of Connecticut, USA, accumulated a collection of hair from 115 historical figures. His set of legendary locks included snippets from Abraham Lincoln, Albert Einstein, and Elvis Presley.

Largest afro

"Afro"—short for "Afro-American" and often called a "natural"—is a hair style popularized by the African-American community in the 1960s. The largest on record belongs to Aevin Dugas (USA), whose afro measured 6.30 in. (16 cm) in height and 4 ft. 7 in. (1.39 m) in circumference on March 31, 2012.

Largest donation of hair

Pilgrims at the Tirupati temple in Andhra Pradesh, India, donate a tonsure—hair shaved from the scalp. An estimated 6.5 million people donate annually, with the help of 600 barbers, and the temple auctions the hair to wigmakers and chemical and fertilizer factories. Tirupati is the **most visited Hindu temple** attracting 30,000–40,000 visitors each day.

Tallest mohican

Kazuhiro Watanabe (Japan) had a high-rise hairdo that measured 44.68 in. (113.5 cm) at Bloc de l'art hair salon, Shibuya, Tokyo, Japan, on October 28, 2011. He's not alone in his fashion: the **largest gathering of people with mohicans** is 257 and was achieved by Today FM's *The Ray D'Arcy Show* in Dublin, Ireland, on February 22, 2013.

¡QUOTE
"Without my beard, I'm not me. I'm pretending to be someone I'm not."

Longest female beard (living)

Vivian Wheeler (USA) had facial hair measuring 10.04 in. (25.5 cm)—from follicle to whisker tip—on April 8, 2011. Vivian began shaving her face at the age of seven, and it was only after four marriages and her mother's death in 1993 that she finally stopped trimming back the facial growth and let her beard grow. She prefers to tie up the beard to allow for her to continue with her day-to-day routines.

The **longest male beard (living)** belongs to Sarwan Singh (Canada), whose combed-out whiskers measured 8 ft. 2.5 in. (2.495 m) in British Columbia, Canada, on September 8, 2011.

Most scissors for a haircut: Zedong Wang (China) cut with 10 pairs of scissors in one hand, controlling each pair, in Beijing, China, on October 31, 2007.

Most expensive haircut: Stuart Phillips (UK), at the Stuart Phillips salon in Covent Garden, London, UK, cut an £8,000 ($16,400) style on October 29, 2007.

Fastest haircut: Ivan Zoot (USA) cut a head of hair in 55 seconds at Roosters Men's Grooming Center in Austin, Texas, USA, on August 22, 2008.

Oldest barber business: Truefitt & Hill, "Gentlemen's Perfumers and Hairdressers," first opened in 1805 at 2 Cross Lane, Long Acre, London, UK.

Highest hairstyle: A tower of real and fake hair reaching 8.73 ft. (2.66 m) was created in an event organized by KLIPP unser Frisör in Wels, Austria, on June 21, 2009.

MEDICAL MARVELS

Richard Lee Norris (USA). The operation gave Norris a complete new face, from his scalp to the bottom of his neck, including both jaws, teeth, and a portion of his tongue.

Longest-lived human cells

On October 4, 1951, Henrietta Lacks (USA, b. August 1, 1920) died from cancer at Johns Hopkins Hospital in Baltimore, Maryland, USA. Cells from her cervical cancer were taken both before and after her death and became the first human cells to survive and divide outside the human body. Known as HeLa cells (*above right*), the descendants of these cells still survive and are used for medical research around the world in areas including cancer research, polio vaccination, and *in vitro* fertilization. Henrietta's cells have been referred to in more than 60,000 research papers.

First brain cell transplant

Doctors from the University of Pittsburgh Medical Center in Pennsylvania, USA, worked to reverse the damage of a stroke experienced by 62-year-old Alma Cerasini (USA), including speech loss and paralysis of her right side, during the first successful brain cell transplant on June 23, 1998.

Longest chain of kidney transplants

A kidney transplant chain links together people who want to donate a kidney to a friend or relative but are unable to do so because they are not a clinical match. The donor instead donates their kidney to a stranger in need of a transplant and the donor's

HANDY MAN
Jifa lost his hands and forearms when a homemade bomb he intended to use for blast fishing detonated accidentally.

First functional homemade double prosthetic arms

On August 14, 2012, UK newspaper *The Daily Telegraph* reported the case of 51-year-old Sun Jifa (China), who had lost both of his hands and forearms in a fishing accident eight years previously. Jifa has spent the years since building a series of prototype prosthetic arms. His current pair, made mostly from scrap metal, contain internal pulleys and wires that he can control with his elbows, allowing him to grip and hold objects, and continue working on his farm.

First successful full-face transplant

Performed by a team of doctors from the Vall d'Hebron University Hospital in Barcelona, Spain, on March 20, 2010, the first ever successful full-face transplant operation took 24 hours to complete. The patient was a 31-year-old man known only as "Oscar," the victim of a shooting accident. His muscles, nose, lips, maxilla, palate, teeth, cheekbones, and mandible were transplanted by means of plastic surgery and microneurovascular reconstructive surgery techniques.

Most extensive face transplant

On March 20, 2012, surgeons at the University of Maryland Medical Center in Baltimore, Maryland, USA, completed 36 hours of surgery on patient

Heaviest triplets (current)

Michelle Lee Wilson (USA) gave birth to triplets with a combined weight of 22 lb. 12.6 oz. (10.33 kg) on July 29, 2003. The triplets—Evan Patrick (8 lb. 9.4 oz.; 3.89 kg), Aiden Cole (7 lb. 5.4 oz.; 3.32 kg) and Lilly Kathryn (6 lb. 13.8 oz.; 3.11 kg)—were delivered within 2 minutes of each other in Englewood, Colorado, USA. Michelle carried the healthy triplets to 36 weeks and 5 days.

intended recipient receives a kidney, in turn, from another stranger who *does* match.

Between August 15 and December 20, 2011, a total of 30 kidney transplants were performed as a result of a chain that stretched from coast to coast across the USA. "Chain 124" began with 44-year-old Rick Ruzzamenti (USA) and ended at Loyola University Medical Center in Illinois, USA, with the final recipient, 46-year-old Don Terry (USA).

Longest surviving heart transplant patient

Tony Huesman (USA, 1957–2009) survived with a single transplanted heart for 30 years 11 months 10 days. Huesman was diagnosed with viral cardiomyopathy at the age of 16 and received a heart transplant operation on August 30, 1978, 11 years after the world's **first heart transplant** was performed in South Africa. He died of cancer on August 9, 2009, at his home in Washington Township, Ohio, USA.

RECORD-BREAKING SURVIVORS

Farthest vertical ski-fall: Bridget Mead (New Zealand) fell nearly 1,312 ft. (400 m) at the 1997 World Extreme Skiing Championships in Valdez, Alaska, USA.

Most lightning strikes: Ex-park ranger Roy C. Sullivan (USA) is the only person to survive being struck by lightning seven times!

Fastest car crash: In 1960, Donald Campbell (UK) crashed *Bluebird CN7* while traveling at a speed of 360 mph (579 km/h) at the Bonneville Salt Flats in Utah, USA.

Farthest fall down an elevator shaft: In 1998, Stuart Jones fell 229 ft. (70 m) down an elevator shaft at the Midland Park Building in Wellington, New Zealand.

Highest percentage of body burns: Tony Yarijanian (USA) survived 90% burns to his body after an accidental explosion in California, USA, on February 15, 2004.

First 3D-printed complete lower jaw implant

In June 2011, an 83-year-old woman underwent surgery at the Orbis Medisch Centrum in Sittard-Geleen, Netherlands, during which she was implanted with a lower jaw created using a 3D printer. It was made from titanium powder fused together using a laser, and was invented by LayerWise in collaboration with scientists at Hasselt University (both Belgium).

First person cured of HIV

It was announced on July 24, 2012 that HIV patient Timothy Ray Brown (USA, *left*) was free of the virus, despite being diagnosed HIV positive in 1995. Brown underwent 11 years of antiretroviral therapy before meeting Gero Hütter (*right*), a German hematologist, in 2007. Hütter transplanted stem cells from a donor who had the CCR5 mutation, which makes cells immune to HIV, and Brown stopped his regular medication. The result is that he is now effectively cured.

of the child's total bodyweight of 6 lb. 8.5 oz. (3 kg)—was excised by a team led by Dr. Palin Khundongbam (India) in Imphal, Manipur, India, on March 17, 2003.

First person to operate a mind-controlled robotic hand

Matthew Nagle (USA, 1979–2007) was paralyzed from the neck down in a knife attack in 2001. On June 22, 2004, at New England Sinai Hospital in Massachusetts, USA, a BrainGate experimental brain-computer

Largest tumor removed

In 1905, Dr. Arthur Spohn's case of an ovarian cyst was estimated to weigh 328 lb. (148.7 kg). It was drained prior to surgical removal of the cyst shell and the patient made a full recovery in Texas, USA.

The **largest tumor removed intact** was a multicystic mass of the right ovary weighing 306 lb. (138.7 kg) by Professor Katherine O'Hanlan and Douglas J. Ramos, MD, of Stanford University Medical Center, California, USA, in October 1991.

Largest facial tumor

A benign tumor on the side of John Burley's (UK) face was removed by the surgeon John Hunter (UK, 1728–93), without anaesthetic, and found to weigh 10 lb. (4.53 kg). The tumor is still displayed in the Hunterian Museum at the Royal College of Surgeons in London, UK.

Largest tumor at birth

A benign cystic hygroma weighing 2 lb. 9 oz. (1.2 kg) was removed from the neck of a baby boy born in India on March 5, 2003. The tumor—which accounted for 40%

Most breast milk donated

Between June 9, 2011 and March 28, 2012, Alicia Richman (USA) donated 694 lb. 11 oz. (315.1 kg) of breast milk, the most donated by any one person, to the Mothers' Milk Bank of North Texas in Fort Worth, Texas, USA. The milk was pumped, stored, and later pasteurized to feed premature infants in local neonatal intensive care units.

interface was attached to the surface of his motor cortex—the area of the brain that would normally control the left arm. The implant was attached to a connector on his skull and linked to a computer. Nagle learned to use the BrainGate, which translated his brain waves and allowed him to move a cursor on a monitor as well as use a robotic hand.

16
Number of days it took Lomas to complete the marathon.

First person to complete a marathon in a robotic walking device

Claire Lomas (UK), who was paralyzed from the waist down in a horse-riding accident in 2007, completed the 2012 Virgin London Marathon using a ReWalk lower body robotic exoskeleton created by Argo Medical Technologies (Israel).

First surgery in microgravity

On September 27, 2006, a team of five doctors led by Dominique Martin successfully removed a benign tumor from the arm of volunteer Philippe Sanchot (both France) in an operation lasting about 10 minutes. The procedure was carried out onboard a modified Airbus A300 flying in parabolas in order to mimic the microgravity environment of space. It was part of an experiment to test the feasibility of performing surgery on astronauts on long-distance space flights.

Longest time without food: Angus Barbieri (UK) survived 382 days, from June 1965 to July 1966, without solid food at Maryfield Hospital in Dundee, UK.

Most hangings: In 1803, Joseph Samuel (Australia) survived three hangings in a row due to various equipment failures, as did John Lee (UK) in 1885.

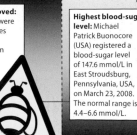

Fastest motorcycle crash: On July 12, 1998, Ron Cook (USA) crashed at an estimated 200 mph (322 km/h) at El Mirage Lake in California, USA.

Most bee stings removed: A total of 2,443 stings were removed from Johannes Relleke (Zimbabwe) at the Kamativi tin mine in Gwaii River, Wankie District, Zimbabwe (then Rhodesia), on January 28, 1962.

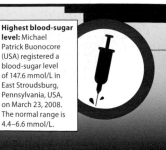

Highest blood-sugar level: Michael Patrick Buonocore (USA) registered a blood-sugar level of 147.6 mmol/L in East Stroudsburg, Pennsylvania, USA, on March 23, 2008. The normal range is 4.4–6.6 mmol/L.

OLDEST

Highest combined age for nine living siblings

The nine living Melis siblings—Consolata, Claudina, Maria, Antonino, Concetta, Adolfo, Vitalio, Fida Vitalia, and Mafalda—born to Francesco Melis (1880–1967) and his wife Eleonora (1889–1952) of Perdasdefogu, Italy, had a combined age of 818 years 205 days, as of June 1, 2012.

1909 in Aberdeenshire, Scotland. Evelyn was born first at 4 p.m. and Edith at 5:30 p.m., according to the birth certificates.

Kin Narita and Gin Kanie (née Yano, Japan, b. August 1, 1892), whose names mean Gold and Silver, were the **oldest female twins ever**. Kin died of heart failure on January 23, 2000 at the age of 107 years; Gin died on February 28, 2001 at 108 years old. The **oldest male twins** ever were Glen and Dale Moyer (USA, b. June 20, 1895), who took the record on January 23, 2000; both men reached 105 years.

Oldest person to abseil

Doris Cicely Long MBE (UK, b. May 18, 1914) abseiled 114 ft. 9 in. (35 m) down the side of Mercantile House in Portsmouth, UK, on May 18, 2013 at the age of 99 years—her fifth successful abseil descent in five years.

Oldest person (ever)

The greatest age to which any human has ever lived is 122 years 164 days by Jeanne Louise Calment (France). Born on February 21, 1875 to Nicolas and Marguerite (neé Gilles), Jeanne died at a nursing home in Arles in France on August 4, 1997. Calment also became the **oldest actress** when she portrayed herself at the age of 114 in *Vincent and Me* (Canada, 1990)—she may have been the last living person to have known Vincent van Gogh—and the **oldest surgery patient**, surviving a hip operation in January 1990 at 114 years 11 months old.

Oldest twins (living)

The oldest living twins are the UK's Edith Ritchie and Evelyn Middleton (née Rennie), who were born on November 15,

61
Number of Japanese prime ministers that have served in Kimura's lifetime!

Largest gathering of centenarians

A tea party attended by 28 people 100 years old or more was hosted by David Amess (UK) at Iveagh Hall in Leigh-on-Sea, Essex, UK, on September 25, 2009.

Largest population of centenarians

The most recent census in the USA counted 53,364 people at the age of 100 and older as of April 1, 2010. This represented 17.3 centenarians per 100,000 people against a total population of 308,745,538.

Oldest living man

Jiroemon Kimura (Japan) was born on April 19, 1897 and, as of April 14, 2011, is the oldest living man, a title he gained at the age of 113 years 360 days. On December 28, 2012, at the age of 115 years 253 days, he became the **oldest man ever**, breaking the record set by Christian Mortensen of Denmark/USA (1882–1998). At the time of going to press (May 15, 2013), Kimura is also the world's **oldest living person**, having just celebrated his 116th birthday. He took the title from Dina Manfredini (USA, 1897–2012) on December 17, 2012.

GUINNESS WORLD RECORDS

CERTIFICATE

The oldest person (male) living is Jiroemon Kimura (Japan) aged 115years and 179days as of 15 October 2012 in Kyotango, Kyoto, Japan

GUINNESS WORLD RECORDS

FOR THE RECORD

Mr. Kimura attributes his longevity to living life in moderation. He wakes up every morning at 6:30 a.m. and until recently enjoyed reading the daily newspaper and watching sumo wrestling on TV. He also puts his good health down to small meals, regular naps, and some good fortune—he comes from a family that enjoyed long life, with four of his siblings living into their 90s and one reaching the age of 100.

SUPERLATIVE SENIORS: MEET THE OLDEST ...

Soccer player: 88-year-old Tércio Mariano de Rezende (Brazil, b. December 31, 1921) played right wing for Goiandira Esporte Clube in Goiás, Brazil.

Kuchipudi dancer: Anuradha Subramanian (USA, b. October 26, 1946) performed at the Stafford Civic Center in Houston, Texas, USA, at the age of 59.

Ballet dancer: Grete Brunvoll (Norway, b. July 27, 1930) still performs regularly into her 80s.

Wing walker: On May 30, 2012, Thomas Lackey (UK, b. May 21, 1920) wing walked above Gloucestershire Airport in Staverton, UK, at the age of 92 years 9 days.

Wakeboarder: Linda Brown (USA, b. December 10, 1945) was 63 years 227 days old when she competed in the Battle of Bull Run Wakeboard Tournament at Smith Mountain Lake, Virginia, USA, on July 25, 2009.

OLDEST LIVING PEOPLE

Below are the 10 oldest living people for whom there is authenticated evidence, usually in the form of a certificate issued at birth. Note that with the exception of Mr. Kimura at No. 1, all those listed are female. The list is maintained by the Gerontology Research Group (USA), a group of "physicians, scientists, and engineers dedicated to the quest to slow and ultimately reverse human aging within the next 20 years".

Name	Nationality	Date of birth	Age
♂ Jiroemon Kimura	Japan	April 19, 1897	116
♀ Misao Okawa	Japan	March 5, 1898	115
♀ Jeralean Talley	USA	May 23, 1899	114
♀ Susannah Jones	USA	July 6, 1899	113
♀ Bernice Madigan	USA	July 24, 1899	113
♀ Soledad Mexia	Mexico/USA	August 13, 1899	113
♀ Evelyn Kozak	USA	August 14, 1899	113
♀ Naomi Conner	USA	August 30, 1899	113
♀ Mitsue Nagasaki	Japan	September 18, 1899	113
♀ Emma Morano	Italy	November 29, 1899	113

Correct as of May 23, 2013

Supercentenarians—those 110 and older—represented 0.6% of the centenarian population.

The country with the **most centenarians per capita** is Japan, with 40.29 per 100,000 people 100 years old or more.

Highest concentration of male centenarians

Villagrande in Sardinia, Italy, is, as of 2012, the village with the highest ratio of male centenarians per capita (among villages with a population of at least 1,000 residents). Villagrande has a population that experienced the highest probability of becoming a centenarian for men born during the years 1876–1911. This probability is known as the extreme longevity index (ELI), and is usually below 0.5% in developed countries; in the case of Villagrande, the EDI is 1.267%.

MOST SIBLINGS TO REACH 100 YEARS OLD

The first recorded case of four centenarian siblings occurred on April 2, 1984, when Lily Beatrice Parsons (née Andrews) reached her 100th birthday, following her three sisters: Florence Eliza White (b. 1874), Maud Annie Spencer (b. 1876), and Eleanor Newton Webber (b. 1880). The family came from Devon in the UK.

Oldest person to circumnavigate the Earth using public transport

Saburo Shochi (Japan, b. August 16, 1906) celebrated his 106th birthday by completing an around-the-world trip using only scheduled public transport. He embarked on his trip on July 16, 2012 and visited six countries, traveling a total of 35,232 miles (56,700 km).

Oldest volunteer

As of February 2013, 111-year-old Violet "Vi" Robbins (Australia, b. February 28, 1902) was working as a volunteer at the Prince of Wales Hospital in Randwick, Sydney, Australia. Vi has been an active volunteer since the 1960s in various organizations in Australia.

100 Age at which Margaret first set a record with a tandem paraglide in October 2007.

Oldest tandem paraglider

Daredevil Margaret McKenzie McAlpine (UK, b. October 30, 1907) was 104 years 168 days old when she completed a tandem paraglide in Karaoğlanoğlu, northern Cyprus, on April 14, 2012.

Oldest living woman

The oldest living woman for whom there is adequate authentication is Japan's Misao Okawa (*above*, née Aoki, b. March 5, 1898), who was 115 years 71 days old as of May 15, 2013. Ms. Okawa was born in Osaka and married her husband Yukio in 1919. She had three children, and now has four grandchildren and six great grandchildren. Her husband died on June 20, 1931—she has been a widow for more than 80 years—and she continues to reside in Higashisumiyoshi-ku in Osaka, in a nursing home.

Ms. Okawa took the title of oldest living woman following the death of 115-year-old Koto Okubo (b. December 24, 1897) on January 12, 2013. Okubo-san passed away in Kawasaki, Kanagawa, Japan, where she lived with her son.

Oldest teacher

Born on December 23, 1912, Father Geoffrey Schneider (Australia) remains an active teacher with St. Aloysius' College in Milsons Point, New South Wales, Australia. As of May 17, 2013, Father Schneider was 100 years 145 days old.

YO, GIRL! What's Ida's secret to long life? Avoid junk food and enjoy gardening, a glass of sherry after lunch, and flirting!

Oldest yoga teacher

The oldest registered yoga teacher is Ida Herbert (Canada, b. August 21, 1916), who remains an active instructor at the age of 95 years 270 days (as of May 16, 2012). Ida retired from a 20-year full-time career teaching yoga at the YMCA in Orillia, Ontario, Canada, but continues to teach a weekly class in the Bayshore Village area of Ontario.

Scuba diver: Saul Moss (Australia, b. July 27, 1924) completed an unassisted dive at Bare Island in Sydney, Australia, on August 1, 2009, at the age of 85 years 14 days.

Bodybuilder (female): E. Wilma Conner (USA, b. September 5, 1935) competed in the 2011 NPC Armbrust Pro Gym Warrior Classic Championships in Loveland, Colorado, USA, at the age of 75 years 349 days.

Active fighter pilot: Squadron Leader Philip Frawley (Australia, b. March 8, 1952) is a fully operational fighter pilot and flying instructor on the staff of 76 Squadron, Royal Australian Air Force, at the age of 60 years 137 days.

Tandem parachute jumper: Estrid Geertsen (Denmark, b. August 1, 1904) made a tandem jump on September 30, 2004 from 13,100 ft. (4,000 m), at the age of 100 years 60 days.

Person to summit Mount Everest: Min Bahadur Sherchan (Nepal, b. June 20, 1931) conquered Everest on May 25, 2008, at the age of 76 years 340 days.

MIND & MEMORY

Fastest time to add 10 10-digit numbers

On November 24, 2012, Naofumi Ogasawara (Japan) added 10 randomly chosen 10-digit numbers, completing the task 10 times in 2 min. 51.1 sec. Ogasawara competed at Memoriad 2012, a mind and memory contest held to coincide with the Olympics. The 2012 event was held at the Belconti Resort Hotel in Antalya, Turkey, on November 24–25, 2012.

Longest binary number sequence memorized in one minute

Jayasimha Ravirala (India) memorized 264 numbers in one minute in the Holy Mary Institute of Technology in Hyderabad, India, on March 8, 2011. He took about nine minutes to recall them perfectly.

The same day, Jayasimha achieved the **longest color sequence memorized**, with 152. Four colors were used and the sequence was recalled in 5 min. 4 sec. On June 22, 2012, he also set the record for the **longest sequence of objects memorized in one minute**, with 40.

Greatest prize money for mathematics

The Clay Mathematics Institute (USA) offered $1 million each for "classic questions that have resisted solution over the years." These are: P versus NP; the Hodge conjecture; the Poincaré conjecture; the Riemann hypothesis (*see above right*); Yang–Mills existence and mass gap; Navier–Stokes existence and smoothness; and the Birch and Swinnerton–Dyer conjecture.

Hardest number problem

Mathematicians regard the validity (or not) of a theorem known as the Riemann hypothesis to be the most important unsolved question in mathematical theory. In 1859, Bernhard Riemann (Germany) put forward a hypothesis involving a convoluted mathematical entity called the Riemann zeta function. The zeroes of this function seem to be linked with the positions of prime numbers (numbers divisible only by themselves and 1). Riemann suggested that the zeroes of the zeta function all lie on a well-defined straight line. He verified the idea for small numbers but failed with a general proof.

If true, it could expand our basic understanding of numbers and how they work.

Most playing cards memorized in 30 minutes

Ben Pridmore (UK) memorized 884 cards (17 packs) at the Derby Memory Championships in Derbyshire, UK, in 2008. He was allowed 30 minutes to memorize cards from a randomly shuffled stack and one hour to recall them in exactly the same order.

FASTEST ...

"Human calculator"

Scott Flansburg (USA) correctly added a randomly selected two-digit number (38) to itself 36 times in 15 seconds without the use of a calculator. He achieved his mental feat on April 27, 2000, on the set of *Guinness World Records* in Wembley, UK.

Time to mentally factorize 20 five-digit numbers

On December 22, 2010, Willem Bouman (Netherlands) factorized 20 random five-digit numbers in 13 min. 39 sec. Factorization involves splitting a number into "factors," numbers which when multiplied together give the original number. Bouman broke his five-digit numbers into their prime factors—divisible by themselves and 1. For example, 3 and 10 are factors of 30; its prime factors are 2, 3, and 5.

Time to memorize a deck of playing cards

Simon Reinhard (*see below left*) needed only 21.19 seconds to memorize and

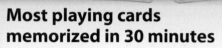

Fastest 10-by-5-digit division

On March 15, 2012, Dr. Amit Garg (USA) divided a 10-digit number by a five-digit number in just 34.5 seconds. This was an average time taken from 10 attempts at randomly chosen numbers made in 5 min. 45 sec.

Most decimal digits memorized in 30 minutes

Simon Reinhard (Germany) memorized 1,400 digits at the German Open on September 16–17, 2011. He had 30 minutes to memorize random digits presented in rows of 40 and an hour to recite them. Simon is pictured above with Memoriad founder Melik Duyar.

RUBIK'S CUBE CRAZY

Most solved while running a marathon: Uli Kilian (Germany) solved 100 while running the 2011 London Marathon in 4 hr. 45 min. 43 sec. on April 17, 2011.

Fastest average 3x3 time in competition: Feliks Zemdegs (Australia) set a time of 7.87 seconds in Melbourne, Australia, on January 29–30, 2011.

Fastest blindfolded solve: Gabriel Alejandro Orozco Casillas (Mexico) set a time of 30.9 seconds at the Tulancingo Open 2010 in Tulancingo, Hidalgo, Mexico, on December 11, 2010.

Fastest time to solve five cubes one-handed: Yumu Tabuchi (Japan) set a time of 1 min. 52.46 sec. in Tokyo, Japan, on March 15, 2010.

Fastest 7x7 solve: Michał Halczuk (Poland) achieved a time of 3 min. 25.91 sec. in Pabianice, Poland, on September 18–19, 2010.

Fastest six-digit-number square-root calculation

On January 3, 2012, Priyanshi Somani (India) averaged 16.3 seconds per calculation in 10 attempts totaling 2 min. 43 sec. at Lourdes Covent School in Surat, India. The 13-year-old, who has competed in international mind sports since she was aged 10, gave the correct answer to eight significant figures.

Pi (π) places memorized

Chao Lu (China) recited pi from memory to 67,890 places at the Northwest A&F University, Shaanxi Province, China, on November 20, 2005. The chemistry student practiced for four years before the 24-hr. 4-min. attempt and was recorded on 26 video tapes.

Random objects memorized

Prijesh Merlin (India) was blindfolded when he recalled 470 random items in the order they were read to him in Kannur, India, on June 23, 2012.

Most names and faces memorized in 15 minutes

Boris Nikolai Konrad (Germany) recalled 201 names and faces at the German Memory Championships at Heilbronn in November 2010. Konrad, a Memory Grand Master ranked world No. 10, works as a neuroscientist at the Max Planck Institute of Psychiatry in Munich, Germany. He also holds the record for the **most birth dates memorized**, with 21 in 2 minutes at the Purist bar in Augsburg, Germany, on February 14, 2011.

recall the order of a deck of cards at the German Open contest held in Heilbronn, Germany, on September 16–17, 2011.

Time to spell 50 words backwards

Shishir Hathwar (India) correctly spelled backward 20 six-letter words, 15 seven-letter words, and 15 eight-letter words in 1 min. 22.53 sec. He was at the Press Club of Bangalore in Bangalore, India, on November 13, 2010.

The total is only slightly less than that of the **most words spoken backward in one minute**, which stands at 71. It was set by Nada Bojkovic (Sweden) at the Nordstan shopping centre in Gothenburg, Sweden, on November 24, 2007.

MOST ...

Crosswords compiled

Roger F. Squires (UK) has compiled 74,634 crosswords as of June 30, 2013, equivalent to more than 2.25 million clues. He turned 81 on February 22, 2013, during the year he completed 50 years as a professional setter. Roger set his 2,000,000th clue in the UK's *Daily Telegraph* newspaper in May 2007, and it read: "Two girls, one on each knee (7)". (*See bottom right for the answer.*)

Roger's puzzles have appeared in 115 publications in 32 countries, including several national newspapers in the UK.

Most historical dates recalled in five minutes

At the Swedish Open Memory Championship in 2011, German memory athlete Johannes Mallow memorized 132 of 140 fictitious historical dates. Contestants have a series of made-up events to memorize. They are then given the list in a different order, and have another 15 minutes to add the correct dates.

Mental calculations in one minute

Chen Ranran (China) performed eight mental calculations on November 2, 2007 on *Zheng Da Zong Yi—Guinness World Records Special* in Beijing, China. Each of her equations had 11 numbers supplied by the World Abacus and Mental Arithmetic Association.

Simultaneous blindfolded chess wins

In 1947, legendary chess player Miguel Najdorf (Argentina) took on 45 players, holding each game simultaneously in his head. Over 23 hr. 25 min. he won 39, drew four, and lost two. Najdorf had been forced to leave his family in Poland at the start of World War II. All died in concentration camps, but Najdorf hoped that if he broke a record, news might reach survivors. He was never contacted.

Weekdays identified from dates in one minute

Given a random date between January 1, 1600 and December 31, 2100, could you work out what day of the week that date fell on? Yusnier Viera Romero (Cuba) identified 93 weekdays from randomly generated dates on December 4, 2010 in Miami, Florida, USA. He was given the dates in the form day–month–year and had he got even one day wrong it would have ended his attempt.

Fastest time to multiply 10 pairs of two eight-digit numbers

Freddis Reyes Hernández (Cuba) multiplied 10 pairs of eight-digit random numbers on November 24, 2012 in Antalya, Turkey, in 3 min. 54.12 sec. The previous month he won the Memoriad trophy at the Mental Calculation World Cup 2012.

Most solved in 24 hours: Milán Baticz (Hungary) solved 4,786 cubes in 24 hours in Budapest, Hungary, on November 15–16, 2008, an average of 3.32 cubes per minute.

Most blindfolded solves: Marcin Kowalczyk (Poland) solved 26 of 29 cubes in 53 min. 1 sec. in Starogard Gdański, Poland, between August 4 and 5, 2012.

Most solved on a unicycle: Adrian Leonard (Ireland), a pilot, completed 28 cubes while pedaling at Mary Peters Track in Belfast, Northern Ireland, UK, on October 6, 2010.

Fastest time to solve two simultaneously underwater: David Calvo (Spain) managed the feat in 1 min. 24 sec. on April 1, 2010.

Fastest time with feet: Anssi Vanhala (Finland) set a time of 42.08 seconds at the Estonian Open in Kose, Estonia, on November 7, 2009.

Crossword compiler answer: Patella

GASTRONAUTS

FASTEST TIME TO EAT …

Three water crackers
On May 9, 2005, Ambrose Mendy (UK) ate three dry water crackers, without the aid of water, in just 34.78 seconds in London, UK.

A raw onion
Peter Czerwinski (Canada) fought back the tears to eat a raw onion in a record 43.53 seconds in Mississauga, Ontario, Canada, on November 2, 2011.

A jam doughnut (no hands)
Oli White (UK) took 33.17 seconds to consume a sugared jam doughnut—without using his hands and without licking his lips, as per the guidelines—on the set of Guinness World Records' YouTube channel, OMG!, in London, UK, on October 25, 2012.

Three éclairs
On April 6, 2012, to mark the end of her run as presenter of *Live with Gabby* on Channel 5 (UK), Gabby Logan challenged her guests Keith Chegwin and Sean Hughes (both UK) to eat three cream and chocolate éclairs in the fastest time. Chegwin (UK) proved to be the fastest, taking just 1 min. 5 sec. and securing the world record.

A Ferrero Rocher (no hands)
Russell Jones (USA) unwrapped and consumed a Ferrero Rocher chocolate—without using his hands—in 11.75 seconds on April 30, 2012 at the Sheraton Chicago in Illinois, USA.

A muffin (no hands)
Mohamed Hossam (Egypt), a visitor to the Guinness World Records "In a Minute" roadshow at the Marina Mall in Kuwait City, Kuwait, on March 2, 2012, consumed a muffin weighing a minimum of 2.1 oz. (60 g) in a record time of 38.6 seconds.

A 12-in pizza
Peter Czerwinski (Canada) ate a 12-in. (30.5-cm) pizza using a knife and fork in 41.31 seconds on GWR's OMG! YouTube channel at Mama's and Papa's Pizzeria in Los Angeles, California, USA, on January 30, 2013.

EGGS-TRAORDINARY EFFORT
Suresh has cracked an impressive total of 17 Guinness World Records.

Most watermelons crushed with the head in one minute
Ahmed Tafzi (Germany) used his head to set a record at the Rose Festival in Saxony-Anhalt, Germany, on May 27, 2011: he headbutted an incredible 43 watermelons in the space of just 60 seconds! Ouch!

Most eggs held in one hand in 30 seconds
Suresh Joachim (Canada) grasped 24 eggs on August 17, 2012, in Mississauga, Ontario, Canada. He equaled the record set by Zachery George (USA) at the Subway restaurant in Parsons, West Virginia, USA, on March 21, 2009. It was very different to Suresh's first record: the **farthest distance covered on foot for a thousand consecutive hours**. Every hour between August 19 and September 29, 1996, he ran a distance of 2.17 miles (3.49 km) in Colombo, Sri Lanka.

A chocolate orange
On February 24, 2013, Marc-Etienne Parent (Canada) unboxed, unwrapped, and ate a Terry's Chocolate Orange in 1 min. 38 sec. in Campbellton, New Brunswick, Canada.

Three bhut jolokia chiles
Birgit Tack (Germany) ate three bhut jolokia ("ghost pepper") chiles in a blistering 1 min. 11 sec. on the set of *Guinness World Records— Wir holen den Rekord nach Deutschland* in Berlin, Germany, on April 2, 2011. With a Scoville rating of 300,000– 1,000,000, bhut jolokias are among the hottest chiles in the world.

A drinking glass
The fastest time to eat a standard, commercially available drinking glass—weighing a minimum of 3.5 oz. (100 g)—is 1 min. 27 sec. by Patesh Talukdar (India) on the set of *Guinness World Records—Ab India Todega* in Mumbai, India, on March 10, 2011. This is not a record you should try at home!

FASTEST EATERS

Hot dogs: Six hot dogs were scoffed in three minutes by Takeru Kobayashi (Japan) on August 25, 2009, in Kashiwa, Japan.

Garlic: A stinky 36 cloves were eaten in one minute by Patrick Bertoletti (USA) in East Dundee, Illinois, USA, on January 14, 2012.

Mince pies: David Cole (UK) ate three mince pies in 1 min. 26 sec. live on ITV's *The Paul O'Grady Show* in London, UK, on December 20, 2005.

Baked beans: 258 baked beans were consumed using a toothpick in five minutes by Gary Eccles (UK) for Comic Relief in Coventry, UK, on March 18, 2011.

Ferrero Rocher: Michael Saleeba (Australia) ate 15 chocolates in 3 min. 59 sec. in Seminyak, Bali, Indonesia, on March 6, 2012.

Fastest time to drink a bottle of ketchup

TV reporter Benedikt Weber (Germany) is a sucker for the red stuff: he slurped up 14 oz. (396 g) of Aro ketchup from a standard glass bottle in just 32.37 seconds, using a straw, on the *Galileo* show in Nuremberg, Germany, on February 17, 2012.

MOST …

Big Macs eaten in a lifetime

In October 2012, fast-food super-fan Donald Gorske (USA) reached a significant milestone in his life: he consumed his 26,000th McDonald's Big Mac. Gorske has eaten at least one Big Mac every day for 40 years.

Chicken nuggets eaten in three minutes

Christian Williams (USA) wolfed down 17.4 oz. (494.9 g) of chicken nuggets in three minutes in San Leandro, California, USA, on August 25, 2012. He was only allowed to use one hand, in accordance with the official guidelines.

Ham sliced in one hour

Diego Hernández Palacios (Spain) trained for three months for his attempt at slicing ham. Using three legs of *jamón de Guijelo*, each weighing 13.2 lb. (6 kg), Palacios cut 2,160 slices—a total weight of 22.13 lb. (10.04 kg)—in Madrid, Spain, on April 12, 2011.

Chocolate truffles made in two minutes

Gino D'Acampo (Italy) made 47 truffles topped with cocoa powder, dry coconut, and confectioners' sugar on ITV's *Let's Do Christmas with Gino & Mel*, UK, broadcast on December 21, 2012.

FOR THE RECORD

An inspiration to record breakers everywhere, Ashrita's many food triumphs include the **fastest time to peel and eat a kiwi** (5.35 seconds on December 10, 2008) and **a lemon** (8.25 seconds on May 3, 2010). *Read more about fantastic Mr. Furman on pp. 94–95.*

Flavors of ice-cream displayed together

Michael and Matthew Casarez (both USA) created 985 ice-cream variations, ranging from vanilla to mango habanero, at Crook's Palace restaurant in Black Hawk, Colorado, USA, on July 17, 2011.

Oysters opened in one minute

Patrick McMurray (Canada) opened 38 oysters during the filming of *Zheng Da Zong Yi* in Beijing, China, on May 21, 2010.

Bananas peeled and eaten in one minute

Patrick Bertoletti (USA) peeled and ate eight bananas without any slipups at Sierra Studios in East Dundee, Illinois, USA, on January 14, 2012.

Fastest time to drink 200 ml of mustard

Ashrita Furman (USA) set yet another record when he drank 6.7 fl. oz. (200 ml) of mustard in a spicy 20.8 seconds at the New York Sri Chinmoy Centre, New York, USA, on December 15, 2011. The mustard was squeezed out of a Plochman's squeeze bottle.

SLICE OF LIFE
Ryan trained as a teacher and combines his skill in martial arts with a career in lecturing.

Most cucumbers cut from the mouth with a sword in one minute

Hayashi the Samurai, aka Ryan Lam (Canada), kept his cool as he sliced 22 cucumbers in half in a minute. To add a further degree of peril, the cucumbers were held in the mouths of his courageous and calm assistants sitting back to back! The terrifying stunt was performed in Rome, Italy, on March 28, 2012.

iQUOTE
"[Hayashi is] very dangerous and compelling to watch …"
—Piers Morgan, *Britain's Got Talent*, 2010

M&M'S with chopsticks: On August 18, 2011, 65 M&M'S were munched in one minute by chopstick-wielding Kathryn Ratcliffe (UK) in Beijing, China, on the set of a *CCTV Guinness World Records Special*.

Grapes: 213 were gobbled in three minutes by veteran record breaker Ashrita Furman (USA) in New York City, USA, on August 16, 2010.

Brussels sprouts: 31 of the wintertime vegetables were consumed in a minute by Linus Urbanec (Sweden) in Rottne, Sweden, on November 26, 2008.

Peas: In three minutes, Mat Hand (UK) ate 211 canned peas using a toothpick in Nottingham, UK, on November 8, 2001.

Jelly doughnuts: Three were put away—without any licking of lips—in just one minute by Patrick Bertoletti (USA) in East Dundee, Illinois, USA, on January 14, 2012.

GREAT GASTRONOMY

Chocolate coin

On November 15, 2012, a chocolate coin weighing 1,450 lb. 10 oz. (658 kg) was unveiled at an event organized by the BF Servizi SRL (Italy) in Bologna, Italy. The giant one-Euro treat measured 6 ft. 5 in. (1.96 m) in diameter—taller than the average adult male—and was 6.69 in. (17 cm) thick.

Custard slice

On June 3, 2012, Flinders Fish and Chips (Australia) used 61 buckets of vanilla custard to make a giant confection weighing 1,120 lb. 3 oz. (508.11 kg) in Flinders, Victoria, Australia.

10,000 Portions that the lavish lasagne was divided into!

Largest lasagne

Created to honor Italy's soccer team in Euro 2012, it took nine hours to bake the world's lengthiest lasagne. The classic meat and pasta dish weighed 10,725 lb. 7 oz. (4,865 kg) and was made by the Magillo restaurant and Makro supermarket (both Poland) in Wieliczka, Poland, on June 20, 2012.

Largest bowl of oatmeal

A giant bowl of oatmeal weighing 3,042 lb. 6 oz. (1,380 kg)—equivalent to 5,500 regular servings—was stirred up by Flahavan's and Waterford Harvest Festival (both Ireland) in Waterford, Ireland, on September 16, 2012.

LARGEST ...

Cheese slice

Halayeb Katilo Co of Egypt served up a supersize slice of Roumy cheese, an Egyptian speciality, on July 13, 2012. It took 18 months to make and weighed 298 lb. 11 oz. (135.5 kg) in Cairo, Egypt.

Largest cookie mosaic

Three-hundred students from Bright School and MoonPie (both USA) made a 1,358.51-sq.-ft. (126.21-m^2) cookie mosaic in Chattanooga, Tennessee, USA, on September 29, 2012, for the school's centennial year. It comprised 16,390 vanilla, chocolate, and banana MoonPie snack cakes.

Fish stew

A fish stew weighing 6,658 lb. (3,020 kg)—the weight of a killer whale—was prepared for students by the University of Massachusetts Dining Services (USA) in Amherst, Massachusetts, USA, on September 3, 2011. Among the ingredients were 1,000 lb. (453 kg) of seafood (such as mussels, lobster, clams, haddock, and salmon) and 1,137 lb. (515 kg) of potatoes.

Fruitcake

Just Bake (India) produced a traditional Christmas plum cake weighing 8,432 lb. 10 oz. (3,825 kg) at Food & Kitchen EXPO 2011 at Tripura Vasini Palace Grounds in Bangalore, Karnataka, India, in December 2011. The cake measured 29 ft. (9 m) long and 19 ft. (6 m) wide—big enough to fill a decent-size dining room!

Enchilada

A tortilla (flat bread) measuring 230 ft. (70 m) had to be made with a specially designed machine to create the world's largest enchilada. The Mexican dish—which means "seasoned with chilli"—contained chicken, avocado, tomato, and onion rolled in a tortilla, and weighed 3,122 lb. (1,416 kg). It was served up at the Explanda de Iztapalapa in Mexico City, Mexico, on October 20, 2010.

Longest ice-cream dessert

A chocolate sundae measuring 670 ft. 1 in. (204.26 m) was created by 160 sweet tooths from The LiGht Youth Group (USA) in Cavalier, North Dakota, USA, on June 9, 2012. The town's main road was closed to make the delicious dessert from 747 lb. (338.83 kg) of vanilla ice-cream and 75 lb. (34 kg) of chocolate syrup.

Fruit salad

McGill Food and Dining Services (Canada) used 250 volunteers to make a dessert weighing 11,197 lb. (5,078.88 kg) at McGill University in Montreal, Quebec, Canada, on August 28, 2012.

Hot cross bun

A hot cross bun weighing 370 lb. (168 kg) was baked by the RSPB

MAGNIFICENT MEALS: THE WORLD'S PRICIEST

Pizza: A pizza with shavings of white truffle (see entry far right) was on the menu for £100 ($178) at Gordon Ramsay's Maze restaurant in London, UK, in 2005.

Sandwich: The von Essen Platinum Club Sandwich, created in 2007 by Daniel Galmiche (UK) at Cliveden hotel in Buckinghamshire, UK, sold for £100 ($200).

Cherries: Aussie Nick Moraitis paid AUS$35,000 ($31,771) for a box of cherries at an auction by Sydney Markets in Australia on October 24, 2007.

Nonjeweled chocolate egg: Created by Japanese and UK chocolatiers, the "golden speckled egg" sold for £7,000 ($11,107) in London, UK, on March 20, 2012.

Hot dog: The California Capitol City Dawg sells for $145.49 at Capitol Dawg in Sacramento, California, USA. It was introduced on May 31, 2012.

Largest hamburger commercially available

Juicys Outlaw Grill in Corvallis, Oregon, USA, serves up a hamburger weighing 777 lb. (352.44 kg)—that's 3,108 regular quarter-pounders! It sells for $5,000 and must be ordered 48 hours in advance.

1,375,000 Calories in Juicys' burger—enough to keep you going for two years!

Mille-feuille

This variant of the custard slice measuring 4,008 ft. 1.2 in. (1,221.67 m) was layered by Gilles Desplanches (Switzerland) in Geneva, Switzerland, on November 11, 2012.

LARGEST SERVING OF ...

Dumplings

The A Chang Meat Dumpling Restaurant (Chinese Taipei) prepared 1,510 lb. 2 oz. (685 kg) of dumplings at Changhua County Stadium in Changhua City, Changhua County, Chinese Taipei, on November 18, 2012.

Mussels

To celebrate its 25th anniversary, the Havfruen fish restaurant of Trondheim, Norway, muscled in on the record-breaking action with a serving of mussels weighing 10,798 lb. (4,898 kg) on August 3, 2012.

Nachos

Supposedly named after their creator, Ignacio Anaya (Mexico), nachos are tortilla chips covered in melted cheese. The largest ever weighed 4,689 lb. (2,126.89 kg), courtesy of Centerplate at the University of Kansas in Lawrence, Kansas, USA, on April 21, 2012.

Largest salad

You should always eat your greens, but even the most dedicated fan of fresh veg might struggle with a salad weighing 41,998 lb. (19,050 kg)! That was the forest of greenery assembled by Kaufland and Salve Club (both Romania) at the Exporom exhibition center in Pantelimon, Bucharest, Romania, on September 23, 2012.

Largest cup of coffee

Aiming to give commuters a boost on the way in to work, De'Longhi (Italy) brewed up a storm with a 3,487.1-gal. (13,200-liter) cup of coffee in London, UK, on November 5, 2012. The cup measured 9 ft. 6 in. (2.9 m) tall and 8 ft. 8 in. (2.65 m) wide.

216,000 Cups of espresso that could be made from the lake of coffee used in the attempt.

Largest bottle of whiskey

A 5-ft. 7-in.-tall (1.7-m) bottle was filled with 60.23 U.S. gal. (228 liters) of The Famous Grouse (UK) at their distillery in The Hosh, Crieff, Perthshire, UK, on August 12, 2012—aka the "Glorious Twelfth," the start of the red grouse shooting season.

and Greenhalghs Bakery (both UK) in Bolton, UK, on April 5, 2012. This spiced fruit bun with a pastry cross is often eaten on Good Friday.

Meat stew

BeefMaster chef Grzegorz Cielecki (Poland) made a 9,011-lb. (4,087-kg) stew—the same weight as a female African elephant—in Chorzów, Poland, on September 9, 2012.

Omelet

The Ferreira do Zêzere city council in Portugal broke a lot of eggs—145,000, to be eggs-act—to make an omelet weighing 14,225 lb. (6,452.35 kg) in Santarém, Portugal, on August 11, 2012.

Polenta

On June 24, 2012, volunteers of Pro Loco Pianello di Cagli (Italy) prepared a polenta weighing 7,848 lb. (3,560 kg) in Pianello di Cagli, Italy.

LONGEST ...

Chikuwa

The Seitoku 140th Anniversary Committee (Japan) made a Chikuwa—a Japanese seafood dish, formed around bamboo into a tube shape—measuring 46 ft. 9 in. (14.27 m) in Kurayoshi, Tottori, Japan, on November 3, 2012.

THE FAMOUS GROUSE

Fungus: The white truffle (*Tuber magnatum pico*) is an edible fungus that sells for about $1,370 per 1 lb. (0.45 kg). The truffles grow underground and are sniffed out by trained dogs.

Pie: A peanut butter and banana pie was bought at auction for $3,100 by Jerry Mumma (USA) in Rich Hill, Missouri, USA, on July 6, 2012.

Caviar: In 2006, the Almas variant of Beluga caviar—"black gold"—sold for around $15,770 per 1 lb. (0.45 kg).

Chocolate: La Madeline au Truffe, created in 2012 by chocolatier Fritz Knipschildt (Denmark), cost $250 each—$2,600 per 1 lb. (0.45 kg)!

Coffee: Kopi luwak coffee sells for about $300 per 1 lb. (0.45 kg). The beans are collected from the excrement of the Sumatran civet cat, which lives in the mountain ranges of Irian Jaya, Indonesia.

PIONEERS

PASSPORT PLEASE!
"What is the purpose of your trip?," asked the customs official who met Wallenda in Canada. "To inspire people," he replied!

Finish: Table Rock Welcome Centre, Canada

Start: Goat Island, USA

1,804 ft. 5 in. (550 m)

173 ft. 10 in. (53 m)

First person to cross the base of Niagara Falls on a tightrope

On June 15, 2012, daredevil and circus legend Nik Wallenda (USA) became the first tightrope walker to cross Niagara Falls at the base—as opposed to crossing over the gorge, upriver, as previous funambulists have done. Wallenda walked 1,804 ft. 5 in. (550 m) from Goat Island in the USA, passing directly over the Falls, to Table Rock in Canada.

The **first person to cross the Niagara Gorge on a tightrope** was Charles Blondin, aka Jean François Gravelet (France, 1824–97), who traversed the 1,100-ft. (335-m) gorge near the location where Rainbow Bridge stands today. This is roughly 1.25 miles (2 km) upriver from the actual Falls.

LEAP OF FAITH

Sky diving reaches a new height

On October 14, 2012, after seven years of planning, the Red Bull Stratos mission came to a dramatic climax. At 9:28 a.m. local time (3:28 p.m. GMT), Felix Baumgartner (Austria) lifted off from Roswell, New Mexico, USA. Destination: the edge of space. Within three hours, Felix would be back on Earth after achieving the **highest jump altitude** (127,852 ft.; 38,969.4 m)*, the **farthest free fall** (119,431.1 ft.; 36,402.6 m), and the **highest speed in free fall** (843.6 mph; 1,357.6 km/h). He also became the **first sky diver to break the sound barrier …**

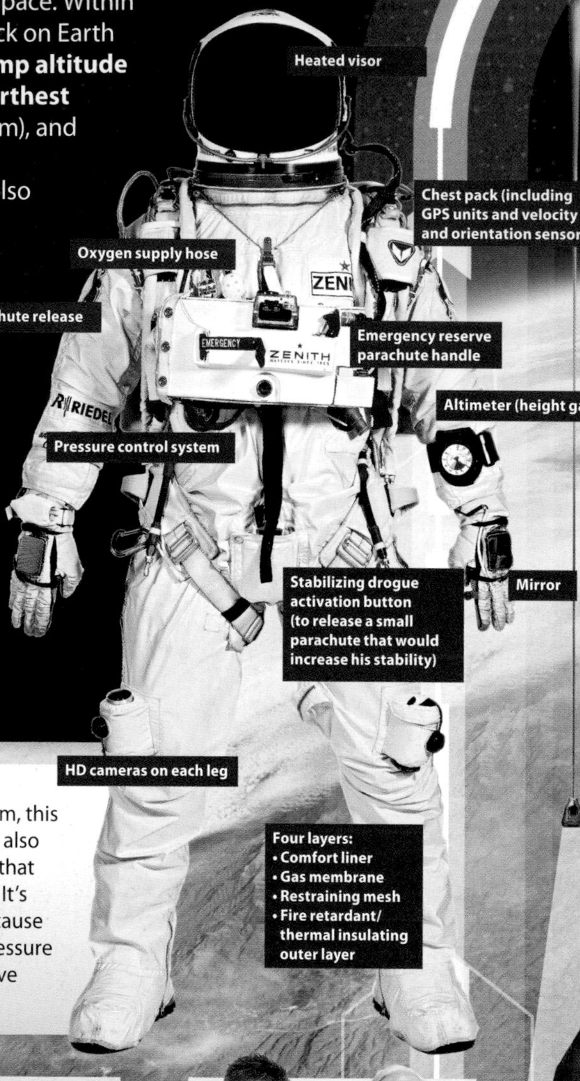

Felix's suit

Felix's stratospheric feat required highly specialized equipment. His special suit, manufactured by the David Clark Company (USA), and gear included an oxygen supply, three parachutes (plus glove mirrors to confirm opening), an altitude gauge, and four GPS devices. His helmet contained a microphone and earphones.

FACT:
Less a suit, more a life-support system, this outfit not only provided oxygen but also protected Felix from temperatures that reached as low as -95.6°F (-70.9°C). It's completely pressurized, too—because at this extreme altitude, the air pressure is so low that Felix's blood would have boiled within his body!

Heated visor

Chest pack (including GPS units and velocity and orientation sensors)

Oxygen supply hose

Main parachute release

Emergency reserve parachute handle

Altimeter (height gauge)

Pressure control system

Stabilizing drogue activation button (to release a small parachute that would increase his stability)

Mirror

HD cameras on each leg

Four layers:
• Comfort liner
• Gas membrane
• Restraining mesh
• Fire retardant/ thermal insulating outer layer

1. THE LAUNCH

Felix would ascend higher than the world altitude record for jet aircraft. His capsule was lifted by a vast helium balloon that at takeoff was 550 ft. (167.6 m)—or around 55 stories—high. It took nearly an hour to inflate with helium, which at jump altitude expanded to completely fill the capacity of nearly 30 million cu. ft. (850,000 m³).

0.00087
Thickness in inches of the balloon that lifted Felix's capsule.

FOR THE RECORD

The main point of contact between Felix and Mission Control during ascent was Joe W. Kittinger (USA, *above right*). On August 16, 1960, Joe set a free-fall record, reaching a top speed of 614 mph (988.1 km/h), and spent nearly 14 minutes in descent.

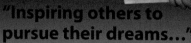

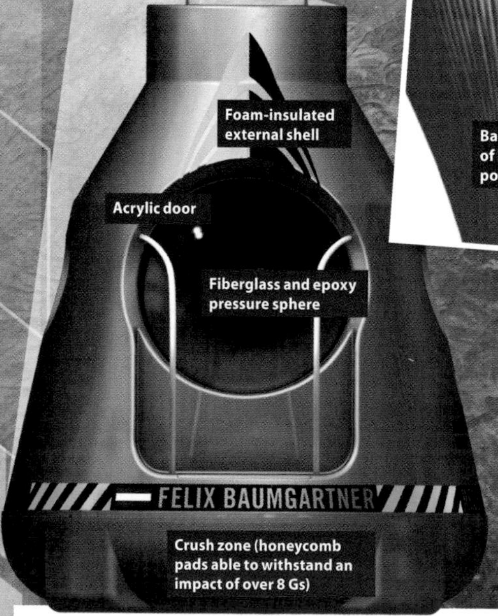

"Inspiring others to pursue their dreams…"

Guinness World Records was proud to present Felix with his official certificate to celebrate and acknowledge his pioneering mission. Here's what he had to say:

"After years of challenges to make this mission a success, *when* you succeed there's a little part of you that thinks, 'Did this really happen?' Our primary goal was always to improve aerospace safety, but receiving the Guinness World Records certificate was a tangible reminder that my supersonic dream had finally become reality.

"It also meant a lot to know that millions of people were right there with us via the live webstream. I continue to hear that the Red Bull Stratos mission is inspiring others around the world to pursue their own dreams, and that's one of the great honors of being considered a record-breaker."

Foam-insulated external shell

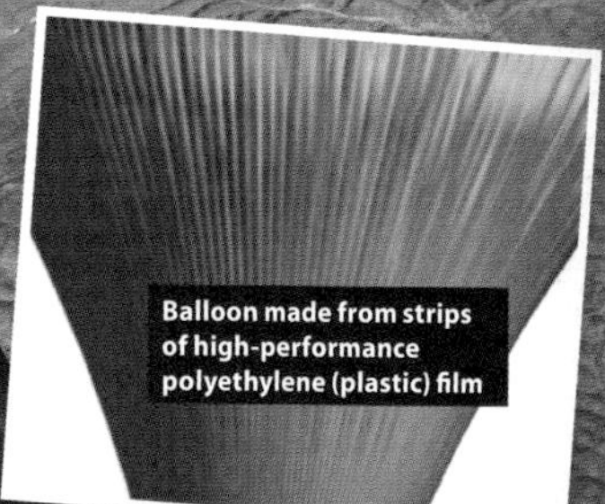

Balloon made from strips of high-performance polyethylene (plastic) film

Acrylic door

Fiberglass and epoxy pressure sphere

FELIX BAUMGARTNER

Crush zone (honeycomb pads able to withstand an impact of over 8 Gs)

2. THE ASCENT

Felix's capsule (*above*) climbed for over two hours—during which time he noticed some unexpected fogging of his visor as he exhaled. He could have aborted the mission at that point but chose not to. When the balloon (detail, *inset*) reached the edge of space, Felix depressurized the capsule and prepared to jump …

* *Ratified by the Fédération Aéronautique Internationale (FAI) as "highest exit altitude"*

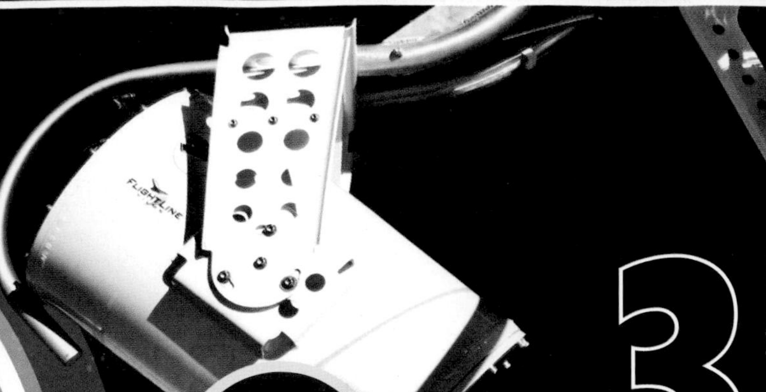

3

15
Number of cameras on the capsule, nine of which were HD.

127,852 FT.
(38,969.4 m)
Felix's jump altitude.

123,800 FT.
(37,734 m)
Unofficial manned balloon altitude record to beat, set by Nicholas Piantanida (USA) on February 2, 1966.

113,740 FT.
(34,668 m)
Official altitude record to beat, set by Malcolm Ross and Victor Prather (both USA) on May 4, 1961.

109,730 FT.
(33,445 m)
Felix reaches the speed of sound.

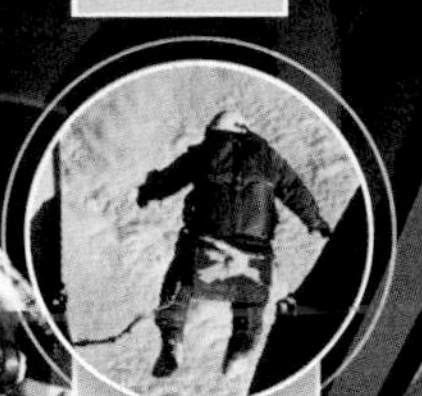

102,800 FT.
(31,333 m)
The previous record for the highest jump, achieved in 1960 by U.S. Air Force Captain Joe W. Kittinger.

130,000 FT. (39,624 M)

120,000 FT. (36,576 M)

110,000 FT. (33,528 M)

100,000 FT. (30,480 M)

90,000 FT. (27,432 M)

80,000 FT. (24,384 M)

70,000 FT. (21,336 M)

3. THE LEAP

Soon after jumping, Felix went into a spin. He could have deployed a stabilizing parachute there and then—but due to his extensive training he was able to regain control without it. His descent was so rapid that he broke the sound barrier, 65 years to the day after Chuck Yeager (USA) became the first man to do so. But Chuck had achieved his feat—the **first supersonic flight**—in a Bell XS-1 rocket aircraft!

4 MIN. 20 SEC.
Length of time Felix spent in free fall.

60,000 FT. (18,288 M)

50,000 FT. (15,240 M)

4. THE LANDING

Felix released his parachute at around 5,000 ft. (1,525 m) above ground level and touched down just 45 miles (72 km) from his place of liftoff. Among those waiting to welcome him was Red Bull Stratos's Technical Project Director, Art Thompson (*below right*).

SUPERSONIC MAN
Felix broke the sound barrier 34 seconds into his free fall and accelerated to 843.6 mph (1,357.6 km/h; Mach 1.25)!

40,000 FT. (12,192 M)

30,000 FT. (9,144 M)

20,000 FT. (6,096 M)

33,333 FT.
Vesna Vulović (Yugoslavia) survived a fall from 33,333 ft. (10,160 m) on January 26, 1972, after the DC-9 she was working aboard blew up—the **highest fall survived without a parachute**.

10,000 FT. (3,048 M)

SEA LEVEL

BY ROAD

Fastest speed in a human-powered vehicle (HPV)

Sam Whittingham (Canada) reached a speed of 82.819 mph (133.284 km/h) in his streamlined recumbent bicycle *Varna Tempest* at the World Human Powered Speed Challenge near Battle Mountain, Nevada, USA, on September 9, 2009. The record was measured for more than 656 ft. (200 m) including a flying start.

FOR THE RECORD

Sam set his speed record on Highway 305, which every year attracts a host of HPV riders. Why? It's North America's flattest, straightest road and lies at an altitude of 4,500 ft. (1,370 m)—resulting in thin air, which helps the racers to go faster.

Longest journey in a wind-powered car

Between January and February 2011, Dirk Gion and Stefan Simmerer (both Germany) traveled 3,100 miles (5,000 km) from Perth to Melbourne in Australia in *Wind Explorer*, a wind-powered vehicle. A wind turbine charged a lithium-ion battery pack to provide propulsion and, when the wind was strong enough, a kite was used to harness the power of the wind.

CIRCUMNAVIGATION

First by car

Racing driver Clärenore Stinnes (Germany), accompanied by movie-maker Carl-Axel Söderström (Sweden), embarked upon what is considered to be the first round-the-world drive on May 25, 1927, setting off from Frankfurt in Germany and finishing just beyond the starting point in Berlin on June 24, 1929, a total of 28,622 miles (46,063 km). The pair drove a 50-hp Adler Standard 6 automobile that was unmodified, except for two lounge seats that were added to give extra comfort. The entire trip took 2 years 1 month and encompassed 23 countries. The following year, Stinnes and Söderström, who had met just two days prior to their departure in 1927, married.

First by hydrogen-powered car

Mercedes-Benz was the first manufacturer to circumnavigate the world with a hydrogen-powered "fuel-cell" vehicle. It took a fleet of three identical cars (based on the company's B-Class hatchback) on a 125-day journey to celebrate Mercedes-Benz's 125th anniversary. The excursion started and finished in Stuttgart, Germany, taking in 14 countries.

Longest journey by car using alternative fuel

From November 15, 2009 to May 4, 2010, Tyson Jerry (Canada, *pictured left*) of the Driven to Sustain project—an educational scheme to teach environmental awareness—drove 30,158.5 miles (48,535.5 km) across North America in a Mitsubishi Delica fueled solely by biodiesel and vegetable oil. Joining Tyson for some of the route was Chloe Whittaker (*right*).

First by amphibious car

Frederick Benjamin "Ben" Carlin (Australia) and his American wife Elinore left Montreal, Canada, in *Half-Safe*, a modified Ford GPA amphibious jeep, on July 24, 1950, intent on traveling around the world over land and sea. It proved to be an eventful trip—Elinore left her husband in India and filed for divorce—but eventually Ben arrived back in Montreal on May 8, 1958, after traveling 39,000 miles (62,765 km) over land and 9,600 miles (15,450 km) by water. For the trans-Pacific stage (Tokyo, Japan, to Anchorage in Alaska, USA), Carlin was joined by *The Japan Times* journalist Boyé Lafayette De Mente.

Fastest by car

The record for the first and fastest man and woman to have circumnavigated the Earth by car covering six continents under the rules applicable in 1989 and 1991 embracing more than an equator's length of driving (24,901 road miles; 40,075 km) is held by Saloo Choudhury and his wife Neena Choudhury (both India). The journey took 69 days 19 hr. 5 min. from September 9 to November 17, 1989. The couple drove a 1989 Hindustan "Contessa Classic," starting and finishing in Delhi, India.

GREATEST DISTANCE DRIVEN ...

In 24 hours

The farthest that a standard production vehicle has been driven in 24 hours is 3,392.64 miles (5,459.92 km), by a team of 13 journalists and test drivers in a Saab Turbo 900 at Talladega Superspeedway in Alabama, USA, on October 19, 1996. The drivers maintained an average speed of 141.36 mph (227.49 km/h) for the full 24 hours. In accordance with the FIA, the international motorsports governing body, the vehicle was randomly selected off the Saab production line.

On two side wheels

The longest distance covered by a vehicle driven on its side on two wheels is 230.57 miles (371.06 km),

LAND SPEED RECORDS

Lunar vehicle:
- 10.5 mph (17 km/h)
- *Apollo 17* rover
- Eugene Cernan (USA)
- December 12, 1972

Edible car:
- 10.69 mph (17.2 km/h)
- Cake vehicle (1:2 replica of a 1933 Indycar Racer)
- Carey Iennaccaro (USA)
- March 4, 2012

Tank:
- 51.10 mph (82.23 km/h)
- S 2000 Scorpion Peacekeeper LC (UK)
- March 26, 2002

Solar-powered vehicle:
- 55.139 mph (88.738 km/h)
- *Sunswift IV*
- Barton Mawer (Australia)
- January 7, 2011

Land yacht:
- 126.1 mph (202.9 km/h)
- *Greenbird*
- Richard Jenkins (UK)
- March 26, 2009

18,592
Hours that the Schmids have spent driving, using 43,736 gal. (165,559 liters) of fuel!

Longest driven journey

As of December 18, 2012, Emil and Liliana Schmid (Switzerland) had covered 413,653 miles (668,485 km) in their Toyota Land Cruiser. The adventurous couple—who have no permanent home—embarked on their epic journey on October 16, 1984, and, to date, have crossed 172 countries and territories.

by Michele Pilia (Italy) in a 1983 BMW 316 mod.E30 1,766 cc at Sant'Elia studio in Cagliari, Italy, on February 26, 2009.

By a solar-powered vehicle

The longest journey by solar electric vehicle is 18,487 miles (29,753 km) and was achieved by the Solar Car Project Hochschule Bochum (Germany), who traveled around the world starting from Adelaide, Australia, on October 26, 2011 and finishing in Mount Barker, Australia, on December 15, 2012.

On a single tank of fuel

The greatest distance driven on a single standard tank of fuel is 1,581.88 miles (2,545.80 km) by a Volkswagen Passat 1.6 TDI BlueMotion, in an event organized by *Auto Motor i Sport* magazine (Croatia). It was driven by Marko Tomac and Ivan Cvetković (both Croatia) within Croatia, between June 27 and 30, 2011. The average fuel consumption was 75.9 mpg (32.2 km/liter), beating the previous distance by a substantial 55.2 miles (88.92 km).

FOR THE RECORD

Irvin paid the equivalent of a whole year's salary for his beloved car, and says he will only sell it if he can get a dollar a mile!

Longest journey by taxi

Leigh Purnell, Paul Archer, and Johno Ellison (all UK) left Covent Garden in London, UK, by taxi on February 17, 2011 and traveled 43,319.5 miles (69,716.12 km) around the globe, returning to Covent Garden on May 11, 2012. The journey, in *Hannah*—a 1992 LTI Fairway FX4 London black taxi cab—clocked up £79,006.80 ($127,530) on the meter. In the process, the team also achieved the **highest altitude by taxi**, reaching 17,143 ft. (5,225.4 m) in Qinghai Province, China, on August 29, 2011.

FOLLOW THAT CAR!
Pictured top to bottom are Leigh, Paul, Johno, and *Hannah* at Angkor Wat, Cambodia; trapped in the snow in Finland; and arriving in Sydney, Australia.

Highest vehicle mileage

A 1966 Volvo P-1800S owned by Irvin Gordon (USA) had clocked up 2,966,000 miles (4,773,314 km) on the odometer as of July 9, 2012. The vehicle is still driven on a daily basis and covers an estimated 85,000–100,000 miles (140,000–160,000 km) per year, owing in part to being driven to numerous car shows in the USA and occasionally overseas. Irvin bought his P-1800S on June 30, 1966 for $4,150 at the age of 25.

TAG NO. 7990
INVOICE DATE 05/10
MILEAGE 2,947,442
COLOR RED #46
DELIVERY DATE 06/2
SELLING 3358
R.O. DATE 05

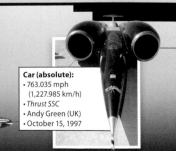

FOR MOTORSPORT RECORDS, TURN TO PP. 248–49

Electric car:
• 307.666 mph (495.140 km/h)
• *Buckeye Bullet 2*
• Roger Schroer (USA)
• August 24, 2010

Diesel-fueled vehicle:
• 350.092 mph (563.418 km/h)
• *JCB DIESELMAX*
• Andy Green (UK)
• August 23, 2006

Motorcycle:
• 376.363 mph (605.697 km/h)
• *Top Oil-Ack Attack* streamliner
• Rocky Robinson (USA)
• September 25, 2010

Wheel-driven vehicle
(i.e., power of the engine is directed to the vehicle's wheels):
• 458.444 mph (737.794 km/h)
• *Vesco Turbinator*
• Don Vesco (USA)
• October 18, 2001

Car (absolute):
• 763.035 mph (1,227.985 km/h)
• *Thrust SSC*
• Andy Green (UK)
• October 15, 1997

BY WATER

of these only the *Vittoria* returned, on September 8, 1522, under the command of navigator Juan Sebastián Elcano and with just 17 of the original crew. Magellan was hacked to death on April 27, 1521 in a fight with natives in Mactan, Philippines.

First nonstop solo circumnavigation of the Americas

Between June 13, 2011 and April 18, 2012, Matt Rutherford (USA) sailed the *St. Brendan* 27,077 miles (43,576 km) from Chesapeake Bay in Maryland, USA, and circumnavigated North and South America. On September 19, 2011, the 27-ft.-long (8.2-m) *St. Brendan* also became the **smallest boat to negotiate the Northwest Passage** in the Arctic Ocean.

First solo nonstop
Male: Robin Knox-Johnston (UK) departed from Falmouth, Cornwall, UK, on June 14, 1968 in the *Sunday Times* Golden Globe Race and returned on April 22, 1969 as the only remaining competitor.
Female: Kay Cottee (Australia) departed from Sydney, Australia, on November 29, 1987 in her 36-ft. (11-m) yacht *First Lady* and returned 189 days later on June 5, 1988.

CIRCUMNAVIGATION

First
While Ferdinand Magellan (Portugal) is often credited with the first around-the-world voyage, he actually died on the way and never completed the journey. He led a fleet of five ships that left Spain on September 20, 1519, but

Fastest circumnavigation sailing solo in a monohull

François Gabart (France) won the 2012–13 Vendée Globe yacht race in 78 days 2 hr. 16 min. in his yacht *MACIF*. He started and finished at Les Sables-d'Olonne, France, from November 10, 2012 to January 27, 2013. At 29, Gabart (b. March 23, 1983) is the **youngest winner of the Vendée Globe yacht race**.

First solo nonstop westward
Male: On August 6, 1971, Chay Blyth (UK) completed a 292-day voyage aboard *British Steel*. The westward route around the world faces prevailing winds and currents that follow the Earth's spin. The more popular route is eastward.
Female: Dee Caffari (UK) took 178 days 3 hr. 5 min. 34 sec. to return to Portsmouth, UK. She sailed in *Aviva*, a monohull measuring 72 ft. (22 m), between November 20, 2005 and May 18, 2006.

Caffari also took part in the Vendée Globe—the eastward-route race—which she finished on February 16, 2009, becoming the **first female to sail nonstop around the world in both directions**.

First solo human-powered circumnavigation

Erden Eruç (Turkey) rowed, kayaked, hiked, and cycled around the world, starting and finishing in Bodega Bay, California, USA. The journey lasted 5 years 11 days 12 hr. 22 min. between July 10, 2007 and July 21, 2012.

Front cabin stores nautical gear, including para-anchor, bottom anchor, lines, fenders, and spares

Cabin-top solar panels charge batteries to power all electronic systems

Main stern cabin

Around-n-over constructed from marine plywood

Internal water ballast helps keep the boat upright

Shaped to aid directional stability

iQUOTE
"The challenge was keeping myself mentally acute, managing discomfort. I'm not trying to conquer nature; I'm trying to be in harmony with it. I'm trying to become the sea."

Side panniers on cycling rig to organize load into easily accessible compartments

Trailer for excess load on land phases of journey

FOR THE RECORD

Individual: Jason Lewis (*opposite page*) completed his human-powered circumnavigation (HPC) five years before Erden, but was accompanied and helped by friends along various stretches of his 46,505-mile (74,842-km) journey.
Solo: Erden (*left*) completed his entire HPC alone—i.e., he is the first person to do it without any accompaniment.

WATER SPEED RECORDS

Human-powered submarine:
- 8.035 knots (9.2 mph; 14.9 km/h)
- OMER 5
- Ecole de Technologie Superieure, University of Quebec, Canada
- June 2007

Human-powered vessel:
- 18.5 knots (21.28 mph; 34.26 km/h) over 328 ft. (100 m)
- Hydrofoil *Decavitator*
- Mark Drela (USA)
- October 27, 1991

Fastest military submarine:
- 40 knots (46 mph; 74 km/h)
- Alfa class (Russia)
- Commissioned 1971

Sail (female):
- 45.83 knots (52.74 mph; 84.88 km/h)
- Mistral 41 board and *Simmer Sail 5.5 SCR*
- Zara Davis (UK)
- November 17, 2012

Sail (male):
- 65.45 knots (75.32 mph; 121.21 km/h) over 1,640 ft. (500 m)
- *Vestas Sailrocket 2*
- Paul Larsen (Australia)
- November 24, 2012

46,504 Miles covered by Jason Lewis in his attempt.

27.75 Average speed in knots attained by Francis Joyon.

First individual human-powered circumnavigation

On July 12, 1994, Jason Lewis (UK) began a 13-year trip from the Greenwich meridian line in London, UK. He walked, cycled, and inline skated across five continents and kayaked, swam, rowed, and pedaled across oceans. He covered more than the circumference of the Earth—24,900 miles (40,075 km)—and finished on October 6, 2007. He was accompanied for parts of the trip by friends and supporters.

3,270 miles (5,262 km) in 55 days. The men, whose record time stood for over 100 years, had expected prize money of $10,000—some $250,000 today—but never received it.

Most rows by one person

Simon Chalk (UK) has made seven ocean rows: the Atlantic east to west in teams of two (1997), five (2007–08), six (2013), eight (2012), and 14 (2011); and the Indian east to west, solo (2003) and in a team of eight (2009).

Oldest to row the Atlantic solo

Pavel Rezvoy (Ukraine, b. November 28, 1938) embarked upon a successful row across the Atlantic east to west solo in *Marion-Lviv* on January 20, 2004 aged 65 years 53 days.

Youngest tandem row across the Indian Ocean

British rowers James Thysse (b. December 8, 1986) and Jamie Facer-Childs (b. July 11, 1987) began a tandem row across the Indian Ocean on April 19, 2009, aboard the *Southern Cross*. James was 22 years 132 days and Jamie was 21 years 282 days. They reached land on July 31, 2009.

Fastest sailing of the Pacific

Olivier de Kersauson (France) sailed 2,925 nautical miles (3,366 miles; 5,417 km) from Los Angeles, California, to Honolulu, Hawaii, USA. He took 4 days 19 hr. 31 min. 37 sec. in November 2005 at an average speed of 19.17 knots (22 mph; 35.5 km/h) in his trimaran *Geronimo*.

Greatest distance sailed solo in 24 hours

Francis Joyon (France) sailed 666.2 nautical miles (766.65 miles; 1,233.8 km) single-handedly in his 95-ft. (29-m) trimaran *IDEC* on July 30–31, 2012. He previously achieved the **fastest circumnavigation sailing solo** at 57 days 13 hr. 34 min. 6 sec. from November 23, 2007 to January 20, 2008.

OCEANS

First row across the Atlantic

New Jersey fishermen George Harbo and Frank Samuelsen (both Norway/USA) crossed the Atlantic west to east, from New York, USA, to the Isles of Scilly, UK. They departed on June 6, 1896 in a skiff measuring 18 ft. (5.48 m) long and arrived on August 1, after rowing

First nonstop row of the Atlantic Ocean both ways

Charles Hedrich (France) rowed from Saint Pierre and Miquelon in the northwestern Atlantic near Canada via the Canary Islands off the coast of Africa to Petite Anse d'Arlet on the Caribbean island of Martinique in a nonstop journey lasting 145 days 10 hr. 57 min. He embarked on his solo and unassisted adventure on July 9, 2012 and finished on December 2, having rowed a total of 6,800 miles (11,000 km) in his boat *Respectons la Terre*.

FARTHEST OPEN WATER ARCTIC OCEAN ROW

Paul Ridley, Collin West, Neal Mueller, and Scott Mortensen (all USA) rowed 1,000 miles (1,600 km) from Inuvik, Canada, to Point Hope, Alaska, in 40 days 3 hr. 7 min. between July 17 and August 26, 2012, onboard a 29-ft. (8.8-m) boat.

Water ski (female):
- 96.54 knots (111.11 mph; 178.8 km/h)
- Dawna Patterson Brice (USA)
- August 21, 1977

Barefoot water skiing:
- 117.95 knots (135.74 mph; 218.44 km/h)
- Scott Pellaton (USA, *pictured during a practise run*)
- November 1, 1989

Formula 1 powerboat:
- 138.36 knots (159.22 mph; 56.25 km/h)
- Lightweight carbon-fiber boat with 153-cu.-in. (2.5-liter) Mercury engine
- Guido Cappellini (Italy)
- April 29, 2005

Propeller-driven boat:
- 229.92 knots (264.58 mph; 425.81 km/h)
- *Problem Child*
- Dale Ishimaru (USA)
- April 21, 2006

Fastest boat:
- 275.97 knots (317.58 mph; 511.11 km/h)
- *Spirit of Australia* hydroplane
- Ken Warby (Australia)
- October 8, 1978

BY ROCK

Oldest person to climb the Seven Summits

Takao Arayama (Japan) conquered all of the Seven Summits—the highest peaks on each continent—when he completed his climb of Kilimanjaro in Tanzania, Africa, on February 18, 2010 at the age of 74 years 138 days.

Most people on Mount Everest on a single day

On May 19, 2012, an unprecedented 234 climbers ascended Everest, the most on a single day, smashing the previous record of 170 set back in 2010. Congestion is a serious issue on the world's **highest mountain**, with 3,721 climbers having reached the summit since it was conquered in 1953 (*see right*). The **deadliest day on Everest** was May 10, 1996, when eight climbers perished in a blizzard.

Fastest time to climb the highest peak in every African country

It took Eamon "Ginge" Fullen (UK) five years to climb the highest peaks in all the countries on the African continent. He finally achieved his task by topping Libya's Bikku Bitti peak (11,076 ft.; 3,376 m) on December 25, 2005.

FASTEST ...

Ascent of Mount Everest

Pemba Dorje Sherpa (Nepal) ascended the south side of Everest in a time of 8 hr. 10 min. on May 21, 2004. Although his time was contested by a rival Sherpa, the Nepalese government and tourist ministry upheld the record.

Ascent of the "8,000ers"

Jerzy "Jurek" Kukuczka (Poland) climbed the 14 peaks higher than

26,246 ft., or 8,000 m, in 7 years 11 months 14 days between October 4, 1979, when he reached the summit of Lhotse (27,939 ft.; 8,516 m) on the Nepal/Tibet border, and September 18, 1987, when he successfully climbed Shisha Pangma (26,335 ft.; 8,027 m) in Tibet.

8,000-m mountain hat trick

The "8,000er hat trick" is the feat of climbing three of the earth's 14 peaks over 26,246 ft., or 8,000 m. In June

First woman to climb Everest twice (one season)

Chhurim Dolma Sherpa (Nepal) scaled Everest twice in a single climbing season—the first time a woman has achieved this remarkable feat. She reached the peak from the Nepal side on May 12, 2012, and again on May 19.

Fastest time to climb Mount Everest and K2

It took Karl Unterkircher (Italy, 1970–2008) just 63 days to climb the two highest peaks on Earth. He summited Everest (29,029 ft.; 8,848 m) on May 24, 2004, and K2 (28,251 ft.; 8,611 m) on July 26, 2004, both without the aid of oxygen.

1983, Erhard Loretan and Marcel Rüedi (both Switzerland) climbed Gasherbrum II, Gasherbrum I, and Broad Peak in 15 days. All three lie on the Pakistani-Chinese border.

Ascent of the Seven Summits

Vernon Tejas (USA) climbed the highest peak on each of the seven continents between January 18 and May 31, 2010—a record time of just 134 days.

FIRST ...

Ascent of Everest

Mount Everest was conquered at 11:30 a.m. on May 29, 1953, when Edmund Percival Hillary (New Zealand) and Tenzing Norgay (India/Tibet) reached the summit. The expedition was led by Henry Cecil John Hunt (UK).

Person to summit two 8,000-m mountains in a day

On May 15, 2012, Michael Horst (USA) crossed from the top of Mount Everest, along the South Col, to the top of Lhotse, the

PEAK PERFORMERS
Ginge and his Chadian guides were the first people to ever climb the remote and inaccessible Libyan peak.

TOP 10 TALLEST PEAKS AND THEIR FIRST CONQUERORS

SEE IT 3D WITH THE FREE APP

1. Mount Everest (29,029 ft.; 8,848 m) Edmund Hillary (New Zealand) and Tenzing Norgay (India/Tibet) on May 29, 1953.

2. K2 (28,251 ft.; 8,611 m) Lino Lacedelli and Achille Compagnoni (both Italy) on July 31, 1954.

3. Kangchenjunga (28,169 ft.; 8,586 m) Joe Brown and George Band (both UK) on May 25, 1955.

4. Lhotse (27,939 ft.; 8,516 m) Ernst Reiss and Fritz Luchsinger (both Switzerland) on May 18, 1956.

5. Makalu (27,837 ft.; 8,485 m) Jean Couzy and Lionel Terray (both France) on May 15, 1955.

fourth-highest peak. This feat is also the **fastest time to reach the summit of two 8,000ers**, taking just over 20 hours.

Ascent of K2 by a woman

Wanda Rutkiewicz (Poland) scaled K2 on June 23, 1986, becoming the first woman to climb the peak.

On May 17, 2010, Edurne Pasaban Lizarribar (Spain) became the **first woman to climb all 14 peaks over 8,000 m (undisputed)** by summiting Shisha Pangma in Tibet. A month earlier, Oh Eun-Sun (South Korea) had claimed this title, but doubt was cast on her summit of Kangchenjunga in 2009 and her record remains disputed.

The **first woman to summit all 8,000ers without oxygen** was Gerlinde Kaltenbrunner (Austria), who made her last summit (K2) on August 23, 2011.

First ascent of Mount Everest by a woman

Junko Tabei (Japan) climbed Mount Everest on May 16, 1975. On June 28, 1992, she became the **first woman to climb the Seven Summits** (the highest peak on each continent) when she topped Puncak Jaya.

Greatest climber of all time?

When it comes to scaling precipitous peaks, few climbers can top Reinhold Messner (Italy), as the table below shows. Other mountaineers may have made more solo climbs, but Messner is the master of high-altitude, high-risk feats. He started at a young age: his father was also a climber, and took him for his first climb—a 3,000-ft. (900-m) peak—when he was at the age of five. The photograph below right shows Messner in 1980 with a picture of Mount Everest. He had just scaled the peak solo and without supplementary oxygen, taking only a small backpack.

OLDEST PERSON TO CLIMB …

Everest

The Japanese alpinist Yuichiro Miura (b. October 12, 1932) made a successful summit of Mount Everest on May 23, 2013 at the age of 80 years 223 days.

Kilimanjaro

Martin Kafer (Switzerland, b. May 10, 1927) topped Mount Kilimanjaro, Tanzania, Africa, at 85 years 144 days old on October 1, 2012.

He made the climb with his wife, Esther Kafer (Switzerland, b. April 23, 1928). The trip saw her become the **oldest woman to climb Mount Kilimanjaro** at the age of 84 years 161 days.

An 8,000-m mountain without bottled oxygen

The only undisputed record holder for this category is Carlos Soria Fontán (Spain, b. February 5, 1939), who topped Gasherbrum I without bottled oxygen on August 3, 2009, at the age of 70 years 179 days.

The Seven Summits (female)

Carolyn "Kay" LeClaire (USA, b. March 8, 1949) completed her ascents of the Seven Summits when she conquered Everest on May 23, 2009, at the age of 60 years 76 days.

KNOW YOUR NOSE

The "Nose" is a ridge that separates the two rock faces of El Capitan. It is the best-known climbing route on the mountain.

24
Climbers who have died on El Capitan since 1905—13 of them on the "Nose."

Fastest time to climb El Capitan

The speediest ascent of El Capitan (7,573 ft.; 2,308 m) in California, USA, via the "Nose" route was achieved by Hans Florine and Alex Honnold (both USA) in 2 hr. 23 min. 51 sec. on June 17, 2012—almost 13 minutes faster than the previous record. Ordinarily, it can take mountaineers up to three days to scale the near-vertical precipice by this route.

Florine also recorded the **fastest time to climb El Capitan solo**, scaling the mountain in 11 hr. 41 min. on July 30, 2005.

RECORD	DETAILS	DATE ACHIEVED
First ascent of Mount Everest without oxygen	Achieved with Peter Habeler (Austria)	May 8, 1978
First solo summit of Mount Everest	It took Messner three days to make the ascent from his base camp at 21,325 ft. (6,500 m)	August 20, 1980
First 8,000-m (26,246-ft.) mountain hat trick	Kangchenjunga on May 6, 1982; Gasherbrum II on July 24, 1982; Broad Peak on August 2, 1982	August 2, 1982
First person to climb all 8,000-m (26,246-ft.) peaks	Began in June 1970. Completed feat by climbing Lhotse on the Nepal/Tibet border	October 16, 1986
First person to climb all 8,000-m (26,246-ft.) peaks without oxygen	Not only was Messner the first to climb all the 8,000ers, he was also the first to do so without supplementary bottled oxygen	October 16, 1986

¡QUOTE

"You learn through failure, not by what we believe are victories."

3D ON THIS PAGE

AUGMENTED REALITY ALERT!

6. Cho Oyu (26,863 ft.; 8,188 m) Josef Jöchler, Herbert Tichy (both Austria), and Pasang Dawa Lama (Nepal/Sherpa) on May 19, 1954.

7. Dhaulagiri I (26,794 ft.; 8,167 m) Kurt Diemberger (Austria), Peter Diener (Germany), Ernst Forrer, Albin Schelbert (both Switzerland), Nawang Dorje, and Nima Dorje (both Nepal/Sherpa) on May 13, 1960.

8. Manaslu (26,781 ft.; 8,163 m) Japanese team led by Yuko Maki on May 9, 1956.

9. Nanga Parbat (26,656 ft.; 8,125 m) Hermann Buhl (Austria) on July 3, 1953.

10. Annapurna I (26,545 ft.; 8,091 m) Maurice Herzog and Louis Lachenal (both France) on June 3, 1950.

BY ICE

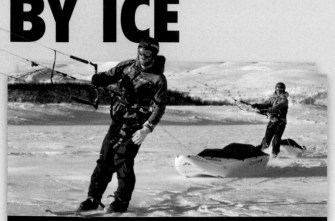

Longest Antarctic snowkiting expedition

On February 3, 2012, Dixie Dansercoer and Sam Deltour (both Belgium) completed their Antarctic ICE Expedition across eastern Antarctica. They carried out their 3,114-mile (5,013-km) trip without any external assistance or the use of motorized vehicles.

NORTH POLE

First to reach the North Pole

The question of who first reached the geographic North Pole has long been a matter of debate. Robert Peary, traveling with Matt Henson (both USA), indicated that he had reached the North Pole on April 6, 1909. Frederick Cook (USA) claimed he had done so a year earlier, on April 21, 1908. Neither claim has been convincingly proven.

The **first undisputed overland journey to the North Pole** ended on April 19, 1968, when expedition leader Ralph Plaisted (USA), accompanied by Walter Pederson, Gerald Pitzl, and Jean Luc Bombardier, reached the Pole after a 42-day expedition by snowmobile over the sea-ice.

First solo expedition

Naomi Uemura (Japan, 1941–84) became the first person to reach the North Pole in a solo trek across the Arctic sea-ice on May 1, 1978. He had traveled 478 miles (770 km), setting out on March 7 from Cape Columbia on Ellesmere Island, Canada.

Børge Ousland (Norway) skied to the North Pole from Mys Arkticheskiy on Russia's Severnaya Zemlya archipelago without external assistance in 52 days from March 2 to April 23, 1994—the **fastest solo trek to the North Pole**. He did not use any form of motorized transport or parafoil kites.

Fastest trek (female), assisted

Catherine Hartley and Fiona Thornewill (both UK) skied to the North Pole—with resupplies—in a time of 55 days from March 11 to May 5, 2001, after setting out from Ward Hunt Island in the Northwest Territories, Canada.

Fastest expedition to the North Pole

A supported and assisted expedition consisting of Tom Avery, George Wells (both UK), Matty McNair, Hugh Dale-Harris (both Canada), and Andrew Gerber (South Africa) reached the North Pole in 36 days 22 hr. 11 min. from March 21 to April 26, 2005. They were attempting to recreate the disputed 1909 expedition of Robert Peary (*see left*). Like Peary, they had four resupplies along the way. *(See right for the fastest trek.)*

Fastest solo trek to the South Pole (female), unsupported, unassisted

Hannah McKeand (UK) skied to the South Pole from the Hercules Inlet at the edge of the Antarctic continent in 39 days 9 hr. 33 min., from November 19 to December 28, 2006.

First long-distance swim at the North Pole

On July 15, 2007, Lewis Gordon Pugh (UK) swam 0.62 mile (1 km) at the North Pole. His dip, in water temperatures of between 29°F and 32°F (-1.7°C and 0°C) and without the aid of a wetsuit, lasted 18 min. 50 sec.

Longest Arctic snowkiting expedition (straight line), unassisted

Adrian Hayes (UK) and adventurers Devon McDiarmid and Derek Crowe (both Canada) traveled by snowkite 1,938 miles (3,120 km) in a straight line, making a vertical crossing of the Greenland ice cap. The trip took 67 days, from May 20 to July 25,

FOR THE RECORD

Once at the Pole, the team (*right*) posed for a photograph that recreated an image of Peary's team (*left*) taken in April 1909. The original image was used as part of Peary's evidence that he had reached the Pole.

EXPLORATION FIRSTS

December 14, 1911—First to reach the South Pole: Party of five men led by Captain Roald Amundsen (Norway).

March 2, 1958—First crossing of Antarctica: Sir Vivian Ernest Fuchs (UK) led a party of 12 on a 99-day trek from Shackleton Base to the Scott Base via the Pole.

April 19, 1968—First undisputed overland journey to the North Pole: Ralph Plaisted (USA) led a team on a 42-day trip with snowmobiles.

May 29, 1969—First crossing of the Arctic: Achieved by the British Trans-Arctic Expedition, led by Wally Herbert (UK).

May 1, 1978—First solo expedition to the North Pole: Japan's Naomi Uemura traveled 478 miles (770 km) alone from Cape Columbia, Canada.

First surface ship at the North Pole

The Soviet (now Russian) nuclear-powered icebreaker *NS Arktika* measured 492 ft. (150 m) long, with a beam of 98 ft. (30 m) and a maximum displacement of 51 million lb. (23,460 tonnes). She began sea trials on November 3, 1974, and operated until 2008. She was capable of breaking through sea-ice up to 16 ft. (5 m) thick and, on August 17, 1977, became the first ship in history to reach the geographic North Pole.

2009. Adrian also set the **fastest time to complete the Three Poles challenge**—conquering Mount Everest and the geographic North and South Poles—at 1 year 217 days. He summited Everest on May 25, 2006, reached the North Pole on April 25, 2007 (from Ward Hunt Island, Canada), and claimed the South Pole from the Hercules Inlet on December 28, 2007.

Fastest trek to the North Pole, supported

David J. P. Pierce Jones (UK), Richard and Tessum Weber (both Canada), and Howard Fairbanks (South Africa) trekked to the North Pole in

FOR THE RECORD

Walk: On foot only, no skis.
Trek: On foot, with skis.
Solo: Journey completed by one person, who at no point is accompanied by any other adventurers.
Individual: Completed by one person, but accompanied at various points on the trip.
Assisted: Help is given along the way in terms of resupplies, food drops, and medical aid.
Supported: Power aids, such as wind (kites), dogs, and motorized vehicles used to provide propulsion.
Overland: A surface journey by any (e.g., motorized) means.

41 days 18 hr. 52 min. from March 3 to April 14, 2010. The team set out on March 3 from 82° 58' 02" N and 77° 23' 3" W and were picked up after reaching the North Pole, 90° N, on April 14, 2010.

SOUTH POLE

First to reach the South Pole

The South Pole was conquered at 11 a.m. on December 14, 1911 by a Norwegian party of five men, led by Captain Roald Amundsen (1872–1928), after a 53-day march with dog sleds from the Bay of Whales.

Fastest overland journey to the South Pole

A team traveling in the *Thomson Reuters Polar Vehicle*—a modified Toyota Tacoma—set a new record for the fastest overland journey to the South Pole, setting off from Patriot Hills, Antarctica, on December 18, 2011 and arriving at their

1,034
Miles covered by Teodor and his fellow trekkers.

destination 1 day, 15 hr. 54 min. later. The UK team comprised two members: Jason De Carteret and Kieron Bradley.

Fastest trek to the South Pole, unsupported, unassisted

Ray Zahab, Kevin Vallely, and Richard Weber (all Canada) reached the South Pole from the Hercules Inlet on January 7, 2009 after a 683.5-mile (1,100-km) speed trek—attaining 10,000 ft. (3,050 m) in just 33 days 23 hr. 30 min.

Fastest solo trek to the South Pole, unsupported, unassisted

On January 13, 2011, 35-year-old Christian Eide (Norway) completed a solo and unsupported trek to the South Pole in a time of 24 days 1 hr. 13 min. He set off on the 715-mile (1,150-km) adventure on December 20, 2010 and opted for the Hercules Inlet route, covering an average of 29 miles (47 km) per day—although on his last day, he managed to ski 56 miles (90 km).

Youngest person to traverse Antarctica

At 20 years 120 days old, Teodor Johansen (Norway, b. August 14, 1991) was the youngest of a team of six who successfully crossed Antarctica in 2011. He started at the Axel Heiberg glacier on November 26, reached the Pole on December 18, and ended his trek—which was assisted and wind-supported—at the Hercules Inlet on January 12, 2012.

Fastest completion of the Three Poles (female)

Cecilie Skog (Norway) reached the three extreme points of the Earth, known as the Three Poles, in just 1 year 336 days: she summited Mount Everest on May 23, 2004, reached the South Pole on December 27, 2005, and, finally, claimed the North Pole on April 24, 2006.

First solo female to traverse Antarctica

Felicity Aston (UK) arrived at the Hercules Inlet on the Ronne ice shelf on January 23, 2012, after a 1,084-mile (1,744-km) journey lasting 59 days. She made the trip from the Ross ice shelf—with resupplies—while pulling two sleds and without the support of kites or any other aids to propulsion.

FOR EXTREME WEATHER, TURN TO P. 22

May 11, 1986—First person to reach the North Pole solo: Dr. Jean-Louis Étienne (France); had the benefit of being resupplied several times on the journey.

May 14, 1989—First person to walk to both Poles: Robert Swan (UK) reached the South Pole on foot on January 11, 1986, and the North on May 14, 1989.

December 27, 1995—First person to walk to both Poles solo and unsupported: Marek Kamiński (Poland) reached the North Pole on May 23, 1995, and the South Pole on December 27, 1995.

May 27, 1997—First all-female polar expedition: Twenty UK women—in five relay teams of four—walked to the North Pole from Ward Hunt Island (Canada), a total distance of 477 miles (768 km).

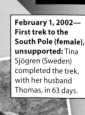

February 1, 2002—First trek to the South Pole (female), unsupported: Tina Sjögren (Sweden) completed the trek, with her husband Thomas, in 63 days.

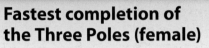

BY AIR

Youngest person to circumnavigate Earth by aircraft

Walter Toledo (Brazil, b. December 4, 1991) flew around the globe in a Piper Malibu Matrix PA-46 from Goiânia, Brazil, between July 8 and August 29, 2012. He was 20 years 269 days old.

AIRPLANE

First transatlantic flight

Albert Cushing Read (USA) and his crew flew from Trepassey Harbour in Newfoundland, Canada, via the Azores, to Lisbon in Portugal from May 16 to 27, 1919.

Major James V. Sullivan and Major Noel F. Widdifield (both USA) crossed the Atlantic in a Lockheed SR-71A Blackbird in 1 hr. 54 min. 56.4 sec. on September 1, 1974—the **fastest transatlantic flight**. The average speed for the 3,461.53-mile (5,570.80-km) New York–London stage was 1,806.96 mph (2,908.02 km/h).

First flight over Everest

On April 3, 1933, two Westland biplanes made the first manned flights over Mount Everest, the **tallest mountain** at 29,029 ft. (8,848 m).

One plane was piloted by Squadron Leader Lord Clydesdale with Colonel L. V. S. Blacker as his observer, while the other was flown by Flight Lieutenant D. F. MacIntyre, whose observer was S. R. Bonnett, a cinematographer.

First solar-powered aircraft

The AstroFlight *Sunrise* was an unmanned experimental electric aircraft designed by Roland Boucher (USA) to fly on solar power. It made its maiden flight on November 4, 1974, from Bicycle Lake on the Fort Irwin military reservation in California, USA, and managed a total of 28 flights before it broke up due to turbulence near cumulus cloud.

Fastest circumnavigation via the poles

Walter H. Mullikin (USA) flew around the world via both geographical poles in 54 hr. 7 min. 12 sec. on October 28–31, 1977, in a Boeing 747 SP. The trip began and ended in San Francisco, USA.

Longest human-powered rotorcraft flight (time)

Colin Gore (USA), a graduate student at the University of Maryland, USA, kept the *Gamera II* human-powered rotorcraft aloft for 1 min. 5.1 sec. at Prince George's Sports & Learning Complex in Landover, Maryland, on August 28, 2012. A rotorcraft uses lift generated by its wings or rotor blades, which revolve around a mast.

HELICOPTER

Fastest circumnavigation

Edward Kasprowicz and crewman Stephen Sheik (both USA) flew around the world in an AgustaWestland Grand helicopter, completing the trip on August 18, 2008 after 11 days 7 hr. 5 min. at an average speed of 84.9 mph (136.7 km/h). They started and finished in New York, USA.

Oldest solo helicopter pilot

On June 28, 2012, Donald Hinkel (USA) completed a solo flight over Oscoda County Airport in

Longest duration of a wing-suit flight

Jhonathan Florez (Colombia) remained airborne in a wing suit above La Guajira, Colombia, for 9 min. 6 sec. on April 20, 2012.

The next day, once more above La Guajira, he achieved the **highest altitude wing-suit jump**, from a height of 37,265 ft. (11,358 m). He is shown (*right*) with his wife, Kaci, and some of his GWR certificates.

AVIATION FIRSTS

First power-driven flight: On December 17, 1903, Orville Wright (USA) flew the chain-driven *Flyer I* for 120 ft. (36.5 m) at an altitude of 8–12 ft. (2.5–3.5 m) near the Kill Devil Hill, Kitty Hawk, North Carolina, USA.

First helicopter flight: On November 13, 1907, Paul Cornu (France) flew an experimental helicopter in untethered flight for the first time, in France.

First balloon flight: Father Bartolomeu de Gusmão (Portugal) invented a model hot-air balloon and flew it indoors at Casa da Índia in Terreiro do Paço, Portugal, on August 8, 1709.

First manned flight: Jean-François Pilâtre de Rozier rose 84 ft. (26 m) into the air on October 15, 1783 in a tethered hot-air balloon built by Joseph-Michel and Jacques-Étienne Montgolfier (all France).

First solo transatlantic flight: At 12:52 p.m. GMT on May 20, 1927, Charles Lindbergh (USA) took off in his monoplane *Spirit of St. Louis* from Long Island in New York, USA. He landed at 10:21 p.m. GMT on May 21, 1927 at Le Bourget airfield in Paris, France, after a 33-hr. 30-min. 29.8-sec. flight.

First skydive without a parachute

Stuntman Gary Connery (UK) used a wing suit to jump from a helicopter at 2,400 ft. (732 m) above Oxfordshire, UK, on May 23, 2012, to become the first skydiver to land safely—into a pile of 18,600 cardboard boxes—without deploying a parachute. Connery shot to fame at the opening ceremony of the 2012 Olympic Games when he jumped out of a helicopter dressed as Queen Elizabeth II.

Mio, Michigan, USA, at the age of 86 years 206 days.

The **oldest active military helicopter pilot** is Major Mike Crabtree (UK), who flew for the Royal Air Force of Oman at the age of 64 years 305 days on October 18, 2012.

First female taikonaut

"Taikonaut" refers to a Chinese astronaut. Liu Yang (China) entered orbit on June 16, 2012 at 10:37 UTC (Coordinated Universal Time) in the *Shenzhou-9* spacecraft. Her mission saw China's first manned docking with its *Tiangong-1* space laboratory.

BALLOON

Greatest altitude in a manned balloon
Malcolm D. Ross and Victor A. Prather (both USA) rose to an altitude of 113,740 ft. (34,668 m) above the Gulf of Mexico, USA, on May 4, 1961, in their balloon *Lee Lewis Memorial*. This was one of the records *not* beaten by Felix Baumgartner during his skydive in 2012 (*see p. 68*) because the balloon must be returned to Earth to satisfy FAI (Fédération Aéronautique Internationale) rules.

First circumnavigation by balloon
Bertrand Piccard (Switzerland) and Brian Jones (UK) completed a nonstop flight in the *Breitling Orbiter 3* on March 20, 1999, flying from Château-d'Oex in Switzerland to the "finishing line" of 9.27°W over Mauritania in North Africa.

Steve Fossett (USA) circled the globe in *Bud Light Spirit of Freedom* from June 9 to July 2, 2002, covering 20,627 miles (33,195 km)— the **first solo circumnavigation in a hot-air balloon**. On July 1, 2002, during this successful attempt, Fossett also achieved a top speed of 200.23 mph (322.25 km/h) in the same craft, giving him the record for the **fastest speed in a hot-air balloon**.

First balloon flight over the North Pole
Ivan André Trifonov (Austria) flew a one-man Thunder and Colt Cloudhopper balloon 0.6 miles (1 km) over the geographic North Pole at 6:30 p.m. GMT on April 20, 1996.

On January 8, 2000, Trifonov also performed the **first balloon flight over the geographic South Pole**, which he crossed at an altitude of 15,000 ft. (4,571 m) with two Spanish crew members, in a Cameron AX 60 – EC-HDB hot-air balloon.

Oldest person to fly in a hot-air balloon
Emma Carroll (née Lanman, USA, May 18, 1895–July 10, 2007) made an hour-long flight in a hot-air balloon at Ottumwa, Iowa, USA, on July 27, 2004, at the age of 109 years 70 days.

FACT:
Two years later, astronaut James Lovell (*left*) went into space again, for the Apollo 13 mission. An oxygen tank exploded onboard, leading to a fire and fears for the crew's safety, but, fortunately, they were able to steer their module safely back to Earth.

First space walk in deep space

Al Worden (USA) was Command Module Pilot on Apollo 15, which launched on July 26, 1971 and returned to Earth on August 7, 1971. At about 198,800 miles (320,000 km) from Earth, Worden performed the first space walk that was not in Low Earth Orbit. It lasted 39 minutes.

First humans to lose contact with Earth

The crew of NASA's Apollo 8 mission—James Lovell, William Anders, and Frank Borman (all USA, *left to right*)— left Earth on December 21, 1968 and became the first people to travel beyond low Earth orbit. At 68 hr. 58 min. 45 sec. into the mission, on December 24, while making their first ever orbit around the dark side of the Moon, the crew lost radio contact with Mission Control in Houston, Texas, for 34 minutes, as scheduled—the first time that any humans had ever lost contact with Earth.

First trans-Pacific flight: The crew of the *Southern Cross* monoplane left Oakland in California, USA, at 8:54 a.m. on May 31, 1928, reaching Brisbane in Queensland, Australia, at 10:50 a.m. on June 9, 1928.

First flight over the South Pole: Pioneering aviator Richard Byrd (USA) flew over the South Pole on November 29, 1929. The round trip to and from the expedition's base on the Ross Ice Shelf took 19 hours.

First flight across the Atlantic solo (female): On May 20–21, 1932, Amelia Earhart (USA) flew from Harbour Grace, Newfoundland, Canada, to Londonderry, Northern Ireland, UK, in 13 hr. 30 min.

First solo circumnavigation by aircraft: Wiley Post (USA) made the first solo flight around the world from July 15 to 22, 1933. He covered 15,596 miles (25,089 km), starting and ending in New York, USA.

First supersonic flight: On October 14, 1947, Captain Charles "Chuck" Elwood Yeager (USA) reached Mach 1.015 (670 mph; 1,078 km/h) over Lake Muroc, California, USA.

CIRCUS

CONTENTS

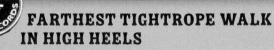

FARTHEST TIGHTROPE WALK IN HIGH HEELS

On January 22, 2013, Chelsea McGuffin (Australia) was in Sydney, New South Wales, Australia, when she crossed a 24-ft. 8-in. (7.52-m) tightrope wearing a pair of shoes with 4.7-in. (12-cm) heels. The wire was 7 ft. 11 in. (2.42 m) from the ground and her heels had a 0.78-in. (2-cm) platform.

TRADITIONAL CIRCUS

FIRST MODERN CIRCUS

Philip Astley (UK), a former cavalry sergeant major turned trick rider, added acrobats, rope dancers, and clowns to his equestrian show in the spring of 1770 at his riding school in London, UK.

"Circus" is Latin for "ring" or "circular," and although Astley rode in a circle, the name "circus" wasn't used until November 4, 1782, when Charles Hughes (UK) opened the Royal Circus. This show, presented in a circular arena 65 ft. (19.7 m) in diameter, referred to a "circus." The name "circus show" had no connection with the much older Roman circus.

1860. It was later (in 1872) taken by William Cameron Coup for his and P. T. Barnum's "P. T. Barnum's Museum, Menagerie, and Circus," and subsequently by all major American circuses. Sanger encouraged the rumor that Britain's Queen Victoria had bestowed a peerage on him for letting her put her head in one of his lion's mouths. His self-title of "Lord" encouraged other circus entrepreneurs to become "Captain", "Sir," and even "King."

1896: First human arrow
Alar the Human Arrow, aka Mary Murphy (UK), was shot from a giant crossbow 40 ft. (12.19 m) through a paper target to a catcher on a trapeze. Mary, of the Flying Zedoras, performed the feat at the Barnum & Bailey Circus in 1896. The following April in Madison Square Garden, New York, USA, the crossbow (the same mechanism as the human cannonball, *see below*) malfunctioned and Mary was knocked out. The press reported the incident with a lurid artist's impression of her unconscious on a platform above the crowd. Her younger sister Frances took over as Alar in 1902.

LARGEST EVER TRAVELING CIRCUS TENT

Ringling Bros. and Barnum & Bailey Circus had a tent covering 91,407 sq. ft. (8,492 m²)—an area equivalent to 32 tennis courts. Consisting of a round top 200 ft. (61 m) in diameter, with five middle sections each 60 ft. (18 m) wide, it was used on tours of the USA from 1921 to 1924.

1904: First cycling loop-the-loop
Trick cycling was introduced by *Les Frères Ancillotti* (Italy)—the Ancillotti Brothers—in 1868. At the Barnum & Bailey Circus in 1904, one of the Ancillottis rode down a ramp and looped-the-loop for the first time. At the head of the loop was a 10-ft. (3.3-m) gap, across which the rider leaped while upside down.

1910: First flying trapeze triple somersault from trapeze to catcher
Key dates for circus feats are often hard to pinpoint—tricks are usually the result of continual practice and, historically, a daily record was not kept. Artists prefer to perform regularly instead of establish one-off records, but we know that at some point in 1910 Ernest Clarke (UK) completed a triple back somersault into the hands of his brother Charles at Ringling Bros. Circus (USA). Clarke attempted his triple somersault regularly in performance but never achieved it consistently. He also worked solo on the far platform, synchronizing his return with the swing of his trapeze.

1826: First circus performed under a canvas big top
Circus entrepreneurs J. Purdy Brown and Lewis Bailey (both USA) used a canvas tent called a "pavilion" for a circus performance in October 1825. Their first series of one-day shows began in May 1826. Few visual representations of circus tents survive before 1847, by which time the tents had grown much larger in diameter or length and evolved visually. The term "big top" began to gain currency by 1883 through the promotion of "P. T. Barnum's Greatest Show on Earth and Great London Circus."

1860: First three-ring circus
"Lord" George Sanger (UK) introduced the system that allowed audiences to watch more than one act at a time in

FIRST HUMAN CANNONBALL

Zazel, aka Rosa Richter (UK), became the first human cannonball on April 2, 1877. She was just 14 years old when she was shot a distance of 30 ft. (6.1 m) at Westminster Aquarium in London, UK. Springs provided the launch, with the explosion being purely theatrical.

MOST TRAVELED CIRCUS

The circus of Giuseppe Chiarini (Italy) toured extensively over Asia, Australasia, Europe, South America, the USA, and the West Indies between its inception in 1856 and the death of Chiarini in 1897. His circus was based in San Francisco, USA.

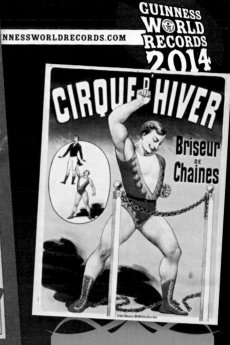

GUINNESS WORLD RECORDS 2014

RINGLING BROS. AND BARNUM & BAILEY CIRCUS

FLYING VAZQUEZ

FIRST FLYING TRAPEZE QUADRUPLE SOMERSAULT

Miguel Vazquez (Mexico) completed a quadruple back somersault from trapeze to catcher during a performance of the Ringling Bros. and Barnum & Bailey Circus in Tucson, Arizona, USA, on July 10, 1982.

1920: First consistent flying trapeze triple somersault

It's one thing to perform a trapeze trick as a result of a lucky fluke, but the mark of a true circus performer is doing it night after night. While Alfredo Codona (Mexico) was not the first trapeze artist to perform a triple back somersault, he was the first to do so consistently. Codona first executed the triple in Chicago, Illinois, USA, at the Sells-Floto Circus on April 3, 1920. He then performed it regularly—with his brother Abelardo as his catcher— until 1933, when he suffered a career-ending injury.

COSTUME KING
The one-piece garment popularized by Jules Léotard was named in his honor in the 1880s.

FIRST FLYING TRAPEZE ARTIST

French gymnast Jules Léotard performed the flying trapeze for the first time on November 12, 1859, at the Cirque d'Hiver in Paris. His father, Jean Léotard, conceived the equipment and Jules leaped alone from trapeze to trapeze. The catcher (and leaps from trapeze to hands of catcher) appeared later, at the end of the 19th century.

OLDEST PERMANENT CIRCUS STILL OPERATING

The Cirque d'Hiver ("Winter Circus") opened in Paris, France, on December 11, 1852. Built by the celebrated architect Jacques Ignace Hittorff for entrepreneur Louis Dejean, it was inaugurated as "Cirque Napoléon" and renamed in 1873. In 1934, it was acquired by the Bouglione circus family and remains under their management.

FIRST TRIPLE-AND-A-HALF BACK SOMERSAULT

Tony Steele (USA) completed a triple-and-a-half back somersault from trapeze to catcher with a leg catch in 1962 in Durango, Mexico, and performed it regularly afterward. Tony began his career at 15, when he ran away from home and joined the circus.

1920: First heel catch on a swinging trapeze

A trapeze performer going into a heel catch will slide their legs over the bar until they are hanging upside down by their heels. The first person to make a catch with two heels on a swinging bar was Winnie Colleano (Australia).

1985: First full twisting pirouette on a swinging trapeze

On June 6, 1985, Elena Panova (b. Elena Nikolaevna Borisova, USSR) of the State Circus School of Moscow gracefully performed a full twisting pirouette from a standing position to an ankle catch in the trapeze ropes. She performed the trick during her professional debut show.

1992: First flying trapeze quadruple somersault from trapeze to catcher (female)

The first female flyer on record to have completed a quadruple back somersault from trapeze to catcher is Jill Pages (USA), who was caught in the hands of her husband, Willy Pages, during a practice session in San Juan, Puerto Rico, on February 19, 1992.

2011: First triple layout somersault on the flying trapeze

The layout somersault is performed straight rather than in a tucked position. Farhad Sadykov, main flyer of the White Birds troupe from Kazakhstan, performed the first triple version at the International Circus Festival of Monte-Carlo in January 2011.

MODERN CIRCUS

LARGEST CIRCUS ORGANIZATION

Cirque du Soleil (Canada) has some 1,300 artists under contract, nine permanent shows in the USA (in Las Vegas and Orlando), 11 traveling productions around the world, and an annual income of approximately $900 million. Founder Guy Laliberté (Canada) started the brand in 1984 with street performers; as of March 2013, he was worth $1.8 billion.

MOST CHEST-STAND FULL-BODY REVOLUTIONS IN A MINUTE

Leilani Franco (UK/Philippines) performed 25 revolutions at the Box Theatre in Soho, London, UK, on March 11, 2013. Leilani [...] th her chest against the floor, her back arched, and her legs stretched over her body with her feet on the ground in front of the face; her legs then made full revolutions around the body, returning to the original starting position each time.

Fastest time to travel 20 m in a contortion roll

On March 11, 2013, expert chest-stander Leilani Franco (*see below left*) achieved the quickest 65 ft. (20 m) in a contortion roll with a time of 17.47 seconds at the Royal Festival Hall in London, UK. In a contortion roll, acrobats start with their feet on the ground, arch backward, and propel themselves forward in a chest-down roll.

Leilani achieved the **fastest 20 m backbend walk** on the same day in 10.05 seconds. Only the hands and feet are on the floor in a backbend, with the arms extended above the head and the back completely arched.

Highest hole jumped through from a trampoline

On March 12, 2012, Charlie Burrows (UK) bounced 6 ft. 7 in. (2 m) and executed a backward pike through a hole that measured 2 sq. ft. 7 sq. in. (80 cm²) in Rome, Italy. He performed backflips along a trampoline to gain momentum and didn't even touch the sides of the hole as he passed through.

TALLEST STACK OF CHAIRS BALANCED ON

Luo Jun (China) from the Zunyi Municipal Acrobatic Troupe did a handstand on a tower of 11 chairs on September 15, 2007 in Beijing, China.

iQUOTE
"I've never seen anything like that in my life."
Simon Cowell, [...]ain's Got [...]Talent

Most motorcycles performing backflips

On February 28, 2013, Nitro Circus—cofounded by action sports star Travis Pastrana (USA)—had 16 motorcyclists backflipping simultaneously at their live show at The O2 arena in London, UK.

Most wheel of death turns in three minutes

Two human-size hamster wheels rotating around a centered pivot are the constituents of a "wheel of death." On November 30, 2011, Zhoukou Acrobatic Troupe's Wan Xiaohua and Zhang Yizhan (both China) performed 42 revolutions in three minutes in Beijing, China.

Most rope jumps on a wheel of death by a pair

Ronald Montes and Jhon Robinson Valencia Lozada (both Colombia) performed a total of 33 rope jumps while riding a wheel of death at the Royal Albert Hall in London, UK, on January 24, 2013, during a live performance of the Cirque du Soleil show Koozå.

Most motorcycles on a globe of death

Ten motorcyclists from Puyang Haoyi Acrobatic Group (China) rode a globe of death in Puyang City, China, on December 5, 2010. As with the wall of death, performers defy gravity as they roar around—but they can also ride up and over the globe's sphere.

LONGEST TIME STANDING ON HANDLEBARS

Ivan Do-Duc (France), an artistic cyclist with Cirque du Soleil, balanced for 1 min. 39.49 sec. on the handlebars of a bicycle. He performed the trick in Milan, Italy, on April 14, 2011, restricting himself to cycling in circles just 33 ft. (10 m) wide.

Longest time to maintain a neck hang

Donovan Jones connected himself to Rebecca Peache (both USA) using an acrobatic support around their necks. He was then raised, upside down, on a trapeze. Rebecca, suspended below him, then spun repeatedly for 1 min. 12.29 sec. in Beijing, China, on August 14, 2011.

Longest time to hang by the teeth

Cirque du Soleil's Igor Zaripov (Russia) dangled by the teeth for 2 min. 32 sec. on the set of Good Morning America in New York, USA, on May 8, 2012.

Most mounts and dismounts from a moving horse in 30 seconds

Liu Wei, from the Zhoukou Acrobatic Troupe, mounted and dismounted a horse 16 times at the Hangzhou Safari Park in Zhejiang Province, China, on November 27, 2010.

RAISING THE BARRE

The acrobat has to be consistently accurate to land safely on the narrow, flexible Russian barre after performing each stunt.

FIRST RUSSIAN BARRE QUADRUPLE SOMERSAULT (FEMALE)

Anna Gosudareva of the Rodion Troupe (both Russia) completed a quadruple back somersault on a Russian barre (a flexible pole) at the International Circus Festival of Monte-Carlo in January 2005. The pole was held aloft by troupe founder Valery Rodion (left) and Aleksandr Mikhaylov.

HOOPSTERS

Hula hoops caught on as a fad in the USA in the 1950s, but hoops have been used for fun and exercise for much longer. Boys in ancient Greece exercised with a bronze ring called a trochus.

MOST FIRE HOOPS SPUN WHILE IN SPLITS POSITION

Pippa "The Ripper" Coram (Australia) spun three burning hula hoops simultaneously while performing the splits at London Wonderground in London, UK, on September 14, 2012. Each hoop was modified with wicks around the perimeter that were doused in gasoline for the attempt.

SIDESHOW ARTS

iQUOTE
"You try to hold your face as horizontal as possible under the torch to avoid the worst part of the flame."

LONGEST SUSTAINED FIRE-TORCH TEETHING

As if fire-eating wasn't hot enough, Carisa Hendrix (Canada) spiced up her attempt further by "teething"—gripping the torch in her teeth without taking a breath, fire side down. She practiced for a month before her 2-min. 1.51-sec. feat on *Lo Show dei Record* in Rome, Italy, on April 12, 2012.

FIRE SKILLS

Most flames blown in one minute
Fredrik Karlsson (Sweden) blew 108 flames at Sergels Torg in Stockholm, Sweden, on November 3, 2012. Firefighter Fredrik is more used to putting fires out, although he also achieved the record for the **longest duration for a continuous fire blow**, set at 9.96 seconds on November 19, 2011.

Most torches extinguished in 30 seconds
Hubertus Wawra (Germany), aka the Master of Hellfire, extinguished 39 fire torches in 30 seconds with his mouth in Mumbai, India, on February 21, 2011.

Most blow torches extinguished with the tongue in one minute
The Space Cowboy (see *above right*) used only his tongue to put out 27 gas blow torches in a minute on September 27, 2012, in London, UK.

Most torches lit and extinguished in one minute
Preacher Muad'dib (UK) lit and put out 83 fire torches in London, UK, on November 18, 2010. He alternated between two fire rods.

He also achieved the **most spins of a fire staff in one minute**, with 150 turns of a 47-in.-long (119-cm) staff in Whitby, UK, on October 31, 2009.

BLADES

Most knives caught in one minute
Ashrita Furman caught 34 Hibben 12-in. (30-cm) knives—thrown by Bipin Larkin (both USA)—one-handed in a minute at the Sri Chinmoy Center in New York City, USA, on May 16, 2012.

Most knives thrown backward around a human target in one minute
Patrick Brumbach (Germany) threw 63 blades around his assistant while facing away from her in Schloß Holte-Stukenbrock, Germany, on August 17, 2011.

iQUOTE
"People have been putting stuff in and out of their noses either for entertainment or for medical reasons for thousands of years."

MOST SWORDS SWALLOWED SIMULTANEOUSLY

The Space Cowboy, aka Chayne Hultgren (Australia), established himself as the world's leading sword swallower when, on September 12, 2012, at the Guoman hotel by Tower Bridge in London, UK, he slid 24 blades—each at least 15 in. (38 cm) long—down his esophagus.

Most balloons burst with throwing knives in one minute
The Space Cowboy (*above*) burst 21 balloons with throwing knives in a minute at Wonderground in London, UK, on August 24, 2012. He was positioned 16 ft. 5 in. (5 m) from the balloons and used 10 knives in total, which he recovered and reused each time.

Most apples cut in the air by sword in one minute
Tsurugi Genzou (Japan) sliced 28 apples thrown into the air with a 26-in.-long (66-cm) blade on the set of *FNS 27HR TV Waratte Iitomo!* at Hizen Yume Kaido in Saga, Japan, on July 22, 2012.

LONGEST METAL COIL PASSED THROUGH THE NOSE AND MOUTH

Andrew Stanton (USA) of the Las Vegas SwingShift SideShow performs as Mr. Screwface. He uses a power drill to insert greased coils of metal where, frankly, they aren't supposed to go. On March 31, 2012, he screwed a 11-ft. 10.91-in.-long (3.63-m) coil through his nose and mouth on the set of *Lo Show dei Record* in Rome, Italy.

MOST CONCRETE BLOCKS BROKEN ON THE STOMACH IN ONE MINUTE

Daniella D'Ville, aka Danielle Martin (UK), laid on a bed of nails at London Wonderground, UK, while eight concrete blocks were smashed, one at a time, on her stomach in one minute by The Great Gordo Gamsby (Australia) on September 14, 2012. Each block measured 3.9 x 17.3 x 8.4 in. (10 x 44 x 21.5 cm) and weighed 12 lb. 12 oz. (5.8 kg). Gordo struck them with a sledgehammer weighing 14 lb. (6.35 kg).

Heaviest vehicle pulled by a sword swallower

Ryan Stock (Canada) swallowed a sword measuring 17 in. (43.18 cm) long and 0.75 in. (2 cm) wide, then attached chains to the hilt and pulled a 2002 Audi A4 for 20 ft.11 in. (6.38 m)—in 20.53 seconds— in Las Vegas, Nevada, USA, on October 28, 2008.

Ryan also set the record for the **heaviest vehicle pulled using a hook through the nasal cavity and mouth**, at 1,598 lb. (725 kg) in Rome, Italy, on March 21, 2012.

WHIPS

Most flowers whip-cracked from the mouth in one minute

The Space Cowboy (see p.86) used a bullwhip to break in half 31 flowers placed, one at a time, in the mouth of Zoe L'Amore (see right) in London, UK, on September 28, 2012.

Most candles extinguished by whip in one minute

The most candles extinguished by cracking a whip in one minute is 78, by Xu Xinguo (China) on the set of a *CCTV Guinness World Records Special* in Beijing, China, on December 10, 2012.

Fastest whip

The whip-cracking speed and accuracy world record is held by Adam Crack, aka Adam Winrich (USA), who hit 10 targets consecutively with a cracking whip in 4.85 seconds at the Bristol Renaissance Faire in Kenosha, Wisconsin, USA, on July 8, 2008.

MOST FANS STOPPED BY TONGUE

Zoe L'Amore, aka Zoe Ellis (Australia), used her tongue to stop 20 electric fans, each with blades 10.6 in. (27 cm) wide, in one minute at London Wonderground, UK, on September 14, 2012. She alternated between two handheld desk fans on full power, stopping each blade entirely before moving to the next.

MOST BAKING SHEETS BUCKLED OVER THE HEAD IN ONE MINUTE

Burnaby Q. Orbax (*far right*) and Sweet Pepper Klopek (both Canada) perform together as the Monsters of Schlock. The dynamic duo took it in turns to bash each other over the head with a total of 55 baking sheets in 60 seconds at Niagara in Ontario, Canada, on August 31, 2012.

1.57 Extent in inches to which the 0.12-in.-thick (3-mm) baking sheets must be buckled in order to count toward the record.

MAGIC

MOST LIVING CREATURES PRODUCED DURING A PERFORMANCE

During their television special *Don't Try This at Home*, filmed in 1990, Penn & Teller (USA) produced more than 80,000 bees in an attempt to represent every animal ever produced by every magician on the planet!

4.69 seconds in Aylestone Leisure Centre, Leicester, UK, on June 9, 2011. She also performed the **most straitjacket escapes in one hour** for *Officially Amazing* (Lion TV), with 49 escapes at the Old Vic Tunnels in London, UK, on January 9, 2013.

Handcuffs blindfolded

On April 10, 2012, Thomas Blacke (USA) escaped from a set of police-issue handcuffs while blindfolded in 3.45 seconds in South Yarmouth, Massachusetts, USA. He also effected the **fastest underwater escape from a pair of handcuffs**—in 3.425 seconds—also in South Yarmouth, on October 25, 2011.

A chain underwater

Weasel Dandaw, aka Daniel Robinson (UK), performed an underwater escape from a chain in 10.76 seconds at the London Studios in London, UK, on September 11, 2004.

FASTEST TIME TO ESCAPE FROM A PAIR OF HANDCUFFS

On January 8, 2011, superstrong stuntman Chad Netherland (USA) escaped from a pair of double-locked handcuffs in just 1.59 seconds in Las Vegas, Nevada, USA. *Check out another macho record by Chad on p. 103.*

Largest magic lesson
Kevin McMahon (UK) gave a magic lesson to 1,063 participants at an event organized by Royal Blind (UK) at Fettes College, Edinburgh, UK, on October 27, 2012.

The **most people taking part in a multivenue magic lesson** is 2,573, by La Fundación Abracadabra de Magos Solidarios (Spain) in 51 hospitals in Spain on December 10, 2010.

Most deadly magic trick
At least 12 people (eight magicians and four bystanders) have died during the bullet-catching trick, in which a marked bullet is loaded into a gun and fired at the magician, who apparently catches the bullet in his teeth. Even

though the feat involves illusionary elements, it is filled with danger. The most famous bullet-catching death was that of Chung Ling Soo (USA, b. William Ellsworth Robinson), shot on stage at the Wood Green Empire, London, UK, on March 23, 1918.

FASTEST ESCAPE FROM ...

A straitjacket
Sofia Romero (UK) escaped from a regulated Posey straitjacket in

Plastic wrap, suspended
Rob Roy Collins (UK) freed himself from 10 layers of plastic wrap—while suspended upside down from a crane—in 27 seconds in Campden, Ontario, Canada, on August 30, 2012.

MOST RABBITS PULLED OUT OF A HAT

Italian magic duo "Jabba," aka Walter Rolfo and Piero Ustignani, pulled 300 fluffy white rabbits out of a magician's hat in less than 30 minutes. They performed this unprecedented version of the classic trick during the Magic Congress in Saint-Vincent, Aosta, Italy, on May 17, 2008.

Prisoner transport irons

Mike Sanford (USA) escaped from a pair of double-locked prisoner transport irons in a time of 1 min. 54.34 sec. at Sammamish, Washington, USA, on October 31, 2004.

MOST ...

Glasses broken during a mind-control illusion

In a classic trick to demonstrate the "power of their minds" at the Masters of Magic convention in Saint-Vincent, Italy, on April 15, 2011, Walter Rolfo and Piero Ustignani (both Italy, *see below left*) broke 66 wine glasses.

Tricks performed underwater in three minutes

The most magic tricks completed underwater in three minutes is 13 by Alessandro Politi (Italy) on the set of *Lo Show dei Record* in Milan, Italy, on April 25, 2009.

Magicians in a magic show

The greatest number of magicians ever assembled for a magic show

is 106, by Magic Circle Germany and Julius Frack (Germany) at the Landestheater Tübingen, Germany, on March 4, 2012.

People to disappear in an illusion

Criss Angel (USA) succeeded in making 100 people "disappear" in an illusion on the set of *Criss Angel: Mindfreak* at the Luxor Hotel and Casino in Las Vegas, Nevada, USA, on May 26, 2010.

FASTEST ESCAPE FROM A STRAITJACKET WHILE SUSPENDED (NO CHAINS)

In just 8.4 seconds, illusionist Lucas Wilson (Canada) managed to wriggle free from a Green Posey straitjacket—while suspended in the air by his ankles at a height of 3 ft. 3 in. (1 m). Lucas performed his upside-down escape at the Holy Trinity Catholic High School in Ontario, Canada, on June 8, 2012.

CHAIN LINK
Lucas also holds the record for the fastest straitjacket escape while suspended and chained!

MOST MAGIC TRICKS ACHIEVED BLINDFOLDED IN ONE MINUTE

Fernando Diaz (Venezuela) performed a total of 17 tricks in one minute while blindfolded on the set of TV show *Buenas Noches* in Caracas, Venezuela, on August 24, 2011. Each of the tricks, including "balloon emerging from a bottle" and "color-changing sponge," had at least two effects or elements and was witnessed by a live audience.

¡QUOTE
"I need to be able to calm myself and not panic, because if I panic then I'm going to mess up the entire thing I've been practicing for."

JUGGLING

MOST REPETITIONS OF THE "BUTTERFLY" IN 3 MINUTES

On November 11, 2012, at NEMO Science Center in the Dutch capital of Amsterdam, Niels Duinker (Netherlands) carried out 212 repetitions of the juggling technique known as the "butterfly." Hand and ball must be kept in permanent contact during the performance of this trick.

Farthest distance traveled on a unicycle while juggling three objects

On August 22, 2011, Ashrita Furman (USA) unicycled a distance of 1.75 miles (2.816 km) while juggling three balls at the Joe Michaels Mile course in Bayside, New York City, USA.

First juggle in space

NASA pilot Donald E. Williams (USA) juggled several pieces of fruit onboard the Space Shuttle *Discovery* on April 15, 1985.

MOST ...

Balls passed by a pair while juggling

Brothers Chris and Andrew Hodge (USA) passed 15 balls between them, making 38 passes (75 total catches), in February 2011.

Bounce-juggling catches by a pair (16 balls)

David Critchfield and John Jones (both USA) kept a 16-ball bounce pattern running for 74 catches on November 13, 2005. Starting with four balls in each hand, both men successively tossed the balls to their partner's opposite hands. Each ball bounced once before being caught and thrown back.

Cigar box end-to-ends in 30 seconds

Despite being known as a form of juggling, in this trick the boxes aren't thrown in the air. They are held out in front of the body—typically one in each hand, with the third held between the other two— and manipulated, most simply by moving one box from the left of the group to the right (an "end-to-end"). The most end-to-ends achieved while juggling three cigar boxes in 30 seconds is 36, by The Great Gordo Gamsby (Australia) at London Wonderground, UK, on September 14, 2012.

LONGEST TIME TO JUGGLE THREE OBJECTS, SUSPENDED UPSIDE DOWN

Quinn Spicker (Canada) achieved the dizzying feat of juggling three objects for 12 min. 50 sec. while suspended upside down at the PNE Garden Auditorium in Vancouver, British Columbia, Canada, on July 22, 2010.

MOST CHAINSAW-JUGGLING CATCHES ON A UNICYCLE

The Space Cowboy, aka Chayne Hultgren (Australia), made eight chainsaw-juggling catches atop a unicycle in Beijing, China, on December 7, 2012.

MOST COMPLETE CHANGEOVERS JUGGLING THREE OBJECTS

Jugglers Matt Baker and Joe Ricci (both USA) made 13 changeovers (passed while leaping over each other) in one minute on the set of *Torihada Scoop 100—New Year SP* in Tokyo, Japan, on January 1, 2012.

MOST CONSECUTIVE MAUL CATCHES

Erik Kloeker (USA) used 2-ft. 3-in.-long (69-cm) mauls (long-handled axes) each weighing 9 lb. 11 oz. (4.3 kg) to perform 86 sequential juggling catches in Newport, Kentucky, USA, on August 30, 2012.

MOST "BACKCROSS" CATCHES IN A ROW (SEVEN OBJECTS)

A "backcross" involves throwing an object so that it passes behind the back to be caught in front of the body by the other hand, then throwing it around the back again to the first hand. Ty Tojo (USA) made 69 backcross catches in a row on February 25, 2013, in Las Vegas, Nevada, USA.

Clubs passed back to back by a pair

Brother-and-sister team Vova and Olga Galchenko (both formerly Russia, now USA) juggled 10 clubs between them while standing back to back during practice sessions in May 2003, in their hometown of Penza, Russia. The duo's best run was 57 passes caught between them.

Individual rotations of clubs juggled while lying down (four clubs)

David Cain (USA) juggled four clubs over his head while lying flat on his back, completing 10 throws and catches, while recording himself in practice at home in Ohio, USA, on November 2, 2012.

Ping-pong balls juggled with the mouth

Tony Fercos (formerly Czechoslovakia, now USA) is able to blow and catch 14 ping-pong balls in succession with his mouth in a single cycle. Each ball is fed into his mouth, "spat" high into the air and caught back in his mouth.

Rings passed by a pair while juggling

In August 2010, Tony Pezzo (USA) and Patrik Elmnert (Sweden) successfully passed 15 rings and made 30 catches while juggling.

MOST BALLS JUGGLED

Ukrainian juggler Alexander Koblikov juggled 14 balls in practice at the 37th International Circus Festival of Monte-Carlo in Monaco on January 16, 2013. Koblikov uses the "multiplex" technique, throwing and catching two (unattached) balls at once. Alex Barron (UK) juggled 11 balls individually on April 3, 2012 at the Roehampton Club in London, UK.

Chainsaw-juggling catches

On September 25, 2011, Ian Stewart (Canada) carried out 94 catches using three fully engaged chainsaws at the Hants County Exhibition in Windsor, Nova Scotia, Canada.

MOST BATONS JUGGLED

Françoise Rochais (France) successfully juggled seven batons in one go in 1999 and still performs with the same number of batons today. She juggles her batons like clubs instead of the typical spinning style used by baton twirlers.

MOST BOWLING BALLS JUGGLED

On November 19, 2011, Milan Roskopf (Slovakia) juggled a total of three bowling balls in front of 350 witnesses. He juggled the balls, each weighing 10 lb. (4.53 kg), for 28.69 seconds at the Prague Juggling Marathon in the Czech Republic.

MOST OBJECTS JUGGLED ON A UNICYCLE

Mikhail Ivanov (Russia), a fourth-generation circus performer, juggled seven balls on a saddleless unicycle ("ultimate wheel") in Ivanovo, Russia, on September 18, 2012. He kept the balls in the air for 12.4 seconds.

Rings flashed between a pair

Rojic Levicky and Victor Teslenko (both Russia) made 18 catches with 18 rings in 2008.

Shaker cups juggled

The feat of juggling 10 shaker cups was first achieved in public in 1980 by John McPeak (USA) at the Nevada Palace casino in Las Vegas, USA. Holding five nested cups in each hand, he threw the stacks of cups into the air simultaneously, sending up four cups from each hand and retaining a fifth cup in his grasp. The flying cups each rotated 360 degrees before landing, in inverse order, back in the cups in his hands.

Most under-leg chainsaw-juggling passes by a pair (one minute)

The Space Cowboy (*see left*) and the Mighty Gareth, aka Gareth Williams (UK), made 40 under-leg chainsaw passes between them in Beijing, China, on December 7, 2012.

MOST FIRECLUBS JUGGLED WHILE SWORD-SWALLOWING

The Great Gordo Gamsby (Australia) juggled three fire clubs while swallowing a sword for 10 seconds at London Wonderground, UK, on September 14, 2012.

PLANNING THE CRAM

The team approached mathematicians from their college for advice on how to fit more than 19 people into the car.

Most people crammed into a Smart Car

Twenty limber members of the Glendale Cheerleading Team (all USA) squeezed into a Smart Car for *Guinness World Records Gone Wild!* in Los Angeles, USA, on September 28, 2011. The members of the team taking part were all female and measured at least 5 ft. (1.52 m) in height.

RECORD ADDICTION

Why break records?

Obtaining just one GWR certificate fulfills a lifetime's ambition for many of us. But others don't stop there. They are the most dedicated, determined, and driven record claimants, and some of them have made hundreds of applications to GWR. Meet the people who have made record-breaking a way of life.

Suresh Joachim, Canada

CHARITABLE ACTS
Suresh's record feats have helped a host of good causes, from the Red Cross to various cancer charities.

MINI BIO

Name: Suresh Joachim
Nationality: Sri Lanka/Canada
Claims: 451
Current records: 17
It's a wrap! On May 22, 2009, Suresh made a full-length feature film, from script to screen, in a record 11 days 23 hr. 45 min.

AN ENDURING SUCCESS

Look down the long list of Suresh's Guinness World Records and one thing becomes clear: he has an insatiable appetite for testing his endurance. Whether he's performing the **longest continuous crawl** (35.18 miles/56.62 km; *far left*) or the **greatest distance dribbling a basketball in 24 hours** (110.29 miles/177.5 km; *center left*), Suresh has worked hard to put himself streets ahead of his competitors.

But he doesn't have to move far to set records. Suresh has spent longer **balancing on one foot** (76 hr. 40 min.; *left*) and **rocking a rocking chair** (75 hr. 3 min.; *above*) than anyone else. In short, this man has truly record-breaking staying power.

Ashrita Furman, USA

MINI BIO

Name: Ashrita Furman
Nationality: USA
Claims: 470
Current records: 155—and counting!
In April 2009, this one-man record-breaking machine became the first (and, to date, only) person to hold 100 GWR titles at once.

LIVING THE DREAM
For Ashrita, breaking records is a way of fulfilling his dreams. As he once proudly stated, "This is my life!"

"I'm gunning for 200 records before I've finished"

ANOTHER DAY, ANOTHER RECORD ...

Ashrita's output includes records for somersaulting, pogo sticking, hopscotch, sack racing, underwater rope jumping, stilt walking, egg-and-spoon racing, and pushing an orange with his nose. Some are exhausting and just a bit strange (**most skips of a rope wearing swim fins in five minutes**: 253; *left*). Some require dexterity and patience (**most M&M's/Smarties eaten blindfolded using chopsticks in one minute**: 20; *above*). Others are simply fun (**most party poppers popped in one minute**: 64, *above left*; **most paper aircraft caught by mouth in one minute**: 16, *right*—achieved with Bipin Larkin [USA]). And by the time you read this, he'll probably have set another one!

SIMPLY SUPERFIT
Judo, boxing, martial arts … it's little wonder that Paddy has often been dubbed "the world's fittest man."

MINI BIO

Name: Paddy Doyle
Nationality: UK
Claims: 128
Current records: 33
Paddy can rightly call himself the toughest man on the planet. And who's going to argue with someone who's endured a record 141 back-to-back martial arts bouts?

🇬🇧 Paddy Doyle, UK

A HARD MAN TO BEAT
This is the face of a man who means business. Since 1987, Paddy has proved himself a push-up master, holding records for one- and two-armed push-ups in various categories and time scales, including the **most push-ups in 12 hours** (19,325) and the exceptionally demanding **most push-ups on the backs of the hands in one minute carrying a 100-lb pack** (26; *left*). He has also recorded the **most squats in one hour** (4,708), the **most full-contact kicks in one hour** (5,750; *far left*), and a record-breaking 29,850 **full-contact punch strikes** in just an hour (*below*). Strength. Speed. Stamina. That's Paddy Doyle in a nutshell.

"Guinness World Records means, to me, the ultimate. Being the best in the world"

☯ Zdeněk Bradáč, Czech Republic

"My passion for breaking records has never stopped— and the greatest challenges are still to come"

THE GREAT ESCAPIST
For Zdeněk, getting out of a pair of handcuffs is as easy as getting out of bed. He currently holds the records for the **most handcuffs unlocked in one minute** (seven) and has registered the **greatest number of escapes from handcuffs in one hour** (627) and **24 hours** (10,625). He's no slouch at the card table either, having recorded both the **fastest time to arrange a deck of shuffled playing cards** (36.16 seconds) and the **most Charlier (one-handed) cuts of a pack of cards in one minute** (73).

The dextrous Zdeněk is also adept at keeping objects aloft, having recorded the **longest duration juggling four objects** (2 hr. 46 min. 48 sec.) and the **most juggling catches of three balls in a minute** (422). As a record breaker, though, Zdeněk himself is hard to catch …

SCUBA DOOBY-DO!
Zdeněk achieved the **longest underwater juggling of three balls** – 1 hr. 30 min. while scuba-diving on February 18, 2011.

MINI BIO

Name: Zdeněk Bradáč
Nationality: Czech Rep.
Claims: 109
Current records: 12
Zdeněk has cast his spell over juggling, escapology, and playing cards. In September 2009, he extricated himself from three pairs of handcuffs in 38.69 seconds—underwater.

BIG STUFF

LARGEST ...

Backpack

With enough room inside to pack the contents of an entire house, the largest backpack measures 34 ft. (10.37 m) high, 25 ft. 7 in. (7.8 m) wide, and 9 ft. 2.2 in. (2.8 m) deep. It was created by Omasu (Saudi Arabia) in Jeddah, Saudi Arabia, on April 4, 2012.

Bag of potato chips

Calbee, Inc. of Japan unveiled a giant bag of chips weighing 1,104 lb. (501 kg)—equivalent in weight to 10 average 14-year-old boys—at the Calbee Chitose Factory in Chitose, Hokkaido, Japan, on July 16, 2012. The bag—a scaled-up version of Calbee's salted crisp packet—measured 15 ft. 8 in. x 13 ft. 9 in. (4.8 x 4.2 m).

Ballpoint pen

Acharya Makunuri Srinivasa (India) presented an 18-ft. 0.5-in.-tall (5.5-m) pen engraved with scenes from Indian mythology in Hyderabad, India, on April 24, 2011.

Book

The largest book measures 16 ft. 4 in. x 26 ft. 5 in. (5 x 8.06 m), weighs approximately 3,306 lb. (1,500 kg), and consists of 429 pages. It was unveiled by the Mshahed International Group in Dubai, UAE, on February 27, 2012.

Bottle of wine

A whopping 12 ft. 2 in. (3.8 m) in height and 3 ft. 3 in. (1 m) in diameter, the largest wine bottle was made by OK Watterfäscht 2011 (Switzerland) and measured in Watt, Gemeinde Regensdorf, Switzerland, on July 9, 2011.

Largest soccer ball

You'd have a lot of trouble finding a goal large enough for this ball ... Made from artificial leather, the largest soccer ball has a diameter of 39 ft. 11.8 in. (12.18 m) and a circumference of 125 ft. 8 in. (38.30 m), and weighs approximately 2,116 lb. (960 kg). It was made by Doha Bank in Doha, Qatar, and displayed in the city's LuLu Hypermarket parking lot on February 12, 2013.

Largest drum kit

Ambitious percussion group Drumartic (Austria) built Big Boom, a massive 5.2:1-scale, fully functional replica kit. It measures 21 ft. (6.5 m) tall by 26 ft. (8 m) wide and was presented, played, and measured in Lienz, Austria, on October 7, 2012.

FOR THE RECORD

Fun four-man team Drumartic, led by Peter Lindsberger, must be pretty strong to handle two giant drumsticks each, not to mention staying in sync without being able to see each other!

BIG BEATS

The diameters of the individual pieces are: bass drum 114 in. (2.9 m); floor tom 83 in. (2.11 m); rack tom 62 in. (1.57 m); snare 73 in. (1.85 m); hi-hat cymbals (two) 68 in. (1.73 m); crash cymbal 78 in. (1.98 m); ride 88 in. (2.24 m).

LARGEST TOYS

Chess piece: A king piece measuring 14 ft. 7 in. (4.46 m) tall and 6 ft. (1.83 m) in diameter around its base, in St. Louis, Missouri, USA, on April 24, 2012.

Video game joy pad: A fully functioning game pad measuring 12 ft. x 5 ft. 3 in. x 1 ft. 8 in. (3.66 x 1.59 x 0.51 m) at Delft University of Technology, Netherlands, in September 2011.

Rag doll: Standing at 15 ft. 2 in. (4.62 m) tall, the doll was made in Genova, Italy, in 2005.

Set of Russian dolls: A 51-piece set, with the largest piece measuring 1 ft. 9.25 in. (53.97 cm) in height. Completed on April 25, 2003, in Cameron, North Carolina, USA.

Whoopee cushion: Made by Steve Mesure (UK) in London, UK, on June 14, 2008, it measured 10 ft. (3.05 m) in diameter.

Largest ridable bicycle

One of many crazy cycling creations crafted by inventor Didi Senft (Germany), this behemoth of a bicycle measures 25 ft. 7.09 in. (7.8 m) long, 12 ft. 1.67 in. (3.7 m) high, has a wheel diameter of 10 ft. 9.92 in. (3.3 m), and weighs 330 lb. (150 kg). It was measured in Pudagla, Germany, on October 2, 2012.

Largest shopping cart

Big enough to hold 250 regular-sized shopping carts, the world's largest measured 54 ft. 5.5 in. (16.6 m) in height from ground to handle. With a basket 31 ft. 5.8 in. (9.6 m) long and 27 ft. (8.23 m) wide, and with wheels 3 ft. 11 in. (1.2 m) in diameter, the trolley took Migros Ticaret A.Ş (Turkey) one month to make from 22,000 lb. (9.9 tonnes) of iron. It was unveiled on June 14, 2012, in Istanbul, Turkey.

Disco ball
A glitterball measuring 32 ft. 9 in. (9.98 m) wide was made by BSG Luxury Group for Bacardi Russia. The ball was displayed at a party in Moscow, Russia, on April 26, 2012.

Dog biscuit
At more than 2,000 times the size of an average doggy treat, a biscuit weighing 617 lb. (279.87 kg) was baked by Hampshire Pet Products (USA) in Joplin, Missouri, USA, on July 8, 2011. It was eventually broken up into pieces and distributed to dogs by the Joplin Humane Society.

Envelope
Addressed to the United Nations and stuffed with messages in support of world peace, the largest envelope measures 36 ft. 1 in. (11.02 m) long and 24 ft. 11 in. (7.61 m) wide. It was created by Aligarh Muslim University (India) in Aligarh, Uttar Pradesh, India, on May 1, 2012.

High-visibility jacket
A hi-vis jacket measuring 45 ft. 6 in. (13.88 m) high and 35 ft. (10.68 m) wide was manufactured by Febelsafe and Secura in Brussels, Belgium, and measured on February 7, 2013. The giant jacket is CE-certified, as required by European health-and-safety regulations!

Inflatable beach ball
Designed to look like a soccer ball, the largest blow-up ball was created by the hypermarket "real,-" (Poland). Its diameter was measured at 51 ft. 10 in. (15.82 m) on May 8, 2012 in Czluchów, Poland.

LARGEST MICROPHONE

Artist David Åberg (Sweden) made a massive mic measuring 14 ft. 9 in. (4.5 m) long with a diameter of 3 ft. 10 in. (1.18 m) across the head. He unveiled his record-breaking creation in Helsingborg, Sweden, on October 19, 2012.

Lollipop
See's Candies celebrated National Lollipop Day in the USA with a 7,003-lb. (3,176.5-kg) version of their signature gourmet chocolate lolly. The 5-ft. 11-in. (1.8-m) treat was created at their factory in Burlingame, California, USA, on July 18, 2012.

Lunch box
Coupons for Change (USA) created a mammoth lunch box to honor Hunger Action Month. It measured 90 x 80 x 40 in. (2.29 x 2.03 x 1.02 m) and was filled with 400 backpacks full of food for needy children in Mountain View, California, USA, on August 15, 2012.

Pencil
Ashrita Furman and members of the Sri Chinmoy Center (both USA) produced a pencil 76 ft. 2.75 in. (23.23 m) long and weighing 21,700 lb. (9.84 tonnes) in New York City, USA, on August 27, 2007.

Postcard
A prodigious postcard measuring 564.89 sq. ft. (52.48 m²) was created by Andrej Maver and Glasbena Agencija GIG (both Slovenia) in Nova Gorica, Slovenia, on August 27, 2012.

ON YOUR BIKE
Infamous on both the Tour de France and Giro d'Italia circuits, Didi is often seen riding one of his creations and always sporting his devil (El Diablo) costume!

Game of Twister: The largest twister board measured 171 ft. 1 in. x 140 ft. 1 in. (52.15 x 42.7 m) and was used for a giant game of Twister on September 1, 2011, in Enschede, Netherlands.

Rocking horse: Measured at 24 ft. 11 in. x 10 ft. 6 in. x 20 ft. (7.6 x 3.22 x 6.1 m), it was made in Tzoran-Kadima, Israel, on September 12, 2010.

Plastic duck: Was 82 ft. (25 m) tall and floated at the port of Saint-Nazaire, France, as part of an art installation from June to September 2007.

Board game: A 2,421-sq.-ft. (225-m²) Monopoly board made by De Eindhovense School (Netherlands) on January 27, 2012.

Hula hoop: Has a diameter of 16 ft. 6.7 in. (5.04 m) and was spun more than three times by Ashrita Furman (USA) in New York City, USA, on September 9, 2010.

COLLECTIONS

LARGEST COLLECTION OF ...

Bottle openers
Marinus Van Doorn shares his home in Veghel, Netherlands, with 33,492 bottle openers as of November 2, 2011.

Fire helmets
As of February 9, 2012, Gert Souer of Haren, Netherlands, had amassed 838 fire helmets.

Garfield memorabilia
Mike Drysdale and Gayle Brennan of Los Angeles, California, USA, have collected 3,000 items related to their favorite comic strip character, Garfield. The couple have turned their home into a shrine to the famous cat. Every corner is crammed with cuddly toys, videos, bedding, pottery, radios, wind-up toys, and other Garfield-related items. The pair have been collecting since 1994.

Jigsaw puzzles
Over the past 26 years, Georgina Gil-Lacuna of Tagaytay City in the Philippines has amassed an unrivalled collection of 1,028 different jigsaw sets. Her largest puzzle has 18,000 pieces.

Largest collection of Iron Maiden memorabilia
Rasmus Stavnsborg (Denmark) had collected 4,168 items of Iron Maiden memorabilia in Karlslunde, Denmark, as of February 9, 2012. Rasmus began listening to the iconic British metal band in 1981 at the age of eight.

Largest collection of toothpaste tubes
Dentist Val Kolpakov (USA) had collected 2,037 toothpaste tubes as of June 15, 2012. His tooth-friendly collection comes from all over the world, including items from Japan, Korea, China, India, and Russia.

Magazines
James Hyman of London, UK, has amassed a collection of 50,953 different magazines. The total was verified on August 1, 2012.

Model motorcycles
Officially counted on May 24, 2012, the largest collection of model motorcycles comprises 1,258 separate items and belongs to David Correia of Norco in California, USA.

Panda-related items
The largest collection of panda-related items belongs to Edo Rajh and Iva Rajh (both Croatia) and takes the form of 1,966 different World Wildlife Fund (WWF) stamps bearing a panda logo. The collection was counted in Zagreb, Croatia, on April 2, 2012.

Three-piece tea sets
Pyrmonter Fuerstentreff (Germany) has collected a grand total of 999 three-piece tea sets, which were displayed in Bad Pyrmont, Germany, on July 7, 2012.

Largest collection of Converse shoes
The most extensive collection of Converse footwear belongs to Joshua Mueller (USA), who owned 1,546 different pairs as of March 8, 2012. Joshua, of Lakewood in Washington, USA, wears his Converse shoes with plastic bags over them to keep them clean!

4.2
Years Joshua could wear a new pair of his shoes every day without repeating!

EVEN MORE COLLECTIONS

Bus tickets: 200,000 unique tickets from 36 countries, as of September 30, 2008. Owned by Ladislav Sejnoha (Czech Republic).

Toasters: 1,284 toasters, belonging to Kenneth Huggins of Columbia, South Carolina, USA, as of July 31, 2012.

Stamps featuring popes: 1,580 stamps, owned by Magnus Andersson (Sweden). Counted at the public library in Falun, Sweden, on November 16, 2010.

Lip balms: 491 diverse lip balms, owned by Eleanor Miller of Tel Aviv, Israel, as of November 29, 2011.

Unprocessed film: 1,250 different analog films as of June 30, 2012, belonging to Ying Nga Chow (Hong Kong) in Hong Kong, China.

COLLECTION	AMOUNT	RECORD HOLDER	DATE COUNTED
Airline sickness bags	6,290	Niek Vermeulen (Netherlands)	February 28, 2012
Batman memorabilia	1,160	Zdravko Genov (Bulgaria)	December 10, 2011
Beer bottles	25,866	Ron Werner (USA)	January 27, 2012
Candles	6,360	Lam Chung Foon (Hong Kong)	December 23, 2011
Chess sets	412	Akın Gökyay (Turkey)	January 30, 2012
Coffee pots	27,390	Robert Dahl (Germany)	November 2, 2012
Cookie jars	2,653	Edith Eva Fuchs (USA)	August 20, 2012
Decorative pins	18,431	Arvind Sinha (India)	May 10, 2010
Letter openers	5,000	Santa Fe College Foundation (USA)	October 25, 2012
Mickey Mouse memorabilia	4,127	Janet Esteves (USA)	March 12, 2012
Military models	2,815	Francisco Sánchez Abril (Spain)	February 16, 2012
Model ambulances	10,648	Siegfried Weinert and Susanne Ottendorfer (both Austria)	April 7, 2012
Model cars	27,777	Nabil Karam (Lebanon)	November 17, 2011
Napkins	50,000	Antónia Kozáková (Slovakia)	August 1, 2012
Pedal-powered model vehicles	400	Phil Collins (UK)	September 4, 2012
Snail-related items	1,377	Professor Henryk Skarżyński, MD, PhD (Poland)	July 15, 2012
Sneakers	2,388 pairs	Jordy Geller (USA)	May 17, 2012
Souvenir plates	621	The Kundin family (Russia)	October 1, 2012
Sugar packets	9,596	Kristen Dennis (USA)	February 11, 2012
Video game screenshots	17,000	Rikardo Granda (Colombia)	30 September 2012
Wind-up toys	1,042	William Keuntje (USA)	November 26, 2011
Wine and champagne labels	16,349	Sophia Vaharis (Greece)	January 17, 2012

Largest collection of Chevrolet memorabilia

Located in Downingtown, Pennsylvania, USA, the most extensive collection of Chevrolet memorabilia belongs to Charles Mallon (USA) and consisted of 2,181 individual Chevrolet items as of April 11, 2012.

Largest collection of vacuum cleaners

When it comes to vacuum cleaners, James Brown (UK) has truly cleaned up! James owned 322 different models as of October 31, 2012, housed at his repair shop Mr. Vacuum Cleaner in Heanor, Derbyshire, UK, and in Hucknall, Nottinghamshire, UK.

OLD SUCKER
James's favorites are the models made by Kirby. His oldest vacuum cleaner is a Hoover 700 made in 1926.

Candy wrappers: 2,048 wrappers, owned by Amanda Destro of Venice, Italy, as of February 16, 2012.

Tea-bag tags: 839 tags, collected by Daniel Szabo of Budapest, Hungary, by September 4, 2011.

Human teeth: 2,000,744 teeth, collected by Brother Giovanni Battista Orsenigo of the Ospedale Fatebenefratelli in Rome, Italy.

Prayer beads: 3,642 prayer bead strings, belonging to Jamal Sleeq of Kuwait City, Kuwait, as of March 9, 2012.

Life belts: 100 individual life belts, collected by José Octavio Busto Iñiguez (USA) as of May 23, 2012.

DAREDEVILS

TIERRA DEL FUEGO '98

Lowest limbo skating over 10 meters

Rohan Kokane (India) limbo-skated under a 33-ft.-long (10-m) line of parked cars on the set of *Lo Show dei Record* in Rome, Italy, on April 4, 2012. The gap between the ground and the cars was just 9.84 in. (25 cm)! This is one record that you should definitely *not* try at home!

LORD OF THE LIMBO
Rohan has also held records for limbo skating beneath 20 cars and blindfold limbo skating.

FARTHEST DISTANCE ...

Firewalking
Trever McGhee (Canada) walked 597 ft. (181.9 m) over embers with a temperature of between 1,214°F and 1,307°F (657.6–853.3°C) at Symons Valley Rodeo Grounds in Calgary, Alberta, Canada, on November 9, 2007.

To throw and catch a running chainsaw
Chayne Hultgren threw a running chainsaw 13 ft. (4 m), at which point it was caught by Gordo Gamsby (both Australia), at London Wonderground, UK, on September 14, 2012. The trigger of the two-stroke Spear & Jackson chainsaw was taped down to keep the blade spinning.

Wall running (parkour)
Amadei Weiland (Germany) ran 11 ft. 5 in. (3.49 m) across a wall on TV's *Guinness World Records—Wir Holen den Rekord nach Deutschland* in Europa Park, Rust, Germany, on July 13, 2012.

Running while on fire
Denni Duesterhoeft (Germany) ran 501 ft. (153 m) while ablaze on the set of the TV show *Das Herbstfest der Überraschungen* (ARD, Germany) in Riesa, Germany, on October 13, 2012.

As a human cannonball
The Bullet, aka David Smith, Jr. (USA), was shot 193 ft. 8 in. (59.05 m) from a cannon on the set of *Lo Show dei Record* in Milan, Italy, on March 10, 2011.

CHECK THIS STOPPIE!
The stoppie was more than 1,100 ft. (335.3 m) long. Jesse was riding a 2004 Suzuki GSXR-750.

Farthest distance in a wing suit

Shinichi Ito (Japan) flew 17.83 miles (28.70 km) in a wing suit above Yolo County, California, USA, on May 26, 2012. His aerial daredevilry gives Shinichi records for both the **greatest absolute distance flown in a wing suit** and the **greatest horizontal distance flown in a wing suit**: 16.71 miles (26.9 km). *(For more air sports, turn to p.222.)*

Fastest motorcycle stoppie

Jesse Toler (USA) carried out a 150-mph (241.4-km/h) stoppie—a front wheelie, performed by skillfully applying the brakes and drawing the bike to a stationary position—at ZMax Dragway during the Charlotte Diesel Super Show in Concord, North Carolina, USA, on October 6, 2012.

RECORD-BREAKING MOVIE STUNTS

Highest stunt free fall on film: 1,100 ft. (335 m) by Dar Robinson (USA), from a ledge at the summit of the CN Tower, Toronto, Canada, for *Highpoint* (Canada, 1982).

Most cars wrecked by a stuntman: 2,003 by Dick Sheppard (UK) over more than 40 years.

Largest movie budget for stunts: More than $3 million, for *Titanic* (USA, 1997).

Most popular Bond movie stunt: A leap from crane to crane in *Casino Royale* (UK/Czech Republic/USA/Germany/The Bahamas, 2006). Source: *Radio Times* poll.

Longest speedboat jump in a movie: 120 ft. (36.5 m) by stuntman Jerry Comeaux (USA) in *Live and Let Die* (UK, 1973).

HOT, HOT, HOT WHEELS
Both cars are modeled on Mattel's Hot Wheels toys. Tanner's is yellow; Greg's is green.

Highest bungee jump into water while on fire

On September 14, 2012, Yoni Roch (France) achieved the doubly dangerous act of performing a bungee jump into water while alight, from a record height of 213 ft. 6 in. (65.09 m) at the Viaduc de la Souleuvre, Normandy, France.

David also attained the **greatest height launched from a cannon**—77 ft. 6 in. (23.62 m)—at the Charlotte Motor Speedway in Concord, North Carolina, USA, on October 15, 2011.

FASTEST ...

Car on ice
Janne Laitinen (Finland) drove a modified Audi RS6 at a speed of 206.05 mph (331.61 km/h) in the Gulf of Bothnia (Baltic "frozen" Sea) in Finland on March 6, 2011.

Car driven blindfolded
Metin Şentürk (Turkey), president of the World Handicapped Foundation, drove blindfolded at 182.03 mph (292.89 km/h) in a Ferrari F430 at the airport in Urfa, Turkey, on March 31, 2010.

Time to jump over three moving cars head-on
Aaron Evans (USA) jumped over three moving vehicles head-on in 29.09 seconds in Los Angeles, California, USA, on July 9, 2012.

Motorcycle wheelie on a tightrope
Johann Traber (Germany) reached a speed of 32.9 mph (53 km/h) while driving a motorcycle along

a tightrope at the Tummelum Festival in Flensburg, Germany, on August 13, 2005.

Speed on a quad bike (ATV)
The highest speed reached on a quad bike, or all-terrain vehicle, given a flying start, is 196.19 mph (315.74 km/h) by Terry Wilmeth (USA) on his ALSR Rocket Raptor version 6.0—a Yamaha 700 Raptor modified with a hybrid rocket thruster —at the Madras Airport in Madras, Oregon, USA, on June 15, 2008.

HIGHEST ...

Ground-supported tightrope walk
On August 7, 1974, Philippe Petit (France) crossed a high-wire strung 1,350 ft. (411 m) above the ground between the towers of the World Trade Center in New York City, USA.

The **highest tightrope crossing by motorcycle** was 426 ft. 6 in. (130 m) high and 2,185 ft. 4 in. (666.1 m) long by Mustafa Danger (Morocco). He rode along a steel cable strung

Highest ramp jump by wheelchair

Aaron Fotheringham (USA) achieved a 23.6-in. (60-cm) ramp jump in his wheelchair in Rome, Italy, on March 24, 2010. Aaron's athleticism has taken him all over the world, inspiring young people and showing off his incredible control and talent with his wheelchair.

Largest loop the loop in a car

Greg Tracy and Tanner Foust (both USA) looped a 60-ft.-diameter (18.29-m) loop for Mattel (USA) in Los Angeles, California, USA, on June 30, 2012. The track was a scaled-up replica of the Hot Wheels Double Dare Snare loop toy and was attempted during X Games 18.

from the Monte Tossal hill to the Gran Hotel Bali in Benidorm, Spain, on October 16, 2010.

The **highest tightrope crossing by bicycle** was 238 ft. (72.5 m) by Nik Wallenda (USA) between the Royal Towers of the Atlantis Paradise Island hotel in Nassau, The Bahamas, on August 28, 2010.

Unassisted static jump into an air cushion
On August 7, 1997, Stig Günther (Denmark) leaped 342 ft. (104.5 m) off a crane onto an air bag measuring 39 x 49 x 14 ft. (12 x 15 x 4.5 m). His impact speed was about 90 mph (145 km/h).

Fastest time to climb the Burj Khalifa unassisted

French climber extraordinaire Alain Robert (France) scaled the Burj Khalifa—at 2,716 ft. (828 m), the world's **tallest building** (see pp. 144–145)—in Dubai, UAE, in 6 hr. 13 min. 55 sec. on March 29, 2011. Emaar Properties, the building's developers, insisted he wore safety equipment for the attempt.

GRIPPING TALE
Alan, aka Spider-Man, wore safety gear this time, but—amazingly—he usually climbs with only his bare hands and rubber shoes.

Most screen swordfights: Christopher Lee (UK) has dueled in 17 movies with foils, swords, lightsabers, and billiard cues.

Highest jump without a parachute on film: 232 ft. (70.71 m) by A. J. Bakunas (USA) in Hooper (USA, 1978). He fell onto an air mattress.

Largest movie stunt explosion: One nine-second blast in Blown Away (USA, 1994) used 720 gal. (2,727 liters) of fuel and 32 bombs, each weighing 16 oz. (453 g).

Most cannon rolls in a car: Seven by stuntman Adam Kirley (UK) in an Aston Martin DBS during filming for Casino Royale (UK, 2006).

Most expensive movie stunt performed in the air: $1 million—Simon Crane (UK) moved between two jets at an altitude of 15,000 ft. (4,572 m) for Cliffhanger (USA, 1993).

MACHO MEN

3.9
Length in inches of each nail—2 in. (5 cm) of each one was hammered into the wood.

iQUOTE
"I've spent my life making painful stunts painfully funny."

HEAVIEST ...

Weight pulled with the tongue

The Great Gordo Gamsby (Australia) pulled a 291-lb. (132-kg) weight for a minimum distance of 32 ft. (10 m) at London Wonderground, UK, on September 16, 2012. Gordo used a hook through his tongue to pull along his glamorous assistant Daniella D'Ville (UK) as she sat on a low-loading trolley.

Weight lifted with the toes

A weight of 51 lb. (23 kg) was lifted by Guy Phillips (UK) in Horning, Norfolk, UK, on May 28, 2011. Firm-footed Guy used a dumbbell fitted with a strap to enable him to use only his toes to hoist the weight.

Weight lifted with the shoulder blades

On the set of a *CCTV Guinness World Records Special* in Beijing, China, on December 8, 2012, Feng Yixi (China) held a 113-lb. 5-oz. (51.4-kg) weight between his shoulder blades and lifted it a minimum of 4 in. (10 cm) from the ground, holding it there for the requisite five seconds.

Vehicle pulled by beard

Sadi Ahmed (Pakistan) attached his beard to a 3,747-lb. (1,700-kg) truck and pulled it over a distance of 16 ft. 5 in. (5 m) at the Punjab Youth Festival in the Lahore Expo Center, Pakistan, on October 21, 2012.

Fastest time to remove five nails with the teeth

Strongman and multiple Guinness World Record-holder René "Golem" Richter (Czech Republic/Germany) ripped five steel nails from a piece of wood in 32.39 seconds on the set of *Lo Show dei Record* on March 28, 2012 using just his teeth. René doesn't do anything special to strengthen or care for his abrasive gnashers—he's simply blessed with naturally tough tusks!

FASTEST ...

Throw of five Atlas stones

Travis Ortmayer (USA) threw five Atlas stones—round weightlifting stones totalling 1,653 lb. 7 oz. (750 kg)—over a 4-ft. 11-in.-tall (1.5-m) obstacle in 15.83 seconds in Milan, Italy, on April 28, 2011.

25-m aircraft pull

On April 21, 2011, Žydrūnas Savickas (Lithuania) pulled an aircraft a distance of 82 ft. (25 m) in 48.97 seconds on the set of *Lo Show dei Record*. To qualify for this record, the aircraft must weigh more than 22,046 lb. (10 tonnes), including the pilot.

FACT:
The car that Igor pulled with his teeth weighed the equivalent of 26 average adult men—or an entire field of soccer players plus the referee and officials!

Heaviest weight lifted using hooks through the forearms

One half of crazy sideshow duo Monsters of Schlock (*see also p. 87*), Burnaby Q. Orbax (Canada) lifted a 31-lb. (14.4-kg) metal cider keg and held it aloft for 10 seconds using meat hooks pierced through the skin of his forearms at London Wonderground, UK, on July 28, 2012.

EXTREMELY TALENTED
Igor is an extreme stunts performer and an aerial acrobat with *Cirque du Soleil*, taking the lead role in many shows.

Fastest time to pull a car a distance of 100 ft. by the teeth

Acrobatic superstar Igor Zaripov (Russia) pulled a vehicle containing a full tank of gasoline and a passenger—weighing a total of 3,627 lb. (1,645 kg)—more than 100 ft. (30 m) by his mouth in just 18.42 seconds in Las Vegas, Nevada, USA, on April 12, 2012.

MIGHTY LIFTERS AND PULLERS

Heaviest weight lifted by neck: Frank Ciavattone (USA) raised an 808-lb. (366.50-kg) weight with his neck on November 15, 2005.

Heaviest weight lifted by a human beard: On April 18, 2012, Antanas Kontrimas (Lithuania) lifted a 139-lb. (63.50-kg) woman with his beard in Rome, Italy.

Heaviest weight lifted by tongue: On August 1, 2008, Thomas Blackthorne (UK) lifted a 27-lb. 8.9-oz. (12.5-kg) weight hooked through a hole in his tongue.

Heaviest weight lifted by both eye sockets: A 52-lb. 14.5-oz. (24-kg) weight was raised by Manjit Singh (UK) in Leicester, UK, on November 15, 2012.

Longest distance traveled while lifting a table with the teeth: Georges Christen (Luxembourg) ran 38 ft. 8 in. (11.8 m) holding a table with a person on top—a total weight of 136 lb. 10 oz (62 kg)—in his teeth in Madrid, Spain, on February 9, 2008.

Longest time restraining two aircraft

Storms, fog, lightning—they can all delay aircraft from taking off. Well, to that list you can add one more phenomenon: the USA's Chad Netherland! On July 7, 2007, Chad prevented the takeoff of two Cessna airplanes pulling in opposite directions for a duration of 1 min. 0.6 sec. at Richard I. Bong Airport in Superior, Wisconsin, USA.

> **iQUOTE**
> "I stay motivated by challenging myself and continually setting new goals."

Hot-water bottle burst

Shaun Jones (UK) blew up a standard hot-water bottle until it burst—using just the power of his lungs—in a record 6.52 seconds for *Lo Show dei Record* in Milan, Italy, on March 31, 2011.

MOST ...

Concrete blocks broken in a single stack

Ali Bahçetepe (Turkey) managed to break a stack of 36 concrete blocks in Muğla, Datça, Turkey, on March 18, 2012.

Stacked benches held between the teeth

On August 19, 2011, Huang Changzhun (China) balanced 17 prestacked benches between his teeth for the duration of 10 seconds on the set of a *CCTV Guinness World Records Special* in Beijing, China.

Iron bars bent in one minute

Alexander Muromskiy (Russia) successfully bent 26 iron bars—each 2 ft. (61 cm) long and 0.47 in. (12 mm) thick—at the Trade Complex Angar Auto in Moscow, Russia, on November 3, 2012.

Ice blocks broken by a human battering ram

J. D. Anderson (USA) was used as a human battering ram to break 13 ice blocks, head first, on the set of *Guinness World Records Gone Wild!* in Los Angeles, California, USA, on July 3, 2012.

Telephone directories ripped apart in two minutes (spine)

On the set of *Zheng Da Zong Yi— Guinness World Records Special* in Beijing, China, on December 21, 2010, Cosimo Ferrucci (Italy) tore 33 telephone directories apart across their spines.

Alexander Muromskiy achieved the equally impressive record of **most telephone directories torn behind the back in three minutes**, tearing 10 at Global City shopping mall in Moscow, Russia, on April 30, 2011.

Baseball bats broken with the back in one minute

Tomi Lotta (Finland) broke 16 baseball bats with his back in Rome, Italy, on March 21, 2012. Lotta, an international strongman, went head-to-head with fellow strength competitor Ákos Nagy (Hungary) for the record attempt.

Most pine boards broken with a backflip kick

In a revolutionary physical feat, Huynh Dang Khoa (Germany) broke a total of five 1-in.-thick (2.54-cm) pine boards in only one minute in Rome, Italy, on March 31, 2012.

Most one-finger push-ups in 30 seconds

Xie Guizhong (China) proved that he has a finger of steel in Beijing, China, on December 8, 2011, when he performed a record 41 one-finger push-ups in 30 seconds. Xie's finger feats don't stop there. On December 11, 2012, in Shenzhen City, China, he achieved the **fastest time pushing a car a distance of 50 m (164 ft.) with one finger**. He took just 47.7 seconds to move the vehicle, which weighed a whopping 4,167 lb. (1,890 kg).

PUSHING THE ENVELOPE

Xie held the previous record for most one-finger push-ups but managed to exceed his own record of 25 when he went head-to-head with a fellow Chinese challenger!

Heaviest train pulled by teeth: Velu Rathakrishnan (Malaysia) pulled a 574,964-lb. (260.8-tonne) train 13 ft. 9 in. (4.2 m) with his teeth at Kuala Lumpur railroad station, Malaysia, in 2003.

Heaviest weight pulled for 100 ft. by a pair: Kevin and Jacob Fast (both Canada) pulled a 153,780-lb. (69,753-kg) fire engine 100 ft. (30 m) in Coubourg, Canada, on June 18, 2011.

Fastest time to pull a car 15 m by "can suction" on the hands: On April 4, 2012, Wei Wei (China) took 23 seconds to pull a car 49 ft. (15 m).

Farthest distance to pull a vehicle with meat hooks in the back: On October 25, 2011, Burnaby Q. Orbax (Canada) heaved an 8,929-lb. (4,050-kg) truck for 366 ft. 6 in. (111.7 m) in Vancouver, Canada.

Heaviest road vehicle pulled by teeth: Igor Zaripov (Russia) tugged a 27,249-lb. (12,360-kg) double-decker bus on *Officially Amazing* in London, UK, on October 15, 2012.

WONDER WOMEN

Heaviest weight pulled with the tongue

Elaine Davidson (UK), the **most pierced woman** (*see p. 46*), pulled a 249-lb. 1.9-oz. (13-kg) weight connected to a meat hook through her tongue. The weight comprised volunteer Grizelda August, plus the low-loader on which she sat and the metal chain attaching the loader to Elaine's tongue.

On the same day, Elaine also held the **most skewers in the tongue**, sliding 14 metal kebab skewers measuring 9.8 in. (25 cm) long and 0.15 in. (4 mm) thick into the hole in her tongue.

Most basketball free throws in one minute

Professional basketball player Ashley Graham (USA) made 40 free throws on the set of *Lo Show dei Record* in Rome, Italy, on March 31, 2012. She was assisted by five male members of Rome's basketball team.

WOMEN ONLY
All the extraordinary world records listed on these pages are in the women's categories only. For outstanding feats of strength and endurance by men, turn back one page.

Heaviest weight lifted with the hair

On April 8, 2011, on the set of *Lo Show dei Record* in Milan, Italy, Anastasia, aka Joanna Sawicka (Poland), was lifted upside-down while supporting the 117-lb. 11-oz. (53.4-kg) weight of another person with her hair.

Fastest time to lift four Atlas Stones

Nina Geria (Ukraine) raised four Atlas Stones in 24.23 seconds in Rome, Italy, on April 18, 2012. The stones weighed 176 lb. (80 kg), 231 lb. (105 kg), 264 lb. (120 kg) and 297 lb. (135 kg) and, as per competition guidelines, were lifted one at a time in increasing order of weight.

Most people lifted and thrown in two minutes

A total of 12 people were lifted and flung by Aneta Florczyk (Poland) on the set of *Guinness World Records* in Madrid, Spain, on December 19, 2008. Florczyk beat Spanish challenger Irene Gutierrez, who threw 10 people.

Highest beer keg toss

On March 12, 2012, the mighty Nina Geria (Ukraine) tossed a beer keg 12 ft. 10 in. (3.90 m) up in the air in Rome, Italy.

Most squats with 130 kg in two minutes

Strongwoman Maria Catharina Adriana Strik (Netherlands) squat-lifted a weight of 286 lb. 9 oz. (130 kg) 29 times in two minutes in Rome, Italy, on April 4, 2012 on the set of *Lo Show dei Record*.

4.04
The difference in seconds between Julia's record and the current women's IAAF 100 m world record!

Fastest 100 m in high heels

Julia Plecher (Germany) sprinted to the finish line in just 14.531 seconds wearing a pair of stylish stilettos on the set of *Guinness World Records: Wir Holen den Rekord nach Deutschland* in Europa Park, Rust, Germany, on July 13, 2012.

MARATHON MAIDENS

Fastest fruit: Sally Orange (UK) achieved a time of 4 hr. 32 min. 28 sec. dressed as her namesake at the Flora London Marathon (UK) on April 26, 2009.

FOR MORE MARATHON FEATS, TURN TO P. 246

Longest crochet chain: Susie Hewer (UK) crocheted a 253-ft.-long (77.4-m) chain while running the Virgin London Marathon (UK) on April 25, 2010.

Fastest superhero: Dressed up as Superwoman, Jill Christie (UK) ran the Virgin London Marathon (UK) on April 25, 2010 in 3 hr. 8 min. 55 sec.

Fastest in military uniform: Sophie Hilaire (USA) ran the Philadelphia Marathon (USA) on November 22, 2009 in just 4 hr. 54 min. 15 sec.

Fastest cartoon character: SpongeBob SquarePants, aka Larissa Tichon (Australia), ran the Blackmores Sydney Marathon (Australia) in 3 hr. 28 min. 26 sec. on September 19, 2010.

GUINNESS WORLD RECORDS 2014

2,981 Total weight in pounds Nina has lifted, pulled, walked, and tossed to earn her five Guinness World Records!

Most telephone directories torn in three minutes

Strongwoman Tina Shelton (USA) tore 21 telephone directories —each with 1,028 pages—from top to bottom at the Ranchland Church in Escondido, California, USA, on February 9, 2007. Tina smashed her previous record of 14, set in Phelan, California, back in September 2006.

Fastest time to break 16 concrete blocks on the body

Taking a real bashing at Cossington sports hall in Leicester, Leicestershire, UK, on November 15, 2012, Asha Rani (India) had 16 concrete blocks placed on top of her, one by one, and broken with a sledgehammer

in 53.828 seconds—all in the name of Guinness World Records Day.

Rani also holds the record for the **heaviest vehicle pulled by the hair**. She tied her hair to a 26,678-lb. 13-oz. (12,101-kg) double-decker bus—more than 210 times her own bodyweight!— and pulled it for a distance of 56 ft. 5 in. (17.2 m) at Humberstone Gate in Leicester, Leicestershire, UK, on August 18, 2012.

Fastest 20-m duck walk carrying 120 kg

Woman of steel Nina Geria (Ukraine) heaved a massive 264-lb. 8.8-oz. (120-kg) weight 65 ft. 7 in. (20 m) in 12.33 seconds on March 28, 2012. Geria also set new records for the **farthest distance to wheelbarrow a car** at 295 ft. 3.3 in. (90 m), on March 31, 2012, and the **longest duration holding Hercules Pillars** (two 485-lb.; 220-kg pillars, plus two 66-lb.; 30-kg chains) at 47.72 seconds, on April 12, 2012. All three records were set in Rome, Italy.

Highest freefall parachute jump

Elvira Fomitcheva (USSR) covered 48,556 ft. (14,800 m) in freefall during a parachute jump over Odessa, Russia (now Ukraine), on October 26, 1977.

Longest time to hold the breath voluntarily

After training for four months and inhaling oxygen for 24 minutes before her attempt, Karoline Mariechen Meyer of Brazil held her breath for an incredible 18 min. 32.59 sec. in the Racer Academy swimming pool in Florianópolis, Brazil, on July 10, 2009.

Longest time on a bed of nails

Miranda, Queen of the Fakirs, aka Geraldine Williams (UK, now Gray), is just one of two women to currently hold a Guinness World Record on a bed of nails (the other is fellow Brit Daniella D'Ville, *see p. 86*). Miranda lay on a bed of sharp nails 6 in. (15.2 cm) tall and spaced 2 in. (5 cm) apart for a record 30 hours in Welwyn Garden City, Hertfordshire, UK, from May 18 to 19, 1977.

Most martial arts kicks in one minute (one leg)

On May 5, 2011, during a simultaneous attempt against another female competitor, Yuka Kobayashi (Japan) high-kicked her way to success 273 times on the set of the television spectacular *100 Beautiful Women Who Have Guinness World Records* at the Shiodome Nihon TV studios in Tokyo, Japan.

Fastest fruit (half marathon): Joanne Singleton (UK) sprinted the Schaumburg Half Marathon Turkey Trot in Schaumburg, Illinois, USA, dressed as a strawberry, in 1 hr. 35 min. 45 sec. on November 26, 2011.

Fastest fairy: Emily Foran (UK) finished in 3 hr. 20 min. 52 sec. at the Virgin London Marathon (UK) on April 17, 2011.

Fastest bottle: Running the MBNA Chester Marathon in Cheshire, UK, on October 9, 2011, Sarah Hayes (UK) achieved a time of 4 hr. 36 min. 19 sec.

Fastest movie character: On April 25, 2010, Alisa Vanlint (UK) ran the Virgin London Marathon (UK) in 3 hr. 53 min. 40 sec. dressed as the bikini-clad Princess Leia from *Star Wars Episode VI: Return of the Jedi*.

Fastest half marathon pushing a stroller: A time of 1 hr. 30 min. 51 sec. was achieved by Nancy Schubring (USA) at the Mike May Races Half Marathon in Vassar, Michigan, USA, on September 15, 2001.

GROUP EFFORTS

10 Usual maximum group size for performing this dance.

GWR DAY NOVEMBER 2012

Largest Kaikottikali dance

Kaikottikali, or Thiruvathirakali, is a folk dance accompanied by singing and clapping, and is traditionally performed by the women of Kerala in India. It was staged by 2,639 participants organized by the Mumbai Pooram Foundation (India) on GWR Day (November 9, 2012) in Dombivli, north of Mumbai, India.

Most people crammed into a photo booth

Seven supple contortionists filled out a photo booth at King's Cross station in London, UK, on July 4, 2012, in an event organized by Photo-Me International (UK). The photo booth was 6 ft. 3 in. (1.92 m) high, 2 ft. 5 in. (0.75 m) deep, and had a width of just 4 ft. 11 in. (1.5 m)—including the space reserved for photo machinery!

LARGEST ...

Tug-of-war tournament
The event motto "winners get bragging rights while losers take a mud bath" aptly describes the annual tug at Rochester Institute of Technology, where 1,574 students took part in the most recent tug organized by Phi Kappa Psi and Zeta Tau Alpha in Rochester, New York, USA, on September 22, 2012.

Human flower
A giant poppy was created by 2,190 people in an event arranged by University Church of England Academy (UK) in Ellesmere Port, Cheshire, UK, on November 9, 2012.

Gathering of "test-tube" children
On October 16, 2011, the Infertility Fund R.O.C. in Taichung, Chinese Taipei, organized a mass gathering of 1,232 children born as a result of artificial insemination.

Trading card tournament
The 100th *Yu-Gi-Oh!* Championship Series involved 4,364 participants at the Long Beach Convention Center in California, USA, from March 23 to 25, 2012.

Largest gathering of people dressed as nuns

How many participants does it take to break a record? Nun—when there are 1,436 of them! Men and women alike had to wear strictly judged habits to mark Nunday in the Irish town of Listowel, County Kerry, on June 30, 2012. The attempt was a fund-raiser for nonprofit organization Pieta House (Ireland).

COSTUMED COLLECTIVES

Pirates: Roger Crouch and the town of Hastings (UK) gathered 14,231 pirates at Pelham Beach, Hastings, East Sussex, UK, on July 22, 2012.

Zombies: 8,027 members of the undead took part in the Zombie Pub Crawl in Minneapolis, Minnesota, USA, on October 13, 2012.

Turkeys: 661 turkeys gathered at the 44th Annual Capital One Bank Dallas YMCA Turkey Trot in Dallas, Texas, USA, on November 24, 2011.

Witches: Pendle Council, Pendleside Hospice, and Pendle Witch Walk (all UK) organized 482 witches at the Barley Village Green in Barley, Lancashire, UK, on August 18, 2012.

Nurses: BBC WM and the Cure Leukaemia charity (both UK) organized for 201 people dressed as nurses to amass in Victoria Square, Birmingham, UK, on February 21, 2012.

MOST PEOPLE...

CATEGORY	PEOPLE	ORGANIZER	LOCATION	EVENT DATE
Wearing red noses	16,092	Credit Union Christmas Pageant	Adelaide, Australia	Nov 12, 2011
Performing a song and dance (multiple venues)	15,122	Salt and Pepper Entertainment (India)	Karnataka, India	Aug 28, 2012
Wearing wigs	12,083	Blatchy's Blues (Australia)	ANZ Stadium, Sydney, New South Wales, Australia	Jun 13, 2012
Running a relay race	8,509	40th Batavierenrace	Nijmegen to Enschede, Netherlands	Apr 28, 2012
Sanitizing their hands	7,675	Saint Gurmeet Ram Rahim Singh Ji Insan and Shah Satnam Ji Green "S" Welfare Force Wing (both India)	SMG Sports Complex, Dera Sacha Sauda Sirsa, Haryana, India	Sep 23, 2012
Playing the mouth harp	1,344	Nikolay Kychkin (Russia)	Yakutsk National Circus, Yakutsk, Republic of Sakha, Russia	Jun 24, 2011
Sitting on one chair (human chair)	1,311	Onojo City (Japan)	Madoka Park in Onojo, Fukuoka, Japan	Oct 28, 2012
Becoming human mattress dominoes	1,150	Höffner Möbelgesellschaft GmbH & Co. KG (Germany)	Gründau-Lieblos, Germany	Aug 12, 2012
Hugging trees	702	Forestry Commission (UK)	Delamere Forest, Cheshire, UK	Sep 11, 2011
Stargazing	683	Mexico	Universidad Nacional Autónoma de México (UNAM), Mexico City, Mexico	Dec 3, 2011
Wearing false moustaches	648	St. Louis Rams (USA)	Edward Jones Dome in St. Louis, Missouri, USA	Sep 16, 2012
Being massaged	641	Department of Health Service Support Ministry of Public Health	Nonthaburi, Thailand	Aug 30, 2012
Performing a hula hoop workout	290	Michelle Clinage (USA)	Allen Elementary School in Hutchinson, Kansas, USA	May 21, 2012
Maypole dancing	173	Victory House (UK)	Hurst Community College, Hampshire, UK	Jul 18, 2012

Largest gathering of storybook characters

Once upon a time— February 17, 2012, to be precise—a record 921 pupils and teachers from the San Agustín School in Valladolid, Spain, dressed up as storybook characters. Staged as part of the school's 50th anniversary celebrations, the event involved characters from 57 different fables and stories.

Most trees planted simultaneously

The charity Love to Live International (India) orchestrated an event in which thousands of volunteers planted an astonishing 99,103 trees in some of the harshest terrain in Ladakh, India, on October 29, 2012.

Most people popping bubble wrap

On January 28, 2013, the Sealed Air Corporation and Hawthorne High School (both USA) assembled 366 people to pop bubble wrap simultaneously in Hawthorne, New Jersey, USA. Hawthorne is known as the birthplace of bubble wrap. The attempt was part of Bubble Wrap Appreciation Day, an event inaugurated by Spirit 95 FM radio station in 2001.

Most people crammed into a new model Mini

Led by Dani Maynard, a team of 28 women calling themselves the David Lloyd Divas (all UK) squeezed into a 2011 Mini Cooper SD on November 15, 2012, in London, UK. Later that day, Dani and her Divas set another record: the **most people crammed into a Mini**—the classic (and smaller) Mini from the 1960s—with 23.

SEE THE VIDEO WITH THE FREE APP

GWR DAY NOVEMBER 2012

AUGMENTED REALITY ALERT! ON THIS PAGE

Ninja Turtles: Nickelodeon Universe (USA) organized a group of 836 Ninja Turtles at the Mall of America in Bloomington, Minnesota, USA, on March 17, 2012.

Cowboy hats: 39,013 folks donned their hats in a gathering organized by Angels Baseball (USA) at Angel Stadium in Anaheim, California, USA, on June 2, 2012.

Star Trek characters: 1,040 sci-fi fans gathered at the Official Star Trek Convention at the Las Vegas Rio Suites Hotel in Las Vegas, USA, on August 13, 2011.

Chefs: 2,847 people dressed up as chefs on January 4, 2013, in an event arranged by the Department of Tourism and Commerce Marketing (United Arab Emirates) in Dubai, UAE.

Nursery rhyme characters: 396 children from Brookmans Park Primary School (UK) dressed as nursery rhyme characters at Village Day 2011 in Brookmans Park, Hertfordshire, UK, on June 18, 2011.

SKATEBOARDING

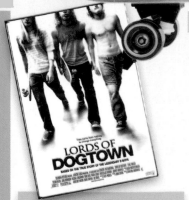

Most successful skateboarding movie

Lords of Dogtown (USA, 2005), directed by Catherine Hardwicke, grossed $13,411,957 at the box office worldwide. Based on the real-life story of the "Z-boys"—a group of Californian skaters who revolutionized the sport in the mid 1970s—it stars Emile Hirsch and the late Heath Ledger.

BOARDS

First skateboards

It is not possible to state exactly who invented the skateboard or when—patents for recreational wheeled boards on which riders propelled themselves forward were first logged in the early 20th century, while by the mid 1950s many skateboarders were making their own boards.

Frank Nasworthy (USA) developed the **first polyurethane wheels** in Encinitas, California,

Oldest surviving skatepark

Construction of Kona Skatepark in Jacksonville, Florida, USA, began in February 1977 and it opened to the public on June 4, 1977. After a brief closure in the late 1970s, the skatepark reopened and remains in full operation today under the long-time ownership of the Ramos family.

USA, in 1970–73—an advance on the hard metal or composite "clay" wheels used previously. Nasworthy formed Cadillac Wheels in 1973 to market his invention, leading to a worldwide resurgence for skateboarding.

Largest skateboard

Designed and produced by Rob Dyrdek and Joe Ciaglia (both USA) in Los Angeles, California, USA, the largest skateboard measured 36 ft. 7 in. (11.14 m) in length, 8 ft. 8 in. (2.63 m) in width, and 3 ft. 7.5 in. (1.10 m) in height. It was unveiled on February 25, 2009, on the MTV series *Rob Dyrdek's Fantasy Factory*. An accomplished boarder, Dyrdek holds 17 Guinness World Records.

Most people riding the same skateboard

In the music video for "Troublemaker" by Weezer, shot in Los Angeles, California, USA, on August 21, 2008, a record 22 people rode the same oversized board.

LONGEST ...

Journey by skateboard

Rob Thomson (New Zealand) covered 7,555 miles (12,159 km) from Leysin, Switzerland, to Shanghai, China, between June 24, 2007 and September 28, 2008.

First skateboarding magazine

In 1964, during the early days of skating, Surfer Publications (USA) released *The Quarterly Skateboarder*, which ran for just four issues. It was resurrected in the 1970s as *Skateboarder*.

Manual (wheelie)

Jeffrey Nolan (Canada) pulled a 712-ft. 3-in. (217.1-m) wheelie on North Augusta Road in Brockville, Ontario, Canada, on June 13, 2012.

Stationary manual

Hlynur Gunnarsson (Iceland) achieved a stationary skateboard manual lasting 7 min. 59.13 sec. at a shopping mall in Reykjavik, Iceland, on October 2, 2011.

Largest skatepark

With 147,466 sq. ft. (13,700 m²) of ridable terrain—bigger than two soccer fields or 52 tennis courts—the SMP Skatepark in Shanghai, China, opened on October 6, 2005 at a cost of $26 million, making it also the world's **most expensive skatepark**.

The park is home to the **largest concrete bowl**, known as the "Mondo Bowl" (*pictured*), which covers an area of 15,231 sq. ft. (1,415 m²), or five times bigger than a tennis court; it also boasts the world's **longest vert ramp**—at 171 ft. (52 m) in length, it's longer than an Olympic-size swimming pool!

FOR THE RECORD

The **first concrete skatepark** was ScatBoard City, later named Skateboard City, which opened in Port Orange, Florida, USA, in February 1976. It contained gentle concrete runs and banks, with none of the bowls, pools, and pipes of later skateparks.

AT THE X GAMES

Most X Games medals: Bagging his first in 1999, Andy Macdonald (USA) has won a total of 19 X Games skateboarding medals.

Youngest X Games athlete: Jagger Eaton (USA, b. February 21, 2001) made his debut at X Games 18 (June 28–July 1, 2012) at the age of 11 years 129 days.

Most men's X Games skateboard vert wins: Between 2002 and 2010, Pierre-Luc Gagnon (Canada) won five vert competitions at the X Games.

Longest ramp jump: Danny Way (USA) made a 79-ft. (24-m) 360 air from a mega ramp at X Games 10 on August 8, 2004.

Most ollie 180s in one minute: Gray Mesa (USA) racked up 17 ollie 180s in a minute at X Games 16 on July 30, 2010.

$280,000
Cost of constructing the "mega ramp."

Largest ramp

In 2006, pro skater Bob Burnquist (USA) had a 360-ft.-long (110-m) mega ramp constructed at his home near San Diego, California, USA. Measuring 75 ft. (23 m) in height with a 180-ft.-long (55-m) launch section and a 30-ft. (9-m) quarter pipe, it enables skaters to reach speeds of 55 mph (88 km/h) and shoot a farther 20 ft. (6 m) or more above the quarter pipe!

One-wheel manual

The longest one-wheel skateboard wheelie on a flat surface is 224 ft. 10 in. (68.54 m) by Stefan Åkesson (Sweden) at the Gallerian shopping center in Stockholm, Sweden, on November 2, 2007.

First …

Ollie: The skateboard "ollie" trick, by which the skateboarder makes the board jump into the air without using their hands, was invented and first performed in 1977 by Alan Gelfand (USA) in Florida, USA. Pictured is Gelfand catching some air in Gainesville, Florida, in July 1979.

Ollie impossible: This extremely difficult trick—in which a flat-ground ollie is combined with the 360-degree vertical rotation of the board around the skater's front or rear foot—was first performed by Rodney Mullen (USA) in 1982. Mullen is considered to be one of the most influential of all street skateboarders.

900: Tony Hawk (USA) became the first person to achieve two-and-a-half airborne rotations, at the X Games on June 27, 1999. He was successful on his 11th attempt in the Best Trick competition.

1080: A month before becoming the **youngest X Games gold medalist (male)** at the age of 12 years 229 days old, Tom Schaar (USA, *right*) pulled off the first three full skateboard rotations while airborne. He achieved this epic feat on a mega ramp in Tehachapi, California, USA, on March 26, 2012.

Handstand

Covering a distance of 2,255 ft. (687.33 m), the longest skateboard handstand was performed by Sam Tartamella (USA) along Nakoma Road in Madison, Wisconsin, USA, on July 21, 1996.

FASTEST …

Speed (standing)

Mischo Erban (Canada) reached an astronomical speed of 80.74 mph (129.94 km/h) at Les Éboulements, Quebec, Canada, on June 18, 2012.

Speed (towed)

The fastest speed for a towed skateboard is 93.2 mph (150 km/h) and was achieved by Steffen Eliassen (Norway) at Rudskogen racetrack in Rakkestad, Norway, on August 24, 2012. Eliassen was towed to the record speed by a Tesla Roadster Sport driven by Øystein Westlie.

50 MILLION
Estimated number of skateboarders worldwide.

Largest full pipe in a skatepark

The Louisville Extreme Park in Kentucky, USA, is home to the biggest full pipe, measuring 24 ft. (7.3 m) in diameter. Constructed of concrete, the park contains 40,000 sq. ft. (3,715 m²) of outdoor skating surface and opened on April 5, 2002.

50-cone slalom

The fastest time to slalom 50 cones with a skateboard is 10.02 seconds and was achieved by Jānis Kuzmins (Latvia) at the Nike Riga Run in Mežaparks, Riga, Latvia, on August 28, 2011.

Kuzmins also holds the record for the **fastest 100-cone slalom**, achieving a time of 20.77 seconds at the same park on September 12, 2010. As before, each cone had to conform to the International Slalom Skateboarding Association regulations, which insist on cones with a minimum base diameter of 5.5 in. (14 cm), and a gap of 5 ft. 3 in. (1.6 m) between each one.

Most ollies in one minute: Jacob Halpin (USA) performed 51 ollies at X Games 18 on June 30, 2012.

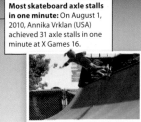

Most skateboard axle stalls in one minute: On August 1, 2010, Annika Vrklan (USA) achieved 31 axle stalls in one minute at X Games 16.

Most women's X Games skateboard vert wins: Rocking a total of three wins at the X Games between 2004 and 2009 was Lyn-Z Adams Hawkins (USA).

Oldest skateboard competitor: Steve Alba (USA) competed in the Park Legends event of the 2010 X Games, at the age of 47 years 176 days.

Fastest 100 m on a skateboard by a dog: Tillman the English Bulldog covered 100 m (328 ft) in 19.678 seconds while visiting X Games 15 on July 30, 2009.

TRIVIAL PURSUITS

Most cones hit with flying disks in one minute

Frisbee phenomenon Brodie Smith (USA) hit eight cones with flying disks in a minute for *Lo Show dei Record* in Rome, Italy, on March 31, 2012. The cones were positioned 32 ft. 9 in. (10 m) from Brodie and 3 ft. 3 in. (1 m) above the ground.

¡QUOTE

"My fans give me the motivation to try harder, try bigger—do crazy things!"

MOST …

Balloons inflated by the nose in one hour

On August 7, 2012, Ashrita Furman (USA) inflated 328 balloons using only his nose in one hour in New York City, USA.

Dominoes toppled in a 3D pyramid

On July 6, 2012, Sinners Domino Production (Germany) toppled 13,486 dominoes in a 3D pyramid at the Wolfgang-Ernst-Gymnasium in Büdingen, Germany.

Beverage can tops torn off with the teeth in one minute

Ryan Stock (Canada) tore off 11 tops from beverage cans in one minute on the set of *Guinness World Records Gone Wild!* in Los Angeles, California, USA, on July 2, 2012.

Highest throw of a playing card

Jordan Barker (UK) hurled a playing card 42 ft. 11.8 in. (13.1 m) into the air on the set of *Officially Amazing* (CBBC/Lion TV) in Tunbridge Wells, UK, on November 5, 2012.

Farthest flip-flop flick using the foot

Phillip Conroy (UK) flicked a flip-flop 111 ft. (33.9 m) from his foot at Hotel Orquidea in Gran Canaria, Spain, on June 10, 2012.

Most spoons balanced on the body

Eitibar Elchiev (Georgia) kept 52 spoons on his body while standing upright on the set of a CCTV *Guinness World Records Special* in Beijing, China, on December 7, 2012. He attributes his success to his unique "sticky" perspiration. Nice!

HONEST EITIBAR

Eitibar has told us that his previous record was miscounted as 55 spoons; it should have been 51. Thanks, Eitibar!

507 MILLION

(Roughly!) Sticky notes it would take to circle Earth.

Most sticky notes on the body

Sarah Greasley (UK) kept 454 sticky notes on her body simultaneously at Magdalene College in Cambridge, UK, on June 17, 2011. A number of sticky notes blew away, owing to the windy weather conditions.

IN A MINUTE …

Most shoes sorted into pairs: 11, by Ercan Metin (Turkey) on February 12, 2010. Equaled by Özgür Taşan (Turkey) on March 26, 2010.

Most clothespins clipped to the face: 51, by Silvio Sabba (Italy) on December 27, 2012.

Most eggs crushed with the head: 142, by Scott Damerow (USA) on July 7, 2012.

Most nails hammered by hand: 31, by Boguslaw Bialek (Spain) on October 8, 2012.

Most T-shirts folded: 23, by Graeme J. Cruden (UK) on March 3, 2009.

EXTRAORDINARY
www.guinness...

GUINNESS
WORLD
RECORDS
2014

38 Thousandths of a second it takes for the classic "Little Nipper" mousetrap to snap!

Most mousetraps released on the tongue in one minute

Canadian hardman Sweet Pepper Klopek released 47 mousetraps on his tongue in 60 seconds in Los Angeles, California, USA, on July 7, 2012. The female record is held by the Painproof Princess, aka Zoe Ellis (Australia, *below*), with 24 traps in London, UK, on September 28, 2012. Ouwth!

Hugs by an individual in one hour
Multiple record holder Jayasimha Ravirala (India) gave out 2,436 hugs in an hour in Tekkali, India, on September 29, 2012.

Golf balls held in one hand
On October 16, 2012, Silvo Sabba (Italy) visited the Guinness World Records Challengers Web site and set a record by holding 27 golf balls in one hand.

FASTEST TIME TO …

Arrange a chess set
Mehak Gul (Pakistan) sorted a chess set into the opening setup for a game in 45.48 seconds during the Punjab Youth Festival at Expo Center Lahore in Pakistan on October 21, 2012.

Build a five-level domino pyramid
The fastest time to construct a five-level domino pyramid is 18.4 seconds, achieved by Silvio Sabba (Italy) in Pioltello, Italy, on December 11, 2012.

Build a three-level house of cards
The speediest time to construct a three-level house of cards is 6.8 seconds, achieved by serial record-breaker Silvio Sabba (Italy) in Pioltello, Italy, on June 26, 2012.

Duct tape a person to a wall
Ashrita Furman duct taped Alec Wilkinson (both USA) to a wall in 32.85 seconds in New York City, USA, on October 2, 2012. Alec stayed taped to the wall for one minute, in accordance with the record guidelines.

Wire a plug
Mian Nouman Anjum (Pakistan) wired an AC power electrical plug in just 35.93 seconds in Lahore, Pakistan, on October 21, 2012.

Party poppers popped in 30 seconds
On October 19, 2012, Alfie Deyes (UK)—one of the stars of the Guinness World Records YouTube channel GWR OMG!—popped a record 29 party poppers in 30 seconds in London, UK. *For the one-minute record, turn to p. 94.*

GWR DAY NOVEMBER 2012

Longest time spinning a basketball on a toothbrush

Michael Kopp (Germany) kept a basketball spinning on the end of a toothbrush for 26.078 seconds at Fliegende Bauten in Hamburg, Germany, on November 14, 2012, to celebrate Guinness World Records Day.

Most toothpicks in a beard

The greatest number of toothpicks placed in a beard is 3,107 by Ed Cahill (Ireland) on Today FM's *Ray D'Arcy Show* in Ireland on September 28, 2012. It took just under three hours for Ed to complete the task, during which he was allowed no assistance.

5.5 inches per year—rate at which a man's whiskers grow.

Longest time in full body contact with snow

Jin Songhao (China) spent a chilling 46 min. 7 sec. in direct, full contact with snow in A'ershan City, Inner Mongolia Autonomous Region, China, on January 17, 2011.

FOR EXTREME WEATHER RECORDS, TURN TO P. 22

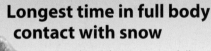

Most coins stacked into a tower: 40, by Abdullah Alasaad (Jordan) on March 3, 2012.

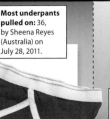

Most underpants pulled on: 36, by Sheena Reyes (Australia) on July 28, 2011.

Tallest coffee cup tower built: 6 ft. 10 in. (209.9 cm), by Silvio Sabba (Italy) on May 29, 2012.

Most socks sorted with one foot: 11 pairs, by Yui Okada (Japan) on June 3, 2012.

Most rubber bands stretched over the face: 82, by Shripad Krishnarao Vaidya (India) on July 19, 2012.

111

BALANCING ACTS

HEAVIEST …

364
Guinness World Records held by Ashrita over the past 25 years.

Car balanced on the head
John Evans (UK) kept a gutted 352-lb. (159.6-kg) Mini car on his head for 33 seconds in London, UK, on May 24, 1999.

Weight balanced on the feet
Guo Shuyan (China) balanced both a large, cast iron urn filled with sand bags and one person—a total of 784 lb. (356 kg)—on his feet on the set of a CCTV *Guinness World Records Special* in Beijing, China, on December 5, 2012.

Weight balanced on the teeth
Frank Simon (USA) balanced a 140-lb. (63.5-kg) refrigerator on his teeth for 10 seconds in Rome, Italy, on May 17, 2007. He also achieved the **longest duration balancing a tire on the teeth**: 31 seconds, achieved in Beijing, China, on June 21, 2009. It was a condition of the record that the tire should weigh at least 110 lb. (50 kg).

LONGEST TIME TO …

Balance on a bicycle at altitude
Xavier Casas Blanch (Andorra) spent 4 hr. 2 min. balanced on his bicycle on the dome of the Hesperia Tower Hotel, 351 ft. (107 m) above street level, in Barcelona, Spain, on September 29, 2011.

Sustain a side wheelie in a manual wheelchair
Extreme wheelchair athlete Aaron "Wheelz" Fotheringham (USA) held a wheelchair on its side wheels for 18.22 seconds in Rome, Italy, on April 12, 2012.

Most pirouettes on pointe on the head
Husband and wife Wu Zhengdan and Wei Baohua (both China)—from the Guangdong Acrobatic Troupe—performed four consecutive pirouettes with Wei atop Wu's head in Rome, Italy, on March 28, 2012. Wu wears a cap with a small groove in it, in which his wife positions her pointe shoe.

MOST …

Bicycles balanced on the chin
On December 8, 2011, in Beijing, China, Sun Chaoyang (China) kept a stack of three adult mountain bicycles on his chin for 30 seconds.

Coins balanced on the face (one minute)
On October 9, 2012, dedicated record breaker Silvio Sabba (Italy) kept 48 coins in place on his face for one minute in Pioltello, Italy.

Eggs balanced by a group
According to the folk culture of Chinese Taipei, anyone who can balance an egg upright on a table or on the ground on the day of the Dragon Boat festival will experience a year of good luck. At an event held on the festival day (June 23, 2012) in Hsinchu, Chinese Taipei, a group of 4,247 people achieved this auspicious feat.

Longest time to balance a chainsaw on the chin
The longest duration spent balancing a chainsaw on the chin is 1 min. 25.01 sec., achieved by serial record breaker Ashrita Furman (USA) at the Sri Chinmoy Center in New York City, USA, on November 12, 2012.

FOR THE RECORD
Outstanding record breaker Ashrita Furman (USA) is the boss of balancing. He currently holds an incredible 24 balance-related records involving everything from pool cues and baseball bats to books, eggs, cigar boxes, and chainsaws. *See more below.*

Farthest distance with a soccer ball balanced on the head
Abdul Halim (Bangladesh) walked for 9.44 miles (15.2 km) with a soccer ball on top of his head at Bangabandhu National Stadium in Dhaka, Bangladesh, on October 22, 2011.

SPLIT TIME
Jacopo was only 18 years old when he set the record. He remained incredibly calm as he maintained the agonizing posture.

Longest time in box splits between two objects
Jacopo Forza (Italy) spent 3 min. 48 sec. in box splits (aka side splits) between two cars for *Lo Show dei Record* in Rome, Italy, on March 28, 2012. The box split is a position in which the legs are extended to the left and right of the torso with the hips square on to create a 180-degree angle.

FACT:
The word "balance" is thought to derive from the Latin *bis* ("twice") and *lanx* ("dish"), referring to the two pans on a set of traditional weighing scales.

ASHRITA BALANCES …

Baseball bat:
9 miles (14.48 km) walked balancing a bat on his finger in Bali, Indonesia, on February 7, 2011.

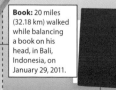

Book: 20 miles (32.18 km) walked while balancing a book on his head, in Bali, Indonesia, on January 29, 2011.

Ladder:
2 min. 50 sec. spent balancing a ladder on his chin, in New York City, USA, on October 2, 2012.

Cigar boxes:
223 boxes balanced on his chin in New York City, USA, on November 12, 2006.

Eggs: 1 min. 15.72 sec. balancing a dozen eggs upright on a kitchen floor in New York City, USA, on April 3, 2012.

Most flips on a beam in one minute

Two talented gymnasts have somersaulted into the record books with an astounding 20 backward flips on a beam in one minute. On March 28, 2012, Giulia Bencini (Italy), seen here at the age of 11, achieved the feat in Rome, Italy. She equaled the record set by Emilie Schutt (France) on the set of *L'Été De Tous Les Records* in Soulac-sur-Mer, France, on August 16, 2005.

FLIPPING FIRST
In 1964, German gymnast Erika Zuchold became the **first woman to perform a back flip on a beam.**

Stairs climbed while balancing a person on the head

Qiaoling Yang climbed 25 stairs while balancing Qiao Deng (both China) on her head on the set of *Zheng Da Zong Yi—Guinness World Records Special* in Beijing, China, on December 18, 2010.

Wine glasses balanced on the chin

Sun Chao Yang (China) balanced a stack of 133 wine glasses on his chin on the set of a CCTV *Guinness World Records Special* in Beijing, China, on December 4, 2012.

Sun's incredible balancing act outclasses—and out-glasses—the record for **most wine glasses held in one hand**, which currently stands at 39 by Reymond Adina (Philippines), who achieved this at the Quatre-Gats restaurant in Barcelona, Spain, on October 24, 2007.

Hula hoop leg rotations in the arabesque position (one minute)

The arabesque involves standing on one leg and stretching the other out at 90 degrees. Rashmi Niranjan Joshi (India) held that pose while turning the hoop on her outstretched leg a total of 104 times on the set of *Guinness World Records—Ab India Todega* in Mumbai, India, on March 15, 2011.

Hats balanced on the head (one minute)

On September 16, 2012, Melanie Devoy (UK) kept 53 hats balanced on her head for one minute at the Hotel Orquidea in Gran Canaria, Spain.

Open umbrellas balanced on the body simultaneously

Liu Lina (China) balanced nine open umbrellas on herself on the set of *Lo Show dei Record* in Milan, Italy, on April 28, 2011. Lying down, she had four on one foot, three on the other, and one on each hand.

31
Record for **most push-ups performed on top of four Swiss balls in one minute**, by Neil in August 2011.

31.5
Distance in feet Chelsea covered by bottle top.

Fastest time to jump across 10 Swiss balls

Neil Whyte (Australia) bounced across 10 Swiss exercise balls, without falling, in 8.31 seconds in Rome, Italy, on April 13, 2012. Neil also set the **farthest jump between two Swiss balls**, clearing 7 ft. 6 in. (2.3 m) in 2006.

Most upright glass bottles walked across

Chelsea McGuffin (Australia) walked across the tops of 51 open and empty champagne bottles on September 20, 2012 in the Spiegeltent ("mirror tent") at London Wonderground in London, UK. The bottles had no support and were freestanding, and Chelsea wore ballet shoes for the attempt.

Lawnmower: Balancing a lawnmower on his chin for 4 min. 12 sec. in New York City, USA, on October 20, 2012.

Milk bottle: Hula hooping for 1 mile (1.6 km) with a milk bottle balanced on his head in 13 min. 37.35 sec. in New York City, USA, on March 11, 2012.

Milk crate stack: 17 crates, weighing 93 lb. 7 oz. (42.4 kg), balanced on his chin for 11.23 seconds in New York City, USA, on June 16, 2006.

Pool cue: 4 hr. 7 min. balancing a pool cue on one finger in New York City, USA, on November 18, 2009.

Beer glasses: 81 beer glasses balanced on his chin for 12.10 seconds in his backyard in New York City, USA, on August 12, 2007.

PERFORMING ARTS

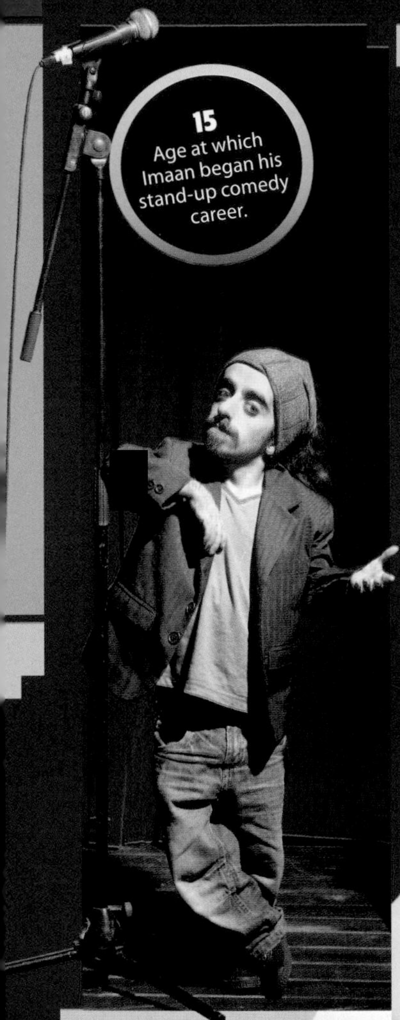

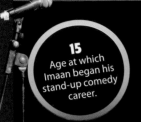

15
Age at which Imaan began his stand-up comedy career.

STAND-UP COMEDY

Most tickets sold

The **highest-grossing stand-up tour per show** was Michael McIntyre's (UK) "Showtime," which in 2012 earned £20.96 million ($32.54 million) from 73 shows, averaging $463,798 per gig.

Longest gig

Highest gig

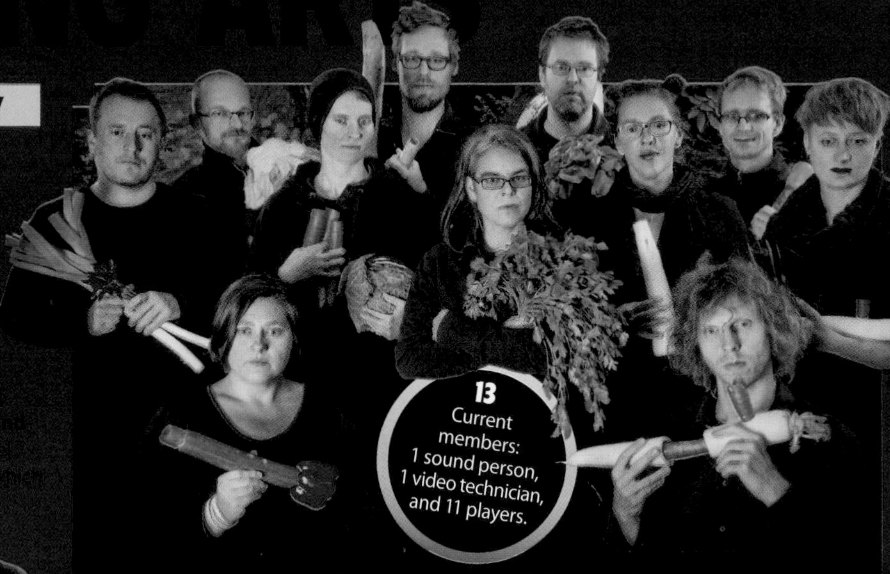

13
Current members:
1 sound person,
1 video technician,
and 11 players.

Most concerts by a vegetable orchestra

The Vegetable Orchestra (Austria) perform using instruments constructed solely from fresh vegetables. Between April 1998 and September 2012, they gave a total of 77 concerts in venues worldwide. The ensemble use a wide range of vegetables to produce their unique sounds, including flutes made from carrots and percussion made from pumpkins.

Longest-running comedy show (same cast)

THEATER

Highest single-week box office gross on Broadway

Longest time in the same West End show

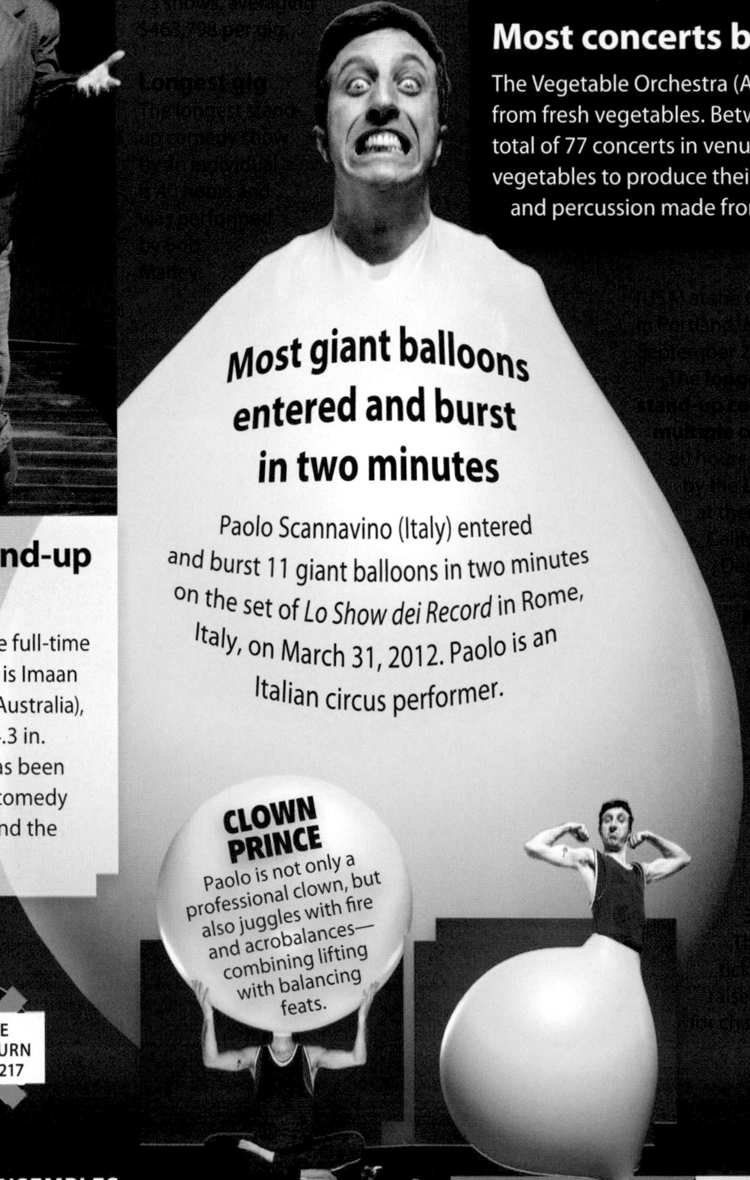

Most giant balloons entered and burst in two minutes

Paolo Scannavino (Italy) entered and burst 11 giant balloons in two minutes on the set of *Lo Show dei Record* in Rome, Italy, on March 31, 2012. Paolo is an Italian circus performer.

CLOWN PRINCE
Paolo is not only a professional clown, but also juggles with fire and acrobalances—combining lifting with balancing feats.

Shortest stand-up comedian

The most diminutive full-time stand-up comedian is Imaan Hadchiti (Lebanon/Australia), who stands at 3 ft. 4.3 in. (102.5 cm). Imaan has been performing on the comedy circuit in Australia and the UK since 2005.

FOR MORE SHOWBIZ, TURN TO PP. 196–217

ASTONISHING ENSEMBLES

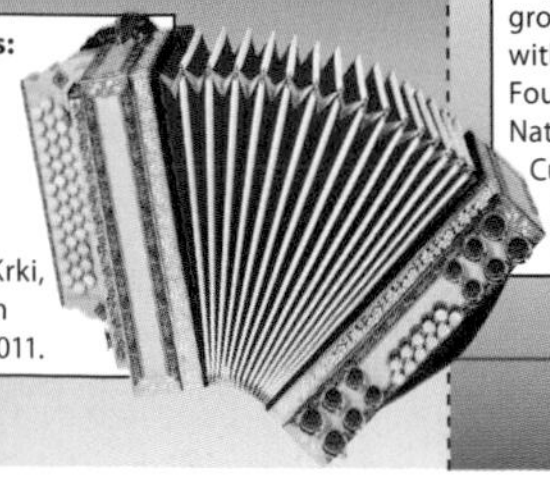

Accordions: 1,137, at the 2011 Panonika Harmonika festival in Cerklje ob Krki, Slovenia, on August 8, 2011.

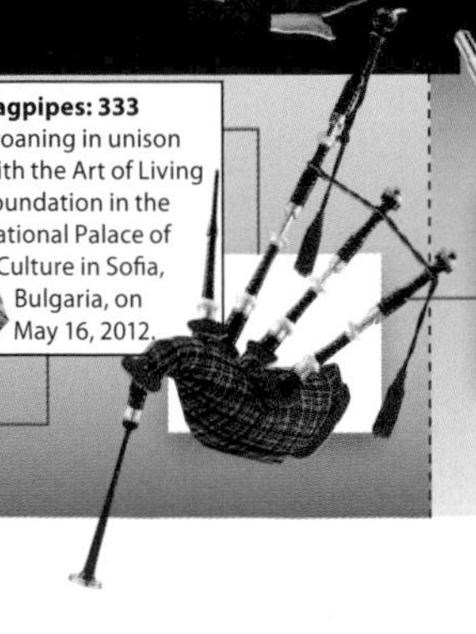

Bagpipes: 333 groaning in unison with the Art of Living Foundation in the National Palace of Culture in Sofia, Bulgaria, on May 16, 2012.

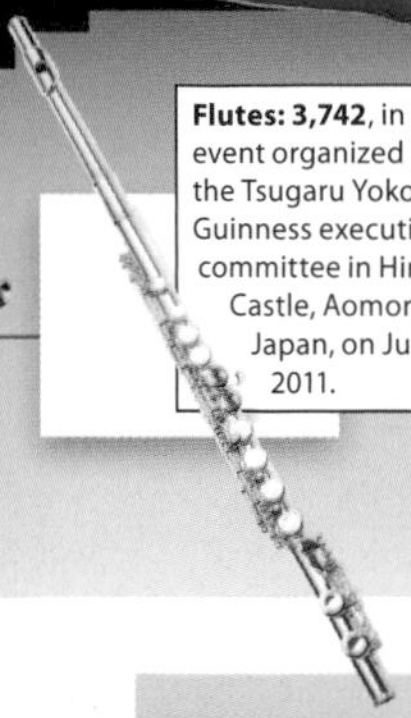

Flutes: 3,742, in an event organized by the Tsugaru Yokobue Guinness executive committee in Hirosaki Castle, Aomori, Japan, on July 31, 2011.

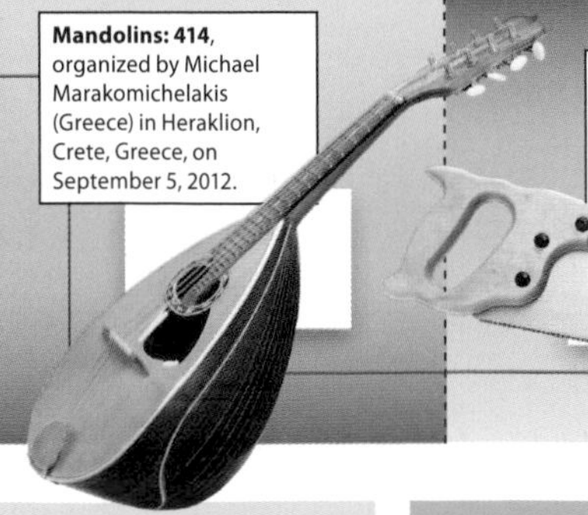

Mandolins: 414, organized by Michael Marakomichelakis (Greece) in Heraklion, Crete, Greece, on September 5, 2012.

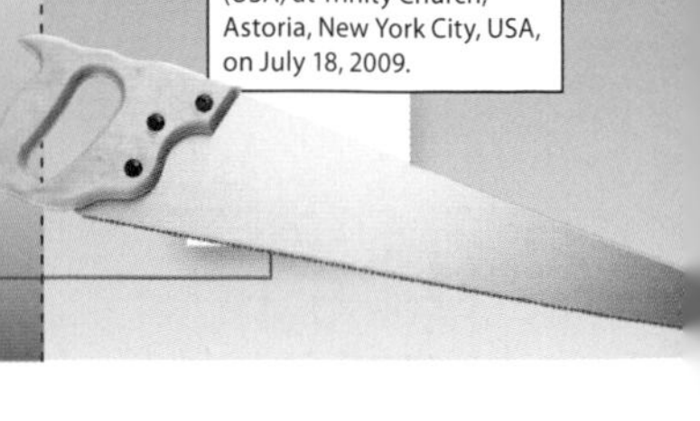

Musical saws: 53, arranged by Natalia "Saw Lady" Paruz (USA) at Trinity Church, Astoria, New York City, USA, on July 18, 2009.

$
Age at which Ethan first began to compose his own music.

Most Laurence Olivier Awards

Matilda the Musical won seven Oliviers in 2012: Best New Musical, collected by writer Dennis Kelly (UK) and composer/lyricist Tim Minchin (Australia); Best Actress in a Musical, shared by the four girls who play Matilda: Cleo Demetriou (Cyprus), Eleanor Worthington-Cox, Kerry Ingram, and Sophia Kiely (all UK); Best Actor, Bertie Carvel in drag as the headmistress; Best Set Design, Rob Howell; Best Theater Choreographer, Peter Darling; Best Sound Design, Simon Baker; and Best Director, Matthew Warchus (all UK).

Youngest musician to headline a solo tour

Ethan Bortnick (USA, b. December 24, 2000) headlined at the Wentz Concert Hall in Naperville, Illinois, USA, on October 3, 2010 at the age of 9 years 9 months 9 days as part of his own tour. The young piano whiz first began playing at the age of three and has been featured on Oprah Winfrey's TV show.

November 25, 2012, there had been 25,007 continuous performances of *The Mousetrap*—the **longest theatrical run** in history.

Longest acting career
Hanna Maron (Israel) was born in 1923 and began acting on stage at the age of four; she continues to perform today in a career spanning 85 years.

Fastest theater production
Youth Theatre Performerz in association with MRL Productions

(both UK) staged the musical *Our House* by Tim Firth—managing all aspects of production, including auditions, choreography sessions, blocking, rehearsals, set and lighting design, and the creation of costumes and props—in just 22 hours at the Princes Theatre in Clacton-on-Sea, Essex, UK, on March 31–April 1, 2012.

DANCE

Longest distance dancing the conga
The longest distance danced in a conga line is 3.41 miles (5.487 km) and was achieved by

14 members of staff from the Salford and Stretford Tesco stores (UK) at Old Trafford in Manchester, UK, on December 2, 2012.

Longest line of dancers
A line of 2,869 dancers organized by the Walkway Over the Hudson charity performed the "Hokey Pokey" dance in Poughkeepsie, New York, USA, on June 9, 2012.

Most 1-2-3 Irish dance steps in 30 seconds
Ben Carolan (Ireland) achieved 43 Irish dance steps known as 1-2-3s in 30 seconds on the set of

Elev8 (RTE) in Dublin, Ireland, on August 3, 2012. The three-step jump is a fundamental of Irish folk dance.

Fastest 20 m moonwalk

Ashiq Baluch (UK, *pictured*) told five fellow Michael Jackson impersonators to "beat it" when he moonwalked 65 ft. 7 in. (20 m) in 7.81 seconds on the set of *Lo Show dei Record* on April 4, 2012. Three contestants were disqualified for not following the strict Jacko technique.

OVER THE MOON
The **fastest 100 m (328 ft.) moonwalk** is 32.06 seconds, achieved by Luo Lantu (China) in Beijing, China, on December 8, 2010.

Saxophones: 1,432, in an event at Houli Horse Farm, Taichung, Chinese Taipei, on August 7, 2011.

Melodicas: 664, by Adile Altınbaş junior high school (Turkey) at Nizip Stadium in Gaziantep, Turkey, on April 23, 2011.

Ukuleles: 2,134, during the Ukulele Picnic set up by Leiland Grow Inc. (Japan) at Yokohama Red Brick Warehouse in Yokohama, Kanagawa, Japan, on July 28, 2012.

Triangles: 574, tinging together with Cambridgeshire Music (UK) in Godmanchester, UK, on May 13, 2012.

Tubas: 502, achieved by TubaChristmas (USA) in Anaheim, California, USA, on December 21, 2007.

Most widespread social network message in 24 hours

On winning the 2012 Presidential election in the USA, Barack Obama (USA) took to Twitter to say "Four more years" and included a photograph of himself embracing wife Michelle. The celebratory announcement had been retweeted 771,635 times by different individuals 24 hours after its first appearance on November 7, 2012.

LARGEST COMPANIES

Identifying the leading companies by market value

As of April 2013, Apple is the most valuable company in a business world that had grown a little bit poorer over the last 12 months. Banks and oil companies, however, continue to head the most profitable sectors overall.

The figures here are based on the *Forbes* Global 2000, a survey of the world's 2,000 most successful companies published each April. Listed are the leading companies in selected sectors, ranked by their market value. So why concentrate on market value? Figures based just on turnover tend to underplay the true size of the banking sector; employee numbers alone can give a false impression about some companies' presence; and profits, as all accountants know, can "disappear" when the time comes to fill in tax returns and so can be an unreliable guide to a company's health.

Market value (also known as "market capitalization") is the share price of a company multiplied by the number of shares that it has issued. In other words, this figure is what investors believe a firm is worth.

Walmart (USA)
Discount stores
Market value: $242.5 billion
Ranking: 7
Walmart (founded in 1962) is the **largest retailer** (*see p. 147*). Its 8,500 warehouse and discount department stores are spread over 15 countries, under various names. In the UK, you'll know them as Asda; for Japan, it's Seiyu, while Indians know Walmart as Best Price.

Caterpillar, aka CAT (USA)
Heavy equipment
Market value: $58.2 billion
Ranking: 97
Caterpillar grew out of the Holt Manufacturing Company, which began producing continuous-track tractors in the early 1900s. Caterpillar was founded in 1925 when Holt merged with rivals the C. L. Best Tractor Company.

$469.16 BILLION
Walmart's annual sales in 2012. (See p. 147.)

Coca-Cola (USA)
Beverages
Market value: $173.1 billion
Ranking: 26
Coca-Cola has been quenching our thirst since 1886 and now incorporates familiar soft drink brands such as Fanta, Sprite, Schweppes, Dr. Pepper, Kia-Ora, Lilt, Coke, and Diet Coke.

Comcast (USA)
Broadcasting and cable
Market value: $106.3 billion
Ranking: 53
Founded in 1963, Comcast provides cable TV, broadband internet, telephone, and even home security services.

Procter & Gamble (USA)
Household/personal care
Market value: $208.5 billion
Ranking: 16
Founded in 1837, Procter & Gamble's products include Head & Shoulders, Braun, BOSS, Daz, Ariel, Duracell, Dreft, Bold, and Pampers.

Sony (Japan)
Consumer electronics
Market value: $17.6 billion
Ranking: 547
Founded in 1946, Sony began as a manufacturer of audio goods, launching Japan's first magnetic-tape recorder (the G-Type) in 1954 and the country's first transistor radio (the TR-55) in 1955. The company later expanded into video, communications, and information technology.

Visa (USA)
Consumer financial services
Market value: $104.8 billion
Ranking: 56
Multinational financial services organization Visa was founded in 1958. It is best known today for its debit and credit cards, through which electronic fund transfers are made.

Amazon.com (USA)
Internet and catalog retail
Market value: $119 billion
Ranking: 43
Online retail phenomenon Amazon.com (founded in 1994) is the **largest online store** (*see p. 146*).

Source: Forbes Global 2000.
All statistics correct as of April 17, 2013

CVS Caremark (USA)
Drug retail
Market value: $66 billion
Ranking: 109
CVS Caremark (founded in 1892) is the USA's largest health-care provider and employs a workforce of 203,000.

FORBES GLOBAL 2000—THE TOP 10

Aside from market value, Forbes magazine—our source for the data on these pages—also ranks companies in terms of three other metrics: sales, profits, and assets. By comparing companies across all four categories combined, Forbes creates its annual Global 2000 list of the largest public companies in the world. The top 10 companies in the 2013 list are as follows:

	COMPANY	SECTOR	SALES	PROFITS	ASSETS	VALUE
1	Industrial and Commercial Bank of China (ICBC)	Major banks	$134.8 bn	$37.8 bn	$2,813.5 bn	$237.3 bn
2	China Construction Bank	Regional banks	$113.1 bn	$30.6 bn	$2,241 bn	$202 bn
3	JPMorgan Chase (USA)	Major banks	$108.2 bn	$21.3 bn	$2,359.1 bn	$191.4 bn
4	General Electric (USA)	Conglomerates	$147.4 bn	$13.6 bn	$685.3 bn	$243.7 bn
5	Exxon Mobil (USA)	Oil and gas operations	$420.7 bn	$44.9 bn	$333.8 bn	$400.4 bn
6	HSBC Holdings (UK)	Major banks	$104.9 bn	$14.3 bn	$2,684.1 bn	$201.3 bn
7	Royal Dutch Shell (Netherlands)	Oil and gas operations	$467.2 bn	$26.6 bn	$360.3 bn	$213.1 bn
8	Agricultural Bank of China	Regional banks	$103 bn	$23 bn	$2,124.2 bn	$150.8 bn
=9	PetroChina	Oil and gas operations	$308.9 bn	$18.3 bn	$347.8 bn	$261.2 bn
=9	Berkshire Hathaway (USA)	Investment services	$162.5 bn	$14.8 bn	$427.5 bn	$252.8 bn

All statistics correct as of April 17, 2013

RANKING
Forbes first scores each company separately by the four metrics, then combines these scores to decide that company's rank on the Global 2000.

Apple (USA)
Computer hardware
Market value: $416.6 billion
Ranking: 1
Apple was founded in 1976. After a difficult period in the 1990s, the company revived spectacularly under CEO Steve Jobs with a host of game-changing products including the iMac, iPod, iPhone, and iPad.

United Parcel Service (USA)
Air courier
Market value: $81.5 billion
Ranking: 81
Courier firm United Parcel Service (UPS) caters to 8.8 million customers daily in 220 countries and territories. Founded in 1907 in Seattle, Washington, USA, UPS has a global workforce of 397,100 employees.

Nestlé (Switzerland)
Food processing
Market value: $233.5 billion
Ranking: 11
Incorporating household brands such as Perrier, Nescafé, Nesquik, Häagen-Dazs, Butterfinger, and KitKat, Nestlé employs a workforce of some 300,000 people. Its founder, Henri Nestlé, was a German pharmacist.

Toyota Motor Corporation (Japan)
Auto and truck manufacturers
Market value: $167.2 billion
Ranking: 29
The world's leading automaker as of 2013—with reported sales of 9.75 million vehicles for the preceding year—Toyota was founded in 1937 by Kiichiro Toyoda. The company produced its 200-millionth vehicle in 2012.

Exxon Mobil (USA)
Oil and gas operations
Market value: $400.4 billion
Ranking: 5
The oil-and-gas giant is also the **largest public company by profit** (see p. 123).

Nike (USA)
Apparel/accessories
Market value: $49.4 billion
Ranking: 160
The sports- and leisurewear giant was founded in 1964.

ICBC (China)
Major banks
Market value: $237.3 billion
Ranking: 9
The Industrial and Commercial Bank of China (ICBC) was founded in 1984. (See also p. 122.)

Johnson & Johnson (USA)
Medical equipment and supplies
Market value: $221.4 billion
Ranking: 13
The multinational company's range includes over-the-counter medicines, baby-care goods, and various skin and hair products. The firm was founded in 1886.

General Electric (USA)
Conglomerates
Market value: $243.7 billion
Ranking: 6
From its foundation in 1892, General Electric has grown to incorporate a variety of sectors including aviation, energy, health-care, and lighting.

McDonald's (USA)
Restaurants
Market value: $99.9 billion
Ranking: 61
The first McDonald's restaurant opened in 1940 and by 1958 the company had sold its 100-millionth burger; the Big Mac appeared 10 years later. By 2011, you could visit a McDonald's restaurant in any one of 119 countries.

Samsung Electronics (South Korea)
Semiconductors
Market value: $174.4 billion
Ranking: 25
Samsung was founded in 1938, operating in a range of areas such as retail, textiles, and food processing. It was not until the 1960s that it began producing the electrical goods for which it is best known today.

Microsoft (USA)
Software and programming
Market value: $234.8 billion
Ranking: 10
Founded by Bill Gates and Paul Allen in 1975, Microsoft is the leading software manufacturer by revenue. Its sales of $72.9 billion are nearly double that of its closest rival, Oracle ($37.1 billion).

Synchronizing the world o

97,811
Microsoft's global workforce, as of March 2013; 57,572 are based in the USA.

POPULATIONS

Most cell phones per capita

The United Arab Emirates has 1,709 cell phones per 1,000 people, according to the latest figures researched for the CIA World Factbook. By 2011, the country had 11.7 million cell phones. In overall terms, the country with the **most cell phones** is China, with 1.04 billion handsets as of July 20, 2012. India is in second place with 890.5 million, and the USA has 300 million.

LARGEST ...

Forced migration
The number of people forcibly transported from Africa to the Americas as slaves between 1501 and 1866 stands at approximately 12.5 million. A similar number may have been transported to Arabian countries but there are no written records. The peak year was 1829, when 117,644 African men, women, and children were moved.

Mass migration
On August 15, 1947, the partition of British India uprooted more than 18 million people. The partition was drawn up arbitrarily along religious lines to create the nation states of India and Pakistan, with a dividing line that ran through the middle of villages.

Partition stirred existing civil and religious tensions between Muslims and Hindus, triggering the **highest casualty rate for a single migration**. At least one million people were killed and 12 million made homeless as Pakistan became home to a majority of Muslims while India became largely Hindu.

Youngest average median population

In 2012, the people of Uganda had the lowest average (median) age of any nation. With an average age of 15.1 years (15 years for men; 15.2 years for women), the people of Uganda are 34.8 years younger than the country with the **oldest average median population**: Monaco.

Democracy
With a population of 1.24 billion, India is the world's largest democracy. The electorate alone was estimated at 714 million for the 2009 national election—more than the combined electorates of the USA and EU. India has a bicameral Parliament, with the upper house made up of 245 seats and the lower house comprised of 545 seats.

Highest birth rate
Based on *Economist* figures for 2005–10, Niger has the highest crude birth rate, with 49.5 births per 1,000 population.

Highest-dwelling nation
Most of Nepal (68 percent) lies in the Mahabharat, Siwalik, and Chure ranges, with a mild climate and an average altitude of 9,843 ft. (3,000 m).

Country with highest percentage of the world's poor

Despite its growing economy, India has 41.01 percent of the world's poor. Overall, it has 1.24 billion citizens, fewer than China, the **most populous country** with more than 1.33 billion citizens, but China has only 22.12 percent of the global population of the poor. Nigeria is third with 8.03 percent but it only has 155.2 million citizens.

$1.25 (or less). The daily wage that the UN defines as poverty.

FOR MORE ON AGING POPULATIONS, TURN TO P. 58

WHAT A WONDERFUL WORLD

Happiest country: Citizens of Costa Rica, asked to rate their own happiness by the World Database of Happiness, averaged 8.5 out of 10.

Highest Environmental Performance Index ranking: Switzerland scored 76.69 (out of 100) in 2012, according to an international forum; factors include biodiversity, agricultural methods, and readiness for climate change.

Highest life expectancy: Citizens in Japan live to an average of 83.7 years. That's 80.1 years for men and 87.2 years for women.

Most energy-efficient country: In 2008, Hong Kong had a 20-GDP-per-unit of energy use (gross-domestic-product-per-kilogram-of-oil-equivalent of energy use).

Largest donor of foreign aid: The USA donated $28.8 billion worth of aid to foreign countries in 2009.

Continent with the highest concentration of human biomass

Of a global population of 7 billion, 6 percent live in North America, but comprise 34 percent of total human biomass due to obesity. Asia has 61 percent of the population but only 13 percent of the biomass. About 2,200 lb. (1 tonne) of human biomass relates to approximately 12 adults in North America and 17 in Asia.

LOWEST ...

Food consumption

The UN's Food and Agriculture Organization has calculated that the people of Sierra Leone and the Democratic Republic of the Congo both consume an average of 1,500 calories per day. This is 39 percent of the average intake for U.S. citizens.

Birth rate

Hong Kong, China, recorded 8.2 births per 1,000 people in 2005–10. Germany had the next lowest birth rate, with 8.4 births per 1,000 people.

Population increase

Bulgaria will have an estimated increase in its population of -0.8 percent (i.e., a 0.8 percent *decrease*) for the period 2010–15. In 2010, there were 7.45 million Bulgarian citizens, a figure the UN predicts will drop to 5.46 million by 2050.

Lowest ratio of men to women

According to estimates published in the 2012 CIA World Factbook, the country in which women most outnumber men is Estonia, where there are just 84 men for every 100 women. The **lowest ratio of women to men** is found in the United Arab Emirates, with 219 men for every 100 women.

MOST ...

Movie theaters per capita

Belarus has more movie theaters per capita than any other country in the world, with one movie theater for every 2,734 inhabitants. In all, the country has 3,780 movie theaters for its population of 10,335,382.

Responses to an e-census

Estonia concluded its first e-census in February 2012 and announced that 66 percent of the population had participated. In Estonia, almost 99 percent of bank transactions are carried out online and 94 percent of tax returns are filed digitally.

Millionaires per capita

Singapore is home to more millionaires than any other country, with 17.1 percent of households worth $1 million or more. This equates to a total of 188,000 households, according to a survey from the Boston Consulting Group for 2011.

Murders per country

Brazil had 43,909 murders according to the United Nations Office of Drugs and Crime 2011 Global Study on Homicide. That works out as 22.7 murders per 100,000 population.

FOR THE RECORD

As of 2005, online journal *BioMedCentral (BMC) Public Health* put the biomass of humans at around 632 billion lb. (287 million tonnes). Of this, 33 billion lb. (15 million tonnes) was due to overweightedness and 7.7 billion lb. (3.5 million tonnes) to obesity.

Combined with mass emigration the figures are set to put strain on the pension system, with an aging population supported by fewer young people.

Personal income tax

The people of Bahrain and Qatar have an income tax rate of nil, regardless of their income. Oil is the backbone of the economies of both countries, providing more than half of government revenues.

Fastest rise in number of graduates

In 1998, there were only one million students in China. By 2004, there were 2,236 colleges and universities and, by 2008, its system was the largest in the world. Between February 2007 and February 2011, a total of 34 million Chinese students graduated, "the fastest such expansion in human history" according to the President of Yale University, Richard C. Levin (USA).

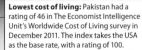
Lowest cost of living: Pakistan had a rating of 46 in The Economist Intelligence Unit's Worldwide Cost of Living survey in December 2011. The index takes the USA as the base rate, with a rating of 100.

Least corrupt country: New Zealand, Denmark, and Finland share a rating of 90 out of 100 in Transparency International's 2012 Corruptions Perception Index.

Lowest rate of infant mortality: Bermuda has an infant mortality rate of 2.5 per 1,000 population. This figure is a 2011 estimate by *The Economist*.

Lowest rate of inflation: Qatar had a rate of -4.9% in consumer price inflation in 2010, according to *The Economist*.

Most peaceful country: Iceland had a score of 1.113 on the Global Peace Index published by the Institute for Economics and Peace.

MONEY & ECONOMICS

30
Percentage of L'Oréal shares owned by the Bettencourt family.

Richest woman

Forbes magazine's April 2013 list of the world's richest people estimated the fortune of French L'Oréal heiress Liliane Bettencourt at more than $30 billion. She last ranked as the richest woman back in 1999.

3
Consecutive years that Helú and his family have been ranked richest in the world.

Richest person

Mexican telecoms giant Carlos Slim Helú and his close family are worth $69 billion. He dominates whole sectors of Mexico's economy, including stakes in banking, airlines, and mining. In 1990, he bought up the main source of his wealth—Mexico's premier telecoms business—when it was privatized.

Highest GDP

According to the World Bank, the USA has a GDP of $14.991 trillion in 2011, making it the leading trading nation. China, in second place, had a GDP of $7.318 trillion.

As of 2011, Monaco had the **highest GDP per citizen**: $171,465 per head. In second place was Luxembourg with $114,232.

Highest budgets

Education: For 2006–11, East Timor (also known as the Democratic Republic of Timor-Leste) devoted 14% of its GDP to schooling.
Health: According to *The Economist*, the U.S. government spent 17.9% of its GDP on healthcare in 2010.

Country with the greatest economic freedom

According to the 2011 Index of Economic Freedom World Rankings, Hong Kong's citizens continue to enjoy what the Index defines as "the fundamental right of every human to control his or her own labor and property. In an economically free society, individuals are free to work, produce, consume, and invest in any way they please, with that freedom both protected by the state and unconstrained by the state."

Largest food company takeover

In February 2013, it was revealed that Warren Buffett, the USA's second wealthiest man after Bill Gates, was the key player in a $28-billion bid to buy the food manufacturer Heinz. The deal—the largest ever announced in the food industry—was welcomed by Heinz's board, but still had to be approved by shareholders as of February 18, 2013.

Safest bank

Evaluating long-term credit ratings from credit agencies as well as banks' actual assets, *Global Finance* magazine rates Germany's KfW Bank the safest in the world. KfW is owned by the German central

government and the *Länder* (the 16 federal states) and has almost all its lending backed by its government—which, in turn, has some of the world's lowest borrowing costs.

Lowest GDP

Gross Domestic Product (GDP) is the value of all final goods and services made within the borders of a country in a year. The Pacific island nation of Tuvalu had a GDP

of just $35,804,372 as of 2011, according to the World Bank.

The **lowest GDP per capita** is $231 in the Democratic Republic of the Congo. Racked by violence and civil war for two decades, the African nation also has the **lowest Gross National Income (GNI) per capita**, with each citizen having just $340 to live on in 2011. In comparison, citizens of Qatar have the **highest GNI per capita**, with an average income of $86,440.

Most indebted person

Jérôme Kerviel (France) was one of the French bank Société Générale's top traders. But that was before he carried out $73 billion of fraudulent and uncovered European stock future trades, exposing his employer to huge losses—and before he was arrested and charged by the French authorities. In October 2012, French courts judged that he owed his former company the astonishing amount of $6.3 billion.

Largest bank

According to *Forbes*, as of April 2013 the largest bank overall (in terms of sales, profits, assets and market value) is the Industrial and Commercial Bank of China (ICBC). Its figures break down as follows: sales, $134.8 billion; profits, $37.8 billion; assets, $2,813.5 billion; market value, $237.3 billion.

TOP 10 LARGEST ECONOMIES BY GDP

1. USA: $14,991,300,000,000

2. China: $7,318,499,269,769

3. Japan: $5,867,154,491,918

4. Germany: $3,600,833,333,333

5. France: $2,773,032,125,000

Source: World Bank, 2011

Most innovative economy

The Global Innovation Index is published yearly by a consortium led by the business school INSEAD and includes the World Intellectual Property Organization—a United Nations agency. Switzerland tops the list for economic innovation, followed by Sweden.

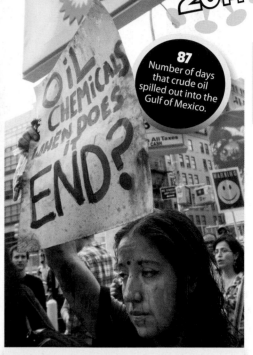

87 Number of days that crude oil spilled out into the Gulf of Mexico.

ASSESSING INNOVATION
The Index considers a range of factors including economies, political institutions, education, infrastructure, and technology.

Mac") buckled during the crisis in the U.S. housing market that broke out in 2007. As a result, both institutions were "bailed out" by being nationalized and refinanced. In 2008, the U.S. Treasury placed a ceiling of $100 billion on each bailout—a limit that was removed in December 2009 as the scale of the crisis became apparent. By late 2012, a total of $187.5 billion had been provided to these stricken giants. The Federal Housing Finance Agency has estimated that the final

Largest public company by profit

As of April 2013, *Forbes* valued oil and gas company Exxon Mobil (USA) at $44.9 billion in profits, with an overall market value of $400.4 billion.

Greatest bank bailout
The U.S. government-sponsored Federal National Mortgage Association (better known as "Fannie Mae," after the initials FNMA) and the Federal Home Loan Mortgage Corporation (aka "Freddie

bill may be as high as $360 billion! Fannie Mae is the **largest company in terms of assets**: $3,226.2 billion as of April 17, 2013, according to *Forbes*.

Greatest trading volume in one day
On October 10, 2008, the New York Stock Exchange (NYSE) Group saw an impressive 7,341,505,961 trades.

Highest economic growth
For 2000–10, Equatorial Guinea saw the highest average annual percentage increase in real GDP, with 17%. In 1999–2009, Zimbabwe saw an annual *decrease* in GDP of 6.1% and thus had the **lowest economic growth**.

Lowest budgets
Education: Congo-Kinshasa and Myanmar have the **lowest budget for education**. Each country devotes just 2% of its GDP to education, according to the latest figures available.
Health: As of 2009, the countries with the **lowest budget for healthcare** are Congo-Brazzaville and Myanmar, with just 2% of their GDP devoted to this sector.

Biggest corporate fine

In April 2010, the Deepwater Horizon oil spill released millions of barrels of crude oil into the Gulf of Mexico, killing 11 workers and wrecking many U.S. businesses. In recompense, BP was ordered to pay $2.4 billion to the U.S. National Fish and Wildlife Foundation, along with a record criminal fine of $1.26 billion. The final bill may be nearer to $4 billion and BP may be subject to $7.8 billion in claims for damages on top of that.

Most expensive election

According to the Center for Responsive Politics, the 2012 Presidential and Congressional elections in the USA were by far the most expensive in democratic history. They weighed in at an extraordinary $6 billion. As the Federal Elections Commission noted, the two presidential hopefuls—Barack Obama and eventual runner-up Mitt Romney (*inset*)—combined spent $30.33 per second.

Largest exporter of arms

In 2011, U.S. arms sales to the rest of the world tripled to $66.3 billion—three-quarters of the global market. The U.S. Congressional Research Service attributed this sharp rise to increased sales to allies in the Persian Gulf.

6. Brazil: $2,476,652,189,880

7. UK: $2,445,408,064,516

8. Italy: $2,193,971,063,086

9. India: $1,872,840,247,709

10. Russian Federation: $1,857,769,676,144

MOST EXPENSIVE ...

£36,000

Cricket bat

A bat belonging to Mahendra Singh Dhoni (India)—the record-breaking captain of the Indian national cricket team—sold at auction for £100,000 ($161,295) to R. K. Global Shares & Securities Ltd. (India) at Dhoni's "East Meets West" charity dinner held in London, UK, on July 18, 2011.

Glove

A glove that once belonged to the singer Michael Jackson (USA) was bought by Ponte 16 Resort (China) for $420,000 at the Hard Rock Cafe in New York City, USA, on November 21, 2009. (*For more outrageously expensive outfits, see below.*)

$420,000

LEGO® brick

A 0.9-oz. (25.6-g) 4 x 2 LEGO brick crafted from 14-carat gold was sold for $12,500 on December 3, 2012 to an anonymous buyer by Brick Envy, Inc. (USA), a speciality LEGO collector Web site.

$12,500

Duck decoys

Two duck decoys carved by A. Elmer Cromwell (USA) sold in a private deal for $1.13 million each on September 20, 2007, in a sale brokered by Stephen O'Brien Jr. Fine Arts in Boston, Massachusetts, USA. The "preening pintail drake" and "sleeping Canada goose" were sold to an anonymous buyer.

Calendar

A calendar featuring costume designs for characters from Lewis Carroll's *Alice's Adventures in Wonderland* was sold to a bidder for £36,000 ($57,848) as part of a fund-raising auction held in aid of the Muir Maxwell Trust and the Fettes Foundation (both UK) at Fettes College, Edinburgh, UK, on July 3, 2011.

Handbag

A Hermès Diamond Birkin handbag sold for $203,150 at a Handbags & Luxury Accessories auction organized by Heritage Auctions in Dallas, Texas, USA, on December 9, 2011.

Cognac (bottle)

An 1858 bottle of Cuvée Leonie (pre-Phylloxera cognac) was sold to Maggie Vong (Hong Kong) by Cognac Croizet Hong Kong Ltd. (China) for 1,000,000 CNY ($156,219) at The Swatch Art Peace Hotel in Shanghai, China, on September 24, 2011.

32,000
Number of Swarovski Element crystals on the HYLA GST.

Downloadable content

A virtual diamond chisel costing £50,000 ($77,000) went on sale on November 6, 2012 in the massively multiplayer online (MMO) video game *Curiosity: What's Inside the Cube?* (22Cans, UK). The game features only a black cube that players hit with virtual chisels, working together to find out what's inside.

Camera

A prototype Leica 35 mm camera was sold to an anonymous buyer for €2.16 million ($2.8 million) at the WestLicht Photographica auction in Vienna, Austria, on May 12, 2012. Only 25 such prototypes were made in 1923.

Computer

The SAGE (Semi-Automatic Ground Environment) system was the **most expensive**, the **largest**—incorporating 56 IBM AN/FSQ-7 computers over an area of 20,000 sq. ft. (1,860 m²)—and **heaviest computer system** (500,000 lb.; 226.8 tonnes) ever built. Created by IBM in association with MIT and RAND, SAGE was completed in 1963 at a cost somewhere between $4 billion and $12 billion at the time—although the majority place the price at $8 billion. It remained operational for more than 20 years.

$21,900

Vacuum cleaner

The jewel-encrusted HYLA GST Swarovski Edition vacuum cleaner costs $21,900. It is made by Hartmut Gassmann (Germany) and HYLA US Gassmann, Inc. (USA) and can be ordered online. As of February 22, 2013, two units had been sold.

€2.16 million

MOST EXPENSIVE ...

Sari: Rs 3,931,627 ($100,021). Sold on January 5, 2008. Made by Chennai Silks, India.

Dress: $4.6 million. Dress worn by Marilyn Monroe (USA) in the movie *The Seven Year Itch* (USA, 1955). Sold on June 18, 2011.

Pop star costume: $300,000. Elvis Presley's (USA) white "peacock" jumpsuit. Sold on August 7, 2008.

Headwear: $277,292. 4th-century-BC winged bronze helmet. Sold on April 28, 2004.

Soccer shirt: £157,750 ($225,109). No. 10 shirt worn by Pelé (Brazil) in 1970 FIFA World Cup final. Sold on March 27, 2002.

$160,000

Check

The original Detective Comics, Inc. payment of $412 to Superman creators Jerry Siegel and Joe Shuster, dated March 1, 1938, was auctioned via the ComicConnect.com (USA) Web site for $160,000 on April 16, 2012. It includes a $130 entry for rights and ownership of the Superman character.

Home speaker system
The $2-million custom-made Transmission Audio Ultimate 15,500-watt speaker array comprises 12 speakers, each 6 ft. 10 in. (2.1 m) high. All are made from aircraft aluminum with piano black or rosewood side finishes and black granite stands.

Internet domain name
The name insure.com was sold in October 2009 to Internet marketing firm QuinStreet for $16 million.

Painting
Paul Cézanne's *The Card Players* was sold to the royal family of Qatar for $250 million in 2011. This painting is one of five in a series by the famed French post-Impressionist painted in the early 1890s.

The **most expensive painting sold at auction** is Edvard Munch's *The Scream* (1895), which was sold on May 2, 2012 to an anonymous buyer at Sotheby's

Gold shirt

On February 6, 2013, Datta Phuge (India) paid 6,615,481 rupees ($120,219) for a custom-made shirt made from 9 lb. 4 oz. (3.20 kg) of 22-carat solid gold in Pimpri Chinchwad, Maharashtra, India. The shirt was created by Ranka Jewellers in two weeks by 15 goldsmiths.

FACT:
There was enough gold left over from the shirt to make a set of rings and a pair of matching cuffs!

in New York, USA, for $119.9 million. The starting price for the painting—which depicts a man holding his head and screaming—was $40 million.

Tuna fish
A bluefin tuna sold for 155,400,000 yen ($1,767,370) at Tsukiji fish market in Chūō, Tokyo, Japan, on January 5, 2013. The fish weighed 489 lb. 6.88 oz. (222 kg).

Rs 6,615,481

$12,970

Cocktail
"The Winston," a cocktail created by Joel Heffernan (Australia), was sold at Club 23 in Melbourne, Australia, on February 7, 2013 for AUS$125,000 ($12,970). The drink—which requires 16 hours of labor owing to its elaborate garnish of chocolate and nutmeg dust—contains 2.1 fl. oz. (60 ml) of Croizet's 1858 Cuvee Leonie cognac (*see left*).

Whiskey
On November 15, 2010, a bottle of 64-year-old Macallan in a special Lalique decanter sold for charity at Sotheby's in New York City, USA, for $460,000.

On November 16, 2000, Norman Shelley (UK) purchased 76 bottles of The Macallan malt whiskey for £231,417.90 ($341,154). This—the **most expensive whiskey collection**—included 76 rare malts, the oldest of which dated from 1856.

£541,250

Olympic memorabilia

The Bréal's Silver Cup—the prize for the marathon at the first modern Olympics in Athens, Greece, in 1896—sold for £541,250 ($861,502) to the Stavros Niarchos Foundation (Greece) on April 18, 2012.

Baseball jersey: $4,415,658. Originally belonged to "Babe Ruth" (USA). Sold on May 20, 2012.

Antique dress: $101,500. 1888 court dress designed by Charles Frederick Worth (UK) and worn by Esther Chapin (USA) when she was presented to Queen Victoria in 1889. Sold on May 3, 2001.

Shoes: $666,000. Ruby slippers worn by Judy Garland (USA) in *The Wizard of Oz* (USA, 1939). Sold on May 24, 2000.

Jacket: £1.1 million ($1.8 million). Calf-leather jacket worn by Michael Jackson (USA) in his 1983 "Thriller" video. Sold on June 26, 2011.

Pair of sneakers: $4,053. High-top Nike Dunks dipped in 18-carat gold, created by Ken Courtney (USA) for fashion show in New York City, USA, in 2007.

MAIL & E-MAIL

Deepest mailbox underwater

Sports divers can post mail in a mailbox located 32 ft. 10 in. (10 m) beneath the waters of Susami Bay, Japan. The box—which is officially part of the Susami Post Office—is checked daily by authorized employees using post-office keys. More than 4,273 undersea mails were collected in the mailbox's first year of operation (1999).

Longest time to deliver a bag of mail

A bag of Indian diplomatic mail was recovered from Mont Blanc in the French Alps, near the site of a 1966 Air India plane crash, by mountain rescue worker Arnaud Christmann and his neighbor Jules Berger on August 21, 2012, some 46 years after it was lost.

Oldest working post office

In 2012, the post office at Sanquhar in Dumfriesshire, UK, celebrated its 300th anniversary. It has been operating continuously since 1712, when it was recorded as being a staging post for mail deliveries by foot and by horseback. Today, it is a popular tourist attraction, and visitors can have their letters stamped with "The World's Oldest Post Office."

Largest e-mail service provider

In June 2012, Google's e-mail service Gmail topped 425 million active monthly accounts, beating off competition from the likes of Yahoo! Mail and Hotmail to become the largest e-mail service provider.

Fastest Internet connection

Between March 27 and 31, 2012 at The Gathering, an annual computer party held at the Vikingskipet Olympic arena in Hamar, Norway, guests could utilize a superspeedy 200-Gbit/s (gigabits per second) connection. E-mail messages were sent at lightning speed, and downloading a high-definition blu-ray movie was possible in just two seconds!

Most expensive stamp

The Swedish "Treskilling" Yellow—a rare stamp that was printed in the wrong color—sold on November 8, 1996 for a staggering CHF2,870,000 ($2,255,403) at David Feldman auctioneers in Geneva, Switzerland.

2,800
Number of students who contributed to the letter.

Longest letter

Students of Brahma Kumaris Youth Wing, a spiritual organization at Gujarat University, India, wrote an epic, 2,841-ft.-long (866-m) letter addressed to God on March 28, 2010 to celebrate their silver jubilee year and the university's diamond jubilee.

First child to be mailed

A few weeks after the U.S. mail service was introduced in 1913, an unnamed baby boy in Ohio was mailed from his parents' house to his grandparents, just one mile away, for the grand sum of 15 cents. The practice of mailing children continued throughout 1914 until the Postmaster issued an order to bar the sending of human beings by the U.S. mail!

Highest post office

The village of Hikkim in Himachal Pradesh, India, is part of the Himalayas and lies at an altitude of 15,500 ft. (4,724 m) above sea level. Hikkim Post Office opened in November 1983 to serve the village's 600 inhabitants and it currently processes 15–20 letters per day and holds savings deposits for around 50 people.

Fastest *Postman Pat* van

A coin-operated *Postman Pat* child's ride, converted to include a racing wheelbase and 500-cc four-stroke engine, completed a quarter-mile drag-racing run at York Raceway in East Yorkshire, UK, on August 30, 2012. It finished in 17.419 seconds, with a terminal speed of 84.28 mph (135.6 km/h).

STAMPS OF AUTHORITY

Most valuable stamp swap: In October 2005, Bill Gross (USA) traded four "Inverted Jenny" airmail stamps—worth a total of $2.97 million—for a 1-cent Z-grill that belonged to Donald Sundman (USA), which was valued in 2005 at $3 million.

Most expensive stamp collection: The Kanai collection of 183 pages of classic issues of Mauritius sold for CHF15,000,000 ($9,982,033) in a single sale by Geneva-based auctioneer David Feldman in Switzerland on November 3, 1993.

First magic society featured on a national stamp: The Royal Mail issued a series of five interactive stamps on March 15, 2005 to commemorate the centenary of the Magic Circle (UK).

First video game featured on a national stamp: In 2000, the U.S. postal service's *Celebrate the Century* series included a 33-cent stamp showing two children playing the Atari 2600 version of *Defender*.

Largest stamp issue: A total of 751.25 million stamps from the 1929 Postal Union Congress commemorative were sold.

Oldest message in a bottle

A drift bottle with number ca'd 646B was recorded by Captain Brown (UK) as being released at 60° 00'N 00° 39'E on June 10, 1914. It was recovered by fisherman Andrew Leaper (UK), skipper of the Lerwick fishing boat Copious, at 60° 6.37'N 00° 25.17'E on April 12, 2012, having spent 97 years 309 days at sea.

computers, and it was Ray who decided to use the @ symbol to separate the recipient's name from their location. The message read: "QWERTYUIOP."

The **first instance of the @ sign** dates back to May 4, 1536, when an Italian merchant used the symbol to refer to amphorae, a unit of measurement.

President with regular e-mail access

When Barack Obama (USA) took office in January 2009, it was announced that he was an avid e-mailer and that he would use e-mail to stay in touch with senior staff and personal friends for the duration of his presidency.

LARGEST ...

National mail service

As of March 31, 2011, India had 154,866 post offices—139,040 of which are in rural areas. It employs more than 466,000 people.

Fastest printing of a postage stamp

To mark the 100th anniversary of their country's first ever stamp, Liechtensteinische Post AG (Liechtenstein) printed a postage stamp in just 57 min. 50 sec. The record attempt was held at the LIBA 2012 Stamp Exhibition in Schaan, Liechtenstein, on August 16, 2012, and the first stamp was purchased by GWR Editor-in-Chief Craig Glenday.

Collection of postal history memorabilia

The Smithsonian Institution's National Postal Museum in Washington, DC, USA, contains a philatelic and postal collection of 13,257,549 items, including stationery and mailboxes. It occupies an area of 75,000 sq. ft. (6,968 m²).

FIRST ...

Airmail flight

On February 18, 1911, just seven years after the Wright brothers made the first ever powered flight, Frenchman Henri Pequet piloted a small biplane transporting 6,500 letters from an airfield in Allahabad to Naini (both India), 6 miles (10 km) away, in about 15 minutes.

E-mail

In 1971, Ray Tomlinson, an engineer at the computer company Bolt, Beranek and Newman in Cambridge, Massachusetts, USA, sent the first e-mail. It was an experiment to see if he could exchange a message between two

Longest time to deliver a letter

In 2008, Janet Barrett (UK), a guesthouse owner in Weymouth, Dorset, UK, received an RSVP to a party invitation addressed to "Percy Bateman" from "Buffy", originally posted on November 29, 1919. It had taken 89 years to be delivered by the Royal Mail.

SPACE SURFING

Composed on an Apple Macintosh Portable, the first space e-mail was sent over the AppleLink network (an online service provided by Apple before the commercialization of the Internet).

First e-mail sent from space

On August 28, 1991, astronauts Shannon Lucid and James C. Adamson (both USA) beamed an e-mail back to Earth from the NASA space shuttle Atlantis. The message read: "Hello Earth! Greetings from the STS-43 Crew. This is the first AppleLink from space. Having a GREAT time, wish you were here ... send cryo and RCS! Hasta la vista, baby ... we'll be back!"

BLAHA BAKER
LUCID ADAMSON LOW

Rarest stamp: Two contenders share the record for rarity: a British Guiana 1-cent "Black on Magenta" of 1856 (*right*, last on the market in 1980) and the Swedish three skilling banco "Treskilling" Yellow of 1855 (*see above*).

Largest stamp mosaic: A mosaic measuring 1,743 sq. ft. (162 m²) was created by volunteers from the South African Post Office and the Hatfield Tuition College (South Africa) at the Tshwane Events Centre in Pretoria, South Africa, between September 12 and October 12, 2010.

Largest stamp collecting organization: With nearly 35,000 members in more than 110 countries, the nonprofit American Philatelic Society is the world's largest society for stamp collectors.

Oldest picture postcard: A card sent by Theodore Hook, Esq. (UK) to himself from Fulham, London, UK, in 1840 features an illustration of post office scribes seated around a giant inkwell.

NEDERLAND
44
eurocent
2007

Largest special-issue stamp: A stamp that measured 1 ft. 11 in. x 1 ft. 7 in. (60 x 49.3 cm) was issued by TNT Post (Netherlands) on November 6, 2007.

SOCIAL NETWORKING

Most viewed online video in 24 hours

The 2013 hit "Gentleman" by PSY, aka Park Jae-sang (South Korea), was viewed 38,409,306 times on April 14, 2013.

Most subscribers on YouTube

As of May 16, 2013, Smosh, the comedy duo of Anthony Padilla and Ian Hecox (both USA), had 9,820,623 YouTube subscribers. The channel (www.youtube.com/user/smosh), which features short comedy clips, is also one of the most viewed on YouTube, with 2,328,054,269 total video views as of May 16, 2013.

Largest video-sharing Web site

YouTube continues to dominate the Internet as the principal source of videos, with more than 4 billion hours of video watched, and 1 billion unique users visiting the site each month, as of May 2013. At the time of writing (May 2013),

TOP-TRENDING TOPICS OF 2012

CATEGORY	SUBJECT	DETAILS
Overall Searches	Whitney Houston (USA)	The untimely death of U.S. singer Whitney Houston (*above*) on February 11, 2012 saw her become the highest-trending topic in the Overall, People, and Performing Artists categories.
People		• PSY's (South Korea) viral hit "Gangnam Style" was the second-highest trend overall, followed by Hurricane Sandy. • Second to Houston in the People category came British royal Kate Middleton. In third place was Canadian student Amanda Todd, whose tragic video went viral in the wake of her death.
Performing Artists		• *The Green Mile* (USA, 1999) star Michael Clarke Duncan, who died on September 3, 2012, was runner-up to Houston in the Performing Artists category. Third came UK pop phenomenon One Direction.
Athletes	Jeremy Lin (USA)	The spectacular rise of U.S. basketball star Jeremy "Linsanity" Lin led the field. Superstar swimmer Michael Phelps (USA) was runner-up; Denver Broncos quarterback Peyton Manning (USA) came in third.
Events	Hurricane Sandy (USA)	The devastation wreaked by Hurricane Sandy was the top-trending event. In second place were photographs of pregnant British royal Kate Middleton. Third came the London 2012 Olympic Games.
Images	One Direction (UK/Ireland)	One Direction prompted the highest picture-related trending on Google in 2012. U.S. actress and singer Selena Gomez was second, followed by Apple's much-anticipated iPhone 5.
Videos	"Gangnam Style"	"Gangnam Style" by PSY (South Korea) beat all, while *Somebody That I Used to Know* by Walk Off the Earth (Canada) was runner-up; Invisible Children, Inc.'s (USA) politically charged *KONY 2012* came third.
Feature Movies	*The Hunger Games* (USA, 2012)	Sci-fi movie *The Hunger Games* took the top spot, followed by the **highest-grossing James Bond movie**—*Skyfall* (UK, 2012, *see p. 203*), with director Ridley Scott's *Prometheus* (UK/USA, 2012) at No. 3.
TV Shows	BBB12 (Rede Globo)	*BBB12* (*Big Brother Brasil 12*) was No. 1; Brazilian soap-opera sensation *Avenida Brasil* came second. *Here Comes Honey Boo Boo*, with child beauty-pageant entrant Alana Thompson, was third.
Consumer Electronics	Apple iPad	Apple's iPad 3 and iPad Mini came first and third respectively in consumer electronics-related trends on Google. In between was Samsung's Galaxy S3 smartphone.

Source: Google – Zeitgeist 2012. Trends on Google Zeitgeist are based on the change in the volume of traffic for any given search term from one year to the next. As such, it is not a measure of the most-searched-for topics but rather those that are rising quickly (i.e. trending).

Most Facebook users by country

The USA had 163,071,460 Facebook users as of March 10, 2013. On the same day, according to the U.S. Census Bureau, the U.S. population was 315,467,468, meaning that 51.69 percent of the nation had a Facebook account. Second in the rankings was Brazil, with 66,552,420 users.

Most Internet users per capita

According to the International Telecommunication Union, Iceland is the country with the highest percentage of individuals using the Internet, at 95.02 percent in 2011.

Most popular Web browser

The Google Chrome browser enjoyed a market share of 39.15 percent as of April 2013, according to http://gs.statcounter.com.

First tweet

Twitter was invented by Jack Dorsey (USA) in 2006 as a microblogging and social networking tool. Users can post text messages, called "tweets," of up to 140 characters, which are sent to their subscribers, or "followers." The very first tweet was posted by Dorsey at 9:50 p.m. Pacific Standard Time (PST) on March 21, 2006 and read "just setting up my twittr."

iQUOTE
"It would be nice to wallpaper the entire interior of my home with GWR certificates"—Misha Collins

Largest media scavenger hunt

Misha Collins (USA) organized the "Greatest International Scavenger Hunt the World Has Ever Seen," with 14,580 participants taking part from October 29 to November 5, 2012. The 151-item checklist included a skydive (*left*), a stormtrooper pool cleaner (*below left*), and a puppet show at a children's hospital (*below right*).

more than 72 hours of video were being added every minute—the equivalent of more than 308,400 full-length movies per week.

Largest online encyclopedia

Wikipedia was founded by Jimmy Wales and Larry Sanger (both USA) as a free online encyclopedia that Internet users can add to and edit. Wikipedia.com was launched on January 15, 2001. As of May 22, 2013, the site featured 4,238,043 articles written in English and more than 37 million articles written altogether, in 285 languages.

Largest online social network

As of March 31, 2013, Facebook was able to boast 1.11 billion monthly active users, with more than 150 billion "friend" connections between them.

The **most "likes" on a Facebook item** as of May 16, 2013 is 4,437,740, as featured on the official page for U.S. President Barack Obama in response to

MOST TWITTER FOLLOWERS FOR A ...

Author: Brazilian author Paulo Coelho has 7,825,671 followers. Among Coelho's work is the best-selling and critically acclaimed novel *The Alchemist*.

Entrepreneur: Microsoft cofounder and renowned philanthropist Bill Gates (USA) has a following of 11,320,473 people.

Actor: Ashton Kutcher (USA) has 14,299,082 followers, the most for any male actor. Ashton also holds the record for the **first person to reach 1 million followers**, which he achieved in 2009.

Reality TV star: Socialite, model, and star of *Keeping up with the Kardashians* and its sequels, Kim Kardashian (USA) has 17,810,657 followers.

Actress: The first Latina actress to earn $1 million in a movie role (for 1998's *Out of Sight*), Jennifer Lopez (USA) has a following of 18,260,631.

*Source: twitaholic.com.
All statistics correct as of May 17, 2013*

200,000,000 in

in

First Google+ Hangout in space

On February 22, 2013, astronauts Kevin Ford, Tom Marshburn (both USA), and Chris Hadfield (Canada) took part in the first Google+ Hangout from space, on the *International Space Station*. The three chatted with their online audience for 20 minutes.

As of May 16, 2013, the **most comments on a Facebook item** is 118,697,614, achieved by Guru Shri Rajendraji Maharaj Jaap Club (India) in response to a post made on March 27, 2012.

Most tweets per second

As midnight struck on New Year's Eve 2012, in the Japan Standard Time Zone, the number of tweets per second from Japan and South Korea hit 33,388. The phenomenon may be partly explained by the Japanese custom of sending New Year's cards, or *nengajo*.

Largest professional online networking site

LinkedIn was launched on May 5, 2003 as a social networking site aimed at business professionals. On January 9, 2013, LinkedIn announced that it had achieved 200 million users worldwide. As of December 31, 2012, it was growing at the rate of two members per second.

British entrepreneur Richard Branson (*right*) has the **most LinkedIn followers**. He was the first member to reach 1 million followers; by March 10, 2013, a total of 1,521,636 people were following him.

his "Four more years" post made on November 7, 2012 (*see p. 116*). The post can be seen here: tinyurl.com/obamalikes

Texas HoldEm Poker (Zynga, 2007) holds the record for the **most "likes" for a game on Facebook**. As of May 16, 2013, the Texas HoldEm Poker page had accrued 70,206,549 "likes."

Bajan sensation Rihanna (b. Robyn Rihanna Fenty) is the undisputed queen of Facebook, with more fans—70,738,592—than any individual on the planet, as of May 16, 2013. During a Facebook Live interview on November 8, 2012 to promote her seventh studio album, *Unapologetic*, the 25-year-old recording artist said of being the **most "liked" person on Facebook** (a title she'd taken from rapper Eminem): "It doesn't feel real … [but] it's exciting to know that [my fans] care."

Most Twitter followers for a pop group

One Direction (UK/Ireland) had amassed 12,130,152 followers on Twitter as of May 16, 2013, through their @onedirection account. The boys also have their own accounts, with Harry Styles (*above right*) leading the way with 12,952,247 followers.

Largest online game of Secret Santa

Web site redditgifts.com (USA) organized the largest online Secret Santa game—where participants send and receive gifts anonymously. Taking place from November 5, 2012 to February 15, 2013, the event included 44,805 participants shipping and receiving gifts.

Most popular social networking game

By January 2011, *CityVille* (Zynga, 2010), Facebook's most popular app, had 84.2 million monthly players.

Most friends on Myspace

From Myspace's 2003 launch until February 2010, cofounder Tom Anderson was made each account's first "friend." As of May 15, 2013, "Myspace Tom" had 11,752,308 friends.

Most money pledged for a Kickstarter project

Kickstarter is a U.S. Web site designed to foster projects paid for by crowd funding. On May 18, 2012, the funding proposal for the Pebble: E-Paper Watch for iPhone and Android closed after reaching $10,266,845 in backing from 68,929 people.

funded with KICK STARTER

28:56
4.08mi
PACE
7:05
min/mi

twelve thirty five

TUE 27

Athlete: Real Madrid *galáctico* Cristiano Ronaldo (Portugal) has amassed a 18,302,613-strong following since joining Twitter six years ago.

TV personality: Comedian and television host Ellen DeGeneres (USA), the star of *The Ellen DeGeneres Show*, has 19,296,433 followers.

Politician: In all, 31,551,812 people follow President Barack Obama (USA). Unusually for such a major public figure, Obama also follows a healthy number of people himself: 662,594.

Female pop singer: Justin Bieber's closest pop rival on Twitter is Lady Gaga (USA). The "Born this Way" star has 37,335,980 followers. Will those Little Monsters (her fans) make her No. 1 in 2014?

Pop singer: Canada's Justin Bieber isn't just the most-followed pop star: as of May 17, 2013, he had the **most followers** outright: 39,206,786 true "Beliebers."

BIG BROTHER

Largest communications surveillance network

Echelon is the electronic eavesdropping network run by the intelligence organizations of the USA, UK, Australia, New Zealand, and Canada. It was founded in 1947 by those nations to share intelligence data. Some analysts estimate that it can intercept some 90% of Internet traffic, as well as monitoring global telephone and satellite communications. Pictured are the radomes—giant golf ball-like satellite covers—used by Echelon at RAF Menwith Hill in North Yorkshire, UK.

First Internet cookies

Http cookies—small pieces of data deposited within your Web browser by Web sites to remember details such as your password or shopping preferences—were invented by Lou Montulli (USA) while working for Netscape in 1994. Their first use on the Internet was on Netscape's own Web site, checking if users were first-time visitors or had used the Web site previously.

First computer worm

Computer worms are a form of malware designed to spread over computer networks. The first such worm was "Creeper," written by Robert Thomas (USA) in 1971 while working for BBN Technologies, USA. It was an experimental self-replicating program designed to demonstrate mobile applications. Creeper infected DEC PDP-10 computers and displayed the following message on the screens of infected computers: "I'm the creeper, catch me if you can!"

The **first worm to spread over the Internet** was the Morris worm, created by Robert Tappan Morris (USA, *see below right*), a student at Cornell University, USA. On November 2, 1988, Morris released

his worm, which went on to disable roughly 10% of all computers connected to the Internet—around 60,000 machines.

First computer worm to target industrial systems

The stuxnet worm was discovered in July 2010. Spreading from PC to PC via a USB stick, it searches for and targets small computers called programmable logic controllers, which are used to control industrial processes. By using default password settings, stuxnet was able to access poorly configured industrial systems and disrupt their settings and operations. Iran—where 60% of the infected computers were located—accused the West of creating stuxnet to attack its nuclear facilities, claiming that centrifuges used in nuclear enrichment had been disrupted as part of a cyber attack.

First computer virus

The first computer program that replicates itself surreptitiously was demonstrated by Fred Cohen, a student at the Massachusetts Institute of Technology, USA, on November 11, 1983. Viruses had been theorized previous to this, but Cohen was the first to write and execute a working code.

First human infected with a computer virus

On May 27, 2010, Mark Gasson (UK) from the University of Reading, UK, announced that he had implanted an RFID (radio-frequency identification) chip into his hand, which he then infected with a computer virus. The chip allowed him to activate his cell phone and pass through security doors. When he passed through a security door, the system that recognized his RFID chip also accepted the virus, which it then passed on to other RFID chips or swipe cards used to activate the door. Gasson's virus was a proof of concept designed to highlight potential threats to implants, such as pacemakers and cochlear implants.

ACTUAL SIZE

First drive-by spam

In January 2012, German e-mail security company Eleven announced their discovery of a new type of malicious e-mail that can infect a PC user with viruses and trojans simply by opening the e-mail. Previously, users could feel safe that e-mails would only infect their machines if they

FOR THE RECORD

E-mail "spam" takes its name from a sketch on the UK TV comedy series *Monty Python's Flying Circus* in which the cast sing the word repeatedly to celebrate "**s**piced **h**am": chopped pork luncheon meat (*right*). In the 1980s, the word was repeated on bulletin boards by abusive users to disrupt online chats.

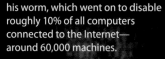

Most prolific spam gang

In November 2009, a U.S. court ordered a gang led by brothers Lane and Shane Atkinson (New Zealand) and Jody Smith (USA) to pay $15.5 million for sending e-mail spam marketing herbal remedies and prescription medicines. The gang controlled a network of 35,000 computers and was alleged to have created one-third of the world's junk mail.

HACKING HALL OF INFAMY

Vladimir Levin (Russia): Accessed accounts of Citibank customers in 1994 and attempted to steal $10.7 million; arrested in 1995 and finally jailed in 1998.

Albert Gonzalez (Cuba/USA): Serving a 20-year jail sentence for hacking into various companies and stealing credit card numbers (as many as 170 million) between 2005 and 2007.

David Smith (USA): Responsible for releasing the "Melissa" virus into the wild in 1999, clogging and shutting down e-mail systems; arrested a week later and sentenced to 10 years.

Gary McKinnon (UK): Alleged by U.S. government to have pulled off "the biggest military computer hack of all time" in 2001–02; claimed to have just been looking for UFOs.

Jonathan James (USA, 1983–2008): Hacked into U.S. Department of Defense systems in 1999; arrested in 2000 and became **first juvenile convicted of a cybercrime**.

1 BILLION:
Estimated number of Web users blocked during the online protests.

Largest Internet protest

SOPA and PIPA (Stop Online Piracy Act and PROTECT IP Act) were two laws proposed in the U.S. Congress that led to widespread protest on the World Wide Web. On January 18, 2012, at least 115,000 Web sites took part by blacking out content or denying access to users. More than 162 million visitors to the English-language version of Wikipedia were greeted by a blocking page that encouraged U.S. users to contact their Congressional representative.

opened an attachment containing the malicious software. This new threat, known as drive-by spam, consists of html e-mails that automatically download malware by using a JavaScript.

Year with the most spam
According to IT security company Symantec, 89.1% of all e-mails sent globally were spam in 2010. This figure dropped to 75.1% in 2011 due to the closure of large botnets, including Rustock. The trend continued

for 2012, when spam accounted for 68% of e-mails. By comparison, 2001 saw just 8% of e-mails containing spam.

First reported rickroll
In May 2007, a URL purporting to link to the first trailer for video game *Grand Theft Auto IV* actually took Web users to the music video of 1980s pop star Rick Astley (UK) singing "Never Gonna Give You Up." This practice—known as "rickrolling"—gradually became a World Wide Web phenomenon, or "meme."

Largest coordinated rickroll protest

On February 10, 2008, in at least 90 cities worldwide, 6,000–8,000 masked members and supporters of the Internet activist group Anonymous gathered as part of Project Chanology, a series of protests against the Church of Scientology. Live rickrolls (*see main text*) were performed by protesters at centers owned by the Church in at least seven cities. Pictured are Anonymous members rallying in support of privacy and human rights in Marseille, France, in October 2012.

First political hacktivism
"Hacktivism" is the term used to describe protests using computer networks in line with a political goal. The first recorded instance of this occurred in October 1989, when computers owned by NASA and the U.S. Department of Energy were penetrated by the Worms Against Nuclear Killers worm. This attack is believed to have originated in Australia and occurred just days before the *Galileo* spacecraft carrying nuclear-powered generators was due to be launched by the space shuttle *Atlantis*.

FACT:
The masks worn by the "hacktivists" of Anonymous depict Guy Fawkes—a member of the Gunpowder Plot to blow up the British parliament in 1605. The mask was designed by artist David Lloyd for the graphic novel *V for Vendetta* by Alan Moore (winner of the **most Eisner Comic Awards**, with nine wins).

FOR THE RECORD
"Big Brother" has entered the language from British author George Orwell (1903–50). In his book *Nineteen Eighty-Four* (1949), Orwell's fictional state of Oceania is ruled with utter authority by a dictator (who may not actually be a single person) known as Big Brother. Part of his party's propaganda is the now-famous phrase "Big Brother is watching you."

Kevin Poulsen (USA): Sentenced to 51 months in jail in 1994 for mail and computer fraud; now a celebrated journalist and author.

Adrian Lamo (USA): Arrested in 2003 after hacking into various media companies' computer systems; served six months detention at his parents' home.

Kevin Mitnick (USA): Security consultant and hacker arrested by FBI in 1995 for wire and computer fraud; served five years in prison.

Michael Calce (Canada): Crippled sites, such as eBay, Amazon, and Yahoo, in 2000; spent eight months in a youth detention center.

Robert Tappan Morris (USA): Created the Morris worm (*see text*); first person convicted under the Computer Fraud and Abuse Act (1984).

PRISONS

Highest population on death row (country)

According to Amnesty International's Annual Report 2012, more than 8,000 prisoners were awaiting execution in Pakistan in 2011—well over twice the number in the USA. The last execution in Pakistan, however, was in 2008.

Largest prison (capacity)

The Silivri Penitentiaries Campus in Silivri, Turkey, houses dangerous criminals. Building started on the high-security prison in 2005 and was completed in 2008. It has capacity for 11,000 inmates but was reported to hold only 8,586 at the start of October 2012. There are 2,677 members of staff.

Largest prison island

Van Diemen's Land—known today as the Australian state of Tasmania—was used by the British as a penal colony in the early 19th century. The island has an area of 26,200 sq. miles (67,800 km²) and at one point housed around 75,000 convicts, representing 40%

Largest prison farm

Covering 18,000 acres (7,300 ha), the Louisiana State Penitentiary, which is surrounded on three sides by the Mississippi River, is a working prison farm in Louisiana, USA. Some 1,624 staff looked after 5,193 prisoners here in the fiscal year 2009–10, on an annual budget of $124,035,534. The farm houses the state's death row and execution chamber and is also the largest maximum-security prison in the USA.

of all the prisoners transported to Australia from the British Isles. Transportation to Van Diemen's Land ceased in 1853.

Largest jailbreak

On February 11, 1979, an Iranian employee of the Electronic Data Systems Corporation led a mob into Ghasr prison, Tehran, Iran, in an effort to rescue two American colleagues. Some 11,000 other inmates seized their chance and staged history's largest jailbreak.

The **largest jailbreak from death row** took place on May 31, 1984, when six inmates escaped from the Mecklenburg Correctional Center in Virginia, USA, pretending that they were removing a bomb. All were caught within a few days and executed over the next 12 years.

Longest-lasting escape

Leonard T. Fristoe (USA) escaped from the Nevada State Prison in Carson City, Nevada, USA, on December 15, 1923. He was turned in by his son on November 15, 1969, at Compton, California,

Largest jail

Rikers Island is the main jail complex for New York City, USA, and comprises 10 jails holding petty criminals, offenders in transit, those unable to get bail, and those serving sentences of one year or less. It has a capacity of nearly 15,000 inmates and is run by 10,432 staff on a budget of $1.08 billion as of 2012. Its average daily inmate population peaked in 2003 at 14,533. The average length of stay is 54 days.

Highest population of prisoners

According to the International Centre for Prison Studies, in 2011 the USA had a record prison population of 2,239,751, and a rate of 716 prisoners for every 100,000 residents— the **most prisoners per capita**. In absolute terms, China is second on the list with 1,640,000 prisoners, but this represents just 121 per 100,000.

BEHIND BARS
As of 2011, the official capacity of U.S. prisons was about 2,134,000; the USA's jails and state and federal prisons totaled 4,575.

FEWER FELONS
The Central African Republic and Comoros share the **lowest prison population rate** of 19 prisoners per 100,000 of the population.

PENAL LONGEVITY

Longest-serving prisoner on Alcatraz: Alvin Karpis (USA) spent 26 years as an inmate of Alcatraz prison in San Francisco Bay, California, USA, from August 1936 to April 1962.

Longest incarceration for a future head of state: Nelson Mandela (President of South Africa, 1994–99) was interned in three prisons from August 5, 1962 to February 11, 1990, a total of 27 years 6 months 6 days.

Longest imprisonment for a leader after being removed from power: Ex-Panamanian general Manuel Noriega (the de facto ruler of Panama from 1983 to 1989) has been imprisoned since his capture by U.S. military forces on January 4, 1990.

Longest-serving executioner: William Calcraft (UK, 1800–79) officiated at nearly every outdoor and indoor hanging at Newgate Prison, London, UK, for 45 years from 1829 to 1874.

Longest sentence for computer hacking: Brian Salcedo (USA) was sentenced to nine years in federal prison on December 16, 2004, for conspiracy and numerous hacking charges after trying to steal credit card information.

Smallest prison

The island of Sark is the smallest of the UK's four main Channel Islands and boasts its own prison, built in 1856. Its maximum capacity is two prisoners.

USA. By then, Leonard was 77 years old and had enjoyed nearly 46 years of freedom under the name of Claude R. Willis.

Most secure form of prison

"Supermax" prisons house the most dangerous criminals. Typically, prisoners stay in their cells, alone, for 23 hours a day with few opportunities for education or relaxation. Meals are passed through a slot in the door and any exercise takes place alone and in a confined area. Contact with staff, other prisoners, or the outside world is censored and minimal. Furniture is made of metal or concrete. Inmates wear handcuffs, belly chains, and leg shackles

when moved out of their cells and the prison's security measures include electronic sensors and laser beams, pressure pads, and the use of guard dogs.

The USA holds 25,000 prisoners in such facilities. No one has yet escaped from a supermax.

Largest prison complex (single building)

The Twin Towers Correctional Facility in Los Angeles, California, USA, has a floor area of 1.5 million sq. ft. (140,000 m²) and is built on a 10-acre (4-ha) site. It includes a medical services building, a transportation bureau, arraignment courts, and, of course, cells for inmates.

Largest prison ship

The largest operational prison ship facility is the 870-bed New York City Prison Barge—aka the Vernon C. Bain Center—situated on the East River in New York City, USA. It forms part of the Rikers Island jail complex. It cost $161 million to build and has been in New York since 1992.

Oldest prisoner released

In 1987, 84-year-old Brij Bihari Pandey (India), a Hindu priest, together with 15 accomplices, murdered four people. His trial lasted more than 20 years and he was handed down a life sentence in 2009. Due to difficulties with his ill health, however, he was released on humanitarian grounds from the Gorakhpur jail in Uttar Pradesh, India, at the age of 108, in June 2011. He died two months later on August 25, 2011.

Bill Wallace (Australia, 1881–1989) is the **oldest prisoner to die in prison**.

He spent the last 63 years of his life in Aradale psychiatric hospital at Ararat, Victoria, Australia, and remained there until his death on July 17, 1989, shortly before his 108th birthday.

Most prison transfers

Between being sentenced in 1971 and his death on September 12, 1998, Lawrence Doyle Conklin (USA) was transferred 117 times between 53 different prison facilities in the USA.

Highest death toll in a prison fire

On February 14–15, 2012, a fire at the Comayagua prison in central Honduras (outside the capital, Tegucigalpa) claimed the lives of at least 358 prisoners and others trapped inside.

Largest women's prison capacity

The Central California Women's Facility—located in Chowchilla, California, USA—is the largest prison dedicated exclusively to women. It is also home to all of California's female death row inmates. As of January 30, 2013, the facility was operating at more than 184.6% of its capacity, housing 3,700 inmates in a complex designed for 2,004 beds.

Longest sentence for playing a video game: In September 2002, Faiz Chopdat (UK) was jailed for four months for playing *Tetris* on his cell phone while on a flight home, "endangering the safety of an aircraft."

Longest period in solitary confinement: By April 17, 2013, Herman Wallace (*left*) and Albert Woodfox (both USA) had spent 41 years in solitary confinement, mainly in the State Penitentiary of Louisiana – known as the Angola Jail – in the USA.

Longest sentence (single count): In 1981, Dudley Wayne Kyzer (USA) was sentenced to 10,000 years for murdering his wife. He received two more life sentences for murdering his mother-in-law and a student.

Longest sentence resulting from an appeal: In 1994, Darron Bennalford Anderson (USA) was found guilty of a number of serious crimes and sentenced to 2,200 years. He appealed, was reconvicted, resentenced, and received an *additional* jail term of 9,000 years, later reduced by 500 years.

Longest time for a dog on death row: Word, a Lhasa Apso mix, was held on canine death row for 8 years 190 days, from May 4, 1993, following two biting incidents.

FARMS & AGRICULTURE

Most combine harvesters direct harvesting simultaneously

The greatest number of combine harvesters working together in one field is 208, achieved by Combines 4 Charity at Gerry Curran's farm, Duleek, County Meath, Ireland, on July 28, 2012.

CROPS AND CEREALS

First domesticated plants

There is some evidence to suggest that rice cultivation began in Korea 15,000 years ago. The oldest known domesticated plants, however, are the eight species of Neolithic founder crop, comprising the flax plant, four species of legume, and three species of cereal. Domesticated by early Holocene

Shortest donkey

KneeHi (b. October 2, 2007) is a brown jack who measured 2 ft. 1 in. (64.2 cm) to the top of the withers at Best Friends Farm in Gainesville, Florida, USA, on July 26, 2011. A registered miniature Mediterranean donkey, KneeHi is owned and cared for by Jim and Frankie Lee and their son Dylan (*pictured*).

400
Approximate top weight of mature miniatures in pounds.

farming communities in southwest Asia's Fertile Crescent region, they date back to 9500 BC.

In June 2006, researchers from Harvard University (USA) and Israel's Bar-Ilan University reported the discovery of nine carbonized figs dated to 11,200–11,400 years ago in an early Neolithic village called Gilgal I, near Jericho in Israel. Researchers believe this particular variety could have been cultivated only with human intervention, making figs the **oldest domesticated fruit crop** and among the first-known examples of agriculture.

Fastest time to plow an acre

The quickest confirmed time for plowing 1 acre (0.404 ha) according to the rules of the United Kingdom Society of Ploughmen is 9 min. 49.88 sec., achieved by Joe Langcake at Hornby Hall Farm in Brougham, Penrith, UK, on October 21, 1989. Joe used a Case IH 7140 Magnum tractor and a Kverneland four-furrow plow.

Most sugarcane cut by hand in eight hours

Roy Wallace (Australia) hand-cut a hefty 110,000 lb. (50 tonnes) of sugarcane in eight hours on October 9, 1961, at a sugar farm in Giru, Australia.

Greatest wheat yield

Mike Solari (New Zealand) harvested 14,000 lb. per acre (15.6 tonnes/ha) of wheat from

Most corn harvested in eight hours

James C (Jay) Justice III (USA) harvested an unprecedented 19,196.59 bushels of corn using one Caterpillar 485 Lexion combine at Catfish Bay Farm in Beckley, West Virginia, USA, on September 14, 2001.

21.9 acres (8.8 ha) on his farm in Otama, Gore, New Zealand, on March 8, 2010.

A yield of 11,000 lb. per acre (12.2 tonnes/ha) of winter barley from 52.6 acres (21.3 ha) was achieved at Stockton Park (Leisure) Limited's Edington Mains Farm in Chirnside, UK, on August 2, 1989, the **greatest barley yield**.

Largest breed of goose

The biggest breed of domestic goose is the African brown, or giant dewlap, goose. Mature ganders average 22 lb. (10 kg) in weight and stand taller than mature females, which average 17 lb. 10 oz. (8 kg).

MOST EXPENSIVE ...

Cow: $1.3 million

Alpaca: $675,000

Sheep: £231,000 ($369,000)

Bull: £126,000 ($199,000)

Draft horse: $112,000

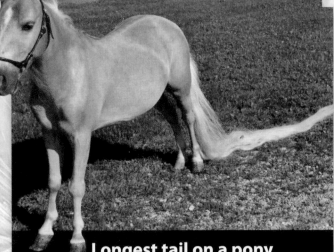

Longest tail on a pony

Golden Shante, aka Topper, a Shetland pony owned by Janine Sparks, has a tail that measured 13 ft. 5 in. (4.08 m) at Brookwood Farm in New Palestine, Indiana, USA, on July 24, 2010.

Largest crop circle

On May 17, 2005, a circle of flattened corn 180 ft. (55 m) in diameter, in the shape of the Bacardi Rum logo, appeared at Dalponte Farms—a large mint farm in Richland, New Jersey, USA. Bacardi buys mint from the farm to use in promotions for the rum-base drink mojito.

ANIMALS

First moose farm

An experimental moose farm was launched in 1949 by Yevgeny Knorre and the staff of the Pechora-Ilych Nature Reserve outside Yaksha in the Komi Republic (USSR, now Russia). However, the first farm entirely devoted to the domestication and rearing of the moose, primarily for milk and cheese production, is Kostroma Moose Farm in Kostroma Oblast, Russia, which was established in 1963. A herd of free-roaming semi-domesticated moose maintained there presently includes 10 to 15 milk-producing moose cows. More than 800 moose have lived on the farm during its existence.

Rarest breed of horse

The least common horse breed is the Abaco Barb. By July 2010, only five individuals existed, all of which were apparently infertile. Once common in The Bahamas, its demise is believed to be due to hunting for food and sport, and poisoning by farming pesticides.

Largest type of domestic turkey

The world's largest standard variety of domestic turkey is the broad breasted white. Adult males (toms) weigh 29–40 lb. (13.5–18 kg) at 20–24 weeks old, and hens at the same age weigh 14–20 lb. (6.5–9 kg).

On account of their size, however, they are unable to breed naturally and so have to be artificially inseminated. The **smallest standard domestic turkey** is the midget white. Adult males weigh around 13 lb. (6 kg), with females at 7–10 lb. (3.5–4.5 kg), making them little larger than the largest domestic chickens.

Heaviest calf

The heaviest live birthweight for a calf is 225 lb. (102 kg) for a Friesian cow at Rockhouse Farm, Bishopston, Swansea, UK, in 1961. The **lightest calf** was a Friesian heifer called Christmas, born on December 25, 1993 in Hutchinson, Minnesota, USA. Christmas weighed 9 lb. (4.1 kg) at birth.

Smallest breed of domestic duck

The call duck, which weighs less than 2 lb. 3 oz. (1 kg), derives its name from its original use. It was initially bred as a decoy to draw wild mallard ducks from the skies into the traps set for them in fens and marshes by hunters.

First cloned horse

The first cloned individual from the horse family, Equidae, was Idaho Gem, a domestic mule. Born on May 4, 2003, he was an identical genetic copy of his brother, Taz, who was a champion racing mule. This historic feat was achieved by adding nuclei from mule cells to eggs from a horse, and was accomplished by scientists from the University of Idaho, USA.

Most breeds for a domestic farm mammal

The domestic sheep (*Ovis aries*) has more breeds than any other species of domestic farm mammal. Worldwide, there are presently more than a thousand distinct breeds of domestic sheep.

Greatest milk yield by a cow in a lifetime

The highest recorded lifetime yield of milk by one cow is 478,163 lb. (216,891 kg) by Smurf—a Holstein cow owned by La Ferme Gillette, Inc., Dairy Farm (Canada) in Embrun, Ontario, Canada.

First domesticated rodent

The earliest domesticated rodent is the guinea pig, or South American cavy (*Cavia porcellus*), which was first bred and maintained as a food animal in the Andes as long ago as 5000 BC.

Goat: NZ$140,000 ($82,600)

Pig: $56,000

Sheepdog: £10,080 ($16,216)

Duck: $2,400

Virtual animal: $1,300 for a pheasant in the video game *FarmVille*

GARDEN GIANTS

Heaviest parsnip

A parsnip weighing in at 17 lb. 4.9 oz. (7.85 kg) was grown by root master David Thomas (UK) and shown at the Malvern Autumn Show at the Three Counties Showground in Worcestershire, UK, on September 23, 2011. "The parsnip is ugly, but it's the biggest!," said David.

Farms Ltd. in Maidstone, Kent, UK, weighed in August 2008.
- **Broccoli:** 35 lb. (15.87 kg), grown by John and Mary Evans of Palmer, Alaska, USA, in 1993.
  - **Celery:** 74 lb. 12 oz. (33.9 kg), grown by Ian Neale (UK), weighed on September 23, 2011 at the Malvern Autumn Show in Worcestershire, UK.
- **Cherry:** 0.76 oz. (21.69 g), grown by Gerardo Maggipinto (Italy), weighed on June 21, 2003.
  - **Cucumber:** 27 lb. 5.3 oz. (12.4 kg), grown by Alfred J. Cobb (UK), presented at the National Amateur Gardening Show's UK National Giant Vegetables Championship in Shepton Mallet, Somerset, UK, on September 5, 2003.
- **Garlic:** 2 lb. 10 oz. (1.19 kg), grown by Robert Kirkpatrick of Eureka, California, USA, in 1985.

Heaviest cabbage

Scott A. Robb's (USA) colossal cabbage tipped the scales at 138.25 lb. (62.71 kg) when presented at the Alaska State Fair in Palmer, Alaska, USA, on August 31, 2012. On hearing the news, Robb exclaimed, "I've been doing it for 21, 22 years and finally I reach the top of the mountain!"

HEAVIEST ...

- **Apple:** 4 lb. 1 oz. (1.849 kg), grown and picked by Chisato Iwasaki (Japan) at his apple farm in Hirosaki City, Japan, on October 24, 2005.
- **Avocado:** 4 lb. 13 oz. (2.19 kg), grown by Gabriel Ramirez Nahim (Venezuela), weighed on January 28, 2009 in Caracas, Venezuela.
- **Beet:** 51 lb. 9.4 oz. (23.4 kg), presented by Ian Neale (UK) of Southport, Wales, UK, at the UK National Giant Vegetables Championship in Shepton Mallet, Somerset, UK, on September 7, 2001.
- **Blueberry:** 0.4 oz (11.28 g), grown by Polana SPZOO in Parczew, Poland, for Winterwood

Largest pumpkin sculpture

Ray Villafane (USA) carved a zombie apocalypse from two giant pumpkins—weighing 1,818 lb. 5 oz. (824.86 kg) and 1,693 lb. (767.9 kg)—in New York, USA, on October 22–23, 2011.

- **Lemon:** 11 lb. 9.7 oz. (5.26 kg), grown by Aharon Shemoel (Israel) in Kfar Zeitim, Israel, weighed on January 8, 2003.
  - **Marrow:** 206.5 lb. (93.7 kg), presented by Bradley Wursten (Netherlands) at the Dutch Giant Vegetable

2,009
Weight in pounds of the **heaviest pumpkin**, grown in 2012 by Ron Wallace (USA, *pictured inset left*).

Championship in Sliedrecht, South Holland, Netherlands, on September 26, 2009.
- **Pear:** 6 lb. 8 oz. (2.95 kg), grown by JA Aichi Toyota Nashi Bukai (Japan) in Toyota, Aichi, Japan, on November 11, 2011.
- **Pineapple:** 18 lb. 4 oz. (8.28 kg), grown by Christine McCallum (Australia) in Bakewell, Australia, harvested in November 2011.
- **Plum:** 11.42 oz. (323.77 g), grown by Minami-Alps City JA Komano Section Kiyo (Japan), measured in Minami-Alps, Yamanashi, Japan, on July 24, 2012.
- **Potato:** 10 lb. 14 oz. (4.98 kg), grown by Peter Glazebrook (UK, *see box right*), weighed at the National Gardening Show, Royal Bath & West Showground in Shepton Mallet, Somerset, UK, on September 4, 2011.
- **Pumpkin:** *See left*.

GREAT OUTDOORS

Longest lawn mower ride: Gary Hatter (USA) rode 14,594.5 miles (23,487.5 km) in 260 days from Portland, Maine, to Daytona Beach, Florida, USA, between May 2000 and February 14, 2001.

Largest garden spade: Yeoman Quality Garden Products (UK) presented a spade measuring 12 ft. 9 in. (3.90 m) tall in Droitwich, UK, on October 4, 2011.

Largest garden gnome: Ron Hale (Canada) made a gnome of his own—25 ft. 11 in. (7.91 m) tall—in 1998.

Largest bird nest box: The Heighley Gate Nursery and Garden Centre built a 6-ft. 10-in.-tall (2.1-m) nest box at Morpeth, UK, in January 2008.

Fastest shed: Edd China's "Gone to Speed" was clocked traveling at 58.41 mph (94 km/h) in Milan, Italy, on April 1, 2011.

TALLEST FRUIT & VEG PLANTS ...

TYPE	HEIGHT	GROWER	YEAR
Basil	10 ft. 11.5 in. (3.34 m)	Anastasia Grigoraki (Greece)	2012
Bean plant	46 ft. 3 in. (14.1 m)	Staton Rorie (USA)	2003
Brussels sprout	9 ft. 3 in. (2.8 m)	Patrice & Steve Allison (USA)	2001
Celery	9 ft. (2.74 m)	Joan Priednieks (UK)	1998
Collard	13 ft. 4 in. (4.06 m)	Woodrow Wilson Granger (USA)	2007
Eggplant	18 ft. 0.5 in. (5.50 m)	Abdul Masfoor (India)	1998
Kale	18 ft. 2 in. (5.54 m)	Gosse Haisma (Australia)	1987
Paddy plant	9 ft. 2 in. (2.8 m)	Tanaji Nikam (India)	2005
Papaya tree	44 ft. (13.4 m)	Prasanta Mal (India)	2003
Parsley	7 ft. 9.38 in. (2.37 m)	David Brenner (USA)	2009
Pepper, sweet	16 ft. (4.87 m)	Laura Liang (USA)	1999
Sugarcane	31 ft. (9.5 m)	M. Venkatesh Gowda (India)	2005
Sweet corn	35 ft. 3 in. (10.74 m)	Jason Karl (USA)	2011
Tomato	65 ft. (19.8 m)	Nutriculture Ltd. (UK)	2000

www.guinnessworl...

GUINNESS WORLD RECORDS 2014

¡QUOTE
"I make my own compost from grass clippings, leaf mold, and potatoes. Potatoes have particular strength—they have an awful lot of nutrients."

Longest cucumber

Ian Neale of Wales, UK, grew a cucumber measuring 42.1 in. (107 cm), as presented in show on September 26, 2011. His rutabaga (*see below right*) caught the eye of rapper and horticulturalist Snoop Dogg (USA), who asked the green-thumbed whiz to his October 2011 Cardiff show to swap gardening tips!

• **Radish:** 68 lb. 9 oz. (31.1 kg), grown by Manabu Oono (Japan), weighed on February 9, 2003 in Kagoshima, Japan.

• **Rutabaga:** 85 lb. 12 oz. (38.92 kg), grown by Ian Neale (UK), weighed at the National Gardening Show in Shepton Mallet, Somerset, UK, on September 4, 2011.
• **Soursop:** 8.14 lb. (3.69 kg), grown by Ken Verosko (USA) in Hawaii, USA, measured on June 8, 2010.
• **Squash:** 1,486 lb. 9 oz. (674.31 kg), grown by Joel Jarvis (Canada), weighed on October 1, 2011 at the Port Elgin Pumpkinfest in Ontario, Canada.
• **Strawberry:** 8.14 oz. (231 g), grown by G. Andersen of Folkestone, Kent, UK, in 1983.

Tallest sunflower

A soaring sunflower grown by Hans-Peter Schiffer (Germany) attained a height of 27 ft. (8.23 m) in Kaarst, Germany, on September 4, 2012. The Lufthansa flight attendant broke his own 2009 record by 8 in (20.32 cm).

Heaviest onion

Peter Glazebrook (UK) shed no tears at presenting an onion weighing 18 lb. 1 oz. (8.195 kg) at the Harrogate Flower Show in North Yorkshire, UK, on September 13, 2012. That day, he also offered up the **longest beet** at 21 ft. (640.5 cm).

118
Average maximum height in inches for varieties of the sunflower.

FOR BIG STUFF TURN TO P. 96

Largest medicinal herb garden: The Guangxi Botanical Garden of Medicinal Plants occupies 498 acres (201.57 ha) and boasts 5,600 varieties of herbs in Nanning City, Guangxi Province, China.

Largest vertical garden: A wall of greenery in Seoul City Hall, South Korea, rose over 16,318 sq. ft. (1,516 m²) when completed on August 31, 2012.

Longest beach garden: The beach at Santos, Brazil, is bordered by a garden that is 3.3 miles (5.3 km) long with a total area of 2,355,143 sq. ft. (218,800 m²).

Garden with most species of tallest trees: The Royal Botanic Gardens in Kew, London, UK, has the tallest known specimen of 138 species of tree.

Largest scented garden: A fragrance garden for the blind covers 88.9 acres (36 ha) at the Kirstenbosch National Botanical Garden on Table Mountain, Cape Town, South Africa.

Most densely populated city

According to the ninth annual edition of the *Demographia World Urban Areas*, published in March 2013, Dhaka in Bangladesh has an estimated population of 14,399,000 people, living in an area of around 125 sq. miles (324 km²). This results in a population density of 115,250 citizens per sq. mile (44,500 citizens per km²).

In this photograph, a massively overcrowded train leaves Dhaka airport rail station ahead of the Muslim festival of Eid al-Adha (also known as the "Festival of Sacrifice"), which takes place at the end of the *hajj*, or pilgrimage to the holy Muslim city of Mecca in Saudi Arabia. Bangladeshi Muslims around the world celebrate by slaughtering sheep, goats, cows, and camels to commemorate the Prophet Abraham's willingness to sacrifice his son Ismail at God's command.

HEART OF ISLAM
The *hajj* draws an average of 2 million people a year, from 140 countries—the **most Muslim pilgrims**. Every Muslim is expected to make the journey at least once in his or her life.

CITY OF THE FUTURE

Imagining the way we will live

Over time, our cities will expand and house more and more people. These urban landscapes will need more energy and more food, new kinds of transport and architecture, and will need to be environmentally sustainable. What will these metropolises look like, and how will they function? For centuries, architects and urban designers have tried to imagine the cities of the future. Here, we look at seven aspects of urban planning and offer an insight into what may be in store—in fact, some of the more extraordinary visions here are already with us!

Transportation

As cities grow and become more complex, traveling could become more time-consuming; pollution levels may well rise, too. One option may lie in evacuated tube transport: capsule-carriages that run in vacuum tubes. There are currently proposals in China for buses that straddle over cars passing underneath (*above*). Meanwhile, vehicles such as the electric Hiriko Fold (*below*), the **first folding car** to enter production, are helping to reduce the impact on the environment and reduce the size of parking spaces.

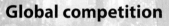

8 ft. 7 in.   6 ft. 9 in.

Global competition

As we become more globally connected, many cities will have to compete with each other to attract residents, businesses, and visitors. Air passengers are predicted to more than double by 2030, so airport connections will become vital.

Eye-catching, iconic buildings also help cities to compete. Examples include the world's **first twisted skyscraper**, the HSB Turning Torso (*above left*) in Malmö, Sweden (2005). Special tourist attractions raise a city's profile, too, such as the 250-acre (101-ha) "Gardens by the Bay" park (*above*) in Singapore (2012). Cities also enhance their prestige by hosting major sporting events, such as the FIFA World Cup and the Olympic Games, both of which are next being staged in Rio de Janeiro, Brazil.

MARTIAN FRONTIER

Mars500, the **longest high-fidelity spaceflight simulation**, ran from 2007 to 2011 in Russia and was an experiment to assess the feasibility of manned missions to Mars.

Planning sustainable communities will be a major priority in the years to come. The main picture on these pages shows a projection for Tianjin Eco-City, a 11.5-sq.-mile (30-km²) site being built some 24.8 miles (40 km) from the centre of Tianjin in China. Designed by Surbana Urban Planning Group, the city will be powered partly through renewable energy sources; desalination and recycled water will cater for at least half of the city's water needs. To minimize carbon emissions, the primary form of transport will be a light-rail transit system, and a waste recycling scheme will also be put in place. It will house an estimated 350,000 people and should be completed in the 2020s.

Extraterrestrial homes

Could we live beyond Earth? A current project by architects Foster and Partners and the European Space Agency is investigating how 3D printing techniques might allow us to construct buildings on the Moon from regolith (lunar soil). Simulated regolith and vacuum chambers have already been used to create mock-ups. Plans are for a four-person residence to shelter inhabitants from dramatic temperature changes, meteorites, and gamma radiation, to be sited at the Moon's southern pole with near-perpetual sunlight on the horizon.

4

Urban designs

The **largest construction by capacity** is currently the Abraj Al Bait Towers (*inset*) in Mecca, Saudi Arabia—a series of towers designed to house 65,000 people. Fantastical urban designs for future architecture, however, have included the 750,000-resident Shimizu Pyramid (*above*) in Tokyo, Japan, proposed in 2004 to be built using nanotube technology. Still on the drawing board are proposals by Foster and Partners for the 26.9-million-sq.-ft. (2.5-million-m^2) Crystal Island in Moscow, Russia, intended to house 30,000 people under one roof.

5

Taller skyscrapers

The **tallest building** today is the 2,716-ft.-high (828-m) Burj Khalifa in Dubai, UAE. But future skyscrapers may climb far higher. Sky City One (*left*), proposed for Changsha in Hunan Province, China, is planned to reach 2,749 ft. (838 m). And the Kingdom Tower in Jeddah, Saudi Arabia, is designed to go beyond 3,280 ft. (1,000 m)!

6

Sustainability

One of the most complex challenges for future cities is how to be sustainable and ecologically minded. New cities will need to utilize sources of alternative energy, such as that from wind, water, and the Sun. The **highest-capacity wind farm** is the Roscoe Wind Farm (*above*) in Texas, USA, with 627 separate wind turbines generating up to 781.5 MW as of 2011. The first billboard that can extract fresh water from humidity in the air recently opened in Lima, Peru (*above right*).

BESPOKE ADVERTISING

Some billboards are now fitted with "perceptive media": face-, gender-, and age-recognition software to assess our tastes.

7

Digital cities

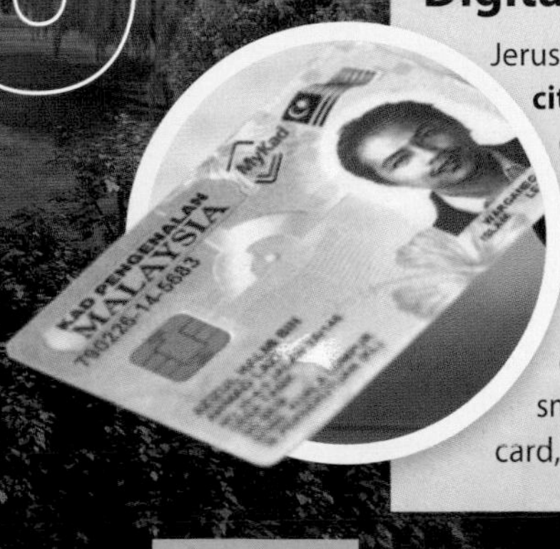

Jerusalem in Israel became the **first fully wi-fi-enabled city** in 2004, and as cities become more digitally connected through ultra high-speed broadband, smartphones, and other communications devices, they will become covered in a largely invisible layer of digital data. This data layer may not change cities a great deal physically, but it will have a massive effect on citizens. Malaysia's MyKad (*left*) is already with us—a smartcard that works as a combined driving licence, ATM card, digital wallet, public transport ticket, and security key.

URBAN SPACES

First Dark Sky City

To protect the view from the Lovell Observatory in Flagstaff, Arizona, USA, the citizens of Flagstaff agreed to tighten regulations regarding light pollution, and in 2001 it was named the first International Dark Sky City.

City with the largest gambling revenue

More than $38 billion was generated by the 35 casinos and other gaming services in Macau, China, in 2012.

Most costly office location

According to research by real-estate firm CBRE released in December 2012, office space in central Hong Kong, China, cost $2,651.24 per m^2 per annum, which is $246.30 per sq. ft.

Largest restaurant

Built in 2002 at a cost of $40 million, the Bawabet Dimashq Restaurant (Damascus Gate Restaurant) in Damascus, Syria, has 6,014 seats. It boasts a 26,909-sq.-ft. (2,500-m^2) kitchen and employs up to 1,800 staff during its busiest periods.

Highest density of white-marble-clad buildings

The Turkmenistan government has redeveloped an 8.5-sq.-mile (22-km^2) area in Ashgabat, its capital, which now boasts 543 new buildings covered with 48,583,619 sq. ft. (4,513,584 m^2) of white marble. The city also has the **most fountain pools in a public place**: 27, as of June 2008, covering 36.5 acres (14.8 ha).

Busiest airport for domestic and international passengers

According to the Airports Council International (ACI), 92,365,860 people flew in or out of Hartsfield-Jackson Atlanta International Airport in Atlanta, Georgia, USA, in 2011.

First buses

The earliest municipal motor omnibus service was inaugurated on April 12, 1903, and ran between Eastbourne railroad station and Meads in East Sussex, UK.

OLDEST BICYCLE PATH

Ocean Parkway in Brooklyn, New York City, USA, was constructed in 1880, following proposals by Frederick Law Olmsted and Calvert Vaux. The pedestrian path was divided to create a separate bicycle path in 1894, and was designated a historic landmark in 1975.

CROWD PLEASER

The Plaza México may be big but the **largest stadium crowd ever** was 199,854 people at a soccer game in the Maracanã Stadium in Rio de Janeiro, Brazil, on July 16, 1950.

Largest bullring

Capable of seating 41,262 people, the largest bullring is Plaza México in Mexico City, Mexico, which opened on February 5, 1946. It covers a total area of 15,629 sq. ft. (1,452 m^2) and has a diameter of 141 ft (43 m). Although primarily used for bullfighting, the arena also hosts boxing matches and concerts.

Oldest museum

The Royal Armouries Museum in the Tower of London, UK, opened its doors to the public in 1660.

Shortest stretch of prohibited parking

A 17-in. (43-cm) stretch of double yellow lines can be found in Stafford Street, Norwich, UK, between a permit parking area for residents and a two-hour waiting zone.

Largest automated parking facility

The Emirates Financial Towers in Dubai, UAE, has an automated parking facility that can store 1,191 autos. It occupies an internal area of 297,150 sq. ft. (27,606 m^2). The parking system is capable of multiple, simultaneous rapid pallet movements and is programmed to control a peak capacity of 360 vehicles per hour. It was completed on June 26, 2011.

Smallest movie house (seats)

The Palast Kino in Radebeul, Germany, has only nine seats. Owned by Johannes Gerhardt (Germany), it opened with Smoke (Germany/USA/Japan, 1995) on October 30, 2006.

TOP 10 MOST LIVABLE CITIES

Source: The Economist Intelligence Unit's global "livability" study. Ratings based on factors including crime rates, transport links, education, freedom of speech, climate, and medical care.

1. Melbourne, Victoria, Australia: 97.5%

2. Vienna, Austria: 97.4%

3. Vancouver, British Columbia, Canada: 97.3%

4. Toronto, Ontario, Canada: 97.2%

=5. Calgary, Alberta, Canada: 96.6%

Widest avenue

Construction of the Avenida 9 de Julio began in Buenos Aires, Argentina, in 1935 and was mostly completed by the 1960s. Its 16 lanes of traffic plus landscaped medians spans some 361 ft. (110 m), occupying more than an entire city block.

Square

Merdeka Square in Jakarta, Indonesia, measures some 9.1 million sq. ft. (850,000 m²)—twice the size of Vatican City, or 1.25 times the size of Disneyland in Anaheim, California, USA.

LONGEST ...

Beer garden

On August 7, 2011, Präsenta GmbH and the Internationales Berliner Bierfestival (both Germany) created a 5,971-ft.-long (1,820-m) beer garden in Berlin, Germany.

Pier

The original wooden pier at Southend-on-Sea in Essex, UK, was opened in 1830 and extended in 1846. The present iron pier is 1.34 miles (2.15 km) long and was opened on July 8, 1889.

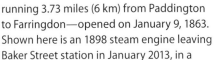

First underground railroad

The first section of the London Underground, UK—a stretch of the Metropolitan Line running 3.73 miles (6 km) from Paddington to Farringdon—opened on January 9, 1863. Shown here is an 1898 steam engine leaving Baker Street station in January 2013, in a re-creation of the first journey on the line.

LARGEST ...

Fountain

The musical fountain at Dadaepo Beach in Busan, South Korea, measures 27,114 sq. ft. (2,519 m²), an area of nearly 10 tennis courts, and was built by the Saha-gu District on May 30, 2009. The water reaches 180 ft. 5 in. (55 m) high and there are 1,046 nozzles and 1,148 lights.

Highway system

The cumulative length of China's National Trunk Highway System (NTHS) came to at least 61,121 miles (98,364 km) by the end of 2012.

Library

The Library of Congress in Washington, D.C., USA, contains more than 151.8 million items. These include some 66.6 million manuscripts, 34.5 million books, 13.4 million photographs, 5.4 million maps, and 3.3 million sound recordings, all kept on about 838 miles (1,349 km) of shelves.

LARGEST TIRE PARK

Nishi Rokugo Koen in Tokyo, Japan, is the largest playground made from old auto tires—more than 3,000 were used to create giant robots, model dinosaurs, swings, tunnels, and climbing frames. It opened in 1969.

Largest indoor theme park

Ferrari World Abu Dhabi on Yas Island, Abu Dhabi, United Arab Emirates, opened on November 4, 2010 and covers 7,534,737 sq. ft. (700,000 m²). The centered 925,700-sq.-ft. (86,000-m²) area lies under a 2,152,700-sq.-ft. (200,000-m²), 64-ft.-high (50-m) roof. Shown below are visitors riding in miniature Ferraris on the opening day.

Urban canal system

Birmingham, UK, has 114 miles (183.5 km) of navigable waterways. Originally 174 miles (280 km) long, the system was begun in 1759.

Walkway

The 4.5-mile-long (7.2-km) Bayshore Boulevard runs alongside Upper Hillsborough Bay in Tampa, Florida, USA. It follows the seawall from Columbus Statue Park to Gandy Boulevard without interruption.

HIT THE ROOF

You could cover 16,750 Ferraris with the aluminum on the roof. The Ferrari logo alone is 213 ft. (65 m) long and covers 32,290 sq. ft. (3,000 m²).

=5. Adelaide, South Australia: 96.6%

7. Sydney, New South Wales, Australia: 96.1%

8. Helsinki, Finland: 96.0%

9. Perth, Western Australia: 95.9%

10. Auckland, New Zealand: 95.7%

TALLEST BUILDINGS

First cut-stone pyramid

The Step Pyramid at Saqqara in Egypt, was built in 2750 BC to entomb the mummified body of the pharaoh Djoser. Once clad in polished white limestone, it was the largest building in the world in its time, rising to 204 ft. (62 m) high with a base of more than 12,917 sq. ft. (1,200 m²).

First skyscraper

The Home Insurance Building in Chicago, Illinois, USA, was erected in 1884–85. The so-called "Father of the Skyscraper" was just 10 stories tall, with its peak at 138 ft. (42 m). Skyscrapers use a steel framework strong enough to support an outer skin made of stone.

Highest mosque

The King Abdullah mosque on the 77th floor of the Kingdom Center building in Riyadh, Saudi Arabia, is 600 ft. (183 m) above ground level and was completed on July 5, 2004.

DEEPEST FOUNDATIONS FOR A BUILDING

The foundations of the Petronas Towers in Kuala Lumpur, Malaysia, are 394 ft. (120 m) deep. The 1,482-ft. 7-in.-tall (451.9-m) towers were the world's tallest building from 1998 to 2004, until overtaken by the 1,666-ft. (508-m) Taipei 101 in Chinese Taipei.

Tallest wooden structure

The 387-ft. (118-m) wooden truss tower in Gliwice, Poland, is the tallest wooden structure currently standing. It was constructed in 1935 and was originally used for radio transmissions, but today it forms part of a cell phone network.

Highest planetarium

The planetarium at the Kōriyama City Fureai Science Center in Fukushima, Japan, is located 342 ft. (104.25 m) above the ground on floors 23 and 24 of the Big-i building. Opened in 2001, the planetarium consists of a tilted dome 75 ft. (23 m) in diameter.

Highest swimming pool

The Ritz-Carlton hotel at the top of the International Commerce Centre (ICC) building in Hong Kong, China, has a swimming pool and spa located on the 188th floor, at a height of 1,556 ft. (474.4 m) above the ground.

TALLEST UNOCCUPIED BUILDING

Construction of the Ryugyong Hotel in Pyongyang, North Korea, was halted in 1992 just after it reached 1,082 ft. (330 m). Since then, the 105-floor shell has remained empty. Building work resumed in April 2008, but at the time of going to press no opening date had been announced.

TALLEST ...

Movie theater

The tallest movie theater complex in the world is the UGC cinema in Glasgow, UK, with an overall height of 203 ft. (62 m). Opening its doors on September 21, 2001, it stands 12 stories high, houses 18 screens, and has a seating capacity of 4,277.

Tallest tower

Japan's Tokyo Sky Tree, formerly known as New Tokyo Tower, rises 2,080 ft. (634 m) to the top of its mast, making it around twice as tall as the Eiffel Tower in Paris, France. Located in Sumida, Tokyo, it opened in May 2012 and serves as a broadcasting and observation tower, and also houses a restaurant. The city's previous broadcasting tower, Tokyo Tower, was no longer tall enough to give complete digital terrestrial TV coverage because it is surrounded by many high-rise buildings.

TOP 10 CITIES WITH THE MOST SKYSCRAPERS

1. Hong Kong, China: 2,354 buildings taller than 328 ft. (100 m), with a combined height of 1,095,262 ft. (333,836 m).

2. New York City, USA: 794 buildings taller than 328 ft., with a combined height of 359,973 ft. (109,720 m).

3. Tokyo, Japan: 556 buildings taller than 328 ft., with a combined height of 239,527 ft. (73,008 m).

4. Shanghai, China: 430 buildings taller than 328 ft., with a combined height of 196,712 ft. (59,958 m).

5. Dubai, UAE: 403 buildings taller than 328 ft., with a combined height of 217,349 ft. (66,248 m).

Tallest building

The Burj Khalifa is 2,716 ft. (828 m) tall. It was developed by Emaar Properties and officially opened in Dubai, UAE, on January 4, 2010. The tower incorporates the **most floors in a building** (160), and is also the **tallest manmade structure ever built on land**.

Leaning tower

The Montreal Olympic Stadium tower in Montreal, Canada, measures 541 ft. (165 m) tall and has a curved angle of 45°. Completed in 1987, the tower is designed to support 75% of the weight of the roof of the main building. While this tower's incline is intentional, the building with the **farthest unintentional lean** is not the famous Leaning Tower of Pisa

TALLEST CONCRETE STRUCTURE

Completed in 2009, the 92-story Trump International Hotel & Tower in Chicago, Illinois, USA, peaks at 1,170 ft. (356 m), or 1,389 ft. (423 m) with the building's spire. The complex houses 486 residential apartments and a 339-room hotel.

TALLEST HOSPITAL

Hong Kong Sanatorium & Hospital—Li Shu Pui building in Happy Valley, Hong Kong, China, stands 487 ft. (148.5 m) tall. The 38-story concrete-and-steel structure was completed in three phases between 1988 and 2008, and has more than 400 beds.

in Italy but the bell tower of the protestant church in Suurhusen, Germany, which leans with an angle of inclination of 5.19° (Pisa leans at just 3.97°).

Lighthouse

Yokohama Marine Tower at Yamashita Park in Yokohama, Japan, is a steel lighthouse that stands 348 ft. (106 m) high. It has a power of 600,000 candelas and a visibility range of 20 miles (32 km), and has an observatory located 328 ft. (100 m) above ground. It was built to mark the 100th anniversary of the first recorded trade between Yokohama and the West in 1854.

FOR THE RECORD

From the 13th century to the end of the 19th century, the world's tallest building was always a church or a cathedral. This pattern was broken in 1901 with the construction of the 548-ft.-tall (167-m) Philadelphia City Hall, USA.

Opera house

The 45-story Civic Opera House in Chicago, Illinois, USA, is an imposing 555-ft.-tall (169-m) limestone skyscraper that can accommodate 3,563 people.

Pyramid

Also known as the Great Pyramid, the pyramid of Khufu at Giza in Egypt was 481 ft. (146.7 m) tall when completed 4,500 years ago; erosion and vandalism have reduced its height to 451 ft. (137.5 m) today.

Steel structure building

Willis Tower in Chicago, Illinois, USA, is a 1,451-ft.-tall (442-m), 108-story office skyscraper

Tallest cemetery

The permanently illuminated Memorial Necrópole Ecumênica in Santos, near São Paulo, Brazil, is 14 stories high and rises 150 ft. (46 m) above ground. The first burial took place here on July 28, 1984. The inset photograph shows additional buildings currently being constructed to make the cemetery even taller.

Tallest wooden pagoda

The Tianning Pagoda in Changzhou, China, stands 504 ft. (153.79 m) high and was completed in 2007. This 13-story pagoda, topped with a soaring golden pinnacle, occupies about 290,625 sq. ft. (27,000 m²) and cost an estimated 300 million yuan ($41 million) to build.

constructed from steel and weighing 444 million lb. (201,848 tonnes). The design incorporates nine steel-unit square tubes in a 3 x 3 tube arrangement. Completed in 1974, it has 4.56 million sq. ft. (423,637 m²) of floor space.

University building

Constructed between 1949 and 1953, the M. V. Lomonosov Moscow State University on Sparrow Hills, south of Moscow, Russia, stands 787 ft. (240 m) tall.

Water tower

The water spheroid at Edmond, Oklahoma, USA, built in 1986, rises to a height of 218 ft. (66.5 m) and has a capacity of 500,077 gal. (1,893,000 liters). The tower was manufactured by CB&I (Chicago Bridge & Iron Company).

Windmill

The tallest *working* traditional windmill is De Noordmolen (now a restaurant) at Schiedam, Netherlands, at 109 ft. (33.33 m).

6. Bangkok, Thailand: 355 buildings taller than 328 ft., with a combined height of 159,898 ft. (48,737 m).

7. Chicago, USA: 341 buildings taller than 328 ft., with a combined height of 158,927 ft. (48,441 m).

8. Guangzhou, China: 295 buildings taller than 328 ft., with a combined height of 140,633 ft. (42,865 m).

9. Seoul, South Korea: 282 buildings taller than 328 ft., with a combined height of 128,963 ft. (39,308 m).

10. Kuala Lumpur, Malaysia: 244 buildings taller than 328 ft., with a combined height of 111,663 ft. (34,035 m).

SHOPPING

Largest online store

Amazon (USA) is the largest online store by revenue, with net sales in 2012 of $61.09 billion. The store has a market value of $119 billion and is ranked 525th in the *Forbes* Global 2000 list of the world's largest companies.

First upside down store

Viktor & Rolf, the Netherlands-base fashion house, created the world's first upside down shop in Milan, Italy, in 2005. Customers enter through an upside down door and encounter chandeliers spouting from the floor, chairs on the parquet-covered ceiling, and even inverted fireplaces. It was created by Dutch owners Viktor Horsting and Rolf Snoeren with Buro Tettero and SZI Design.

LARGEST ...

Commercial building

In terms of floor area, the world's largest commercial building under one roof is the flower-auction building Bloemenveiling Aalsmeer in Aalsmeer, Netherlands. The floor surface of the building measures (8.423 million sq. ft. (782,599 m²), enough floor space to accommodate 14 Great Pyramids.

Department store

The Shinsegae ("New World") department store at Centum City in the Haeundae-gu district of Busan, South Korea, covers

Oldest candy shop

The aptly named "Oldest Sweet Shop in England" in Pateley Bridge, North Yorkshire, UK, first opened its doors in 1827 and has sold candies continuously right up to the present day. (The "1661" on the lintel refers to the date of the building.) Most of the candies are still made in traditional copper pans and using molds that are, in some cases, more than 100 years old.

Largest online music store

By October 2011, Apple's iTunes Store had sold more than 16 billion songs for digital download. By late 2012, it had more than 400 million active purchasers, accounting for 29% of all worldwide music sales.

3.16 million sq. ft. (293,905 m²)—an area equivalent to more than 50 soccer fields. The store opened on March 3, 2009 and, in addition to its luxury brand concessions, contains a spa, a roof garden, and a 60-tee golf driving range.

In-store shop facade

The three-story Galeries Lafayette (France) store, in the Morocco Mall in Casablanca, Morocco, has an in-store shop facade covering a total area of 36,402.68 sq. ft. (3,381.92 m²). The store, developed and managed by Groupe Aksal (Morocco), was designed by Davide

Padoa of Design International (UK) and inaugurated in November 2011.

Illuminated facade

Mall Taman Anggrek in Grogol Petamburan, West Jakarta, Indonesia, has a curved continuous LED-illuminated facade that covers 93,380 sq. ft. (8,675.3 m²) and displays full-color animated video images. At night, the whole front wall of the building glows with the light of 862,920 pixels. The installation was completed on February 29, 2012.

First shopping mall

The world's first shopping mall—that is, a large number of separate stores grouped together under a covered roof—was at Trajan's Forum in ancient Rome, Italy. Designed by architect Apollodorus of Damascus and built between AD 100 and 112, the forum included a market area with 150 stores and offices arranged over six gallery levels.

TOP 10 LARGEST STORES BY GROSS LEASABLE AREA

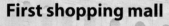

1. New South China Mall
Dongguan, China
6.4 million sq. ft. (600,153 m²)

2. Golden Resources Mall
Beijing, China
6 million sq. ft. (557,419 m²)

3. SM City North Edsa
Quezon City, Philippines
5.19 million sq. ft. (482,878 m²)

4. 1 Utama
Selangor, Malaysia
5 million sq. ft. (465,000 m²)

5. CentralWorld
Bangkok, Thailand
4.62 million sq. ft. (429,500 m²)

Shopping bag

A cloth bag measuring 275 ft. (83.82 m) high (minus handles) and 125 ft. (38.10 m) wide was made by Raj Bahadur (India) and displayed in Ghaziabad, India, in February 2009.

The **largest paper shopping bag** was presented by the hypermarket chain Kaufland (Romania) in Bucharest, Romania, on May 18, 2009. The bag—made from recycled paper—measured 13 ft. 8 in. x 21 ft. 8 in. x 5 ft. 10 in. (4.18 x 6.62 x 1.79 m).

Price tag

A price tag measuring 11 ft. 9 in. (3.60 m) long and 16 ft. 7 in. (5.07 m) wide was made by Forum Ankara Outlet and Media Markt in Ankara, Turkey, on March 28, 2010. The giant tag was hung from an ad for a refrigerator outside the mall.

Motorized shopping cart

Monster Kart is an oversize cart constructed by Frederick Reifsteck

Highest annual revenue for a department store

Harrods in London, UK, reported a revenue of £1.01 billion ($1.63 billion) for the year ending January 29, 2011. The iconic department store—the largest in Europe—was acquired by Qatar Holdings in 2010 for a reported £1.5 billion ($2.3 billion).

FOR THE RECORD

Harrods is the store of choice if you want to buy record-breaking items, such as the **most expensive bathtub**—a £530,000 ($845,000) tub cut from a 20,000-lb. (9.07-tonne) Amazonian crystal stone!

(USA) from stainless steel and fitted with a 900-hp 454 Chevrolet motor. The motorized and drivable cart measures 27 ft. (8.23 m) long, 15 ft. (4.57 m) tall, and 8 ft. (2.43 m) wide and was displayed at South Wales, New York, USA, on April 2, 2012. (For the **largest shopping cart**, see p. 97.)

The **fastest motorized shopping cart** achieved a speed of 42.87 mph (69 km/h) and was created by Tesco PLC and The Big Kick at the Tesco Extra store in Hatfield, Hertfordshire, UK, on November 17, 2011.

Most expensive store rent

For the first time in 11 years, Fifth Avenue in New York, USA, lost its claim to be the most expensive area in the world in which to rent store space. In 2012, the yearly rent in Causeway Bay, Hong Kong, China, was $2,630 per square foot.

Largest shopping center

Based on gross leasable area (GLA), the New South China Mall in Dongguan, China, is the largest, with 6.4 million sq. ft. (600,153 m²) of available retail space. The **largest mall by total area**, however, is the Dubai Mall in the UAE (*pictured*), which covers 12.1 million sq. ft. (1,124,000 m²).

Underground shopping center

The PATH walkway in Toronto, Canada, has 16.7 miles (27 km) of shopping arcades with 4 million sq. ft. (371,600 m²) of retail space accommodating around 1,200 stores and services. More than 50 buildings, five subway stations, and a rail terminal are accessible through the complex.

Parking lot

The parking lot at West Edmonton Mall in Alberta, Canada, can hold 20,000 vehicles, with overflow facilities in an adjoining park for 10,000 more autos. West Edmonton Mall is the largest shopping complex in North America.

Largest retailer

Walmart (USA) had total global sales of $469.16 billion in 2012. Headquartered in Bentonville, Arksansas, USA, the Walmart group has 10,818 stores in 27 countries and employs 2.2 million staff.

WHAT'S IN A NAME?

IKEA is an acronym formed from **I**ngvar **K**amprad (the founder's name), **E**lmtaryd (the name of his farm), and **A**gunnaryd (his home town).

Largest furniture retailer

Founded by Ingvar Kamprad in Sweden in 1943, IKEA had a worldwide revenue of €25.173 billion ($32.59 billion) in 2011. The furniture giant—which employs 131,000 staff across 332 stores in 38 countries—sells a range of 9,500 products, and in 2011 welcomed 655 million visits from customers.

=6. Persian Gulf Complex
Shiraz, Iran
4.52 million sq. ft. (420,000 m²)

=6. Mid Valley Megamall
Kuala Lumpur, Malaysia
4.52 million sq. ft. (420,000 m²)

=6. Istanbul Cevahir
Istanbul, Turkey
4.52 million sq. ft. (420,000 m²)

9. The Dubai Mall
Dubai, United Arab Emirates
3.77 million sq. ft. (350,224 m²)

10. West Edmonton Mall
Edmonton, Alberta, Canada
3.76 million sq. ft. (350,000 m²)

Source: Emporis

UPS & DOWNS

First moving walkway

The 1893 World's Columbian Exposition in Chicago, Illinois, USA, featured the first and **longest ever** moving walkway. Riders could stand while moving at 2 mph (3.2 km/h) or sit on benches and travel at 4 mph (6.4 km/h). Operated by the Columbian Movable Sidewalk Company, the walkway – destroyed by fire in 1894 – moved visitors arriving by steamboats and ran 0.6 miles (1 km) along a pier to the Exposition entrance.

a temporary elevator car at the Midland Park Building, Wellington, New Zealand, in May 1998. Despite multiple injuries, he survived.

Betty Lou Oliver (USA) survived the **longest fall in an elevator**, a plunge of 75 stories (more than 1,000 ft.; 300 m) in the Empire State Building in New York, USA, on July 28, 1945. Oliver ended up in the basement—her impact was cushioned by severed cables piling up in a springlike spiral on the floor. Air pressure slowed the elevator in the relatively airtight shaft.

Worst elevator disaster

A gold mine elevator at Vaal Reefs, South Africa, fell 1,600 ft. (490 m) on May 10, 1995, killing 105 people. The accident was caused by a locomotive entering the wrong tunnel and plunging down a shaft, landing on top of the elevator.

First elevator for cyclists

The Trampe Bicycle Lift in Trondheim, Norway, opened in 1993. Riders placed their right leg on a footrest and were pushed 426 ft. (130 m) up the 1-in-5-gradient Brubakken Hill at nearly 5 mph (8 km/h). It was replaced with the similar "CycloCable" system in 2013.

Tallest elevator

In a single descent, the elevator at AngloGold Ashanti's Mponeng gold mine in South Africa drops an astonishing 7,490 ft. (2,283 m)—more than 4.5 times farther than the elevators in the world's **tallest building**, the Burj Khalifa (*see below*). This journey takes just three minutes. A second elevator then takes miners lower, to 11,800 ft. (3,597 m). It ferries 4,000 workers to the mine.

Highest fall down an elevator shaft

Stuart Jones (New Zealand) fell 23 stories—a distance of 229 ft. (70 m)—down an elevator shaft while working on the roof of

Highest single elevator rise in a building

The main elevator in the Burj Khalifa skyscraper in Dubai, UAE, climbs 1,654 ft. (504 m) in a single ascent. Other elevators then take visitors higher up. The building officially opened on September 4, 2010. To find out more about the Burj—the **tallest building**— see p. 144.

- Houses 57 elevators and eight escalators
- Includes double-deck elevators, with a capacity of 12 to 14 people per cabin, for those traveling to the observation deck at Level 124
- Incorporates three "sky lobbies" on levels 43, 76, and 123: intermediate floors at which passengers can leave an express elevator and join a local elevator, which will stop on every floor in one section of the building
- No single elevator gives access to all floors in the building

40 Seconds it takes the two elevators to reach the 89th floor at 1,253 ft. (382 m) from the ground.

Fastest elevator in a building

Two high-speed elevators installed by Toshiba Elevator and Building Systems (Japan) in the Taipei 101 skyscraper in Chinese Taipei can reach 37.6 mph (60.6 km/h). Their atmospheric-pressure regulatory systems help to avoid "ear popping" in the occupants.

Largest grain elevator

A single-unit grain elevator operated by DeBruce Grain Inc. in Wichita, Kansas, USA, consists of 310 elevators arranged in a triple row on each side of the central loading tower. The unit is 2,717 ft. (828 m) long and 100 ft. (30.5 m) wide. Each tank is 120 ft. (37 m) high and has an internal diameter of 30 ft. (9.1 m), giving a total storage capacity in excess of 20 million bushels (7.3 million hectoliters) of wheat. (A hectoliter is 100 liters.) It is estimated that this is enough to supply the flour for all the bread consumed in the USA for six weeks.

Fastest moving walkway

A high-speed moving walkway (or "travelator") at Montparnasse metro station in Paris, France, moved commuters at 5.6 mph (9 km/h), around three times faster than regular walkways. The 590-ft.-long (180-m) unit was installed in 2003 but taken out of service in 2009 due to passenger falls and system breakdowns. A regular walkway opened in 2011.

EXTRAORDINARY ELEVATORS

AquaDom, Berlin-Mitte, Germany: An 82-ft.-tall (25-m) clear elevator in the center of an aquarium—the **tallest aquarium to contain an elevator.**

Volkswagen Autostadt silos, Wolfsburg, Germany: The **fastest automated parking facility** uses robotic "shuttles" in two 20-story, 157-ft.-tall (48-m) towers to deliver an auto in 45 seconds.

Falkirk Wheel, Falkirk, UK: The **largest rotating boat lift** ferries boats between the Union Canal and the Forth and Clyde canal.

Paternoster elevator, University of Sheffield, UK: A chain of 38 constantly moving, open-sided cabins in the university's 256-ft.-tall (78-m) Arts Tower. It is the **largest paternoster elevator**.

Louvre elevator, Paris, France: An open-topped, hydraulically powered elevator with slide-out walkway

Spiral escalator

The first fully operational spiral or curved escalator was presented at a trade fair site in Osaka, Japan, in 1985. Installed by the Mitsubishi Electric Corporation, it was much more complex and expensive than a conventional escalator owing to multiple center points and other engineering challenges.

Escalator

Jesse W. Reno (USA) created the first escalator as an amusement ride at the Old Iron Pier on Coney Island, New York City, USA, in September 1895. His "inclined elevator" had a vertical rise of 7 ft. (2.1 m) and an inclination of 25°. Riders sat on cast-iron slats atop a belt moving at a speed of 75 ft. (22.8 m) per minute.

Longest escalator ride

Suresh Joachim Arulanantham (Sri Lanka/Canada) traveled a total distance of 140 miles (225.44 km) on up and down escalators at Westfield Shoppingtown in Burwood, New South Wales, Australia. His record-breaking ride lasted for 145 hr. 57 min., from May 25 to 31, 1998.

Shortest escalator

A moving walkway at Okadaya More's shopping mall at Kawasaki-shi, Japan, has a vertical height of just 2 ft. 8 in. (83.4 cm). It was installed by Hitachi Ltd.

Most escalators in a metro system

The metro subway system in Washington, DC, USA, incorporates 557 escalators maintained by a team of 90 contracted technicians.

FIRST ...

Safety elevator

The first safety elevator—that is, one built with a ratchet fail-safe mechanism to prevent the cabin from falling if the cable breaks—was designed by Elisha Graves Otis (USA) and demonstrated in the New York Crystal Palace building, USA, in 1854.

The **first building to have a permanent safety elevator** was the E. V. Haughwout emporium at 488–492 Broadway, New York City, in 1857. The steam-driven Otis elevator ferried shoppers between the department store's five stories.

Scenic elevator

The first scenic (glass wall-climber) elevator attached to the outside of a building was installed in 1956 at El Cortez hotel, San Diego, USA, by its then owner Harry Handlery. Designed by Polish-American architect C. J. "Pat" Paderewski, the 15-floor elevator was known as the *Starlight Express*.

Tallest elevator-testing facility

The Tytyri High-Rise Elevator Laboratory in Lohja, Finland, is a testing facility that descends 1,090 ft. (333 m) down a limestone mine. Installed by KONE (Finland), it is designed to test high-speed elevators—up to speeds of 56 ft. per sec. (17 m/s)—for buildings more than 656 ft. (200 m) tall.

LONGEST ...

Escalator system

Hong Kong's Central Hillside Escalator Link is a 2,624-ft.-long (800-m) set of moving walkways. It carries commuters between the Mid-Levels district and Central Market close to the waterfront on Hong Kong Island, China.

Metro escalator

Located in St. Petersburg, Russia, the Admiralteyskaya station has four parallel escalators, each with a rise of 225 ft. 8 in. (68.6 m) and 770 steps. The station was inaugurated in December 2011.

Moving walkway (current)

Underneath the parks and gardens of The Domain in Sydney, Australia, is a 679-ft.-long (207-m) moving walkway. Officially opened on June 9, 1961 and constructed by the Sydney Botanic Gardens Trust as a futuristic novelty, it was rebuilt in 1994. The gently inclined walkway moves at 1.5 mph (2.4 km/h).

Ski lift

The gondola (cable car) ski lift at Grindelwald–Männlichen in Switzerland is 3.88 miles (6.239 km) long. The ride is in two parts, but it is possible to ride the entire length without changing gondola.

Tallest outdoor elevator

The upper 562 ft. 4 in. (171.4 m) of the 1,070-ft. (326-m) glass-sided Bailong ("Hundred Dragons") elevator is above ground and built on the side of a quartzite cliff in the Zhangjiajie National Forest Park in Hunan Province, China.

Oregon City municipal elevator, Oregon, USA: Transports passengers up or down a 130-ft.-tall (39-m) cliff, between the two levels of the city, in 15 seconds.

CN Tower, Toronto, Canada: Controlled by electrical charge, the glass floor panels turn opaque at the beginning and end of each 1,136-ft. (346-m) ride in the **tallest elevator drop with a glass floor**.

Rising Tide elevator, MS *Oasis of the Seas*: A combined elevator and bar linking two levels on the ship—the **first elevator with a bar**.

Strépy-Thieu boat lift, Le Roeulx, Belgium: Links the Meuse and Scheldt rivers. The **tallest boat lift**, with a vertical travel of 240 ft. (73.15 m), it can lift barges of 2.9 million lb. (1,350 tonnes) in weight.

Umeda Hankyu Building elevator, Osaka, Japan: 11 ft. 2 in. x 9 ft. 2 in. (3.3 x 2.8 m) elevator can carry 80 passengers—the **largest passenger capacity for an elevator in an office building**.

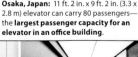

HOTELS

5.4 MILLION
Weight in pounds of The Marmara's rotating attic.

NOVEL INSPIRATION
The hotel is named after French novelist Jules Verne, author of Twenty Thousand Leagues Under the Sea.

First sand hotel

In the summer of 2008, vacationers on Weymouth beach in Dorset, UK, were able to spend the night in a hotel made entirely of sand. In total, 600 hours were needed to build the open-air, 161-sq.-ft. (15-m²) sandcastle hotel. A family room with a full and single bed was available for £10 ($21) a night. The hotel was the brainchild of sculptor Mark Anderson (UK), who was commissioned by the Web site LateRooms.com.

Highest-altitude hotel

Hotel Everest View above Namche, Nepal—the village closest to Everest base camp—is located at an altitude of 13,000 ft. (3,962 m).

Hotel with most restaurants

The Venetian Resort Hotel Casino which opened in May 1999 in Las Vegas, Nevada, USA, has 17 different restaurants (*see right*).

First rotating hotel

The Marmara in Antalya, Turkey, has 24 bedrooms in its rotating top section, which offers views across the Mediterranean and Bey Mountains. The entire section floats in 956,000 lb. (433 tonnes) of water in a special underground pool and is moved by just six 1-kW electric motors. The water reduces friction as the loft rotates each day. Construction of the 18-story hotel was completed in 2005 at a cost of $22 million. It was designed by Hillier Architecture and structural engineers MEP.

First underwater hotel

Guests dive down 21 ft. (6.4 m) to the front door of Jules' Undersea Lodge in Emerald Lagoon, Key Largo, Florida, USA. The lodge features two bedrooms and an 8- x 20-ft. (2.4- x 6-m) lounge. Originally built as an undersea research laboratory, the lodge was developed as a hotel by Ian Koblick and Neil Monney (both USA) and opened in 1986. Its past guests have included former Canadian Prime Minister Pierre Trudeau and rock star Steven Tyler, lead singer of Aerosmith.

Largest hotelier

Wyndham Hotels and Resorts is the world's largest hotel chain, operating more than 7,250 hotels in 50 countries under its banner. With headquarters at Parsippany in New Jersey, USA, the group's chains include Wyndham, Ramada, Days Inn, Howard Johnson, Planet Hollywood, and Travelodge. Its revenues in 2012 came to $4.5 billion.

Most fountains at a hotel

There are more than 1,000 fountains on the 12-acre (4.8-ha) artificial lake at the Bellagio hotel in Las Vegas, Nevada, USA—that's an area equivalent to almost 70 tennis courts! The fountains shoot water 243 ft. (73 m) into the air, accompanied by surround-sound music and a light display that features 4,000 programmed lights.

Most northerly hotel

The northernmost full-service hotel is the Radisson Blu Polar Hotel Spitsbergen in Longyearbyen, Svalbard, Norway. Svalbard consists of several islands from Bjørnøya in the south to Rossøya in the north, Europe's most northerly point.

Largest hotel Rolls-Royce fleet

The Peninsula Hotels Group has 28 Rolls-Royce vehicles worldwide. It runs 14 Rolls-Royce Phantom extended-wheelbase limousines in Hong Kong (*pictured*) as well as a 1936 Phantom II Sedanca De-Ville. Two Phantoms are used in Beijing; four Phantoms and a 1934 Phantom II Sedanca De-Ville in Shanghai; two Phantoms and a 1934 Phantom II Sedanca De-Ville in Tokyo; two Silver Spurs in Bangkok and another Rolls-Royce in Beverly Hills. All are painted in a dark green livery.

TOP 10 MOST EXPENSIVE HOTEL SUITES

1. Royal Penthouse at the President Wilson hotel, Geneva, Switzerland: $65,000 per night—the **most expensive hotel room**. Features marble bathroom, Steinway grand piano, private terrace and views over Lake Geneva.

2. Royal Villa at the Grand Resort Lagonissi, Athens, Greece: $45,000 per night. Includes wooden terrace, butler's quarters and private path leading to the beach.

3. Hugh Hefner Villa (now Two-Story Sky Villa) at the Palms Casino Resort, Las Vegas, USA: $40,000 per night. Featuring cantilevered pool, revolving bed and space to entertain 250 friends!

4. Ty Warner Penthouse at the Four Seasons, New York City, USA: $35,000 per night. Includes floor-to-ceiling windows providing a 360-degree view of Manhattan, nine rooms, and cut-glass chandeliers.

5. Royal Plaza Suite at The Plaza hotel, New York City, USA: $30,000 per night. Features library, private dining room for 12 people and in-suite gym.

Source: travel.usnews.com

806
Rooms in Tower 1. Tower 2 is scheduled to open in 2015.

Largest salt hotel

The 16-bedroom Palacio de Sal, on the salt flats of the Salar de Uyuni in Bolivia, incorporates floors, walls, ceilings, tables, chairs, beds, and a golf course all made of salt. Even its dip pool is filled with salt water. The present hotel was rebuilt in 2007 from around one million 13.77-in. (35-cm) blocks of salt weighing a total of 22 million lb. (10,000 tonnes). The blocks are held together using a cementlike paste of water and salt.

Oldest hotel

The Nisiyama Onsen Keiunkan in Hayakawa, Yamanashi Prefecture, Japan, is a hot-spring hotel that has been operating since AD 705.

Smallest hotel

The Eh'häusl hotel in Amberg, Germany, has an overall floor space of 570 sq. ft. (53 m²). Sandwiched between two larger buildings, the hotel is too small to accommodate more than two guests at any time.

Tallest stained-glass window

Perhaps surprisingly, the tallest stained-glass window isn't in a great cathedral. You'll find the 135-ft.-tall (41.14-m), 29-ft. 6-in.-wide (9-m), back-lit glass mural in the atrium of the Ramada hotel in Dubai, UAE. It was installed in 1979.

LARGEST ...

Hotel lobby

The lobby at the Hyatt Regency in San Francisco, California, USA, is 350 ft. long (107 m) and 160 ft. wide (49 m), and at 170 ft. tall (52 m) is the height of a 15-story building.

Ice structure

Located 120 miles (200 km) north of the Arctic Circle, the ICEHOTEL in Jukkasjärvi, Sweden, has been rebuilt

every December since 1990 and has a floor area of 43,000–54,000 sq. ft. (4,000–5,000 m²). In the winter of 2012–13, it included an ice reception, ice bar, ice church, and bedrooms with themes such as "Dragon Nest", "Iceberg," and "Whitewater."

Spa resort

Mission Hills Haikou has an area of 1,897,499 sq. ft. (176,284.14 m²) and is located in Haikou, Hainan, China. The facility was measured on October 17, 2012.

Casino

Guests at the 3,000-suite Venetian Macao casino-hotel resort in Macau, China, can play on 3,400 slot machines or at 870 gaming tables in a gambling area covering 550,000 sq. ft. (51,100 m²)—bigger than nine football fields!

Largest hotel

Built in two phases from 1999 to 2008, the Venetian and Palazzo complex at Las Vegas in Nevada, USA, includes 7,017 rooms and features an indoor canal in its shopping mall. It was designed by architects KlingStubbins (Venetian) and HKS (Palazzo) and is owned by Las Vegas Sands Corp.

FOR THE RECORD

The Marriott Marquis (*right*) is the tallest building to exclusively house a hotel. However, there are taller constructions that offer hotel accommodation. Such "mixed-use" hotels are those in which at least 15% of the overall floor usage is for a purpose other than hotel accommodation, such as shops, residences, and offices.

Tallest hotel

The J. W. Marriott Marquis Dubai, UAE, formerly known as Emirates Park Towers Hotel & Spa, is the tallest hotel, standing at 1,165 ft. (355.35 m) from ground level to the top of its mast. The hotel consists of two 77-floor twin towers, the first of which opened on November 11, 2012.

=6. Presidential Suite at the Ritz Carlton, Tokyo, Japan: $25,000 per night. Includes views of Mount Fuji, club concierge and access to the Ritz-Carlton Club Lounge.

=6. Bridge Suites, Royal Towers at Atlantis, Paradise Island, The Bahamas: $25,000 per night. Features a grand piano, 22-carat-gold chandelier and permanent staff of seven.

8. Royal Suite at the Burj Al Arab, Dubai, UAE: $22,900 per night. Includes revolving four-poster bed, private movie theater, library and personal elevator.

9. Imperial Suite at Park Hyatt Paris Vendôme, France: $19,000 per night. Comes with spa bathroom (including massage table) and 13-ft.-high (4-m) ceilings.

10. Ambassador's Bure at Wakaya Club & Spa, Fiji: $4,900 per night. Features spa, private pool and private ocean access.

HOUSES & HOMES

Largest Hollywood home

The house at 594 Mapleton Drive in Los Angeles, California, USA, occupies an area of 56,550 sq. ft. (5,253 m²). It was extended by Aaron Spelling (USA), producer of such TV series as *Charlie's Angels* and *Beverly Hills 90210*, to 123 rooms including a gymnasium, bowling alley, swimming pool, and skating rink.

FOR THE RECORD

Prior to Antilia (*see below*), the most expensive house was Hearst Castle (*above*) in San Simeon, California, USA, built for William Randolph Hearst (USA) in 1939. It has more than 100 rooms, a 104-ft.-long (32-m) heated swimming pool, and a garage for 25 limousines.

Three rooftop helipads with a panoramic view of the city of Mumbai

Antilia contains nine high-speed elevators to access its various sections; two elevators are for parking areas, three are for guest rooms, two are for the family, and two are for service

Primarily a steel-and-glass structure, the house features six stories of family residences to house the owner, his wife, mother, and three children; they are based on the top six floors of the house

Maintenance floor

ANCIENT INSPIRATION
Antilia is named after a mythical Atlantic isle. The design of the house was meant to abide by old Hindu architectural principles.

Guest bedrooms

Narrowest house

Keret House in Warsaw, Poland, is 3 ft. 0.2 in. (92 cm) at its narrowest and 4 ft. 11.8 in. (1.52 m) at its widest. Designed by Jakub Szczęsny of Polish architects Centrala, it has a floor area of 151 sq. ft. (14 m²). Instead of stairs, a ladder links the bedroom, kitchen, and bathroom.

Most northerly home

The world's northernmost year-round homes are for the five permanent residents of the Alert settlement on Ellesmere Island in the Canadian Arctic, just 507 miles (817 km) from the North Pole. Inhabited since 1950, Alert accommodates a weather station and signals intelligence base.

The **most southerly permanent human habitation** is the U.S. Amundsen-Scott South Polar Station, completed in 1957 and replaced in 1975. Tourists visiting the base in the summer months have access to a store, bank, and post office.

Oldest houses

The houses at the neolithic settlement of Çatalhöyük in modern Turkey date from 7,500–5,700 BC. Between 5,000 and 8,000 residents occupied the mud-brick homes here. The buildings were entered via rooftop holes that also served for smoke ventilation.

Largest underground house

Microsoft billionaire Bill Gates (USA) lives in an earth-sheltered mansion overlooking Lake Washington in Medina, Washington, USA. Designed by James Cutler and Peter Bohlin, the building, much of which is underground, occupies 66,000 sq. ft. (6,100 m²) of space and was completed in 1995. The mansion contains seven bedrooms, 24 bathrooms, six kitchens, a 60-ft. (18-m) pool, a 2,500-sq.-ft. (230-m²) gym, a trampoline room, and a complex computer-managed environmental, data, and entertainment system.

The two-story fitness center incorporates a swimming pool, spa, and gymnasium

Tallest house

Owned by Mukesh Ambani (India, *seen above with his wife Nita*) and completed in 2010, Antilia is 568 ft. (173 m) tall. The triple-height spacing of the 27 floors makes the building as tall as a typical 60-story office tower. It is also the **largest house**, with a living floor area of 400,000 sq. ft. (37,000 m²). Exact expenditure is unclear, but its ultimate cost was close to $2 billion, making it the **most expensive house ever built**.

Outdoor yard

10 TALLEST RESIDENTIAL BUILDINGS

1. Princess Tower
Dubai, UAE:
1,356 ft. (413.4 m).
World's **tallest residential building**.

2. 23 Marina
Dubai, UAE:
1,295 ft. (395 m).

3. The Domain
Abu Dhabi, UAE:
1,253 ft. (382 m).

4. Elite Residence
Dubai, UAE:
1,246 ft. (380 m).

5. The Torch
Dubai, UAE:
1,131 ft. (345 m).

Source: Emporis.com

Farthest building relocation

In August 2006, Warkentin Building Movers, Inc. (Canada) successfully drove a house 1,205 miles (1,650 km) across Canada from McAuley in Manitoba to a location near Athabasca in Alberta. The 1,400-sq.-ft. (130-m²) house was delivered in perfect shape after 40 hours of driving.

554
Aircraft at Spruce Creek, including planes, helicopters, and ultralights.

Largest fly-in community

Spruce Creek is a private group of houses with exclusive access to airplane hangars and a runway (also known as an airpark) near Daytona Beach in Florida, USA. On a 1,350-acre (550-ha) site (*right*), more than 5,000 residents share 700 hangars, a 0.76-mile (1.22-km) runway, and 14 miles (22.5 km) of paved taxiways, as well as fueling and repair facilities.

Tallest residential-only building

Princess Tower in Dubai in the United Arab Emirates (UAE) is 1,356 ft. (413.4 m) tall and was completed in 2012. The highest occupied floor stands at 1,171 ft. (356.9 m).

Highest residential apartments

The Burj Khalifa in Dubai, UAE, developed by Emaar Properties and opened on January 4, 2010, has the highest residential floor at 1,263 ft. (385 m). The Khalifa Tower combines hotel, residential, and corporate space. Floors 77–108 are residential.

If nonterrestrial locations are taken into account, the **highest-altitude home**, providing a place of residence for periods of several months or more, is the *International Space Station* (*ISS*) at an orbit of between 205 miles (330 km) and 255 miles (410 km) above Earth. First launched in 1998, the *ISS* usually has six scientists and astronauts living aboard at any one time.

Smallest temporary house

The aptly named One-Sqm-House was designed by German architect Van Bo Le-Mentzel in 2012.

Largest inhabited castle

Windsor Castle, the British Royal Family residence at Windsor in Berkshire, UK, is originally of 12th-century construction. It is built in the form of a waisted parallelogram measuring 1,890 x 540 ft. (576 x 164 m).

Tilting the self-build wooden structure on its side lets the single resident lie down to sleep, while four wheels allow the lightweight 88-lb. 3-oz. (40-kg) microhouse to move to new locations.

Most rooms in a house

The house with the most rooms is Knole near Sevenoaks in Kent, UK, which is believed to have had 365 rooms, one for each day of the year. Built around seven courtyards, its total depth from front to back is about 400 ft. (120 m). Constructed in 1456 by Thomas Bourchier, Archbishop of Canterbury, the house was extended by Thomas Sackville, 1st Earl of Dorset, ca. 1603–08. Today, Knole is administered by the National Trust.

Longest time to live in one residence

Florence Knapp (October 10, 1873–January 11, 1988) of Montgomery Township, Pennsylvania, USA, lived in the same house for 110 years.

Highest house valuation

The largest amount of money for which a house has been advertised is $165 million asked for a former home of newspaper tycoon William Randolph Hearst. The 75,000-sq.-ft. (6,967-m²) villa is set in 6.5 acres (2.6 ha) of land in Beverly Hills, California, USA, and boasts 29 bedrooms, 40 bathrooms, three swimming pools, and a nightclub. It featured in the movie *The Godfather* (USA, 1972).

Most lights on a residential property

Timothy, Grace, Emily, Daniel, and John Gay (USA) arranged 346,283 lights on their home in Lagrangeville, New York, USA, on November 23, 2012. The display, named ERDAJT Holiday Light Display after the first and middle initials of the family's children, is synchronized to 154 songs.

Largest spherical house

Casa Bola in São Paulo, Brazil, is owned by businessman Lucas Longo. The giant red steel-frame house measures 32 ft. (9.75 m) across and is split over three levels. The two bedrooms, kitchen, and bathroom are joined by a continuous curved ramp. Casa Bola also boasts custom-made curved doors, cupboards, and furniture.

LIKE FATHER, LIKE SON
Casa Bola was built in 1980 by architect Eduardo Longo—Lucas's father—who also built himself a round house in the city.

6. Q1 Tower
Gold Coast, Australia: 1,058 ft. (322.5 m); Australia's tallest residential building.

7. Ocean Heights
Dubai, UAE: 1,017 ft. (310 m).

8. Infinity Tower
Dubai, UAE: 1,007 ft. (307 m).

9. East Pacific Center Tower A (*far left*)
Shenzhen, China: 1,004 ft. (306 m).

10. Etihad Tower 2
Abu Dhabi, UAE: 1,000 ft. (305 m).

PALACES

Largest socialist state palace

The Palace of the Parliament in Bucharest, Romania, was mostly built between 1984 and 1989, during the rule of the Romanian Communist Party and its then head Nicolae Ceaușescu. The building measures 890 x 790 ft. (270 x 240 m) and rises 282 ft. (86 m) above ground, with another 302 ft. (92 m) devoted to subterranean levels. It has 1,100 rooms and parking spaces for 20,000 autos across a 3,700,000-sq.-ft. (340,000-m²) floor area.

First royal palace
A whitewashed mud-brick—or possibly limestone—palace was built in the 31st century BC for Hor-Aha, the second pharaoh of the First Dynasty, in Memphis, Egypt. Hor-Aha also had the outside of his tomb—located at Abydos—decorated to resemble a palace facade.

Oldest hedge maze
The hedge maze at Hampton Court Palace in Surrey, UK, was built for King William III and Mary II of England. It was designed by royal gardeners George London and Henry Wise (both UK) and planted in 1690 using hornbeam (*Carpinus betulus*) for the hedges. The maze covers 0.5 acres (0.2 ha) and its path is 2,624 ft. (800 m) long.

Largest palace garden
In the late 17th century, André Le Nôtre (France) created a magnificent garden for King Louis XIV at the Palace of Versailles, near Paris, France. The gardens and parkland cover more than 1,976 acres (800 ha), of which the famous formal garden covers 247 acres (100 ha).

Heaviest building
The Palace of the Parliament in Bucharest, Romania, is constructed from 1.5 billion lb. (700,000 tonnes) of steel and bronze combined with 35.3 million cu. ft. (1 million m³) of marble, 7.7 million lb. (3,500 tonnes) of crystal glass, and 31.7 million cu. ft. (900,000 m³) of wood.

Largest palace used as an art gallery

The Louvre Palace in Paris, France, was largely built and modified by the kings of France between 1364 and 1756. Later developments and additions have given the palace a size of 2,260,421 sq. ft. (210,000 m²). The famous glass pyramid designed by architect I. M. Pei was added to the Louvre courtyard in 1989.

Largest palace

The Imperial Palace in central Beijing, China, covers a 178-acre (72-ha) rectangle measuring 3,150 x 2,460 ft. (961 x 753 m). Construction took place between 1407–20 under Ming emperor Zhu Di and his three architects, Hsu Tai, Yuan An, and Feng Chiao, and it involved more than one million workers. Today, the site comprises around 980 buildings with 8,886 rooms. The last emperor of China, Puyi, went into exile in 1924. The palace became a World Heritage Site in 1987.

Highest-altitude palace

The Potala Palace in Lhasa, Tibet, is situated 12,139 ft. (3,700 m) above sea level on the side of the Red Mountain in the Lhasa Valley. Construction began in 1645 under the Great Fifth Dalai Lama. The palace covers an area of 1,312 x 1,148 ft. (400 x 350 m).

Largest hypostyle hall
The hypostyle (pillared) hall of the temple of Amun-Re at Karnak in Egypt had a roof supported by 134 giant columns and has an overall area of around 54,000 sq. ft. (5,000 m²). This is large enough to house nearly 26 tennis courts—or the cathedral of Nôtre Dame in Paris! It was commissioned by Ramses I in around 1290 BC.

Largest palace harem
The Imperial Harem wing at the Topkapı Palace of the Ottoman Empire (1299–1923) in what is now Istanbul, Turkey, was constructed in various stages from 1459 onward. With 400 rooms spread over several buildings, many designed by the Ottoman architect Mimar Sinan, it is the largest harem—the enclosed quarters in a polygamous household that are reserved for women and forbidden to men. Often called "the golden cage,"

TOP 10 RICHEST ROYALS (BY NET WORTH)

1. Bhumibol Adulyadej, King of Thailand
$30 billion

Source: Forbes.com. All figures accurate as of 2010, the year of the last such survey

2. Haji Hassanal Bolkiah, Sultan of Brunei
$20 billion

3. Abdullah bin Abdulaziz Al Saud, King of Saudi Arabia
$18 billion

4. Khalifa bin Zayed Al Nahyan, President of the United Arab Emirates
$15 billion

5. Mohammed bin Rashid Al Maktoum, Prime Minister of the UAE
$4.5 billion

built between 1729 and 1735. The 180- x 59-ft. (55- x 18-m) baroque riding hall allows for elaborate displays of equestrian dressage by the famous white Lipizzan horses and their skilled riders.

Most art gallery space

A visitor would have to walk 15 miles (24 km) to visit each of the 322 galleries of the Winter Palace within the State Hermitage Museum in St. Petersburg, Russia. The galleries house almost three million works of art and archaeological objects.

19
Height in feet of the palace. Its sofas, chairs, wine glasses, and clock were all made from ice, too.

First ice palace

Anna Ivanovna, Empress of Russia, commissioned an ice palace in St. Petersburg, Russia, during the winter of 1739–40. Architect Piotr Eropkin and scientist Georg Wolfgang Krafft used huge ice blocks measuring 52 ft. 6 in. (16 m) long by 16 ft. 5 in. (5 m) wide, joined together with frozen water, to build the palace. The city recreates the ice palace every winter.

Largest palace created single-handedly

The Palais Idéal in Hauterives, France, was made by local mailman Joseph-Ferdinand Cheval between 1879 and 1912. The finished palace measures 85 ft. (26 m) long, 40 ft. (12 m) wide, and 35 ft. (11 m) high.

FOR THE RECORD

Cheval (*see above*) put in more than 93,000 hours of labor to create his dream palace. He used local stones, pebbles, seashells, and snail shells, cemented together by more than 3,500 bags of lime mortar. The Palais Idéal incorporates a terrace, gallery, tower, temple, tomb, cupola, sculptures, spiral staircase, and fountain.

the Imperial Harem housed the sultan's mother ("Valide Sultana"), concubines, wives, relatives, and children, along with eunuchs, consorts, and court favorites.

Largest palace riding school

The Spanish Riding School at the Hofburg Palace in Vienna, Austria, was designed by Joseph Emanuel Fischer von Erlach (Austria) and

Largest religious palace

Construction of the Papal Palace (also known as the Apostolic Palace or Vatican Palace) at the Vatican in Vatican City, took place mainly between 1471 and 1605. Covering 1,743,753 sq. ft. (162,000 m^2), it contains the Papal Apartments, offices of the Roman Catholic Church and Holy See, chapels, Vatican Library, museums, and art galleries.

Tallest ice building

An ice palace completed in January 1992 in St. Paul, Minnesota, USA, for the Winter Carnival incorporated 18,000 blocks of ice weighing 10.8 million lb. (4,900 tonnes). Built by TMK Construction Specialties Inc., it was 166 ft. 8 in. (50.8 m) high. St. Paul's inaugural Winter Carnival was staged in 1886; one of its most popular attractions was the city's first ice palace.

Most valuable carpet

Created for the audience hall of the Sassanian palace at Ctesiphon, Iraq, the Spring Carpet of Khosrow consisted of about 7,000 sq. ft. (650 m^2) of silk and gold thread encrusted with emeralds. The carpet was cut up as booty by looters in AD 635, but historians believe that it must originally have been worth around $195 million.

Largest residential palace

The 1,788-room Istana Nurul Iman near Bandar Seri Begawan in Brunei is home to the Sultan of Brunei and the seat of the Brunei government. It covers 2,152,782 sq. ft. (200,000 m^2).

INVITE ONLY
The Imperial Palace is often referred to as the "Forbidden City," because permission to enter or leave had to come from the emperor himself.

6. Hans-Adam II, Prince of Liechtenstein
$3.3 billion

7. Mohammed VI, King of Morocco
$2.5 billion

8. Hamad bin Khalifa Al Thani, Emir of Qatar
$2.4 billion

9. Albert II, Prince of Monaco
$1 billion

10. Karim al-Husseini, Aga Khan IV
$800 million

Tallest ridable motorcycle

A fully functioning motorcycle constructed by Fabio Reggiani (Italy) measured 16 ft. 8 in. (5.10 m) tall, from the ground to the top of the handlebars, and 32 ft. 10 in. (10.03 m) in length. It was ridden over a 328-ft. (100-m) course at Montecchio Emilia, Italy, on March 24, 2012. The bike is powered by a 5.7L V8 motor, and is steered using a series of levers operated by the rider standing on a platform in front of the rear wheel.

SEE THE
VIDEO
WITH THE
FREE APP

AUGMENTED REALITY ALERT!

ON THIS PAGE

FIRE CHIEF
GASOLINE

HARLEY-DAVIDSON

RAISING THE *CONCORDIA*

A record-breaking salvage operation

On January 13, 2012, in calm seas, the cruise ship *Costa Concordia* hit a submerged reef by the coast of the Isola del Giglio, an island off the west coast of Italy. The reef ripped a 164-ft.-long (50-m) tear in the *Concordia*'s port side, and the ship grounded some 1,640 ft. (500 m) from shore. Of the 3,229 passengers and 1,023 crew, 30 people died; another two are still missing, presumed dead.

On April 21, 2012, Italian authorities announced that salvage companies Titan Salvage and Micoperi would attempt to refloat and remove the wreck, so it can be safely broken up in port, in the **largest ship refloating project**.

Before the accident

Under the command of Captain Francesco Schettino (*right*), the *Costa Concordia* had deviated from her planned route, allegedly as a publicity stunt to perform a "salute" to islanders on Isola del Giglio. The captain abandoned ship early, breaking the maritime tradition that all passengers and crew should evacuate first.

Costa Concordia

In operation since 2005, the *Costa Concordia* has a gross tonnage (GT)—a measure of its total internal volume—of 125,814, and is 952 ft. (290.2 m) long. Within one hour of being struck, it had listed starboard at an angle of 70 degrees, and became stranded in 65 ft. (20 m) of water. Boats and helicopters were used to rescue survivors, and teams of rescuers boarded the ship with the task of searching all 1,500 cabins and 13 public decks. The search and rescue effort lasted several months before being called off.

COSTA CONCORDIA SPEC.	
Builder	Fincantieri Sestri Ponente (Italy)
Cost	€450 million ($570 million)
Launched	September 2, 2005
Maiden voyage	July 14, 2006 (christened: July 7, 2006)
Capsized	January 13, 2012
Displacement	113.2 million lb. (51,387 tonnes); 125,814 GT
Length	952 ft. (290.2 m)
Beam	116 ft. 6 in. (35.5 m)
Power	101,380 hp. (75,600 kW)
Capacity	3,780 passengers; 1,100 crew

Divers explore

Exploring the capsized ship was a hazardous enterprise for the divers. They had to wear sealed wetsuits, because normal gear would not protect them from any chemicals, fuel, or other pollutants leaking from the ship.

GUINNESS WORLD RECORDS 2014

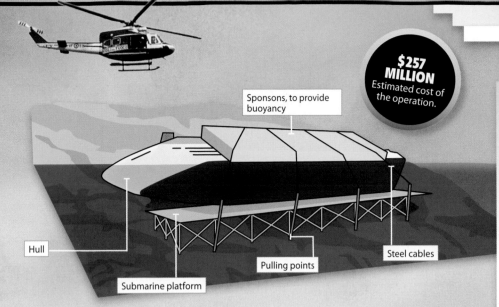

$257 MILLION
Estimated cost of the operation.

Sponsons, to provide buoyancy

Hull

Submarine platform

Pulling points

Steel cables

Salvage

Crews have begun work to recover the wreck of the *Costa Concordia*. Declared a total loss, she will eventually be scrapped.

The plan: Once the ship has been stabilized, grout bags are laid beneath the hull to provide support and help the ship pivot to prevent more movement. A subsea platform is then installed and 15 sponsons are welded to the port side for buoyancy. The ship is partly raised by crane, and another 15 sponsons are attached to the starboard side. The cables are removed and the ship floats free.

SHIPWRECKS & SALVAGES

Oldest shipwreck	A wooden, single-mast sailing ship wrecked off Uluburun near Kaş in southern Turkey and dated to the 14th century BC (Late Bronze Age). Discovered in 1982. Carried an extensive cargo of copper, tin, and glass ingots, jars of resin, gold and silver jewelry, nuts, and spices. (*Pictured right is a full-size replica built and scuttled for research purposes in 2009.*)
Largest wreck	The 708 million-lb. (321,186-tonne) VLCC (very large crude carrier) *Energy Determination* blew up and broke in two in the Strait of Hormuz, Persian Gulf, on December 12, 1979. The ship was not carrying any cargo at the time but its hull value was $58 million.
Most valuable wreck	The *Nuestra Señora de Atocha* sank in 1622 off the Key West coast in Florida, USA; found on July 20, 1985 along with its cargo of 96,434 lb. (43.7 tonnes) of gold and silver, and some 70 lb. (31.75 kg) of emeralds. Also recovered were 20 bronze cannon (*pictured right*).
Deepest wreck	On November 28, 1996, Blue Water Recoveries (UK) discovered the wreck of the SS *Rio Grande* at the bottom of the South Atlantic Ocean. The wreck, a World War II German blockade runner, lies at a depth of 18,904 ft. (5,762 m).
Deepest salvage from a shipwreck	Blue Water Recoveries (UK) salvaged 394,627 lb. (179 tonnes) of blister copper and tin ingots from the SS *Alpherat*, from a depth of 12,370 ft. (3,770 m) in the Mediterranean just east of Malta, in February 1997.
Deepest commercial salvage	On July 21, 1961, the US spacecraft *Liberty Bell 7*—part of the U.S. Mercury-Redstone 4 mission—splashed down in the Atlantic Ocean and sank before it could be recovered. (*Pictured right is the helicopter sent to rescue the sole astronaut, Virgil I. "Gus" Grissom.*) The spacecraft lay in more than 15,000 ft. (4,500 m) of water before being commercially salvaged by the ship *Ocean Project* on July 20, 1999.
Deepest salvage with divers	A team of 12 divers worked on the wreck of HM cruiser *Edinburgh*—sunk on May 2, 1942 in the Barents Sea off northern Norway—in 803 ft. (245 m) of water. Over 31 days (from September 7 to October 7, 1981), they recovered a total of 460 gold ingots.

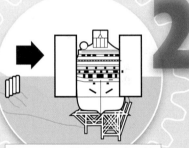

1 *Concordia* is pulled upright on her port side

2 Sponsons are added to the other side

3 The cables are removed. Now buoyant, the ship should float free

Refloating

In April 2013, the last of 30 giant sponsons (hollow steel boxes) were attached to the ship. Pumped full of air, these will act as "arm bands," allowing the ship to be refloated above an artificial seabed built from bags of cement and steel platforms.

AVIATION

MOVING EXPERIENCE
The A380's huge wings are 34% larger than those of a Boeing 747—so long that their tips "flap" about 13 ft. (4 m) during takeoff.

First female-owned flying school

Katherine Stinson (USA) was the fourth woman to earn a pilot's license in the USA. She learned to fly in 1911 and soon afterward began exhibition flying. In 1916, she and her family founded the Stinson School of Flying in San Antonio, Texas, USA.

Largest airspace company

In 2012, Boeing (USA) reported sales of $81.7 billion, profits of $3.9 billion, and a market value of $65.36 billion—all record figures in the airspace sector. Founded in 1916, Boeing today has a workforce of about 174,400 people.

The Boeing Everett facility in Washington, USA, where the aircraft are assembled, is the **largest factory** in the world. Opened in 1967, the factory has expanded twice in its history and today has a total volume of 472 million cu. ft. (13.3 million m³), covering a floor area of 4.3 million sq. ft. (399,480 m²)—large enough to house most of the Vatican City, which covers an area of 4.7 million sq. ft. (440,000 m²), or voluminous enough to accommodate the Great Pyramid at Giza in Egypt five times over!

Largest aviation deal

On January 11, 2011, the European aircraft company Airbus signed a deal with the Indian airline Indigo for 180 aircraft: 30 of its Airbus A320s and 150 of the new Airbus A320NEO (New Engine Option) variant—the biggest deal by number of aircraft in commercial aviation history. Overall, the deal is valued at $15.6 billion.

Largest flying-boat formation to cross the Atlantic

On July 1, 1933, Italian General Italo Balbo commanded a formation flight of 24 Savoia-Marchetti S.55X flying boats from Europe to the USA. Flying from Orbetello in Tuscany, Italy, the aircraft routed over the Alps, and then in stages via Iceland, Greenland, and Labrador to Lake Michigan, Chicago, USA. They arrived on July 15 after a 5,750-mile (9,200-km) flight and more than 48 hours of flying time.

Highest passenger capacity for an aircraft

The double-deck Airbus A380, manufactured by EADS (Airbus SAS), first flew in Toulouse, France, on April 27, 2005. The jet airliner has a nominal seating capacity of 555, but a potential capacity of 853 depending on the interior fuselage fit. It has a wingspan of 261 ft. 8 in. (79.8 m) and a range of 9,750 miles (15,700 km; 8,470 nautical miles). *Above left:* an A380 is delivered to the Emirates airline in Hamburg in 2008. *Above right*: one of the aircraft's luxurious interiors.

First electric tilt-rotor aircraft

On March 5, 2013, helicopter constructor AgustaWestland—part of the Italian Finmeccanica group—unveiled Project Zero: the first electric-powered tilt-rotor aircraft. This unique craft can transition from hovering flight to forward flight by means of two integrated rotors that tilt 90 degrees. The rotors are set within the wingspan instead of at the end of the wing, as is the case in conventionally powered tilt-rotor aircraft.

Smallest aircraft

The biplane *Bumble Bee Two*, built by Robert H. Starr (USA), was 8 ft. 10 in. (2.69 m) long, with a wingspan of 5 ft. 6 in. (1.68 m), and weighed 396 lb. (179.6 kg) empty. It was capable of carrying one person, but on May 8, 1988, after flying to a height of 400 ft. (120 m), it crashed and was destroyed; although injured, the pilot made a full recovery. The highest speed it attained was 190 mph (306 km/h).

GIANTS IN THE SKY

Heaviest aircraft in service: The Antonov An-225 "Mriya" ("Dream") has a maximum takeoff weight of 1.4 million lb. (640 tonnes). Only two were ever built.

Heaviest aircraft in production: The Airbus A380 weighs in at 1.2 million lb. (560 tonnes).

Heaviest bomber in service: The Russian Tupolev Tu-160 "Blackjack" bomber has a maximum takeoff weight of 606,000 lb. (275 tonnes) and a maximum speed of around Mach 2.05 (1,350 mph; 2,200 km/h).

Largest propeller-driven aircraft: The Russian Antonov An-22 (NATO code-name "Cock") had a wingspan of 211 ft. (64.4 m) and a maximum takeoff weight of 550,000 lb. (250 tonnes).

Largest bomber by wingspan: The American 10-engined Convair B-36J "Peacemaker" had a wingspan of 230 ft. (70.1 m). The aircraft, which had a maximum takeoff weight of 410,000 lb. (185 tonnes), was replaced by the Boeing B-52 in the late 1950s.

FOR THE RECORD

The **first aircraft to fly on solar power** was the *AstroFlight Sunrise*. The unmanned experimental electric aircraft first flew on November 4, 1974, from Bicycle Lake on the Fort Irwin military reservation in California, USA.

First manned solar flight

Thirteen-year-old Marshall MacCready (USA) made the first manned solar-powered flight, in *Gossamer Penguin* on May 18, 1980 at Shafter Airport near Bakersfield in California, USA. He was chosen as the pilot because of his light weight—just 80 lb. (36.2 kg).

FIRST ...

Takeoff from water

On March 28, 1910, the inventor Henri Fabre (France) took off from Lake Berre in Martigues, France, in his hydroplane, nicknamed *Le Canard* ("The Duck"). Powered by a 50-hp rotary engine, the plane flew for 1,650 ft. (502 m) at a height of around 6 ft. (1.8 m).

Landing on a ship

On January 18, 1911, pilot Eugene B. Ely (USA) landed a Curtis Pusher aircraft on a wooden platform mounted on the quarterdeck of the USS *Pennsylvania* in San Francisco Bay, California, USA. Ely used ropes weighed down by sand-filled

seabags and hooks attached to the plane to halt his landing run.

On August 2, 1917, Squadron Commander E. H. Dunning of the British Royal Naval Air Service landed a Sopwith Pup on the aircraft carrier HMS *Furious* while it was at sea in Scapa Flow, Orkney, UK—the **first landing on a moving ship**.

Parachute jump from an aircraft

Captain Albert Berry of the U.S. Army jumped from a Benoist biplane over Jefferson Barracks in St. Louis, Missouri, USA, on March 1, 1912, from a height of 1,500 ft. (460 m).

First flight attendant

Heinrich Kubis (Germany) began attending to passengers onboard the DELAG Zeppelin LZ-10 *Schwaben* in March 1912. He also took the role of chief steward on the 72-passenger LZ-129 *Hindenburg*, and was onboard when it burst into flames at Lakehurst in New Jersey, USA, on May 6, 1937. He escaped by jumping out of a window as the cabin neared the ground.

Solo east-west flight across the Atlantic

Starting on August 18, 1932 from Portmarnock Strand in Dublin, Ireland, Captain Jim Mollinson (UK) flew solo across the Atlantic Ocean in a de Havilland DH80A Puss Moth named *The Heart's Content*. He landed at Pennfield in New Brunswick, Canada, on August 19, 1932.

Manned flight by solar- and battery-powered aircraft

Designed and built by the American Larry Mauro, the *Mauro Solar Riser* flew for about 0.5 miles (0.8 km), reaching a maximum height of 40 ft. (12 m) on April 29, 1979 at Flabob Airport in Riverside, California, USA.

Longest production run for a military aircraft

The Hercules C-130 has enjoyed the longest continuously operating production line of any military aircraft. Manufactured by U.S. company Lockheed Martin, the Hercules first flew on August 23, 1954, and deliveries began in December 1956. The picture above shows a C-130 assembly line.

2,437 Number of Hercules C-130s produced as of March 7, 2013.

Largest helicopter: The Russian Mil Mi-12 was 121 ft. 4 in. (37 m) long, had a maximum takeoff weight of 227,000 lb. (103.3 tonnes), and a rotor diameter of 219 ft. 10 in. (67 m). It first flew in 1968 but due to technical problems it never went into production.

Largest flying boat: Boeing's Model 314 "Clipper" aircraft were the largest flying boats ever to carry passengers in commercial service, with a wingspan of 152 ft. (46.3 m), a length of 106 ft. (32.3 m), and a maximum takeoff weight of 84,000 lb. (38.1 tonnes).

Largest military flying boat: The Martin JRM-3 "Mars" has a wingspan of 200 ft. (61 m) and a maximum takeoff weight of 162,000 lb. (73.5 tonnes). Five were built for the U.S. Navy in the 1940s, of which one remains in service as a water bomber.

Largest helicopter in service: The Russian Mil Mi-26 first flew in 1977. It has a crew of five and a maximum takeoff weight of 123,000 lb. (56 tonnes).

Largest biplane in service: The Antonov An-2/An-3 has a wingspan of 61 ft. 7 in. (18.8 m) and a maximum takeoff weight of 12,800 lb. (5.8 tonnes). It was first manufactured in 1947 and can typically accommodate 12 people.

CONSTRUCTION VEHICLES

First mechanical excavator

William Smith Otis (USA) patented the steam shovel in 1839. The device resembled a modern-day hydraulic excavator with a wheeled chassis and a digger arm and bucket. It was powered by a steam engine and transferred power to the shovel bucket via pulleys.

Largest high-reach demolition excavator

High-reach demolition excavators are used for knocking down tall buildings. Euro Demolition have one consisting of a Caterpillar 5110B excavator with a Rusch TUHD 90-5 boom that can demolish buildings of 295 ft. (90 m) in height.

Heaviest weight lifted by a crane

A barge, ballasted with water and weighing 44 million lb. (20,133 tonnes), was lifted by the Taisun crane at Yantai Raffles shipyard in Yantai, China, on April 18, 2008. The crane is used to install modules onto vessels.

LARGEST ...

Bulldozer

The Komatsu D575A Super Dozer weighs 336,425 lb. (152.6 tonnes) and has been in production since 1991. It has a capacity of 2,437 cu. ft. (69 m³) and

3,360
Power output in kilowatts from its SAE J1995 engine.

Largest mobile industrial machine

The F60 conveyor bridge is 1,647 ft. (502 m) long and is used to move overburden (the rock and earth above coal in opencut mines) by conveyor belt. Five of these railed bridges were built in the 1980s by the German firm TAKRAF. Each is 262 ft. (80 m) high and 787 ft. (240 m) wide and moves material at up to 42 ft. (13 m) per minute.

Largest hydraulic shovel excavator

In October 2012, Caterpillar unveiled its new Cat 6120B H FS. With a bucket volume of 1,589–2,295 cu. ft. (45–65 m³), it is able to load up a Caterpillar 797F 800,278-lb. (363-tonne) truck in as little as three passes. The 6120B is also the first hydraulic shovel to utilize "hybrid" technology, taking energy from the shovel's swing as it decelerates and storing it in high-efficiency capacitors. In total, the shovel excavator weighs a huge 27.9 million lb. (1,270 tonnes).

a blade measuring 24 ft. 3 in. x 10 ft. 8 in. (7.4 x 3.25 m). The pusher is 38 ft. 5 in. (11.72 m) long and moves on caterpillar tracks.

Two-axle dump truck

The T 282B, manufactured by Liebherr in Virginia, USA, has a capacity of 800,278 lb. (363 tonnes). The truck was introduced in 2004 and is 47 ft. 6 in. (14.5 m) long, 28 ft. 10 in. (8.8 m) wide, 24 ft. 3 in. (7.4 m) high, and when empty weighs more than 441,000 lb. (200 tonnes).

Fork truck

Three counterbalanced fork trucks capable of lifting 198,000 lb. (90 tonnes) were made by Kalmar LMV (Sweden) in 1991 to build water pipelines in Libya. Each fork truck weighed 256,838 lb. (116,500 kg) and measured 54.1 ft. (16.6 m) long and 15.9 ft. (4.85 m) wide.

Tallest telescopic crane

The Liebherr LTM 11200-9.1 has a maximum boom length of 328 ft. (100 m). The boom consists of eight nested sections of steel tube that extend like a mariner's telescope. The truck-mounted boom is able to lift weights of 2.4 million lb. (1,088 tonnes).

65.6
Length in feet of the crane's nine-axle carrier vehicle.

TOP 10 CONSTRUCTION MANUFACTURERS BY SALES

Data from KHL Group/Statista.com

1. Caterpillar (USA): $35.30 billion
Founded 1925; had its roots in Benjamin Holt's pioneering tractor design.

2. Komatsu (Japan): $21.75 billion
Founded 1921; began as a mining equipment maker.

3. Volvo (Sweden): $10.01 billion
Founded 1927; ÖV4 production line auto was the first product.

4. Hitachi (Japan): $10 billion
Founded 1910; in 1924, it made the first large-scale DC electric locomotive in Japan.

5. Liebherr (Switzerland): $7.93 billion
Founded 1949; Hans Liebherr started with his first mobile, easy-assemble tower crane.

SHEAR POWER

A demolition shear is a pair of powerful scissors mounted on a long, robot-like arm. It is used for snipping apart large metal structures.

Largest demolition shear

The Genesis 2500 demolition shear is fitted to a Rusch Triple 34-25 excavator arm, giving it a reach of 111.55 ft. (34 m). Norwegian demolition contractor AF Decom built it in 2009 to munch its way through sections of disused North Sea oil platforms. The machine's arm is jointed into three sections for extra maneuverability and is built from steel.

country's Defense Research & Development Establishment in Pune, Maharashtra. It has bridge sections that unfurl to span gaps in the road or bodies of water, allowing for vehicles and equipment to cross. It consists of five truck-mounted sections—each 49 ft. (15 m) long—that can be deployed in 100 minutes to create a "road" 13 ft. (4 m) wide.

Tower crane jib

Zoomlion Heavy Industry Science & Technology Development Co., Ltd. (China) built a crane with a jib (boom/arm) that measured 363 ft. 1.47 in. (110.68 m) in length

Most advanced space construction robot

Canadarm2 has an arm with a reach of 57.7 ft. (17.6 m) that is used to fit new *International Space Station* modules into place. The arm is double-ended, enabling it to crawl end-over-end across the station. It can easily overcome the inertia of payloads up to 225,700 lb. (116 tonnes).

Tunnel boring machine

Bertha the borer has a cutting head measuring 57.5 ft. (17.5 m) in diameter and is scheduled to drill the State Route 99 tunnel beneath Seattle in Washington, USA. The cutter consists of a large steel face with 600 small cutting disks that grind rock. Manufactured by Japanese engineering firm Hitachi Zosen, it measures 300 ft. (91 m) long and weighs 14 million lb. (6,350 tonnes).

LONGEST ...

Mobile bridge system

The Sarvatra mobile bridging system has a maximum span of 246 ft. (75 m) and was developed in 1994 for the Indian Army by the

Most heavily armored combat bulldozer

The fortified version of the Caterpillar D9 is operated by the Israel Defense Forces. Nicknamed the Doobi (Hebrew for "teddy bear"), it carries a colossal 33,069 lb. (15 tonnes) of armor to deflect rocket-propelled grenades.

992 Pounds of explosives that D9s have reportedly withstood on duty.

when measured in Changde, Hunan Province, China, on August 28, 2012.

Zoomlion also set the record for the **longest truck-mounted crane jib** at 331 ft. 11 in. (101.18 m), measured in Changsha, Hunan Province, on September 28, 2012. The seven-section boom is used to pump concrete on large construction sites.

Fastest wheel loader

With its many modifications, including wheels instead of the more usual caterpillar tracks, a Volvo L60G PCP wheel loader reached 75 mph (120 km/h) on a 1.12-mile (1.8-km) stretch of runway at Sweden's Eskilstuna Airport on September 13, 2012. Its top speed prior to the refit was 28 mph (46 km/h).

6. Sany (China): $7.86 billion Founded 1989; early products centered on welding materials in its factory.

7. Zoomlion (China): $7.17 billion Founded 1992; concrete pumps formed its first product line in 1993.

8. Terex (USA): $6.51 billion Founded 1933; originally the Euclid company, making haul trucks.

9. Doosan (South Korea): $5.83 billion Founded 1896; the 117-year-old company is South Korea's oldest.

10. John Deere (USA): $5.37 billion Founded 1837; blacksmith John Deere started with just one store.

CHAIRS

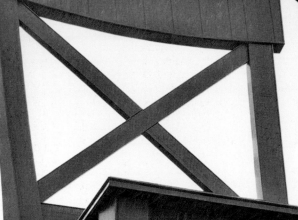

First domestic chair in space

In 2004, artist Simon Faithfull (UK) sent a domestic chair 18.6 miles (30 km) into the air as part of the *Artists' Airshow* exhibition. Attached to a weather balloon, the chair—and Faithfull's film of its rise into the stratosphere—formed an artwork called *Escape Vehicle No. 6*.

First execution by electric chair

William Kemmler (USA) was the first person ever to be executed using an electric chair. Kemmler was sentenced to death for murdering his lover Tillie Ziegler with an ax in 1888 and electrocuted by alternating current on August 6, 1890 in Auburn Prison, New York, USA. It took eight minutes and two attempts to kill him—first with 1,000 volts, then with 2,000 volts.

Largest structure made from cotton swabs

Monika Veidt of Schönebeck, Germany, constructed an armchair using 61,422 cotton swabs on April 18, 2002. The chair also has a matching lamp and coffee table made entirely out of cotton swabs.

FOR THE RECORD

You can find tall chairs in Lucena, Spain (85 ft. 4 in.; 26 m), Nürnberg, Germany (82 ft.; 25 m), Manzano, Italy (65 ft.; 20 m), Washington, D.C., USA (53 ft. 4 in.; 16.25 m); and Anniston, Alabama, USA (33 ft.; 10 m).

Most expensive sofa

One of Israeli-born British artist Ron Arad's stainless steel "D" sofas sold for $409,000 at Phillips de Pury in New York City, USA, on December 13, 2007.

A pair of chairs designed by Robert Adam and built by Thomas Chippendale (both UK) sold at Christie's in London, UK, for £1.7 million ($2.8 million) on July 3, 1997, the **most expensive chairs** ever sold.

HOW TALL?
The chair is about the height of five adult giraffes, or three-quarters the size of the Statue of Liberty in New York Harbor, USA.

Largest chair

Measuring 98 ft. 5 in. (30 m) tall, the largest chair ever made was created by XXXLutz together with Holzleimbauwerk Wiehag GmbH (both Austria). The colossal seat was completed and presented in Sankt Florian, Austria, on February 9, 2009.

SUPERLATIVE SEATING

Most expensive chair: An armchair that belonged to French designer Yves Saint Laurent sold for € 21.9 million ($28 million) at Christie's in Paris, France, in February 2009.

Lightest chair: Massimiliano Della Monaca's (Italy) carbon fiber chair *Estrema* can support up to 220 lb. (100 kg)—but it weighs just 1 lb. 5.7 oz. (0.617 kg).

Largest collection of miniature chairs: As of March 13, 2008, Barbara Hartsfield's (USA) collection of miniature chairs numbered 3,000.

First mass-produced plastic chair: The Bofinger chair (BA 1171), designed by Helmut Bätzner (Germany) in 1964, was produced from 1966.

First beanbag chair: *Sacco* was created in 1969 by Italian designers Piero Gatti, Cesare Paolini, and Franco Teodoro.

Largest inflatable furniture

This outsize couch measured 67 ft. 3 in. (20.5 m) long, 26 ft. 6 in. (8.10 m) wide and high, and had a volume of 28,287 cu. ft. (801 m³). Built by Jacobs Krönung (Germany) in four separate parts, it was presented in Bremen, Germany, on April 14, 2009.

Longest Samson's chair

The longest static wall sit—aka Samson's chair, in which you lean against a wall in a sitting position—is an excruciating 11 hr. 51 min. 14 sec. by Dr. Thienna Ho (Vietnam) at the World Team USA gymnasium in San Francisco, California, USA, on December 20, 2008.

Largest chair dance

The largest sitting dance routine involved 271 participants at The Stiletto Gym by FIMB Yoga and Wellness Center (USA) in Riverside, Missouri, USA, on November 5, 2011.

Most people doing chair-base exercise

On National Grandparents Day on September 9, 2012, a total of 262 people took part in a "cane-fu" lesson: a low-impact martial arts-base activity that teaches seniors simple self-defense techniques. The class took place at Silvera for Seniors in Calgary, Alberta, Canada, where the oldest participant was 98-year-old Hazel Gehring.

Tallest hydrofoil (airchair) ridden

William Blair (UK) has created and successfully ridden a 10-ft 9.1-in.-tall (3.28-m) hydrofoil chair behind a motorboat, for more than 330 ft.

Largest game of musical chairs

On August 5, 1989, a game of musical chairs began with 8,238 people at the Anglo-Chinese School in Singapore. Three-and-a-half hours later, the game ended with winner Xu Chong Wei on the last chair.

20
Number of local furniture factories that worked together to create the couch.

Fastest dining set

Fast Food is a drivable dining set that achieved a top speed of 113.8 mph (183.14 km/h)—taken as the average of two runs in opposite directions—at Santa Pod Raceway in Northamptonshire, UK, on September 5, 2010. It was invented, and driven, by Perry Watkins (UK).

Longest sofa

The lengthiest couch measured 2,920 ft. (890.25 m) and was manufactured by furniture factories in Sykkylven, Norway, on June 14, 2009. The sofa was displayed on the Sykkylvsbrua, a bridge that crosses the fjord of Sykkylven, and was more than 10 times longer than the previous record holder.

13,227
Weight in pounds of this giant deck chair—it's more than a bull elephant.

Largest deck chair

One way to guarantee yourself space on the beach is to take along the largest deck chair. Measuring 31 ft. 4 in. (9.57 m) long, 18 ft. 11 in. (5.77 m) wide, and 27 ft. 5 in. (8.36 m) tall, this super-size seat was made by Pimm's (UK) and displayed in Bournemouth, UK, on March 22, 2012. Its designer, Stuart Murdoch, is shown above.

STEP INSIDE SOME EXTRAORDINARY HOMES ON P. 152

Oldest surviving upholstered furniture: This chair and footstool was upholstered by craftsman John Casbert in 1661 for the then Bishop of London, William Juxon.

Fastest sofa: Glenn Suter of New South Wales, Australia, drove his couch at 101.36 mph (163.117 km/h) on September 26, 2011.

Largest rocking chair: A 42-ft.-tall (12.83-m) rocker built by Dan Sanzaro (USA) was measured in Cuba, Missouri, USA, on September 4, 2008.

Tallest human chair stack: The Peking Acrobats (China) achieved a 21-ft.-tall (6.4-m) human chair stack in Los Angeles, California, USA, in October 1999.

First cantilever chair: Architect Mart Stam (Netherlands) built his iconic chair (self-supporting with no back legs) from old gas pipes in 1926.

BRICK BY BRICK

Fastest robot to solve a Rubik's cube

On November 11, 2011, the CubeStormer II, commissioned by ARM Holdings and built by Mike Dobson and David Gilday (all UK) from four LEGO Mindstorms NXT kits, completed a scrambled cube in just 5.270 seconds in London, UK. That's 0.28 seconds faster than Mats Valk (Netherlands) who, as of March 2013, was the fastest human solver.

Smallest movie set (commercially available)

The LEGO Steven Spielberg MovieMaker Set, launched on April 1, 2001, supplies kids with everything needed to build an entire mini movie set measuring 9.84 x 10.03 in. (25 x 25.5 cm). Fans can then create their own movie with the LEGO PC movie camera and editing software.

Most LEGO Ninjago spinner competitions in 24 hours (multiple venues)

Ninjago is a popular ninja figurine battle game and cartoon show created by LEGO. On February 17, 2012, the most devout Ninjago enthusiasts gathered at 44 LEGO stores across North America for a 24-hour competition frenzy. A total of 18,559 competitions were battled out and completed using the competitors' personalized characters.

LARGEST …

Picture built with LEGO

More than two million multicolor bricks were used by 5,000 children to create an image of the 26 cantons of Switzerland. It measured 1,646 sq. ft. (153 m²) and was created by LEGO GmbH (Germany) in collaboration with Manor AG and Pro Juventute (both Switzerland) at the Suisse Toy in Bern, Switzerland, on October 6, 2012. The motto of the record attempt was, "Children are building the future of Switzerland".

Collection of LEGO sets

Kyle Ugone of Yuma, Arizona, USA, owns the world's most extensive LEGO collection, boasting a staggering 1,091 complete sets as of July 23, 2011.

Toy-building lesson (multiple venues)

A total of 287 LEGO fans each learned to make a train engine with a trolley using 82 pieces at an event organized by Merlin Entertainments Group Ltd (UK). The building lessons took place simultaneously at nine LEGOLAND® Discovery Centres worldwide and at the LEGOLAND Windsor resort on November 15, 2012.

LONGEST …

Span of a LEGO bridge

At 45 ft. 11 in. (14 m) in length, the bridge built by visitors to the "SteinZeit im Phaeno" ("Stone Age in Phaeno") exhibition in Wolfsburg, Germany, on October 6, 2008 took LEGO modeling to new lengths. The construction was supervised by LEGO experts René Hoffmeister and Klaas H. Meijaard.

LEGO structure

Built in the shape of a gigantic millipede, the longest LEGO structure measured 5,179 ft. 10 in. (1,578.81 m)—roughly the same length as 32 Olympic swimming pools—and consisted of 2,901,760 parts. The record was set in Grugliasco, Turin, Italy, on February 13, 2005.

Tallest LEGO® tower

The tallest structure built from interlocking plastic bricks is the 106-ft. 7-in.-tall (32.5-m) tower built from LEGO in Prague, Czech Republic, to mark the 80th anniversary of the LEGO company's history. Rower Miroslava Knapková clicked the final brick into place on September 9, 2012 at the end of a four-day build. An estimated 500,000 bricks were used in the construction.

HIGH AND MIGHTY

LEGO have a long-running tradition of building towers around the world—the first one appeared in London in 1988, measuring 49 ft. (15.2 m).

AWESOME E-REX-TION

The T-rex featured as the largest item in Sawaya's touring LEGO exhibition, The Art of the Brick, and was built over the summer of 2011 "in honor of the thousands of children who enjoy the art of LEGO building."

Largest LEGO dinosaur skeleton

At 20 ft. (6 m) in length and comprising 80,020 pieces, *Dinosaur Skeleton* by Nathan Sawaya (USA) is an actual-size *Tyrannosaurus rex* skeleton—the largest complete skeleton made from LEGO bricks.

FACT: More than 400 billion LEGO bricks have been produced since 1949—that's enough, when stacked, to connect the Earth and Moon 10 times over!

TOP 10 LARGEST LEGO SETS …

1. Currently topping the brick-building charts is the LEGO Taj Mahal model, released in 2008 with a whopping total of 5,922 pieces!

2. Issued in 2007, the Star Wars Ultimate Collector's *Millennium Falcon* comes in at a close second with 5,195 pieces.

3. London's Tower Bridge set takes third position; released in 2010, it contains 4,287 parts.

4. Sporting 3,803 pieces, the popular Star Wars Death Star is up next and was first released in 2008.

5. The Death Star II follows closely, unleashed in 2005 with 3,441 individual parts.

Most contributors to a sculpture

Cartoon Network employed Kevin Cooper (UK) to design a huge LEGO sculpture of new character "Bloxx" from *Ben 10: Omniverse* with help from no less than 18,556 contributors. It incorporated 240,000 bricks and was built across nine locations in the UK from August 4 to October 4, 2012.

TALLEST ...

In 2009, Guinness World Records opened a series of categories based on the tallest LEGO tower built in various time spans, by individuals or teams of two, and using one hand or two. Current records include:

• **One minute, two hands**: On June 5, 2010, Andy Parsons (UK) assembled a stack of 131 LEGO bricks in 60 seconds at Butlin's in Minehead, Somerset, UK.
• **One minute, one hand**: The following year, on December 26,

2011 at Butlin's in Skegness, Lincolnshire, UK, fellow Brit Chris Challis erected a stack that reached 48 bricks tall in one minute using just one hand.
• **30 seconds, one hand**: Viktor Nikitoviæ (Netherlands) built a 28-brick-tall tower in 30 seconds using just one hand at the NEMO Museum in Amsterdam, Netherlands, on November 11, 2012. The finished tower stretched to a height of 10.63 in. (27 cm).
• **30 seconds, team of two**: A 31-brick tower was erected by Madelyn and Maddox Corcoran (both USA) at Moss Park in Orlando, Florida, USA, on November 4, 2012.

LEGO LODGINGS
This mammoth LEGO mansion sprawls across two whole floors, with a total of four rooms. It even has LEGO "stained glass" windows!

Largest LEGO house

At 15 ft. 4 in. (4.69 m) high, 30 ft. 9 in. (9.39 m) long, and 18 ft. 10 in. (5.75 m) wide, the biggest house built with plastic bricks was completed by 1,200 volunteers along with James May (UK) for *James May's Toy Stories* in Dorking, Surrey, UK, on September 17, 2009.

915 MILLION
Different ways to combine six LEGO bricks.

FOR THE RECORD

LEGO *Star Wars II: The Original Trilogy* features 50 characters unique to the game and lets players mix and match body parts to create more than a million customized characters. It has the **most playable characters in an action-adventure video game**.

Largest LEGO Technic set

This 1:12.5-scale Mercedes-Benz Unimog U 400 truck is the largest LEGO Technic set available to buy in the stores and is comprised of 2,048 pieces. The truck features a pneumatically powered articulated crane with working grabber and a recovery winch at the front.

FANTASTIC PLAS-TECH
The Unimog boasts functional steering, four-wheel drive, and suspension, as well as a detailed engine.

Largest display of LEGO *Star Wars* clone troopers

LEGO (UK) amassed an unrivalled army of 35,210 Star Wars LEGO clone trooper minifigures on June 27, 2008 in Slough, Berkshire, UK. The fearsome array, headed up by a LEGO Darth Vader, took six-and-a-half hours to create.

6. Scaling the dizzy heights of advanced models is the Eiffel Tower set with 3,428 pieces, first issued back in 2007.

7. Spinning into seventh place is the Grand Carousel model, released in 2009 with 3,263 parts.

8. The Star Wars Imperial Star Destroyer contains 3,096 components and made its first appearance in 2002.

9. The Statue of Liberty model is 2 ft. 9 in. (0.76 m) tall and built using 2,882 pieces. It was released in 2000.

10. In 2005, the (not to scale) New York Skyline set burst onto the market with 2,747 components, including autos, a ferry, and even a monorail.

MARINE ENGINEERING

Heaviest object lifted at sea

The crane vessel Saipem 7000 (Italy), broke the offshore weightlifting record when it transported a 26 million-lb (12,150-tonne) single integrated deck (SID) from a heavy-transport carrier to the Sabratha platform in Libya's Bahar Essalam field in October 2004. The lift took just four hours to complete, helped by near-perfect weather conditions in the Mediterranean Sea.

First self-elevating offshore wind farm construction vessel

The Turbine Installation Vessel (TIV) *MPI Resolution* was built in Qinhuangdao, China. It measures 428 ft. long x 125 ft. wide (130.5 x 38 m) and can operate in water 16–114 ft. (5–35 m) deep. Its six legs let the ship jack itself up out of the water to become a stable platform for constructing offshore wind farms.

Most powerful undersea rock trencher

The RT-1, built by Soil Machine Dynamics Ltd. (UK), is a 352,739-lb. (160-tonne) tracked unmanned vehicle designed to dig trenches up to 6 ft. 6 in. (2 m) deep on the seabed to protect undersea pipelines. It has 2,350 kilowatts of power and measures 52 ft. 6 in. long x 42 ft. 7 in. wide x 24 ft. 7 in. high (16 x 13 x 7.5 m).

Largest offshore gas platform

The Troll A, an offshore gas platform located off Norway in the North Sea, is the **heaviest man-made mobile object**. The dry weight of its gravity base structure is 1.4 billion lb. (656,000 tonnes). Standing 1,210 ft. (369 m) tall, it was made from (8,652,090 cu. ft. (245,000 m³) of concrete and 220 million lb. (100,000 tonnes) of steel (equivalent to 15 Eiffel Towers).

Largest offshore wind farm

The Greater Gabbard wind farm has 140 Siemens SWT-3.6-107 turbines capable of generating 500 megawatts of electricity. It is in the North Sea, 15.53 miles (25 km) from the UK, and transmits power via three 28-mile (45-km) cables.

Largest offshore oil-containment boom

Developed by Ro-Clean Desmi, the Ro-Boom 3500 has a deflated width of 11 ft. 6 in. (3.5 m). The deflated width of such booms normally ranges from 1 ft. 7 in. to 6 ft. 7 in. (0.5–2 m). The importance of this device is underlined by the fact that each year, 83 million gallons (3.77 billion liters) of oil spill into the world's oceans.

Largest floating crane ship

Operated by Heerema Marine Contractors (Netherlands), *Thialf* is a 661-ft.-long (201.6-m) semisubmersible, sea-going barge with a total lifting capacity of 31 million lb. (14,200 tonnes).

Thialf carries two 311-ft.-tall (95-m) cranes capable of lifting objects in tandem. The lower section of *Thialf*'s hull can be flooded, increasing its draft (i.e., causing it to float lower in the sea) by 65 ft. (20 m). This massive addition to the weight of the vessel creates the stability necessary to lift such massive loads, and also lets *Thialf* operate in rough seas.

WORSE THINGS HAPPEN AT SEA

Longest journey in a lifeboat: 800 miles (1,300 km), from Elephant Island to South Georgia, Antarctica, in 17 days (arriving May 19, 1916), by Sir Ernest Shackleton (UK) and five of his men in the *James Caird* lifeboat.

Worst ferry disaster: *Doña Paz* sank on December 21, 1987. Officially had 1,500 passengers but may have carried as many as 4,000. Only 24 survived.

Largest scuttling of ships: On November 27, 1942, in Toulon, France, 73 ships of the French fleet were sunk to avoid capture by German forces.

Longest time adrift at sea alone: 133 days (November 23, 1942 to April 5, 1943) by Second Steward Poon Lim (b. Hong Kong) of the UK Merchant Navy.

Most civilians rescued at sea: 4,296 Japanese civilians, rescued by American cargo ship USS *Brevard* (AK-164) on January 23, 1946.

ENGINEERING

www.guinnessworldrecords.

GUINNESS
WORLD
RECORDS
2014

Deepest spar platform by ocean depth

The *Perdido* oil drilling and production platform is moored in 8,000 ft. (2,438 m) of water. It has a cylindrical design, with most of its structure underwater to provide stability. Operated by Shell, it was delivered to the Gulf of Mexico in August 2008 and began extraction of oil and gas on March 31, 2010.

LONGEST ...

Offshore gas pipeline
The Nord Stream pipeline consists of a pair of parallel natural gas pipelines running for 759 miles (1,222 km) under the Baltic Sea. On October 8, 2012, both pipes became operational for the first time, connecting Vyborg, Russia, to Greifswald, Germany. The pipeline can transport 2 trillion cu. ft. (55 billion m³) of gas per year.

Submarine fiber-optic cable
Light forms the basis for all communications in the modern world, with many thousands of miles of fiber-optic cables lying at the bottom of the world's oceans. The longest of

Oldest offshore lighthouse

Bell Rock Lighthouse was built by British civil engineer Robert Stevenson and completed in 1811 on Bell Rock, a 426- x 229-ft. (130- x 70-m) sandstone reef some 11 miles (18 km) off the east coast of Scotland. The granite and sandstone lighthouse measures 115 ft. (35.3 m) from its foundation to the top of its lightroom.

DEEPEST ...

Oil well
Before its blowout in 2010—which led to the worst oil spill in U.S. history—the *Deepwater Horizon* semisubmersible rig achieved a vertical drilling depth of 33,011 ft. (10,062 m) at the Tiber oil field in the Gulf of Mexico.

Water in which a drillship has operated
On April 11, 2011, offshore drilling company Transocean (USA) announced that its ultradeepwater drillship *Dhirubhai Deepwater KG2* had drilled into the ocean bed in 10,193 ft. (3,107 m) of water off the Indian coast.

736
Number of workers that *Thialf* can accommodate at one time. The structure also houses a helipad suitable for a Boeing Chinook 234.

Deepest ocean drilling by seabed depth

On September 9, 2012, while drilling in the Pacific Ocean off the coast of Japan's Shimokita Peninsula, the Japanese research vessel *Chikyū* achieved a drilling depth of 8,090 ft. (2,466 m) below the seabed. That's nearly eight times greater than the height of the Eiffel Tower.

all these light pipes is the Sea-Me-We 3 (Southeast Asia-Middle East-Western Europe). Measuring 24,000 miles (39,000 km) long, it is operated by India's Tata Communications and was fully commissioned in late 2000.

Underwater power cable
A 358.8-mile-long (577.5-km) underwater power cable connects the Norwegian power grid at Feda with the Dutch power grid at Eemshaven. It was inaugurated on September 11, 2008. The single cable weighs 25 lb. per ft. (37.5 kg per m); the double cable weighs 57 lb. per ft. (85 kg per m).

THIALF

Worst accidental explosion on a ship: 1,635 people died when explosives-laden freighter *Mont Blanc* hit another ship in Halifax Harbour, Nova Scotia, Canada, on December 6, 1917.

Worst nuclear submarine disaster: Russian nuclear submarine K-219 sank in Atlantic Ocean on October 6, 1986, carrying two nuclear reactors and 16 nuclear missiles.

Worst offshore oil disaster death toll: Fire on *Piper Alpha* oil production platform in North Sea on July 6, 1988; 167 people killed out of a crew of 225.

Worst oil spill ever: "Lakeview Gusher" began March 14, 1910, at Midway-Sunset Oil Field, California, USA. Lasted 18 months. Released some 9 million barrels (378 million gal; 1.43 billion liters) of oil.

Worst yacht race disaster: 23 boats sunk or abandoned from August 13 to 15, 1979, in a Force-11 gale during the 28th Fastnet Race. Nineteen people died.

REMARKABLE RIDES

40 Passenger capacity of *Midnight Rider*, served by a crew of four.

were all operated simultaneously, making the ground vibrate with a velocity of 0.25 in./sec. (6.325 mm/sec). The result was the equivalent of a 661-lb. (300-kg) high-explosive charge detonating at a distance of 1,640 ft. (500 m) from the seismograph. The event was organized by *Fast Car* magazine and www.talkaudio.co.uk (both UK).

Hairiest car

Maria Lucia Mugno (Italy) owns a hirsute Fiat 500 covered with 220 lb. (100 kg) of natural hair. It was presented and measured on the set of *Lo Show dei Record* in Rome, Italy, on March 4, 2010,

Heaviest limousine

Midnight Rider weighs in at a hefty 50,560 lb. (22,933 kg). This 70-ft.-long (21.3-m), 13-ft. 8-in.-high (4.1-m) behemoth was designed by Michael Machado and Pamela Bartholemew (both USA, *above*) in California, USA, and began operating on September 3, 2004. *Midnight Rider* incorporates three lounges and a separate bar, and its interior decor is based on that of railroad Pullman cars, which were popular from the mid-19th century onward. Its horn plays the tune of "Midnight Rider" by The Allman Brothers.

Lightest car

Louis Borsi (UK) has built and driven a 21-lb. (9.5-kg) car with a 2.5-cc engine, capable of reaching 15 mph (25 km/h).

Longest car

With features including a king-size water bed and a swimming pool with diving board, the longest car is a 100-ft.-long (30.5-m), 26-wheel limousine designed by Jay Ohrberg (USA). Its design

allows for the vehicle to bend in the middle, although it can also be driven as a rigid vehicle. It was originally built for use in movies and advertising.

Largest car horn ensemble

As part of the seventh Pausaer Trabant race in Ebersgrün, Germany, staged on June 12, 2011, a group of 212 cars assembled to honk the children's song "All My Ducklings." The event was organized by Trabant Club Pausa e.V. (Germany).

Largest car seat

In September 2004, a supersize car seat 11 ft. 2 in. (3.4 m) high, 7 ft. 2 in. (2.17 m) wide, and 8 ft. 4 in. (2.54 m) deep was created for the *Lust am Auto* exhibition in Mannheim, Germany. The seat was acquired at auction by Hemhofen Primary School in Hemhofen, Bavaria, Germany, and measured on December 10, 2006.

Largest motorized model car

Sheikh Hamad bin Hamdan Al Nahyan (UAE) created an outsized, motorized model of a Willy Jeep 44 ft. 8.4 in. (13.62 m) long, 20 ft. 3.6 in. (6.18 m) wide, and 21 ft. 2.4 in. (6.46 m) high—built

at a scale of 4:1. It was measured at the Emirates National Auto Museum in Abu Dhabi, UAE, on November 3, 2010.

Largest "earthquake" caused by car stereos

On October 22, 2008, at the Santa Pod Raceway in Northampton, UK, the stereo systems in 22 cars

Fastest baby carriage

Colin Furze (UK) has built a motorized baby carriage capable of reaching a speed of 53.46 mph (86.04 km/h). It was tested at Shakespeare County Raceway in Stratford-upon-Avon, UK, on October 14, 2012. (*For another of Colin's amazing rides, go to p. 173.*)

(For another of Colin's amazing rides, go to p. 173.)

Longest ramp jump in a limousine

Michael Hughes (USA) jumped a distance of 103 ft. (31.39 m) in a 6,500-lb.

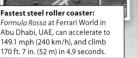

TOAST OF THE COASTERS

Tallest steel roller coaster: *Kingda Ka* at Six Flags Great Adventure near Jackson in New Jersey, USA, reaches a maximum height of 456 ft. (139 m).

Longest drop on a wooden roller coaster: *El Toro* at Six Flags Great Adventure near Jackson, New Jersey, USA, includes a drop of 176 ft. (54 m). It is 188 ft. (57.3 m) tall at its peak.

Fastest steel roller coaster: *Formula Rossa* at Ferrari World in Abu Dhabi, UAE, can accelerate to 149.1 mph (240 km/h), and climb 170 ft. 7 in. (52 m) in 4.9 seconds.

Longest steel roller coaster: *Steel Dragon 2000* at Nagashima Spaland in Mie, Japan, is 8,133 ft. (2,479 m) long and has a maximum height of 311 ft. 8 in. (95 m).

Longest wooden roller coaster: *The Beast* at Kings Island in Ohio, USA, is 7,400 ft. (2,286 m) long.

Longest mobility scooter

Made by Orchard Mobility (UK), the *Limobilizer* is a 9-ft. 6-in.-long (2.9-m) mobility scooter. It was measured at Somerset College in Taunton, Somerset, UK, on October 25, 2012.

(3-tonne) Lincoln Town Car stretch limousine at Perris Auto Speedway in Perris, California, USA, on September 28, 2002.

Tallest limousine
Built by Gary and Shirley Duval (both Australia), the tallest limousine measures 10 ft. 11 in. (3.33 m) from the ground to the roof. It has two separate engines and an eight-wheel independent suspension system and sits on eight monster-truck tires. It took a little over 4,000 hours to complete.

FASTEST ...

Amphibious car
Powered by an engine based on the LS Corvette power train, the *WaterCar Python* has a maximum speed of 60 mph (96 km/h; 52 knots) on water and can accelerate from 0 to 60 mph

(0–96.5 km/h) in 4.5 seconds on land. The *Python* is hand-built to order, with prices starting from $200,000.

Lawnmower
Don Wales (UK) of Project Runningblade drove a lawnmower at a speed of 87.83 mph (141.35 km/h) in Pendine, Carmarthenshire, UK, on May 23, 2010.

Mobile bed
The fastest mobile bed was created and driven by Edd China (UK) and reached a speed of 69 mph (111 km/h) along a private road in London, UK, on November 7, 2008 as part of Guinness World Records Day.

The talented Edd also built the **fastest office**, capable of a top speed of 87 mph (140 km/h). Edd drove the desk across

Westminster Bridge and into the City of London, UK, on November 9, 2006, to mark Guinness World Records Day that year. (*For yet another of Edd's creations, see right.*)

Mobility scooter
The highest speed reached on a mobility scooter is 82.67 mph (133.04 km/h) and was achieved by Klaus Nissen Petersen (Denmark) at Danmarks Hurtigste Bil, in Vandel, Denmark, on June 3, 2012.

Monster truck
Randy Moore (USA) drove an Aaron's Outdoors monster truck at 96.80 mph (155.78 km/h) at the zMAX Dragway, Charlotte Motor Speedway, in North Carolina, USA, on March 17, 2012.

Fastest milk float

Developed by the all-UK team of mechanic (and multiple record holder) Edd China (*pictured*), driver Tom Onslow-Cole, and eBay Motors, the fastest milk float hit a speed of 77.53 mph (124.77 km/h) in Wokingham, UK, on October 18, 2012. The attempt was part of eBay Motors' sponsorship of the West Surrey Racing team.

Towed toilet
Brewton McCluskey (USA) reached a speed of 52.01 mph (83.7 km/h) on a towed toilet (built atop a modified go-cart) at the South Georgia Motorsports Park in Adel, USA, on April 4, 2011.

Police car
The 2009 Lamborghini Gallardo LP560-4 has a top speed of 230 mph (370 km/h). Just 30 officers are permitted to drive the car, which is used primarily on the highway between Salerno and Reggio Calabria in Italy.

Smallest roadworthy car

Austin Coulson (USA) has constructed a car that was measured at just 2 ft. 1 in. (63.5 cm) high, 2 ft. 1.75 in. (65.41 cm) wide, and 4 ft. 1.75 in. (126.47 cm) long in Carrollton, Texas, USA, on September 7, 2012.

It's not the **lowest roadworthy car**, though. That honor goes to *Mirai*, which is just 1 ft. 6 in. (45.2 cm) from the ground to its highest part. *Mirai* was created by Hideki Mori (Japan) and students on the automobile engineering course at Okayama Sanyo High School in Asakuchi, Japan, on November 15, 2010.

The speed limit in mph that Austin can legally drive his car on the roads.

FOR THE RECORD

The paintwork on Austin's pint-size ride is themed after the P51 Mustang military aircraft, and the sides are inscribed with the tail numbers of a ship that his grandfather served on during World War II.

Steepest steel roller coaster: *Takabisha* at Fujikyu Highland amusement park (aka Fuji-Q Highland amusement park) in Fujiyoshida City, Japan, inclines 121 degrees for 11 ft. 1 in. (3.4 m).

Steepest wooden roller coaster: *Outlaw Run* at Silver Dollar City, Branson, Missouri, USA, has a drop of 81 degrees.

Most track inversions in a roller coaster: *The Smiler* at Alton Towers in Staffordshire, UK, boasts 14 inversions along its 3,839-ft. (1,170-m) track.

Oldest roller coaster: *Leap-the-Dips* at Lakemont Park in Altoona, Pennsylvania, USA, opened in 1902. It was closed for restoration from 1985 to 1999 but today is fully operational.

Oldest continuously operating roller coaster: *The Scenic Railway* at Luna Park in St. Kilda, Melbourne, Victoria, Australia, opened to the public on December 13, 1912 and has been in operation ever since.

MOTORCYCLES

aerodynamic "streamliner," although Assen's bike—a Suzuki GSX1300R Hayabusa —was "partially streamlined," meaning that he was not completely enclosed by the fairings (bodywork).

The **fastest speed on a conventional motorcycle by a female** is 232.522 mph (374.208 km/h) by Leslie Porterfield (USA)—also riding a Hayabusa at the Bonneville Salt Flats—on September 5, 2008.

First motorcycle

The earliest internal-combustion-engine motorized bicycle was a wooden-frame machine built at Bad Cannstatt, Germany, between October and November 1885 by Gottlieb Daimler and first ridden by Wilhelm Maybach (both Germany). It had a top speed of 12 mph (19 km/h) and generated 0.5 hp (0.37 kW) from its single-cylinder 264-cc four-stroke engine at 700 rpm.

FASTEST ...

Motorcycle (streamliner)
On September 25, 2010, Rocky Robinson (USA) achieved an average speed of 376.363 mph (605.697 km/h) in his *Top Oil-Ack Attack* streamliner over 0.6 miles (1 km) at the Bonneville Salt Flats in Utah, USA.

Motorcycle (conventional)
Richard Assen (New Zealand) achieved a speed of 261.315 mph (420.546 km/h) on a conventional motorcycle at the Bonneville Salt Flats in Utah, USA, on September 23, 2011. "Conventional" refers to a normal production bike, as opposed to an

Monocycle
Kerry McLean (USA) reached 57 mph (91.7 km/h) on a monocycle at Irwindale in California, USA, on January 10, 2001. He used a 48-in.-wide (1.22-m) 40-hp (30-kW) monowheel—a large wheel that revolves around a track, inside which the rider and engine are housed.

Tandem motorcycle
The highest speed achieved by a rider and a pillion passenger

Fastest motorcycle (piston engine)

The MV Agusta F4 R 312 is the fastest piston-engine (as opposed to jet-engine) production motorcycle, with a top speed of 193.88 mph (312 km/h, hence the "312" in its name). Pistons—in this case, made from titanium—convert pressure into a rotating motion that drives the back wheel.

is 181.426 mph (291.98 km/h) by Erin Hunter and Andy Sills (both USA), who rode a BMW S1000RR at the Bonneville Salt Flats in Utah, USA, on September 20, 2011. The pair did two timed runs in opposite directions and took turns as rider/passenger.

FACT:
It's not surprising that the Y2K is the fastest and most powerful motorcycle when you know that the Rolls-Royce Allison 250 gas turbine engine that powers this road monster was previously used in Bell JetRanger helicopters!

Fastest production motorcycle

Powered by a Rolls-Royce Allison gas turbine engine, the MTT Turbine Superbike has a highest recorded speed of 227 mph (365 km/h), although MTT claim to have registered speeds "in excess of 250 mph [402 km/h]". The reason for its superlative speed is the 286 hp (213 kW) of power supplied at the rear wheel, with 425 lb./ft. (577 Nm) of torque at 2,000 rpm, making it the **most powerful production motorcycle ever**.

When it went on sale in 2004, the MTT Turbine Superbike cost $185,000, making it the **most expensive production motorcycle ever**.

FOR MORE ON MOTORSPORTS, TURN TO P. 248

STUNTS AND SKILLS

Most motorcycle pirouettes in 30 seconds: Horst Hoffmann (Germany) performed 21 spins during the Centro Festival in Oberhausen, Germany, on September 9, 2006.

Largest simultaneous burnout: The Harleystunts and Smokey Mountain Harley-Davidson team achieved 213 burnouts in Maryville, Tennessee, USA, on August 26, 2006.

Most consecutive yoga positions on a motorcycle: On the set of *Guinness World Records—Ab India Todega*, 23 yoga positions were displayed by Yogaraj C. P. (India) in Mumbai, India, on February 17, 2011.

Most people on one motorcycle: The Army Service Corps Motorcycle Display Team Tornadoes (all India) squeezed 54 members on one bike at Air Force Station Yelahanka in Bangalore, India, on November 28, 2010.

Fastest wheelie on ice: At Lake Koshkonong in Wisconsin, USA, on February 5, 2011, Ryan Suchanek (USA) pulled off a 95-mph (152.89-km/h) wheelie on ice.

Heaviest motorcycle

The mighty *Panzerbike* was built by Tilo and Wilfried Niebel of Harzer Bike Schmiede in Zilly, Germany, and weighed 10,470 lb. (4.749 tonnes) on November 23, 2007, making it the heaviest motorcycle. At 17 ft. 4 in. (5.28 m) long and 7 ft. 6 in. (2.29 m) tall, and powered by a Russian tank engine, the bike took a team of mechanics and welders almost a year to construct.

Motorcycle hearse
Rev. Ray Biddiss (UK) achieved 114.1 mph (227.08 km/h) on his Triumph Rocket 2,340-cc motorcycle hearse at Elvington Airfield in York, UK, on May 10, 2011.

Mobility scooter
After upgrading the motor on his mobility scooter, Klaus Nissen Petersen (Denmark) reached 82.67 mph (133.04 km/h) at Danmarks Hurtigste Bil in Vandel, Denmark, on June 3, 2012.

RIDES

Highest altitude reached
Six members of the North Calcutta Disha Motorcycle Club (all India) reached an altitude of 20,488 ft.

(6,245 m) while riding their Hero Hondas on the Chang Chenmo range near Marsemikla in India on August 29, 2008. The altitude was confirmed using GPS and verified by the chief of the Indian border patrol.

Farthest distance traveled by motorcycle in 24 hours
L. Russell "Rusty" Vaughn (USA) rode 2,019.4 miles (3,249.9 km) in 24 hours on his 2010 Harley-Davidson Electra Glide Ultra Limited FLHTK at Continental's Uvalde Proving Grounds in Texas, USA, between August 9 and 10, 2011.

Fastest speed by a jet-powered motorcycle

Officially certified by the IHRA (International Hot Rod Association), Kevin Martin's (USA) speed peaked at 202.55 mph (325.97 km/h) on the *Ballistic Eagle* jet-powered motorcycle at the Spring Nationals at Rockingham Speedway in North Carolina, USA, on April 24, 2009.

Longest motorcycle

With enough seating for 25 people, the longest motorcycle is 72 ft. 2 in. (22 m) long and was created by Direct Bikes Ltd. and Colin Furze (both UK). It was presented and measured at Saltby Aerodrome in Leicestershire, UK, on July 27, 2011.

34.79 Miles per hour that the longest motorcycle has achieved.

First mass-production motorcycle
The German motorcycle factory Hildebrand & Wolfmüller opened in 1894 and in its first two years produced more than 1,000 bikes, each with a water-cooled 1,488-cc (90.8-cu.-in.) twin-cylinder four-stroke engine.

Most expensive motorcycle sold at auction
Sold for £291,200 ($464,835), excluding commissions or tax, the 1922 Brough Superior SS80, known as *Old Bill*, was sold by H&H Classic Auctions (UK) at the Imperial War Museum in Cambridgeshire, UK, on October 23, 2012.

Motorcycle with largest engine capacity
The Triumph Rocket III is powered by a three-cylinder 2,294-cc (140-cu.-in.) engine, the largest ever fitted to a production bike. It creates 140 hp (104 kW) of power and 147 lb./ft. (200 Nm) of torque, more than most sedan autos.

Most powerful production motorcycle
The Vyrus 987 C3 4V "Kompressor" produces a claimed 213 hp (157.3 kW) and has a 1,198-cc (73.110-cu.-in.) engine sourced from the Ducati 1098R with a supercharger fitted to increase the power.

Fastest electric motorcycle
The SWIGZ Electric Superbike Prototype (USA) achieved a speed of 196.912 mph (316.899 km/h) with a running start when ridden by Chip Yates (USA) at the Bonneville Salt Flats in Utah, USA, on August 30, 2011.

Fastest time to cross 21 oil drums on a trials motorcycle: Jake Whitaker (NZ) crossed 21 drums in 10.933 seconds in Beijing, China, on December 16, 2011.

Smallest distance between airplane and motorcycle during a midair crossing: A distance of 7 ft. 11.28 in. (2.42 m) was achieved by Veres Zoltán and Gulyás Kiss Zoltán (both Hungary) in Etyek, Hungary, on September 7, 2008.

Longest stoppie (nose wheelie) on a motorcross bike: Gary Harding (USA) nose-wheelied for a distance of 282 ft. 10 in. (86.2 m) on a Kawasaki KX250T8F at Mason Dixon Dragway in Boonsboro, Maryland, USA, on August 22, 2010.

Fastest speed while blindfolded: Billy Baxter (UK) reached 164.87 mph (265.33 km/h) while riding a 1,200-cc Kawasaki Ninja blindfolded at RAF (now MoD) Boscombe Down in Wiltshire, UK, on August 2, 2003.

Longest stoppie (nose wheelie) on a motorcycle by two people: Craig Jones (UK) achieved 1,000 ft. (305 m) carrying Wing Tat Chui (UK, b. Hong Kong) at Donington Park race circuit, Derby, UK, on May 8, 2006.

PLANE CRASHES

First pilot to die in a powered aircraft crash

On September 7, 1909, in Juvisy-sur-Orge, France, Eugène Lefebvre (France, *above*), engineer and pilot for the Wright Company, crashed the plane he was testing. He was the first pilot—and the second person ever—to die in a crash. The **first fatal airplane crash** occurred on September 17, 1908, when Thomas E. Selfridge (USA) died in a plane piloted by flight pioneer Orville Wright.

First black box aircraft data recorder

In 1956, Dr. David Warren (Australia) designed a crash-survivable prototype called the ARL Flight Memory Unit to record a flight crew's conversation and other data prior to a crash. Dr. Warren was working at the Defence and Science Technological Organization's Aeronautical Research Laboratories in Melbourne, Australia. His interest in electronics was prompted by his father giving him a crystal radio set in 1934 when he was nine. Shortly afterward, his father was killed in one of Australia's

Most dangerous place to fly

The 2012 *Annual Review* of the International Air Transport Association reported that air travel in Africa is nine times more dangerous than the global average. Measured in aircraft destroyed or written off per million flights, Africa had, in 2011, an accident rate of 3.27—although this was 56% improved on the previous year's figures.

first air disasters, the loss of the de Havilland 86 *Miss Hobart* in the Bass Strait south of Victoria, between Australia and Tasmania.

First airplane crash caused by a dog

On November 29, 1976, an unrestrained German Shepherd dog onboard a Piper 32-300 Air Taxi operated by Grand Canyon Air interfered with the controls. The dog perished, along with the pilot and lone passenger.

Safest year for jet airliner crashes

According to the 2012 *Annual Review* of the International Air Transport Association (IATA), the accident rate for Western-built jet aircraft in 2011 was the lowest ever. Measured in hull losses (aircraft destroyed or written off) per million flights, the rate was 0.37, or one hull loss for every 2.7 million flights—an improvement of 39% over the previous record low set in 2010. Statistically, the accident rate is now so low that someone taking one flight a day could expect 14,000 years of trouble-free flying.

Most successful aircraft ditching

Airliners have landed on water in emergency without casualties before, but the largest number of survivors in a 100% success scenario were the 155 passengers and crew of U.S. Airways Airbus A320 Flight 1549. Captain Chesley "Sully" Sullenberger's aircraft experienced a series of bird strikes soon after taking off from New York's LaGuardia Airport on January 15, 2009. The engines cut out but the aircraft ditched on the Hudson River without serious injury to passengers.

38,000 Pounds of thrust from each of Concorde's four engines. They were the most powerful pure jet engines flying commercially.

Highest death toll in a supersonic aircraft

The first and only crash of a Concorde took place on July 25, 2000, when an Air France Concorde crash killed 113 people—100 passengers, 9 crew members, and 4 people on the ground. Flight 4590 hit a hotel near the town of Gonesse, north of Paris, France. The Concorde had taken off from Paris Charles de Gaulle Airport but was brought down by an explosion in one of its fuel tanks, which was pierced by rubber from a burst tire thrown out at high speed. In turn, the tire had been punctured by a piece of metal on the runway.

FOR AVIATION, TURN TO P. 160

MOST FATAL AVIATION DISASTERS

Source: planecrashinfo.com

1. New York, USA, September 11, 2001: 2,907 deaths American B767, United Airlines B767; terrorist attack. Listed by planecrashinfo.com as one incident; total includes ground fatalities

2. Tenerife, Canary Islands, March 27, 1977: 583 deaths Pan Am B747, KLM B747; runway collision (*see above right*)

3. Mount Osutaka, Japan, August 12, 1985: 520 deaths Japan Airlines B747; mechanical failure

4. New Delhi, India, November 12, 1996: 349 deaths Saudi B747, Kazakh IL76; midair collision (*see above right*)

5. Bois d'Ermenonville, France, March 3, 1974: 346 deaths Turkish Airlines DC10; mechanical failure

Highest death toll from an aircraft ground collision

On March 27, 1977, two Boeing 747s collided on the runway at Tenerife in the Canary Islands, killing 583 people. A KLM aircraft attempted to take off without clearance and collided with a Pan Am 747, which was taxiing against the flow of traffic on the runway in poor visibility.

First airplane crash caused by a crocodile

A crocodile was smuggled inside a sports bag onto an internal flight from Kinshasa to Bandundu in the Democratic Republic of the Congo on August 25, 2010. When the reptile escaped, panicked passengers rushed the cockpit, unbalancing the Let L-410 Turbolet plane. With 20 passengers and crew killed, the crocodile was among only two survivors, but it was killed afterward with a machete.

Most frequent aviation accident category

The International Civil Aviation Authority 2011 *State of Global Aviation Safety Report* confirms that runway incidents accounted for 59% of accidents in 2005–10. The accident most likely to lead to fatalities, however, was loss of control in-flight, representing 29% of all fatalities and 4% of accidents.

Worst midair collision

On November 12, 1996, a Saudi Boeing 747 and Air Kazakhstan freighter struck each other near Delhi International Airport, India, killing 349 people. This was the worst midair death toll—23 crew and 289 passengers on the Saudi aircraft and 10 crew and 27 passengers on the Ilyushin freighter.

Most fighter planes lost in one peacetime sortie

The British Royal Air Force lost six of eight Hawker Hunter combat aircraft on February 8, 1956 at RAF West Raynham, UK. They were due to undertake air combat training at 45,000 ft. but were diverted because of poor weather to RAF Marham. A sudden deterioration in visibility precluded safe visual approaches and there was not enough time to effect spaced radar approaches. Four pilots ejected when they ran out of fuel, one crash-landed and survived, and another pilot was killed. Two aircraft landed successfully.

Most fatal helicopter crash

On August 19, 2002, Chechnyan separatists fired a missile at an overloaded Mi-26 helicopter. It crashed into a minefield, killing 127 passengers and crew. Chechnyan Doku Dzhantemirov was later found guilty by a Russian court of terrorism and sentenced to life imprisonment.

FOR THE RECORD

The survival rate for aircraft accidents is 95.7%, according to a survey of all accidents involving commercial U.S. air carriers between 1983 and 2000. The study was conducted by the National Transportation Safety Board in the USA. Of 53,487 people involved in an accident, 51,207 survived.

FLIGHT 191

On August 2, 1985, violent winds hit a Lockheed L-1011 TriStar 1; 134 on board died when the plane crashed near Dallas/Fort Worth International Airport in Texas, USA.

Worst year for aviation fatalities

The year 1985 was the worst for plane-crash deaths, although the actual figure differs depending on the source. According to planecrashinfo.com, which maintains an aviation accident database, 2,670 people were killed in crashes in that year. Three accidents accounted for 1,105 fatalities: Air India Flight 182 (329 fatalities), Japan Airlines Flight 123 (520), and Canada's Arrow Air Flight 1285 (256). Pictured are the remains of Delta Flight 191 (*see right*).

6. Atlantic Ocean, 110 miles (177 km) west of Ireland, June 23, 1985: 329 deaths
Air India B747; bomb

7. Riyadh, Saudi Arabia, August 19, 1980: 301 deaths
Saudi Arabian Airlines L1011; fire and smoke

8. Persian Gulf near Bandar Abbas, July 3, 1988: 290 deaths
Iran Air A300; shot down by U.S. missiles

9. Shahdad, Iran, February 19, 2003: 275 deaths
Islamic Revolutionary Guards Corps IL-76MD; adverse weather

10. Chicago, Illinois, USA, May 25, 1979: 273 deaths
American Airlines DC10; mechanical failure

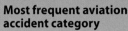

SHIPS

Largest ocean liner

Today's large passenger ships are used mostly for recreational cruises, but the RMS *Queen Mary 2*, whose maiden voyage began on January 12, 2004, was designed as a true ocean liner. She measures 1,131 ft. (345 m) long with a beam of 134 ft. (41 m) and can travel at 29.5 knots (33.9 mph; 54.6 km/h).

Fastest operational class of warship

First commissioned in 1999, the Royal Norwegian Navy's Skjold class stealth missile corvettes can exceed 60 knots (69 mph; 110 km/h). The sixth Skjold class ship, KNM *Gnist*, was delivered in November 2012.

The **highest speed attained by a destroyer** was 45.25 knots (52 mph; 83.42 km/h) by the 6.4-million-lb. (2,900-tonne) French ship *Le Terrible* in 1935.

Largest container ship by capacity

Although slightly smaller in dimensions than the Maersk E-class ships, the CMA GCM *Marco Polo* has a higher cargo capacity. She measures 1,300 x 177 ft. (396 x 54 m) but can carry 16,020 TEU (20-ft. equivalent units)—this unit is based on the dimensions of a standard 20-ft.-long (6-m) cargo container. *Marco Polo* began her first voyage on November 7, 2012.

First surface ship to reach the North Pole

The Soviet nuclear-powered ice-breaker NS *Arktika* began sea trials on November 3, 1974 and operated until 2008. She was capable of breaking through sea ice 16 ft. (5 m) thick, and on August 17, 1977 became the first ship in history to reach the geographic North Pole.

LARGEST ...

Concrete ship still afloat

The SS *Peralta* was built as an oil tanker and launched in 1921. She is 420 ft. (128 m) long with a beam of 50 ft. 6 in. (15.4 m) and a gross tonnage (internal volume) of 6,144. The ship now serves as a floating breakwater to protect a log storage area on the Powell River in British Columbia, Canada.

Ship ever built

At 1,504 ft. (458.45 m) long, the ultralarge crude carrier (ULCC) *Seawise Giant*—later named *Happy Giant*, *Jahre Viking*, *Knock Nevis,* and *Mont*—weighed 1,245 million lb. (564,763 tonnes) deadweight. The term "deadweight" refers to the weight a ship can safely carry, including

First double-acting tanker

Completed in 2002, the MT *Tempera* is the first tanker to use the double-acting technique, whereby a ship travels backward while ice-breaking. This technique is used as the necessary hull design to travel forward while ice-breaking is inefficient in open water. The ship is driven by azimuth thrusters, which can be turned around 180 degrees to propel it backward.

Largest bulk carrier ship

The *Vale Beijing* and *Vale Qingdao* were constructed by South Korean shipbuilder STX Offshore & Shipbuilding and took their first loads in December 2011 and June 2012, respectively. Each can carry some 891 million lb. (404,389 tonnes) of ore.

KNOW YOUR LINERS
Ocean liners transfer people between two set destinations. By contrast, cruise ships are used purely for leisure purposes.

LARGEST BY DISPLACEMENT

Aircraft carrier (under construction): USS *Gerald R. Ford* (USA). Length ca. 1,092 ft. (333 m); beam (greatest width) ca. 147 ft. (45 m); full-load displacement ca. 222 million lb. (101,000 tonnes).

Battleship: *Yamato* (*pictured*) and *Musashi* (both Japan). Length 863 ft. (263 m); beam 127 ft. (38.7 m); full-load displacement 157 million lb. (71,111 tonnes).

Hospital ship: USNS *Mercy* (*pictured*) and USNS *Comfort* (both USA). Length 894 ft. (272.5 m); beam 105 ft. 8 in. (32.2 m); full-load displacement 138 million lb. (62,922 tonnes).

Battle cruiser: Admiral class (UK). Length 860 ft. 6 in. (262.3 m); beam 104 ft. (31.7 m); full-load displacement 108 million lb. (49,136 tonnes).

Amphibious assault ship: Wasp class (USA). Length 843 ft. (257 m); full-load displacement 81 million lb. (36,740 tonnes).

cargo and crew. When she was scrapped in 2010, she became the **largest ship scrapped**—at the Alang Ship-Breaking Yard in India.

Shipwreck
The 708 million-lb. (321,186-tonne) deadweight very large crude carrier (VLCC) *Energy Determination* blew up and broke in two in the Strait of Hormuz in the Persian Gulf on December 12, 1979. Its hull value was $58 million.

The **most valuable shipwreck** was found by treasure hunter Mel Fisher (USA) off the Key West coast in Florida, USA, on July 20, 1985. The ship *Nuestra Señora de Atocha* was carrying 881,841 lb. (40 tonnes) of gold and silver and approximately 70 lb. (31.75 kg) of emeralds when it went down in a hurricane in September 1622 with 265 people onboard, of whom only five survived.

Largest pipe-laying ship
The MV *Solitaire* has a deadweight tonnage of 281 million lb. (127,435 tonnes). She was constructed as a bulk carrier in 1972 but was converted to a pipe-laying ship in 1998. The *Solitaire* measures 984 ft. (300 m) long—1,302 ft. (397 m) including pipe-laying equipment—with a beam of 133 ft. (40.6 m), and can carry 49 million lb. (22,000 tonnes) of pipe, which she can lay at a rate of 5.5 miles (9 km) per day.

Largest cruise ship
MS *Allure of the Seas* is 1,187 ft. (362 m) long, 215 ft. (66 m) wide, and has a gross tonnage (volume of its enclosed spaces) of 225,282. It towers 213 ft. (65 m) above the waterline.

The *Allure of the Seas* incorporates 16 passenger decks and can accommodate 6,318 guests. It has a maximum speed of 22 knots (25.3 mph; 40.7 km/h). The photograph above right shows the outdoor shopping mall and guest suites; to the right, the ship's promenade gallery is pictured. Among many amenities the ship boasts a spa, an ice cream parlor and a nightclub.

LONGEST …

Container ship
With a length of 1,300 ft. (397 m), a beam of 183 ft. (56 m), and a depth from deck edge to keel of 98 ft. (30 m), the MV *Emma Maersk* is the largest container vessel. It carries a crew of 30 and has a speed in excess of 25 knots (28.7 mph; 47.2 km/h). It can carry more than 11,000 containers.

Naval vessel
The USS *Enterprise* (CVN-65), which was commissioned in 1961 and in service until 2012, measures 1,122 ft. (342 m) long, although with a smaller displacement than the later Nimitz-class carriers. *Enterprise* is unique among carriers—another five of her class were planned but never built. She had a capacity of 5,828 people, including the crew and air wing, which comprised around 60 aircraft with a maximum of 90. She was also the **first nuclear-powered aircraft carrier**.

Cruise liner
The SS *Norway*, which has a gross tonnage of 76,049, is 1,035 ft. (315.53 m) long and can accommodate 2,032 passengers and 900 crew. She was built as the SS *France* in 1960 and renamed after purchase in June 1979 by Knut Kloster (Norway). The *Norway* is normally employed on cruises in the Caribbean and is based in Miami, Florida, USA.

Sailing ship
The French-owned sister ships *Club Med 1* and *2* are each 613 ft. (187 m) long. They have five aluminum masts and 30,100 sq. ft. (2,800 m²) of computer-controlled polyester sails. Each caters for around 400 passengers. With their relatively small sail area and powerful engines, the ships are technically motor-sailers.

Submarine: 941 Akula class (Russia). NATO designation: "Typhoon." Length 562 ft. 7 in. (171.5 m); dived displacement 58 million lb. (26,500 tonnes).

Attack submarine: Oscar II class (USSR). Length 505 ft. (154 m); full-load displacement 37 million lb. (16,600 tonnes).

Wing-in-ground effect vehicle*: "Caspian Sea Monster" (USSR). Length 348 ft. (106 m); wingspan 131 ft. (40 m); weight 1.19 million lb. (540 tonnes).

*vehicle whose wings are close to the ground, or water, in flight

Hovercraft: Zubr class (Russia). NATO designation: "Pomornik." Length 187 ft. (57 m); beam 73.1 ft. (22.3 m); full-load displacement 1.17 million lb. (535 tonnes).

Hydrofoil: *Aleksandr Kuhanovich* (USSR). NATO designation: "Babochka." Full-load displacement of more than 882,000 lb. (400 tonnes).

SEE THE VIDEO WITH THE FREE APP

MASSIVE MONSTER

Fanny—aka Project Tradinno (a portmanteau of "tradition" and "innovation")—is a 24,250-lb. (11-tonne) dragon powered by a 2.0-liter turbo diesel engine with 140 hp!

AUGMENTED REALITY ALERT!

ON THIS PAGE

Largest walking robot

Measuring 51 ft. 6 in. (15.72 m) in length, 40 ft. 5 in. (12.33 m) in width, and 26 ft. 10 in. (8.20 m) in height, the biggest four-legged walking robot was unleashed by Zollner Elektronik AG (Germany) in Zandt, Germany, on September 27, 2012. The mighty mechatronic beast—pictured below without its scaly covering—is radio remote-controlled and was created to feature in Germany's longest-running folk play!

MISSION TO MARS

Largest Martian rover: Exploring the "Red Planet"

Curiosity is the fourth rover to land successfully on Mars, after NASA's *Sojourner* (1997), *Spirit*, and *Opportunity* rovers (both 2004). Around 9 ft. 10 in. (3 m) long and with a mass of 1,982 lb. (899 kg), *Curiosity* is the size of a small auto and about twice the size of the biggest previous rovers. It is capable of traveling 656 ft. (200 m) per day over the rough Martian terrain. It landed in Gale crater on August 6, 2012—a location that scientists selected because it seemed a likely zone in which to find evidence of past conditions on the "Red Planet" that could have supported life.

6,144 Different wavelengths of ultraviolet, visible, and infrared light that can be recorded.

"Seven minutes of terror"

This is what the NASA mission scientists and engineers dubbed *Curiosity*'s landing sequence. The audacious landing employed a technique never before used in planetary exploration. First, the spacecraft used its heat shield to slow down as it entered the Martian atmosphere. After deploying a parachute to slow down farther, the spacecraft jettisoned the parachute, slowed again using retro rockets, and lowered the rover on a cable. After gently dropping the rover onto the surface, the spacecraft's tether to the rover was cut, and the tether flew away sideways before impacting to avoid crashing onto the rover itself.

BORING RECORD Pictured here is the first hole drilled on Mars for sample collection; it measures just 0.63 in. (1.6 cm) across and 2.5 in. (6.4 cm) deep.

Curiosity's rock zapper

Sharing the rover's mast with its MastCam, the ChemCam contains a 1,067-nanometer infrared laser that can vaporize small amounts of rock as far as 23 ft. (7 m) from the rover. The rock vapor from these brief laser pulses is analyzed through observation of the spectra of light they emit.

FOR THE RECORD

Is Mars jinxed? Of the 40 missions to Mars since 1960, 22 have failed. The "Great Galactic Ghoul" is a mythical monster often invoked to explain the disasters, as it munches on Mars probes. No other planet has seen so many failed missions, some of which are listed below.

Layered terrain at Mount Sharp

Aeolis Mons (Mount Sharp) is the central peak in Gale Crater. Rising 18,000 ft. (5,500 m) above the crater floor, it is the ultimate destination for *Curiosity*. The panorama from the rover's Mast Camera (MastCam) shows distinct horizontal layers in the mountain; inset is a close-up of a small broken rock with blue-white material exposed.

FAILED MISSIONS TO MARS

To date, the number of successful Martian exploration missions is put by NASA at 16 (with a further two partial successes). Some of the lowlights include:

PROBE	ORIGIN	LAUNCH DATE	WHAT HAPPENED?
Phobos-Grunt	Russia	November 8, 2011	Spacecraft thrusters failed to fire; remains in Earth orbit
Beagle 2	Europe	June 2, 2003	Carried to Mars by *Mars Express* but lost on landing
Mars Polar Lander	USA	January 3, 1999	Contact lost upon arrival at Mars
Mars Climate Orbiter	USA	December 11, 1998	Crashed into Mars instead of entering orbit due to a mix-up between imperial and metric unit calculations; cost $327.6 million, making it **most expensive conversion error** of all time
Nozomi	Japan	July 4, 1998	Failed to enter Mars orbit
Mars '96	Russia	November 16, 1996	Engine failure in Earth orbit
Mars Observer	USA	September 25, 1992	Contact lost three days before arriving at Mars
Phobos 1 and 2	USSR	July 7 and 12, 1988	Contact lost with both landers and orbiters
Mars 3	USSR	May 28, 1971	Lander operated for just 20 seconds on the surface before contact was lost
Zond 2	USSR	November 30, 1964	Successful flyby of Mars but failed radio meant no data was received on Earth
Mariner 3	USA	November 5, 1964	Flyby mission failed after launch malfunction; remains in solar orbit
Mars 1	USSR	November 1, 1962	Enjoyed 61 days of radio transmissions during flyby until antenna orientation system failed
Mars 1M No. 1 and No. 2	USSR	October 10 and 14, 1960	Both probes experienced control-system failures and reached just 75 miles (120 km) before breaking up

SCIENCE & TECHNOLOGY
www.guinnessworldrecords.com

GUINNESS
WORLD
RECORDS
2014

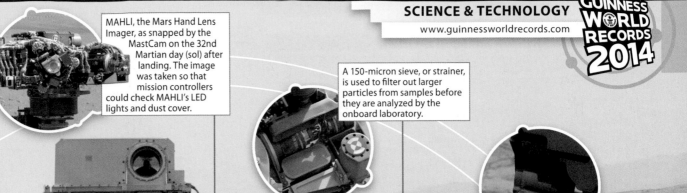

MAHLI, the Mars Hand Lens Imager, as snapped by the MastCam on the 32nd Martian day (sol) after landing. The image was taken so that mission controllers could check MAHLI's LED lights and dust cover.

A 150-micron sieve, or strainer, is used to filter out larger particles from samples before they are analyzed by the onboard laboratory.

The 1.77-in.-wide (4.5-cm) scoop contains the first sample obtained by the rover's drill. This gray-green powder is from a rock nicknamed "John Klein."

1.5
Distance in miles *Curiosity* was from its landing target—not bad after 350 million miles (563 million km)!

The first sample of dust and sand collected by the robot arm appears as a white smudge on the surface of the rover's observation tray. Martian wind may have shifted the sample from the center.

Martian self-portrait

Curiosity is a nuclear-powered rover. A radio-isotope thermal generator produces heat, which is converted onboard to 125 watts of electrical power. This is used for all of the rover's instruments and propulsion, as well as for keeping its systems warm.

The rover is seen here in a "self-portrait" digitally sewn together from images taken by its Hand Lens Imager (MAHLI), located on the robot arm.

Samples of powdered Martian rock and soil are funneled into the CheMin instrument through this 1.37-in.-wide (3.5-cm) hole. CheMin fires X-rays at the samples to determine chemical compositions.

Curiosity has six 19.6-in.-wide (50-cm) wheels, which use a rocker-bogie suspension system. The front and rear wheels can be steered independently, letting the rover perform turns on the spot. They give *Curiosity* an average speed of around 100 ft. (30 m) per hour.

SPACE TELESCOPES

measures 8 ft. 10 in. x 15 ft. 5 in. (2.7 x 4.7 m), with a mass upon launch of 2,320 lb. (1,052 kg). Since its launch, it has followed Earth in a heliocentric orbit and used its 4-ft. 6-in.-wide (1.4-m) mirror and 95-megapixel camera to identify 2,740 planet candidates orbiting 2,036 stars, as of January 2013.

Largest infrared space telescope

The European Space Agency's (ESA) Herschel space observatory launched on May 14, 2009. It measures 24 ft. 7 in. x 13 ft. (7.5 x 4 m) with a mass on launch of 7,500 lb. (3,400 kg). Its 11-ft. 5-in. (3.5-m) reflector is the **largest mirror sent into space**. From a location ca. 0.9 million miles (1.5 million km) from Earth, it has performed observations at far infrared and submillimeter wavelengths. Its spectral range let Herschel see through dust clouds that hide galactic centers and star-forming regions.

Longest exposure by the Hubble space telescope

The Hubble extreme deep field is a composite photograph that was released on September 25, 2012. It combines a decade's worth of observations of a small patch of sky in the constellation of Fornax, totaling more than 2 million seconds of exposure time. The image contains around 5,500 separate galaxies.

First detection of cosmic gamma-ray bursts

The Vela satellites were developed by the USA to monitor Earth for nuclear tests that contravened the 1963 Partial Test Ban Treaty. On July 2, 1967, Velas 3 and 4 detected a flash of gamma rays that did not match the signature of any known nuclear test. Although the Velas were not designed to be astronomical instruments, they had accidentally discovered gamma-ray bursts, which we now know are associated with supernovae in distant galaxies. This discovery remained classified until 1973.

Most comets discovered by a spacecraft

The ESA/NASA spacecraft SOHO (solar and heliospheric observatory) was launched in December 1995 to study the Sun from L1—the place between the Sun and Earth where the gravities of the two bodies cancel each other out. As of October 2012, SOHO had discovered 2,378 comets, although these discoveries have been purely serendipitous.

Largest planet-hunter space telescope

NASA's Kepler space telescope was launched on March 7, 2009 on a Delta II rocket from Cape Canaveral, USA. The spacecraft

Most manned missions to a space telescope

The Hubble space telescope (HST) is the only space observatory designed to be visited and serviced by astronauts. The first mission was STS-61 in December 1993, during which astronauts repaired a spherical aberration in its primary mirror. Four more Space Shuttle missions to Hubble occurred in February 1997, December 1999, March 2002, and May 2009.

First lunar observatory

Apollo 16, the penultimate manned mission to the Moon, spent almost three days on the Descartes Highlands from April 21, 1972. Among the experiments deployed was the far ultraviolet camera/spectrograph. It used a 3-in. (7.6-cm) telescope to image objects such as Earth, nebulae, and star clusters. The instrument was deployed in the lunar module's shadow to prevent overheating.

STILL UP THERE... Although the film from the far ultraviolet camera was returned to Earth for processing, the telescope remains on the Moon.

HISTORIC SPACE TELESCOPES

Hubble space telescope: Equipped with 7-ft. 9-in. (2.4-m) reflecting mirror. Launched: April 24, 1990 on the Space Shuttle. Deployed: April 25, 1990.

Chandra X-ray telescope: Features high-resolution camera (HRC); advanced CCD imaging spectrometer (ACIS); low- and high-energy transmission grating spectrometers (LETGS and HETGS, respectively). Launched: July 23, 1999.

XMM-Newton telescope: Equipped with three X-ray telescopes. Launched: December 10, 1999 by an Arianne 5 rocket.

Integral gamma-ray observatory: Incorporates X-ray monitor, optical monitoring camera, gamma-ray spectrometer, and gamma-ray imager. Launched: October 17, 2002.

Fermi gamma-ray space telescope: Carries gamma-ray burst monitor and large area telescope. Launched: June 11, 2008.

Coldest space telescope

The ESA's *Planck* spacecraft is a space observatory designed to study the cosmic microwave background. To detect this faint radiation—echoes of the first light ever released, shortly after the big bang—the spacecraft's instruments need to be very cold. Launched on May 14, 2009, *Planck* uses active refrigeration along with a shield to protect it from the Sun to reach its operating temperature of -459.49°F (-273.05°C), one-tenth of a degree above absolute zero.

FOR THE RECORD

The 18 segments of the *James Webb* mirror are made from gold-coated beryllium (₄Be), a relatively rare element. Combined, the mirrors have an area more than five-and-a-half times greater than *Hubble*'s.

Nearest celestial body imaged by the *Hubble* space telescope

On April 16, 1999, astronomers revealed the first image of the Moon taken with the *Hubble* space telescope. The image was taken while the telescope's spectrograph was measuring the colors of sunlight reflected from the lunar surface. The image is a close-up of the Copernicus crater, showing features just 278 ft. (85 m) across. The Moon, our nearest celestial neighbor, is 238,855 miles (384,400 km) from Earth.

Hubble, the **largest space telescope**, weighs 24,250 lb. (11 tonnes) and is 43 ft. (13.1 m) in overall length, with a 7-ft 9-in (2.4-m) reflector. At a cost of $2.1 billion, it is also the **most expensive telescope**.

Most powerful X-ray telescope

Launched in July 1999, the *Chandra* X-ray telescope has resolving power equivalent to the ability to read a STOP sign at a distance of 12 miles (19 km). Its extreme sensitivity is possible because of the size and smoothness of the mirrors. If the U.S. state of Colorado were as smooth as *Chandra*'s mirrors, the 14,110-ft. (4,299-m) mountain Pikes Peak would stand less than 1 in. (2.2 cm) tall.

With a mass of 50,161 lb. (22,753 kg), the *Chandra* telescope also represents the **heaviest payload launched by the Space Shuttle**.

Largest radio space telescope

On July 18, 2011, Russia launched *Spektr-R* from the Baikonur Cosmodrome, Kazakhstan. It is designed to work in tandem with ground-based radio telescopes, using a technique called interferometry. Upon reaching space, it unfurled a 33-ft.-diameter (10-m) radio dish of 27 carbon-fiber "petals."

Largest space mirror under construction

NASA's *James Webb* space telescope is set to succeed the *Hubble* space telescope. Its primary mirror will consist of 18 hexagonal segments with a combined diameter of 21 ft. 4 in. (6.5 m) and a light-collecting surface area of 269 sq. ft. (25 m²).

FOR MORE MOONS, FOCUS ON P. 186

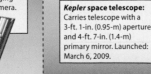

Granat (formerly known as Astron 2): Incorporated gamma radiation telescope, X-ray telescope and spectroscope. Launched: January 12, 1989. Ended transmissions: November 27, 1998.

Herschel telescope (formerly known as FIRST): Incorporates 11-ft. 5-in.-diameter (3.5-m) mirror. Launched: May 14, 2009.

Planck telescope: 4 ft. 11 in. (1.5 m) in diameter. Equipped with the low-frequency instrument (LFI) and high-frequency instrument (HFI). Launched: May 14, 2009.

Spitzer infrared space telescope: Incorporates 2-ft. 9-in.-diameter (85-cm) telescope. Includes infrared spectrograph, multiband imaging photometer, infrared array camera. Launched: August 25, 2003.

Kepler space telescope: Carries telescope with a 3-ft. 1-in. (0.95-m) aperture and 4-ft. 7-in. (1.4-m) primary mirror. Launched: March 6, 2009.

= Size of an astronaut relative to the size of each space telescope.

COMMERCIAL SPACE

RESTING PLACE IN SPACE
The U.S. company Celestis, which organized the event below, has carried out burials in space since 1997.

$30 MILLION
Total Google Lunar X Prize award money offered.

Largest X Prize

On September 13, 2007, Google and the X Prize Foundation announced the Google Lunar X Prize, a competition for privately funded lunar exploration. Of several awards offered, the largest—$20 million—will be awarded to the first privately funded team to produce a robot that lands on the Moon and travels 1,640 ft. (500 m) across its surface. All awards will expire at the end of 2015, or when they have been claimed.

First commercial astronaut

After the first successful space flight of Scaled Composites' (USA) *SpaceShipOne* on June 21, 2004, her pilot, Mike Melvill (USA), was awarded the first commercial astronaut wings by the U.S. Federal Aviation Administration.

As of February 2013, the only other individual to be awarded commercial astronaut wings is Brian Binnie (USA), for his successful flight of *SpaceShipOne* on October 4, 2004. (*See "Space Tourism Milestones" below.*)

First commercial filmed in space

An advertising campaign for Tnuva milk, showing cosmonaut Vasily Tsibliyev (Russia) drinking milk aboard the *Mir* space station, was broadcast on August 22, 1997.

This occasion also marked the first time that milk in liquid form had been sent into space.

Heaviest commercial satellite

The weightiest commercial satellite is *TerreStar-1*, with a launch mass, including propellant, of 15,220 lb. (6,903.8 kg). It was constructed by Space Systems/Loral (USA) and is now operated by Dish Network Corporation (USA). *TerreStar-1* was launched on July 1, 2009 by an Arianespace Ariane 5 ECA booster and will serve as a communications satellite for around 15 years.

Highest-capacity communications satellite

The *ViaSat-1* communications satellite has a proven throughput (the amount of information a system can deal with in a given period) of 134 Gbps (gigabits per second). Launched from Baikonur Cosmodrome in Kazakhstan on

October 19, 2011, aboard a Proton Breeze M rocket, the satellite is in geostationary orbit above North America at a longitude of 115.1° W.

Largest global navigation system

Global navigation systems are constellations of Earth-orbiting satellites that allow users to pinpoint their location on the Earth using triangulation—a way of calculating

Largest inflatable space habitat

Built by Bigelow Aerospace (USA), *Genesis I* and *Genesis II* (seen right, in orbit) are unmanned inflatables to demonstrate future manned space-module technology. They are 14 ft. 5 in. (4.4 m) long and 8 ft. 4 in. (2.54 m) in diameter, with a pressurized internal volume of 406.1 cu. ft. (11.5 m^3). *Genesis I* and *II* were launched on July 12, 2006 and June 28, 2007, respectively.

FIRST ASTEROID MINING COMPANY

Officially founded in November 2010, Arkyd Astronautics is a U.S.-based company (now a subsidiary of Planetary Resources Inc.) unveiled at a press conference on April 24, 2012 at the Museum of Flight in Seattle, Washington, USA. Planetary Resources Inc. is a private company that intends to exploit mineral wealth in asteroids. Its investors include movie director James Cameron (Canada), Google cofounder Larry Page (USA), and entrepreneur and space tourist Charles Simonyi (USA, b. Hungary, *see below*).

Largest space burial

On May 22, 2012, the Dragon C2+ mission began with the launch of a Falcon 9 rocket. The second stage of the rocket carried a canister containing samples of the cremated remains of 308 people, including U.S. astronaut Gordon Cooper and Canadian actor James Doohan, who portrayed "Scotty" in *Star Trek*.

SPACE TOURISM MILESTONES

First civilian in space (female): As well as being the first civilian in space, Valentina Tereshkova also became the **first woman in space** when she took part in the *Vostok 6* orbital flight on June 16–19, 1963.

First civilian in space (male): Konstantin Feoktistov (Russia) made his only space flight on board *Voskhod 1* from October 12 to 13, 1964.

First space tourist (male): American businessman Dennis Tito was the first space tourist. Tito's trip to the *ISS* lasted from April 28 to May 6, 2001.

First privately funded manned space flight: On June 21, 2004, Mike Melvill (USA) flew *SpaceShipOne* to an altitude of 62.21 miles (100.12 km), taking off and landing at Mojave Airport in California, USA.

Highest altitude by a commercial astronaut: On October 4, 2004, Brian Binnie (USA) flew *SpaceShipOne* to 69.58 miles (111.99 km) above the Mojave Desert, California, USA. This was the plane's third and final space flight.

GUINNESS WORLD RECORDS 2014

First commercial payload launched on a Space Shuttle

When the Space Shuttle *Columbia* launched on November 11, 1982, it carried two commercial communications satellites in its cargo bay. *SBS 3* and *Anik C3* were owned by Satellite Business Systems (USA) and Telesat Canada respectively. The mission, STS-5, was the fifth flight in the U.S. Space Shuttle program.

400
Transmissions (TV, phone, and communication signals) by *Telstar 1* in its first six months.

First active direct relay communications satellite

Built by Bell Telephone Laboratories (USA), *Telstar 1* was launched on July 10, 1962. This roughly spherical satellite measured 2 ft. 10.5 in. (87.6 cm) across and was equipped with solar cells and batteries to actively relay intercontinental communications on Earth. It ceased operations on February 21, 1963.

the relative position of a point by referring to other, known, points. The USA's Global Positioning System (GPS) uses 31 satellites while Russia's GLONASS uses 24 satellites, each in orbits that provide 100% coverage of the Earth's surface. China's BeiDou service employs 14 satellites and provides navigation coverage for Asia, with the goal of growing to 35 satellites. Europe's Galileo system is expected to be fully operational by 2019, with 30 satellites. GPS and GLONASS became fully operational in 1994 and 1995 respectively.

Most active artificial satellites in one orbital zone

As of December 2012, there were 1,046 active operational satellites orbiting the Earth. Low Earth orbit is defined as the region around the Earth up to an altitude of around 1,060 miles (1,700 km). With 503 active and operational satellites, this is the most

crowded zone for satellites. Geosynchronous orbit, at an altitude of approximately 22,180 miles (35,700 km), is occupied by some 432 active and operational satellites.

Largest marine space-launch platform

The *Odyssey* launch platform, owned and operated by Sea Launch (USA), is a self-propelled, semisubmersible rocket launchpad measuring 436 ft. (132.8 m) long and 220 ft. (67 m) wide. This former North Sea oil platform provides accommodation for 68 crew and has been operating as a commercial space launch facility since its inaugural launch in March 1999.

PANEL SHOW
The two prominent "wings" of the Dragon capsule are equipped with eight solar panels to provide power for the craft.

First resupply mission to the *ISS* by a private company

On May 22, 2012, U.S. private space company SpaceX launched the Dragon C2+ mission to the *International Space Station* (*ISS*). An unmanned Dragon capsule blasted off from Cape Canaveral in Florida, USA, atop a Falcon 9 rocket and rendezvoused with the *ISS*; the Dragon capsule was captured by the station's robot arm on May 25 (*see left*). *ISS* crew unloaded the capsule's cargo and refilled it with items to be returned to Earth. After nearly six days docked with the *ISS*, the Dragon capsule uncoupled and splashed down in the Pacific Ocean (*pictured above*).

First space tourist (female): On September 18, 2006, Anousheh Ansari (Iran) lifted off in the Soyuz TMA-9 capsule on a 10-day visit to the *International Space Station* (*ISS*).

Most visits into space by a tourist: Charles Simonyi (USA, b. Hungary) made his first space trip on April 7, 2007. At 60 years old, he made a second voyage, departing on March 26, 2009. Both trips were to the *ISS*.

Most expensive tourist trip: As of 2009, a visit to the *ISS* cost $20–35 million. Since 2001, seven individuals, including Guy Laliberté (Canada), the founder of Cirque du Soleil (*below, second from left in bottom row*), have made the trip.

First commercial passenger spaceplane: *SpaceShipTwo* made its inaugural test flight on March 23, 2010. Richard Branson's (UK) Virgin Galactic is planning to use such aircraft to fly space tourists to the edge of the Earth's atmosphere.

First purpose-built commercial spaceport: Located in New Mexico, USA, Spaceport America has been constructed to facilitate commercial ventures in space, including tourism, and officially opened in October 2011. Twelve suborbital launches had taken place here as of August 2012.

MOONS

Largest moon compared to its planet

At 2,158 miles (3,474 km) across, Earth's moon is 0.27 times the diameter of Earth. Our Moon is the largest of the three moons in the inner solar system and the only other world to be visited by humans. We only ever see the same side of the Moon from Earth—the far side remains turned away from us.

Dwarf planet with the most moons

Pluto—which lost its status as a true planet in 2006 and is now a "dwarf"—has five moons. They are: Charon, discovered in 1978, Nix and Hydra, discovered in 2005, and two others discovered in 2011 and 2012 and provisionally named S/2011 P 1 and S/2012 P 1. Many scientists regard Charon as a binary dwarf planet.

Closest moon to a planet

The Martian satellite Phobos is 5,827 miles (9,378 km) from the center of Mars—equal to 3,716 miles (5,981 km) above the surface.

Smoothest surface in the solar system

Jupiter's large icy moon Europa has the smoothest surface of any solid body in the solar system. The only prominent relief on its surface takes the form of ridges a few hundred yards in height.

1.49
Distance in inches that the Moon moves away from Earth every year.

Planet with the most moons

As of 2013, a total of 67 natural satellites have been discovered orbiting Jupiter. Saturn has the second greatest number of moons, with 62. Earth, Mars, Uranus, Neptune, and Pluto (dwarf planet) have 1, 2, 27, 13, and 5 moons respectively. Most of the Jovian and Saturnian moons are small, irregularly shaped bodies of ice and rock, and many are almost certainly captured asteroids.

First pictures from the Moon

The first images from the surface of Earth's moon were taken by the Soviet robotic lander *Luna 9* (*right*). Launched on January 31, 1966, the small probe landed on February 3 and transmitted data until February 7.

First men on the Moon

Neil Alden Armstrong (USA, *above*), commander of the Apollo 11 mission, became the first man to set foot on the Moon, on the Sea of Tranquility, at 10:56:15 p.m. Eastern Daylight Time (EDT) on July 20, 1969 (02:56:15 GMT/Greenwich Mean Time on July 21, 1969). He was followed out of the lunar module *Eagle* by Colonel Edwin Eugene "Buzz" Aldrin, Jr. (USA, *right*). Only 10 others, listed below, have ever walked on the Moon.

Farthest moon from a planet

Neso, the 13th moon of Neptune, was observed on August 14, 2002 and recognized as Neptune's moon in 2003. It orbits the planet at an average distance of 30,055,664 miles (48,370,000 km), taking 25.66 years to complete one orbit. Neso measures about 37.28 miles (60 km) across.

Deepest crater in the solar system

The far-side South Pole-Aitken impact crater on Earth's moon is 1,400 miles (2,250 km) in diameter and on average 39,000 ft. (12,000 m) deep below its rim. By comparison, London is approximately 35 miles (56 km) from east to west—40 times smaller—and Everest, the world's **highest mountain**, would fit inside the crater with more than 10,000 ft. (3,000 m) to spare.

THE OTHER MEN ON THE MOON

All dates GMT
All nationalities USA

1969

3. Pete Conrad:
Apollo 12
Walked on Moon:
Nov 19–20, 1969
Age at first lunar walk:
39 years 5 months 17 days

4. Alan Bean: Apollo 12
Walked on Moon:
Nov 19–20, 1969
Age at first lunar walk: 37 years 8 months 4 days

5. Alan Shepard:
Apollo 14
Walked on Moon:
Feb 5–6, 1971
Age at first lunar walk: 47 years 2 months 18 days; Shepard became the **oldest person to walk on the Moon** on February 5, 1971

6. Edgar Mitchell: Apollo 14
Walked on Moon:
Feb 5–6, 1971
Age at first lunar walk: 40 years 4 months 19 days

7. David Scott:
Apollo 15
Walked on Moon:
Jul 31–Aug 2, 1971
Age at first lunar walk: 39 years 1 month 25 days

Largest extraterrestrial lakes

In January 2004, radar images from the NASA/ESA *Cassini* mission revealed about 75 liquid methane lakes near the north pole of Saturn's moon Titan. The largest are 68 miles (110 km) wide. Titan is also home to the **largest methane sea**, Kraken Mare, a body 727 miles (1,170 km) across with an area similar to that of the Caspian Sea on Earth (143,550 sq. miles; 371,800 km²).

Most powerful volcano in the solar system

Loki, an active volcano on Jupiter's moon Io, emits more heat than all of Earth's active volcanoes put together. Its huge caldera (volcanic crater) is more than 4,000 sq. miles (10,000 km²) in area and is regularly flooded with molten lava.

Coldest observed geological activity

Active geysers of frigid nitrogen gas erupt several miles high into the thin atmosphere of Neptune's large moon Triton. With a surface temperature of -391°F (-235°C), Triton's lakes of water are frozen as hard as steel.

Most volcanically active body in the solar system

Enormous volcanic eruption plumes—some of them reaching several hundred miles into space—issue from the surface of Io, one of Jupiter's moons. This activity is driven by tidal energy inside Io, which results from gravitational interactions between Jupiter, Io, and one of the other moons, Europa.

Only six planets in our solar system have moons. Below are the largest moons of each planet.

Moon (Earth)
In comparison to Earth:
Mean radius: 0.2727
Mass: 0.0123
Volume: 0.020

Phobos (Mars)
In comparison to Earth:
Mean radius: 0.0017
Mass: 0.0000000018
Volume: 0.000000005

Ganymede (Jupiter)
Largest moon in the solar system
In comparison to Earth:
Mean radius: 0.413
Mass: 0.025
Volume: 0.0704

Titan (Saturn)
In comparison to Earth:
Mean radius: 0.404
Mass: 0.0225
Volume: 0.066

Titania (Uranus)
In comparison to Earth:
Mean radius: 0.1235
Mass: 0.00059
Volume: 0.0019

Triton (Neptune)
In comparison to Earth:
Mean radius: 0.2122
Mass: 0.0036
Volume: 0.0096

Most craters on any moon

The most heavily cratered moon is Callisto, the outermost of Jupiter's four large moons, an ancient relic whose surface is 100% covered with impact craters. No evidence of any other geological processes has been discovered. Callisto is around the same size as Mercury, with a diameter of 3,000 miles (4,800 km).

Largest ice plumes

Cryovolcanism is the eruption of cold material such as nitrogen, water, or methane. Active cryovolcanism on Enceladus, Saturn's sixth-largest moon, had been predicted after the geologically young surface of this icy moon was revealed by the two *Voyager* spacecraft in the early 1980s. In 2005, the *Cassini* spacecraft showed huge plumes of water ice—at least as tall as Enceladus's 313-mile (505-km) diameter—that had erupted above the moon's south pole.

FOR THE RECORD

From January 16 to June 23, 1973, the Soviet *Lunokhod 2* rover traveled 23 miles (37 km) across the eastern edge of Mare Serenitatis (Sea of Serenity) on the Moon. This is the **greatest distance traveled on another world**.

FIRST ...

Asteroid found with a moon

In 1993, NASA's *Galileo* spacecraft passed the asteroid Ida, en route to Jupiter. When images from the flyby were examined by scientists, on February 17, 1994, they discovered that Ida, which is 33.3 miles (53.6 km) along its longest axis, has its own natural satellite. This moon—assigned the name Dactyl, a creature from Greek mythology—measures just 1 x 0.9 x 0.7 miles (1.6 x 1.4 x 1.2 km) and orbits Ida once every 20 hours.

Discovery of extraterrestrial volcanism

Shortly after *Voyager 1*'s encounter with Jupiter on March 5, 1979, navigation engineer Linda Morabito (USA, b. Canada) discovered an anomalous crescent protruding from the moon Io while examining images. Although it first appeared to be another moon behind Io, the crescent was soon confirmed to be above a part of Io that looked like a volcano. Morabito had discovered the first active volcano on a world other than Earth.

TURN TO P. 12 FOR RECORDS ABOUT EARTH

1971

8. James Irwin:
Apollo 15
Walked on Moon: Jul 31–Aug 2, 1971
Age at first lunar walk: 41 years 4 months 14 days

9. John Young:
Apollo 16
Walked on Moon: Apr 21–23, 1972
Age at first lunar walk: 41 years 6 months 28 days

10. Charles Duke: Apollo 16
Walked on Moon: Apr 21–23, 1972
Age at first lunar walk: 36 years 6 months 18 days—making him the **youngest man to walk on the Moon**

11. Eugene Cernan:
Apollo 17
Walked on Moon: Dec 11–14, 1972
Age at first lunar walk: 38 years 9 months 7 days; although he was 11th to land, when stepping off the lunar surface on December 14, 1972 Cernan became the **last man on the Moon**

1972

12. Harrison Schmitt:
Apollo 17
Walked on Moon: Dec 11–14, 1972
Age at first lunar walk: 37 years 5 months 8 days

ELECTRICITY

First battery

The "Parthian batteries" are two clay jars found in 1936 in a tomb near modern-day Baghdad, Iraq. Dating to ca. 200 BC, their tops were sealed with an asphalt plug that held a copper tube in place. A thin iron rod was inserted and hung in the center of the tube without touching it. By filling the jar with acidic liquids, such as vinegar or fruit juice, a small current of 1.5–2 volts (V) was produced, thus forming the first battery.

First electrical power station

The world's first electrical power station was built in 1878 by Sigmund Schuckert in Ettal, Bavaria, Germany. Using 24 dynamos powered by a steam-driven engine, the privately owned station provided power to illuminate the gardens of the Linderhof Palace near Ettal.

The **first public power station** was at 57 Holborn Viaduct, London, UK. Built by the Edison Electric Light Station company, it opened in January 1882 and supplied power to light the Holborn Viaduct and local businesses.

Largest Tesla coil

Invented by Nikola Tesla (USA, b. Serbia) around 1891, the Tesla coil is a method of generating high-voltage, low-current electricity. Tesla coils are most commonly used to produce lightning displays at science museums and in science classes. The largest operational Tesla coil is the 130-kilowatt (kW) two-coil system mounted on top of a 38-ft.-tall (12-m) sculpture at Gibbs Farm in Kaipara Harbour, New Zealand.

Largest Van de Graaff generator

The world's largest Van de Graaff generator is currently housed at the Museum of Science in Boston, Massachusetts, USA, and once had a very real use in exploring atomic science. Built by the physicist Dr. Robert J. Van de Graaff (USA) in the 1930s, the generator has two conjoined 15-ft. (4.5-m) aluminum spheres standing on columns 22 ft. (6.7 m) tall and can generate 2 million V.

6,613
Weight in tons of each of the main generators.

Largest hydroelectric power station output

Completed on July 4, 2012, the Three Gorges Dam project in Yiling District, Yichang, Hubei Province, China, has a generation capacity of 22,500 megawatts (MW). The hydroelectric-generation station on the Yangtze River comprises 32 main generators, each capable of 700-MW-generation capacity, and two smaller 50-MW generators that provide power for the plant facility.

ELECTRICAL LANDMARKS

1752 | **1800** | **1808** | **1821** | **1837**

1752: To test the electrical properties of lightning, Benjamin Franklin (USA) flies a kite in a thunderstorm. When it is struck by lightning, Franklin collects the electrical charge.

1800: Alessandro Volta (Italy) invents the Voltaic Pile, the first battery to produce a constant and reliable electrical current.

1808: Humphry Davy (UK) invents the **first "arc lamp"**—a piece of carbon that glowed when attached to a battery by wires.

1821: The **first electric motor** is invented by Michael Faraday (UK).

1837: Thomas Davenport (USA) creates the industrial electric motor, now widely used in electrical appliances.

Most powerful battery

Providing 36 megawatt hours (MWh) of energy storage, the world's most powerful battery is housed in a dedicated building larger than a soccer field and was commissioned in Zhangbei, Hebei Province, China. The battery regulates and stores energy produced from local 100-MW wind turbines and 40-MW solar photovoltaic panels that can power 12,000 homes for up to an hour in the event of total grid failure.

Most powerful tidal power station

The Sihwa Lake Tidal Power Station in South Korea opened on August 4, 2011. Making use of a seawall defense built in 1994 for flood management, the tidal barrage uses 25.4-MW submerged turbines—10 in all—that give the power station an output capacity of 254 MW.

Highest electrical current in the universe

Cosmic jets are produced when ordinary matter is expelled at tremendous speed from the core of active galaxies. Experts believe they are fueled by large black holes; matter is compressed into small volumes until it gains enough energy to be flung off into space.

Scientists at the University of Toronto, Canada, have discovered an electrical current measuring 1,000,000,000,000,000,000 amps generated by a cosmic jet in a galaxy called 3C303, more than 2 billion light-years away. The jet—thought to be some 150,000 light-years long (greater than the diameter of the Milky Way)—is probably caused by magnetic fields from a huge black hole.

In the picture above, Galaxy 3C303 is indicated by the red spot on the left. The red arrow indicates the direction of the jet.

Highest operating transmission voltage

Running at 1,150 kilovolts (kV), the Ekibastuz–Kokshetau power transmission line in Kazakhstan is the highest operational transmission line voltage in the world. Built in the Soviet Union era as power line 1101, the overhead lines run for 268 miles (432 km) and are mounted on pylons with an average height of 200 ft. (60 m).

LONGEST ...

Man-made spark

The multimillion-volt impulse Marx generator at the Siberian Power Research Institute (SIBNIIE) in Novosibirsk, Russia, uses 896 storage capacitors to impart 1.225 million joules of energy per discharge of the generator. This results in spectacular arcs of electrical lightning jumping a 230-ft. (70-m) gap with an arc path length estimated at 492 ft. (150 m).

Human electrical circuit

Staff and pupils of Merrill Middle School, Oshkosh, Wisconsin, USA, formed a world-beating electrical circuit on June 2, 2010. It consisted of 378 people and was powered by a low-voltage powerball.

Tallest electricity pylon

Completed in 2010, the Damaoshan pylon carries power cables from Mount Damaoshan, Zhejiang Province, to the Zhoushan Islands (both China). Its lattice tower is 1,213 ft. (370 m) high, weighs 13.2 million lb. (5,999 tonnes), and has a capacity of 600,000 kW per day.

Most electricity generated by bicycles in an hour

The greatest amount of electricity produced by cyclists in one hour is 4,630 watt hours (Wh), achieved by Siemens (Australia and New Zealand) in Melbourne, Victoria, Australia, on December 11, 2012.

Power line

The longest High Voltage Direct Current (HVDC) power line is the Rio Madeira link in Brazil. It runs for more than 1,550 miles (2,500 km) between Porto Velho and São Paulo. The line transfers hydroelectric power from the Itaipu Dam to São Paulo across large portions of Amazonian rain forest.

The **longest time to build a power line** is nine years. Costing around $1 billion, the Inga–Shaba Extra High Voltage DC Intertie project started in 1973 and was completed in 1982. The line links the Inga hydroelectric-generation station with the mining intensive mineral fields within the province of Katanga (formerly Shaba) in the Democratic Republic of the Congo.

1844: Samuel Morse (USA) invents the electric telegraph, a machine that could transmit long-distance messages across wire.

1878: Joseph Swan (UK) creates the **first incandescent lightbulb** (also called an "electric lamp"), although it burns out quickly.

1879: After many experiments, Thomas Edison (USA) invents an incandescent lightbulb that can be used for about 40 hours without burning out.

1948: The first transistor is developed by scientists at Bell Telephone Laboratories in New Jersey, USA.

1954: Nuclear power plant APS-1 in Obninsk, USSR (now Russia), begins generating electricity for commercial use. It is the **longest-operating nuclear power station**.

PERIODIC TABLE

It's really quite elementary ...

On March 6, 1869, Russian chemist Dmitri Ivanovich Mendeleev presented *The Dependence Between the Properties of the Atomic Weights of the Elements* (*see right*)—the **first periodic table of elements**—to the Russian Chemical Society. His document demonstrated how elements could be arranged in order of atomic weight—the combined mass of the three types of particle (protons, neutrons, and electrons) that make up an atom. He also showed how elements could be grouped together when they had similar properties—metals with metals, for example.

FOR THE RECORD

Every element on these pages is listed with its atomic number (the number of protons in the nucleus of each atom that makes up that element) and its abbreviated chemical symbol.

Radon $_{86}$Rn
Densest element to remain a gas in free air
Radon is the heaviest of the naturally occurring noble gases on the Periodic Table. Its density is about 0.60 lb. per cu. ft. (9.73 kg/m³), about eight times the density of Earth's atmosphere at sea level (0.075 lb. per cu. ft.; 1.217 kg/m³).

AW 222   100 ml

Radon
(Rn - gaseous)

For medical use only!

NOBLE IDEA
"Noble" gases—neon, argon, xenon, radon, krypton, and helium—are colorless and odorless with low chemical reactivity.

Lithium $_3$Li
Least dense metal
At room temperature, the least dense metal is lithium at 0.3083 oz. per cu. in. (0.5334 g/cm³)—or about half the density of water. When alloyed with metals such as aluminum or copper, it can produce lightweight, hard-wearing metals. It is also used in the manufacture of batteries.

Iron $_{26}$Fe
Most common element on Earth by mass
Of the Earth's total mass, 32.1% is made up of iron, with the planet's core comprising of 88.8% iron (which gives the Earth its strong magnetic field). The core itself is around 35% of Earth's total mass.

Hydrogen $_1$H
Most common element in the human body by number of atoms
Combined with oxygen as water (*molecule below*), hydrogen atoms represent 63% of the number of atoms that make up a person.

65
Percent of total body mass comprised of oxygen—the **most common element in the body by mass**.

Silver $_{47}$Ag
Element with the highest electrical conductivity
At room temperature, silver has an electrical conductivity of 6.29 x 10⁷ S·m⁻³ (siemens per meter—a unit of measurement to indicate how well a material can transport an electrical charge). It is widely used in jewelry, tableware, and coins, but also in electrical contacts and in mirrors. As a precious metal it is very expensive, however, which is why copper wire is more commonly used as a conductor of electricity.
Silver also has the **highest thermal conductivity** of any element, at 429 W·m⁻¹·K⁻¹. Thermal conductivity is a measure of how well heat travels through an element, and is written as watts per meter kelvin.

TOP 10 MOST COMMON ELEMENTS IN THE UNIVERSE

1. Hydrogen $_1$H (73.9%): Used in petroleum and chemical industries, and for food processing. Once used to lift airships, though today helium is considered safer.

2. Helium $_2$He (24%): Serves as a coolant for nuclear reactors and to pressurize liquid-fuel rockets; used to inflate balloons.

3. Oxygen $_8$O (1.07%): Used in rocket fuel oxidant and in oxyacetylene welding; utilized in hospitals to help patients' breathing.

4. Carbon $_6$C (0.46%): Allotropes include diamond and graphite (used for lubrication; as a pigment in printing ink and India ink; and in pencils.)

5. Neon $_{10}$Ne (0.134%): Used in advertising signs, television tubes, high-voltage indicators, and as a cryogenic refrigerant.

Berkelium $_{97}$Bk
Rarest element on Earth
Estimates of the amount of the radioactive element berkelium in the Earth's crust at any one time are of the order of between 10 and 50 atoms, making it the rarest naturally occurring element on the planet.

Osmium $_{76}$Os
Densest naturally occurring element
The density of osmium is 13.05 oz. per cu. in. (22.59 g/cm³), which is around double that of lead (6.55 oz. per cu. in.; 11.34 g/cm³). Because of the toxic nature of oxides of osmium, it is rarely used in natural form and is most commonly used as an alloy with other metals.

Tin $_{50}$Sn
Largest number of stable isotopes in one element
Every element in the Periodic Table has variations of itself called isotopes. Isotopes only differ from the basic element by the number of neutrons within the nucleus of the atom. Isotopes can be stable or unstable, and decay by emitting radiation. Tin has the most stable isotopes, with 10.

Polonium $_{84}$Po
Most radioactive naturally occurring element
Samples of polonium are often seen to glow blue due to the intense radiation ionizing gas particles around the sample. The rate of decay is such that a small sample of polonium will reach temperatures of around 932°F (500°C), and the resulting radiation can kill a human.

Helium $_2$He
Lowest melting point of any element
Uniquely, helium remains a liquid at Absolute Zero (0K, or -459.67°F; -273.15°C) at atmospheric pressure. Even solid helium is unusual: it "looks" very much like liquid helium (above right) and can be compressed to 60% of its solid volume—some 100 times more compressible than water.

Carbon $_6$C
Element with the most allotropes
Some elements appear in differing forms, in terms of structure, color, or chemical properties. The various versions of an element are called allotropes. Carbon has seven allotropes: graphite, diamond (*left*), amorphous carbon, lonsdaleite, carbyne, fullerenes, and carbon nanotubes.

0.0005
Percentage of helium in the Earth's atmosphere.

Gold $_{79}$Au
Most malleable element
A metal's malleability is a measure of how much it can be stretched or hammered thin. Gold is the most malleable element: gold leaf can be produced to a thickness of just 0.000098 in. (0.0025 mm). It is widely used to gild furniture, to edge the pages of books, and in jewelry manufacture.

GOOD TO GLOW
Tungsten is used widely for filaments in bulbs and lamps as it can be heated to glow by high electrical current without melting.

Tungsten $_{74}$W
Highest melting point of any element
The metal tungsten makes the transition from solid to liquid at 6,170°F (3,410°C). Carbon is often cited as having a higher melting point at 6,422°F (3,550°C), but does not truly melt to a liquid form at normal atmospheric pressures: it sublimates directly to a gas.

6. Iron $_{26}$Fe (0.109%): Widely used in construction, often in the form of alloyed steel; used in machinery, hulls of large ships, automobile parts, and stainless steel.

7. Nitrogen $_7$N (0.097%): Forms a chemical component of ammonia (used in fertilizer and to create nitric acid) and used as a refrigerant to freeze and transport food; also used to inflate aircraft tires.

8. Silicon $_{14}$Si (0.065%): Widely used in computer chips and to make transistors and solid-state electronic devices; also used to make bricks and concrete.

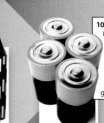

9. Magnesium $_{12}$Mg (0.058%): An ingredient in pyrotechnics and flares; once used in flash photography; used in alloys by the aviation, automobile, and armament industries.

10. Sulfur $_{16}$S (0.044%): Used in the synthesis of sulfuric acid, widely used to produce fertilizer; used in batteries as "battery acid," and to make gunpowder.

Percentages are relative totals given as parts per million, e.g. carbon = 4,600 parts/million

PHOTOGRAPHY

Longest extraterrestrial river system photographed

In December 2012, NASA's *Cassini* spacecraft photographed a river network more than 200 miles (322 km) long on Titan, Saturn's largest moon. Titan is an icy world with no liquid water—the river is believed to comprise liquid hydrocarbons ethane and methane.

he created as an act of protest. Bayard believed he had never received his rightful credit for inventing photography. Instead, the process was attributed to Louis-Jacques-Mandé Daguerre (France) and William Henry Fox Talbot (UK).

Most expensive photograph at auction

Rhein II, a photograph of the Rhine under gray skies taken by German artist Andreas Gursky, fetched $4,338,500, including the buyer's premium, at a Christie's auction held in New York City, USA, on November 8, 2011.

Smallest object photographed

In July 2012, physicists at Griffith University, Australia, announced that they had photographed an atom. They used an electric field to trap an "ion" of the element ytterbium, then shone light on the trapped ion and used a superhigh-resolution microscope to get an image of the shadow cast by the ion. This was recorded on a CCD—a kind of electronic photographic film. An ytterbium ion has a diameter of approximately 400 picometers—that's just 0.4 millionths of one twenty-fifth of an inch!

Farthest camera from Earth

As of January 2013, NASA's *Voyager 1* spacecraft was 11.5 billion miles (18.5 billion km) from our planet. Launched in 1977, the probe carries two cameras known collectively as the Imaging Science System.

Longest photographic exposure

Photographic exposures usually last a fraction of a second—the camera's shutter opening and closing rapidly to let a carefully measured amount of light fall on the film. But German artist Michael Wesely carried out a photographic exposure lasting an astonishing 34 months— almost three years. The resulting photograph, taken between 2001 and 2003, captures the demolition and reconstruction of New York's Museum of Modern Art in a single frame. Wesely employs filters that dramatically reduce the quantity of light getting through to the film, allowing him to leave the shutter open for inordinately long periods.

Most flashbulbs used to take a photograph

Jason Groupp (USA) took a photo using 300 flashbulbs in Cincinnati, Ohio, USA, on May 8, 2011.

First hoax photograph

In *Self-Portrait as a Drowned Man* (1840), French photographic pioneer Hippolyte Bayard depicts himself slumped to one side and apparently deceased, in an image

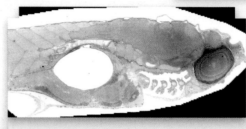

Largest digital image

A compound digital image of a 0.06-in.-long (1.5-mm) slice of zebrafish embryo measuring 921,600 × 380,928 pixels (a total of 351,063,244,800, equal to 281 gigapixels of data) was composited from 26,434 electron microscopy images by Frank G. A. Faas and his colleagues at Leiden University Medical Center, Netherlands, in December 2010.

Most successful instant camera

In 1947, Edwin Land (USA), founder of the Polaroid Corporation, created a system of one-step photography that used the principle of diffusion transfer to reproduce the image recorded by the camera lens directly onto a photosensitive surface. Polaroid stopped making the film used for the camera's technology in 2008.

LARGEST ...

Photograph

On December 18, 2000, Shinichi Yamamoto (Japan) printed a photograph 475 ft. 8 in. (145 m) long and 14 in. (35.6 cm) wide.

Largest panoramic image

A 320-gigapixel image, photographed from the BT Tower in London, UK, by 360Cities (UK), comprises 48,640 individual frames collated into a single panorama. If printed at normal resolution, the panorama would be 320 ft. (98 m) across and 78 ft. (24 m) tall—almost as big as Buckingham Palace.

PHOTOGRAPHIC FIRSTS

Oldest known surviving photograph: By Joseph Niépce (France), in 1827. It shows the view from the window of his home.

First known photograph to include a human: *Boulevard du Temple*, Paris, France, by Louis-Jacques Mandé Daguerre (France) ca. 1838.

First durable color photograph: Made on May 5, 1861, using a three-color method invented by James Clerk Maxwell (UK). The photograph of three color separations of a tartan ribbon was taken by Thomas Sutton (UK).

First X-ray: Taken by Wilhelm Röntgen (Germany), inventor of the process, on December 22, 1895 at the University of Würzburg, Germany.

First infrared photograph: Taken by Professor Robert Williams Wood (USA), it appeared in the October 1910 *Photographic Journal* of the Royal Photographic Society (RPS) and depicted a landscape by infrared light.

0.588 TRILLION
Rate of frames per second that this camera can record.

Fastest camera

In December 2011, the Massachusetts Institute of Technology, USA, revealed a camera that takes images with an exposure of 1.7 trillionths of a second. The team are able to use the technique to create movies that show light moving.

The panoramic image was taken from a negative 100 ft. (30.5 m) long and 2.75 in. (7 cm) wide.

Pinhole camera

In June 2006, an airplane hangar 45 x 160 x 80 ft. (13.7 x 48.7 x 24.3 m) in size was used as a pinhole camera to create a photograph that measured 31 ft. 7 in. x 111 ft. (9.6 x 33.8 m). The record was organized by The Legacy Project in El Toro, California, USA. The exposure time lasted 35 minutes.

CCTV camera

A close-circuit TV camera measuring 14 ft. 11 in. (4.56 m) long, 5 ft. 6 in. (1.7 m) wide, and 5 ft. 2 in. (1.6 m) tall was created by Darwin Lestari Tan and PT

TelView Technology (both Indonesia) in Bandung, Indonesia, on July 10, 2011.

Daguerreotype

Created by David Burder (UK), *Big Bertha* is a 6.5-sq.-ft. (2-m²) daguerreotype camera capable of taking images measuring up to 1.9 x 6.9 ft. (0.6 x 2.12 m). Burder created a daguerreotype at this size on November 18, 2003 for the BBC's *Industrial Road Show* (UK). The daguerreotype got its name from its inventor, Louis-Jacques Mandé Daguerre.

Simultaneous photography exhibition

An exhibition of Martin Parr's (UK) work entitled *Common Sense* could be viewed at 41 galleries around the world on April 1, 1999.

Photography competition

The "Wiki Loves Monuments 2011" competition, which was organized by Vereniging Wikimedia Nederland and ran from July 1 to September 31, 2011, attracted 168,208 entries.

Largest collection of instant cameras

As of May 2011, Wong Ting Man (Hong Kong) owned 1,042 instant cameras capable of producing a finished, hard-copy photo with no need for separate printing or processing. He began collecting in 1992.

5
Total number of 20x24 cameras that have been built by Polaroid.

Largest Polaroid camera

In 1976, the Polaroid Corporation built the first prototype of the largest Polaroid camera still in use today: the 20x24. This camera—which produces instant photos measuring 20 x 24 in. (50.8 x 70 cm)—weighs 235 lb. (107 kg) and is moved around on a wheeled base.

First digital image: Created by Russell A. Kirsch (USA) in 1957 at the National Bureau of Standards in Washington, DC, USA. The image was of his baby son, Walden.

First full-view photo of Earth: Taken by NASA satellite ATS-3 on November 10, 1967 while in orbit 23,000 miles (37,000 km) above Brazil.

First JPEG: "JPEG" stands for Joint Photographic Experts Group—one of the best-known digital image formats. The first JPEGS were a set of four test images used by the JPEG Group, created on June 18, 1987, in Copenhagen, Denmark.

First image of a sprite: Sprites are electrical flashes that shoot from the tops of thunderstorms up to altitudes 62 miles (100 km) above Earth's surface. The first image of one was taken, accidentally, in 1989 by a low-level-light TV camera.

First camera to photograph an object it cannot see: In "ghost imaging," a special flash produces pairs of photons. One lights the object, the other enters the camera lens. An image of the object is formed in the camera—although its light has never been in direct contact with the object. First announced May 2008.

SCIENCE FRONTIERS

Most sensitive listening device

In January 2012, scientists at the Ludwig Maximilian University of Munich, Germany, published details of the most sensitive listening device known so far. They suspended gold nanoparticles just 60 nanometers across in a water droplet and trapped one within a laser beam. They then observed it as other nearby particles in the droplet were heated by a different laser beam. The resulting pressure or sound waves were picked up by the first nanoparticle, corresponding to a sensitivity of around -60 decibels. This is equivalent to one-millionth of that detectable by the human ear.

19.6
Diameter in feet of the hole a meteor fragment punched into ice on Lake Chebarkul in Russia.

Greatest measured impact on Earth

On February 15, 2013, a ca. 55-ft.-wide (17-m) meteor entered the atmosphere at about 40,390 mph (65,000 km/h) and exploded some 20–30 miles (30–50 km) above Chelyabinsk in central Russia. Infrasonic waves from the fireball were recorded at 17 stations in the Comprehensive Nuclear-Test-Ban Treaty Organization's International Monitoring System. The impact, equivalent to about 500 kilotons of TNT, was the largest recorded on Earth since the 1908 Tunguska impact, and the largest overall measured with modern instruments.

First telecommunication using neutrinos

Subatomic neutrino particles pass through matter easily because they rarely interact with it. Scientists at Fermilab in Batavia, Illinois, USA, successfully used a beam of neutrinos to send a message to a detector for the first time. The message, which spelled "neutrino," was sent more than 0.62 miles (1 km), including 787 ft. (240 m) through solid rock, at a data rate of 0.1 bits per second. The team announced its achievement on March 13, 2012.

Thinnest glass

In January 2012, an international team of scientists announced their accidental creation of silica glass measuring just three atoms thick. Silica glass is composed of silicon dioxide (SiO_2), which is two atoms of oxygen with one of silicon. This new discovery can be regarded as 2D glass, because three atoms is the minimum thickness of SiO_2.

Largest known prime number

A prime number, a natural number that can only be divided without a remainder by 1 and itself, was discovered on January 25, 2013 by Curtis Cooper (USA), a professor of computer science at the University of Central Missouri in Warrensburg, Missouri, USA. The number is $2^{57,885,161} - 1$ and has 17,425,170 digits.

Strongest bite of a land animal

In February 2012, scientists from the Universities of Liverpool and Manchester (both UK) published their discovery of the power of the jaws of *Tyrannosaurus rex*. They made a 3D computer model of a *T. rex* skull using a laser scanner and then digitally mapped muscles onto it. By making the digital muscles snap the jaws shut, the team estimated that the maximum force generated (at the back teeth) was up to 57,000 N— equivalent to the force of a medium-size elephant sitting on the ground.

Highest manmade temperature

Scientists at CERN's Large Hadron Collider in Geneva, Switzerland, announced on August 13, 2012 that they had achieved temperatures of more than 5 trillion K and perhaps as high as 5.5 trillion K (more than 800 million times hotter than the surface of the Sun). The team had been using the ALICE experiment to smash together lead ions at 99% of the speed of light to create a quark-gluon plasma—an exotic state of matter believed to have filled the universe just after the Big Bang.

FACT:
Kelvin (K) is the SI unit of temperature. It is an absolute scale based on the temperature below which it is impossible to go (0 K, equal to -459.67°F; -273.15°C). It was proposed by and named after William Thomson, 1st Baron Kelvin (UK, 1824–1907).

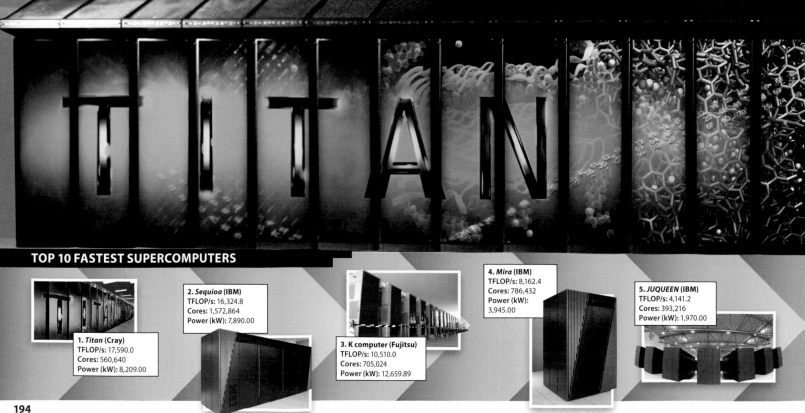

TOP 10 FASTEST SUPERCOMPUTERS

1. Titan (Cray)
TFLOP/s: 17,590.0
Cores: 560,640
Power (kW): 8,209.00

2. Sequioa (IBM)
TFLOP/s: 16,324.8
Cores: 1,572,864
Power (kW): 7,890.00

3. K computer (Fujitsu)
TFLOP/s: 10,510.0
Cores: 705,024
Power (kW): 12,659.89

4. Mira (IBM)
TFLOP/s: 8,162.4
Cores: 786,432
Power (kW): 3,945.00

5. JUQUEEN (IBM)
TFLOP/s: 4,141.2
Cores: 393,216
Power (kW): 1,970.00

Most accurate kilogram

The kilogram is the only base SI unit of measurement whose definition is still grounded on a physical prototype: an 1889 cylinder made of platinum and iridium maintained at the Bureau International des Poids et Mesures at Sèvres near Paris, France. Scientists are currently attempting to change the definition of the kilogram by linking it to precise measurements of a known physical constant referred to as Planck's constant.

Nearest extrasolar planet

In October 2012, astronomers using the European Southern Observatory's La Silla Observatory in Chile announced their discovery of a planet in the closest star system to our own. Alpha Centauri B, at 4.37 light-years from the Sun, is one of three stars that comprise the Alpha Centauri system. Orbiting this star at a distance of just 3.7 million miles (6 million km), Alpha Centauri Bb is a small planet with a mass slightly greater than Earth's. It takes just 3 days 5 hr. 39 min. to complete one orbit of its parent star, and has an estimated surface temperature of around 2,192°F (1,200°C).

Largest asteroid visited by spacecraft

NASA's *Dawn* spacecraft is an unmanned probe whose mission is to explore the two biggest asteroids in the main asteroid belt between Mars and Jupiter. On August 11, 2011, *Dawn* arrived at asteroid 4 Vesta, which has an average diameter of 326.4 miles (525.4 km) and is also classed as a dwarf planet. It spent just over a year orbiting the asteroid before departing on September 4, 2012 on a trajectory that will allow it to rendezvous with and orbit the even larger asteroid 1 Ceres in early 2015.

Longest-operating Earth-observation satellite

Landsat 5 is an Earth-observation satellite developed by NASA and launched on March 1, 1984 from Vandenberg Air Force Base in California, USA. Managed by the National Oceanic and Atmospheric Administration (1984–2000) and by the U.S. Geological Survey (USGS, 2001–13) as part of the Landsat Program, it has completed more than 150,000 orbits of Earth and sent back more than 2.5 million images of Earth's surface. On December 21, 2012, the USGS announced *Landsat 5* was to be decommissioned after the failure of a gyroscope.

Largest mecha robot controlled by smartphone

Kuratas, a diesel-powered mecha (walking) robot measuring 13 ft. (4 m) tall and weighing 8,000 lb. (3.62 tonnes), can be controlled by a "robot pilot" from inside the "cockpit" or operated remotely using a 3G smartphone. The robot was unveiled by inventor Kōgorō Kurata (Japan) at Wonder Festival in Tokyo, Japan, on July 29, 2012, and is available for a cool ¥100 million ($1.3 million) from Suidobashi Heavy Industry (Japan).

Fastest computer

Titan, a Cray XK7 at the Oak Ridge National Laboratory in Tennessee, USA, can achieve 17,590 TFLOP/s (**T**rillion **FL**oating-point **OP**erations per second) on the Linpack Benchmark using 560,640 cores. Titan achieved first place in the TOP500 list of the world's most powerful supercomputers when the 40th list of rankings was released on November 12, 2012 (*see below*).

DOES COMPUTE
The TOP500 project ranks computers based on the speed at which they can solve linear equations, known as the Linpack Benchmark.

6. *SuperMUC* (IBM)
TFLOP/s: 2,897.0
Cores: 147,456
Power (kW): 3,422.67

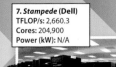

7. *Stampede* (Dell)
TFLOP/s: 2,660.3
Cores: 204,900
Power (kW): N/A

8. *Tianhe-1A* (NUDT)
TFLOP/s: 2,566.0
Cores: 186,368
Power (kW): 4,040.00

9. *Fermi* (IBM)
TFLOP/s: 1,725.5
Cores: 163,840
Power (kW): 821.88

10. *DARPA Trial Subset* (IBM)
TFLOP/s: 1,515.0
Cores: 63,360
Power (kW): 3,575.63

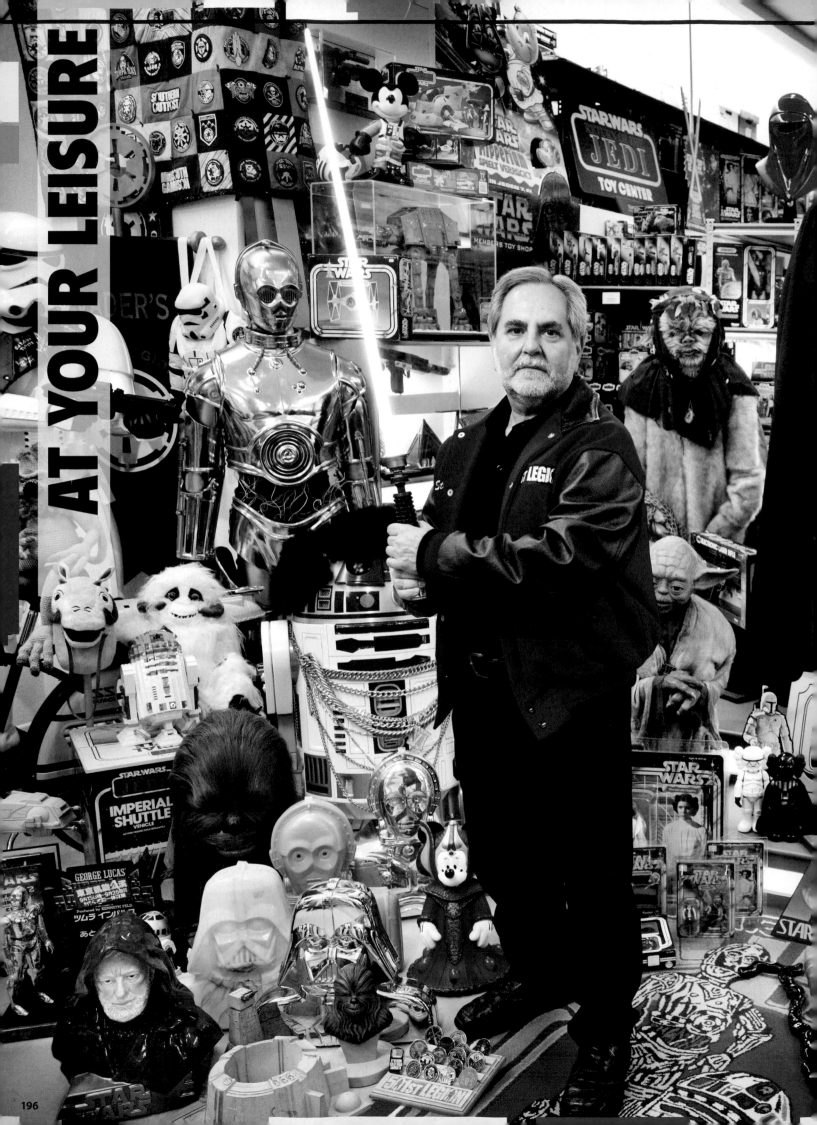

GUINNESS WORLD RECORDS 2014

Largest collection of *Star Wars* memorabilia

Steve Sansweet (USA) has amassed an estimated 300,000 unique items at Rancho Obi-Wan in northern California, USA. As of May 15, 2013, a total of 90,546 items have been accurately audited and cataloged—a number sufficient enough, however, to beat the previous Guinness World Records figure by a factor of four. Sansweet estimates that the cataloging process will take years to complete, as his collection continues to grow.

FORCE FAN
Steve was Director of Content Management and Head of Fan Relations at Lucasfilm for 15 years and continues to advise the company on its interaction with fans.

VIRAL VIDEOS

Taking over the world, one view at a time

"Viral" videos are well named. They spread across the Internet faster than you can type "You've got to see these kittens, they're *sooo* cute!" Such popularity has seen the business of uploading videos become professionalized, and only the homemade "Charlie bit my finger—again!" makes it into YouTube's all-time Top 10. The chart is otherwise dominated by music videos, but for the first time pop is a truly global phenomenon. It's no longer true that everything comes from the West and the USA in particular. As a result of online videos, stars such as a certain stylish South Korean can rack up more than a billion views in less than six months.

Video uploading remains a powerful hybrid of 21st-century technology and personal recommendation that has the potential to bring down a government ... or simply embarrass grandma.

TOP 10 YOUTUBE CHANNELS BY SUBSCRIBERS			
CHANNEL	**WHAT IS IT?**	**SUBS**	**VIEWS**
Smosh	Comedy sketches by Ian Hecox and Anthony Padilla (both USA)	9,781,472	2,323,432,710
Jenna Marbles	Comedy alter ego of Jenna Mourey (USA)	8,780,770	1,103,995,980
NEW VIDEO EVERY TUESDAY	Comment and comedy from Ray William Johnson (USA)	8,704,762	2,293,529,143
nigahiga	Observational comedy from Ryan Higa (USA)	8,252,930	1,436,187,701
Rihanna	Pop videos and behind-the-scenes footage from the Barbados songstress	8,104,461	3,630,912,069
BECOME A BRO TODAY!	Video game commentary from PewDiePie, aka Felix Kjellberg (Sweden)	7,701,817	1,598,921,599
Machinima	U.S. video gaming network featuring news, trailers, and demos	7,580,450	4,217,963,856
Hola Soy German (video todos los viernes)	Quirky observations and comedy from Germán Alejandro Garmendia Aranís (Chile)	6,780,904	482,609,012
OneDirectionVEVO's channel	Pop videos and chat with the world's biggest boy band	6,438,005	1,536,384,997
BrandonJLa / freddiew	Special effects-rich short movies with a video game flavor by Brandon J. Laatsch (USA)	5,453,961	834,061,819

Source: Socialbakers. Statistics correct as of May 14, 2013

1. "Gangnam Style"
PSY
1,598,585,367 views
Official music video, uploaded July 15, 2012

10 MILLION
Number of daily views of "Gangnam Style" at its peak.

3. "On the Floor"
Jennifer Lopez featuring Pitbull
668,860,098 views
Official music video, uploaded March 3, 2011

4. "Love the Way You Lie"
Eminem featuring Rihanna
560,292,597 views
Official music video, uploaded August 5, 2010

5. "Party Rock Anthem"
LMFAO featuring Lauren Bennett and GoonRock
540,403,117 views
Official music video, uploaded March 8, 2011

6. "Charlie bit my finger—again!"
525,007,126 views
Home video, uploaded May 22, 2007

TOP 10 MOST VIEWED YOUTUBE VIDEOS 2012

VIDEO TITLE	USER	UPLOADED	VIEWS
PSY—GANGNAM STYLE	officialpsy	Jul 15, 2012	971.5 million
Somebody That I Used to Know—Walk off the Earth (Gotye—Cover)	walkofftheearth	Feb 14, 2012	140.2 million
KONY 2012	invisiblechildreninc	Mar 7, 2012	94.5 million
"Call Me Maybe" by Carly Rae Jepsen—Feat. Justin Bieber, Selena, Ashley Tisdale & MORE!	CarlosPenaTV	Feb 18, 2012	54.9 million
Barack Obama vs Mitt Romney. Epic Rap Battles Of History Season 2	ERB	Oct 15, 2012	45.4 million
A DRAMATIC SURPRISE ON A QUIET SQUARE	turnerbenelux	Apr 11, 2012	39.6 million
WHY YOU ASKING ALL THEM QUESTIONS? .. #FCHW	SpokenReasons	Jan 21, 2012	39.5 million
Crystallize—Lindsey Stirling (Dubstep Violin Original Song)	lindseystomp	Feb 23, 2012	38.5 million
Facebook Parenting: For the troubled teen	Tommy Jordan	Feb 8, 2012	35.5 million
Felix Baumgartner's supersonic freefall from 128,000 ft.—Mission Highlights	redbull	Oct 14, 2012	30.6 million

Source: YouTube

38,114,277 Shares of "On the Floor" by Jennifer Lopez, the **most shared video** according to viral-video chart unrulymedia.com, as of May 14, 2013.

15 MB OF FAME In 2012, the number of Web users who uploaded at least one clip to a video-sharing site grew from 21 percent to 27 percent.

2. "Baby" Justin Bieber featuring Ludacris 857,398,511 views Official music video, uploaded February 19, 2010

CHARTING SUCCESS In 2013, the U.S. Billboard Hot 100 began to include video views in the formula it uses for compiling the chart.

FACT: YouTube statistics April 23, 2005: "Me at the Zoo" (first video, uploaded by cofounder Jawed Karim) 2013: 1 billion users and 4 billion monthly hours of viewing Views outside USA: 70 percent 99 percent of views: from 30 percent of videos 2 billion hits: On Obama and Romney in U.S. election year 2012

7. "Waka Waka (This Time for Africa)" Shakira 524,443,371 views Official 2010 FIFA World Cup song, uploaded June 4, 2010

8. "Bad Romance" Lady Gaga 518,440,711 views Official music video, uploaded November 23, 2009

9. "Ai Se Eu Te Pego" Michel Teló 501,025,764 views Official music video, uploaded July 25, 2011

10. "Call Me Maybe" Carly Rae Jepsen 455,334,605 views Official music video, uploaded March 1, 2012

Source: YouTube, May 14, 2013

ADVERTISING

Most expensive billboard

A site at the entrance of the Burj Khalifa in Dubai, UAE, became host to the most expensive single billboard advert in June 2012 when energy drinks company Go Fast and Skydive Dubai combined forces to promote their services with the aid of a man wearing a jet pack. The 30-second stunt, during which Jet Pack Man flew around the billboard, cost an estimated $15,000.

First classified advertising

Thomas Newcomb's *Publick Adviser* (London, UK, May 19–September 28, 1657) was the first newspaper devoted entirely to advertising, aimed at "all persons that are any way connected in matter of buying and selling".

First brand manager

Thomas J. Barratt (UK) can be considered the world's first brand manager, joining the firm A&F Pears—manufacturers of Pears soap—in 1865. Credited as the "father of modern advertising", he took a systematic approach and combined attractive images by leading artists of the day—such as the Pre-Raphaelite painter John Everett Millais (UK)—with memorable slogans to promote the Pears soap brand.

Largest audience for a livestream advertisement

On October 14, 2012, around 8 million people logged onto YouTube to watch Felix Baumgartner (Austria) make his record-breaking skydive to Earth (*see p. 68*), the natural conclusion of the seven-year, $20-million Red Bull Stratos project. The live-stream event, which featured extensive use of the sponsor's logo and branding, would have been even larger had demand not outstripped server capabilities.

Oldest existing advertising

An advertisement for a book-seller was found among the rubble preserved at Pompeii, the city near Naples in Italy that was destroyed and buried by ash in the eruption of Mount Vesuvius in AD 79. Prior to this, inscriptions by Babylonian merchants dating back to 3000 BC can be considered the first "written" advertisements.

First public TV ad

The first advertisement ever broadcast on public television was on NBC's WNBT station in New York, USA, on July 1, 1941. The product being promoted was a Bulova watch, and the slot cost all of $9 to fill—equivalent to just $141 today.

First banner ads

Banner ads—advertisements embedded into Web sites and delivered by an ad server—were launched on October 27, 1994

Highest fee paid to an actor for an advert

On October 15, 2012, Brad Pitt (USA, *above right*) became the first male face of the perfume Chanel No. 5, earning the actor a record $7 million.

   Nicole Kidman (Australia, *above*), who also promoted Chanel No. 5, was paid $3.71 million in 2004, the **highest fee paid to an actress for an advertising campaign**.

First newspaper ad

Samuel Pecke's *Perfect Diurnall*, a newspaper published in London, UK, in the 17th century, first carried advertisements from November 1646 for sixpence per insertion. The first ads were for books, then later expanded to medical cures and vermin extermination.

First TV advertising

The use of television to promote a product can be traced to the Hairdressing Fair of Fashion held in November 1930 in London, UK, when hairstylists Messrs Eugene Ltd. of Dover Street (UK) used closed-circuit TV to promote their permanent waving technique.

Longest-running ad campaign

Smokey Bear first appeared on a public-service fire-prevention advert on August 9, 1944 with his famous warning: "Only You Can Prevent Forest Fires". The campaign has continued, with minor variations, to the present day.

INTERBRAND'S "BEST GLOBAL BRANDS 2012"

1. COCA-COLA: $77,839 million
"A name that is more universally recognized than any other in the world."

2. APPLE: $76,568 million
"Few companies have captured our imagination, inspired such devotion …"

3. IBM: $75,532 million
"… consistently ranked as one of the world's most innovative, profitable, and sustainable brands …"

4. GOOGLE: $69,726 million
"While opinions are mixed on Google+ and Google's other various innovations, overall, the search giant has had a productive year."

5. MICROSOFT: $57,853 million
"Still one of the world's most recognized technology brands … found itself in a bit of a holding pattern in 2012 …"

Most expensive advertising slot

A 30-second ad slot during 2013's Super Bowl XLVII cost $3.8 million, making it the most expensive in the history of television. The cost was up by $300,000 on the previous year and has been rising steadily—despite recession—with each passing year. Advertisers this year included Taco Bell, Samsung, and Doritos (*pictured*).

TOP 10 MOST SHARED SUPER BOWL ADS		
BRAND	**ADVERT**	**SHARES**
Volkswagen	*The Force* (2011)	465,824
Budweiser	*Respect 9/11* (2002)	426,691
Old Spice	*The Man Your Man Could Smell Like* (2010)	413,138
Doritos	*House Rules* (2010)	279,149
e*trade	*Girlfriend* (2010)	49,323
Budweiser	*Whassup?* (2010)	31,870
Snickers	*Betty White* (2010)	19,989
Apple	*1984* (1984)	18,787
Doritos	*Snack Attack Samurai* (2010)	17,180
Audi	*Green Car* (2010)	17,008

Based on the number of times a Super Bowl ad has been shared on YouTube—the world's largest video sharing site—as of February 3, 2013

on the HotWired Web site, an early offshoot of *Wired* magazine. In total, 14 of the clickable 468 x 60-pixel ads were launched that day for various companies, although the banner for AT&T that was included in this batch—"Have you ever clicked your mouse right here? You will"—is believed to have been the first ever seen online.

Largest advertising revenue for an Olympic Games

On July 25, 2012, NBC Universal (USA) became the first broadcaster to earn more than $1 billion in TV advertising revenue for its Olympic Games coverage. This exceeds the $850 million earned during the Beijing Games in 2008, and represents ad revenue from 5,535 hours of footage scheduled across NBC, Telemundo, and various cable affiliates.

GLOBAL AD $PEND
In 2012, $495 billion was spent on advertising globally—that's $70 for every single human on Earth!

Largest fine for a tracking cookie

In August 2012, Internet search giant Google was fined $22.5 million by the U.S. Federal Trade Commission after the company illegally tracked Apple iPhone, iPad, and Mac users in an attempt to tailor advertising specific to each

Most advertisements in an election campaign

In the run-up to the U.S. Presidential Election held on November 6, 2012, Americans were bombarded with in excess of one million political advertisements, the most ever aired during an election. A study by the Wesleyan Media Project discovered that the advertising for the two candidates in the presidential race, Mitt Romney and Barack Obama (both USA, *pictured*), far exceeded that of any previous political campaign.

individual. Google was accused of deliberately circumventing privacy protections on Apple's Safari Web browser, which were designed to stop "cookies" being used to track movement between Web sites. Google has refused to acknowledge any responsibility in the matter, claiming that the cookies were placed "by accident."

91 ft. 10 in. (28 m)

WHAT IF THE WORLD'S FASTEST MAN WENT EVEN FASTER?

20 ft. 4 in. (6.2 m)

2.7
Seconds it would take Usain Bolt, who features on the billboard, to run from end to end!

EVERYDAY AT NISSAN

WE TURN WHAT IF INTO WHAT IS.

Largest illuminated indoor advertising sign

A billboard with an area of 1,874 sq. ft. (174.17 m²) and illuminated with 183,024 LEDs was installed by Nissan Motor Co. (Japan) at Dubai International Airport, UAE, on February 4, 2013.

6. GE: $43,682 million
"… GE pulled the ultimate trump card. In 2012, the brand launched GE Works, an integrated communications platform …"

7. McDONALDS: $40,062 million
"… exceptional brand management, significant global presence … and admirable approach to consumer engagement."

8. INTEL: $39,385 million
"… the last year has been filled with change, big bets, and the continued quest to remain at the forefront of the ceaseless computing revolution …"

9. SAMSUNG: $32,893 million
"… one of the biggest successes of 2012, marked by a meteoric 40% rise in brand value …"

10. TOYOTA: $30,280 million
"… resilience of the Toyota brand seems to have … helped the carmaker in reclaiming its global leadership position."

Figures based on Interbrand's estimation of the value of each brand

MOVIES

FOR THE RECORD

The Master (*right*) was the first movie in 16 years to be shot in 65-mm (using Panavision System 65 cameras), but few screens are equipped to project this size; four of the five movie theaters showed it in 70-mm, while the fifth opted to show a 35-mm version. *The Master* holds the live-action record; the **highest per-screen gross of all time** is an incredible $793,376 from just two screens showing Disney's animation *The Lion King* (USA, 1994).

Highest-grossing opening weekend for a live-action movie (per screen)

The Master (USA, 2012) opened in just five movie theaters and grossed an average of $145,949 per screen. Written, directed, and produced by Paul Thomas Anderson (USA), the movie stars Joaquin Phoenix as a drifter who joins a cult led by "The Master," played by Philip Seymour Hoffman.

Most Oscar wins for Actor in a Leading Role

At the Oscars on February 24, 2013, Daniel Day-Lewis (UK) became the first performer to win three awards in the Actor in a Leading Role category when he picked up a statuette for his portrayal of Abraham Lincoln in 2012's *Lincoln* (USA; *above, bottom*). He had previously won for playing Christy Brown (*above, top*) in *My Left Foot* (Ireland, 1989), and Daniel Plainview (*above, center*) in *There Will Be Blood* (USA, 2007).

Highest box-office movie gross—opening weekend

Marvel's *The Avengers* (USA, 2012) took $207,438,708 in U.S. movie houses on its opening weekend of May 4–6, 2012, beating the record previously set by *Harry Potter and the Deathly Hallows: Part II* (UK/USA, 2011).

The movie also secured records for: **highest average gross per screen**, taking $47,698 from each of its 4,349 locations during its "wide" opening weekend in the USA; **highest-grossing opening week** (and **highest-grossing week** in movie history), taking $803.3 million worldwide; **highest 10-day gross**, at $1.07 billion by May 13, 2012; **fastest movie to earn $500 million** (two days); and in absolute terms, the **fastest entertainment property to gross $1 billion** (*see p. 208*).

Largest budget-to-box-office ratio

With a production budget of just $15,000 and a total worldwide gross of $196,681,656, Oren Peli's (Israel/USA) *Paranormal Activity* (2009) achieved a phenomenal budget/box office ratio of 1:13,112—that is, it earned $13,112 for every $1 spent.

Largest attendance at a movie screening

The premiere of the feature documentary *Honor Flight* (USA, 2012) was attended by 28,442 people. The movie was made by Freethink Media for the Stars and Stripes Honor Flight charity (both USA) and shown at Miller Park stadium in Milwaukee, Wisconsin, USA, on August 11, 2012.

Highest-grossing opening weekend for a 2D movie

The Dark Knight Rises (USA/UK, 2012)—starring Tom Hardy (UK, *above*) as the villainous Bane and Christian Bale (UK, *inset*) as the eponymous superhero—took $160,887,295 on its opening weekend, on July 20–22, 2012.

TOP 10 HOLLYWOOD HIGHEST EARNERS

Source: Forbes, based on estimated earnings between May 2011 and May 2012

1. Tom Cruise (USA)
$75 million

=2. Leonardo DiCaprio (USA)
$37 million

=2. Adam Sandler (USA)
$37 million

4. Dwayne Johnson (USA)
$36 million

5. Kristen Stewart (USA)
$34.5 million

YOUNGEST NOMINEE: BEST ACTRESS OSCAR

Nine-year-old Quvenzhané Wallis (USA, b. August 28, 2003) became the youngest actress ever to receive an Oscar nomination. She made the short list in the Actress in a Leading Role category for her performance in *Beasts of the Southern Wild* (USA, 2012).

OLDEST NOMINEE: BEST ACTRESS OSCAR

Emmanuelle Riva (France, b. February 24, 1927) earned an Oscar nomination for Actress in a Leading Role in 2012 for *Amour* (France/Germany/Austria, 2012). Riva was 84 years old when she played the role, and the awards ceremony took place on her 86th birthday.

Most directors of one movie

The multi-language independent feature movie *The Owner* (2012) had 25 directors from 13 countries. The movie follows a backpack on its journey around the world, interweaving a variety of cultures, languages, and film styles into one single narrative. The movie premiered around the world on May 25, 2012.

First Bond theme song to win an Oscar

The theme tune for the James Bond movie of the same name, "Skyfall" – written by Adele, aka Adele Adkins, and Paul Epworth (both UK) – was the first Bond song ever to win an Oscar for Best Original Song.

Least successful Bond movie

Despite an all-star cast, *Casino Royale* (1967), Charles Feldman's (USA) surrealist spoof of the Bond series, grossed $277,841,894 when adjusted for 2012 inflation, making it the least successful Bond movie.

FACT: Jackie also holds a record for the **most stunts by a living actor**. He made his debut in 1962 at the age of eight and has been in more than 110 movies since 1972. He performs his own stunts and has so far broken his nose (three times), both cheekbones, most of his fingers, and his skull.

Highest box-office gross for an actor

As of May 2012, actor Samuel L. Jackson (USA) had appeared in 75 theatrically released movies, grossing at least $9.5 billion worldwide. With his slate of movies in 2013, he will no doubt push this record over $10 billion soon.

Most countries considered for Best Foreign Language Oscar

Prior to the unveiling of the 2012 Oscar nominations, the Academy of Motion Picture Arts and Sciences (AMPAS) announced that they had received submissions for the Best Foreign Language Film from a record 71 countries, including entries from Burkina Faso, Iceland, Albania, and Afghanistan, and the first ever submissions from Greenland, Malaysia, and Kenya.

Longest uncut movie

Agadam (India, 2012) runs unedited for 2 hr. 3 min. 30 sec. (excluding opening and end credits). It was produced by Last Bench Boys Productions (India) and premiered on April 7, 2013.

Most credits in a movie

Hong Kong superstar Jackie Chan was credited with 15 roles for *Chinese Zodiac* (China, 2012): writer, director, actor, producer, executive producer, cinematographer, art director, unit production manager, catering coordinator, stunt coordinator, gaffer, composer, props, stunts, and theme-tune vocalist.

Highest-grossing James Bond movie

Even adjusting for inflation, *Skyfall* (UK/USA, 2012), starring Daniel Craig as James Bond, is a bigger blockbuster than any previous entry in the James Bond series. Its total worldwide gross of $1.108 billion surpasses *Thunderball* (UK, 1965), which would have grossed $1.047 billion when adjusted for inflation.

SKYFALL WINDFALL
Skyfall is the 7th highest-grossing movie ever, the most successful UK movie, and the most successful movie shown in UK movie houses.

6. Cameron Diaz (USA) $34 million

7. Ben Stiller (USA) $33 million

=8. Sacha Baron Cohen (UK) $30 million

=8. Johnny Depp (USA) $30 million

=8. Will Smith (USA) $30 million

SPECIAL EFFECTS

Twice (USA), was rushed out to capitalize on the new 3D craze and wowed audiences with its scenes of spiders, fists, and dead bodies that seemed to leap right out of the screen!

Biggest 3D opening weekend

The 3D release of The Avengers (USA, 2012) grossed $207,438,708 in the USA during the weekend of its release on May 4–6, 2012. It was the **largest opening weekend** of all time for a movie, 3D or otherwise.

Largest attendance at a 3D movie screening

A total of 6,819 movie lovers enjoyed the German première of Men in Black 3 (USA, 2012) in an event organized by Sony Pictures and o2 at o2 World in Berlin, Germany, on May 14, 2012.

First film shot at 48 fps

The first major feature to be filmed and projected at 48 frames per second (fps)—instead of the regular 24 fps—was Peter Jackson's The Hobbit: An Unexpected Journey (US/NZ, 2012). Filming at such a high frame rate results in a smoother, sharper image and, in Jackson's words, "a much more lifelike and comfortable viewing experience."

Highest-grossing 3D movie

Avatar (USA, 2009)—filmed and released in digital 3D—is the **highest-grossing movie of all time**, having reaped an eye-popping $2,782,275,172 globally. Directed by James Cameron (Canada, below), Avatar was the result of the **largest motion-capture project**, with a total of three years of live-action filming by Giant Studios (USA). The success of the movie means that Cameron is, technically, the **most successful 3D moviemaker** (see below).

Most expensive 3D movie

Although Avatar (see above) is said to be the most expensive movie ever made, its official budget was "just" $237 million. The highest budget posted for a 3D movie is $260 million for Disney's animation Tangled (USA, 2010). (See also p. 206.)

3D MOVIES

First 3D movie by a major studio

Columbia Pictures became the first big studio to venture into the 3D movie market, with Man in the Dark (USA, 1953) on April 9, 1953. The movie, a remake of the 1936 film noir The Man Who Lived

Widest opening for a 3D movie

On its opening weekend, July 15–17, 2011, Harry Potter and the Deathly Hallows: Part 2 (USA, 2011) was released on 4,375 screens in the USA and on another 17,000 worldwide. It also achieved the **highest opening-day box-office gross**, taking $91,071,119 in the USA alone.

Most successful 3D moviemaker

Despite having made only one 3D movie, James Cameron (Canada) is the most successful 3D moviemaker in terms of international box-office revenue, with Avatar (2009) remaining the **highest-grossing movie of all time** (see above). He is also director of the **most billion-dollar movies** with two (Avatar and Titanic), a record he shares with Christopher Nolan (USA) and Peter Jackson (New Zealand).

However, for moviemakers with three or more 3D titles to their name, Robert Zemeckis (USA) is the **most successful**, with Beowulf (USA, 2007), The Polar Express (USA, 2004), and A Christmas Carol (USA, 2009) grossing more than $829 million combined. Zemeckis, a pioneer of modern 3D cinema, revolutionized moviemaking with the development of groundbreaking motion-capture technology. He is also the second-highest-grossing director of all time.

FX FIRSTS

Movie special-effects studio: Built in 1896 in Montreuil-sous-Bois, Paris (France), by French special-effects moviemaker and illusionist Georges Méliès, the facility was a hybrid photography studio and stage with theatrical mechanisms.

Film shot using special effects: The silent, minute-long Execution of Mary, Queen of Scots (USA, 1895) was the first piece of film footage to use stop-action, giving the impression of a beheading.

First use of double exposure in a movie: In George Albert Smith's (UK) Santa Claus (UK, 1898), a simple scene was depicted of two sleeping children, with the arrival of Santa Claus superimposed in a circle in the same shot.

Use of the Schüfftan process in a movie: Devised by Eugen Schüfftan (Germany) in 1923, it was first used in Die Nibelungen (Germany, 1924) and most famously used in Metropolis (Germany, 1927), pictured here. Models were made of huge cityscapes and a mirror mounted in front of the camera to reflect the miniatures.

Oscar for special effects: The Rains Came (USA, 1939) won an Oscar for its epic flood scenes. A split-screen combination of live action and miniatures was used and overseen by 20th Century Fox's Fred Sersen (Czechoslovakia).

Most expensive live-action 3D movie

Based on the book *A Princess of Mars* (1917) by Edgar Rice Burroughs (USA), the sci-fi adventure movie *John Carter* (USA, 2012)—directed by Andrew Stanton (USA)—had a budget of $250 million, due in part to its large cast of fantastical, other-worldly creatures.

Most extensive digital character

Created by Industrial Light & Magic (ILM) for *Transformers: Dark of the Moon* (USA, 2011), the Decepticon serpent *Colossus* is the largest and most complex digital character ever to appear in a film, comprising 86,000 pieces of geometry and 30 million polygons. The giant, tentacled drilling machine features in a complex scene in which it destroys a Chicago skyscraper.

Most extensive digital object

The "Orrery"—an interactive three-dimensional map of the universe—was created for Ridley Scott's *Prometheus* (USA/UK, 2012) using between 80 and 100 million polygons.

First 3D movie to generate a sequel

Most early 3D movies were single productions designed to exploit the new format, but Universal's *The Creature from the Black Lagoon* (USA, 1954), featuring the "terrifying" Gill-man monster, proved sufficiently successful to spawn a sequel—*Revenge of the Creature* (USA, 1955), also shot and released in 3D.

The scene was constructed over the course of seven months by a team of 80 special-effects artists and technicians from Australian company Fuel VFX.

CGI (COMPUTER-GENERATED IMAGERY)

First CGI character with realistic fur

Visual-effects company Industrial Light & Magic (ILM, USA) created digitally rendered, realistic fur for Kitty the saber-toothed tiger, a character that featured in the live-action movie version of *The Flintstones* (USA, 1994).

First movie with digital water

Pioneering the use of software to imitate water was DreamWorks' *Antz* (USA, 1998). Powerful, physics-base simulations were created to achieve realistic effects. Prior to this, fluid effects were painstakingly drawn, frame by frame, using graphics programs.

Most Oscars won for makeup

Rick Baker (USA) has won seven Academy Awards® throughout his career. The first was for *An American Werewolf in London* (1981) at the 54th Academy Awards on March 29, 1982, and the most recent at the 83rd Academy Awards for *The Wolfman* (2010) on February 27, 2011.

12
Number of Oscar nominations Rick has received to date.

MAKEUP

Most multidiscipline technical Oscars won

Richard Taylor (New Zealand), effects supervisor at Weta Workshop in Wellington, New Zealand, has won technical Oscars across a record three disciplines: Visual Effects for *King Kong* (NZ/USA/Ger, 2005) and Costume Design and Makeup for *The Return of the King* (USA/NZ/Ger, 2003).

Most special-effect makeup characters portrayed

Appearing in a vast array of sci-fi movies and series since 1989—such as *Star Trek*, *Babylon 5*, *Sliders*, and *Alien Nation*—actor Bill Blair (USA) has donned extensive SFX makeup to play 202 characters as of May 6, 2011.

3D movie in color: Audiences had to wear colored filter glasses to witness *Bwana Devil* (USA, 1952), the spectacular tale of two man-eating lions, written and directed by Arch Oboler (USA).

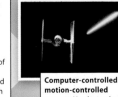

Computer-controlled motion-controlled camera: Used to make *Star Wars* (USA, 1977), it was capable of memorizing and repeating sophisticated camera movements.

Computer-generated character in a major blockbuster movie: The T-1000 Terminator, nemesis of Arnold Schwarzenegger's character in *Terminator 2: Judgment Day* (1991), was created by ILM (USA) using Silicon Graphics computers.

Movie produced entirely using computer-generated sets: *Able Edwards* (USA, 2004) was produced by Graham Robertson (USA) and first shown at the South by Southwest Film Festival in Austin, Texas, USA, on March 15, 2004. The movie combined real actors shot against a green screen.

Movie in digital 3D: *Chicken Little* (USA, 2005) was the first mainstream cinematic release to be distributed in a digital, stereographic 3D format. Unlike earlier titles, it could be watched with or without polarizing glasses.

ANIMATION

Most successful animation studio

Since the studio's first feature-length animation, *Antz* (USA, 1998), DreamWorks Animation SKG (USA) have produced movies with a total gross of $10,436,283,235 worldwide, eclipsing even the $9,266,841,464 generated by Disney (USA) over more than 76 years. Shown here is the cast of *Madagascar 3* (2012).

Most prolific animation studio

Although Disney has produced more animated feature movies overall (67 in the 76 years since *Snow White and the Seven Dwarfs* first hit movie theaters), DreamWorks Animation SKG has maintained a faster work rate, releasing 25 titles since 1998—an average of 1.8 movies per year. Disney currently has an average of 0.9 feature movies per year.

Most expensive motion-capture animation

The 3D motion-capture version of *A Christmas Carol* (USA, 2009), directed by Robert Zemeckis (USA), cost $200 million to produce. In this process, actors' performances are captured on video—usually in 3D—then mapped onto digital characters that mirror the actors' movements.

Most Oscar wins for Best Animated Feature

Since the Best Animated Feature category was first introduced at the Oscars in 2001, Pixar (USA) have won 7 of the 13 awards, for *Finding Nemo* (2003), *The Incredibles* (2004), *Brave* (2012), and a four-year run of success with *Ratatouille* (2007), *WALL•E* (2008), *Up* (2009), and *Toy Story 3* (2010).

Highest-grossing stop-motion animated movie

Chicken Run (UK, 2000) had grossed $225 million worldwide by December 31, 2000. The movie was created by Aardman Animations (UK), the studio behind the successful Wallace & Gromit stop-motion shorts and feature movies.

25
Animated features made by DreamWorks since 1998.

TANGLED TALES
Tangled was the 50th movie in Disney's "Animated Classics" series. *Snow White and the Seven Dwarfs* (1937) was the first.

FAME-MOUSE
On November 13, 1978, Disney's iconic Mickey Mouse became the **first fictional character on the Hollywood Walk of Fame.**

Most expensive animated movie

As of February 2013, *Tangled* (USA, 2010) is the most expensive animated movie ever made, with a budget of $260 million. The reimagining of the Rapunzel fairy tale had the fifth biggest budget of any movie, and is the only animation in the top 20 list of the most expensive movies of all time.

ANIMATED LANDMARKS

First 2D animation: *Humorous Phases of Funny Faces* (USA, 1906), by J. Stuart Blackton (USA, b. UK), a series of caricatures drawn in white chalk on a blackboard, shot one frame at a time, then wiped clean and redrawn.

First prime-time animation show: *The Flintstones*, created by William Hanna and Joseph Barbera; debuted on ABC Television (USA) in September 1960.

First use of computer-generated (CG) animation in a major motion picture: *Tron* (USA, 1982).

First motion-capture animation in a video game: *Prince of Persia*, created in 1989 by designer and programmer Jordan Mechner (USA).

Biggest-selling animation soundtrack: *The Lion King* (USA, 1994), with 7.84 million confirmed sales in the USA and in excess of 10 million units sold worldwide.

2
Days it took Danny Elfman to write the famous *Simpsons* theme tune in 1989.

AT YOU... ...RE
www.guinnessw... ...om

GUINNESS WORLD RECORDS 2014

First anime to win an Oscar

Studio Ghibli's *Spirited Away* (2001) won Best Animated Feature at the 75th Academy Awards. The movie is the **highest-grossing anime**, taking $274.9 million worldwide, and the **highest-grossing foreign-language animation**. It is also the highest-grossing Japanese movie of any kind.

Most consecutive Oscar wins

The Best Short Subject (Cartoons) category was introduced at the 1932 Academy Awards and Walt Disney Productions won the award for the next eight years.

AT THE BOX OFFICE

Fastest $100-million gross for an animation

Only two animated movies have grossed $100 million within three days of their release: *Shrek the Third* (USA, 2007) and *Toy Story 3* (USA, 2010) hit the $100-million mark on May 18, 2007 and June 18, 2010, respectively.

Most successful 3D animation

Toy Story 3 (USA, 2010) has earned $1.06 billion globally since its opening on June 18, 2010. The movie also enjoyed the **most successful opening weekend for a 3D animation**, taking $110,307,189 from its first weekend. In all, 12 feature-length 3D animations were

produced in 2010, the **most animated 3D features released in one year**.

Toy Story 3 is also the **first animated movie to gross $1 billion** at the worldwide box office, achieving the landmark total by 30 August 2010. This also makes it the **highest-grossing computer-animated feature movie**.

Most successful foreign-language animation studio

Founded in Koganei, Tokyo, in 1985, Japan's Studio Ghibli is the most profitable animation

studio based outside the USA. It has produced 18 feature movies, but the nine titles the studio has released since *Princess Mononoke* (1997) marked a new distribution deal with Disney/Buena Vista (USA) and have grossed more than $1 billion worldwide.

Longest-running sitcom

The current longest-running sitcom on U.S. television is *The Simpsons* (FOX), which completed its 23rd series in spring 2012. Its 500th episode was broadcast on February 19, 2012. In 2011, the show was renewed for another two seasons and so will reach the historic landmark of achieving 25 seasons on air in 2013–14.

Most Oscar nominations for an animated movie

WALL·E (USA, 2008) was nominated for six Academy Awards in six categories: Best Animated Feature, Original Screenplay, Score, Song, Sound Mixing, and Sound Editing. It won Best Animated Feature.

The **first animated movie to win an Oscar** was the eight-minute "Silly Symphony" cartoon *Flowers and Trees* (inset) at the fifth Academy Awards in 1932. It won Walt Disney an Oscar for Best Short Subject (Cartoons), a category only introduced that year.

A WALT DISNEY
SILLY SYMPHONY
FLOWERS AND TREES

Highest average gross for a studio

Pixar have produced 13 feature movies since 1995, which have grossed $7.8 billion worldwide at an average of $601,707,296 per title.

6
Weeks it took *WALL·E* to gross $200 million in the USA.

First feature-length computer-animated movie: *Toy Story* (USA, 1995).

First use of CARI animation: *Dragonheart* (USA, 1996) featured Industrial Light & Magic's (USA) CARI ("caricature") animation to render skin and muscle tissue effects on animated characters.

First computer-generated animated movie with photorealistic characters: *Final Fantasy: The Spirits Within* (USA, 2001).

First animation to be Oscar-nominated for Best Foreign Language Movie: *Vals Im Bashir* (Waltz with Bashir) (Israel/Germany/France/USA, 2008), directed by Ari Folman (Israel).

First animated feature made in stereoscopic 3D: *Monsters vs. Aliens* (USA, 2009), created in a stereoscopic format instead of being converted to 3D after completion.

SUPERHEROES

First female superhero

The first female to appear in print as a superhero was Fantomah, a shape-shifting ancient Egyptian princess created by Barclay Flagg (aka Fletcher Hanks, USA) for *Jungle Comics* No. 2, published in February 1940. The first masked and costumed superheroine (and of "natural" birth) was The Woman in Red, created by Richard Hughes and George Mandel (both USA) for *Thrilling Comics* No. 2, published in March 1940.

Most expensive comic

A near-mint copy of *Action Comics* No. 1, published in 1938 and featuring the first appearance of Superman, was bought anonymously via auction Web site ComicConnect.com for $2.16 million, inclusive of the seller's premium, on November 30, 2011.

Widest release for a superhero movie (single country)

The Dark Knight Rises (USA, 2012) opened at 4,404 movie houses in the USA on July 20, 2012, a release beaten only by *The Twilight Saga: Eclipse* (USA, 2010) at 4,468 cinemas and *Harry Potter and the Half-Blood Prince* (UK/USA, 2009) at 4,455.

Highest-grossing reboot

In a comparison by Box Office Mojo of movies that have been "rebooted," *The Amazing Spider-Man* (USA, 2012) proved to be the most successful, grossing $262,030,663 and beating off *Star Trek* (USA, 2009), *Batman Begins* (USA, 2005), and *Casino Royale* (UK, 2006) among others.

HIGHLY ADAPTABLE
With eight full-length live-action movies to his name as of 2012, Batman is the **most adapted comic-book character**.

A FIRE WILL RISE
THE DARK KNIGHT RISES

Best-selling comic-book video game

The Man of Steel may have been the **first superhero to feature in his own video game** (*Superman* was released for the Atari 2600 in 1979), but the biggest selling comic-inspired game of all time is *Batman: Arkham City* (Rocksteady, 2011), which had sold 7.19 million copies as of September 2012.

First superhero

The Phantom was created in 1936 by the cartoonist Lee Falk (USA) two years before Superman. The Phantom newspaper strip featured the adventures of Kit Walker, who sported a mask and a figure-hugging purple outfit.

The **first superhero to die** was The Comet, aka John Dickering, created by Jack Cole (USA) for *Pep Comics* in January 1940 and killed off 17 issues later in July 1941, when he was shot by henchmen sent by his nemesis, Big Boy Malone.

FOR THE RECORD

The **longest-running monthly comic** is *Detective Comics*, printed continuously by DC Comics in the USA since issue No. 1 in March 1937. The comic introduced Batman in issue No. 27 in May 1939.

Highest-grossing superhero movie

Marvel's *The Avengers* (USA, 2012) took $1,511,757,910 at the international box office in its 22 weeks on general release between May 4 and October 4, 2012.

The star-packed flick is also the **fastest movie to gross $1 billion**, doing so just 10 days after it went on general release.

62
Number of live-action movies based on Marvel comic books as of 2012.

TOP 10 BOX-OFFICE SUPERHEROES

1. Batman: $3,718 million

Source: Box Office Mojo. Figures combined from all films (1978–2013) in which these characters take the lead role. Accurate as of January 2013.

2. Spider-Man: $3,248 million

3. X-Men: $1,890 million

4. The Avengers: $1,511 million

5. Iron Man: $1,209 million

AT YOUR LEISURE

www.guinnessworldrecord[s]

GUINNESS
WORLD
RECORDS
2014

The **highest-grossing superheroine movie** is *Catwoman* (USA, 2004), starring Halle Berry (USA), which earned $82,102,379 at the global box office. Despite this, the movie was a critical and commercial flop, failing to make back its estimated $100-million budget.

Most people dressed as superheroes
In an event organized by Paramount Studios to promote the Dreamworks movie *Megamind* (USA, 2010), 1,580 participants dressed up as superheroes in Los Angeles, California, USA, on October 2, 2010.

Most people dressed as Superman

The largest gathering of people dressed as Superman was 437, achieved by Nexen Inc. (Canada) at the Nexen Inc. headquarters in Calgary, Alberta, Canada, on September 28, 2011. Nexen used the record attempt to kick off their United Way fundraising campaign (titled "Be a Superhero").

Largest collection of Superman memorabilia

Herbert Chavez (Philippines) has a supersize collection of Superman-related items, comprising 1,253 individual objects as of February 22, 2012. He has even had extensive plastic surgery to make him resemble the superhero.

FOR THE RECORD

Stan Lee—born Stanley Lieber in 1922—cocreated the iconic Spider-Man with artist Steve Ditko (USA) in 1962. Among his many plaudits, Lee has a star on the Hollywood Walk of Fame.

Most movies from the work of a comics creator

Stan Lee's (USA) creations had been adapted into Hollywood movies a record 18 times as of February 2013. Pictured here are the stars of *X-Men: First Class* (USA, 2011)—the most successful of the *X-Men* movies.

Best-selling comic

X-Men 1 (Marvel Comics, 1991), created by Chris Claremont (UK) and Jim Lee (USA), sold 8.1 million copies. Lee designed four variant covers, published simultaneously with the date October 1991. A month later, another edition combined the variants as a gatefold cover.

$492,937.50
The highest price for a copy of the first issue of *X-Men* from 1963, sold by Heritage Auctions (USA) on July 26, 2012.

First television superhero

Superman became the first comic superhero with his own TV series when *The Adventures of Superman*, starring George Reeves (USA), syndicated in 1952. Reeves's Superman suit sold for $129,800 at the Profiles in History auction in Los Angeles, California, USA, on July 31, 2003, the **most expensive costume from a TV series sold at auction**.

Most expensive movie based on a comic-book character

With a budget estimated to be in excess of $270 million, Bryan Singer's (USA) *Superman Returns* (USA, 2006) is the most expensive movie based on a comic character.

X-CEPTIONAL
As of June 28, 2012, Eric Jaskolka (USA) owns the **largest collection of X-Men memorabilia**, numbering 15,400 items.

6. The Hulk: $1,133 million

7. The Incredibles: $631 million

8. Hancock: $624 million

9. The Fantastic Four: $619 million

10. Superman: $484 million

209

POP MUSIC

First album to top the global chart for two consecutive years

21 by Adele (UK, b. Adele Adkins) sold 18.1 million copies in 2011 and 8.3 million copies in 2012. Worldwide sales of 26.4 million copies to the end of 2012 put it among the 50 biggest-selling albums of all time.

Youngest *X Factor* judge

Demi Lovato (USA, b. August 20, 1992, *above left*) was 19 years 278 days old when she began filming the second season of *The X Factor USA* alongside Simon Cowell, L. A. Reid, and Britney Spears on May 24, 2012. Lovato mentored the Young Adults category but failed to reach the final with any of her acts.

Most BRIT awards won

Robbie Williams (UK) has won 17 BRIT awards in total, including solo awards and those that he won with Take That.

The **most BRIT awards won by a group** is eight and is held jointly by Coldplay and Take That (both UK). Coldplay equaled the record set by Take That between 1993 and 2011 when they won Best Live Act in 2013. Their awards include three for Best British Group.

Most music videos on one album

Kono Hi no Chime wo Wasurenai (*I Don't Forget Today's Chime*), the debut album by SKE48 (Japan), was released in their homeland in September 2012. Its bonus DVD had 63 music videos to showcase the vocal talents of each of the 63 members.

First solo female with two million-selling weeks on U.S. albums chart

The third and fourth studio albums by country-pop princess Taylor Swift (USA)—*Speak Now* in November 2010 and *Red* in November 2012—both sold more than one million copies in their first week on sale. They sold 1.04 million and 1.20 million copies respectively.

1.31 MILLION
Copies of *Oops!... I Did it Again* sold by Britney Spears in March 2000—the only female artist to top Taylor on release.

Fastest-selling digital single

Taylor Swift's "We Are Never Ever Getting Back Together," from her album *Red* (2012), debuted at No. 1 on iTunes' singles sales chart just 50 minutes after it was released on August 14, 2012. It sold 623,000 units in its first week.

Most digital tracks sold in one country in one week

A record 55.74 million digital songs were sold in the USA in the week ending December 30, 2012, with Taylor Swift's "I Knew You Were Trouble" (582,000 copies sold) leading the charge. This one-week surge took total digital sales in the USA in 2012 to a record 1.336 billion.

Most consecutive weeks on UK singles chart (multiple singles)

Dating back to the No. 1 debut of "Run This Town" on September 12, 2009, Rihanna (Barbados, b. Robyn Rihanna Fenty) had spent 187 consecutive weeks in the UK Top 75 as of April 6, 2013.

The prolific hit-maker, who has sold in excess of 100 million records during her career, has charted with 29 different tracks since September 2009, 22 of those as a solo or lead vocalist.

TWITTER-WOO
Rihanna had 29,600,637 followers on Twitter as of May 15, 2013.

TOP 10 HIGHEST-PAID MUSICIANS (2011–12)

1. Dr. Dre, aka Andre Young (USA), $110 million

2. Roger Waters (UK), $88 million

3. Elton John (UK), $80 million

4. U2 (Ireland), $78 million

5. Take That (UK), $69 million

AT YOU
www.guinn...........om

GUINNESS
WORLD
RECORDS
2014

341,000 first-week digital sales of "Live While We're Young".

Highest debut by a UK group on the U.S. singles chart

One Direction—from left: Harry Styles, Zayn Malik, Liam Payne, Louis Tomlinson (all UK), and Niall Horan (Ireland)—debuted at No. 3 on the U.S. chart on October 20, 2012 with "Live While We're Young", the highest debut by an all- or predominantly British group in the 55-year history of the *Billboard* Hot 100.

Simon Cowell (UK) appeared on the first seven series in the UK (2004–10) and the first two series in the USA (2011–12). Louis Walsh (Ireland) has starred in all nine UK series to date (2004–12). The reality TV music show has been broadcast in 39 territories worldwide since its UK debut in 2004.

Most winners mentored
Morgan, aka Marco Castoldi (Italy), has mentored four winners of the Italian version of *The X Factor*: Aram Quartet, Matteo Becucci, Marco

Highest-charting UK single by an unsigned musician

"Forever Yours" by Alex Day (UK) debuted at No. 4 on December 31, 2011. Alex, 24, is a video blogger who uses social networks to promote his music. He has charted solo with the 2012 singles "Lady Godiva" and "Stupid Stupid" and with Chartjackers ("I've Got Nothing," 2009) and Sons of Admirals ("Here Comes My Baby," 2010). As of May 15, 2013, Alex's YouTube channel, *nerimon*, had attracted 112,087,217 views.

Most viewed music video
"Gangnam Style" by South Korean pop star PSY (b. Park Jae-sang) is the most viewed music video online, as well as the **most viewed video of any kind** (*see p. 198*). As of May 14, 2013, the video had racked up an astonishing 1,598,585,367 views on YouTube.

Most popular Facebook music app
In March 2013, there were a reported 25.94 million monthly active users and 9.05 million daily active users of music-streaming service Spotify (Sweden) on Facebook. In November 2012, *Music Week* said that 62.6 million songs had been played 22 billion times on all Facebook music apps, equating to 210,000 years' worth of music.

Largest Harlem Shake
American indie rock duo Matt & Kim (aka Matt Johnson and Kim Schifino) got in on the Harlem Shake dance craze—based on Baauer's (USA, b. Harry Rodrigues) 2012 single "Harlem Shake"—when their crowd of 3,344 performed it at Rensselaer Polytechnic Institute's Houston Field House arena in Troy, New York, USA, on February 11, 2013.

MOST YOUTUBE VIEWS FOR AN UNSIGNED MUSICIAN

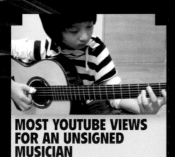

Finger-picking guitar videos by "jwcfree," aka Sungha Jung (South Korea, *above*), had been viewed 677,173,291 times by May 15, 2013. The record for **most YouTube views for an unsigned female musician** is held by Venetian Princess, aka Jodie Rivera (USA), who had 385,708,717 views as of May 15, 2013.

Most consecutive UK Top 10 weeks for a debut album
Our Version of Events by Emeli Sandé (UK) spent its 63rd successive week inside the UK Top 10 – including 10 weeks at No.1 – on May 4, 2013. She broke a record which had stood for 50 years, beating the achievement of The Beatles' *Please Please Me*, with 62 consecutive weeks following its release in March 1963.

THE X FACTOR

Most appearances by a judge
Two judges or mentors have appeared in nine series of *The X Factor* to date. Deviser

Mengoni, and, most recently, Chiara Galiazzo in the 2012 series.

Youngest winning judge
Charice (Philippines, b. Charmaine Pempengco, May 10, 1992) was 20 years 150 days old when she mentored K. Z. Tandingan (b. Kristine Tandingan) to victory in the first season of *The X Factor Philippines* on October 7, 2012.

Youngest solo artist to have five U.S. No. 1 albums

Justin Bieber (Canada, b. March 1, 1994) hit No. 1 with *My World 2.0* (2010), *Never Say Never: The Remixes* (2011), *Under the Mistletoe* (2011), *Believe* (2012), and *Believe Acoustic* (2013) before his 19th birthday. On October 22, 2012, he became the **first musician with a music channel viewed three billion times**. As of May 15, 2013, his total YouTube views were 3,699,424,545.

6. Bon Jovi (USA), $60 million

7. Britney Spears (USA), $58 million

=8. Paul McCartney (UK)
=8. Taylor Swift (USA), $57 million

=10. Justin Bieber (Canada)
=10. Toby Keith (USA), $55 million

Source: Forbes.com
Based on total earnings from May 2011 to May 2012

LIVE CONCERTS

4
Number of days it took Simpson to travel from London, UK, to Oymyakon.

164 ft. (50 m) high and measuring 229,000 sq. ft. (2,694 m²). The steel spaceshiplike stage required 120 trucks to transport and cost between £15 and £20 million ($23–30 million). Each of The Claw's "legs" boasted a sound system powerful enough for an entire arena, 72 separate subwoofers, and its own lighting. Three of the behemoths were built.

Most live concerts in 24 hours (multiple cities)

The Flaming Lips (USA) played eight concerts at various cities in the USA over the course of one 24-hour period as part of the O Music Awards on June 27–28, 2012. The band played for at least 15 minutes in each city before boarding their tour bus and heading to the next destination.

First fatal stage dive by a musician

Bad Beat Revue frontman Patrick Sherry (UK) died of head injuries after jumping from the stage at the Warehouse club in Leeds, UK, on July 20, 2005. The charismatic 29-year-old vocalist fractured his skull when he plunged

Coldest concert

Charlie Simpson (UK) performed a gig at a temperature of -22°F (-30°C) in Oymyakon, Russia, on November 24, 2012. Simpson played for locals of this remote Siberian village—famed for being the **coldest permanently inhabited place** on Earth.

headfirst from a lighting gantry while performing the closing track during the Club NME show.

Largest reward for the return of a stage prop

During a performance on April 27, 2008 by Roger Waters (UK, *see below*) at the Coachella Valley Music and Arts Festival in Indio, California, USA, a giant inflatable pig broke free from its tethers. Organizers offered a $10,000 reward and four lifetime Coachella tickets (potentially worth $36,900) for the safe return of the stage prop, which was a popular fixture at the former Pink Floyd bassist's shows. The 40-ft.-long (12-m) "capitalist pig" was found two days later as "crumpled heaps of shredded, spray-painted plastic" approximately 9 miles (14 km) away in La Quinta, California, USA.

Largest audience

Rod Stewart (UK) attracted an estimated 4.2 million fans to the Copacabana beach in Rio de Janeiro, Brazil, on New Year's Eve in 1994, the largest nonpaying concert audience—although it was suggested that some people may have come solely to see the fireworks at midnight. At the same location, on February 18, 2006,

The Rolling Stones (UK) played to an estimated 2 million fans.

In the same city, at the Maracanã Stadium, both Paul McCartney (UK) and Tina Turner (USA) played to an estimated 180,000–184,000 people, the **largest paying audience for a solo artist**. The former Beatle played on April 21, 1990, while Turner took to the stage on January 16, 1988.

The Molson Canadian Rocks for Toronto concert held on July 30, 2003 at Downsview Park in Toronto, Ontario, Canada, was seen by a crowd of 489,176, the **largest paying audience for one bill**. Acts included The Flaming Lips (USA), AC/DC (Australia) and Justin Timberlake (USA).

Largest stage rig

Between 2009 and 2011, on their 360° Tour, U2 (Ireland) played under "The Claw," a four-legged structure

HIGHEST DEMAND FOR CONCERT TICKETS

Led Zeppelin's (UK) only reunion show at London's O2 arena on December 10, 2007 attracted more than 20 million ticket requests. Such was the demand for the 18,000 tickets available that they were selling for as much as £1,800 ($3,654) on eBay—more than 14 times their original price of £125 ($253).

Largest audience for a music tour in 12 months

Based on the average attendance for the first 122 shows of The Rolling Stones' (UK) 134-date "Voodoo Lounge Tour," an estimated 5,769,258 people—or 47,289 people per concert—attended the spectacle worldwide between August 1, 1994 and August 1, 1995.

TOP 10 HIGHEST-GROSSING TOURS OF 2012

1. Madonna
Cities/shows: 67/88
Gross: $296.1 million

2. Bruce Springsteen & The E Street Band
Cities/shows: 66/81
Gross: $210.2 million

3. Roger Waters
Cities/shows: 48/72
Gross: $186.4 million

4. Coldplay
Cities/shows: 49/67
Gross: $171.3 million

5. Lady Gaga
Cities/shows: 50/80
Gross: $161.4 million

Source: www.pollstarpro.com

First rock 'n' roll concert

The Moondog Coronation Ball at the Cleveland Arena in Ohio, USA, on March 21, 1952 has been described as the "Big Bang of rock 'n' roll." The concert was organized by DJ Alan Freed and music store owner Leo Mintz and headlined by saxophonist Paul Williams and his Hucklebuckers (all USA). The event was abandoned after about 30 minutes due to overcrowding and rioting after more than 20,000 revelers stormed the 9,950-seat venue.

Most births at a concert

Four births—in addition to four well-publicized deaths—were reported by the American Red Cross at the infamous and chaotic Altamont Speedway (now Altamont Raceway Park) concert headlined by The Rolling Stones and attended by 300,000 revelers in Tracy, California, USA, on December 6, 1969.

FIRST BAND TO DESTROY THEIR INSTRUMENTS

During a performance at The Railway Hotel in Harrow, London, UK, in 1964, guitarist Pete Townshend of The Who (UK) "finished off" his Rickenbacker after accidentally breaking the neck of the guitar on the venue's low ceiling.

Oldest annual popular music festival

The UK's Reading Festival started out as the nomadic National Jazz (& Blues) Festival before moving to its permanent home in Reading in 1971. The three-day event has been staged since 1961, although in 1984 and 1985 the local council reclaimed the site for development and it was canceled when an alternative venue could not be found.

The **oldest annual popular music festival in continuous existence** is the Pinkpop Festival, held

Longest concert rider

In 1982–83, Van Halen (USA) embarked on a 98-date American tour with a 53-page typewritten list of demands that featured requests such as five rooms with a "pleasant temperature," herring in sour cream, 44 assorted sandwiches, and M&M's (but no brown ones). Not simply a frivolous demand, the rider was a way of determining whether their contract had been read carefully.

FIRST STADIUM TOUR BY A MUSICIAN

Elvis Presley (USA, 1935–77) established the blueprint for stadium concerts with a five-date tour of the Pacific Northwest in August and September 1957. The first of these shows is regarded as rock's first real stadium concert.

Most expensive concert VIP package

The reserved, front-row "Diamond VIP Experience" tickets for Bon Jovi's (USA) 2010 "Circle" tour were individually priced at $1,875. The package included a collectable concert chair ("You sit in it. You watch the show in it. You take it home with you."), preshow hospitality, and a fully autographed tour programme.

for the last 43 consecutive years in Limburg, Netherlands. Attracting more than 2 million visitors and 644 different acts since 1970, Pinkpop has an average annual attendance of almost 50,000.

Most live albums
The Grateful Dead (USA) have been the source of 121 official, full-length live albums since 1969. Of these, 105 have been released since they disbanded in 1995.

6. Cirque du Soleil—"Michael Jackson: The Immortal"
Cities/shows: 74/172
Gross: $140.2 million

7. Kenny Chesney & Tim McGraw
Cities/shows: 22/23
Gross: $96.5 million

8. Metallica
Cities/shows: 21/30
Gross: $86.1 million

9. Elton John
Cities/shows: 78/95
Gross: $69.9 million

10. Red Hot Chili Peppers
Cities/shows: 72/77
Gross: $57.8 million

TV

First 3D broadcast of the Queen's Christmas message

On December 25, 2012, the annual Christmas message from Queen Elizabeth II (UK) was broadcast in 3D for the first time. "We wanted to do something a bit different and special in this Jubilee year," explained a spokesman for Buckingham Palace, "so doing it for the first time in 3D seemed a good thing, technology-wise, to do."

Highest annual earnings for a television personality

Female: Despite her income dropping $125 million from the previous year, Oprah Winfrey (USA) still earned $165 million between May 2011 and May 2012, according to *Forbes* magazine, meaning she remains TV's highest earner. Oprah's prime concerns are her production company Harpo—responsible for *Dr. Phil*, *Rachael Ray*, *The Dr. Oz Show*, and Discovery's OWN (the Oprah Winfrey Network)—her magazine *O*, and radio station *Oprah Radio* on XM Satellite Radio.

Most-viewed factual TV show

Airing in 212 different territories worldwide, the UK's *Top Gear* (BBC) is the most widely watched factual program on TV. The motoring show began in 1977 and relaunched in 2002. It is currently hosted by Jeremy Clarkson (*above*), Richard Hammond, and James May (all UK).

Male: For the year ending May 1, 2012, the highest-earning male television personality—and indeed the highest earning man on TV in any capacity, including acting—is Simon Cowell (UK). The founder of SYCO Entertainment (UK/USA), Cowell took home $90 million from his role as a judge on *The X Factor USA* and from his management of musical acts such as One Direction (UK), who found fame on the British version of the show.

Longest screen kiss on a TV show

Lasting for a lip-smacking 3 min. 28 sec., Malik Anthony and Merilee Rhoden (both USA) kissed fully on the lips on *The Jeff Probst Show* in Los Angeles, California, USA. The episode aired on Valentine's Day, February 14, 2013.

Most durable presenter

Amateur astronomer Sir Patrick Moore (UK, 1923–2012) hosted the monthly sky-watching series and **longest-running show hosted by the same presenter**, *The Sky at Night* (BBC), from the very first edition in 1957 until the 722nd episode, "Reaching for the Stars", which aired on January 7, 2013.

Highest rate of TV viewing (country)

The average viewer in the USA watched 293 minutes of TV every day in 2011, according to Ofcom, the UK's regulator for the communications industry. Italy is in second place at 253 minutes, followed by the UK at 242 minutes.

Largest penetration of Internet TV

When it comes to watching or catching up on television over the Internet, the UK leads the world. According to Ofcom's (UK) *7th*

Highest-rated TV series

Based on published critical reviews, *Breaking Bad* (AMC, 2008–13) garnered a metascore of 99 out of 100 on Web site Metacritic.com in 2013. The series stars Bryan Cranston (USA) as Walter White, a high-school chemistry teacher diagnosed with lung cancer who undergoes a midlife crisis and turns to drug dealing. Created by Vince Gilligan (USA), it is a Sony Pictures television production broadcast on the cable channel AMC.

NOT BAD AT ALL
Breaking Bad also has the distinction of being the **highest-rated TV series ever**, owing to its unprecedented Metacritic score.

PROLIFIC PRESENTERS

Deepest broadcast on television by a presenter: Alastair Fothergill (UK) broadcast at a depth of 1.5 miles (2.4 km) underwater on *Abyss Live* (BBC, UK) on September 29, 2002.

First TV announcer (male): In 1936, radio personality Leslie Mitchell (1905–85) became the first of three TV presenters chosen for the BBC's fledgling television service.

Most durable "blooper" presenter: Denis Norden CBE (UK, b. February 6, 1922) presented blooper shows for 29 years. He first hosted *It'll be Alright on the Night* on September 18, 1977, and presented his last show, *All the Best from Denis Norden*, in September 2006.

Most episodes of *Who Wants to be a Millionaire?* hosted: Presenter Gerry Scotti, aka Virginio Scotti (Italy), has hosted 1,593 episodes, as certified on *Lo Show dei Record* in Milan, Italy, on May 5, 2011.

Youngest TV presenter: Luis Tanner (Australia, b. May 9, 1998) first hosted *Cooking for Kids with Luis* (Nickelodeon) on October 25, 2004 aged 6 years 168 days.

GUINNESS WORLD RECORDS 2014

HIGHEST-PAID ACTRESS PER TV EPISODE

The 14th series of *Law & Order: Special Victims Unit* (NBC) returned to U.S. screens in September 2012, enabling Mariska Hargitay (USA) to regain her title as the highest-paid actress per episode, with an estimated $500,000 per show.

HIGHEST-PAID ACTOR PER TV EPISODE

Ashton Kutcher (USA) nets at least $700,000 per episode for the sitcom *Two and a Half Men* (CBS). Kutcher replaced the previous record holder, Charlie Sheen (USA), on the show. Sheen earned $1.2 million an episode for his time in the role.

NBC paid $1.2 billion alone for the right to broadcast the London 2012 Olympics.

Most-pirated TV show

According to the TorrentFreak file-sharing weblog, the most downloaded TV show is HBO's epic medieval fantasy *Game of Thrones*, the most popular episode of which was accessed 4,280,000 times in 2012. The average number of downloads per episode of series 2 was 3.9 million.

Longest TV career for an entertainer (female)

Actress Betty Marion White Ludden (USA, b. January 17, 1922), better known as Betty White, made her television debut in 1939 and is still appearing on screen aged 91 years 39 days old, as of February 25, 2013. Her career has spanned 74 years.

International Communications Market Report, almost a quarter of British Internet users (23%) claim to take advantage of TV services over the net on a weekly basis, driven by the ease of access to online TV catch-up services such as BBC iPlayer, Sky Go, and 4OD.

Longest-running sci-fi series

As of May 18, 2013, a total of 798 episodes of *Doctor Who* (BBC, UK) have been aired. This total includes 239 story arcs and a full-length TV movie but does not include spoofs, spin-offs, or webisodes. Filming for the eighth series of the revamped format, once again starring Matt Smith (UK) as the Eleventh Doctor, is scheduled for September 2013.

Most comprehensive Olympic coverage

The multiplatform digital coverage of London 2012 saw the event become the most comprehensively covered Olympics ever. A total of 5,535 hours of coverage from London was available from NBC (USA) across NBC Sports Network, MSNBC, CNBC, Bravo, Telemundo, and NBCOlympics.com, while BBC Sport (UK) broadcast 2,500 hours of coverage on television and online—with up to 24 high-definition live streams, and Web pages for every athlete, country, sport, and venue. In China, CCTV provided 610 million streams to iPads, smartphones, and connected devices alone.

In June 2011, the U.S. broadcaster NBC agreed to a $4.38-billion contract with the International Olympic Committee to show the Olympic Games on television in the USA from 2014 to 2020—the **most expensive Olympic rights deal**.

74
Number of years that Bruce Forsyth has been appearing on television.

Longest TV career for an entertainer (male)

Sir Bruce Forsyth (UK) made his debut in 1939 as an 11-year-old on the BBC (UK) show *Come and Be Televised* and hosted his first show, *Sunday Night at the London Palladium* (ATV/ITV), in 1958. His most recent appearance was in 2012, cohosting a *Strictly Come Dancing Christmas Special* (BBC).

Longest TV shopping presenting marathon

Presenter Steve Macdonald (UK) broadcast live for 25 hr. 2 min. on the set of shopping program *Price Drop* in London, UK, on October 28, 2012.

Most-portrayed human literary character on screen

Sherlock Holmes has been portrayed in movies and on TV more than any other human character from literature. As of April 2012, Holmes had been incarnated at least 254 times in various movies and TV shows. The **most portrayed character** of any kind is the Devil, who had featured in 849 movies and TV episodes as of the same date.

Most expensive Batman memorabilia sold at auction

A Batmobile used in the 1960s *Batman* TV series (ABC, USA, 1966–68) sold at the Barrett-Jackson automobile auction in Scottsdale, Arizona, USA, on January 19, 2013 for $4,620,000, inclusive of premium.

$1
Price for which auto customizer George Barris bought a Lincoln Futura in 1965. Fifteen days and $15,000 later, he had transformed it into the Batmobile!

Most hours on U.S. TV: In a career spanning 52 years as of September 15, 2011, presenter Regis Philbin (USA) accumulated 16,746 hours of air time.

Most powerful person in TV: *Forbes* magazine lists Oprah Winfrey (USA, b. 1954) as the most powerful person in television, owing largely to her own TV network.

Richest presenter of reality TV: Richard Branson (UK), star of the 2004 reality TV show *The Rebel Billionaire: Branson's Quest for the Best* (FOX, USA), is worth an estimated $4.6 billion.

Most TV talk shows hosted by the same presenter: Japanese presenter Tetsuko Kuroyanagi has hosted 9,486 episodes of her daily show *Tetsuko no Heya* ("Tetsuko's Room") since it was first broadcast by TV Asahi (Japan) on February 2, 1976.

Longest career as a TV naturalist: Celebrating 60 years in broadcasting in 2012, Sir David Attenborough joined the BBC (both UK) in 1952 and presented his first show, *Zoo Quest*, in 1954.

VIDEO GAMES

MARKADE

Bret has been collecting. He began his games museum in 2005.

Smallest arcade machine

Mark Slevinsky (Canada) has created a diminutive but fully playable arcade machine measuring just 4.88 x 2.05 x 2.36 in. (124 x 52 x 60 mm). The computer engineer built it from scratch in 2009 and wrote his own operating system, FunkOS, to program its *Tetris*, *Space Invaders*, and *Breakout* clones.

Largest collection of video game memorabilia

In 1989, eight-year-old Brett Martin's (USA) parents gave him a 1.6-in.-tall (4-cm) Mario holding a mushroom. As of October 2012, Brett had amassed a treasure trove of 8,030 gaming items, which he stores at his Video Game Memorabilia Museum (videogamemm.com). The Mario inflatable (*left*) comes from a store display, and is one of Nintendo's earliest and rarest Mario marketing items. More merchandise was produced for Mario than for any other games character, although Link is Brett's favorite.

Fastest time for a video game to gross $1 billion

Within 16 days of release, *Call of Duty: Modern Warfare 3* (Infinity Ward/Sledgehammer Games, 2011) had grossed $1 billion.

Longest-running video game series

Spanning 32 years 3 months between its first and most recent releases, *Flight Simulator* is the longest-running series of them all as of September 2012. Originally released by developer subLOGIC in October 1979 for the Apple II, the game was subsequently acquired by Microsoft and distributed for PCs as *Flight Simulator 1.00* in 1982. It now boasts 16 main series titles.

Most Super Mario Kart world records

Thirteen-year-old Leyla Hasso (UK) wasn't born when Super Mario Kart (Nintendo EAD) was released in 1992, but by September 19, 2012, she held 30 out of 40 possible time trial records on the PAL version. That's 26 more records than her closest rival Tanja Brönnecke (Germany).

Fastest-selling PC game

Diablo III (Blizzard, 2012) sold 3.5 million copies in its first 24 hours after launch, with 4.7 million players on day one. This doesn't include the 1.2 million players who received the game for free as part of a *World of Warcraft* Annual Pass promotion.

Fastest-selling sports game

Soccer game *FIFA 13* (EA Canada, 2012) sold 4.5 million units within a week.

Longest home run in *Wii Sports*

Brandon Christof (Canada) hit a 662-ft. (201.7-m) home run in *Wii Sports* (Nintendo, 2006) in Shakespeare, Ontario, Canada, on November 4, 2012, beating his own record of 649 ft. (197.8 m).

Highest margin of victory vs. computer on *FIFA 12*

When it comes to *FIFA 12* (EA Canada, 2011), Jacob Gaby (UK, *left*) is in a league of his own. On August 20, 2012, he set the record for the highest margin of victory against a computer, winning 189–0 playing as FC Barcelona against Fulham FC in Bushey, Hertfordshire, UK.

BEST-SELLING GAMES BY GENRE

Sports: *Wii Sports* (Nintendo, 2006)—80.91 million copies

All figures from VGChartz.com, as of January 15, 2013

Platform: *Super Mario Bros.* (Nintendo, 1985)—40.24 million

Racing: *Mario Kart Wii* (Nintendo, 2008)—33.33 million

Role-playing: *Pokémon Red/Green/Blue Version* (Game Freak, 1996)—31.37 million

Shooter: *Call of Duty: Modern Warfare 3* (Infinity Ward/Sledgehammer Games, 2011)—29.67 million

Largest game of *Pong*

Atari, Inc. (USA) created a game of *Pong* on a display with an area of 41,748 sq. ft. (3,878 m²) at the Marriott Hotel in Kansas City, Missouri, USA, on November 16, 2012.

First video game world championships

Cosponsored by Twin Galaxies and *That's Incredible* (ABC, USA), the North American Video Game Olympics took place in Ottumwa, Iowa, USA, on January 8–9, 1983. The event featured five current titles—*Frogger*, *Millipede*, *Joust*, *Super PAC-Man*, and *Donkey Kong Jr.*—and a field of 19 rival video gamers. The eventual victor, and the **first video game world champion**, was Ben Gold (USA).

Most polygons per auto in a racing video game

The race for ever-increasing reality in video game auto graphics is driving developers to increase the number of polygons—the discrete 2D shapes used to build the vehicles and other objects.

The previous polygon record holder was PS3 title *Gran Turismo 5* (Polyphony Digital, 2010), with 400,000 polygons per vehicle. *Forza Motorsport 4* has now comfortably eclipsed this figure by doubling it with 800,000 polygons per racer.

MOST CRITICALLY ACCLAIMED GAMES

The following list of records is based on Metacritic ratings as of March 19, 2013. Where more than one game shares the highest ranking, the record has been awarded to the game with the greater number of reviews.

N64: *The Legend of Zelda: Ocarina of Time* . . . . 99% (Nintendo, 1998)
Xbox 360: *Grand Theft Auto IV* 98% (Rockstar Games, 2008)
PS3: *Grand Theft Auto IV* 98% (Rockstar Games, 2008)
PS1: *Tony Hawk's Pro Skater 2* . . . . . 98% (Activision, 2000)

Highest-earning *Call of Duty* player

Will "BigTymer" Johnson (USA) is the top-earning *Call of Duty* player. Between 2009 and 2012, Will made $135,000 from four different *Call of Duty* titles on the Major League Gaming Pro Circuit. Will has been playing competitively online since 2009. In play, he prefers to use his index finger instead of his thumb to press buttons—that way, he never has to stop aiming.

DUTY TO BE CHARITABLE
Call of Duty publisher Activision has created a nonprofit foundation to help find work for U.S. war veterans.

GAMER ON TRACK
Jann now has an international racing licence and drives for Nissan in the Blancpain Endurance Series.

Youngest winner of GT Academy to turn pro

Jann Mardenborough (UK) won the 2011 GT Academy, an initiative set up by Nissan and PlayStation to bring together the best *Gran Turismo* gamers and let them drive a pro racing auto. At 19 years old at the time of his win, Jann is the youngest winner of GT Academy.

Wii: *Super Mario Galaxy 2* . . . . . 97% (Nintendo, 2010)
Xbox: *Halo: Combat Evolved* . . 97% (Microsoft Game Studios, 2001)
PS2: *Grand Theft Auto III* . . . . . . 97% (Rockstar Games, 2001)
PC: *Half-Life 2* . . . . 96% (VU Games, 2004)
iOS: *World of Goo HD* . . . . 96% (2D Boy, 2010)
Game Boy Advance: *The Legend of Zelda: A Link to the Past* . . . . . . 95% (Nintendo, 2002)
3DS: *The Legend of Zelda: Ocarina of Time 3D* . . . . 94% (Nintendo, 2011)
PS Vita: *Persona 4 Golden* . . . . . 93% (Atlus Co., 2012)
DS: *Grand Theft Auto: Chinatown Wars* . . . . 93% (Rockstar Games, 2009)
PSP: *God of War: Chains of Olympus* . . . . 91% (SCEA, 2008)
Wii U: *Runner2: Future Legend of Rhythm Alien* . . . . 91% (Gaijin Games, 2013)

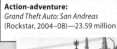

Action-adventure:
Grand Theft Auto: San Andreas (Rockstar, 2004–08)—23.59 million

Simulation:
The Sims (Maxis, 2000–03) —14.91 million

Casual gaming: *Just Dance 3* (Ubisoft, 2011)—12.06 million

Fighting: *Super Smash Bros. Brawl* (Nintendo, 2008)— 11.49 million

MMORPG:
World of Warcraft (Blizzard Entertainment, 2004)—6.25 million

MESSI BEGINNINGS
So eager was FC Barcelona's coach to sign the young Messi that he wrote a contract on the only piece of paper he had: a napkin!

CONTENTS

Most wins of the FIFA Ballon d'Or

The Fédération Internationale de Football Association (FIFA) Ballon d'Or is awarded to the most outstanding soccer player of the previous season, as voted for by coaches, captains, and sports journalists. On January 7, 2013, Lionel Messi (Argentina) was awarded this prestigious "Golden Ball" trophy for a fourth time; he is shown above receiving the award in consecutive years, starting in 2009. The remarkable Messi also scored the **most goals in a calendar year**—a total of 91, including goals for both his club and his country, but excluding friendly matches—reached when he scored in a 3–1 victory over Valladolid in La Liga, the top Spanish league, on December 22, 2012.

WACKY WORLD SPORTS

Global tour of alternative sporting achievements

Why do some sports, such as synchronized swimming or discus throwing, make it into global sporting championships such as the Olympics, while others are relegated to regional obscurity? Why is rhythmic gymnastics more of a "sport" than, say, mashed potato wrestling or winkle spitting? Why the triple jump but not the canal jump? At Guinness World Records, all record claimants are equals, so here we celebrate some of the more esoteric and unusual contests and championships. You may not find all of these events on ESPN, but they are nevertheless worthy of a superlative or two ...

Farthest cow pat toss: The question of whether dry cow pats—or "chips"—may be molded into spheres affects records in this sport. The greatest distance under the "nonsphericalized and 100% organic" rule of 1970 is 266 ft. (81.1 m). It was set by Steve Urner (USA) at the Mountain Festival in Tehachapi, California, USA, on August 14, 1981.

Fastest time in the Wife Carrying World Championships: Margo Uusorg and Sandra Kullas (both Estonia) completed the 831-ft 8-in. (253.5-m) obstacle course in Sonkajärvi, Finland, in 56.9 seconds on July 1, 2006. This is the best time since a minimum wife weight was first set in 2002.

Longest-running pumpkin boat race: The Pumpkin Regatta and Parade has been held annually since 1999 in Windsor, Nova Scotia, Canada. PVC (Personal Vegetable Crafts) are paraded before the race, which is contested over a 2,624-ft. (800-m) stretch across Lake Pesaquid in hollowed-out giant pumpkins. Vessels can be motorized or paddled.

Farthest distance to hurl a haggis: Lorne Coltart (UK) from Perthshire in Scotland threw a haggis 217 ft. (66 m) at the Bearsden & Milngavie Highland Games, Scotland, UK, on June 11, 2011. His throw was so long that the measuring tape ran out.

Longest-running finger wrestling contest: *Fingerhakeln* has been staged in Bavaria, Germany, since the 14th century, when rivals competed for women's favors. Today, wrestlers compete for weight titles in the Finger Wrestling Championships held in various towns. Competitors try to pull rivals seated opposite across a table between them, using a finger lash wrapped around each contestant's digit.

FACT:
A pit measuring about 20 x 10 ft. (6 x 3 m) wide and more than 1 ft. (30 cm) deep is filled with mashed potatoes for the event, and old flakes or potato sweepings are used to avoid wastage.

Most wins of the Mashed Potato Wrestling Championships: Steve-O Gratin, aka Steve Barone (USA), founded the Mashed Potato Wrestling Federation. Steve, pictured above left with Rowdy Roddy Potato Head, has won the Championships a total of four times, from 2006 to 2008 in Barnesville, Minnesota, and Clark, South Dakota, USA.

Most consecutive World Pea-Shooting Championships: These Championships are held every year in Witcham, Cambridgeshire, UK. They have been won three times by three people, most recently by David Hollis (UK) in 1999–2001.

Largest game of kingyo sukui: The art of scooping up goldfish with a delicate paper scooper—or *poi*—was conducted on a grand scale on August 4, 2002, with 60,000 goldfish, 15,000 medaka (Japanese killifish), and 2,641 gallons (10,000 liters) of water. The event was organized by Masaaki Tanaka of the guild of Fujisawa-Ginza-Doyokai in Kanagawa, Japan.

RECORD	LOCATION & DATE	UNITS	HOLDER
Largest annual food fight	Tomato festival and fight in Buñol, Valencia, Spain; record set 2009	275,500 lb. (125 tonnes)	La Tomatina (Spain)
Largest conker championships	The sport is run in the UK every year; record set October 9, 2011	395 conker wielders	Hampstead Heath Education Centre (UK)
Largest water balloon fight	University of Kentucky, USA, 175,141 balloons; August 27, 2011	8,957 fighters	Christian Student Fellowship (USA)
First sheep counting championships	Sheep ran past entrants in 2002 in New South Wales, Australia	277 counted	Peter Desailly (Australia)
Largest shaving cream pie fight	Organized in Dallas, Texas, USA, on July 31, 2012	714 fighters	Ringling Bros. and Barnum & Bailey (USA)
Farthest thrown cell phone (male)	2007 UK Mobile Throwing Championships	314 ft. 5 in. (95.83 m)	Chris Hughff (UK)
Farthest thrown cell phone (female)	2006 UK Mobile Throwing Championships	175 ft. 7 in. (53.52 m)	Jan Singleton (UK)
Most worms charmed	2009 World Worm Charming Championships, UK	567 worms	Sophie Smith (UK)
Largest water pistol fight	2007 celebrations of the patron of Valladolid, Spain	2,671 shooters	Coordinadora de Peñas de Valladolid (Spain)
Farthest spitting of a cherry pit	International Cherry Pit-Spitting Championship, USA, 2004	93.54 ft. (28.51 m)	Brian Krause (USA)

Fastest morse code transmission: In June 2005, Andrei Bindasov (Belarus) tapped 230 morse code marks of mixed text as part of the International Amateur Radio Union's sixth world championship in high-speed telegraphy in Primorsko, Bulgaria.

Longest kiiking swing shaft: Kiiking's aim is to make a 360-degree revolution on a swing, and the longer the shaft, the better. Andrus Aasamäe (Estonia) used a swing shaft measuring 23 ft. (7.02 m) in Haapsalu, Estonia, on August 21, 2004.

28 Gold medals won—out of a possible 34—by US robots at the 2005 RogoGames.

Farthest distance to spit a periwinkle: Alain Jourden (France) spat a snail to defend the Winkle Spitting World Championship title with a spit of 34 ft. 1.4 in. (10.4 m). He was in Moguériec, France, on July 16, 2006.

Largest robot competition: A total of 646 engineers, 466 robots, and 13 countries took part in the 2005 RoboGames held at San Francisco State University in California, USA. Events included soccer with reprogrammed Aibo robot dogs, robo-sumo wrestling, bipedal racing, fire fighting, and musical artistry.

Farthest canal jump: Bart Helmholt (Netherlands) jumped a distance of 70 ft. 6.84 in. (21.51 m) across water using an aluminum pole on August 27, 2011 in Linschoten, Netherlands, in the Dutch Championships. The sport is known locally as *fierljeppen* (far leaping).

Longest-running man vs. horse race: The Man vs. Horse Marathon has been held annually since 1980 in Llanwrtyd Wells, Wales, UK. The race takes place over 22 miles (35.4 km) of rugged terrain. It was first staged to answer a pub debate over who was faster. Because the course has been altered over the years to make horse and rider more evenly matched with runner, the contest has become closer. Runners have won twice, in 2004 and 2007.

FOR A SPORTS ROUNDUP, TURN TO P. 262

Longest-running cockroach race: Races have been held at the Story Bridge Hotel in Brisbane, Australia, on January 26 since 1980. The cockroaches are released in the middle of a circular track, and the first to the edge is the winner.

AIR SPORTS

IN REVIEW In terms of air sports, the year 2012 was evolutionary rather than revolutionary, with significant refinements in technology and individual skills allowing more than 200 new world records to be set. Significantly, paragliding, hang gliding, and wing-suit flying have moved on in bounds, enabling aviators to perform feats only possible in conventional aircraft until fairly recently.

To achieve 568 consecutive infinity tumbles in a paraglider is testament not only to the refinement of paraglider design but also to true mastery of the parachute-like wing. The record for the **farthest distance flown in a hang glider** is similarly impressive. At 474 miles (764 km), it approaches the records set by conventional gliders in the early 1960s! The barriers to entry of these sports are lower than ever, which—along with improving capabilities—promises exciting times ahead.

iQUOTE
"Fifteen minutes seem to last forever. You're there in a fight: one more, one more, one more …"

GLIDING

Highest flight
Male: The absolute altitude record in a glider is 50,721 ft. (15,460 m) by Steve Fossett (USA) over El Calafate in Argentina on August 29, 2006.
Female: The women's single-seater world record for absolute altitude is 41,460 ft. (12,637 m) by Sabrina Jackintell (USA) over Black Forest Gliderport in Colorado Springs, USA, on February 14, 1979.

Greatest free triangle distance
Male: Klaus Ohlmann (Germany) flew 1,091 miles (1,756.1 km) in an open-class glider over Chapelco, Argentina, on January 12, 2011. Ohlmann (*below*) currently holds 18 FAI-ratified world records in the Open Glider class, and has held 36 records over his gliding career.
Female: Susanne Schödel (Germany) covered a triangular distance of 660 miles (1,062.5 km) over Bitterwasser, Namibia, on December 20, 2011.

Longest distance over a triangular course
Male: Klaus Ohlmann covered 1,087 miles (1,750.6 km) over Chapelco, Argentina, on January 12, 2011.
Female: Pamela Hawkins (UK) flew 644 miles (1,036.56 km) from Tocumwal in New South Wales, Australia, on December 25, 1998. She also holds the **longest free distance** record, flying 670 miles (1,078.2 km) on January 5, 2003.

Farthest out-and-return
Male: Klaus Ohlmann made a round-trip flight of 1,395 miles (2,245.6 km) from Chapelco in Argentina on December 2, 2003.

Female: Reiko Morinaka (Japan) achieved 737 miles (1,187 km), also from Chapelco in Argentina, on December 30, 2004.

PARAGLIDING

Farthest flight
Male: The farthest straight distance achieved by a paraglider is 312 miles (502.9 km) by Nevil Hulett (South Africa) at Copperton, South Africa, on December 14, 2008.
Female: Seiko Fukuoka-Naville (Japan) piloted her Niviuk Icepeak 6 paraglider 208 miles (336 km) in a 10-hour flight from Quixadá in Brazil on November 20, 2012.

Farthest out-and-return
Male: Arduino Persello (Italy) covered 175 miles (282.4 km) from Sorica in Slovenia to Longarone in Italy and back on June 27, 2012.
Female: Nicole Fedele (Italy) flew 102 miles (164.6 km)—from Sorica in Slovenia to Piombada in Italy and back—on August 19, 2009.

FLY FAST
On December 22, 2006, Ohlmann reached the **fastest speed in a glider**—190.6 mph (306.8 km/h)—above Zapala, Argentina.

Greatest free distance in a glider

On January 12, 2010, Klaus Ohlmann (Germany) flew a Schempp-Hirth Nimbus-4DM glider for 1,402 miles (2,256.9 km) at El Calafate, Argentina. The term "free distance" denotes a course comprising just one straight-line leg, with declared start and finish points and no turn points.

Most consecutive infinity tumbles paragliding

Infinity tumbling is a looplike maneuver in which the pilot and paraglider describe a circle vertically. It is a very difficult exercise to perform, one that involves balancing momentum and aerodynamic forces. Horacio Llorens (Spain), a four-time paragliding world champion, managed 568 consecutive loops on December 21, 2012 after jumping from a helicopter at 19,700 ft. (6,000 m) and deploying his rig, lines first, from a bag secured to the floor of the helicopter. He made his attempt in the skies over the Tak'alik Ab'aj archaeological site in Guatemala.

FOR THE RECORD

For every lap-and-a-half Horacio Llorens made (*see above*), he lost 33 ft. (10 m) in height. He experienced forces of 6G with each rotation and had to keep his head buried on his chest to protect his neck, meaning that he had to "feel," instead of see, his position and progress.

Fastest speed in a 1,750–3,000-kg piston engine aircraft over 15 km

On April 23, 2012, Will Whiteside (USA) flew over a 9.3-mile (15-km) stretch of the Interstate 505 highway, west of Sacramento, California, USA, in his World War II-era Russian Yakovlev YAK-3 aircraft at an average speed of 381.53 mph (614.02 km/h). No aircraft with piston engines in the 3,858–6,614-lb. (1,750–3,000-kg) weight bracket has ever flown faster.

Farthest straight distance to a declared goal

Male: Brazil's Sol team—Frank Brown, Donizete Lemos, Samuel Nascimento, and Marcelo Prieto—all individually achieved a straight-line record of 261 miles (420.3 km) from Quixadá to Ceará in Brazil on October 26, 2012.
Female: Kamira Pereira Rodrigues (Brazil) flew 177 miles (285.3 km) from Quixadá to Castelo do Piauí in Brazil on November 14, 2009.

HANG GLIDING

Farthest distance flown

Male: Dustin Martin (USA) and Jon Durand (Australia) set off from Zapata in Texas, USA, on July 4, 2012, with Martin flying his Wills Wing T2C and Durand his Moyes Delta Litespeed RX 3.5. Both beat the previous record of 435 miles (700.6 km), but it was Martin who landed 1.8 miles (3 km) farther on than Durand in Lubbock, Texas, 474 miles (764 km) from the starting point.

Female: The women's FAI straight-line distance record is 250 miles (403.5 km), by Kari Castle (USA) out of Zapata in Texas, USA, on July 28, 2001.

Fastest speed over a 62-mile triangular course

Male: Dustin Martin flew around a 62-mile (100-km) triangular circuit from Zapata in Texas, USA, on July 26, 2009, achieving an average speed of 30.4 mph (49 km/h).
Female: On December 31, 1998, New Zealand's Tascha McLellan clocked an average speed over a triangular course from Forbes in New South Wales, Australia, of 19.1 mph (30.81 km/h).

PARACHUTING

Farthest distance canopy piloting

Also known as swooping, canopy piloting involves a skydiver deploying the parachute (canopy) at 5,000 ft. (1,524 m), then entering a steep rotating dive before leveling out and completing a course.
Male: Nick Batsch (USA) piloted his canopy a distance of 498 ft. (151.95 m) on June 15, 2012, above Rockmart in Georgia, USA, the farthest achieved in competition (G1 subclass). He also holds the **absolute farthest canopy piloting** (G2) record, having covered 729 ft. (222.45 m) over Longmont in Colorado, USA, on July 29, 2011.
Female: The day prior to Batsch's competition record, on June 14, 2012, fellow American Jessica Edgeington achieved the women's distance record of 394 ft. (120.18 m), also over Rockmart, Georgia. Like Batsch, she also holds the **absolute farthest canopy**

Farthest declared-goal distance in a hang glider

This discipline requires the hang glider pilot to declare the distance flown before takeoff and then achieve that distance (as opposed to taking a semi-random route defined by air currents). Jon Durand (Australia) achieved a flight of 346 miles (557 km) from Zapata to Sterling City in Texas, USA, on July 17, 2012.

Farthest journey by powered paraglider

Miroslav Oros (Czech Republic) made a 5,674-mile (9,132-km) trip in a powered paraglider across his homeland, starting in Sazená and ending in Lipová-lázně, from April 1 to June 30, 2011.

piloting G2 record (female), set the day after her male counterpart (July 30, 2011) at Longmont, Colorado, with a distance of 552 ft. (168.32 m).

Largest heads-down vertical formation

General: The largest heads-down vertical skydiving formation record in the FAI's performance subclass (G2) was set by a mixed team of 138 skydivers falling heads down in a snowflake pattern on August 3, 2012 at a skydiving festival near Chicago, Illinois, USA.
Female: The women-only record stands at 41 vertical parachutists over Eloy in Arizona, USA, on November 26, 2010.

MOST WORLD CHAMPIONSHIPS WON

Aerobatics (male)	2	Petr Jirmus (Czechoslovakia): 1984, 1986
		Sergei Rakhmanin (Russia): 2003, 2005
Aerobatics (female)	6	Svetlana Kapanina (Russia): 1996, 1998, 2001, 2003, 2005, 2007
Glider aerobatics (team)	9	Poland: 1985, 1987, 1989, 1991, 1993, 1999, 2001, 2003, 2011
Glider aerobatics (individual)	7	Jerzy Makula (Poland): 1985, 1987, 1989, 1991, 1993, 1999, 2011
Gliding	3	George Lee (UK): 1976, 1978, 1981
		Ingo Renner (Australia): 1983, 1985, 1987
Hang gliding (male)	4	Manfred Ruhmer (Austria): 1999, 2001, 2003, 2013
Hang gliding (female)	5	Corinna Schwiegershausen (Germany): 1998, 2004, 2006, 2008, 2013
Paragliding (male)	1	Seven men have each won one title
Paragliding (female)	3	Petra Krausova-Slívová (Slovenia): 2003, 2007, 2011
Paragliding (team)	7	Switzerland: 1991, 1993, 1995, 1997, 2001, 2003, 2005
Paragliding accuracy (male)	2	Matjaž Ferarič (Slovenia): 2003, 2007
Paragliding accuracy (female)	2	Markéta Tomášková (Czech Republic): 2005, 2011
Paragliding accuracy (team)	4	Slovenia: 2003, 2005, 2007, 2011

Statistics correct as of March 27, 2013

AIR FLAIR
Jon started on tandem hang gliders at the age of 9, with his dad, and first flew solo at the age of 14. He has spent more than 10,000 hours airborne.

FOOTBALL

IN REVIEW The 93rd season of the NFL featured the successful comebacks of injured superstars Peyton Manning and Adrian Peterson, as well as the launch of the 2012 rookie quarterback class of Andrew Luck, Russell Wilson, and Robert Griffin III. Meanwhile, a well-established quarterback, Drew Brees of the New Orleans Saints, extended his mark of throwing at least one touchdown pass in 54 consecutive games, the longest streak in league history.

In the Super Bowl, the Baltimore Ravens, coached by John Harbaugh, outlasted the Jim Harbaugh-coached San Francisco 49ers, 34–31, in February 2013 as two brothers squared off on opposite sidelines for the first time in a Super Bowl matchup. The game was suspended for 34 minutes by a stadium power outage inside the Superdome in New Orleans. The lights went off immediately after Baltimore's Jacoby Jones returned the second-half kickoff 108 yards, a Super Bowl record for a touchdown. Ray Lewis, the Ravens' emotional leader, won his second Super Bowl ring 12 years after the first. No other player has waited longer between titles.

NFL SEASONS

Fewest team turnovers
The fewest turnovers in an NFL 16-game season was by the New England Patriots (USA) in 2010 at 10. This was matched by the San Francisco 49ers (USA) in 2011—the team's first season under Jim Harbaugh and Trent Baalke.

Fewest fumbles by a team
The New Orleans Saints (USA) lost six fumbles in 2011. That year they gained 7,474 offensive yards, the **most offensive yards by a team**.

Most 100-yard receiving games by an individual
When Calvin Johnson (*see above right*) recorded his 11th 100-yard receiving game on December 22, 2012, he equaled the mark set by Michael Irvin of the Dallas Cowboys (both USA) in 1995.

Most field goals converted of 50 yards or more
Blair Walsh (USA) converted 10 goals while place-kicking for the Minnesota Vikings in 2012. While at the University of Georgia, Athens, USA, Walsh's conversions of long field goal attempts lent him the nickname "Athens Assassin."

Most pass attempts
Matthew Stafford (USA) made 727 pass attempts as quarterback for the Detroit Lions in 2012.

Most passing yards in a first season
Andrew Luck (USA) recorded 4,374 passing yards in his first season with the Indianapolis Colts in 2012. He also set the record for **most yards passing in a game by a rookie quarterback**, with 433, in a win over the Miami Dolphins on November 4, 2012.

Most tight end receptions
Jason Witten (USA) was playing for the Dallas Cowboys in 2012 when he made 110 catches. On October 28, 2012, he made the **most catches by a tight end in a game**, with 18.

$132 MILLION
Maximum value of Johnson's seven-year contract with the Detroit Lions.

Most yards gained receiving in an NFL season

Calvin Johnson (USA) gained 1,964 yards receiving while playing for the Detroit Lions in 2012. He is also the **first NFL player with at least 1,600 receiving yards in consecutive seasons**, playing for the Lions in 2011 and 2012. In 2012, he played the **most consecutive games with 10 or more catches**: a total of four games.

Most consecutive seasons with at least 40 touchdown passes by a quarterback

In 2011–12, Drew Brees (USA) of the New Orleans Saints became the first player in NFL history with at least 40 touchdown passes in consecutive seasons. Only one other player has made more than 40 touchdown passes in any two seasons— Dan Marino. And only five other players have ever topped 40 in one season: Tom Brady, Peyton Manning, Aaron Rodgers, Kurt Warner, and Matthew Stafford.

Most yards gained by both teams in a playoff

The most yards gained in a game by two teams is 1,038. It was most recently achieved by the New Orleans Saints (626—the **most yards gained by a team in an NFL playoff**) and the Detroit Lions (412) on January 7, 2012 (*pictured here*), equaling the record set on December 30, 1995 by the Buffalo Bills (536) and the Miami Dolphins (502).

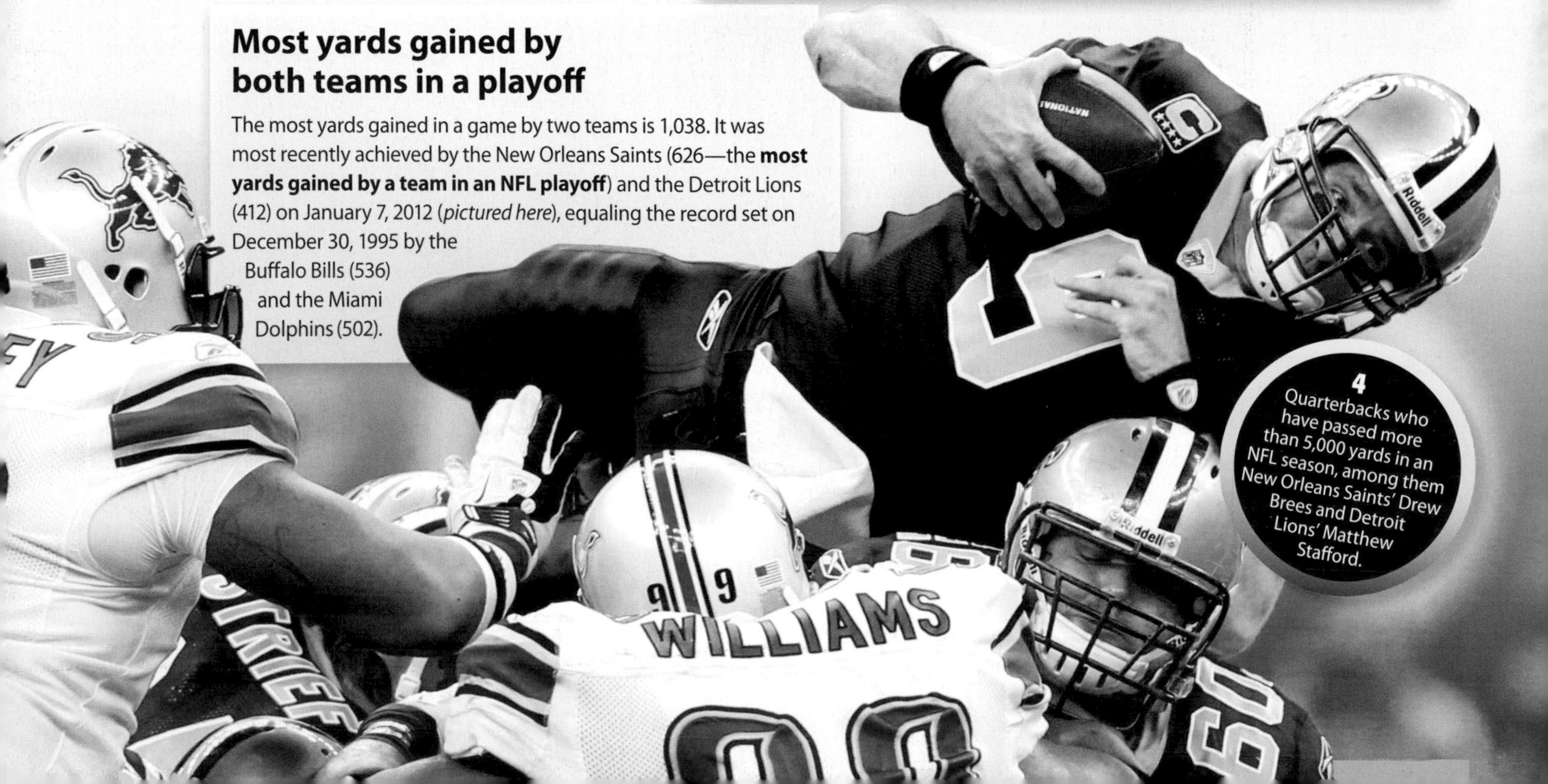

4
Quarterbacks who have passed more than 5,000 yards in an NFL season, among them New Orleans Saints' Drew Brees and Detroit Lions' Matthew Stafford.

SUPER BOWL SUPERLATIVES

Most Super Bowls won	6	Pittsburgh Steelers	Oldest head coach to win	65 years 159 days	Tom Coughlin (USA, b. August 31, 1946), New York Giants	
Longest touchdown yardage	108	Jacoby Jones (USA), Baltimore Ravens, February 3, 2013	Oldest player to score	42 years 11 days	Matt Stover (USA, b. January 27, 1968), Indianapolis Colts	
Highest attendance	103,985	XIV, January 20, 1980, Pittsburgh Steelers vs. LA Rams	Youngest player	21 years 155 days	Jamal Lewis (USA, b. August 26, 1979), Baltimore Ravens	
Most consecutive initial pass completions	9	Eli Manning (USA), New York Giants, February 5, 2012	Most career yards gained receiving	589	Jerry Rice (USA), San Francisco 49ers and Oakland Raiders	
Most career field goals	7	Adam Vinatieri (USA), New England Patriots and Indianapolis Colts	Most game yards gained passing	414	Kurt Warner (USA), St. Louis Rams	
Most career passes completed	127	Tom Brady (USA), New England Patriots	Most career touchdown passes	11	Joe Montana (USA), San Francisco 49ers	

Most consecutive pass completions in a Super Bowl game

Tom Brady (USA) made 16 pass completions for the New England Patriots against the New York Giants on February 5, 2012 in Super Bowl XLVI. He also shares the **most passes completed in a Super Bowl game** (32) with Drew Brees.

Most fumbles forced by an individual in a season

Osi Umenyiora (UK) of the New York Giants made 10 forced fumbles in the 2010 season. It was equaled in the 2012 season by Charles Tillman (USA) of the Chicago Bears, who recorded the **most fumbles forced by an individual in a game**, with four against the Tennessee Titans on November 4, 2012.

Longest NFL field goal

A field goal of 63 yards has been booted through the uprights four times, most recently by David Akers (USA, *above*) of the San Francisco 49ers on September 9, 2012. He joined Sebastian Janikowski (Poland) of the Oakland Raiders, Jason Elam (USA) of the Denver Broncos, and Tom Dempsey (USA) of the New Orleans Saints.

NFL CAREERS

Most field goals of 50 yards or more

Jason Hanson (USA) has made 52 successful field goals of 50 yards or more while place-kicking for the Detroit Lions since 1992. As of March 2013, he is the **oldest active NFL player**.

Most points

Place-kicker Morten Andersen (Denmark), nicknamed "The Great Dane," racked up 2,544 points over a 25-year career that began in 1982 with the New Orleans Saints.

Most touchdowns

Multiple record holder Jerry Rice (USA) scored 208 touchdowns between 1985 and 2004 playing for the San Francisco 49ers, the Oakland Raiders, and the Seattle Seahawks.

Longest kickoff return for a touchdown

Jacoby Jones (USA) made a return of 108 yards for a touchdown for the Baltimore Ravens on October 14, 2012, and again at Super Bowl XLVII on February 3, 2013 (*see also Super Bowl Superlatives, above*). He equaled the distance of Ellis Hobbs (USA) on September 9, 2007, and Randall Cobb (USA) on September 8, 2011.

Most career touchdowns by a tight end

Tony Gonzalez (USA) made 103 touchdown catches while playing for the Kansas City Chiefs and Atlanta Falcons from 1997 through the 2012 season.

FOR SOCCER, TURN TO P. 254

TRACK & FIELD

IN REVIEW Retaining an Olympic title in track and field marks an athlete out as truly great, and two people joined the exclusive club in 2012. Jamaica's Usain Bolt defended his 100 m and 200 m titles, and with his 200 m victory he became the first man in Olympic history to win two golds in the event. Ethiopia's Tirunesh Dibaba defended her 10,000 m title and, together with her 5,000 m gold from Beijing, her achievements rank among the best ever.

Jessica Ennis shouldered the expectation of the home nation in the heptathlon and delivered one of the standout performances of the Games. And no review would be complete without David Rudisha's astonishing 800 m performance. The Kenyan flyer burned up the London track, winning one of the most electrifying middle-distance races of all time.

title in the 10,000 m at London 2012 with a time of 30 min. 20.75 sec. Four years earlier, her time at the Beijing Games was 29 min. 54.66 sec.

Back in November 2009, Dibaba also set a time of 46 min. 28 sec.— the **fastest 15 km road run**.

Youngest 800 m medalist

Timothy Kitum (Kenya, b. November 20, 1994) won bronze in the men's 800 m final in London, UK, on August 9, 2012, at the age of 17 years 263 days.

OLYMPICS AND PARALYMPICS

First win of 100 m and 200 m sprints at successive games

Usain Bolt (Jamaica) achieved the historic "double double" at the 2012 Olympics in London, UK, with 9.63 seconds in the 100 m on August 5 and 19.32 seconds in the 200 m on August 9. Four years earlier in Beijing, China, he ran the 100 m in 9.69 seconds on August 16 and the 200 m in 19.30 seconds on August 20. Bolt equaled the record set by Carl Lewis (USA) for the **most wins of the 100 m at the Olympics**. Lewis won in 1984 and 1988 with a record time of 9.92 seconds.

Most female 10,000 m golds

Multiple record holder Tirunesh Dibaba (Ethiopia) defended her

Most European Championship 5,000 m golds

Mo Farah (UK) is the only athlete to win more than one 5,000 m title at the European Athletics Championships, in Barcelona in 2010 and Helsinki (*above*) in 2012.

MEN'S OUTDOOR TRACK EVENTS

Event	Time	Name (Nationality)	Date
100 m	9.58	Usain Bolt (Jamaica)	Aug 16, 2009
200 m	19.19	Usain Bolt (Jamaica)	Aug 20, 2009
400 m	43.18	Michael Johnson (USA)	Aug 26, 1999
800 m	1:40.91	David Rudisha (Kenya)	Aug 9, 2012
1,000 m	2:11.96	Noah Ngeny (Kenya)	Sep 5, 1999
1,500 m	3:26.00	Hicham El Guerrouj (Morocco)	Jul 14, 1998
1 mile	3:43.13	Hicham El Guerrouj (Morocco)	Jul 7, 1999
2,000 m	4:44.79	Hicham El Guerrouj (Morocco)	Sep 7, 1999
3,000 m	7:20.67	Daniel Komen (Kenya)	Sep 1, 1996
5,000 m	12:37.35	Kenenisa Bekele (Ethiopia)	May 31, 2004
10,000 m	26:17.53	Kenenisa Bekele (Ethiopia)	Aug 26, 2005
20,000 m	56:26.00	Haile Gebrselassie (Ethiopia)	Jun 26, 2007
25,000 m	1:12:25.4	Moses Cheruiyot Mosop (Kenya)	Jun 3, 2011
30,000 m	1:26:47.4	Moses Cheruiyot Mosop (Kenya)	Jun 3, 2011
3,000 m steeplechase	7:53.63	Saif Saaeed Shaheen (Qatar)	Sep 3, 2004
110 m hurdles	12.80	Aries Merritt (USA)	Sep 7, 2012
400 m hurdles	46.78	Kevin Young (USA)	Aug 6, 1992
4 x 100 m relay	36.84	Jamaica (Yohan Blake, Nesta Carter, Michael Frater, Usain Bolt)	Aug 11, 2012
4 x 200 m relay	1:18.68	Santa Monica Track Club, USA (Michael Marsh, Leroy Burrell, Floyd Heard, Carl Lewis)	Apr 17, 1994
4 x 400 m relay	2:54.29	USA (Andrew Valmon, Quincy Watts, Harry Reynolds, Michael Johnson)	Aug 22, 1993
4 x 800 m relay	7:02.43	Kenya (Joseph Mutua, William Yiampoy, Ismael Kombich, Wilfred Bungei)	Aug 25, 2006
4 x 1,500 m relay	14:36.23	Kenya (Geoffrey Rono, Augustine Choge, William Tanui, Gideon Gathimba)	Sep 4, 2009

MEN'S OUTDOOR FIELD EVENTS

Event	Distance/Points	Name (Nationality)	Date
High jump	8 ft. 0.45 in. (2.45 m)	Javier Sotomayor (Cuba)	Jul 27, 1993
Pole vault	20 ft. 1.73 in. (6.14 m)	Sergei Bubka (Ukraine)	Jul 31, 1994
Long jump	29 ft. 4.36 in. (8.95 m)	Mike Powell (USA)	Aug 30, 1991
Triple jump	60 ft. 0.78 in. (18.29 m)	Jonathan Edwards (UK)	Aug 7, 1995
Shot	75 ft. 10.23 in. (23.12 m)	Randy Barnes (USA)	May 20, 1990
Discus	243 ft. 0.53 in. (74.08 m)	Jürgen Schult (Germany)	Jun 6, 1986
Hammer	284 ft. 7 in. (86.74 m)	Yuriy Sedykh (Russia)	Aug 30, 1986
Javelin	323 ft. 1.16 in. (98.48 m)	Jan Železný (Czech Republic)	May 25, 1996
Decathlon	9,039 points	Ashton Eaton (USA)	Jun 23, 2012

Statistics correct as of April 9, 2013

FOR MARATHON RUNNING, TURN TO P. 246

Fastest 100 m (T44)

Male: Paralympian Jonnie Peacock (UK) ran 10.85 seconds for the men's 100 m T44 (single below-knee amputation) at Indianapolis, USA, on July 1, 2012. Peacock also holds the Paralympic record, clocking 10.90 seconds in the final in London, UK, on September 6, 2012. **Female:** April Holmes (USA) ran the women's 100 m in 12.98 seconds in Atlanta, USA, on July 1, 2006. She, too, is the Paralympic record holder, clocking 13.13 seconds in Athens, Greece, on September 22, 2004.

Fastest 200 m (T42)

Male: Richard Whitehead (UK) set a time of 24.38 seconds in the T42 (single above-knee amputation or combined arm/leg amputations) 200 m in London, UK, on September 1, 2012.

Fastest 4 x 100 m relay (female)

The American 4 x 100 m relay team (*from left*, Carmelita Jeter, Bianca Knight, Allyson Felix, and Tianna Madison, all USA) took a record that had stood for almost 27 years when they clocked 40.82 seconds in London, UK, on August 10, 2012. The previous 4 x 100 m relay record (41.37 seconds) was set by East Germany in Canberra, Australia, on October 6, 1985.

WOMEN'S OUTDOOR TRACK EVENTS

Event	Time	Name (Nationality)	Date
100 m	10.49	Florence Griffith-Joyner (USA)	Jul 16, 1988
200 m	21.34	Florence Griffith-Joyner (USA)	Sep 29, 1988
400 m	47.60	Marita Koch (GDR)	Oct 6, 1985
800 m	1:53.28	Jarmila Kratochvílová (Czech Republic)	Jul 26, 1983
1,000 m	2:28.98	Svetlana Masterkova (Russia)	Aug 23, 1996
1,500 m	3:50.46	Qu Yunxia (China)	Sep 11, 1993
1 mile	4:12.56	Svetlana Masterkova (Russia)	Aug 14, 1996
2,000 m	5:25.36	Sonia O'Sullivan (Ireland)	Jul 8, 1994
3,000 m	8:06.11	Wang Junxia (China)	Sep 13, 1993
5,000 m	14:11.15	Tirunesh Dibaba (Ethiopia)	Jun 6, 2008
10,000 m	29:31.78	Wang Junxia (China)	Sep 8, 1993
20,000 m	1:05:26.60	Tegla Loroupe (Kenya)	Sep 3, 2000
25,000 m	1:27:05.90	Tegla Loroupe (Kenya)	Sep 21, 2002
30,000 m	1:45:50.00	Tegla Loroupe (Kenya)	Jun 6, 2003
3,000 m steeplechase	8:58.81	Gulnara Samitova-Galkina (Russia)	Aug 17, 2008
100 m hurdles	12.21	Yordanka Donkova (Bulgaria)	Aug 20, 1988
400 m hurdles	52.34	Yuliya Pechonkina (Russia)	Aug 8, 2003
4 x 100 m relay	40.82	USA (Allyson Felix, Carmelita Jeter, Bianca Knight, Tianna Madison)	Aug 10, 2012
4 x 200 m relay	1:27.46	United States "Blue" (LaTasha Jenkins, LaTasha Colander-Richardson, Nanceen Perry, Marion Jones)	Apr 29, 2000
4 x 400 m relay	3:15.17	USSR (Tatyana Ledovskaya, Olga Nazarova, Maria Pinigina, Olga Bryzgina)	Oct 1, 1988
4 x 800 m relay	7:50.17	USSR (Nadezhda Olizarenko, Lyubov Gurina, Lyudmila Borisova, Irina Podyalovskaya)	Aug 5, 1984

WOMEN'S OUTDOOR FIELD EVENTS

Event	Distance/Points	Name (Nationality)	Date
High jump	6 ft. 10.28 in. (2.09 m)	Stefka Kostadinova (Bulgaria)	Aug 30, 1987
Pole vault	16 ft. 7.21 in. (5.06 m)	Yelena Isinbayeva (Russia)	Aug 28, 2009
Long jump	24 ft. 8.06 in. (7.52 m)	Galina Chistyakova (USSR)	Jun 11, 1988
Triple jump	50 ft. 10.23 in. (15.50 m)	Inessa Kravets (Ukraine)	Aug 10, 1995
Shot	74 ft. 2.94 in. (22.63 m)	Natalya Lisovskaya (USSR)	Jun 7, 1987
Discus	252 ft. (76.80 m)	Gabriele Reinsch (GDR)	Jul 9, 1988
Hammer	260 ft. 6.76 in. (79.42 m)	Betty Heidler (Germany)	May 25, 2011
Javelin	253 ft. 6 in. (72.28 m)	Barbora Špotáková (Czech Republic)	Sep 13, 2008
Heptathlon	7,291 points	Jackie Joyner-Kersee (USA)	Sep 24, 1988
Decathlon	8,358 points	Austra Skujytė (Lithuania)	Apr 15, 2005

Statistics correct as of April 9, 2013

Female: Kelly Cartwright (Australia) recorded 35.98 seconds at the Adelaide Track Classic in Australia on January 28, 2012.

Fastest 100 m (T34)
Male: Olympic record holder Walid Ktila (Tunisia) secured the world record in the 100 m T34 (cerebral palsy, wheelchair) with a time of 15.69 seconds in Kuwait City, Kuwait, on January 17, 2012.
Female: Hannah Cockroft (UK) set the world record at 17.60 seconds in Nottwil, Switzerland, on May 20, 2012, and the Paralympic record at 18.06 seconds in London, UK, on August 31, 2012.

Farthest club throw (F51)
Male: Željko Dimitrijević (Serbia) achieved a throw of 88 ft. 2.28 in. (26.88 m) in the F51 class at London, UK, on August 31, 2012. The club throw involves throwing a wooden club and is the Paralympic equivalent of the hammer throw.

It is contested by athletes with cerebral palsy (F31, F32), and wheelchair-bound competitors (F51) throw from a seated position.
Female: Catherine O'Neill (Ireland) achieved a throw of 51 ft. 11.28 in. (15.83 m) in Nové Město nad Metují, Czech Republic, on August 18, 2001.

IAAF WORLD CHAMPIONSHIPS

Most medals won (team)
The USA have won a total of 275 medals at the IAAF World Championships (inaugurated 1983): 132 gold, 74 silver, and 69 bronze (all record totals).

Most medals won
Male: Carl Lewis (USA) won 10 medals between 1983 and 1991: eight gold (a record he shares with Michael Johnson, 1991–99), one silver, and one bronze.

Female: Merlene Ottey (Jamaica) won 14 medals at the World Championships—three gold, four silver, and seven bronze.

Most javelin wins
Male: Jan Železný (Czech Republic) won the IAAF men's javelin in 1993, 1995, and 2001. He also won the **most gold medals at the Olympics for javelin (male)** with victories in 1992, 1996, and 2000.
Female: Trine Hattestad (Norway) and Mirela Manjani (Greece) both won the IAAF women's javelin twice, in 1993 and 1997, and in 1999 and 2003, respectively.

Most cross country wins
Male: Kenya claimed 24 victories in World Championship cross country running (first held in 1973) between 1986 and 2011.
Female: Kenya also holds the women's record, with 10 wins between 1991 and 2011.

Highest indoor pole vault (female)
Jenn Suhr (USA) vaulted to 16 ft. 5.64 in. (5.02 m) in Albuquerque, New Mexico, USA, on March 2, 2013. The London 2012 gold medalist beat the 16 ft. 5.28 in. (5.01 m) set by Yelena Isinbayeva (Russia) in February 2012. The **highest indoor pole vault (male)** is 20 ft. 2.12 in. (6.15 m) by Sergei Bubka (Ukraine) on February 21, 1993.

1968
Year in which David's father, Daniel, won silver in the 4 x 100 m Olympic relay.

Most points in male indoor heptathlon
Ashton Eaton (USA) racked up 6,645 points in Istanbul, Turkey, on March 10, 2012. One of the world's best all-rounders, he recorded: **60 m**, 6.79 seconds; **long jump**, 26 ft. 9.24 in. (8.16 m); **shot put**, 47 ft. 9.24 in. (14.56 m); **high jump**, 6 ft. 7.92 in. (2.03 m); **60 m hurdles**, 7.68 seconds; **pole vault**, 17 ft. 0.72 in. (5.20 m); **1,000 m**, 2 min. 32.77 sec.

Fastest men's 800 m
David Rudisha (Kenya) clocked 1 min. 40.91 sec. to win the Olympic 800 m final in London on August 9, 2012. He beat his own world record of 1 min. 41.01 sec., set in Rieti, Italy, on August 29, 2010.

BALL SPORTS

IN REVIEW At London 2012, there were wins in field hockey for the German men's and Dutch women's teams, while the Netherlands' victory at the Riverbank Arena at the Olympic Park saw them equal Australia's record of three golds. Germany took gold in the men's beach volleyball event, and the USA—whose team featured the record-breaking Misty May-Treanor and Kerri Walsh Jennings—won the women's tournament.

Elsewhere, Irene van Dyk made her 212th international appearance for New Zealand's national netball team, and the Netherlands continued to dominate korfball in both world and European competitions. Iran were thwarted in their pursuit of a record-breaking sixth Paralympic men's sitting volleyball gold by Bosnia and Herzegovina, while China extended their winning sequence with a third consecutive victory.

FACT:
Lacrosse derives from centuries-old Native American games. These were often staged between different tribes, sometimes involving hundreds of players, and could last for days.

AUSTRALIAN FOOTBALL LEAGUE (AFL)

Most consecutive Grand Final wins
The Brisbane Lions won the AFL Grand Final three times in 2001–03.
The **largest attendance at an AFL Grand Final** is 121,696 at the Melbourne Cricket Ground in Victoria, Australia, on September 26, 1970.

Longest winning streak
The most consecutive games won in the AFL Premiership is 23, by Geelong between 1952 and 1953.

Most goals in an AFL career
Tony Lockett (Australia) scored a grand total of 1,360 goals in 281 games from 1983 to 2002.

CANADIAN FOOTBALL LEAGUE (CFL)

Longest regular-season field goal
Paul McCallum (Canada) kicked a 62-yard field goal for Saskatchewan Roughriders vs. Edmonton Eskimos on October 27, 2001.

Most career pass attempts by a quarterback
Anthony Calvillo (USA) made 9,241 pass attempts playing for the Las Vegas Posse, Hamilton Tiger-Cats, and Montreal Alouettes from 1994 to 2012. Calvillo has broken many records in his 18-year CFL career to date. For the same three teams, he has made the **most career pass completions** (5,777), the **most career touchdown passes** (449), and the **most career yards passing** (78,494), all from 1994 to 2012.
The prolific Calvillo has also recorded the **most pass completions in a game** (44), for the Alouettes against Hamilton on October 4, 2008, and the **most pass completions in the Grey Cup** (179), again for the Alouettes.
The **most receiving yards in a career** is 15,787, by Geroy Simon (USA) for the Winnipeg Blue Bombers and BC Lions since 1999.

Most wins of the Hockey Champions Trophy

Male: Australia have won the men's Hockey Champions Trophy (inaugurated in 1978) an unprecedented 13 times, in 1983–85, 1989–90, 1993, 1999, 2005, and 2008–12.
Female: The most wins of the women's Hockey Champions Trophy—first held in 1987—is six, a record shared by two teams. Australia won in 1991, 1993, 1995, 1997, 1999, and 2003, while the Netherlands won in 1987, 2000, 2004–05, 2007, and 2011.

FIELD HOCKEY

Most EuroHockey Nations Championships won
Male: The EuroHockey Nations Championship is the premier international field hockey competition in Europe. The most championship wins is seven, by Germany (formerly West Germany) between 1970 and 2011.
Female: The Netherlands have claimed eight wins in the women's game between 1984 and 2011.

Most career international hockey appearances
Male: Two-times Olympic champion Teun de Nooijer (Netherlands) appeared for his country 431 times between 1994 and January 25, 2011.
Female: The most international appearances by a women is 425, by Natascha Keller (Germany) from 1994 to 2012.

Largest victory in an Olympic match
Male: The third match in the 1932 Olympic tournament ended with India beating the USA 24–1.
Female: South Africa vs. Team USA at the Riverbank Arena in London, UK, on August 6, 2012 ended 7–0 to South Africa.

LACROSSE

Most international appearances (female)
Vivien Jones (UK) played in 97 internationals (85 for Wales, 9 for the Celts, and 3 for Great Britain) from 1977 to 2001.

Most Major League Lacrosse titles

The Chesapeake Bayhawks (USA) have won four Major League Lacrosse (MLL) titles, in 2001, 2003, 2010, and 2012. They won their first two titles as the Baltimore Bayhawks before relocating the franchise to Washington, D.C. and playing as the Washington Bayhawks in 2007–09 and the Chesapeake Bayhawks from 2010.

NET GAIN
Drew Westervelt (left) of the Chesapeake Bayhawks and Chris O'Dougherty of the Denver Outlaws on August 26, 2012 in Boston, Massachusetts, USA.

CHAMPIONSHIPS, CUPS, AND TITLES		
Australian Football League (AFL) premierships (Victorian Football League first held 1897; superseded by AFL 1990)	16	Carlton
		Essendon
Beach Volleyball World Championships (male)	5	Brazil
Beach Volleyball World Championships (female)	4	USA
		Brazil
Gaelic Football Sam Maguire Cups	36	Kerry
Handball World Championships (male)	4	Sweden
		Romania
		France
Handball World Championships (female)	4	Russia
Indoor Lacrosse World Championships	3	Canada
Korfball World Championships	8	The Netherlands
Statistics correct as of March 25, 2013		

GUINNESS WORLD RECORDS 2014

Most Olympic field hockey golds

Female: The Dutch women's hockey team (*above*) secured their third gold at London 2012, having previously won in 1984 and 2008. The record is shared with Australia, who won in 1988, 1996, and 2000.
Male: India won the men's gold eight times between 1928 and 1980.

Largest victory margin in an MLL Championship game

The Baltimore Bayhawks beat the Long Island Lizards 21–12 in Columbus, Ohio, USA, in 2001.

Most goals in an MLL career

Mark Millon (USA) racked up 206 MLL career goals for the Baltimore Bayhawks and the Boston Cannons in 2001–05.

NETBALL

Most Commonwealth Games titles

Two countries have won two Commonwealth Games titles: Australia in 1998 and 2002, and New Zealand in 2006 and 2010. Netball has been contested four times at the Commonwealth Games: in Kuala Lumpur, Malaysia, in 1998; in Manchester, UK, in 2002; in Melbourne, Australia, in 2006; and, in Delhi, India, in 2010.

Most World Series wins

New Zealand has won the Netball World Series twice, in 2009 and 2010. This international competition features modified rules and is played every year by the top six teams in the world.

The **highest team score in a Netball World Series final** is 33 points by England against New Zealand in Liverpool, UK, on November 27, 2011. England beat reigning champions New Zealand 33–26.

Most World Netball Championship wins

Australia has won the World Netball Championships an unprecedented 10 times, in 1963, 1971, 1975, 1979, 1983, 1991, 1995, 1999, 2007, and 2011. The championships were instituted in 1963.

Most African Handball Championship wins

Male: Tunisia won the African Handball Nations Championship nine times between 1974 and 2012. Pictured is Denmark's Lasse Svan (*left*) and Tunisia's Kamel Alouini on January 20, 2013.

Female: In the women's sport, Angola won 11 times between 1989 and 2012.

VOLLEYBALL

Largest volleyball tournament

The 39th Amateur Athletic Union (AAU) Girls' Junior National Volleyball Championships were staged at the Orange County Convention Center and ESPN Wide World of Sports in Orlando, Florida, USA, from June 19 to 27, 2012. The 16-club division featured a record 2,631 competitors in 192 teams.

Most Volleyball World Grand Champions Cup wins

Brazil has won the Fédération Internationale de Volleyball (FIVB) World Grand Champions Cup three times, in 1997, 2005, and 2009.

Most Beach Volleyball World Championships

Male: The Brazilian men's pair has won the title five times, in 1997, 1999, 2003, 2005, and 2011.
Female: Two teams have each won the title four times: the USA in 2003, 2005, 2007, and 2009, and Brazil in 1997, 1999, 2001, and 2011. The Beach Volleyball World Championships are held every two years.

Most Paralympic sitting volleyball gold medals

Male: Iran has won the Paralympic sitting volleyball competition five times, in 1988, 1992, 1996, 2000, and 2008.
Female: The most golds won in the women's Paralympic sitting volleyball tournament is three by China, in 2004, 2008, and 2012.

Most international netball appearances

From 1994 to 2012, South African-born Irene van Dyk played in 211 international netball games. She played 72 games for her home country (1994–99), and since 2000 has appeared 139 times for her adopted nation of New Zealand.

TURTLE-Y AMAZING
Misty, nicknamed "The Turtle," holds the record for the **highest earnings in a beach volleyball career** at $2,132,733!

Most beach volleyball tournament titles (female)

Misty May-Treanor (USA) retired in July 2012 after securing gold at the London Olympics (*see above*). She ended her career with more tournament victories than any other player, having notched up 112 wins since April 2000.

BASEBALL

IN REVIEW It's been a terrific year for Major League Baseball (MLB). The San Francisco Giants won the World Series in October 2012, powered by Pablo Sandoval (Venezuela), who hit three home runs in a World Series game, something only four players had ever done before. Josh Hamilton (USA), who hit four home runs in one game for the Texas Rangers in May, gave the most impressive power surge during the regular season.

Jamie Moyer (USA), pitching for the Colorado Rockies in April 2012, became the Major League's oldest winner at 49 years 151 days, displacing a record held by Jack Quinn (USA, 49 years 70 days) for 80 years. Moyer added one more win in May to push the record to 49 years 180 days. In that game, he also recorded a two-run single, becoming the oldest player with a run batted in.

The 2012 season was also notable for one of the strangest no-hit games ever recorded. The Seattle Mariners accomplished the feat in June by using a combination of six different pitchers, the first time so many pitchers had been used to record a no-hit game since June 2003.

Most walk-off home runs in a career

A game-ending or walk-off home run is a home run on the final pitch of the game that results in a victory for the home team. Jim Thome (USA) has hit 13 of them while playing for the Cleveland Indians, Philadelphia Phillies, Chicago White Sox, Los Angeles Dodgers, Minnesota Twins, and Baltimore Orioles since 1991. He recorded the 13th on June 23, 2012, while playing for the Phillies.

Most home runs in a game

The greatest number of home runs struck in an MLB game is four. This outstanding feat has been accomplished by 16 players, most recently by Josh Hamilton (USA) while playing for the Texas Rangers against the Baltimore Orioles on May 8, 2012.

Most Major League franchises played for

Octavio Dotel (Dominican Republic) has played for 13 different teams since making his debut in 1999. Dotel has played for the New York Mets, Houston Astros, Oakland Athletics, New York Yankees, Kansas City Royals, Atlanta Braves, Chicago White Sox, Pittsburgh Pirates, Los Angeles Dodgers, Colorado Rockies, Toronto Blue Jays, St. Louis Cardinals, and Detroit Tigers.

BATTERS

Longest postseason hitless streak

In 2012, Robinson Canó (Dominican Republic) made 26 consecutive hitless plate appearances while playing for the New York Yankees, with whom he made his Major League debut in 2005. His batting average was down to .075.

Most career runs batted in by a designated hitter

David Ortiz (Dominican Republic) has batted in 1,147 runs in his career with the Minnesota Twins and Boston Red Sox since 1997. Nicknamed "Big Papi," he also recorded the **most home runs by a designated hitter in a career**, with 353 while playing for the same two teams.

Most career home runs

The greatest number of home runs in an MLB career—and the **most career home runs by a left-handed batter**—is 762, by Barry Bonds (USA, b. July 24, 1964) playing for the Pittsburgh Pirates and San Francisco Giants in 1986–2007. In 2007, he also became the **oldest person to start an All-Star baseball match**, at 42 years 351 days on July 10, 2007.

Bonds jointly holds the record for the **most home runs hit in a single postseason**, with eight, playing for the San Francisco Giants in 2002. The record was equaled by Carlos Beltrán (Puerto Rico) playing for the Houston Astros in 2004 and Nelson Cruz (Dominican Republic), playing for the Texas Rangers in the 2011 postseason.

Most home runs batting left- and right-handed in the same game

Mark Teixeira (USA) has scored switch-hit home runs (batted both left- and right-handed) 13 times for the Texas Rangers, Atlanta Braves, Los Angeles Angels, and New York Yankees since 2003.

Most consecutive seasons of 30 or more home runs from a career start

Albert Pujols (Dominican Republic) recorded 12 consecutive seasons of scoring 30 or more home runs while playing for the St. Louis Cardinals and Anaheim Angels of Los Angeles from 2001 to 2012.

Most home runs hit in a World Series game

Four players have hit three home runs in a World Series game. Pablo Sandoval (Venezuela, *pictured*) for the San Francisco Giants in 2012; Albert Pujols (Dominican Republic) for the St. Louis Cardinals in 2011; Reggie Jackson (USA) for the New York Yankees in 1977; and "Babe" Ruth (USA) for the New York Yankees in 1926 and 1928.

BIRTH OF THE WORLD SERIES
The Boston Americans overcame the Pittsburgh Pirates 5–3 to clinch the first official "Fall Classic" in 1903.

MAJOR LEAGUE BASEBALL (MLB) WORLD SERIES RECORDS

Team		
Most titles (first awarded in 1903)	27	New York Yankees
Most consecutive victories	5	New York Yankees, 1949–53
Largest cumulative attendance	420,784	Six games between Los Angeles Dodgers and Chicago White Sox, October 1–8, 1959; Dodgers won 4–2
Individual		
Most home runs	5	Chase Utley (USA) of Philadelphia Phillies, 2009 World Series against New York Yankees; Reggie Jackson (USA) of New York Yankees, 1977 World Series against Los Angeles Dodgers
Most games pitched	24	Mariano Rivera (Panama) of New York Yankees in 1996, 1998, 1999, 2000, 2001, 2003, and 2009
Most MVP awards	2	Sanford "Sandy" Koufax, 1963, 1965; Robert "Bob" Gibson, 1964, 1967; Reginald Martinez "Reggie" Jackson (all USA), 1973, 1977

Statistics correct as of the end of the 2012 season

Most games finished by a pitcher

Mariano Rivera (Panama) has finished 892 games for the New York Yankees since 1995.

Rivera's total of 1,051 games with the Yankees represents the **most games pitched with one team**.

The prolific pitcher also holds the record for **most career saves**, with 608 achieved during his spell with the Yankees since 1995.

Pujols shares the record for the **most runs batted in during a World Series game**—six—which he scored for the St. Louis Cardinals in Game 3 of the 2011 World Series on October 22. He equaled the mark held by Bobby Richardson (USA) for the New York Yankees in Game 1 of the 1960 World Series on October 5, and Hideki Matsui (Japan) for the New York Yankees in Game 6 of the 2009 World Series on November 4.

Most career grand slam home runs

Two players have scored 23 grand slam home runs: Lou Gehrig (USA, *inset*) for the New York Yankees in 1923–39 and Alex Rodriguez (USA, *main picture*) for the Seattle Mariners, Texas Rangers, and New York Yankees since 1994.

PITCHERS

First pitcher to save 600 games

Trevor Hoffman (USA) saved a total of 601 games for the Florida Marlins, San Diego Padres, and Milwaukee Brewers from 1993 to 2010.

Longest opening-day game

The Toronto Blue Jays (Canada) defeated the Cleveland Indians (USA) 7–4 in 16 innings (*see right*) in the longest opening-day game in Major League history on April 5, 2012.

BLUE JAYS -VS- **Indians**
WP-L. PEREZ (1-0)
LP-J. ASENCIO (0-1)
HOME RUNS
HANNAHAN 3-RUN HR(1) IN THE 2ND
BAUTISTA SOLO HR(1) IN THE 4TH, 2 RBI
ARENCIBIA 3-RUN HR(1) IN THE 16TH
ATTENDANCE - 43,190   TIME - 5:14

Most pitchers used in a no-hit game

Two teams have used six pitchers in a no-hit game: the Houston Astros against the New York Yankees on June 11, 2003, and the Seattle Mariners against the Los Angeles Dodgers (all USA) on June 8, 2012.

Lowest earned-run average

Pitching for the Tampa Bay Rays in 2012, Fernando Rodney (Dominican Republic) set an earned-run average (ERA) of 0.60, a record for an individual pitching at least 50 innings in a season.

93.2 Average speed in mph of Kimbrel's fastball in the 2012 season.

Most home runs allowed by a pitcher

Jamie Moyer (USA) conceded 522 home runs from 1986 to 2012 while playing for the Chicago Cubs, Texas Rangers, St. Louis Cardinals, Baltimore Orioles, Seattle Mariners, Boston Red Sox, Philadelphia Phillies, and Colorado Rockies.

TEAMS

Most home wins to start a season

The Los Angeles Dodgers (USA) won their first 13 home games to start the 2009 season, surpassing the previous mark of 12 straight by the Detroit Tigers in 1911.

By contrast, from 1993 to 2012, the unfortunate Pittsburgh Pirates (USA) registered the **most consecutive losing seasons**, with 20.

Most runs

The Texas Rangers (USA) set a modern (since 1900) single-game record by scoring 30 runs in a 30–3 victory over the Baltimore Orioles on August 22, 2007.

The **most grand slam home runs hit by a team in one game** is three, by the New York Yankees (USA) in a 22–9 victory over the Oakland Athletics on August 25, 2011. The grand slam home runs were hit by Robinson Canó (Dominican Republic), Russell Martin (Canada), and Curtis Granderson (USA).

Fewest errors at second base

The MLB record for the **most consecutive games played by a second baseman without an error** is 141, by Darwin Barney (USA, *above*) while playing for the Chicago Cubs in 2012 and Plácido Polanco (Dominican Republic) while playing for the Detroit Tigers in 2007.

First pitcher to strike out half the batters in one season

Craig Kimbrel (USA) of the Atlanta Braves is the only pitcher to date in Major League history to fan at least half of the batters he faced in a season. Kimbrel recorded 116 strikeouts while facing 231 batters in 2012. His 16.7 strikeouts per nine innings is also a Major League record.

BASKETBALL

IN REVIEW The USA continued to dominate Olympic basketball, with the men's team securing a record 14th gold and the women's team taking their record seventh gold (and record fifth consecutively) at London 2012.

FIBA celebrated their 80th anniversary and announced that the 17th Basketball World Cup, taking place in Madrid, Spain, will be the last on the current four-year cycle, to avoid overlap with the FIFA World Cup. FIBA will shift to a new cycle starting in 2019.

In the NBA, the 67th season got off to a dramatic start with the LA Lakers ousting head coach Mike Brown after five games and LeBron James becoming the youngest player to reach 20,000 career points. In the women's game, Notre Dame beat Ohio State 57–51 in November 2012—in the first women's game on an aircraft carrier!

25.5
Career season average points per game scored by Kobe.

Youngest player to score 30,000 points

Kobe Bryant (USA, b. August 23, 1978) was 34 years 104 days old when he reached 30,000 points during Los Angeles Lakers' 103–87 win over the New Orleans Hornets on December 5, 2012. He is the youngest of five to reach the total: Wilt Chamberlain was 35, Kareem Abdul-Jabbar and Karl Malone were each 36, and Michael Jordan was 38.

Most blocked shots in an NBA playoff game

Three players have blocked 10 shots in a playoff: Hakeem Olajuwon (Nigeria/USA), Mark Eaton (USA), and most recently Andrew Bynum (USA, *above*), playing for the Los Angeles Lakers against the Denver Nuggets on April 29, 2012.

Most Olympic golds (men)
The USA won 14 of the 18 Olympic men's basketball tournaments staged between 1936 and 2012. They went unbeaten in seven consecutive finals between 1936 and 1968 and returned to winning ways at Montreal 1976. In 2012, they defeated Spain 107–100 in London, UK, on August 12. The USSR (1972 and 1988), Yugoslavia (1980), and Argentina (2004) are the only other teams to have won the men's Olympic final.

Highest margin of victory in an Olympic final (female)
The USA won their fifth consecutive Olympic gold medal at the London 2012 Games when they swept aside France 86–50 on August 11. Their 36-point margin of victory was the largest in the 36-year history of women's Olympic basketball. This was the team's seventh title, the **most women's basketball Olympic golds**, yet it's an Australian player who has racked up **most career points in women's Olympic matches**. Lauren Jackson has scored 550 points since making her Olympic debut at the 2000 Games in Sydney, Australia.

NBA

Fastest time for a coach to win 100 matches
Tom Thibodeau (USA) racked up 100 career victories in 130 games, one game fewer than the previous record set by Avery Johnson, coach of the Dallas Mavericks in 2006. Thibodeau's milestone victory occurred during the Chicago Bulls' 85–59 win over the Orlando Magic on March 19, 2012.

Most consecutive 50-win seasons by a team
The San Antonio Spurs (USA) finished the 2011–12 season with a 50–16 record, topping 50 games for a 13th consecutive season.

Most minutes played without converting a free throw in a season
During the 2011–12 season, Josh Childress (USA) played 34 games totaling 491 minutes for the Phoenix Suns without a free throw. He was 0–2 from the free throw line.

Longest post-season team losing streak
The New York Knicks' (USA) run of 13 losses began in the 2000–01 postseason and only ended during the 2011–12 playoffs with an 89–87 win over the Miami Heat.

Worst winning percentage by a team in a season
The Charlotte Bobcats (USA) compiled a 7–59 record in the 2011–12 season with a percentage of just 0.106.

First to record 20,000 points, 8,000 assists, and 2,000 steals
Gary Payton (USA), playing for the Boston Celtics, scored his 20,000th career point against the Portland Trailblazers on November 10, 2004 to break the treble barrier.

Most free throw attempts in an NBA game

Dwight Howard (USA) was playing for the Orlando Magic in a 117–109 victory over the Golden State Warriors on January 12, 2012 when he shot 39 free throws. Howard converted 21 of the 39 attempts and surpassed the 34 set by Wilt Chamberlain for the Philadelphia Warriors against the St. Louis Hawks on February 22, 1962.

14,812 Career minutes played by Katie Smith since 1998.

Most minutes played in a WNBA career

Tina Thompson (USA, *left*) had played 15,112 minutes by February 20, 2013. Her Seattle Storm colleague Katie Smith (USA, *right*) has played the **most minutes per game in a WNBA career**, with 33.1.

the previous record of nine by the Los Angeles Sparks in 2001 and 2003. In 2012, the Minnesota Lynx also set the **highest field goal percentage in a game**, with 0.695 during a 107–86 victory over the Tulsa Shock on July 10, 2012. The Lynx converted 41 of 59 field goal attempts.

Most free throws in a career

Tamika Catchings (USA) has played for the Indiana Fever since 2002, in which time she has made 1,573 free throws. As well as contributing to the USA's 2012 wins as part of the Olympic team, she has also recorded the **most steals in a career**, with 845. As a high-school player in 1997, she was the first of just two players to record a quintuple double—that is, five totals in double figures for points, rebounds, assists, steals, and blocked shots, though this feat has never been done at college or professional level.

Most games played in a career

Tangela Smith (USA) has played in 463 games for the Sacramento Monarchs, Charlotte Sting, Phoenix Mercury, Indiana Fever, and San Antonio Silver Stars since 1998. She has started 400 games.

Most three-point field goals attempted by an individual (NBA career)

Ray Allen (USA) had attempted 6,980 three-point goals as of February 19, 2013. He had made 2,797 of those goals by the same date, the **most three-point goals in an NBA career**, playing for the Milwaukee Bucks, Seattle SuperSonics, Boston Celtics, and Miami Heat.

FOR THE RECORD

Ray Allen has also been an actor. He won praise for his role as hot young prospect Jesus Shuttlesworth in Spike Lee's *He Got Game* (USA, 1998).

WNBA

Fewest games to reach 1,000 career rebounds

Tina Charles (USA) required 89 games to reach 1,000 career rebounds, besting Yolanda Griffith's (USA) record of 92. She has played for the Connecticut Sun since being No. 1 draft pick in 2010.

Largest half-time lead

Tina Charles' team, the Connecticut Sun (USA), led 61–27 over the New York Liberty on June 15, 2012, and won 97–55. The Sun's half-time margin bested Seattle Storm's 33-point margin (60–27) against the Tulsa Shock on August 7, 2010.

Most assists in a career

Ticha Penicheiro (Portugal) provided 2,599 assists in 454 games playing for the Sacramento Monarchs, Los Angeles Sparks, and Chicago Sky since 1998. She also holds the record for **most assists per game**, with 5.7.

Most consecutive wins to begin a season

The Minnesota Lynx (USA) began 2012 in style with 10 wins, breaking

FIBA, NBA & WNBA

FIBA (International Basketball Federation)

Most FIBA World Championships (first held in 1950)	5	Yugoslavia/Serbia
	4	USA
	3	USSR
Most FIBA Women's World Championships (first held in 1953)	8	USA
	6	USSR
	1	Australia

NBA (National Basketball Association)

Most NBA titles (first held in 1946–47)	17	Boston Celtics (USA)
	16	Minneapolis/Los Angeles Lakers (USA)
	6	Chicago Bulls (USA)
Most NBA minutes played	57,446	Kareem Abdul-Jabbar (USA)
	54,852	Karl Malone (USA)
	50,000	Elvin Hayes (USA)
Most NBA free throws made	9,787	Karl Malone (USA)
	8,531	Moses Malone (USA)
	7,737	Kobe Bryant (USA)

WNBA (Women's National Basketball Association)

Most WNBA titles (first held in 1997)	4	Houston Comets (USA)
	3	Detroit Shock (USA)
	2	Los Angeles Sparks (USA)
		Phoenix Mercury (USA)
		Seattle Storm (USA)
Most WNBA minutes played	15,112	Tina Thompson (USA)
	14,821	Katie Smith (USA)
	13,546	Taj McWilliams-Franklin (USA)
Most WNBA free throws made	1,573	Tamika Catchings (USA)
	1,477	Lisa Leslie (USA)
	1,412	Katie Smith (USA)

Correct as of February 20, 2013

FOR MORE AMERICAN SPORT, TURN TO P. 224

BOXING

24
Number of Tavoris Cloud's previous undefeated professional bouts.

IN REVIEW The 2012 London Olympics introduced boxing to a wider audience than ever, due largely to the introduction of women's categories—a decision that broke down "one of the last bastions of Olympic equality," according to the London Organising Committee of the Olympic and Paralympic Games. In the professional ranks, the Klitschko brothers Wladimir and Vitali (Ukraine) held onto their heavyweight titles with an iron grip, while five-division champion Floyd Mayweather, Jr. (USA) remained undefeated.

Meanwhile, a bright star is shining on the horizon in the shape of American Andre Ward, who is undefeated in 26 bouts and is now the WBA super world super-middleweight champion and WBC world super-middleweight champion. This title holder certainly could be a future record breaker.

Oldest boxing world champion

On March 9, 2013, Bernard Hopkins (USA, b. January 15, 1965, *above left*) became the oldest man to win a major version of a world championship when, at the age of 48 years 53 days, he outpointed reigning champion Tavoris Cloud (USA, *above right*) for the IBF world light-heavyweight crown over 12 rounds at the Barclays Center in Brooklyn, New York, USA.

Fewest fights to win the world heavyweight championship

On February 15, 1978, Leon Spinks (USA) outpointed title holder Muhammad Ali (USA, born Cassius Marcellus Clay, Jr.) over 15 rounds at the Hilton Sports Pavilion in Las Vegas, USA, to capture the title in just his eighth professional contest.

Longest time between world heavyweight titles

George Foreman (USA) won the world heavyweight crown on January 22, 1973 against Joe Frazier (USA) in two rounds in Kingston, Jamaica. He then lost the title when he was knocked out in round eight on October 30, 1974 in

Fewest punches in a 12-round title fight

Randall Bailey (USA, *above left*) lost his IBF world welterweight title to Devon Alexander (USA, *above right*) by way of a 12-round points decision at the Barclays Center in Brooklyn, New York, USA, on October 20, 2012. During the bout, CompuBox registered that Bailey landed just 45 punches. The fight was originally scheduled for September 8, but was delayed after Bailey was injured in sparring.

Kinshasa, Democratic Republic of the Congo, by Muhammad Ali (USA). Foreman regained the WBA and IBF versions of the championship 20 years later on November 5, 1994, when knocking out title holder Michael Moorer (USA) in round 10 in Las Vegas, USA. (*See above right for more on Foreman.*)

First siblings to hold world heavyweight titles simultaneously

Vitali Klitschko regained the WBC title on October 11, 2008, when his brother Wladimir (both Ukraine) was WBO, IBF, and IBO champion.

First undefeated heavyweight world champion

With a total of 49 wins, Rocky Marciano (USA, b. Rocco Francis Marchegiano, 1923–69) is the first —and only—world heavyweight champion to have won every fight of his professional career, which lasted from March 17, 1947 to September 21, 1955.

Shortest heavyweight champion

At 5 ft. 7 in. (170.18 cm), Tommy Burns (Canada), who outpointed Marvin Hart (USA) over 20 rounds for the world championship on February 23, 1906, was the shortest ever heavyweight title winner.

First one-handed boxer

Michael Costantino (USA) was born without a right hand and made his professional debut in the cruiserweight division on October 27, 2012, in Brooklyn,

FOR THE RECORD

With 27 bouts in total, Joe Louis (USA, May 13, 1914–April 12, 1981) participated in the **most world heavyweight title bouts**. Louis first won the title on June 22, 1937, and went on to make 25 successful defenses until his comeback (and 27th title bout) on September 27, 1950, whereby he failed to regain the world crown when outpointed by holder Ezzard Charles over 15 rounds.

Youngest winner of the world heavyweight title

Mike Tyson (USA, b. June 30, 1966, *left*) became the youngest person to win a version of the heavyweight title, at the age of 20 years 145 days. He stopped reigning champion Trevor Berbick (Canada, *below*) in two rounds to capture the WBC crown on November 22, 1986 at the Hilton Hotel in Las Vegas, USA.

SPORTS

www.guinnessworldrecords.com

GUINNESS
WORLD
RECORDS
2014

18
Age gap in years between Foreman and Moorer when the two met at the MGM Grand in 1994.

Oldest world heavyweight champion

At the age of 45 years 299 days, "Big George" Foreman (USA, b. January 10, 1949, *above right*) became the oldest world heavyweight boxing champion when he knocked out title holder Michael Moorer (USA). He floored "Double M" in round 10 at the MGM Grand in Las Vegas, USA, on November 5, 1994, regaining the title that Muhammad Ali had taken from him in the "Rumble in the Jungle" 20 years earlier.

Spanish boxer ever—won the WBA crown from previous title holder Felix Sturm (Germany) on July 15, 2006 at the record age of 38 years 115 days. He stopped Sturm in round 10 at the Color Line Arena in Hamburg, Germany.

Most consecutive world super-middleweight title defenses

Joe Calzaghe (UK) and Sven Ottke (Germany) both made 21 title defenses. Calzaghe achieved the feat when he beat Mikkel Kessler (Denmark) in Cardiff, UK, on November 3, 2007, while Ottke achieved his 21st triumph, over Armand Krajnc (Sweden), on March 27, 2004 in Germany.

Most punches thrown in a championship match

U.S.-born Mexican fighter Antonio Margarito threw 1,675 punches in a 12-round WBO welterweight title match against Joshua Clottey (Ghana) in Atlantic City, New Jersey, USA, on December 2, 2006.

First winner of all super-middleweight boxing titles

Joe Calzaghe (UK), who retired on February 5, 2009, was the first boxer to have held all four major versions of the world super-middleweight titles during his career. The respective titles are the WBO, IBF, WBC, and WBA.

Most consecutive rounds

Gerry Cronnelly (Ireland) boxed 123 rounds against 42 opponents at the Raheen Woods Hotel in Athenry, County Galway, Ireland, on October 20, 2012.

First female Olympic boxing gold medal

Flyweight Nicola Adams (UK) defeated China's Ren Cancan 16–7 over four two-minute rounds in the first ever Olympic women's boxing final, staged at the ExCeL arena in London, UK, on August 9, 2012.

The **youngest female boxing gold medalist** is Claressa Shields (USA, b. March 17, 1995), who was just 17 years 145 days old when she defeated Nadezhda Torlopova (Russia) in the middleweight (75 kg) final on August 9, 2012.

New York, USA, stopping his opponent Nathan Ortiz (USA) in round two. While Costantino is registered as light-heavyweight, this contest took place at the higher weight limit.

Oldest world middleweight champion

Javier Castillejo (Spain, b. March 22, 1968)—who is generally regarded as the greatest

LORD OF THE RING
As of May 2013, Mayweather is an undefeated champion, winning 44 out of 44 fights.

iQUOTE
"I've had boxing gloves on since before I could walk and been in gyms all my life."

FOR THE RECORD

On September 21, 1985, Michael Spinks (*above right*) outpointed Larry Holmes (both USA) over 15 rounds to win the IBF version of the world championship at the Riviera hotel and casino in Las Vegas, USA. In doing so, he became the **first world light-heavyweight title holder to win a world heavyweight crown**.

Highest annual earnings for a boxer

Floyd Mayweather, Jr. (USA) is not only the highest-earning boxer but also the **highest-earning athlete** of any kind. According to *Forbes'* 2012 list, he earned $85 million for winning just two fights. The first was a challenge for the WBC world welterweight crown on September 17, 2011 against Victor Ortiz (USA), which brought in $40 million. The second was the title challenge for the WBA world super light-middleweight crown on May 5, 2012 against Miguel Cotto (Puerto Rico).

COMBAT SPORTS

IN REVIEW London 2012 saw three wrestlers each win third consecutive Olympic gold medals. Saori Yoshida and Kaori Icho (both Japan) won the women's freestyle lightweight and middleweight contests respectively. Uzbekistan's Artur Taymazov added a London gold to those he won at Athens and Beijing.

In taekwondo, South Korea continued to dominate with Olympic medals for both the men's and women's teams.

The Ultimate Fighting Championship (UFC) had its first female champion: "Rowdy" Ronda Rousey (USA). Elsewhere, UFC legend Anderson "The Spider" Silva (Brazil) racked up the **most middleweight division wins**, **most consecutive fight wins**, and **most knockouts**. Do not mess with this man!

FENCING

First Olympian and Paralympian medalist
Only one athlete has won medals at both the Summer Olympic and Paralympic Games. Fencer Pál Szekeres (Hungary) won bronze in the men's team foil at the Olympic Games in Seoul, South Korea, in 1988. Injured in a bus accident in 1991, he took up wheelchair fencing and won gold in the individual foil in Barcelona, Spain, in 1992 and in the individual foil and individual saber in Atlanta, USA, in 1996. He also won three bronze medals as a Paralympian, in the individual foil at Sydney 2000 in Australia and Beijing 2008 in China, and in the individual saber at Athens 2004 in Greece.

Most Olympic fencing medals
Male: Edoardo Mangiarotti (Italy) won 13 Olympic medals—six gold, five silver, and two bronze—for foil and épée from 1936 to 1960.

FACT:
The earliest mention of a combat sport in the ancient Olympic Games was in 648 BC, when pankration, a mixed martial art that involved wrestling and boxing, was contested.

Female: Valentina Vezzali (Italy) has won nine Olympic fencing medals: six gold, one silver, and two bronze. She won gold in the team foil and silver in the individual foil at Atlanta 1996; gold in the individual and team foil at Sydney 2000; gold in the individual foil at Athens 2004; and gold in the individual foil and bronze in the team foil at Beijing 2008. Finally, at London 2012, she won gold in the team foil and bronze in the individual foil.

Vezzali's three individual foil wins at the 2000, 2004, and 2008 Games mean she also holds the

Most Olympic freestyle wrestling gold medals (female)

Saori Yoshida (Japan, *above*) has won three golds in the lightweight division, at the Athens 2004, Beijing 2008, and London 2012 Games. Middleweight wrestler Kaori Icho (Japan) has also won three golds, at the same Games.

record for the **most consecutive Olympic gold medals in individual foil fencing (female)**.

UFC

Most consecutive UFC wins
The Ultimate Fighting Championship (UFC) is a mixed martial arts competition contested across eight weight categories. The greatest number of back-to-back UFC fight wins is 17, by Anderson "The Spider" Silva (Brazil) between 2006 and 2012. Silva

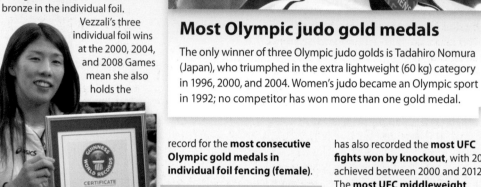

Most Olympic judo gold medals

The only winner of three Olympic judo golds is Tadahiro Nomura (Japan), who triumphed in the extra lightweight (60 kg) category in 1996, 2000, and 2004. Women's judo became an Olympic sport in 1992; no competitor has won more than one gold medal.

has also recorded the **most UFC fights won by knockout**, with 20 achieved between 2000 and 2012. The **most UFC middleweight championship bouts won** by an individual fighter is 11, again by the redoubtable Silva between 2006 and 2012. Silva's record comprises the original title win along with 10 successful defenses.

The **most UFC welterweight championship bouts** won by an individual fighter is 10, by Georges St-Pierre (Canada) between 2006 and 2012.

Most Olympic taekwondo flyweight gold medals (female)

Wu Jingyu (China) has picked up two Olympic gold medals in the women's taekwondo flyweight (49 kg) division, at Beijing 2008 and London 2012.

ANCIENT ROOTS
Taekwondo (meaning "the art of the foot and the hand") is a Korean martial art and dates back some 2,000 years.

TOUGH MEN? HIT P. 102. TOUGH WOMEN? HIT P. 104

Most UFC featherweight championships

The greatest number of UFC featherweight championship bouts won by a fighter is four, by José Aldo (Brazil) between 2011 and 2013. This record comprises the original title win along with three successful defenses.

JUDO

Most World Judo Championships (female)
Japan have won the World Judo Championships team contest three times, in 2002, 2008, and 2012.

Oldest Olympic judo gold medalist
At the age of 33 years 118 days, Dae-Nam Song (South Korea, b. April 5, 1979) won Olympic gold in the men's judo 90 kg category at the ExCeL in London, UK, on August 1, 2012. Song defeated Asley González (Cuba) in the final, with the winning *waza-ari* score coming courtesy of a throw in the "golden score" extra-time period.

Longest pro wrestling match

Shockwave Impact Wrestling (USA) promoted the Ultimate Iron Man Match—a 12-hour professional wrestling match—at the Shelby County Fairgrounds in Sidney, Ohio, USA, on November 6, 2010. Six fighters took part in the contest. *Above*, Dark Angel (aka Mike White) squares up to the masked American Kickboxer II (aka Brandon Overholser, both USA).

MOST OLYMPIC COMBAT SPORTS GOLD MEDALS

Fencing (female)	6	Valentina Vezzali (Italy): 2000, 2004, and 2008 (individual); 1996, 2000, and 2012 (team)
Fencing (male)	7	Aladár Gerevich (Hungary): 1948 (individual); 1932, 1936, 1948, 1952, 1956, and 1960 (team)
Judo (female)	1	(See p. 236.)
Judo (male)	3	(See p. 236.)
Taekwondo (female)	2	Chen Yi-an (Taiwan): 1988 and 1992
		Hwang Kyung-seon (South Korea): 2008 and 2012
Taekwondo (male)	2	Ha Tae-kyung (South Korea): 1988 and 1992
Wrestling, Freestyle (female)	3	Kaori Icho (Japan), 63 kg: 2004, 2008, and 2012
		Saori Yoshida (Japan), 55 kg: 2004, 2008, and 2012 (see p. 236)
Wrestling, Freestyle (male)	3	Aleksandr Medved (Belarus): 1964, 1968, and 1972
		Buvaysa Saytiev (Russia): 1996, 2004, and 2008
		Artur Taymazov (Uzbekistan): 2004, 2008, and 2012
Wrestling, Greco-Roman (male)	3	Carl Westergren (Sweden): 1920, 1924, and 1932
		Aleksandr Karelin (Russia): 1988, 1992, and 1996

Statistics correct as of April 15, 2013

First female UFC champion

Ronda Rousey (USA) was announced as the first women's UFC bantamweight champion at a press conference in Seattle, Washington, USA, on December 6, 2012. She defended her title against Liz Carmouche (USA) at UFC 157 in Anaheim, California, USA, on February 23, 2013.

TAEKWONDO

Most popular martial art
According to Taekwondo Chungdokwan, the British branch of the World Taekwondo Federation, approximately 50 million people worldwide practice the martial art of taekwondo, the national sport of South Korea.

Most World Taekwondo Championships
Male: South Korea won this title 19 times from 1973 to 2009.
Female: South Korea also hold the female record, with 12 championship wins from 1997 to 2011.

Most Olympic taekwondo middleweight gold medals (female)
Hwang Kyung-seon (South Korea) has won the women's Olympic taekwondo middleweight (67 kg) division twice, at the Beijing 2008 and London 2012 Games.

Youngest Olympic taekwondo medalist (male)
Alexey Denisenko (Russia, b. August 30, 1993) won a bronze medal in the men's 58 kg division at London 2012 on August 8, 2012, at the age of 18 years 344 days.

WRESTLING

Most Olympic freestyle wrestling super-heavyweight gold medals (male)
The greatest gold-medal haul by a male wrestler at the Olympic Games in the super-heavyweight division is three, by Artur Taymazov (Uzbekistan) at Athens 2004, Beijing 2008, and London 2012.

Most Freestyle Wrestling World Championships (male)
Two competitors have each won these championships seven times: Aleksandr Medved (Belarus) in the +100 kg class between 1962 and 1971, and Valentin Jordanov (Bulgaria) in the 55 kg class between 1983 and 1995.

15
Lisa's age when she set the record; previously it had been 7 ft. 0.6 in. (2.15 m).

Highest unassisted martial arts kick (female)

Lisa Coolen (Netherlands) performed an unassisted, 7-ft. 8-in.-high (2.35-m) martial arts kick at the Sportcomplex in de Bandert in Echt, Netherlands, on May 12, 2012. She performed a jumping front kick, a taekwondo move also known as *twimyo ap chagi*.

CRICKET

31
Forbes's ranking of Dhoni in the list of richest sportspeople, as of June 2012.

IN REVIEW The past year has seen England captain Alastair Cook and Australia's Michael Clarke lead from the front with extraordinary feats of patience and endurance, while Shikhar Dhawan (India) compiled the **fastest hundred by a batsman on Test debut** (85 balls).

Rahul Dravid (India), Ricky Ponting (Australia), and Andrew Strauss (England) all announced their retirements in 2012, while the finest player of his generation—"Little Master" Sachin Tendulkar (India)—bowed out of ODIs with an unprecedented 18,426 runs (at an average of 44.83), 49 hundreds, and 96 fifties to his name from 452 innings.

The West Indies won the World T20 (their first major trophy since 2004) and South Africa became the team to beat in all three formats of the game. The Australians added February's World Cup to the World T20 crown they won in October 2012 to remain the dominant force in women's cricket.

iQUOTE
"If you don't perform, you don't deserve to win anything."

Highest-paid cricketer

Mahendra Singh Dhoni, captain of the Indian cricket team, earned $26.5 million in the year to June 2012, according to *Forbes* magazine. His cricket-related pay was dwarfed by the $23 million he made from endorsements from companies such as Reebok and Sony.

FIRST ...

Player to hit a six off the first ball of a Test match
Chris Gayle (Jamaica) swatted Bangladesh paceman Sohag Gazi over the boundary rope from the first delivery of the 2,051st Test match, which started in Mirpur, Bangladesh, on November 13, 2012.

Team to successfully defend a World T20 title
Australia retained the International Cricket Council (ICC) Women's World Twenty20 crown when they beat England by four runs at the Premadasa Stadium in Colombo, Sri Lanka, on October 7, 2012.

Test team to declare their first innings and lose by an innings
Late on the first day of the 2nd Test against India at Rajiv Gandhi International Stadium in Hyderabad, India, on March 2, 2013, Australia declared their first innings on 237 for 9. In reply, India made 503 all out in their first innings, to lead by 266 runs. On the fourth day of the match, Australia were all out for 131, losing by an innings and 135 runs.

Most wickets in a T20 International

Sri Lankan off-spinner Ajantha Mendis is the only cricketer to have claimed six wickets in a Twenty20 (T20) International match—and he's done it twice. On August 8, 2011, he took six wickets for 16 runs from four overs against Australia at Pallekele International Cricket Stadium, Sri Lanka. On September 18, 2012 at the ICC World Twenty20, again in Sri Lanka, he took six wickets for eight runs from four overs.

MOST ...

"Ducks" in Twenty20 cricket
As of March 22, 2013, the most scores of 0 recorded by an individual batsman in Twenty20

RUNS, WICKETS, AND CATCHES

Test matches		
Most runs	15,837	Sachin Tendulkar (India), 1989–2013
Most wickets	800	Muttiah Muralitharan (Sri Lanka), 1992–2010
Most catches (fielder)	210	Rahul Dravid (India), 1996–2012
One-Day Internationals		
Most runs	18,426	Sachin Tendulkar (India), 1989–2012
Most wickets	534	Muttiah Muralitharan (Sri Lanka), 1993–2011
Most catches (fielder)	195	Mahela Jayawardene (Sri Lanka), 1998–2013
Twenty20 Internationals		
Most runs	1,814	Brendon McCullum (New Zealand), 2005–13
Most wickets	74	Umar Gul (Pakistan), 2007–13
Most catches (fielder)	33	Ross Taylor (New Zealand), 2006–13

Statistics correct as of March 22, 2013

First player to score five centuries in first five Test matches as captain

Alastair Cook's first five Test matches as England's captain saw the prolific left-hander register scores of 173, 109 not out, 176, 122, and 190. His 190, scored in the first innings of the 3rd Test against India in Kolkata on December 6–7, 2012, made him the youngest player to score 7,000 Test runs (at 27 years 347 days old) and England's leading century maker, with 23 hundreds.

First national team to be ranked top in all formats

When South Africa defeated England in a One-Day International (ODI) at the Ageas Bowl, Southampton, UK, on August 28, 2012, they became the first team in the history of international cricket to be ranked as the ICC's top Test, ODI, and T20 side simultaneously.

International matches is seven by Luke Wright (England). The middle-order batsman made his seven ducks in 36 innings.

Fifties in a Twenty20 career
Brendon McCullum (New Zealand) took his tally of Twenty20 International half-centuries to 12 (including two he converted into centuries) when he smashed 74 runs from just 38 balls against England at Seddon Park, Hamilton, New Zealand, on February 12, 2013.

Centuries in international cricket
Sachin Tendulkar (India) scored 100 centuries in Test matches and ODIs between August 14, 1990 and March 16, 2012.

Test matches as captain
Graeme Smith (South Africa) became the first cricketer to make 100 Test match appearances as captain when he led out the

Proteas for the 1st Test against Pakistan on home soil in Johannesburg on his 32nd birthday, February 1, 2013. As of February 4 that year, Smith had won 48 of his 100 matches as captain and scored 26 Test match hundreds.

Test match deliveries faced
Rahul Dravid (India) has squared up to 31,258 balls in his Test career. The right-handed batsman played the last of his 164 Test matches against Australia in Adelaide in January 2012.

Most dismissals by a wicket-keeper

A. B. de Villiers (South Africa, *pictured*) and Jack Russell (England) have both taken 11 catches in a Test match. Russell's came against hosts South Africa at New Wanderers Stadium in Johannesburg on November 30 and December 2–3, 1995. De Villiers matched the feat against Pakistan at the same venue on February 2–4, 2013.

WOMEN'S CRICKET

Most wins of the ICC Women's World Cup
The Women's World Cup has been staged on 10 occasions since 1973. Australia have won a record six times, in 1978, 1982, 1988, 1997, 2005, and 2013.

Most women's ODI runs
England captain Charlotte Edwards scored her 4,845th run in women's One-Day Internationals when defending World Cup champions England beat India at the 2013 World Cup in Mumbai, India, on February 3.

Most aggregate runs in a women's ODI
Australia (289 for 6) chased down New Zealand's 288 for 6 with 20 balls to spare at the North Sydney Oval in Australia on December 14, 2012 to produce a women's ODI record match aggregate of 577 runs.

Most Test double centuries in a single year

Australian Test captain Michael Clarke scored an unbeaten double century on the opening day of the 2nd Test between Australia and South Africa in Adelaide, Australia, on November 22, 2012 to notch up his fourth score of 200 or more in 2012. In the calendar year, Clarke scored 1,595 Test runs, averaging 106.33 runs per innings.

Most runs in a Twenty20 International

Brendon McCullum hit 123 runs for New Zealand against Bangladesh during the ICC World Twenty20 in Pallekele, Sri Lanka, on September 21, 2012. He plundered seven sixes and 11 fours in a 58-ball knock.

Most runs in a Twenty20 World Cup career

Mahela Jayawardene (Sri Lanka) has scored 858 runs in 25 innings, at an average of 40.85 runs per innings, in the four ICC World Twenty20 tournaments (2007, 2009, 2010, and 2012) held to date. He's shown here launching another ball toward the boundary, watched by West Indian wicket-keeper Denesh Ramdin, during the 2012 ICC World Twenty20 final in Colombo, Sri Lanka.

ALL HAIL MAHELA
In 2006, Jayawardene made the highest Test score by a Sri Lankan—374—against South Africa in Sri Lanka.

CYCLING

IN REVIEW The world of cycling was highly newsworthy during 2012—and not always for the most honorable of reasons. That fall, one of the sport's biggest names—the USA's Lance Armstrong—was embroiled in jaw-dropping revelations about enhancing his performance in races. However, this news could not overshadow the record-breaking triumphs of the 2012 summer, headed by the achievements of Bradley Wiggins (UK). He became the first person to win the Tour de France and an Olympic gold medal in the same year, a feat that earned him a knighthood in the 2013 New Year Honours.

Another UK leading light, Sir Chris Hoy, announced his retirement on April 18, 2013, having won a fifth gold medal at London 2012, an Olympic record for a track cyclist. With 12 medals, Team GB dominated cycling, winning gold in eight of the 18 events; no other nation managed more than one gold.

OLYMPICS

Fastest team 500 m unpaced standing start (female)
Gong Jinjie and Guo Shuang (both China) clocked a time of 32.422 seconds for the unpaced 500 m (standing start) at the Velodrome in London, UK, on August 2, 2012.

Fastest 4 km team pursuit (male)
Great Britain (Steven Burke, Ed Clancy, Peter Kennaugh, and Geraint Thomas) set a time of 3 min 51.659 sec in the men's 4 km team pursuit, taking Olympic gold on August 3, 2012.

29
Gold medals for Team GB at London 2012. The USA won most golds overall: 46.

Most vertical feet cycled in 48 hours

Jacob Zurl (Austria) climbed the equivalent of 94,452 ft. (28,789 m) by bicycle in 48 hours on Oberschöcklweg in Weinitzen, Austria, on April 20–22, 2012. He covered 164 laps of a 1.12-mile (1.8-km) course that rose 5,752 ft. (1,753.2 m) at an average gradient of 9.8 percent.

Fastest circumnavigation by bicycle
Alan Bate (UK) took just 127 days to circle the globe, cycling a distance of 18,310.47 miles (29,467.91 km) and traveling more than 26,475.8 miles (42,608.76 km) overall, including transfers. The journey lasted from March 31 to August 4, 2010, starting and finishing at the Grand Palace in Bangkok, Thailand.

Highest-altitude bicycle race
The 310-mile-long (500-km) I Ruta Internacional de la Alpaca reaches 15,987 ft. (4,873 m) above sea level between Juliaca and Ayaviri in Peru. The inaugural race was held from November 25 to 28, 2010.

Highest score for single indoor artistic cycling
In artistic cycling, athletes perform a five-minute routine of tricks (exercises) on fixed-gear bicycles in front of judges, and are awarded points according to the quality of their performance.
Male: The highest score recorded by a rider in the men's single event is 208.91, by David Schnabel (Germany), achieved in Kagoshima, Japan, on November 6, 2011.
Female: Sandra Beck (Germany) scored 181 points in the women's single artistic cycling discipline during a competition in Erlenbach, Germany, on November 17, 2012. Beck is a five-time Indoor Cycling World Championships silver medalist (2005, 2008–09, 2011–12).

Most Olympic track cycling gold medals won

Sir Chris Hoy (UK) won five Olympic track cycling gold medals: the 1-km time trial at Athens 2004; the individual sprint, team sprint, and Keirin at Beijing 2008; and the team sprint at London 2012.

Fastest 750 m unpaced standing start (male)
Great Britain (Philip Hindes, Jason Kenny, and Sir Chris Hoy) set a new world record time of 42.6 seconds to win Olympic gold in this event at the Velodrome in London, UK, on August 2, 2012.

Most road race medals (male)
Cyclist Alexander Vinokourov (Kazakhstan) claimed his second Olympic road race medal by winning the 155-mile (250-km) endurance event at the London 2012 Olympic Games. His first road race medal came at the Sydney 2000 Games, when he won silver.

Most road cycling gold medals
Kristin Armstrong (USA) became the first person to successfully defend an Olympic cycling road title (time trial or road race) when she won the women's time trial event at the London 2012 Olympic Games on August 1, four years after claiming time trial gold in Beijing, China, on August 13, 2008. Armstrong (USA, b. August 11, 1973) became the **oldest winner of an Olympic road cycling gold medal** when, at 38 years 356 days old, she successfully defended her time trial title at London 2012, completing the 18-mile (29-km) course in 37 min. 34.82 sec.

Oldest Olympic cross-country mountain biking medalist (female)
Sabine Spitz (Germany, b. December 27, 1971) won a silver medal in the Olympic cross-country mountain-biking event at Hadleigh Farm, Essex, UK, on August 11, 2012 at the age of 40 years 228 days. Cross-country cycling became an Olympic sport at Atlanta 1996.

Youngest Olympic cross-country mountain biker

Julie Bresset (France, b. June 9, 1989) is the youngest winner of a medal in Olympic cross-country mountain biking after triumphing in the women's 2.9-mile (4.8-km) race, at the age of 23 years 63 days, at Hadleigh Farm in Essex, UK, on August 11, 2012.

Fastest 3 km team pursuit (female)

Great Britain (Dani King, Laura Trott, and Joanna Rowsell) clocked 3 min. 14.051 sec. to win Olympic gold in the women's 3-km (1.8-mile) team pursuit at the Velodrome in London, UK, on August 4, 2012. The trio smashed their own world record of 3 min. 15.669 sec., set in the qualifying round the day before.

Youngest gold medalist in track cycling (female)

Laura Trott (UK, b. April 24, 1992) was 20 years 102 days old when she claimed Olympic gold in the women's team pursuit at London 2012 (see box above).

UCI (UNION CYCLISTE INTERNATIONALE)

Fastest individual 500 m unpaced standing start (female)

Anna Meares (Australia) rode 500 m (1,640 ft.) in 33.010 seconds at the UCI World Track Cycling Championships on April 8, 2012 in Melbourne, Australia.

Fastest 200 m unpaced flying start (female)

On January 19, 2013, at the UCI Track Cycling World Cup in Aguascalientes,

Most competitors in the UCI BMX World Championships

The 2005 UCI BMX World Championships, held from July 29 to 31 at the Palais Omnisport de Paris-Bercy, France, drew 2,560 competitors from 39 countries.

Most wins of the UCI BMX World Championships

Male: Kyle Bennett (USA) has won the championships three times, in 2002–03 and 2007.
Female: Two riders share this record. Argentina's Gabriela Diaz won three UCI BMX World Championships, in 2001–02 and 2004. Shanaze Reade (UK) equaled the feat in 2007–08 and 2010.

Mexico, Tianshi Zhong (China) rode the 200 m (656 ft.) flying start in 10.573 seconds.

TOUR DE FRANCE		
Most wins (First held in 1903. The yellow jersey for overall winner was first formally awarded in 1919)	5	Jacques Anquetil (France): 1957, 1961–64
		Bernard Hinault (France): 1978–79, 1981–82, 1985
		Miguel Indurain (Spain): 1991–95
		Eddy Merckx (Belgium): 1969–72, 1974
	3	Louison Bobet (France): 1953–55
		Greg LeMond (USA): 1986, 1989–90
		Philippe Thys (Belgium): 1913–14, 1920

Statistics correct as of April 15, 2013

First cyclist to win the Tour de France and an Olympic gold medal in the same year

Bradley Wiggins (UK) capped a memorable summer for British cycling when he eased to victory in the men's time trial at the London Olympic Games on August 1, 2012 (pictured right), just 10 days after becoming the first British rider to win the Tour de France (below). His time trial win, in 50 min. 39 sec., gave Wiggins a seventh Olympic cycling medal.

Most successful country at the UCI Track World Championships

As of March 22, 2013, France had won 353 medals at the UCI Track World Championships, a haul comprising 129 gold, 107 silver, and 117 bronze medals. Second-placed Great Britain lies some way behind, with 218 medals. The event was first staged, for amateurs, in Chicago, USA, in 1893.

QUOTE
"...s the stuff of ... As a child ... ...gined that ...'d be in ...is position."

FOR THE RECORD

Their victories at London 2012 saw Bradley Wiggins and Chris Hoy become the most decorated British Olympic Games athletes of all time. Each now has seven Olympic medals. Wiggins has four gold, one silver, and two bronze medals; Hoy has six golds and one silver medal. Both men were knighted for their Olympic achievements.

GOLF

IN REVIEW The past year has seen Rory McIlroy smashing records, winning events on the USPGA Tour, and topping the money list. He's part of a new crop of young stars, with China's Guan Tianlang and Andy Zhang, and Lydia Ko from New Zealand, all of whom made waves in the sport at the age of just 15 or under. Of the old guard, Tiger Woods seems back to his best, while Ernie Els and Phil Mickelson keep racking up tournament wins.

The 2012 Ryder Cup at Medinah Country Club, Illinois, USA, was unforgettable. Led by Ian Poulter (UK), Europe made one of the greatest comebacks in the history of the 85-year-old contest, recovering from 10–4 down to win 14½ points to 13½ in a match dubbed the "Miracle of Medinah."

Lowest 18-hole score
Rhein Gibson (Australia) set a score of 55 at the par-71 course at River Oaks Golf Club in Edmond, Oklahoma, USA, on May 12, 2012. Rhein's round included two eagles and 12 birdies, and the rest of his holes came in at par for the course.

Fastest time to play a round of golf on each continent
Heinrich du Preez (South Africa) played 18-hole rounds of golf on each of the continents (excluding Antarctica) in 119 hr. 48 min. from May 22 to 27, 2007. He started at noon in Pretoria, South Africa, and moved to Germany, Argentina, the USA, and Australia, then finished his marathon session at 11.48 a.m. at a golf course in Bangkok, Thailand.

$68,877,458
Phil Mickelson's PGA career earnings.

Most PGA Tour victories by a left-hander

Phil Mickelson (USA) is right-handed in everything except golf, and won 41 tournaments playing left-handed between 1998 and 2013. "Lefty" Mickelson also holds the record for the **most major tournament victories by a left-hander**, winning the U.S. Masters in 2004, 2006, and 2010 and the PGA Championship in 2005.

Highest career earnings on the PGA Tour

As of March 8, 2013, Tiger Woods's (USA) PGA Tour earnings had reached $102,122,300. Woods has the **highest annual earnings for a golfer**, with $59.4 million accrued in winnings and endorsements as of June 2012, according to *Forbes*. They rank him No. 3 in the 2012 list of the highest-paid athletes.

Largest lesson
Golf PARa Todos ("Golf FORe Everyone") taught 1,073 participants at the El Camaleón golf course in Playa del Carmen, Quintana Roo, Mexico, on January 23, 2011.

Airport with the largest golf course
Don Mueang International Airport in Bangkok, Thailand, has an 18-hole golf course between its two main runways. It belongs to the Royal Thai Air Force and there is no fence around the course.

Largest putting green
Spring Lake Golf Resort in Sebring, Florida, USA, has a putting green measuring an entire acre (42,070 sq. ft.; 3,908 m²)—more than 15 times the size of a tennis court. The green is located on the ninth hole of the Osprey course.

Youngest LPGA tour winner

Lydia Ko (New Zealand, b. April 24, 1997) was 15 years 122 days when she won the CN Canadian Women's Open at Vancouver Golf Club, Canada, in August 2012.

RYDER CUP

Most consecutive Ryder Cup team wins
The USA has twice managed to win the biennial Ryder Cup seven times in a row. The first run was from 1935 to 1955 (there was no competition during World War II) and the second was in 1971–83.

Youngest Ryder Cup captain
Legendary player Arnold Palmer (USA) was 34 years 31 days when he captained the U.S. team at East Lake Country Club in Atlanta, Georgia, USA, in 1963.

PGA

Highest European Senior Tour career earnings
By March 12, 2013, Carl Mason (UK) had earned €2,403,565 ($3,200,436) in a career that started back in 2003.

Longest putt (tournament)
Jack Nicklaus (USA) recorded a putt of 110 ft. (33.5 m) in the 1964 Tournament of Champions. In the 1992 PGA Championship, this was matched by Nick Price (Zimbabwe).

CHASING JACK
Tiger Woods was 37 in December 2012. At the same age in 1977, Jack Nicklaus (USA) had also won 14 majors and started 60 as a pro. He went on to win four more. Can Woods beat his record?

MOST WINS AND LOWEST ROUNDS

British Open

Most wins	6	Harry Vardon (UK)
Lowest total score (72 holes)	267 (66, 68, 69, 64)	Greg Norman (Australia), Royal St. George's, July 15–18, 1993

US Open

Most wins	4	Willie Anderson (UK)
		Bobby Jones, Jr (USA)
		Ben Hogan (USA)
		Jack Nicklaus (USA)
Lowest total score (72 holes)	268 (65, 66, 68, 69)	Rory McIlroy (UK), Congressional Country Club, Bethesda, Maryland, USA, June 16–19, 2011

US Masters

Most wins	6	Jack Nicklaus (USA)
Lowest total score (72 holes)	270 (70, 66, 65, 69)	Tiger Woods (USA), August National Golf Club, April 10–13, 1997

Statistics correct as of May 15, 2013

Oldest European Tour winner

On November 18, 2012, Miguel Ángel Jiménez (Spain, b. January 5, 1964) won the UBS Hong Kong Open—part of the European Tour since 2001—at the age of 48 years 318 days. The win was Jiménez's third in the event, following wins in 2005 and 2008, and extended his own record for **most European Tour wins by a player at the age 40 or over** to 12.

$1,710,000 Prize money that goes to the winner.

Greatest prize money for a golf tournament

The annual Professional Golfers' Association Tour Players Championship, which takes place at Sawgrass in Florida, USA, has a total prize pool of $9,500,000. Matt Kuchar (USA, *pictured*) took the top spot in 2012.

Most Asian Tour wins

Thongchai Jaidee (Thailand) won 13 events on the Asian Tour between 2000 and 2010. The Tour began in 1995 and is the main tour in the region apart from Japan, which has its own organization.

Lowest score under par in the LPGA Championship

A score below par of -19 has been recorded by two golfers: Cristie Kerr (USA) in 2010 and Yani Tseng (Taiwan) in 2011. Both scores were set at Locust Hill Country Club in Pittsford, New York, USA.

Youngest U.S. Masters player

Guan Tianlang (China, b. October 25, 1998) was just 14 years 169 days old when he teed off at the U.S. Masters in Augusta, Georgia, USA, on April 11, 2013. Guan also holds records for the **youngest U.S. Masters qualifier** at the age of 14 years 12 days old, and the **youngest golfer on the PGA European Tour** when, on April 19, 2012, he played the Volvo China Open at 13 years 177 days old.

OPEN

Youngest player

Andy Zhang (China, b. December 14, 1997) was 14 years 183 days old when he played the 2012 U.S. Open at the Olympic Club in San Francisco, California, USA, on June 14.

Greatest winning margin in the Women's British Open

Fast-rising young star Jiyai Shin (South Korea) finished with rounds of 71, 64, 71 and 73 to win by nine strokes at the Royal Liverpool Golf Club near Hoylake, Merseyside, UK, on September 13–16, 2012.

Most U.S. Women's Open titles won

Elizabeth "Betsy" Rawls and Mary "Mickey" Wright (both USA) each won four U.S. Women's Open titles. Betsy won hers in 1951, 1953, 1957, and 1960, while Mickey, who won 13 major championships, took the U.S. Women's Open title in 1958, 1959, 1961, and 1964.

Most money won in a rookie season on the Ladies European Tour

Carlota Ciganda (Spain) won €251,289.95 ($335,764) in 2012. In a phenomenal debut season, she also won the tour's Player of the Year and Rookie of the Year awards and the Order of Merit, awarded to the tour's leading money winner.

MASTERS

Most birdies recorded in a U.S. Masters round

Anthony Kim (USA) scored 11 birdies in his second round at the Augusta National in Georgia, USA, on April 10, 2009.

First Masters hole-in-one

Ross Somerville (Canada) made history when he aced the 16th hole at the Augusta National in Georgia, USA, on March 22, 1934.

¡QUOTE "I really don't like being put on a pedestal ... I'm always quite keen to break the ice, to just be normal."

Highest career earnings on the European Tour

As of March 8, 2013, Ernie Els (South Africa) had earned €28,384,297 ($39,016,800) on the European Tour since 1989. He also holds the record for the **lowest score under par at a PGA Tour event after 72 holes**, with 31 under par at the 2003 Mercedes Championships at Kapalua Resort on Maui, Hawaii, USA, on January 12.

ICE HOCKEY

IN REVIEW Russia defeated all 10 of its opponents en route to winning the gold medal at the 76th Ice Hockey World Championships in May 2012. Russia became the first undefeated champion since the Soviet Union team in 1989. It was Russia's third gold medal in the last five years and 26th overall (including as the Soviet Union). The tournament's top scorer, Russia's Evgeni Malkin (who plays in the NHL for the Pittsburgh Penguins), was named the most valuable player of the tournament.

In the NHL, a lockout caused by labor strife resulted in a shortened 2012–13 season, from 82 to 48 games. When the regular season finally got underway, the Chicago Blackhawks came flying out of the gate to set an NHL record for best start to a season, playing their first 24 games without a loss in regulation time (as of March 6, 2013).

contract paid $67.5 million, while Kovalchuk's is for $100 million.

Longest home winning streak by an NHL team

The Detroit Red Wings (USA) set an NHL record with 23 consecutive home wins during the 2011–12 season. This beat the previous mark of 20 held by the Boston Bruins in 1929–30 and matched by the Philadelphia Flyers in 1975–76.

MOST …

Consecutive goals in an ice hockey match

Ralph DeLeo (USA) scored 10 consecutive goals for Boston Technical against Roxbury Memorial (both USA) in the Greater Boston Senior League at the Boston Tech Arena in Massachusetts, USA, on January 10, 1953.

Highest attendance for an ice hockey match

The largest confirmed audience for a game of ice hockey was 104,173 people at "The Big Chill at the Big House" between the University of Michigan and Michigan State University (both USA) at Michigan Stadium in Ann Arbor, Michigan, USA, on December 11, 2010.

Highest score in an international ice hockey match

Slovakia beat Bulgaria 82–0 in a pre-Olympic women's qualification game at Liepāja in Latvia on September 6, 2008.

Longest NHL contract

Two ice hockey players have signed 15-year contracts: Rick DiPietro (USA), with the New York Islanders on September 12, 2006, and Ilya Kovalchuk (Russia), with the New Jersey Devils on September 3, 2010. DiPietro's

Most NHL games played for one team

Nicklas Lidström (Sweden) played a total of 1,564 games for the Detroit Red Wings from the 1991–92 season to 2011–12. During that time, he won four Stanley Cups with the team and was named the NHL's top defenseman on seven occasions.

Career wins by a goaltender

The most regular-season wins by a goaltender is 656, by Martin Brodeur (Canada) playing for the New Jersey Devils since the 1993–94 season.

Other NHL records held by the prolific Brodeur include: the **most regular-season games played by a goaltender** (1,191), the **most regular-season shots faced by a goaltender** (29,915), the **most minutes played in an NHL ice**

Most shootouts by a team in an NHL season

The Minnesota Wild (USA) were involved in 20 shootouts during the 2011–12 season, matching the record for tiebreakers in a single season set by the Phoenix Coyotes (USA) in 2009–10.

FOR THE RECORD

The Minnesota Wild joined the NHL for the 2000–01 season, captained by Sean O'Donnell. Their first goal was scored by Marián Gáborík against the Mighty Ducks of Anaheim. In 2007–08, Gáborík went on to score the most goals by a Wild player in a season: 42.

CUP AND SOURCE
The NHL's Stanley Cup is named after Lord Stanley, a Governor General of Canada. He donated the first cup (actually a bowl) in 1892.

NATIONAL HOCKEY LEAGUE

Most Stanley Cup appearances	34	Montreal Canadiens (Canada), 1916–93
Most Stanley Cup wins	24	Montreal Canadiens (Canada), 1930–93
Most matches played	1,767	Gordie Howe (Canada), for Detroit Red Wings and Hartford Whalers, 1946–80
Most goals scored	894	Wayne Gretzky (Canada) for Edmonton Oilers, LA Kings, St. Louis Blues, and New York Rangers
Most saves made	27,312	Martin Brodeur (Canada), for New Jersey Devils, 1991–present
Longest winning streak	17	Pittsburgh Penguins (USA), March 9 to April 10, 1993
Most goals in a game by one player	7	Joe Malone (Canada), for Quebec Bulldogs vs. Toronto St. Patricks on January 31, 1920
Most goals in a game by a team	16	Montreal Canadiens (Canada), in a 16–3 victory over Quebec Bulldogs on March 3, 1920

Correct as of February 5, 2013

hockey season (4,697 minutes, in 2006–07), the **most postseason shutouts by a goaltender in playoffs** (24), and the **most shutouts by a goaltender** (119). All were set with the Devils.

Consecutive years in the Stanley Cup playoffs

Two players have participated in NHL playoffs in a record 20 consecutive seasons. They are: Larry Robinson (Canada), playing for the Montreal Canadiens and Los Angeles Kings from the 1972–73 season to the 1991–92 season, and Nicklas Lidström (Sweden), playing for the Detroit Red Wings from the 1991–92 season to the 2011–12 season.

Goals scored in an NHL season by a team

The Edmonton Oilers (Canada) scored 446 goals during the 1983–84 season.

The **most goals scored in an NHL season by a player** is 92, by Wayne Gretzky (Canada) for the Edmonton Oilers in 1981–82.

Goals scored in overtime

Jaromir Jágr (Czech Republic) holds the NHL record for the most goals scored in overtime with 16, achieved while playing for the Pittsburgh Penguins, Washington Capitals, New York Rangers, and Philadelphia Flyers from the 1990–91 season to 2011–12.

Ice hockey gold medals at the Winter Olympics

Two teams have won a record eight gold medals in ice hockey at the Winter Olympics. The feat was first achieved by the USSR (last gold medal in 1992) and later matched by Canada at the 2010 Vancouver Winter Olympics.

The **most ice hockey gold medals won at the Winter Olympics by a female team** is three and was achieved by Canada at the 2002, 2006, and 2010 Games.

17
Kovalchuk's number—a tribute to late, great Russian player Valeri Kharlamov, who also wore it.

Most saves by an NHL goaltender in a regular-season shutout

Mike Smith (Canada) of the Phoenix Coyotes pulled off an impressive 54 saves in a shutout in a 2–0 victory against the Columbus Blue Jackets on April 3, 2012.

FACT:
Ilya's father started training him for sport soon after his third birthday. By the age of 18, Ilya was the youngest ice hockey pro at the 2002 Winter Olympics.

Losses by a team in overtime

In the 2011–12 season, the Florida Panthers lost 18 games in overtime, matching the mark set by the Tampa Bay Lightning (both USA) in 2008–09.

Matches consecutively scoring the winning goal

Newsy Lalonde (Canada) scored the winner five times playing for the Montreal Canadiens in February 1921. Just behind him is Daniel Alfredsson (Sweden), who became only the second NHL player to score four straight game winners while playing for the Ottawa Senators from January 9 to January 16, 2007.

Teams played for during an NHL career

Mike Sillinger (Canada) joined 12 teams in a 17-year career from 1990 to 2009: Columbus Blue Jackets, Detroit Red Wings, Florida Panthers, Mighty Ducks of Anaheim, Nashville Predators, New York Islanders, Philadelphia Flyers, Phoenix Coyotes, St. Louis Blues, Tampa Bay Lightning, Ottawa Senators, and Vancouver Canucks.

CHILL OUT—WINTER SPORTS ARE ON P. 260.

Most game-winning shootout goals scored in an NHL season

New Jersey Devils winger and alternate captain Ilya Kovalchuk (Russia) set an NHL record with seven game-deciding shootout goals during the 2011–12 season. This is the most ever by a player in a single season since the league adopted the tiebreaker in 2005.

MARATHONS

IN REVIEW African athletes continue to set the pace in marathon events, recording fast times and winning races worldwide. Kenyans Patrick Makau and Geoffrey Mutai each set new marathon records this year. A Ugandan athlete took Olympic glory on the Mall at London 2012, as Stephen Kiprotich won his country's only gold medal of the Games.

The Kenyan trio of Edna Kiplagat, Priscah Jeptoo, and Sharon Cherop made history at the World Championships in Daegu with the **first clean sweep in the marathon event**. Jeptoo also won silver at London 2012. And we were all moved by the tragic events at the 2013 Boston Marathon. Runners at the start of the 2013 London Marathon observed a 30-second silence, and many wore black ribbons in memory of the victims.

summer Paralympics. It was jointly hosted by Stoke Mandeville, UK, and New York City, USA. Around 3,000 athletes competed in all.

Most southerly marathon
The Antarctic Ice Marathon, which is held on the Antarctic mainland, takes place at a latitude of 80° south. It has been held annually since 2006.

The **most northerly marathon** is the North Pole Marathon, held annually at the geographic North Pole since 2002.

Fastest time to complete a marathon on each continent

Wendelin Lauxen (Germany, *main picture*) ran a marathon on each of the seven continents in 21 days 5 hr. 33 min. from October 31 to November 21, 2012. Not tough enough for you? The **fastest time to run a marathon and ultramarathon on each continent** is 1 year 217 days, by Andrei Rosu (Romania, *inset*) from July 31, 2010 to March 4, 2012.

First London Marathon
Regarded by many as the world's premier marathon, the London Marathon was first staged on March 29, 1981.

The **first New York Marathon** took place on September 13, 1970 in Central Park. A total of 126 men and one woman started the race. The men's event was won by Gary Muhrcke (USA) in a time of 2 hr. 31 min. 38 sec. The female competitor did not finish.

First wheelchair marathon at the Paralympic Games
The inaugural wheelchair marathon was staged at the 1984

4
Record wins by Fearnley in the wheelchair event at the New York City Marathon.

Fastest London Wheelchair Marathon

Female: Amanda McGrory (USA) raced home in 1 hr. 46 min. 31 sec. on April 22, 2011.

Male: Australia's Kurt Fearnley completed the London Wheelchair Marathon on April 26, 2009 in 1 hr. 28 min. 57 sec.

Most marathons in a calendar year
R. L. "Larry" Macon (USA) ran a total of 157 marathons between January 1 and December 31, 2012.

Most wins of the London Wheelchair Marathon
Male: David Weir (UK) has triumphed in the London Wheelchair Marathon six times altogether, in 2002, 2006–08, and 2011–12.
Female: The women's record for most victories in the London Wheelchair Marathon is also six, achieved by Tanni Grey-Thompson (UK) in 1992, 1994, 1996, 1998, and 2001–02.

FASTEST ...

Berlin Marathon
Male: The fastest time to run the Berlin Marathon by a male athlete is 2 hr. 3 min. 38 sec., by Patrick Makau Musyoki (Kenya) on September 25, 2011. Makau's time is also the **fastest marathon ever run**—an average speed of 4 min. 42.9 sec. per mile—smashing the previous record by 21 seconds.

RUNNING LONDON
More than 36,000 runners competed in the 2013 London Marathon; just 7,747 ran in the inaugural London Marathon.

2013 VIRGIN LONDON MARATHON: NEW WORLD RECORDS

While marathon running is a serious business for elite athletes, such as those featured above, for others it is a great excuse to have some fun—and where better to have it than at the world's premier marathon event: the London Marathon? Pictured below are some of the colorful characters who took part this year, listed in order of their times.

Carrying an 80-lb. pack
Roscoe Nash (UK)
5 hr. 58 min. 58 sec.

Longest scarf knitted while running a marathon
Susie Hewer (UK)
6 ft. 8.7 in. (2.05 m)
5 hr. 54 min. 23 sec.

Dribbling a soccer ball
Alan Simeoni (UK)
5 hr. 10 min. 46 sec.

Shoe
Lucie Barney (UK)
4 hr. 40 min. 56 sec.

Internal organ (female)
Katherine Stephens (UK), as a brain
4 hr. 28 min. 36 sec.

Mascot (female)
Wendy Shaw (UK), as Alfie, Guide Dogs mascot
4 hr. 2 min. 56 sec.

Doctor (female)
Fiona Jenkinson (UK)
3 hr. 59 min. 15 sec.

Internal organ (male)
Alan Blair (UK), as a heart
3 hr. 48 min. 34 sec.

Nurse's uniform (female)
Emma Blair (UK)
3 hr. 48 min. 34 sec.

Military dress (male)
Olivier Hamar (France), as Napoleon
3 hr. 47 min. 14 sec.

Full-body animal costume (male)
Bruce Moore (UK), as a gorilla
3 hr. 31 min. 36 sec.

Largest women's marathon

The Nagoya Women's Marathon 2013, which was held in Nagoya, Aichi, Japan, on March 10, had a record 14,554 participants—an increase on the 13,114 runners who took part in 2012. The 2013 winner was Ryoko Kizaki (Japan) in a time of 2 hr. 23 min. 34 sec.—17 seconds ahead of runner-up Berhane Dibaba's (Ethiopia) time of 2 hr. 23 min. 51 sec.

Female: Mizuki Noguchi (Japan) is the fastest woman to run the Berlin Marathon, setting a time of 2 hr. 19 min. 12 sec. on September 25, 2005.

Chicago Marathon
Male: Samuel Kamau Wanjiru (Kenya, 1986–2011) completed the Chicago Marathon in 2 hr. 5 min. 41 sec. on October 11, 2009. Seven months earlier, on April 26, he ran the **fastest London Marathon (male)**, in 2 hr. 5 min. 10 sec.
Female: On October 13, 2002, Paula Radcliffe (UK) ran the Chicago Marathon in a world record time of 2 hr. 17 min. 18 sec. She went on to break the record for the **fastest London Marathon by a female**—which was also the **fastest marathon ever run by a female**—finishing in a time of 2 hr. 15 min. 25 sec. on April 13, 2003.

New York Marathon
Male: The fastest time to complete the New York Marathon by a male is 2 hr. 5 min. 6 sec., by Geoffery Mutai (Kenya) on November 6, 2011.
Female: Kenya's Margaret Okayo completed the New York Marathon in 2 hr. 22 min. 31 sec. on November 2, 2003.

Wheelchair marathon (T52)
Thomas Geierspichler (Austria) won gold in the men's T52-class marathon (no lower limb function) in 1 hr. 40 min. 7 sec. in Beijing, China, on September 17, 2008.

Wheelchair marathon (T54)
Male: Heinz Frei (Switzerland) won the men's T54 marathon (for racers with spinal cord injuries) in a time of 1 hr. 20 min. 14 sec. in Ōita, Japan, on October 31, 1999.

Female: Wakako Tsuchida (Japan) set a time of 1 hr. 38 min. 32 sec. in Ōita, Japan, on November 11, 2001.

Marathon run backward
In a record-breaking feat of reverse athleticism, China's Xu Zhenjun completed the Beijing International Marathon in China by running backward in 3 hr. 43 min. 39 sec. on October 17, 2004.

Marathon by a linked team
Tied together at the waist with elastic cords, runners Les Newell, Aaron Burgess, Darrell Bellinger, Chris Bedford, and Julian

First Athletics World Championships marathon clean sweep

Kenya won all three medals at the Athletics World Championships in Daegu, South Korea, on August 27, 2011—a first for either the men's or women's marathon event. Pictured from left to right are: Priscah Jeptoo (silver); Edna Kiplagat (gold); Sharon Cherop (bronze).

Fastest T12 marathon

Alberto Suárez Laso (Spain, *above center*) won the T12 (visual impairment) men's marathon in 2 hr. 24 min. 50 sec. at the Paralympic Games in London, UK, on September 9, 2012.

Richardson (all UK) crossed the line at the Abingdon Marathon in Abingdon, Oxfordshire, UK, on October 21, 2012 in a time of 2 hr. 57 min. 7 sec. The team ranged from 28 to 48 years old and raised nearly £2,000 ($3,200) for Mates 'n' Dates, a local charity for adults with learning disabilities.

Marathon barefoot
On September 10, 1960, Abebe Bikila (Ethiopia) ran the marathon at the Olympics in Rome, Italy, barefoot, in a time of 2 hr. 15 min. 16.2 sec. Bikila ran without shoes because the sponsor, Adidas, could not find him a pair that fitted comfortably. Luckily, the Ethiopian—who was a member of the Imperial Bodyguard—had trained barefoot and so decided to compete in the same manner.

Martial arts suit (female)
Victoria Carter (UK)
3 hr. 30 min. 14 sec.

Carrying a 40-lb. pack
Mike Ellicock (UK)
3 hr. 25 min. 21 sec.

Wetsuit
David Ross (UK)
3 hr. 25 min. 0 sec.

Insect (female)
Laura Bartlett (UK), as a bee
3 hr. 24 min. 10 sec.

Astronaut
Subhashis Basu (UK)
3 hr. 19 min. 37 sec.

School uniform (female)
Sophie Wood (UK)
3 hr. 14 min. 34 sec.

School uniform (male)
Sam Hull (UK)
3 hr. 2 min. 53 sec.

Lifeguard
Carl Smith (UK)
3 hr. 0 min. 1 sec.

Business suit (male)
Joe Elliot (UK)
2 hr. 58 min. 3 sec.

Sailor
Stephen Richardson (UK)
2 hr. 52 min. 32 sec.

Nurse's uniform (male)
Michael Harris (UK)
2 hr. 48 min. 24 sec.

Movie character costume (male)
David Stone (UK), as Captain Jack Sparrow
2 hr. 42 min. 52 sec.

MOTORSPORTS

IN REVIEW German legend Michael Schumacher took his final checkered flag at the 2012 Brazilian Grand Prix, ending the most successful Formula One career ever.

The Dakar Rally goes from strength to strength in its alternative home in South America. French team Stéphane Peterhansel and Jean-Paul Cottret still dominate the Car category, while the Bike, Truck, and Quad categories have all delivered thrilling races. In the World Rally Championship, Sébastien Loeb is now pedal to the metal for a 10th consecutive title.

In NASCAR, Brad Keselowski claimed the Sprint Cup for the first time, winning five races. Elsewhere, Audi scored another 24 Hours of Le Mans victory, but still has some way to go to match Porsche's record in this event.

Most fastest laps in a career
Between August 25, 1991 and July 22, 2012, F1 legend Michael Schumacher (Germany) recorded 77 fastest laps.

Most wins in a season by a rookie
Two drivers have won four F1 races in their debut season, most recently Lewis Hamilton (UK) in 2007. Jacques Villeneuve (Canada) set the same record in 1996.

Most points in a season
Sebastian Vettel (Germany, *below*) secured 392 points in the 2011 season.

POLE POSITION
Pictured is the Action Express Racing Porsche crossing the finish line to win the Grand-Am Rolex 24 at Daytona in January 2010.

Most wins at the 24 Hours of Daytona race by a manufacturer
Porsche (Germany) won the 24 Hours of Daytona race 22 times between 1968 and 2010, with 11 consecutive wins in 1977–87.

FORMULA ONE (F1)

Most consecutive Grand Prix wins
Alberto Ascari (Italy) won the last six races of the 1952 season and the first race of the 1953 season for Ferrari (Italy). Michael Schumacher (Germany, *see opposite page*) also secured seven consecutive wins in the 2004 season, again in a Ferrari.

Fastest speed in a Grand Prix
Juan Pablo Montoya (Colombia) reached a speed of 231.5 mph (372.6 km/h) in a McLaren-Mercedes at Monza in the Italian Grand Prix on September 4, 2005. Montoya began the race in pole position and led from start to finish.

Youngest F1 champion
Sebastian Vettel (Germany, b. July 3, 1987) won the Abu Dhabi Grand Prix in the UAE on November 14, 2010 at the age of 23 years 134 days. In 2007, aged 19 years 349 days, he became the **youngest driver to claim an F1 point**, and in 2008 the **youngest to win an F1 race**, aged 21 years 72 days.

Most points without a race win
Driving for Prost, Sauber, Jordan, Williams, BMW Sauber, and Renault between 2000 and 2011, Nick Heidfeld (Germany) picked up 259 points without winning a single Grand Prix race.

ISLE OF MAN TT

Most wins in a year
The greatest number of events won in a single year at the Isle of Man TT (Tourist Trophy) is five, by Ian Hutchinson (UK) in 2010. His record-breaking victories came in the Senior, Superbike, Superstock, and Supersport 1 and 2 events.

These five wins also give Hutchinson the record for the **most consecutive wins at the Isle of Man TT**.

Fastest TT Senior lap
Riding a Honda CBR1000RR in the TT Senior class, John McGuinness (UK) completed one lap in a time of 17 min. 12.30 sec., in 2009.

The **fastest lap in the TT Superbike class** is 17 min. 12.83 sec. by Conor Cummins (UK) on a Kawasaki ZX-10R in 2010.

In 2012, riding a MotoCzysz E1PC, Michael Rutter (UK) recorded the **fastest lap in the electric-powered TT Zero class**, with a time of 21 min. 45.33 sec.

The **fastest ever lap by a woman** at the 37.73-mile (60.75-km) Isle of Man TT is 18 min. 52.42 sec., at an average speed of 119.94 mph (193.03 km/h), by Jenny Tinmouth (UK) on June 11, 2010.

80
Usual pit lane speed limit in mph for Formula One cars.

Fastest F1 pit stop
Infinity Red Bull Racing (Austria) carried out a 2.05-second pit stop for Mark Webber's car in the Malaysian Grand Prix at Sepang International Circuit, Sepang, Malaysia, on March 24, 2013.

(341.92 km/h), by Greg Anderson (USA) at Concord, North Carolina, USA, on March 27, 2010.

The **fastest speed in Pro Stock motorcycle drag racing** is 197.65 mph (318.08 km/h), by Michael Phillips (USA) at Baton Rouge in Louisiana, USA, on July 18, 2010. The **fastest speed by a Top Fuel drag racer** is 337.58 mph (543.16 km/h), by Anthony Schumacher (USA) in Brainerd, Minnesota, USA, on August 13, 2005.

Most WRC race wins

Sébastien Loeb (France) won 78 individual World Rally Championship (WRC) races, driving for the Citroën World Rally Team, between 2002 and May 4, 2013.

Most Top Fuel championships

Joe Amato (USA) won five NHRA Top Fuel championships, in 1984, 1988, and 1990–92.

68
The **most F1 pole positions in a career**, a record still held by Michael Schumacher.

NASCAR

Most races won in a season

There are four major races in the National Association for Stock Car Auto Racing (NASCAR) series: Daytona 500 (first held 1959), Winston 500 (first held in 1970), Coca-Cola 600 (first held 1960), and Southern 500 (first held 1950). The most race wins is three, by Dave Pearson in 1976, Bill Elliott in 1985, and Jeff Gordon in 1997 (all USA). In 1969, LeeRoy Yarbrough (USA) won the three races contested that year.

Most consecutive race wins

Richard Petty (USA) recorded 10 victories in a row in 1967.

Eight drivers have achieved four wins, the **most consecutive race wins in the modern era** (since 1972). The most recent of these is Jimmie Johnson (USA) in 2007.

Most consecutive championships won

Jimmie Johnson and Cale Yarborough (both USA) have won three consecutive NASCAR Cup championships. Johnson won his third straight title in 2008; Yarborough accomplished the same feat between 1976 and 1978.

Youngest race winner

Joey Logano (USA, b. May 24, 1990) was 19 years 35 days old when he won the Lenox Industrial Tools 301 at New Hampshire Motor Speedway, USA, on June 28, 2009.

NHRA (NATIONAL HOT ROD ASSOCIATION)

Fastest speed in Pro Stock (Car) NHRA drag racing

The highest terminal velocity for a gasoline-driven, piston-engine car (Pro Stock) is 212.46 mph

MOST CHAMPIONSHIP WINS

Formula One		
Most World Drivers' Championships (first awarded in 1950)	7	Michael Schumacher (Germany) in 1994–95 and 2000–04
	5	Juan Manuel Fangio (Argentina) in 1951 and 1954–57
	4	Alain Prost (France) in 1985–86, 1989, and 1993
Most World Constructors' Championships (first awarded in 1958)	16	Ferrari (Italy) in 1961, 1964, 1975–77, 1979, 1982–83, 1999–2004, and 2007–08
	9	Williams (UK) in 1980–81, 1986–87, 1992–94, and 1996–97
	8	McLaren (UK) in 1974, 1984–85, 1988–91, and 1998
NASCAR (National Association for Stock Car Auto Racing)		
Most Sprint Cup Series Drivers' Championships (first awarded in 1949)	7	Richard Petty (USA) in 1964, 1967, 1971–72, 1974–75, and 1979
		Dale Earnhardt, Sr (USA) in 1980, 1986–87, 1990–91, and 1993–94
	5	Jimmie Johnson (USA) in 2006–10
	4	Jeff Gordon (USA) in 1995, 1997–98, and 2001
Rallying		
Most World Rally Championships (first awarded in 1977)	9	Sébastien Loeb (France) in 2004–12
	4	Juha Kankkunen (Finland) in 1986–87, 1991, and 1993
		Tommi Mäkinen (Finland) in 1996–99
	2	Walter Röhrl (Germany) in 1980 and 1982
		Miki Biasion (Italy) in 1988–89
		Carlos Sainz (Spain) in 1990 and 1992
		Marcus Grönholm (Finland) in 2000 and 2002

Statistics correct as of March 18, 2013

Most points by an F1 driver

Between August 25, 1991 and November 25, 2012, Michael Schumacher (Germany) racked up 1,566 points in his Formula One career. His 91 Grand Prix victories between 1992 and 2006 represent the **most F1 Grand Prix wins by a driver**. He also retains the record for **most wins in a season by a driver**, with 13 victories in 2004.

Most Dakar Rally quad bike wins by a manufacturer

Yamaha (Japan) supplied the winning machine in all five stagings of the Dakar Rally ATV/quad bike event, from its institution in 2009 to 2013.

WINNING WAYS
Here, Alejandro Patronelli (Argentina) drives his Yamaha Raptor 700 to victory in the 2012 Dakar Rally in Chile.

RACKET SPORTS

IN REVIEW A golden age of men's singles tennis shows no sign of ending. Contests between Roger Federer, Rafael Nadal, Novak Djokovic, and now Andy Murray often rank in the list of greatest matches of all time. In women's tennis, Serena Williams continues to forge one of the greatest careers the sport has seen, completing the Golden Grand Slam in both singles and doubles when she won the London 2012 Olympic singles. Not only that, she cruised to the gold medal, beating Maria Sharapova by a record margin.

Malaysia's Nicol David won an incredible seventh squash World Open title, while China continued its dominance in badminton and table tennis with another gold rush at London 2012.

SQUASH

Most European Team Squash Championships
Between 1978 and 2012, England's men won 37 European Team Championships. Their most recent win was a 3–0 victory over France on May 5, 2012. England achieved the double in 2012, with the women's team beating Ireland 2–1 and upping their record for the **most wins of the European Women's Team Squash Championships** to 34 (since 1973).

Largest squash racket
The Qatar Squash Federation unveiled a racket 22 ft. 3 in. (6.80 m) long and 7 ft. (2.15 m) wide in Doha, Qatar, on December 7, 2012.

Most Olympic table tennis golds (men)

Ma Lin (China), the International Table Tennis Federation (ITTF) No. 6, took Olympic gold on three occasions: in the 2004 men's doubles and the men's singles and team categories in 2008. He was part of the 2012 China team that won the Swaythling Cup for the 18th time—the **most wins of the World Table Tennis Championships by a team (male)**, beating Germany 3–0 in the final.

Longest squash marathon
Guy Fotherby and Darren Withey (both UK) played a singles match lasting 31 hr. 35 min. 34 sec. at Racquets Fitness Centre in Thame, Oxfordshire, UK, on January 13–14, 2012.

The **most consecutive opponents in squash singles** was 69 by Ian Charles (UK) at the David Lloyd club in Cardiff, UK, on May 7–8, 2011. Ian required 31 hr. 55 min. to challenge all 69 opponents.

Most badminton World Team Championships won (female)

China has won the Uber Cup (instituted 1956) on 12 occasions (1984, 1986, 1988, 1990, 1992, 1998, 2000, 2002, 2004, 2006, 2008, and 2012). Shown here is Wang Xin in the 2012 Uber Cup final in Wuhan, Hubei Province, China.

BADMINTON

First badminton player to retain an Olympic singles title (male)
Lin Dan (China)—winner of the **most World Championships men's singles titles** with four—became the first man to win back-to-back badminton singles titles at the Olympic Games when he defeated Lee Chong Wei (Malaysia) 15–21, 21–10, 21–19 at Wembley Arena, London, UK, on August 5, 2012.

Most Olympic badminton medals won by a country

China took eight medals (five gold, two silver, one bronze) at London 2012, winning all possible gold medals over both male and female events. Since badminton joined the Olympics in 1992, China has won an unprecedented total of 38 medals.

Most Olympic badminton medals won

The most medals won by an individual player is four, by Gao Ling (China). She won mixed doubles gold in 2000 and 2004, women's doubles bronze in 2000, and women's doubles silver in 2004.

TENNIS

Fewest games lost in a women's singles Olympic tennis final
In the most one-sided women's singles Olympic tennis final ever, Serena Williams (USA) lost only one game against Maria Sharapova (Russia). Williams won the gold medal at Wimbledon, UK, on August 4, 2012, 6–0, 6–1.

In 2012, Williams made history again with the **first singles and doubles Golden Grand Slam**, completing one of tennis' greatest-ever achievements when she won the women's singles at the Olympics in London, UK. She became the first tennis player, male or female, to complete both singles and doubles career Golden Slams—winning all four major tournaments plus the Olympic gold in both disciplines. (*See right for more tennis.*)

World squash titles

Nicol David (Malaysia) has achieved the **most consecutive women's World Championships** (four), the **most Women's Squash Association (WSA) Player of the Year awards** (six), and the **most Women's World Open titles** (seven).

14
Lin's age when he joined the Chinese national table tennis team.

RACKET SPORTS WORLD CHAMPIONS

Tennis		
Most men's ATP* titles won indoors	53	Jimmy Connors (USA) in 1972–89
Most men's ATP titles won outdoors	56	Guillermo Vilas (Argentina) in 1973–83 and Roger Federer (Switzerland) in 2002–12
Table tennis		
Most men's World Team Cup wins	6	China in 1991, 1994, 2007, 2009, 2010, and 2011
Most women's World Team Cup wins	7	China in 1990–91, 1995, 2007, and 2009–11
Badminton		
Most World Championship titles overall	5	Park Joo-bong (South Korea): men's doubles, 1985 and 1991, and mixed doubles, 1985, 1989, and 1991
Squash		
Most World Open wins	8	Jansher Khan (Pakistan) in 1987, 1989–90, 1992–96

Statistics correct as of the end of the 2012 season   **ATP = Association of Tennis Professionals*

First golden set in a tennis Grand Slam

When a player wins a set without conceding a point, it is known as a "golden set." Yaroslava Shvedova (Kazakhstan) was the first person to complete a golden set in a Grand Slam, in her Wimbledon match against Sara Errani (Italy) on June 30, 2012. The unseeded Kazakh won 24 consecutive points in the first set of her third-round match against 10th seed and 2012 French Open runner-up Errani, hitting 14 winners in the process. Shvedova won 6–0, 6–4, but

was beaten by the championship's eventual winner, Serena Williams (USA), in the next round.

Fastest serve

Samuel Groth (Australia)—ranked No. 189 in the world—served a 163.4-mph (263-km/h) ace in Busan, South Korea, on May 9, 2012 during a match against Uladzimir Ignatik of Belarus.

The **fastest serve at Wimbledon** in London, UK, was achieved on June 23, 2010, when Taylor Dent (USA) delivered a "bullet" at 148 mph (238 km/h).

Highest total attendance at the Australian Open

The Australian Open tennis championships saw a total attendance of 686,006 at Melbourne Park, Australia, from January 16 to 29, 2012. This tournament marked the 100th staging of the men's singles championship.

First tennis player to win three successive Australian Open titles

Novak Djokovic (Serbia)—the ATP world No. 1—secured his third successive Australian Open title when he beat Andy Murray (UK) 6–7, 7–6, 6–3, 6–2 in the final at Melbourne Park, Melbourne, Australia, on January 27, 2013.

Wheelchair tennis wins

Dutch player Esther Vergeer won a record-breaking four Paralympic gold medals—one each at the 2000, 2004, 2008, and 2012 Games. The prolific Vergeer, who announced her retirement in February 2013, also holds the records for **most consecutive women's wheelchair singles matches won** (470) and **most wins of the wheelchair World Championships** (10).

Oldest female tennis world No. 1

The oldest female tennis player ranked No. 1 by the Association of Tennis Professionals (ATP) is Serena Williams (USA, b. September 26, 1981), who became the highest seeded women's player on February 18, 2013 at the age of 31 years 145 days. As of March 18, 2013, Serena also holds the female record for the **highest earnings in a tennis career** (*see below*).

MOST OLYMPIC WINS

Superstar tennis sisters Serena and Venus Williams (both USA) have each won four Olympic tennis titles, sharing the record for **most Olympic gold medals**. The sisters also share the record for **most Olympic tennis doubles titles** with Reginald Doherty (UK, 1872–1910). Each of them has won three times.

SMASH AND GRAB

Serena—who has spent 19 years on tour—is the only female athlete to have earned more than $35 million in prize money.

RUGBY

IN REVIEW A new international rugby union contest kicked off in 2012 as Argentina joined Tri-Nations teams New Zealand, Australia, and South Africa to form The Rugby Championship. New Zealand won the inaugural title, but underdogs Argentina pulled off a fantastic 16–16 draw against South Africa.

In the Six Nations, Ireland's Ronan O'Gara, who announced his retirement on May 18, 2013, extended his points-scoring record, while teammate Brian O'Driscoll became the leading try scorer in Five and Six Nations. In Sevens, New Zealand continued to dominate the International Rugby Board (IRB) World Series with a 10th title. In the women's game, England won an eighth Six Nations in 2012, and Ireland surprised many in 2013 with their first ever title.

Rugby league records tumbled, too, as England won another European Cup in 2012, making it 12 in total. In the English domestic game, Leeds Rhinos' Danny McGuire scored his 200th Super League try, becoming the league's all-time top try scorer.

UNION

Highest attendance for an international match
A total of 109,874 spectators saw New Zealand defeat Australia 39–35 at Stadium Australia in Sydney on July 15, 2000.

Highest score
On November 17, 1973, in a Danish rugby union match, Comet beat Lindo 194–0. The **highest score in an international rugby union match** saw Hong Kong beat Singapore 164–13 in a World Cup qualifying match in Kuala Lumpur, Malaysia, on October 27, 1994.

177 Points scored by New Zealand in the first Rugby Championship tournament.

Most Rugby Championship matches won
During the inaugural staging of the Rugby Championship in 2012, New Zealand won all six of their matches, beating Australia, South Africa, and Argentina both home and away. Pictured above, New Zealand's Liam Messam wins a line-out ball in the match against the Springboks at FNB Stadium in Johannesburg, South Africa, on October 6, 2012.

Most World Cup wins
Three teams have each won the Rugby World Cup twice: New Zealand (1987 and 2011), Australia (1991 and 1999), and South Africa (1995 and 2007). The **most Women's Rugby World Cup titles** is four, by New Zealand in 1998, 2002, 2006, and 2010.

Most consecutive Tri-Nations wins
The greatest number of successive wins of the Rugby Union Tri-Nations (The Rugby Championship since 2012) is four, by New Zealand between 2005 and 2008.

Most wins of the IRB Player of the Year award
Richie McCaw (New Zealand, *above*) has won the International Rugby Board (IRB) Player of the Year award on three occasions, in 2006, 2009, and 2010.

The **most wins of the IRB Coach of the Year award** is five by Graham Henry (New Zealand) in 2005–06, 2008, and 2010–11.

Most wins of the Home/Five/Six Nations Championships
England and Wales have each recorded 26 outright wins of the Rugby Union Six Nations Championship (previously the Home Nations and Five Nations). Wales won most recently in 2013, matching England's record.

Most wins by a team in the Six Nations Championship
England and France jointly hold the record for the most wins by a team, with 47 apiece between 2000 and 2013. France have recorded 1,798 points and 175 tries, and England have scored 1,923 points and 200 tries.

Most conversions in an international career
As of May 16, 2013, Dan Carter (New Zealand) had kicked 245 conversions in 94 matches for the All Blacks.

Highest margin of victory in a Heineken Cup final
Leinster (Ireland) beat Ulster (UK) 42–14 at Twickenham, UK, on May 19, 2012; the 28-point margin of victory is the largest in rugby union Heineken Cup finals history. The match was watched by 81,774 spectators: the **largest attendance for a rugby union Heineken Cup final**.

Most drop goals in an international career
Jonny Wilkinson (UK) scored 36 drop goals from 97 matches for England and the British and Irish Lions from 1998 to 2011. Jonny has also kicked the **most penalties in an international rugby union career**, with 255 goals in his 97 matches from 1998 to 2011.

Wilkinson is the **leading scorer in World Cup matches**, with 277 points in 19 games from 1999 to 2011. His tally comprises 1 try, 28 conversions, 58 penalties, and 14 drop goals.

Finally, as of December 4, 2012, Wilkinson had made the **most career conversions in the Five/Six Nations Championships**, with 89 from 43 matches between April 4, 1998 and March 13, 2011.

Most tries scored in a Super League career
The greatest number of tries scored by a player in rugby league Super League matches is 205 by Danny McGuire (UK) for Leeds Rhinos between 2002 and April 19, 2013. His senior debut for the Rhinos came on July 6, 2001, against the Salford City Reds.

CAPPED CAPTAIN

O'Driscoll captained Ireland and the British and Irish Lions 84 times from 2002 to 2012, the **most international caps won as captain.**

Most tries in a Five/Six Nations Championship career

The greatest number of tries scored by an individual player in a Five/Six Nations career is 26 by Brian O'Driscoll (Ireland) in matches played between February 5, 2000 and March 16, 2013.

Most IRB Sevens World Series titles

The International Rugby Board (IRB) Sevens World Series, which began in 1999, has been won 10 times by New Zealand, in 2000–05, 2007–08, and 2011–12.

The **most tries by a player in IRB Sevens tournaments** is 230 by Santiago Gómez Cora (Argentina) from 1999 to 2009.

LEAGUE

Highest attendance

A crowd of 107,558 saw the National Rugby League Grand Final at Stadium Australia in Sydney, New South Wales, Australia, on September 26, 1999, when Melbourne defeated St. George Illawarra 20–18.

MOST GRAND SLAMS

Two teams have each won three Six Nations Championship Grand Slams. France were the winners in 2002, 2004, and 2010; Wales were victorious in 2005, 2008, and 2012. Pictured above, Welsh captain Sam Warburton celebrates his team's 16–9 victory over France at the Millennium Stadium in Cardiff, UK, on March 17, 2012.

Highest score

Ngāti Pikiao of Rotorua beat Tokoroa United 148–0 in a Bay of Plenty rugby league under-17s league match at Pikiao, New Zealand, on July 10, 1994.

The **highest score in an international rugby league match** is France's 120–0 defeat of Serbia and Montenegro during the Mediterranean Cup in Beirut, Lebanon, on October 22, 2003.

Most Challenge Cup wins

Wigan have won the rugby league Challenge Cup 18 times, in 1924, 1929, 1948, 1951, 1958–59, 1965, 1985, 1988–95, 2002, and 2011.

Most Super League titles

Leeds Rhinos have won six rugby league Super League titles, in 2004, 2007–09, and 2011–12.

MOST INTERNATIONAL ...		
Rugby union		
Caps	139	George Gregan (Australia), 1994–2007
Points	1,342	Dan Carter (New Zealand), 2003–present
Tries	69	Daisuke Ohata (Japan), 1996–2006
Rugby league		
Caps	59	Darren Lockyer (Australia), 1998–2011
Points	278	Mal Meninga (Australia), 1982–94
Tries	41	Mick Sullivan (UK), 1954–63

Statistics correct as of April 17, 2013

Most Four Nations wins

The rugby league Four Nations competition (inaugurated in 2009) involves Australia, New Zealand, and England, plus one invited nation. Australia have won the competition twice, beating England both times in 2009 and 2011.

Most consecutive State of Origin matches played

Australians Johnathan Thurston (*pictured*) and Greg Larson each played 24 consecutive State of Origin rugby league matches for Queensland. Larson's matches were in 1991–98; Thurston's came in 2005–12.

Most State of Origin series wins

The State of Origin series has been played annually between Queensland and New South Wales since 1982. Queensland won 17 series between 1982 and 2012, while New South Wales won 12 times. Two series—1999 and 2002—were drawn. In both cases, the holder was Queensland, and they retained the trophy. Queensland have won the last seven contests, from 2006 to 2012.

FACT:

Ronan O'Gara (*below left*) was born in San Diego, California, USA, in 1977 but moved to Cork in Ireland at a young age. He won his first international cap in 2000.

Most appearances in a Six Nations career

Ronan O'Gara (Ireland) has racked up a host of rugby union records in the Six Nations Championship since 2000. Ronan has the record for the most match appearances by a player in a Six Nations career, with 63 between February 19, 2000 and February 24, 2013. His points tally of 557 represents the **most points scored by a player in a Six Nations career**, in matches between February 19, 2000 and March 16, 2013. O'Gara has also scored the **most penalties by a player in a Six Nations career**, with 109 penalties between February 19, 2000 and February 10, 2013.

CLUB SOCCER

IN REVIEW Lionel Messi is rewriting the record books at Barcelona, itself one of the greatest clubs in the world with 22 domestic La Liga titles since 1929. In January 2013, the skilled striker won a record fourth consecutive Ballon d'Or award, heading a 1-2-3 for Spanish club soccer with Real Madrid's Cristiano Ronaldo in second and Messi's Barcelona team-mate Andrés Iniesta in third. The award recognized Messi's incredible total of 91 goals in 2012—79 of which were scored for Barcelona at a ratio of more than one goal per game.

Not to be outdone, two Manchester United veterans set records in longevity and excellence. Sir Alex Ferguson—who retired in May 2013—drove the Red Devils to win more league titles than any club in the history of the English game, while Ryan Giggs plays on at the highest level into his 40s.

CHAMPIONS LEAGUE

Most goals (individual)
Two players have each scored 14 times in a UEFA Champions League (formerly European Cup) season. The first player to do so was José Altafini (Brazil) while playing for AC Milan during the 1962–63 season. This was equaled by Lionel Messi (Argentina) for Barcelona in the 2011–12 season.

Most Champions League games managed

Sir Alex Ferguson (UK) oversaw his 190th Champions League game as manager of Manchester United when his team played against Real Madrid in a 2012–13 UEFA Champions League tie on March 5, 2013.

Most valuable soccer club
According to money magazine *Forbes*, Manchester United (UK) had a market capitalization of $2.2 billion as of April 2012.

The team also enjoyed the **longest unbeaten run in the UEFA Champions League**. Between September 19, 2007 and May 5, 2009, they played 25 matches without losing.

Most goals in one La Liga season
In the 2011–12 season, Lionel Messi (Argentina) scored 50 goals for Barcelona in 37 games. He is also the **first player to have scored more than one hat-trick in a Champions League season**. His first came against Viktoria Plzeň on November 1, 2011, the second against Bayer Leverkusen on March 7, 2012.

Most consecutive Premier League appearances

The greatest number of consecutive Premier League appearances is 310, by Brad Friedel (USA) for Blackburn Rovers, Aston Villa, and Tottenham Hotspur between August 14, 2004 and September 29, 2012.

Most goals by a goalkeeper
Rogério Ceni (Brazil) scored 93 goals for São Paulo FC from 1997 to 2010. Ceni regularly takes free kicks and penalties for the club.

Most goals scored in European club competitions
Raúl González Blanco (Spain) scored 76 times for Real Madrid and Schalke 04 in the Champions

League, Super Cup, and Europa Cup from 1995–96 to the end of the 2011–12 season. From 1997–98 to the end of the 2010–11 season Raúl also scored at least one goal for 14 seasons in a row—the **most consecutive Champions League seasons scored in**.

Largest tournament
Held in Mexico from January 2 to December 11, 2011, Copa Telmex 2011 featured 181,909 players and 10,799 teams. The **largest soccer tournament (female)** was Copa Telmex 2012, contested by 27,768 players and 1,542 teams.

Most clubs played for
Zlatan Ibrahimović (Sweden) has played—and scored—for six clubs in the Champions League: Ajax, Juventus, Inter Milan, Barcelona, AC Milan, and Paris Saint-Germain, from 2002 to 2012 (*see opposite*).

Most times hosting the Champions League final
Wembley Stadium in London, UK, has hosted the final of European soccer's top club competition seven times, in 1963, 1968, 1971, 1978, 1992, 2011, and 2013.

Fastest hattrick
Bafétimbi Gomis (France) scored a hattrick in seven minutes for Olympique Lyonnais vs. Dinamo Zagreb at Stadion Maksimir in Croatia on December 7, 2011.

First player to appear in every Premier League season

Uniquely, Manchester United's Ryan Giggs (UK) has played in all 21 seasons of the Premier League since it began in 1992–93. He is also the **first—and only—player to score in every Premier League season**, with 109 goals as of February 28, 2013.

NATIONAL SOCCER LEAGUES: MOST WINS OF THE...

Division		
Scottish top division (Football League, 1890–91 to 1997–98; Premier League, 1998–99 to present)	54	Rangers
Egyptian Premier League	36	Al Ahly
Argentinian Primera División	34	River Plate
Portugese top division (Primeira Liga, 1934–35 to 1937–38 and 1999–2000 to present; Primeira Divisão, 1938–39 to 1998–99)	32	Benfica
Spanish Primera División aka **La Liga**	32	Real Madrid
Dutch top division (Netherlands Football League Championship, 1888–89 to 1955–56; Eredivisie 1956–present)	32	Ajax
Italian Serie A	27	Juventus
German Bundesliga	22	Bayern Munich
English top division (Football League, 1888–89 to 1891–92; Football League First Division, 1892–93 to 1991–92; Premier League, 1992–93 to present)	20	Manchester United
Japanese J League Division 1	7	Kashima Antlers

Figures correct as of May 20, 2013

Most Bundesliga goals by a foreign player

Claudio Pizarro (Peru) scored 160 goals for Werder Bremen and Bayern Munich in Germany's Bundesliga in 1999–2012.

Most hattricks

Alan Shearer (UK) scored 11 hattricks in his career playing for Blackburn Rovers and Newcastle United from 1992 to 2006.

Most goals in a debut season

In the 1999–2000 season, Kevin Phillips (UK) scored 30 goals for Sunderland. It was Phillips' third season playing for The Black Cats but his first for them as a Premier League side.

PREMIER LEAGUE

Most titles by a manager

Sir Alex Ferguson (*see left*) has won 13 Premier League titles as manager of Manchester United, in 1992–93, 1993–94, 1995–96, 1996–97, 1998–99, 1999–2000, 2000–01, 2002–03, 2006–07, 2007–08, 2008–09, 2010–11, and 2012–13.

Ferguson has managed Manchester United for every one of the 21 seasons that the league has been in existence—an achievement that also makes him the **longest-serving Premier League manager**.

Most seasons as top scorer

Playing for Arsenal between 1999 and 2007, Thierry Henry (France) was the Premier League's top scorer for a record four seasons. He scored 21 goals in 2001–02, 30 in 2003–04, and 25 in both 2004–05 and 2005–06.

Most goals in La Liga by a foreign player

Hugo Sánchez (Mexico, *left*) scored a still-unmatched 234 goals in the Spanish La Liga playing for Atlético Madrid, Real Madrid, and Rayo Vallecano from 1981 to 1994.

Most Premier League goals by a foreign player

Thierry Henry (France) scored 175 goals for Arsenal. He scored 174 of these during his eight seasons with the team (1999–2007), and one goal while on loan to them in 2012.

Most goals in a match

Four players have netted five goals in a Premier League game: Andy Cole (UK) for Manchester United vs. Ipswich at Old Trafford in Manchester, UK, on March 4, 1995; Alan Shearer (UK) for Newcastle United vs. Sheffield Wednesday at St. James's Park in Newcastle, UK, on September 19, 1999; Jermain Defoe (UK) for Tottenham Hotspur vs. Wigan Athletic at White Hart Lane in London, UK, on November 22, 2009; and Dimitar Berbatov (Bulgaria) for Manchester United vs. Blackburn Rovers at Old Trafford on November 27, 2010.

Most clean sheets

Keeper David James (UK) played 170 games without conceding a goal playing for Liverpool, Aston Villa, West Ham, Manchester City, and Portsmouth from August 16, 1992 to March 1, 2010.

261
Goals Ibrahimović has scored for club and country as of March 2013.

Highest combined fees

As of March 2013, Zlatan Ibrahimović (Sweden) has cost $173.4 million in transfer fees. His moves were: Malmo to Ajax (July 2001); Ajax to Juventus (August 2004); Juventus to Inter Milan (August 2006); Inter Milan to Barcelona (July 2009); Barcelona to AC Milan (August 2010); and AC Milan to Paris Saint-Germain (July 2012). He is shown here in the strips of his last six teams, in order, from Ajax (*far left*) to Paris Saint-Germain (*far right*).

INTERNATIONAL SOCCER

IN REVIEW The Spanish national team is now regarded as one of the greatest sides ever, and they've got the records to prove it. Their ultimate goal will be to retain the FIFA World Cup in Brazil in 2014, a feat no team has achieved since 1962, and the host nation—among other contenders—stand in their way.

Egyptian skipper Ahmed Hassan became the most capped player in international football history when he made his 184th appearance, surpassing the mark of Saudi Arabia's Mohamed Al-Deayea. It's no coincidence that Hassan's incredible career has run alongside his nation's recent Africa Cup of Nations victories. Hassan has played in eight tournaments, winning four—a phenomenal strike rate.

Finally, all eyes turn to Brazil for the 20th World Cup. On home soil, can Brazil win an unprecedented sixth title?

Between 2006 and 2010, Egypt went unbeaten for a string of 18 matches, the **longest unbeaten run in the Africa Cup of Nations**.

Most goals

Samuel Eto'o (Cameroon) scored 18 goals for Cameroon in Africa Cup of Nations tournaments between 1996 and 2010.

The **most goals scored in a single Africa Cup of Nations tournament** is nine, by Ndaye Mulamba for Zaire (now the Democratic Republic of the Congo) from March 3 to 14, 1974 in Egypt.

Most goals in a women's Olympic tournament

Christine Sinclair (Canada) scored six goals at London 2012, from July 25 to August 9, 2012.

The **most goals by a national team in a women's Olympic soccer tournament** is 16 by the USA, also at London 2012.

COPA AMÉRICA

Oldest international soccer competition

The South American Championship (Copa América since 1975) is organized by the South American Football Confederation, CONMEBOL. It was first held in Argentina in 1916.

The **most wins of the Copa América** is 15 by Uruguay, from 1916 to 2011. "La Celeste", as they are known defeated Paraguay 3–0 in the final at Estadio Monumental in Buenos Aires, Argentina, on July 24, 2011.

Most goals scored

Two soccer players have each scored 17 goals in Copa América tournaments: Norberto Méndez (Argentina) between 1945 and 1956, and Zizinho (Brazil) between 1941 and 1953.

Most wins at the European Championships

Germany (West Germany 1960–88) won 23 matches at the Union of European Football Associations (UEFA) European Championships between 1960 and 2012; they won the overall event three times, in 1972, 1980, and 1996—the **most wins of the UEFA Championships**.

Fastest Olympic soccer goal

Oribe Peralta (Mexico) scored the fastest goal in Olympic men's soccer competition—and, indeed, any FIFA tournament finals—when he scored after just 28 seconds against Brazil at Wembley Stadium, London, UK, on August 11, 2012.

Fastest hattrick in international soccer

Japanese international Masashi "Gon" Nakayama scored a hattrick in 3 min. 15 sec. against Brunei during an Asian Cup qualifying match on February 16, 2000.

AFRICA CUP OF NATIONS

Most wins

Egypt has won the Africa Cup of Nations seven times: in 1957, 1959, 1986, 1998, 2006, 2008, and 2010.

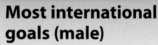

Most international goals (male)

Ali Daei (Iran) scored 109 goals from 1993 to 2006. However, the absolute record for the **most career international goals scored (male or female)** is 158, by Mia Hamm (USA) from 1987 to 2004.

Longest career as a FIFA referee

Sarkis Demirdjian (Lebanon) remained an official Fédération Internationale de Football Association (FIFA) referee for 20 years 10 months, from September 1962 to July 1983.

Longest unbeaten run in international soccer

Brazil went unbeaten for 35 games (December 16, 1993–January 18, 1996), a feat later matched by Spain (October 11, 2006–June 20, 2009).

Most penalties missed by a player in an international soccer game

Martín Palermo (Argentina) missed three penalties during his team's defeat by Colombia in the 1999 Copa América in Paraguay on July 4.

Most international caps

Midfielder/winger Ahmed Hassan made an unprecedented 184 international appearances for Egypt's national team between December 29, 1995 and June 1, 2012.

Youngest player at the Euro finals

Jetro Willems (Netherlands, b. March 30, 1994) played for his country against Denmark, at the age of 18 years 71 days, in the UEFA European Championships match at Metalist Stadium in Kharkiv, Ukraine, on June 9, 2012.

GOAL! With his first goal for PSV Eindhoven against NEC Nijmegen on April 22, 2012, Willems became the youngest scorer in the Eredivisie, the top Dutch league.

3
FIFA World Cups that Casillas has played in (2002, 2006 and 2010).

The **oldest goalscorer in a UEFA European Championships** is Ivica Vastić (Austria), who was at the age of 38 years 256 days when he scored a penalty for Austria vs. Poland at Ernst-Happel-Stadion in Vienna, Austria, on June 12, 2008.

Most international clean sheets

The most international matches in which a goalkeeper has not conceded a goal is 82, by Iker Casillas, for current World and European champions Spain, between 2000 and 2012.

FIFA WOMEN'S WORLD CUP

Most wins
The German female national team won its second FIFA World Cup at the 2007 tournament in Shanghai, China; they had also won in 2003. Their achievement equals that of the USA, winners in 1991 and 1999.

Most appearances
Kristine Lilly (USA), Bente Nordby (Norway), Miraildes Maciel Mota "Formiga" (Brazil), Birgit Prinz (Germany), and Homare Sawa (Japan) have each appeared five times at Women's World Cups.

Greatest winning margin in a Euro final

With goals from David Silva (*above right*), Jordi Alba, Fernando Torres, and Juan Mata, Spain beat Italy 4–0 in the final of the European Championships at the Olympic Stadium in Kiev, Ukraine, on July 1, 2012.

UEFA EUROPEAN CHAMPIONSHIPS

Most matches played
As of 2012, Germany (aka West Germany, 1960–88) have played a record 43 matches at the European Championships.

Fastest goal
Dmitri Kirichenko (Russia) scored 1 min. 7 sec. after the start of the Greece vs. Russia match in the group stages of the UEFA European Championships at the Estádio do Algarve in Faro-Loulé, Portugal, on June 20, 2004.

Most goals in a tournament
Michel Platini (France) scored nine goals in the European Championship finals in France from June 12 to 27, 1984.

FACT:
Brazil has made the **most appearances at the FIFA World Cup finals**, being the only team to have qualified for all 19 tournaments since the very first one in 1930.

Highest attendance
Held jointly in Poland and Ukraine from June 8 to July 1, 2012, Euro 2012 attracted 1,440,896 fans.

Youngest goalscorer
Johan Vonlanthen (b. 1 February 1986) was 18 years 141 days old when he scored for Switzerland vs. France in Coimbra, Portugal, on June 21, 2004.

FIFA WORLD CUP

Individual		Holder	Location	Date(s)
Fastest goal	11 seconds	Hakan Şükür, for Turkey vs. South Korea	Daegu, South Korea	June 29, 2002
Most goals	15	Ronaldo (Brazil)	France (four)	1998
			Japan and South Korea (eight)	2002
			Germany (three)	2006
First hattrick	USA vs. Paraguay	Bert Patenaude (USA)	Estadio Gran Parque Central, Montevideo, Uruguay	July 17, 1930
Most hattricks	2	Sándor Kocsis (Hungary)	Switzerland	1954
		Just Fontaine (France)	Sweden	1958
		Gerd Müller (West Germany)	Mexico	1970
		Gabriel Batistuta (Argentina)	USA	1994
			France	1998

Team		Holder	Location	Date(s)
Longest time with a clean sheet	559 minutes	Switzerland	Various	1994–2010 (seven World Cup matches)
Most consecutive wins	11	Brazil	Japan/South Korea and Germany	From June 3, 2002 (2–1 win vs. Turkey) to June 27, 2006 (3–0 win vs. Ghana)
Most goals in one tournament	27	Hungary	Switzerland	1954
Most goals overall	210	Brazil	Various	1930–2010

Most goals by one player
Germany's Birgit Prinz has scored 14 goals in FIFA Women's World Cup matches. Her last goal was against Brazil in the final at the Hongkou Stadium in Shanghai, China, on September 30, 2007.

Latest goal in a final
Homare Sawa scored in the 117th minute of Japan's victory over the USA at the 2011 FIFA Women's World Cup in Frankfurt, Germany. The extra-time goal tied the match at 2–2, with Japan triumphing 3–1 on penalties to capture the nation's first World Cup.

Most FIFA World Cup wins

Brazil has won the World Cup five times: 1958, 1962, 1970, 1994, and 2002 (*pictured*). Brazil's game against Uruguay on July 16, 1950, at the Maracanã Stadium in Rio de Janeiro, Brazil, drew 199,854 fans—the **largest crowd at a World Cup match**.

WATER SPORTS

IN REVIEW In swimming, Ryan Lochte (USA) is the man to beat in the 100-m and 200-m short-course medley events after setting records at the World Championships in Turkey. His USA team had a great 2012 Olympics, too, topping the swimming medal table with 16 golds from 31 in total.

The daredevil sport of cliff diving continues to be dominated by England's Gary Hunt, who won his third consecutive World Series title. The event has only been staged three times, so this makes him the only man to have won it to date.

In sailing, Sir Ben Ainslie won an unparalleled fifth gold medal at the Olympics, collected another World Sailor of the Year accolade, and is all set to head up a British challenge for the America's Cup.

Fastest ILSF 100-m rescue medley

The fastest International Life Saving Federation (ILSF) 100-m rescue medley is 1 min. 11.23 sec., by Samantha Lee (Australia) in Adelaide, Australia, on November 8, 2012. Competitors swim 50-m freestyle, then turn, dive, and swim underwater to a submerged manikin located at 20 m (men) and 15 m (women) below the surface. The competitor surfaces the manikin within the 5-m pickup line and then carries it the remaining distance to the edge of the pool.

Fastest short-course 100-m medley

Ryan Lochte (USA) swam the 100-m individual medley in 50.71 seconds on December 15, 2012, at the FINA World Championships in Istanbul, Turkey. At the same event, he also swam the **fastest 200-m medley**, finishing in 1 min. 49.63 sec.

Most wins of the Red Bull Cliff Diving World Series

Gary Hunt (UK) won the Cliff Diving World Series on three consecutive occasions between 2010 and 2012. The Series was inaugurated in 2010. He was also the **first diver to execute a running takeoff in a cliff-diving competition**, launching into four front-pike somersaults with two-and-a-half twists during the inaugural World Series event at Polignano a Mare in Italy on August 8, 2010.

SWIMMING

Most consecutive Olympic swimming golds in one event

Male: Michael Phelps (USA) won the 200-m individual medley at London 2012 to become the first man to win three consecutive Olympic gold medals in a single swimming event. Phelps is the **most decorated Olympian of all time**, winning 22 medals (18 gold, two silver and two bronze) at Athens 2004, Beijing 2008 and London 2012.
Female: Two women share this record: Dawn Fraser (Australia) in the 100-m freestyle in 1956–64 and Krisztina Egerszegi (Hungary) in the 200-m backstroke in 1988–96.

Most Olympic swimming medals won (female)

Three women have won 12 Olympic swimming medals: Dara Torres (USA) won four each of gold, silver, and bronze in 1984–2008; Jenny Thompson (USA) won eight gold, three silver, and one bronze in 1992–2004; and Natalie Coughlin (USA) won three gold, four silver, and five bronze medals in 2004–12.

Free diving—variable weight (female)

On June 6, 2012, Natalia Molchanova (Russia) recorded the deepest free dive by a woman with a depth of 416 ft. 8 in. (127 m) in Sharm el-Sheikh, Egypt. Another free-dive record set in 2012 was the **deepest constant-weight dive**: Alexey Molchanov (Russia) dived to 413 ft. 5 in. (126 m) in The Bahamas on November 20, 2012.

DIVING

Most Olympic diving medals won

Male: Dmitri Sautin (Russia) won eight Olympic diving medals: two gold, two silver, and four bronze between 1992 and 2008. The year before his first Olympic appearance, Sautin was stabbed multiple times in a street fight but recovered in time to win a bronze at Barcelona 1992.
Female: Two Chinese divers share this record with six medals: Guo Jingjing (2000–08) and Wu Minxia (2004–12).

Most FINA Diving World Series 10 m platform wins

Male: Qui Bo (China) has won gold in the World Series 10-m platform event three times (2009–11).
Female: Chen Ruolin (China) has won four 10-m golds (2007–12).

Most wins of the Diving World Series 3-m springboard

Male: Qin Kai (China) won the FINA Diving World Series men's 3-m springboard event four times, in 2007 and 2009–11.
Female: He Zi (China) won the World Series women's 3-m springboard title four times, in 2009–12.

Most consecutive Olympic gold medals in one event (absolute)

Male: The most successive gold medal wins in Olympic history is six by Aladár Gerevich (Hungary), who was a member of the winning sabre fencing team in 1932–60.

1 The USA women's water polo team world ranking as of March 19, 2013.

Most women's Water Polo World League wins

The USA have won seven out of nine FINA Water Polo World League contests, securing victories in 2004, 2006–07, and 2009–12. The League has been contested every year since 2004, with Greece winning in 2005 and Russia in 2008.

WATER SPORTS RECORDS SET AT THE LONDON 2012 OLYMPICS

Swimming		
1,500-m freestyle long-course (male)	14:31.02	Sun Yang (China)
100-m breaststroke (male)	58.46	Cameron van der Burgh (South Africa)
200-m backstroke (female)	2:04.06	Melissa "Missy" Franklin (USA)
200-m breaststroke (female)	2:19.59	Rebecca Soni (USA)
100-m butterfly (female)	55.98	Dana Vollmer (USA)
400-m individual medley (female)	4:28.43	Ye Shiwen (China)
4 x 100-m medley relay (female)	3:52.05	USA (Franklin, Soni, Vollmer, Allison Schmitt)
Water polo		
Most points scored (male, team)	21	Serbia vs. Great Britain (21–7); shared with Russia (September 27, 2000)
Rowing		
Fastest coxless pairs (male)	6:08.50	Eric Murray and Hamish Bond (New Zealand)
Most double sculls medals won	3	Slovenia (Luka Špik and Iztok Čop, 2000–12)

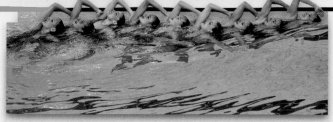

SPORTS

www.guinnessworldrecords.com

GUINNESS
WORLD
RECORDS
2014

Most Synchronized Swimming World Trophy wins by a team

Spain have clocked up the most wins of the Synchronized Swimming World Trophy by a national team with three in total in 2008, 2010, and 2011. The FINA-organized World Trophy has been contested annually since 2006.

Female: Diver Wu Minxia (China) became only the sixth female Olympian in history to win a gold medal in the same individual event at three consecutive Olympic Games when she won the synchronized 3-m springboard event in 2012. The other five women to achieve this are: gymnast Larisa Latynina (Soviet Union, now Russia), team event, 1956–64; swimmer Dawn Fraser (Australia), 100-m freestyle, 1956–64; swimmer Krisztina Egerszegi (Hungary), 200-m backstroke, 1988–96; equestrian Anky van Grunsven (Netherlands), individual dressage, 2000–08; and fencer Valentina Vezzali (Italy), foil, 2000–08.

SYNCHRONIZED SWIMMING

Most synchronized swimming Olympic golds won

Individual: Anastasia Davydova (Russia) has won five Olympic gold medals in synchronized swimming. She secured titles in the duet competition at Athens 2004 and Beijing 2008 and the team event at Athens 2004, Beijing 2008, and London 2012. Her most recent success was as a member of the nine-woman Russian team who won gold at the Aquatics Centre, London, UK, on August 10, 2012.

Team: Russia won eight Olympic gold medals in synchronized swimming between 2000 and 2012—a clean sweep of every duets and team event in that period. At the 2012 Games in London, UK, Natalia Ishchenko and Svetlana Romashina picked up gold medals in the duets competition, and the pair were part of the nine-woman team who claimed Olympic gold in the team event on August 10, 2012.

Fastest row coxed eights

At the World Rowing Cup in Lucerne, Switzerland, on May 25, 2012, two records were set. The USA women's coxed eights—Esther Lofgren, Zsuzsanna Francia, Jamie Redman, Amanda Polk, Meghan Musnicki, Taylor Ritzel, Caroline Lind, Caryn Davies, and cox Mary Whipple (*above*)—recorded a time of 5 min. 54.17 sec., and the Canadian men's coxed eights—Gabriel Bergen, Douglas Csima, Rob Gibson, Conlin McCabe, Malcolm Howard, Andrew Byrnes, Jeremiah Brown, Will Crothers, and cox Brian Price—set a time of 5 min. 19.35 sec.

OLYMPIC SAILING

Sailing has featured in the Olympics since the very first Games in 1896 but the 1896 races were canceled due to bad weather.

Most ISAF World Sailor of the Year awards

The most wins of the International Sailing Federation (ISAF) World Sailor of the Year award (male category) is four by Ben Ainslie (UK), in 1998, 2002, 2008, and 2012. Ben also holds the prestigious record for the **most Olympic gold medals in sailing**, winning four gold medals at four successive Olympic Games from 2000 to 2012.

FACT:

Divers receive a score of 0–10 for each dive. Judges take into account starting position, takeoff, flight, and entry. A score of 0 is deemed "completely failed" and 10 is "excellent."

Youngest medalist at a FINA Diving World Cup

Tom Daley (UK, b. May 21, 1994) is the youngest medalist at a FINA Diving World Cup. He was 13 years 277 days old when he won bronze in the 10-m synchro competition in Beijing, China, on February 22, 2008.

SPEED SAILING

Fastest 500-m outright

Male: Paul Larsen (Australia) covered 500 m in 14.85 seconds—a record speed of 65.45 knots (75.32 mph; 121.21 km/h)—in the *Vestas Sailrocket 2* hydrofoil in Walvis Bay, Namibia, on November 24, 2012.

Female: The fastest speed reached by a woman under sail on water by any craft over a 500-m timed run was set by windsurfer Zara Davis (UK), who achieved 45.83 knots (52.74 mph; 84.87 km/h)—using a Mistral 41 board and Simmer Sail 5.5 SCR—in Lüderitz, Namibia, on November 17, 2012.

FOR MORE SAILING ACHIEVEMENTS, TURN TO P. 72

WINTER SPORTS

298.8
Distance in feet (243.5 m) of Gregor's personal best, achieved in Norway in 2011.

IN REVIEW US skier Lindsey Vonn dominated in the mountains, recording the best-ever season's performance in 2012. In 2013, she won her sixth consecutive downhill title and is now just one title behind Austrian legend Annemarie Moser-Pröll (1971–75; 1978–79).

On the ice, Scotland won its fourth European Mixed Curling Championships, while Canada's women added to their World Championships wins. In the skeleton, Latvia's Martins Dukurs won a fourth title, while Elena Nikitina (Russia) dominated the women's event at the European Championships. Speed skaters Lee Sang-hwa and Christine Nesbitt set records in 500 m and 1,000 m respectively. Michel Mulder and Heather Richardson posted record points in their sprints.

SLEDDING

Most wins of the Bobsled World Championships
Germany has logged a record 20 wins in the two-man bobsled World Championships. (For the women's record, see opposite page.)

Most bobsled Olympic gold medals won (country)
Germany has won 16 Olympic bobsled gold medals. The most recent win was by Kevin Kuske and André Lange in the two-man event in Vancouver, Canada, in 2010. Both men now hold the record for the **most bobsled Olympic golds** with four apiece.

Most ski jumping World Cup victories in a season

Gregor Schlierenzauer (Austria) secured a record 13 individual World Cup competition victories (out of 27 events) in the 2008–09 season. This equates to 2,083 points, the **most points scored in a single ski jumping World Cup season**.

Fastest Cresta Run
The Cresta Run in St. Moritz, Switzerland, is a 3,977-ft.-long (1,212-m) ice run with a drop of 514 ft. (157 m). Racers hurtle down the track head-first on toboggans, just a couple of inches above the ground. The fastest time recorded in competition is 50.09 seconds (54.13 mph; 87.11 km/h) by James Sunley (UK) on February 13, 1999.

161
Podium places achieved by Vonn in her career to date.

SKATING

Fewest points for speed skating long track sprint combination
Male: Michel Mulder (Netherlands) scored 136.790 points in the long track sprint combination event—over 500/1,000/500/1,000 m—at Salt Lake City, USA, on January 26–27, 2013.
Female: Heather Richardson (USA) scored 147.735 points in the combination at Calgary, Canada, on January 19–20, 2013.

Most wins of the snowmobiling International 500
The International 500—aka the "I-500"—is staged at Sault Ste. Marie in Michigan, USA, and is the largest and longest snowmobile race in the world. Corey Davidson (USA) is the sport's pre-eminent figure, having won a record seven times between 1998 and 2011.

During the 1996 race, a temperature of -31°F (-35°C) was recorded, making it the **coldest International 500** ever staged.

Most points in a women's World Cup skiing season

Lindsey Vonn (USA) scored 1,980 points in the 2011/12 World Cup skiing season. She also holds the record for the **most consecutive women's downhill skiing World Cup titles**. In 2013, she won a record sixth consecutive downhill title to surpass the achievement of Annemarie Moser-Pröll (Austria), who won five straight titles (1971–75).

Fastest women's 1,000 m skating

On January 28, 2012, Canadian speed skater Christine Nesbitt completed a 1,000-m race at Calgary's Olympic Oval in Canada in 1 min. 12.68 sec., shaving 0.43 seconds off the previous record. With Kristina Groves and Brittany Schussler, Nesbitt also shares the record for the **fastest women's team pursuit**, with a time of 2 min. 55.79 sec. on December 6, 2009, also set in Calgary.

WINTER OLYMPICS MEDAL WINNERS

Men				
Most medals	12	Bjørn Dæhlie (Norway)	Cross-country skiing	1992–98
Most gold medals	8	Bjørn Dæhlie (Norway)	Cross-country skiing	1992–98
Most gold medals at one Games	5	Eric Heiden (USA)	Speed skating	1980
Most individual medals	9	Bjørn Dæhlie (Norway)	Cross-country skiing	1992–98
Women				
Most medals	10	Raisa Smetanina (USSR/Unified)	Cross-country skiing	1976–92
Most gold medals	6	Lidiya Skoblikova (USSR)	Speed skating	1960–64
Most gold medals at one Games	4	Lidiya Skoblikova (USSR)	Speed skating	1964
Most individual medals	8	Karin Kania (GDR)	Speed skating	1980–88
		Claudia Pechstein (Germany)	Speed skating	1992–2006
		Gunda Niemann-Stirnemann (Germany)	Speed skating	1992–98

Correct as of January 2013

Most women's bobsled World Championship wins

Since a women's World Championships was introduced in 2000, Germany has won the two-women title seven times, in 2000, 2003–05, 2007–08, and 2011. Pictured are Germany's Sandra Kiriasis and Berit Wiacker in 2011.

SKIING

Most Super G World Cup race wins by an individual

Male: The most race wins of the downhill skiing Super Giant Slalom World Cup, aka Super G, is 23 by Hermann Maier (Austria) from 1996 to 2009.

Female: The most celebrated female in Super G is Lindsey Vonn (USA), with 20 race wins in 2006–13.

Oldest winner of a ski jumping World Cup competition

Takanobu Okabe (Japan, b. October 26, 1970) was 38 years 135 days old when he won at Kuopio, Finland, on March 10, 2009.

The **youngest winner of a ski jumping World Cup competition** is Steve Collins (Canada), who was 15 years 362 days old when he won at Lahti, also in Finland, on March 9, 1980.

Longest ski jump

Male: The longest competitive ski jump by a man is 808 ft. (246.5 m), by Johan Remen Evensen (Norway) at Vikersund, Norway, on February 11, 2011.

CHAIRWOMAN OF THE BOARD
Karine was hailed as the greatest ever female snowboarder before her tragically early death on Mont Blanc in 2009.

Most snowboarding World Cup wins

Female: The most World Cup wins is 20, by Karine Ruby (France, *above*, 1978–2009), between 1995 and 2004.

Male: Mathieu Bozzetto (France) won the men's World Cup six times between 1999 and 2002.

Female: The longest ski jump by a woman is 418 ft. 4 in. (127.5 m) by Anette Sagen (Norway), who achieved the distance at Oslo, Norway, on March 14, 2004.

Most successful Nordic skier

Male: In Nordic skiing, the skier's boot is not attached to the skis (unlike downhill skiing). The first Nordic World Ski Championships were those of the 1924 Winter Olympics in Chamonix, France, and the greatest number of titles won (including Olympics) is 17, by Norway's Bjørn Dæhlie.

Female: The most Nordic titles won by a woman is also 17, by Yelena Välbe (Russia), with 10 individual and seven relay wins from 1989 to 1998. With an additional seven silver and bronze medals, her total of 24 is also a record.

Fastest 5 km barefoot on ice

On February 12, 2012, Kai Martin (Germany) completed a 3.1-mile-long (5-km) barefoot race held on a deep-frozen prepared snow track at the Van der Valk Alpincenter ski resort in Wittenburg, Germany, in a winning time of 23 min. 42.16 sec.

Fastest 500 m long track speed skating

Male: In long track skating, competitors race in pairs but against the clock (short track is raced in larger groups). Jeremy Wotherspoon (Canada) clocked a time of 34.03 seconds in the 500 m at Salt Lake City, Utah, USA, on November 9, 2007.

Female: On January 20, 2013, at Calgary in Canada, Lee Sang-hwa (South Korea) completed 500 m in a time of 36.80 seconds.

Fastest 500 m short track speed skating

Male: John Robert "J. R." Celski (USA) recorded a time of 39.937 seconds in Calgary, Alberta, Canada, on October 21, 2012.

Female: Meng Wang (China) completed the distance in 42.60 seconds in Beijing, China, on November 29, 2008.

Most consecutive wins of the bobsled skeleton

Male: Martins Dukurs (Latvia, *pictured*) won his fourth consecutive skeleton (face-down toboggan) World Cup in 2013.

Female: Alex Coomber (UK, née Hamilton) won the women's skeleton World Cup a record three times—consecutively—from 2000 to 2002.

Most World Curling Championship titles won (country)

Canada has won the World Curling Championships more times than any other nation. The men's team won a record 34 times (1959–2012), while the women have notched up 15 wins (1980–2008). Pictured is Canada's Wayne Middaugh at the 2012 event.

FOR PIONEERS ON ICE, TURN TO P. 76

SPORTS ROUNDUP

IN REVIEW As our packed sports section draws to a close, we have set aside these pages to bring you the best of the rest. These are the competitors who weren't in sports with their own features in this year's book but who have nevertheless turned in outstanding performances in their chosen arena. Many 2012 records—such as almost all weightlifting feats—have come from the Olympic Games in London, but there are plenty of other sports from all over the world to highlight, from kabaddi to darts by way of snooker and archery.

Most career ranking titles won in snooker

In a professional snooker career that began in 1985 at the age of just 16, Stephen Hendry (UK, b. January 13, 1969) won 36 ranking titles, including seven World Championships and five UK Championships. On April 29, 1990, he became the **youngest professional snooker world champion** at the age of just 21 years 106 days.

Among his many other achievements, Hendry went on to set the **most century breaks in a professional career** (775), the **longest unbeaten run** in competition (36 games from March 17, 1990 to January 3, 1991), and the **most competitive 147 breaks** (11, a total matched by Ronnie O'Sullivan, UK). His retirement came on May 1, 2012, following a 13–2 defeat to Stephen Maguire (UK) at the World Championship in Sheffield, UK.

Longest Olympic gold-winning run by a country

Two countries have won golds in an Olympic discipline at eight consecutive summer Games. The USA won the men's 4 x 100 m medley relay in the pool from 1984 to 2012 inclusive, and male Kenyan runners won the 3,000 m steeplechase in the same time frame.

Fastest 100 km barefoot

Wayne Botha (New Zealand) ran 100 km (62.14 miles) in 11 hr. 14 min. 3 sec. on October 6, 2012 at the 15th Annual Sri Chinmoy 24-Hour race in Auckland, New Zealand.

Trap shooting

The trap is named after the devices that launch clay targets. Shooters do not know which of three traps will release next and they are allowed to take only two shots at each target.

Male: The maximum score is 125 and has been hit nine times, most recently by Giovanni Pellielo (Italy) in Al Ain, United Arab Emirates, on April 18, 2013.

Female: Jessica Rossi (Italy) scored 99 out of a possible 100 to win gold at London 2012 on August 4.

ISSF shooting, 10 m air rifle standing (SH1)

Male: Chao Dong (China) scored 596 points at the Paralympic Games in London, UK, on August 31, 2012. He equaled the record achieved by Jonas Jakobsson (Sweden) at the Paralympic Games in Beijing, China, on September 8, 2008. SH1 shooters can support the weight of their firearm.

Female: Im-Yeon Kim (South Korea) scored 399 points in Seoul, South Korea, on July 6, 2002.

Most participants at a summer Paralympics

The London 2012 Paralympic Games saw 4,200 athletes from 166 countries competing in 503 medal events in 20 different sports. Among them was British swimmer Ellie Simmonds, who recorded the **fastest 200 m individual medley (SM6)** on September 3, 2012, in a time of 3 min. 5.39 sec.—almost 9 seconds clear of her nearest rival.

Most Olympic shooting gold medals won (female)

Kim Rhode (USA) won her third Olympic shooting gold medal at London 2012 in the skeet on July 29. In doing so, she equaled the **most Olympic shooting medals won (female)**, with five, between 1996 and 2012—a feat first achieved by Marina Logvinenko (Russia), who won five medals, including two golds, between 1988 and 1996.

Most points in women's individual compound archery

On August 11, 2010, Danielle Brown (UK) scored a record 697 points in Vichy, France, in the women's individual compound archery. Competing in the Open class in September 2012, Danielle successfully defended her Paralympic gold, beating UK teammate Mel Clarke in the final. In 2013 her achievements were recognized with an MBE for services to archery. In her home town of Skipton, Yorkshire, UK, the Post Office honored her with a mailbox painted gold.

5
Total number of 17-year-olds who have qualified for the World Championship.

Youngest snooker player to qualify for the WPBSA World Championship

Luca Brecel (Belgium, b. March 8, 1995) was 17 years 38 days old when he qualified for the 2012 World Professional Billiards and Snooker Association (WPBSA) World Championship at the Crucible Theatre in Sheffield, UK. Brecel broke the record held by Stephen Hendry (*see left*), who was almost two months older when he qualified for his Crucible debut in 1986.

Most Olympic shooting medals won (male)

Carl Townsend Osburn (USA) recorded 11 shooting medals in the Games of 1912, 1920, and 1924. His tally comprised of five gold, four silver and two bronze medals.

Youngest Olympic weightlifting gold medalist (female)

Zulfiya Chinshanlo (Kazakhstan, b. July 25, 1993) was 19 years 4 days old when she won gold at the London 2012 Olympic Games with a snatch of 95 kg and a 131-kg clean and jerk for a total of 226 kg in the women's 53 kg category (*see below*) on July 29. The 117-lb. (53.07-kg) Chinshanlo lifted two-and-a-half times her own bodyweight.

LONGEST DOUBLES DARTS MARATHON

Dave Abbott (*pictured*), Gary Collins, Mark Collins, and Stephen Morrison (all UK) played darts for 38 hr. 2 min. at the Capel St. Mary Village Club near Ipswich, Suffolk, UK, on May 25–26, 2012. The group scored seven maximum 180s during their marathon session.

Most points scored in individual recurve archery (ST)

Male: Timur Tuchinov (Russia) scored 659 points in London, UK, on May 4, 2012. Archers in this Paralympic event are classed as standing (ST), as opposed to the W1 and W2 classes who compete in a seated position.
Female: Fangxia Gao (China) holds the women's record. She scored 641 points in Guangzhou, China, on December 13, 2010.

Most men's kabaddi World Cup wins

Kabaddi is a popular South Asian contact sport in which two teams take turns to send a "raider" to

FOR THE RECORD

Olympic Games history wasn't only made in competition. London 2012 also recorded the **highest bill**, at £8.4 billion ($13.01 billion); **most drugs tests**, with 5,000; **most expensive pint of beer** (£7.23; $11.20); **heaviest gold medals**, at 14.53 oz. (412 g); **first time all participating nations sent female athletes**; **first time male and female athletes competed in each sport** (26 sports; 204 nations); **largest global audience for a Paralympics**, with an estimated 4 billion.

Heaviest weightlifting 94 kg total (male)

Ilya Ilyin (Kazakhstan) lifted a combined score of 418 kg (233 kg clean and jerk, 185 kg snatch) in the 94 kg division in London, UK, on August 4, 2012 to retain his Olympic gold. With the 233-kg weight, he also set the record for the **heaviest weightlifting 94 kg clean and jerk (male)**.

THIN ICE
The "short program" is the first of two parts in figure skating, and is the more technical of the two. The second program is known as free skating.

Highest score in a figure skating short program (men)

Patrick Chan (Canada) scored 98.37 points on March 13 at the 2013 World Figure Skating Championships in London, Ontario, Canada. He broke his own record of 93.02 points set on April 27, 2011.

the other's area, tag players, and return without being wrestled to the ground. Kabaddi originated in India, and it is the Indian men's team who have won all three World Cups since its institution in 2010, through to 2012.

Most Asian Games kabaddi wins (male)

The Indian men's team have recorded the most wins at the Asian Games with six, in 1990, 1994, 1998, 2002, 2006, and 2010.

RECENT WEIGHTLIFTING MILESTONES

Category	Weight	Name & Nationality	Date	Location
Male				
62 kg snatch	153 kg	Kim Un Guk (North Korea)—equaled Shi Zhiyong's (China) 2002 record	Jul 30, 2012	London, UK
62 kg total	327 kg	Kim Un Guk (North Korea)	Jul 30, 2012	London, UK
77 kg snatch	175 kg	Lu Xiaojun (China)	Aug 1, 2012	London, UK
77 kg total	379 kg	Lu Xiaojun (China)	Aug 1, 2012	London, UK
94 kg clean & jerk	233 kg	Ilya Ilyin (Kazakhstan)	Aug 4, 2012	London, UK
94 kg total	418 kg	Ilya Ilyin (Kazakhstan)	Aug 4, 2012	London, UK
Female				
53 kg clean & jerk	131 kg	Zulfiya Chinshanlo (Kazakhstan)	Jul 29, 2012	London, UK
75+ kg snatch	151 kg	Tatiana Kashirina (Russia)	Aug 5, 2012	London, UK
75+ kg clean & jerk	188 kg	Meng Suping (China)	Nov 9, 2012	Eilat, Israel
75+ kg total	333 kg	Zhou Lulu (China)	Aug 5, 2012	London, UK

Statistics correct as of May 16, 2013

406
Total kilograms lifted by Ilya in Beijing, China, in 2008 for his first Olympic gold.

FOR MORE MACHO MEN, SEE P. 102

ACKNOWLEDGMENTS

Guinness World Records would like to thank the following for their help in compiling this edition:

Patrick Abrahart; Across the Pond (Julie, Rob, Aaron, Esther, Karen, Reese, James, Tom, Beki, Laura, Nicola); Carmen Maria Alfonzo Portillo; Asatsu-DK Inc. (Motonori Iwasaki, Shinsuke Sakuma, Keiichiro Misumi); Ash Inc.; James (Masha) Ashdown; Charlotte Atkins; Eric Atkins; Freya Atkins; Simon Atkins; Base79 (Richard, Lucy, Ashley, Jana, Jamie); Dr George Beccaloni, Natural History Museum; Oliver Beatson; Clark Bernat, Manager, Niagara Falls Museums, Canada; Bender Helper Impact (Mark Karges, Crystal McCoy, Eric Zuerndorfer, Jerry Griffin); Jack Bennetts; Anisa Bhatti; Christopher Bingham; Michelle A Blackley, Communications Manager, Niagara Tourism and Convention Corporation, USA; Blue Peter; Luke and Joseph Boatfield; Alfie Boulton-Fay; Chiara Bragato; Patrick Bragato; Donald J Brightsmith; British Sumo Association (Steve Pateman); Bucks Consultants; Marcus Butler; C Squared; Hayley Jane Campbell; Caroline Carr; Charlie Carter Steel; Rob Cave; CBBC (Joe, Cheryl, Kez); CCTV (Li Xing, Wang Qiao); Camille Chambers; Clara Chambers; Georgina Charles; Louise Chisholm; Finn Chisholm; Dr Phibul Choompolpaisal; Scott Christie; The Chunichi Shimbun (Tadao Sawada); Dr L Stephen Coles, Gerontology Research Group; Mark Collins; Colo; Comic Relief; Paul Conneally, International Telecommunication Union; Connection Cars (Rob and Tracey Dunkerley); Juan Cornejo, PhD; Jeff Cowton, The Wordsworth Trust; Dr Kate Crosby; Charlie Crowe; Fred Dahlinger, Jr; Adam "Maldini" Davidson; Ceri Davies; Deft Productions (Sophie Davidson); Denmaur Independent Papers Limited (Julian Townsend); Heather Dennis; Alfie Deyes; Mildred Dimery; Discover Dogs; Emlyn Dodd; East London Gymnastics (Jamie Atkinson); Dave Eaton; Europroduzione/Veralia (Marco, Renato, Carlo); Amelia Ewen; Toby Ewen; Eyeworks Germany (Michael, Guido, Kaethe, Martin); Helen Fair, Research Associate, International Centre for Prison Studies; Benjamin Fall; Rebecca Fall; The Fells (Tim, Sue, Simon, Joanna, Becca); Daniel Fernandez; FJT Logistics Limited (Ray Harper, Gavin Hennessy); James Fleetham; Esteve Font Canadell; Formulation Inc. (Sakura, Marcus); Denice Fredriksson (The Vegetable Orchestra); Sarah Freiermuth, The Coral Reef Alliance; Sue Frith, Society of Ploughmen; Frontier International (Satoru Kanda); Justin Garvanovic, European Coaster Club; Arjun Gautam; Rhea Gautam; Yash-Raj Gautam; Jack Geary; Gerontology Research Group; Gerosa Group; Reece Gibbs; Ferran Gil; Damien Gildea; Prof Stephen Gill; Mike Gilmore; Annabelle Ginger; Ryan and Brandon Greenwood; Victoria Grimsell; Markus Gusset, PhD, World Association of Zoos and Aquariums; Gym Media International (Eckhard Herholz); Christian Hamel; Hampshire Sports and Prestige Cars (Richard Johnston); Jamie Hannaford, National River Flow Archive, Centre for Ecology & Hydrology; Sophie Alexia Hannah Alfonzo; Harlem Globetrotters International, Inc. (Brett Meister); Ruby Hayes; Claire Haywood; Dr Haze, Circus of Horrors; Bob Headland; Mark Heaton, Rapido3D; Matilda Heaton; High Noon Entertainment (Jim, Rachel, Stephen, Burt, Paul, Brent, Lauren); The Himalayan Database; Marsha Hoover; Hoovercat; Cheryl Howe; Oliver Howe; Colin Hughes; ICM (Michael and Greg); IMG (John, Alex, Anna, Lisa); Image Science & Analysis Laboratory, NASA Johnson Space Center; Integrated Colour Editions Europe (Roger Hawkins, Susie Hawkins, Clare Merryfield); Margaret Johnson, Nezahat Gökyiğit Botanic Garden (NGBG); Res Kahraman, FMG; Alex Keeler; Tony Kirkham, Royal Botanic Gardens, Kew; Granville Kirkup; Dan Koehl; Alan Küffer, Australian Bird & Bat Banding Scheme; Martina Lacey; Tom and Noodle Langridge; Orla Langton; Thea Langton; Frederick Horace Lazell; Deborah E Legge, Researcher, Niagara Falls Museums, Canada; Lion Television (Richard, Jeremy, Simon, Dougie, Sue, Patsy); London Gymnastics (Anne McNeill); London Pet Show; London Tattoo Convention; London Toy Fair; London Wonderground; Loose Women; Sean Macaulay; Ciara Mackey; Sarah and Martin Mackey; Theresa Mackey; Esperanza Magpantay, International Telecommunication Union; Mail Online (Steven Lawrence); Christian de Marliave; Missy Matilda; Dave McAleer; Trish Medalen; Miditech India (Nivedith, Niret); Scott Mills; Tamsin Mitchell; Suzanne Moase, Curator, Niagara Falls Museums, Canada; Florence Molloy; Harriet Molloy; Joshua Molloy; Sophie Molloy; Colin Monteath; Veronica Murrey, Administrator, International Centre for Prison Studies; Stefano Musacchi, Università di Bologna; Prof Susan Naquin, Princeton University; James Ng; The Nichols Clan (James, Jennifer, Jessica, Jack); Dr Lukas Nickel; Zhu Ning (Cherry); NTV Europe (Miki Matsukawa and Chieko Otsuka); Official Charts Company; Phil Olsen; Roland J Oosterbaan (www.waterlog.info); Robert Opie, The Museum of Brands, Packaging and Advertising; Consetta Parker (Rancho Obi Wan); Finlay Paterson; Louise Paterson; Andrew Peacock; Charlotte Peacock; David Peacock; Caitlin Penny; Katharina Pesch; Steve Pitron; Joseph Postman, National Clonal Germplasm Repository; Matt Poulton; Press Association (Cherry Wilson); John Pricci (HorseRaceInsider.com); Abigail Prime; Izzy Prime; Miriam Randall; Ross Rattray; Re:fine Group; Red Bull; John Reed, World Speed Sailing Records Council; Martyn Richards; Tom Richards; Jane Robertson, Hawk Conservancy Trust; Dan "Stork" Roddick PhD, World Flying Disc Federation (WFDF); Florian Ruth; Prof Walter H Sakai; Nick Seston; Bill Sharp, Billabong XXL Global Big Wave Awards; Ang Tshering Sherpa; Samantha Shutts (and all at Columbus Zoo); Lyle Spatz (Chairman, Baseball Records Committee, Society for American Baseball Research); Spectratek Technologies, Inc. (Terry Conway, Mike Foster); Glenn Speer; Bill Spindler; Jack Steel; Daisy Steel; Lily Steel; Chelsie Stegemiller; Ray Stevenson; Stora Enso Kabel; Joe Sugg; The Sun (Lee Price and David Lowe); Prof Kathryn Sutherland; Lilah Simone Swalsky; Dale Swan, Anna Swan Museum, Creamery Square Heritage Centre; Prof Peta Tait; Charlie Taylor; Daisy Taylor; Holly Taylor; This Morning; Spencer Thrower; TNR; truTV (Marc, Darren, Angel, Stephen, Simmy, Jim, Marissa); Prof Diana Twede; Virgin (Philippa Russ); Virgin London Marathon (Nicola Okey, Tiffany Osbourne, Fran Ridler); Helmut Wahl; Charlie Wainwright; Muhammad Isa Waley, British Library; Roy Walmsley, World Prison Brief Director, International Centre for Prison Studies; Thom Walton; Richard Weigl; Susan Westermayer; Westfield shopping centre (Grace Charge, Denise Moore); Anna Wharton; Alex White; Oli White; Catherine Wieser, International Canoe Federation (ICF); Dr Dave Williams, National Space Science Data Center (NSSDC); Emily Williams (and all at Lake Roosevelt High School, Coulee Dam, Washington); Rhys Williams, British Horseracing Authority (BHA); Elizabeth Wilson, HarperCollinsPublishers; Nick Wojek; Dr Elizabeth Wood, Marine Conservation Society; Dr Frances Wood, British Library; Lydia Wood; Patricia Wood; Worcestershire Farriery Services (Matt Burrows); Rueben George Wylie-Deacon; Tobias Hugh Wylie-Deacon; Xujing Cai; YouTube (Billy, Rosie); Zippy Productions (Mitsue Matsuoka); Zodiak Kids (Karen, Delphine, Gary); Zodiak Rights (Matthew, Barnaby, Andreas).

PICTURE CREDITS

1: Paul Michael Hughes/GWR **4:** Science Photo Library **7:** Robbie Reynolds; Mark Yeoman; Owen Billcliffe **8:** Franco Russo; Matt Crossick/PA; Matt Crossick/PA; Matt Crossick/PA **9:** Simon Jones; Ken McKay; Matt Crossick/PA **6 (USA):** Mathieu Young **7 (USA):** Scott Gries/AP; Lyn Hughes/GWR; Lyn Hughes/GWR **8 (USA):** Carol Kaelson; Cindy Ord/Getty Images **6 (Canada):** James Ellerker/GWR; Michael G Manoukian **7 (Canada):** James Ellerker/GWR; James Ellerker/GWR **9 (Canada):** Paul Michael Hughes/GWR **6:** Rob Lindblade **7 (Australia):** Joe Murphy; Joe Murphy; Hector Calara **8 (Australia):** Max Fleet/NewsMail **9 (Australia):** Otago Daily Times; Mark Metcalfe/Getty Images **10:** Paul Michael Hughes/GWR **11:** Mathieu Young; Gustavo Ferrari/GWR **12:** Toru Yamanaka/Getty Images **14:** Buckminster Fuller Institute; Getty Images; David Tipling **15:** Chris McGrath/Getty Images; Getty Images; Jimin Lai/Getty Images; Jacky Naegelen/Reuters **16:** Getty Images; Getty Images; Getty Images; Getty Images; Juan Barreto/Getty Images; Getty Images; Getty Images; Getty Images; Getty Images **17:** Getty Images; Getty Images; Science Photo Library; William Foley/Getty Images; Getty Images; Getty Images; Getty Images; Getty Images **18:** Alamy; Getty Images; Getty Images; Getty Images; Getty Images; Getty Images; Getty Images **19:** Getty Images; Arlan Naeg/Getty Images; Getty Images; Getty Images; Getty Images; Jacky Naegelen/Reuters; Getty Images **20:** Christina Dicken/News-Leader; Photoshot; AP/PA; Florin Iorganda/Reuters; Getty Images; NOAA; Getty Images; Getty Images; Getty Images **21:** Photoshot; SuperStock; Mario Tama/Getty Images; Michael Appleton/Getty Images; Getty Images; Getty Images; Getty Images; Getty Images; Getty Images; Getty Images **22:** Antony Njuguna/Reuters; Getty Images; Reuters; Alamy; Getty Images; Getty Images; Bryan and Cherry Alexander **23:** Corbis; Paul Chiasson/AP/PA; NASA; Getty Images; Montana State University; Getty Images; Getty Images; David Gubler **24:** James Ellerker/GWR **28:** Getty Images; Kevin Scott Ramos/GWR; Science Photo Library; NHPA/Photoshot; Getty Images; The Reptile Zoo; Robert Valentic/Nature PL; Getty Images; Getty Images; Bristow; Getty Images **29:** Getty Images; Chime Tsetan; Rex Features; Mark Conlin/Alamy; Ho New/Reuters; Blair Hedges/Penn State; Getty Images; Getty Images; Getty Images; Mario Lutz **30:** Lawrence Lawry/Science Photo Library; Alex Wild; Dave Pinson/Robert Harding; Jeff Rotman/NaturePL; Michael Dunning/Getty Images; Francesco Tomasinelli / Natural Visions; Getty Images; Vincent C Chen; Getty Images; Andreas Viklund; Getty Images; Getty Images **31:** Ken Lucas/Ardea; NHPA/Photoshot; Mark Moffett/FLPA; Nick Gordon/Ardea; L Kimsey and M Ohl; Superstock; Dan Hershman; Getty Images; Getty Images; Getty Images **32:** Corbis; Science Photo Library; Corbis; Getty Images; Getty Images; Piotr Naskrecki/Getty Images; Getty Images; Maurizio Gigli; Geert-Jan Roebers/WNF; Brian V Brown **33:** John Abbott/NaturePL; Claus Meyer/FLPA; Photoshot; Getty Images; Getty Images; PA; The Natural History Museum, London / Natural History Museum; Renzo Mazzaro **34:** Gerard Lacz/Rex Features; Anup Shah/Getty Images; Jonathan Doster/Getty Images; Sulaiman Salikan; Getty Images; Fotolia; Getty Images; Getty Images; Getty Images **35:** Getty Images; Sergey Gorshkov/Corbis; I Shpilenok/Still Pictures; Edwin Giesbers/NaturePL; Leon Werdinger/Alamy; Dave Watts/Alamy; Getty Images; Getty Images; Getty Images; Getty Images **36:** Alamy; Rex Features; Rex Features; Dr Robert Mitchell; Getty Images; MBARI **37:** Elisa Gudrun/EHF; A & J Visage/Getty Images; Black Hills Institute; JAMSTEC; Australian Museum; Gaetan Borgonie/Ghent University **38:** Roslan Rahman/Getty Images; Graham S Jones/AP/PA; Getty Images; Justin Limoges **39:** Getty Images; Justin Limoges; Joe Maierhauser; Alamy; Alamy; John MacDougall/Getty Images **40:** James Ellerker/GWR; Tom Gannam/AP/PA; Susan Sternberg; Getty Images; Getty Images; Daniel Munoz/Reuters; Ronald Grant **41:** Roy Van Der Vegt/Rex Features; Paul Michael Hughes/GWR; Andy Anderson/K9 Storm; Si Barber/Eyevine; Getty Images; Getty Images **42:** James Ellerker/GWR; Anita Maric/SWNS; Reuters; Ronald Mackechnie/GWR **43:** AA Rabbits; Ryan Schude/GWR; Getty Images; Rex Features **44:** Paul Michael Hughes/GWR **46:** Javier Pierini/GWR; Paul Michael Hughes/GWR **47:** Paul Michael Hughes/GWR; Paul Michael Hughes/GWR; Paul Michael Hughes/GWR **48:** Rob Fraser/GWR; Paul Michael Hughes/GWR; Getty Images; Getty Images; Getty Images; Getty Images **49:** Sanjib Ghosh/GWR; Paul Michael Hughes/GWR; Getty Images; Getty Images; Getty Images; Getty Images; Getty Images; Getty Images **50:** Ryan Schude/GWR; Ronald Mackechnie/GWR; Phil Robertson/GWR; John Wright/GWR; Drew Gardner/GWR; Paul Michael Hughes/GWR; Drew Gardner/GWR **51:** Ronald Mackechnie/GWR; Ryan Schude/GWR; Paul Michael Hughes/GWR; Paul Michael Hughes/GWR; Drew Gardner/GWR; Ronald Mackechnie/GWR; Paul Michael Hughes/GWR **52:** Gustavo Ferrari/GWR; Kevin Scott Ramos/GWR; Neil Mackenzie; John Wright/GWR; **53:** Getty Images; Ryan Schude/GWR; Tim Anderson/GWR **54:** Richard Bradbury/GWR; Paul Michael Hughes/GWR **55:** Paul Michael Hughes/GWR; Paul Michael Hughes/GWR; James Ellerker/GWR **56:** Rex Features; Wellcome Images; Photoshot; Sheng Li/Reuters **57:** Splash news; Gerard Julien/Getty Images; John Phillips/Getty Images **58:** Ettore Loi/Getty Images **59:** Richard Lautens/GetStock **60:** Memoriad; Caters; Memoriad; **61:** Jens Wolf/EPA; See Li/Corbis; Memoriad; Belfast Telegraph; **62:** Paul Michael Hughes/GWR; James Ellerker/GWR; Paul Michael Hughes/GWR **63:** Richard Bradbury/GWR; Sam Christmas/GWR; Paul Michael Hughes/GWR **64:** Jacek Bednarczyk/EPA; Tony McDaniel; Paul Michael Hughes/GWR **65:** Bogdan Cristel/Reuters; Derek Fett; WENN; Paul Michael Hughes/GWR; Getty Images; Getty Images; Getty Images **66:** AP/PA **67:** Brigitte Dusseau/Getty Images **68:** Red Bull; Red Bull; Getty Images; Andreas Rentz/Getty Images; Red Bull **69:** Red Bull; Red Bull; Getty Images; Red Bull; Robert W Kelley/Getty Images; AFP **70:** Lorne Bridgman; Ho New/Reuters; NASA **71:** Seth Wenig/AP/PA; Seth Wenig/AP/PA; Seth Wenig/AP/PA; Getty Images; Getty Images **72:** Jean-Sebastien Evarard/Getty Images **73:** Don Emmert/Getty Images; Jean-Micel Andre/Getty Images; Getty Images; Getty Images **74:** Kenji Kondo/AP/PA; EPA; Prakash Mathema/Getty Images; Getty Images; Getty Images; Getty Images; Getty Images; Getty Images **75:** Michele Falzone/Getty Images; Paul Hara; AP/PA; Getty Images; Getty Images; Getty Images; Getty Images; Getty Images; Getty Images; Getty Images **76:** Antarctic ICE; Getty Images; Getty Images; Getty Images; Getty Images; Getty Images **77:** Richard Bradbury/GWR; TopFoto **78:** Getty Images; Getty Images; Getty Images; Getty Images **79:** Getty Images; Getty Images; Getty Images; Getty Images; NASA; NASA; Getty Images; Getty Images; Getty Images; Getty Images; Getty Images **80:** Paul Michael Hughes/GWR **82:** The British Library/Getty Images **83:** Bibliotheque Nationale de France; Getty Images **84:** Ranald Mackechnie/GWR **85:** David Munn/Getty Images; Paul Michael Hughes/GWR **86:** Paul Michael Hughes/GWR; Paul Michael Hughes/GWR; Paul Michael Hughes/GWR **87:** Paul Michael Hughes/GWR; Paul Michael Hughes/GWR; Paul Michael Hughes/GWR **89:** James Ellerker/GWR **90:** Richard Faverty/Beckett Studios; Paul Michael Hughes/GWR; Il Mauri; Eric Evers **91:** Fabrini Crisci; Paul Michael Hughes/GWR **92:** Ryan Schude/GWR **94:** James Ellerker/GWR; Sam Christmas/GWR **95:** Sam Christmas/GWR; Silvie Lintimerov **96:** Richard Bradbury/GWR; Ranald Mackechnie/GWR; Mykel Nicolaou/GWR **97:** Richard Bradbury/GWR; Robin F Pronk; Getty Images **99:** Charlie Mallon; Ranald Mackechnie/GWR **100:** Paul Michel Hughes/GWR; James Ellerker/GWR; Getty Images; Getty Images; 20th Century Fox; Sony Pictures; United Artists **101:** Kent Horner/WENN; Paul Michael Hughes/GWR; Emmanuel Aguirre/Getty Images; Ranald Mackechnie/GWR; Warner Brothers/Getty Images; Alamy; Sony Pictures; Columbia TriStar **102:** Paul Michael Hughes/GWR; Paul Michael Hughes/GWR; John Wright/GWR; Paul Michael Hughes/GWR **103:** Ranald Mackechnie/GWR; Paul Michael Hughes/GWR; Paul Michael Hughes/GWR; Vincent Thian/AP/PA; Paul Michael Hughes/GWR; **104:** Paul Michael Hughes/GWR; Paul Michael Hughes/GWR; Paul Michael Hughes/GWR **105:** Paul Michael Hughes/GWR; Ranald Mackechnie/GWR **106:** Subhash Sharma/GWR; Brendan Landy **107:** Frank Rumpenhorst/EPA; Sukree Sukplang/Reuters; Diane Bondareff/AP/PA; Paul Michael Hughes/GWR; Steve Niedorf; **108:** Kimberly Roberts; Brian Fick; Paul Michael Hughes/GWR; Getty Images; **109:** Sandy Huffaker/Eyevine; Jim Goodrich; Getty Images; Getty Images; Paul Michael Hughes/GWR **110:** Paul Michael Hughes/GWR; Paul Michael Hughes/GWR; Getty Images; Getty Images; Getty Images **111:** Paul Michael Hughes/GWR; Rex Features; Getty Images; Getty Images; Getty Images; Getty Images **112:** Sam Christmas/GWR; Paul Michael Hughes/GWR; Paul Michael Hughes/GWR; Sam Christmas/GWR; Getty Images; Getty Images; Getty Images; Getty Images **113:** Paul Michael Hughes/GWR; Paul Michael Hughes/GWR; Paul Michael Hughes/GWR; Getty Images; Getty Images; Getty Images **114:** Paul Michael Hughes/GWR; Richard Bradbury/GWR; Paul Michael Hughes/GWR; Getty Images; Getty Images; Getty Images; Getty Images; Getty Images **115:** Paul Michael Hughes/GWR; David Livingston/Getty Images; Paul Michael Hughes/GWR; Getty Images; Getty Images; Getty Images; Getty Images **117:** Jewel Samad/Getty Images **118:** Paul Michael Hughes/GWR **120:** Getty Images; Roberto Schmidt/Getty Images; Daniel Berehulak/Getty Images; Getty Images; Getty Images; Getty Images; Getty Images **121:** Mario Tama/Getty Images; William Andrew/Getty Images; Getty Images; Getty Images; Getty Images; Getty Images; Getty Images; Getty Images **122:** Francois Durand/Getty Images; Marcelo A Salinas/Getty Images; Getty Images; Alamy; Getty Images; Getty Images; Getty Images **123:** Arnd Wiegmann/Reuters; Richard Levine/Alamy; Mladen Antonov/Getty Images; Darren McCollester/Getty Images; Rex Features; Getty Images **124:** Lou Bustamante/Profiles in History; Getty Images; Christie's; Getty Images **125:** Comic Connect; Alex Coppel/Rex Features; EuroPics; Louisa Gouliamaki/Getty Images; SCP Auctions; Getty Images; Getty Images **126:** Daniel Acker/Getty Images; Stu Stretton **127:** Eddy Risch; NASA; BNPS **128:** Getty Images; Michael Caulfield/Getty Image; Getty Images; Getty Images **129:** Getty Images; Getty Images; Getty Images; Getty Images; Getty Images; Getty Images **130:** PA; Shaun Curry/Getty Images **131:** Stan Honda/Getty Images; Anne Christine Poujoulat/Getty Images; Erin Lubin/Getty Images; Dan Callister/

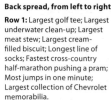

Getty Images; Graham Hughes/PA **132:** Corbis; Sophie Elbaz/Corbis; Lucy Nicholson/Reuters; Getty Images **133:** Doug Houghton/ Alamy; Damian Dovarganes/AP/ PA; Lea Suzuki/Corbis; Jon Super/ PA **134:** PA; James Ellerker/GWR; Alamy; Getty Images; Tim Scrivener; Tim Scrivener/Rex Features **135:** Getty Images; SuperStock; Getty Images; Eric Isselée/lifeonwhite.com; Getty Images; Jonathan Pow; Grant Brereton **136:** Ranald Mackechnie/ GWR **137:** Fran Stothard/SWNS; John Giles/PA; Yang Chul Won; Getty Images; Getty Images **138:** Rafiquar Rahman/Reuters **140:** AP/PA; Alamy **141:** Ernesto Benavides/Getty Images; Fayez Nureldine/Getty Images **142:** Mauricio Ramos/SuperStock; Getty Images; Getty Images; Getty Images; Getty Images; Getty Images **143:** Chad Ehlers/Getty Images; Dan Istitene/Getty Images; Corbis; Ho New/Reuters; Ahmed Jadallah/Reuters; Getty Images; Getty Images; Getty Images; Getty Images; Getty Images **144:** Getty Images; Tomasz Górny; Getty Images; Getty Images; Getty Images; Getty Images; Getty Images; Getty Images **145:** Alisdair Miller; Michael Snell/Alamy; Getty Images; Getty Images; Getty Images; Getty Images; Getty Images **146:** Matt Cardy/Getty Images; Sylvain Sonnet/Corbis; Getty Images; Getty Images; Ramon F Velasquez; Tee Meng; Mark Fischer **147:** Jumana El Heloueh/Reuters; Dan Kitwood/ Getty Images; Getty Images; John Gress/Reuters; So Hing-Keung/ Corbis; Matthew Staver/Getty Images; Photo Parsi; Getty Images **148:** SuperStock; Tom Bonaventure/Getty Images; Getty Images; Getty Images; Getty Images; Getty Images **149:** Coal Miki; Mark Evans/Rex Features; Getty Images; Exclusive Pics; Getty Images; Jean-Marie Hoornaert **150:** Stephen Frink/Corbis; Richard Ellis/Alamy **151:** Simon Gerzina/Alamy **152:** Rex Features; Wojtek Radwanski/Getty Images; Kacper Pempel/Reuters; Reed Saxon/AP/PA; AP/PA; Rafiq Maqboo/AP/PA; Getty Images **153:** Carlos Bravo; Getty Images; Fernando Caro; Chad Breece/ Getty Images; Aedas **154:** Getty Images; Getty Images; Getty Images; Getty Images; Getty Images; Getty Images; Getty Images; Getty Images **155:** Fuste Raga/SuperStock; Reuters; Getty Images; Frank Rollitz/Rex Features; Getty Images; Getty Images; Getty Images; Getty Images; Getty Images **156:** Richard Bradbury/GWR **158:** Vincenzo Pinto/Getty Images; Getty Images; Paul Hanna/Reuters; John Cantlie/ Getty Images; Reuters; Paul Hanna/Reuters **159:** Reuters Graphics; Getty Images; Paul Hermans; NASA; EPA **160:** Corbis; Martin Rose/Getty Images; Getty Images; Getty Images; Sergey Krivchikov; Oleg Belyakov; Getty Images **161:** Alamy; Getty Images **162:** Eigenes Werk; J-H Janßen; Getty Images **163:** NASA; Getty Images; Getty Images **164:** Richard Bradbury/GWR; V&A Images **165:** Rex Features; Rex Features **166:** Alamy; Martin Divisek/Getty Images; Lego **167:** Tim Anderson; PA; PA; PA **168:** Jan Berghuis; Frank Hurley; Japanese American Relocation Photograph Collection **169:** AP/ PA; Alamy; Getty Images **170:** Paul Michael Hughes/GWR; John Wright/GWR; Ranald Mackechnie/ GWR; Getty Images **171:** James Ellerker/GWR **172:** Deutsches Zweirad- und NSU-Museum; Marco Stepniak **173:** John Wright/ GWR; Geoffrey Robinson/Rex Features; Alamy **174:** Reuters; Toshihiko Sato/AP/PA; Rex Features; Rex Features; Getty Images; Getty Images; Getty Images; Getty Images; Getty Images **175:** PA; Robert Nickelsberg/Getty Images; Getty Images; Getty Images **176:** Robert Holmes; Michel Verdure; Getty Images; Getty Images **177:** Reuters; Getty Images; Paulo Whitaker/Reuters; Getty Images **178:** Richard Bradbury/GWR **179:** Zollner Elektronik **180:** NASA; NASA **181:** NASA **182:** ESA; NASA; NASA; NASA; Historic Spacecraft **183:** ESA; NASA **184:** Robyn Beck/Getty Images; Robyn Beck/Getty Images; Stephen Brashear/Getty Images; NASA; NASA; Getty Images; Getty Images; Getty Images; **185:** NASA; SpaceX; NASA; NASA; Getty Images **186:** NASA; NASA; NASA; NASA; NASA; Getty Images; NASA; NASA **187:** NASA; NASA; NASA; NASA; NASA **188:** TopFoto; Science Photo Library; Getty Images; Getty Images; Getty Images; Getty Images; Getty Images **189:** Lang Lang/Reuters; AFP; Getty Images; Getty Images; Getty Images; Getty Images; Getty Images **190:** Don Bayley/Getty Images; Getty Images; Heinrich Pniok; Science Photo Library; Getty Images; Heinrich Pniok; Getty Images; Getty Images; Getty Images; Getty Images; Getty Images **191:** Oakridge National Laboratory; Heinrich Pniok; Getty Images; Getty Images; Getty Images; Fotolia; Getty Images; Getty Images; Getty Images; Getty Images; Getty Images; Getty Images **192:** NASA; Jeff Martin/360cities **193:** Time Out Hong Kong; Evan Kafka **194:** PA; Getty Images **195:** BIPM; Kim Kyung Hoon/Reuters; Getty Images **196:** Ryan Schude/GWR **198:** Paul Michael Hughes/GWR **199:** Matt Crossick **200:** Splash News; Red Bull; WENN **201:** Melina Mara/Getty Images **202:** A.M.P.A.S./Rex Features; Rex Features; Miramax Films; The Weinstein Company; 20th Century Fox; Warner Bros; Warner Bros; Getty Images; Getty Images; Getty Images; Getty Images; Getty Images **203:** Cinereach; Les Films du Losange; Rex Features; Eon Productions; Eon Productions; Getty Images; Getty Images; Getty Images; Getty Images; Getty Images **204:** 20th Century Fox; 20th Century Fox; Warner Bros.; Getty Images **205:** Walt Disney Pictures; Universal/Kobal; Universal/Kobal; Ryan Schude/ GWR; Lucasfilm; TriStar Pictures; Graphic Films; Walt Disney Pictures **206:** DreamWorks Animation; Aardman Animations; Walt Disney Pictures; Kobal; Walt Disney Pictures **207:** Studio Ghibli; Walt Disney Pictures; Walt Disney Pictures; Universal Pictures; Columbia Pictures; Razor Film Produktion GmbH; DreamWorks Animation **208:** Columbia Pictures; Marvel Studios **209:** Jay Directo/Getty Images; 20th Century Fox **210:** Rex Features; Ash Newell; Jason Merritt/Getty Images; Getty Images; Getty Images; Getty Images; Getty Images **211:** John Urbano; Getty Images; Getty Images; Getty Images; Getty Images; Getty Images; Getty Images **212:** Monica McKlinski/ Getty Images; Monica McKlinski/ Getty Images; Cate Gillon/Getty Images; Paul Natkin/Getty Images; Getty Images; Getty Images; Getty Images; Getty Images **213:** Getty Images; Richard E Aaron/Getty Images; Getty Images; Kevin Mazur/Getty Images; Getty Images; Getty Images; Getty Images; Getty Images; Getty Images **214:** Paul Michael Hughes/GWR; Roger Bamber/Rex Features; Getty Images; Getty Images; Getty Images; Getty Images; Getty Images **215:** Rex Features; Sonja Flemming/Getty Images; Angela Weiss/Getty Images; Corbis; Paul Michael Hughes/GWR; Jana DeHart; Getty Images; Getty Images; Getty Images; Getty Images; Getty Images **216:** James Ellerker/GWR; James Ellerker/GWR; Paul Michael Hughes/GWR **217:** James Ellerker/ GWR; Richard Bradbury/GWR **218:** Gustau Nacarino/Reuters **219:** Getty Images **220:** Rex Features; Taina Rissanen/Rex Features; Andrew Vaughan/AP/PA; Roberto Cavieres; Frank Leonhardt/Getty Images; Geoffrey Robinson/Rex Features **221:** Jasper Juinen/Getty Images; Brandon Wade/Invision; Fred Tanneau/Getty Images; Kathy deWitt/Alamy; Thomas Niedermueller/Getty Images; Jonathan Wood/Getty Images **222:** Camilo Rozo/Red Bull; John Stapels/Red Bull **223:** Mark Watson/Red Bull **224:** Mike Stone/Reuters; Jonathan Bachman/Reuters; Jeff Haynes/ Reuters **225:** Getty Images; Jim McIsaac/Getty Images; Andy Lyons/Getty Images; Michael Zagaris/Getty Images; Joe Robbins/Getty Images; Doug Kapustin/Getty Images; Streeter Lecka/Getty Images **226:** Getty Images; Getty Images **227:** Mike Hewitt/Getty Images; Ian Walton/ Getty Images; Eric Feferberg/ Getty Images **228:** Michael Dodge/Getty Images; Jim Rogash/ Getty Images **229:** Mike Hewitt/ Getty Images; Jose Jordan/Getty Images; Hagen Hopkins/Getty Images; Nhat V Meyer/AP/PA **230:** Patrick Semansky/AP/PA; Getty Images; Getty Images; Getty Images; Getty Images; Christian Petersen/Getty Images **231:** Getty Images; Chris Trotman/Getty Images; Mark Duncan/AP/ PA; Jason Miller/Getty Images; Christian Petersen/ Getty Images; Jim McIsaac/ Getty Images **232:** Stacy Revere/Getty Images; Andrew D Bernstein/Getty Images; Rocky Widner/Getty Images **233:** Terrence Vaccaro/ Getty Images; Nathaniel S Butler/ Getty Images **234:** Getty Images; Al Bello/Getty Images; Getty Images; Getty Images **235:** John Gurzinski/Getty Images; John Gichigi/Getty Images; Ethan Miller/Getty Images; Robert Riger/ Getty Images **236:** Franck Fife/ Getty Images; Getty Images **237:** Josh Hedges/Getty Images; Jim Kemper/Getty Images **238:** Dinuka Liyanawatte/Reuters; Danish Siddiqui/Reuters; Matthew Lewis/Getty Images **239:** Carl Court/Getty Images; Duif du Toit/ Getty Images; Getty Images; Graham Crouch/Getty Images; Matthew Lewis/Getty Images **240:** Bryn Lennon/Getty Images; Leon Neal/Getty Images; Clive Brunskill/Getty Images **241:** Odd Andersen/Getty Images; Alexander Nemenov/Getty Images; Doug Pensinger/Getty Images; Carl De Souza/Getty Images **242:** Lucy Nicholson/ Reuters; Hunter Martin/Getty Images; Harry How/Getty Images **243:** Mike Ehrmann/Getty Images; Chris Keane/Reuters; Matthew Lewis/Getty Images; Stuart Franklin/Getty Images **244:** Frederick Breedon/Getty Images; David E Klutho/Getty Images **245:** Norm Hall/Getty Images; Frederick Breedon/Getty Images **246:** Ben Stansall/Getty Images; Steve Bardens/Getty Images **247:** Bryn Lennon/Getty Images; Chris McGrath/Getty Images **248:** Sam Greenwood/ Getty Images; Nelson Almeida/ Getty Images; Ranald Mackechnie/GWR **249:** Getty Images; Mark Ralston/Getty Images; Ruben Sprich/Reuters; Philippe Desmazes/Getty Images **250:** Michael Regan/Getty Images; Liu Jin/Getty Images; Squashpics.com; AP/PA **251:** Michael Dodge/Getty Images; Helene Wiesenhaan/ Getty Images; Clive Brunskill/ Getty Images **252:** Duif du Toit/ Getty Images; Getty Images; Hannah Johnston/Getty Images; Hamish Blair/Getty Images **253:** Adrian Dennis/Getty Images; Cameron Spencer/Getty Images; Stu Forster/Getty Images; David Rogers/Getty Images **254:** Andrew Yates/Getty Images; Ben Stansall/Getty Images; John Peters/Manchester United FC **255:** Getty Images; Getty Images; Shaun Botterill/Getty Images; Alex Livesey/Getty Images; Getty Images; Getty Images; Liu Jin/ Getty Images; Giuseppe Cacace/ Getty Images; David Ramos/Getty Images **256:** Quinn Rooney/Getty Images; Patrik Stollarz/Getty Images; Shaun Botterill/Getty Images; Paul Gilham/Getty Images; Getty Images **257:** Pedro Ugarte/Getty Images; Martin Rose/Getty Images; Hannah Johnston/Getty Images; Antonio Scorza/Getty Images **258:** Getty Images; Red Bull; Kimmo Lahtinen; Lintao Zhang/Getty Images **259:** Feng Li/Getty Images; Martin Rose/Getty Images; Feng Li/Getty Images; Mark Dadswell/Getty Images **260:** Alexander Hassenstein/ Getty Images; Alexis Boichard/ Getty Images; Jeff McIntosh/ AP/PA **261:** Frank Augstein/ AP/PA; Jeff J Mitchell/ Reuters; Markus Scholz/EPA; George Frey/Getty Images; Arnd Wiegmann/Reuters **262:** Harry Engels/ Getty Images; Adrian Dennis/Getty Images **263:** Andrew Yates/Getty Images; Dave Sandford/Getty Images; Yuri Cortez/Getty Images **270:** Frank Quirarte/Billabong XXL **272:** David Ovenden; Cyril Almeras.

ENDPAPERS

Front spread, from left to right

Row 1: Largest energy-efficiency lesson; Most eggs cracked with one hand in one hour; Largest cream tea party; Longest BBQ marathon; Largest streamer string fight; Oldest golf club president; Largest soccer ball mosaic.

Row 2: Longest cake roll; Most bottle caps removed with the head in one minute; Largest loop-the-loop in a car; Fastest motorcycle wheelie on ice; Largest sampa dance; Fastest time to duck tape (duct tape) a person to a wall; Jesse Hoagland's World Record Project.

Row 3: Largest bikini parade; Largest painting made by footprints; Fastest 100 m on spring-loaded stilts; Largest serving of mashed potato; Most lip balms; Most Parmesan cheese wheels cracked simultaneously.

Row 4: Longest marathon playing wheelchair basketball; Largest collection of bottle openers; Most individual rotations of clubs juggled while lying down (four clubs); Most players in a five-a-side soccer exhibition match; First "1080" on a skateboard; Youngest X Games athlete; Largest collection of jigsaw puzzles.

Row 5: Largest polenta; Fastest 10 km pushing a pram; Largest magic lesson; Most cars washed in eight hours (multiple venues); Largest pumpkin pie; Largest flag skydiving; Largest devil's knot.

Back spread, from left to right

Row 1: Largest golf tee; Largest underwater clean-up; Largest meat stew; Largest cream-filled biscuit; Longest line of socks; Fastest cross-country half-marathon pushing a pram; Most jumps in one minute; Largest collection of Chevrolet memorabilia.

Row 2: Most Lego® Ninjago spinner competitions in 24 hours (multiple venues); Largest cookery lesson; Largest dim sum meal; Largest human smiley; Most sandcastles built in one hour; Most people to disappear in an illusion; Most chillies chopped in 30 seconds.

Row 3: Most bottle caps removed with the head in one minute; Most people arm wrestling; Heaviest plum; Largest sequin mosaic; Largest bikini parade; Longest kiss; Most magicians in a magic show.

Row 4: Largest gathering of people dressed as cows; Largest custard slice; Loudest bark by a dog; Most BMX cliffhanger spins (one foot on the handlebars) in one minute; Longest time in plank position; Farthest distance dribbling a hockey ball.

Row 5: Heaviest cabbage; Largest display of lit menorahs; Largest gathering of people dressed as Star Trek characters; Largest human star; Largest collection of magic sets; Largest speed mixer; Longest zipline course.

7,346 Number of Guinness World Records books it would take to match the weight of the **largest carnivorous dinosaur!**

STOP PRESS

1833 pounds of chocolate that went into the sculpture.

First to photograph every bird of paradise species

All 39 recognized species of birds of paradise were photographed by Dr Tim Laman (Japan), in a quest that lasted eight years. *Birds of Paradise: Revealing the World's Most Extraordinary Birds* featuring the photographs, was published on October 23, 2012.

Largest free-floating soap bubble (indoors)

SamSam BubbleMan, aka Sam Heath (UK), made a free-floating soap bubble with a volume of 117 cu. ft. (3.3 m³) on January 11, 2013 at the Hinde Street Methodist Church in London, UK, for the BBC TV show *Officially Amazing*.

Largest word search puzzle

Mel Crow (USA) used 51,000 letters arranged in 204 columns and 250 rows to form more than 5,500 words and phrases in a puzzle presented as a 10 x 15.5-ft. (3 x 4.7-m) poster at the Eagle Gate College campus in Utah, USA, on January 18, 2013. The searchable list of words and phrases included famous actors and a list of 200 additional secret words and phrases to be found but not listed. The puzzle was made available by Tate Publishing & Enterprises as a digital download and can be accessed via tinyurl.com/melcrow.

Youngest golfer on the PGA European Tour

Chinese teenager Ye Wo-cheng (b. September 2, 2000) was 12 years 242 days old when he played the Volvo China Open at Binhai Lake Golf Club, China, on May 2, 2013.

Most UK Top 10 singles from one album

On April 27, 2013, Calvin Harris (UK) scored an unprecedented eighth Top 10 hit from his 2012 album

Longest chocolate sculpture

Andrew Farrugia (Malta) sculptured a chocolate train measuring 111 ft. 8 in. (34.05 m) long. It included an old-fashioned steam locomotive at one end and a more modern style of engine at the other, and also featured individual coaches. The edible express was unveiled in Brussels-South railroad station in Belgium on November 19, 2012.

Longest kiss

Ekkachai and Laksana Tiranarat (both Thailand) locked lips for an incredible 58 hr. 35 min. 58 sec. in Pattaya, Thailand, on February 12–14, 2013. The superlative smooch earned the couple 100,000 baht ($3,380) in cash and two diamond rings in the Valentine's Day contest.

Fastest coffee-powered vehicle

Martin Bacon (UK) built and drove a bean-fired car that attained an average speed of 65.53 mph (105.45 km/h) in Stockport, UK, on February 19, 2013. The challenge was backed by the Co-op supermarket to mark 10 years of Fairtrade coffee in their stores.

Longest domestic cat ever

Mymains Stewart Gilligan, aka "Stewie," was a Maine Coon who measured 48.5 in. (123 cm) long. Previously the **longest cat (domestic)**, a record he'd held since August 28, 2010, he was certified the longest ever cat in 2013. Sadly, we were told that Stewie, owned by Robin Hendrickson and Erik Brandsness (USA), died in January 2013.

Fastest century in professional cricket

Chris Gayle (Jamaica) smashed a century from just 30 balls while playing for Royal Challengers Bangalore against Pune Warriors in the Indian Premier League in Bangalore, India, on April 23, 2013. Gayle's destructive knock of 175 not out featured 13 fours and 17 sixes. The hosts amassed 263 for 5 in their 20 overs and won the contest by 130 runs.

Largest wave surfed (paddle in)

On December 21, 2012, Shawn Dollar (USA) rode a wave measuring 61 ft. (18.5 m) from trough to crest at Cortes Bank, a reef 100 miles (166 km) west of San Diego, California, USA. His feat was confirmed in May 2013 by the Billabong XXL Global Big Wave Awards committee, which awarded him the Pacifico Paddle Award and the XXL Biggest Wave title, accompanied by $30,000 in prize money.

Largest shoe

Electric sekki (Hong Kong) created a shoe measuring 21 ft. (6.4 m) long, 7 ft. 10 in. (2.39 m) wide, and 5 ft. 5 in. (1.65 m) high on April 12, 2013. The shoe was made in Hong Kong, China, by Electric sekki's Peter Solomon and Amiee Squires-Wills. They received their certificate from Adjudicator Charlie Wharton (*left*). Shoe manufacturer Superga's Marco Boglione is pictured right.

SHOE SHOW
The oversize footwear was put on display at the Harbour City shopping center from April 12 to May 12, 2013 in Hong Kong, China.

Most Laurence Olivier award wins

The Curious Incident of the Dog in the Night-Time, adapted by Simon Stephens from Mark Haddon's (both UK) novel of the same name, equalled the total of seven Oliviers won by *Matilda the Musical* (see p.115) on April 29, 2013. Its haul included Best New Play, Best Actor, and Best Director.

18 Months when "I Need Your Love," featuring Ellie Goulding, reached No. 7. Among other hits from the album were two UK No. 1s: "We Found Love," featuring Rihanna, and "Sweet Nothing," featuring Florence Welch from Florence + the Machine. Michael Jackson (USA) previously held the title with his seven Top 10 hits from both *Bad* (1987) and *Dangerous* (1991).

Longest ongoing pilgrimage

Arthur Blessitt (USA) has been walking since December 25, 1969 and claims the greatest distance for a round-the-world pilgrimage,

Most skateboard ollies in one minute

Gabriel Peña (USA) performed 72 ollies in a minute in Houston, Texas, USA, on April 7, 2013. Find out more about ollies— who invented them, what they are, and who has done the most—on p. 108.

having covered 40,235 miles (64,752 km) as of April 24, 2013. He has visited all seven continents, including Antarctica, and crossed 321 nations, island groups, and territories while carrying a 12-ft.-tall (3.7-m) wooden cross and preaching from the Bible.

Fastest time to type a text message (SMS) on a touch-screen cell phone

Mark Encarnación (USA) typed a 160-character text message (SMS) using a touch-screen cell phone in 20.53 seconds outside the Microsoft Studios in Redmond, Washington, USA, on April 24, 2013.

Most expensive work by a living artist sold at auction

The painting *Domplatz, Mailand* (1968) by Gerhard Richter (Germany) sold for $37.1 million on May 15, 2013 at Christie's in New York City, USA. It was bought by Don Bryant, founder of Napa Valley's Bryant Family Vineyard. The previous holder, *Benefits Supervisor Sleeping* (1995) by British artist Lucian Freud, fetched $33.64 million on 13 May 2008.

FACT:
Morgan is the third dog to hold this record since the category was opened in 2012. She towers over most dogs, including her little Terrier friend here, and beat the previous record holder Bella (see p. 40) by 1.25 in. (3.22 cm).

Tallest living female dog

Morgan the Great Dane—who lives with Dave and Cathy Payne in Strathroy-Caradoc, Ontario, Canada—was measured at 3 ft. 2.5 in. (98.15 cm) tall to the shoulder on January 9, 2013. The 200-lb. (90.7-kg), four-year-old gentle giant eats seven cups of dry food (kibble) and two cups of wet food every day.

Most business cards collected in 24 hours

James Fleetham of C Squared (UK) collected a total of 402 business cards at The Festival of Media Global 2013 in Montreux, Switzerland, on April 29–30, 2013. As per the guidelines, James had to make personal networking interactions with each of the card holders, under the watchful eye of an adjudicator.

3
Miles of shoreline along which the fireworks were launched.

Largest firework display

Kuwait marked the 50th anniversary of the ratification of its constitution with a bang—well, 77,282 to be exact—as Kuwait City let off the largest firework display on November 10, 2012. The record-breaking display started at 8 p.m., lasted 64 minutes, and included a light and sound show.

ARE YOUR FEET OFFICIALLY AMAZING?

Record-breaking is free and open to everyone, so why not fulfil a life's ambition and get your name in the record books? Find out how here:

officiallyamazing.tv/feet

HUNGRY FOR MORE?
GET YOUR CLAWS ON MORE INCREDIBLE RECORDS

TAKE THE CHALLENGE
Want to try a record right now? Head over to **guinnessworldrecord. com/challengers** and choose your challenge!

UNLOCK YOUR FREE EBOOK

Access extra bonus content on your favorite records. Enter our competition and take the chance to be a record-breaker too. Download it for free now!

guinnessworldrecords.com/ freebook

GAMER'S EDITION 2014

Look out for the latest edition of our annual book dedicated to video gaming. It's full of the latest high scores, speed runs and technical achievements.

guinnessworldrecords.com/ gamers

DOWNLOAD OUR EBOOKS

Explore your favourite records on your digital device. Check out our range of eBooks available from your digital retailer.

guinnessworldrecords.com/ ebooks

 /GuinnessWorldRecords

 /GWRnews

 /GuinnessWorldRecords